AUGUSTINE

IN HIS OWN WORDS

D1565843

AUGUSTINE

IN HIS OWN WORDS

EDITED BY WILLIAM HARMLESS, S. J.

The Catholic University of America Press
Washington, D. C.

REGIS COLLEGE LIBRARY
100 Wellesley Street West
Toronto, Ontario
Canada M5S 2Z5

BR
65
A52
E6
2010

Copyright © 2010
The Catholic University of America Press
All rights reserved

The paper used in this publication meets the minimum requirements of
American National Standards for Information Science—Permanence of Paper for
Printed Library Materials, ANSI Z39.48-1984.
∞

Library of Congress Cataloging-in-Publication Data
Augustine, Saint, Bishop of Hippo.
[Selections. English. 2010]
Augustine in his own words / edited by William Harmless.
p. cm.
Includes bibliographical references (p.   ) and indexes.
ISBN 978-0-8132-1743-7 (pbk. : alk. paper)
I. Harmless, William, 1953–   II. Title.
BR65.A52E6 2010b
270.2—dc22
2010011081

For Wayne Conway

CONTENTS

List of Illustrations   viii
Introduction: Of Portraits, Voices, and the Art of Mosaic   ix
Abbreviations   xxiii
The Works of Augustine: Texts and Translations   xxvii

1   *Confessions*   1

2   Augustine the Philosopher   39

3   Augustine the Bishop   78

4   Augustine the Preacher   122

5   Augustine the Exegete   156

6   Controversies (I): Against the Manichees   201

7   Controversies (II): Against the Donatists   232

8   Augustine the Theologian: *On the Trinity*   274

9   Controversies (III): *On the City of God, Against the Pagans*   315

10   Controversies (IV): Against the Pelagians   373

    Epilogue   437

Chronology: The Life and Major Works of Augustine   441
Suggestions for Further Reading   447
Index of Scripture   469
Index of Augustinian Texts   475
Index of Other Ancient Authors and Texts   480
Index of Persons and Subjects   482

ILLUSTRATIONS

Vittore Carpaccio, *St. Augustine in His Study*   x

Map, Fourth-Century Italy and
Roman North Africa   xliv

Map, Augustine's North Africa   79

Photograph, The Ruins of Augustine's
Basilica Pacis   123

INTRODUCTION
Of Portraits, Voices, and the Art of Mosaic

Medieval and Renaissance artists loved to imagine the great saints of the past, how they looked, how they dressed, how they lived. St. Augustine (354–430) was an occasional subject. Most artistic renderings of him, whether in paintings or illuminated manuscripts or stained glass windows, are rather workmanlike.[1] But there is one great portrait of him. It is a large oil painting by Vittore Carpaccio (c. 1460–c. 1526), entitled *Saint Augustine in His Study*.[2] Carpaccio portrays Augustine seated behind a desk, stylus in hand, his right arm raised in the air, poised between thoughts, ready to transcribe the next great theological inspiration. Scattered about his desk and beneath his feet are books, some piled up, others lying open, all expensively bound. He sits completely alone in a spacious, elegant study. The room's high ceiling is ornately paneled. In the background is a small private chapel, located in a niche, with an episcopal miter left behind on the altar and an episcopal crosier leaning up against the wall. Augustine himself is given a European's face, bearded, fair-skinned.[3] He is dressed in the refined robes of a Renaissance bishop and gazes out not at us, but to the left, at some scene visible through the nearby window or, more likely, at some far-off horizon beyond the senses' grasp.

It is a wonderfully dramatic image. It is also almost entirely wrong. What's wrong with it? First, Augustine was no European. He was an African, a native of Thagaste (now Souk Ahras in Algeria), and he spent nearly 35 years of his life as the bishop of a second-rate, bustling North African port city, Hippo Regius (now Annaba on the Algerian-Tunisian border). His contemporaries acclaimed him one of the great masters of the Latin language,

1. See Joseph C. Schnaubelt and Frederick Van Fleteren, eds., *Augustine in Iconography: History and Legend*, Augustinian Historical Institute Series, vol. 4 (New York: Peter Lang Publishing, 1999).
2. This painting graces the cover of two of the finest contemporary scholarly studies of Augustine: Allan Fitzgerald's *Augustine Through the Ages: An Encyclopedia* (Grand Rapids: Eerdmans, 1999), and Peter Brown's *Augustine of Hippo: A Biography*, rev. ed. (Berkeley: University of California Press, 2000).
3. Patricia Fortini Brown, "Carpaccio's St. *Augustine in His Study*: A Portrait Within a Portrait," *Augustine in Iconography*, 507–37, argues that Carpaccio based his Augustine figure on the appearance of Cardinal Bessarion (1403–1473), bishop of Nicaea, who spent key parts of his career in Venice.

Vittore Carpaccio (c. 1460–c. 1526), St. *Augustine in His Study* (Scuola di S. Giorgio degli Schiavoni, Venice). Scala / Art Resource, NY. Used with permission.

but he spoke it with a detectable African accent.[4] He was proud of his African heritage, and he owed much in both theology and piety to traditions of North African Christianity.[5] Augustine the bishop had neither miter nor crosier. He said no private masses and had no private chapel. Nor did he wear distinctive episcopal garb. There was, at the time, no settled uniform for clergy. Augustine, by his own account, spurned fineries and dressed with great simplicity, likely in the rough robes of a monk. Carpaccio's image is wrong in other ways as well. It is almost impossible to imagine the historical Augustine spending long hours alone writing. He seems everywhere and always surrounded by people, by close friends and clamoring parishioners: preaching extemporaneously to large and noisy crowds in Hippo and Carthage; listening in frustration to lawsuits between contentious local litigants; chewing over the Bible with his monks and clergy as they shared their common meals; or deliberating long hours in council with his fellow North African bishops. Augustine was certainly an author, but few writings were likely written with his own pen. He mostly spoke his books, dictating them, often late at night, to stenographers who worked on the staff of his government-supported church. We think of Augustine as a great writer, but contemporaries knew him as a great talker. He was, in fact, a talker by profession, a highly trained and enormously gifted orator. He certainly consulted books, but most often cited them, especially the Bible, from his prodigious memory.

Pictures cannot capture that voice of his. The historical Augustine comes down to us as all voice. One hears through that voice, through that endless flow of sonorous words, an intellect at times fierce and combative, but more often penetrating and restless, always searching, always probing. But what catches our ear, as it caught the ear of his first hearers, is the heart beneath that voice, that uncanny ability of his to speak across the centuries, heart to heart, his heart to ours.

The book you have in your hand offers, in its own way, a portrait of Augustine. Its materials are not paint on a canvas, but words on a page. Its words are mostly Augustine's own. In these pages, I try and let Augustine tell his own story in his own words. In the process, I hope to help readers tune their ears to the melodies of his speech and to the swirl of his mind. His was an agitated eloquence, and he used it to ponder and wrestle aloud with life's

---

4. In *De ordine* 2.17.45 (BA 4/2:296), Augustine complains that "even I, for whom a thorough study of these matters [of pronunciation and diction] has been a dire necessity, am nevertheless censured by the Italians for my pronunciation of many words" (trans. Russell, FOTC 5:321).

5. See J. Kevin Coyle, "The Self-Identity of North African Christians in Augustine's Time," *Augustinus Afer: Saint Augustin: africanité et universalité: Actes du colloque international Alger-Annaba, 1–7 avril 2001*, ed. Pierre-Yves Fux, Jean-Michel Roessli, and Otto Wermelinger (Fribourg: Éditions Universitaires Fribourg Suisse, 2003), 61–74.

mysteries, both those glimpsed in the epic of human history and those astir in the depths of the human heart. But Augustine's center and passion was another far greater mystery, the God he met in his Bible and in his heart.

This book is an introduction, intended for first-time readers of Augustine. I do not presume readers know anything much, or anything at all, about his life, world, or thought. For nearly two decades, I have worked to introduce undergraduates, graduates, and many, many others to the art of reading Augustine. A book is not a classroom, of course, but the years of teaching have alerted me to needs that newcomers often have. The challenge is how best to enter into his life, thought, and world. That world of his, the world of Late Antiquity, is both dauntingly intricate and deceptively remote from our own. To enter it, one needs certain basics and a measure of sympathy. Augustine himself used to ask readers for a certain benefit of the doubt when starting out:

> Let everyone who reads these pages move along with me when he is equally sure of things. When he is equally hesitant, let him delve into them along with me. When he realizes the error is his, let him come back to me. When it is mine, let him call me back. And so let us go forward together, along the road charity lays out, setting our sights on the One of whom it is said: "Seek His face always" (Ps 104:4).[6]

I do not think the book you have in your hands is the only one you will need. It is best read alongside one or more of the remarkable scholarly introductions to Augustine's life and theology. All the same, it is one thing to read about him and quite another thing to read him. Augustine can be difficult at times, but that does not lessen the need to hear him in his own words and on his own terms.

Often those who seek Augustine himself are content to work their way through his *Confessions* (*Confessiones*). It is one of the unquestioned masterpieces of world literature and offers a brilliant evocation of his early career and his inner life. It is also one-sided. In *Confessions*, we hear Augustine the middle-aged bishop tell us of Augustine the thirty-something convert—and tell us of himself in all the glaring clarity of retrospect. *Confessions* may be brilliant, but it tells us about only a modest portion of his life and offers but a small glimpse into his restless and wide-ranging mind.

This book sketches a broader, fuller portrait by gathering Augustine's many sides into a single volume. It brings together, one might argue, not a single portrait of Augustine, but rather a portrait gallery, a gathering of the many Augustines under one roof. *Confessions* is certainly here, but only as a

---

6. *De Trinitate* 1.3.5 (CCL 50:32); my trans. On this, see Robert Wilken, *The Spirit of Early Christian Thought: Seeking the Face of God* (New Haven: Yale University Press, 2003), 80–109.

starting point. To seek the complete Augustine, we will have to venture into his complete works, his sprawling *opera omnia*. To do so much in so few pages requires balancing breadth and brevity.

What is that breadth? Well, in 426, near the end of his career, Augustine catalogued his lifetime's work in a treatise entitled *Reconsiderations* (*Retractationes*). In it, he lists a staggering 93 books! (And before he died in 430, he authored a few more). Some of these are what we would now call essays, but many others are books of enormous length. *The City of God* (*De civitate Dei*) alone stretches out, in standard English translations, to nearly 1500 pages. His final book, *Against Julian, an Unfinished Work* (*Contra Julianum opus imperfectum*), is over 800 pages and, as the title indicates, was left incomplete. Augustine never got around to cataloguing his nearly 300 letters (published recently in four volumes). Nor did he catalogue his nearly 600 *Sermons to the People* (*Sermones ad populum*, published recently in eleven volumes), his 124 sermons on John's Gospel (*In Johannis evangelium tractatus*, published in five volumes), nor his sermons on each of the 150 Psalms (*Enarrationes in Psalmos*, published in six volumes). All told, his surviving corpus is the largest of any ancient author.

Augustine's eloquent long-windedness overwhelms not only newcomers, but even experts, both ancient and modern. Possidius of Calama, Augustine's good friend and earliest biographer, knew how daunting the task could be. Soon after Augustine's death, Possidius put together his own comprehensive catalogue of Augustine's works, what he called the *Indiculum*, "the little index."[7] Possidius too felt overwhelmed and solemnly pronounced on the impossibility of mastering Augustine's output: "So many articles were dictated and published by Augustine, and so many topics discussed in church, written down and amended, either against various heretics or expounded from the canonical books for the edification of the Church's holy sons and daughters, that scarcely any student could read and know them all."[8] A few centuries later, Isidore of Seville put it more bluntly: that anyone who claimed to have read the entire corpus of Augustine was a liar.[9]

It is a daunting prospect, therefore, to try and survey so much and to do it so briefly. This book assembles a modest but wide-ranging harvest of Augustinian texts and collects them into ten chapters. Older anthologies used to

7. For the text of the *Indiculum*, see Wilhelm Geerlings, ed., *Possidius: Vita Augustini*, AOW (Paderborn: Ferdinand Schöningh, 2005), 114–37. For a discussion, see François Dolbeau, "La survie des œuvres d'Augustin: Remarques sur l'*Indiculum* attribué à Possidius et sur la bibliothèque d'Anségise," *Augustin et la prédication en Afrique: Recherches sur divers sermons authentiques, apocryphes ou anonymes*, CEASA 179 (Paris: Institut d'Études Augustiniennes, 2005), 475–94.

8. Possidius, *Vita s. Augustini* 18 (Geerlings, 62); trans. Muller, FOTC 15:95–96.

9. Isidore of Seville, *Versus* [in *Bibliotheca*] VII (CCL 113A:219).

use the categories of systematic theology ("God," "the soul," "faith," "grace," "sacraments," etc.) as a way to organize Augustine's thought.[10] Such an outline is misleading. It leaves the false impression that Augustine was a systematic theologian. It also wrenches texts out of their context, or rather their many varied contexts: literary, social, historical, and religious. His words were addressed not to us nor to all eternity, but to specific audiences at specific moments for specific reasons. I have chosen, therefore, to stay close to the obvious divisions within Augustine's literary corpus. I devote one chapter to each of his best-known masterpieces (*Confessions, On the Trinity, City of God*) and one chapter to each of his best-known controversies (against Manichees, Donatists, and Pelagians). I also explore overlooked sides of his life, namely, his routine work as a bishop, as a preacher, and as an interpreter of the Bible. Each of these three topics also gets its own chapter. I've ordered all this to follow the course of his career, its historical unfolding. His thought, I believe, is best seen as a moving target, not a brilliant fixity.

Let me spell out this outline more fully. Chronology shapes the basic flow. Chapter 1 focuses on his *Confessions*. It gathers the best-known passages and surveys his early career as a student, a teacher, and an orator up through his famous conversion in Milan in August 386 and his baptism at the Easter vigil in April 387. Chapter 2 explores his earliest writings, works composed between 386 and 391, dialogues such as *Against the Skeptics* (*Contra Academicos*) and treatises such as *On True Religion* (*De vera religione*). Some were begun in Milan, while he was still a professional orator and still a catechumen; others date from his days as a baptized "servant of God," retired and living on his family property in Thagaste. These early texts hover around issues that we today would call philosophical.

Chapter 3 focuses on Augustine the bishop. For this, I draw especially on two sources: Possidius's early biography and Augustine's own letters. These let us glimpse his day-to-day life—its routine rhythms, its weighty responsibilities, its newsworthy crises. His work as a pastor was the linchpin and the catalyst for his voluminous writings. Remaining chapters explore individual threads and specific battles that defined his episcopal career. As a bishop, he preached, of course. He did so often and at length. Chapter 4, therefore, surveys Augustine the preacher. We will look at a few complete sermons and a sprinkling of excerpts. These I intertwine with his theoretical reflections on the art of preaching, drawing especially on Book 4 of his *On Christian Teaching* (*De doctrina christiana*). Augustine's preaching focused, of course, on the Bi-

---

10. For example, Erich Przywara, ed., *An Augustinian Synthesis* (New York: Sheed and Ward, 1945); Vernon J. Bourke, ed., *The Essential Augustine* (Indianapolis: Hackett, 1974).

ble. Chapter 5, therefore, explores Augustine the exegete. Here again, I inter-twine examples of his practical exegesis with his more theoretical reflections, drawing especially on Books 1–3 of *On Christian Teaching*.

We today think of Augustine mainly as a theologian. He was that, but he was no academic. His theological works sprang from pastoral concerns and clashes. He was also, by training and by temperament, a debater. His theology was crafted in the searing fires of controversy. This "kiln" gives his theology its distinctive coloration and contours and occasional hard edges. Four controversies shape his career. Chapter 6 looks at the first of these, his debate with the Manichees. Manicheism was a gnostic religion founded in the third century by a Persian prophet, Mani, and spread east to China and west into the Roman Empire. Augustine himself had been a Manichee for nearly a decade. One thread of *Confessions* is a debate with his former co-religionists, but *Confessions* is only the best known of his anti-Manichean writings. This debate drew on his best energies in the 390s.

Chapter 7 looks at a second controversy, his debate with the Donatists. North African Christians had divided into two rival churches, Catholic and Donatist. The Donatists were, for much of the fourth century, the larger, but had severed communion with other Christians around the Empire. Here we will see a sampling of Augustine's letters, pamphlets, and provocative sermons, as they poured forth against a violent backdrop of religious terrorism and spasms of government repression. This debate occupied his best energies, both pastoral and theological, through the first decade of the 400s, climaxing in the Conference of Carthage in 411, where the schism was ended by government edict.

Chapter 8 steps away from controversy—at least, the face-to-face variety—and surveys the second of Augustine's masterpieces, *On the Trinity* (*De Trinitate*). This work, written in fits and starts between 400 and 422, addresses the central Christian mystery, "the Trinity who God is," as Augustine used to put it.[11] The issue is this: How can Christians call Jesus "God" and call the Holy Spirit "God" and not end up with three gods? The question had been a burning one for much of the fourth century. Augustine was committed to the Council of Nicaea (325), its creed and its defenders, and used this work as a way to think through its implications. His synthesis would deeply influence the theological tradition of the medieval West and beyond. I highlight here his unique contributions, especially the search for the impress of Trinity within each of us.

Chapter 9 returns to controversy and looks at his third masterpiece, *On*

---

11. *De Trinitate* 15.6.10; 15.17.28 (CCL 50A:473, 502).

the *City of God*. Its subtitle, *Against the Pagans*, names its polemical focus. Its writing was sparked by the Gothic sack of Rome in 410. Pagans interpreted the sack as the gods' punishment for the Christian banning of sacrifices to Rome's ancient divine protectors. Augustine defended Christianity against the charges, launching his massive rebuttal in 413 and completing it, after many interruptions, in 426. His guiding concept is of two cities, the City of God and the earthly city, and he uses it as a framework to think through the epic course of human history, to probe the meaning of society and government, law and justice, war and peace, and much, much else.

Chapter 10 explores Augustine's final controversy, a long-running and bitter debate with the Pelagians. Pelagius (c. 350–c. 425) was an ascetic who worked as a spiritual advisor to Rome's aristocratic elite and was horrified by Augustine's views on grace. Around 411, Augustine was drawn into the fight by close friends who were alarmed by Pelagius's sharp-witted disciple, Caelestius, who once sought ordination in Carthage and ended up accused of heresy. Only later and only slowly did Augustine engage Pelagius himself. The clash became an international *cause célèbre* and occupied Augustine's best energies through the 410s. After Pelagius's final condemnation in 418, Augustine continued being drawn into controversy by Julian of Eclanum, an Italian bishop who chose exile over seconding the papal condemnation of Pelagius. This no-holds-barred battle with Julian never let up. The two continued exchanging long and venomous treatises through the 420s. Virtually to the day he died, Augustine felt compelled to answer Julian's attacks, leaving no taunt unanswered.

That defines the breadth. What about the brevity? Seeing the big picture is never easy; seeing it briefly is doubly difficult. I have worked to keep chapters to a manageable length, roughly 30 to 40 pages, something that one might read in a single sitting. One exception is the chapter on *City of God*, which is longer, though this should come as no surprise, given the work's epic length and scope. A second is the final chapter on the Pelagians, which excerpts from a corpus of literature several times the size of *City of God*. Keeping things brief has been a difficult task, especially since I have had, for each chapter, to choose from original sources that run on for many hundreds of pages. Within individual chapters, I have chosen brief excerpts, each running from one to five pages in length. Each excerpt gets its own brief introduction that highlights its context and, on occasion, its distinctiveness.

Of the hundreds of possibilities, why choose the ones I did? My overarching concern was to include Augustine's "greatest hits," all the best known and most often quoted texts. To help with this, I have consulted working Augustinian scholars as well as the vast scholarship on Augustine they have produced. I have also looked, along the way, for hidden gems, passages that only experts might know of. Few would realize, for example, that Augustine gives his best brief summary of Manicheism in a late letter (*ep.* 238) or that he once tacked a brilliant point-by-point contrast between Manichean and Catholic views onto an early commentary on Genesis. I introduce each of the four chapters on Augustine's controversies with excerpts from his opponents. It helps to hear a Manichee or a Donatist or a Pelagian speak in his own voice about his own concerns before we hear Augustine's rebuttal.

Why such brief excerpts? Years in the classroom have taught me that newcomers do best when they watch their diet of ancient texts and limit themselves to smaller morsels. Brief excerpts tend to invite closer examination. While this book is intended for a broad range of readers, some will grapple with it in the rough-and-tumble of the classroom, where texts can be probed, pondered, dissected, argued over, and, if need be, argued with. My all-too-brief introductions to individual excerpts are no more than points of entry. These texts invite, indeed require, fuller commentary.

What guides the flow? That depends. It varies from chapter to chapter, from topic to topic. Sometimes Augustine's own text shapes the sequence, as in Chapter 1 on *Confessions*. Other times the order is roughly chronological, as in Chapter 3 on Augustine the bishop. Still other times it follows the point-counterpoint of controversy, as in Chapter 10 on the Pelagian debate. But often the choice is intuitive. I have thought of this project as piecing together a vast mosaic whose fragments, in the end, offer a portrait. Mosaics, after all, are collections of small, brilliantly colored stones known as *tesserae*. When skillfully assembled, *tesserae* come together to create intricate designs and gleaming portraits. The metaphor of mosaic-making is quite apt since mosaic was among the most popular and the most artistically accomplished art forms practiced in Augustine's North Africa.[12] The floor of his basilica had a patchwork of mosaics. Augustine himself once compared God's ordering of creation to the aesthetic of the mosaic artist: "If a person were to look at an intricate pavement so narrowly as to see only the single *tessera*, he would say the artist, lacking a sense of composition, had set the little pieces at haphazard, since he could not take in at once the whole pattern, inlaid to form a single image of beauty."[13] The challenge mosaic-artists face, as Augustine notes, is to create a coherent portrait from seemingly haphazard little pieces,

12. Aïcha Ben Abed, *Tunisian Mosaics: Treasures from Roman Africa* (Los Angeles: Getty Conservation Institute, 2006); Katherine M. D. Dunbabin, *The Mosaics of Roman North Africa: Studies in Iconography and Patronage*, Oxford Monographs on Classical Archaeology (Oxford: Clarendon Press/Oxford University Press, 1978).

13. *De ordine* 1.1.2 (BA 4/2:72-74); trans. Garry Wills, *Saint Augustine*, Penguin Lives (New York: Viking Penguin, 1993), 3.

to make them all fit together well enough for viewers, once they stand back, to see a unified image. The same challenge faces editors.

In constructing this Augustinian mosaic, I have had several exemplars in view. One has been David Ford's and Mike Higton's anthology, entitled *Jesus*.[14] It gathers a wide-ranging variety of 1- to 2-page excerpts drawn from theological texts, ecumenical councils, mystical writings, hymns, apocryphal texts, poems, and much else, about Jesus. An older model, well known to patristic scholars, is J. Stevenson's classic two-volume compilation, *A New Eusebius* and *Creeds, Councils, and Controversies*.[15] Stevenson assembled snippets from a wide range of hard-to-find materials: acts of Christian martyrs, conciliar documents, fragments from heretics and persecutors, inscriptions on coins and catacombs, snatches of gossip in scattered letters. The final result is a brilliant mosaic of early Christianity. Augustine, I believe, deserves a mosaic of comparable luster.

I want this book to serve as a hospitable entry into Augustine's writings and world, and hope it encourages readers to explore beyond its pages. I have, therefore, appended an annotated bibliography, which offers a broad sampling of scholarly studies that readers may want to turn to next. I also hope readers will begin exploring Augustine's individual works in their entirety. To aid that, I have assembled a listing of his complete works, both the Latin originals and the major English translations, arranged according to their Latin titles. I realize that many readers may not know any Latin, but it is important that they gradually learn to recognize the Latin titles in order to follow scholarly discussions and to chase down references.

This book, as I noted, is for newcomers. I take both consolation and certain cues from Augustine himself, who was deeply attuned to the needs of beginners and who once composed a brief, brilliant treatise entitled *On Catechizing Beginners* (*De catechizandis rudibus*). He wrote the work at the request of Deogratias, a deacon from Carthage. In it, he stressed that teaching beginners is both a noble task and an intricate art form. He reminded Deogratias of the experience of taking friends on a tour of one's hometown and the nearby countryside, noting how "we, who have been in the habit of passing this landscape by without any enjoyment, find our own delight renewed by their delight at the novelty of it all." And if, he added, long familiarity has cooled our enthusiasm, then we should be "renewed in their newness" and "catch fire in their fire." Good teaching, he believed, springs from a myste-

---

14. David Ford and Mike Higton, eds., *Jesus*, Oxford Readers (New York: Oxford University Press, 2002).

15. J. Stevenson, ed., *A New Eusebius: Documents Illustrative of the History of the Church to AD 337* and *Creeds, Councils, Controversies: Documents Illustrative of the History of the Church AD 337–461*, rev. ed. W. H. C. Frend (London: SPCK, 1987, 1989).

rious, heartfelt sympathy between teacher and learner: "For so great is this feeling of compassion that when people are touched by us as we speak and we by them as they learn, we dwell each in the other, and so it is as if they speak in us what they hear while we, in some way, learn in them what we teach."[16] That, I hope, has guided what I have gathered here. I agree with Augustine: Beginners are the best of teachers, and what we do, we do for love.

⸙

A Note on the Translations: The genesis of this book came about several years ago, when David McGonagle, Director of the Catholic University of America Press, asked whether I would be interested in putting together a new Augustine reader by drawing on the 30 volumes of Augustine's works previously published in the eminent Fathers of the Church (FOTC) series. This, I knew at once, was a great opportunity. I also knew that one could not, without further ado, simply pick and choose from those 30 volumes. The Fathers of the Church series offered a valuable starting point and a solid core, but its volumes were not, of themselves, sufficient to survey the breadth of Augustine's corpus. None of his *Expositions of the Psalms* appear in the series, nor does it include any of his anti-Donatist treatises; and it has only a small selection of his *Sermons to the People*. There are, as well, many other smaller gaps. In addition, many of the Augustine volumes were translated in the 1940s and 1950s and sometimes use a style and word choice that now seems awkward and outdated. In a number of cases, older translations have been superseded because new critical editions of Augustine's Latin text have been published. My general policy has been to make use, wherever possible, of the FOTC volumes, but I have taken the liberty of altering those earlier translations wherever needed. To insure accuracy, I have checked each excerpt against the best edition of the Latin text, as well as against one or more recent translations in English or French. Many passages required at least a few small amendments. In a number of cases, I have used the FOTC translation as a starting point and then thoroughly reworked sentences and often whole paragraphs. In these instances, I note that the passage is not "translated by so-and-so," but is "based on so-and-so's translation." About one third of this book consists of my own new translations; the remainder are either drawn from or are much revised versions of the FOTC.

Translating Augustine is demanding. He was, by talent and training, an orator. His words are often melodious. There are rhymes, alliterations, long chains of balanced antitheses, all sorts of baroque embellishments. Such musicality was part of the orator's craft, and Augustine carefully and con-

---

16. *De catechizandis rudibus* 12.17 (CCL 46:141); my trans.

sciously cultivated it. His word-choice also routinely plays on complex chains of images, some drawn from the Bible, some from the world around him, so that ideas move along as much by metaphor as by logic. These qualities defy easy translation, but, here and there, they can be captured in English, if only roughly and sporadically. I have tried, wherever possible, to give readers some taste of both his musicality and his poetics.

There is much else about Augustine's Latin that is difficult to render in idiomatic English. Like many Latin speakers, he had a fondness for long, winding periodic sentences. While these can, with difficulty, be replicated in English, the English version tends to come off as unwieldy, obtuse, and abstract, while the Latin originals are models of terse elegance and clarity. On occasion, I have broken down such sentences into shorter units; other times, I have replicated their length, tying them together by repeating a key word that appears but once in the Latin original, but which serves as the linchpin linking the chain of clauses. My concern is that the English be as readable as possible. Latin grammar is not English grammar, and readers are meeting Augustine in English, not Latin. An obvious point perhaps, but one not always honored by translators. Augustine's own bottom line was clarity. I have tried to honor that. I have translated as much for the ear as for the eye. Augustine spoke his works out loud, and that orality needs to be respected and translated where possible. At several junctures, I encourage readers to read the texts aloud, and, while they are in English and not Latin, some of Augustine's oral flair does come through, even in translation.

I should also add that Latin as a language is, to some extent, word-poor. This means that a single Latin word can possess many different meanings. Augustine often exploited this. As a translator, one has to make choices. What does one do when it is clear that Augustine wanted to exploit a single word's multiple meanings? I have, in certain cases, chosen to use several words where Augustine uses but one. Also hard to capture is tone. Augustine's letters display a diplomat's flair and finesse and adopt a stately rhetorical style. In his controversial works, his voice can shift rapidly, much the way an able lawyer's does, now interrogating witnesses, now probing the evidence, now appealing to the jury. His sermons vary even more widely in tone and style, sometimes using an intricate elegance, other times adopting a conversational informality. To translate this more popular touch, I resort to occasional contractions, even the occasional slang, to give some equivalent to Augustine's tone.

Augustine's prose is saturated with biblical quotations, biblical allusions, biblical echoes. It is hard to decide how best to cite these. One runs the risk of cluttering the text with parenthetical references or glutting the bottom of the page with footnotes. James O'Donnell, in his edition of *Confessions*, took the opposite tack, removing not only all biblical references from the Latin text, but also all quotation marks.[17] This "clean" look does give a fairer visual approximation of what Augustine's original layout looked like and helpfully reminds readers that the insertion of all such references into the text is the work of later editors. It also reminds readers that Augustine spoke "Bible," that he, quite literally, made the Bible's words his own words. I have, however, followed the more traditional course, namely, that whenever Augustine explicitly quotes a biblical text, I mark it as such and put the reference in parentheses within the text (rather than in a footnote). The harder task involved deciding when and how to mark allusions and paraphrases. I have kept these to a minimum. In clear and important instances, I insert a parenthetical reference, but without quotation marks and without any "cf."

The Bible that Augustine drew most upon was the so-called Vetus Latina, or "Old Latin" versions. The Old Testament of these early Latin Bibles had been translated (sometimes poorly) not from the Hebrew original, as one finds in modern Bibles, but from the ancient Greek translation known as the Septuagint. As a result, Augustine's biblical quotations do not consistently match modern versions. The translations given here reflect the Bible Augustine knew. Discrepancies between Augustine's Bible and ours are most frequent and obvious when he quotes the Psalms. It is important to be aware that the Septuagint's numbering of Psalms 9 through 147 is one behind modern numbering, and so they have been marked throughout the text. I sort out these matters in the index of biblical references at the end of the book. It seemed better to do that than to give a double citation for each Psalm reference within the text itself.

While this anthology draws on translations from a variety of translators, I have imposed a consistent spelling of proper names and of terms. I have followed as much as possible what has become the defining standard for contemporary Augustinian studies, namely, Allan Fitzgerald's *Augustine Through the Ages: An Encyclopedia*. I have followed Fitzgerald's decisions on almost all scores: spelling of names, the titles of Augustine's works, choice of terminology, abbreviations, and much else.

I must thank a number of colleagues who kindly read drafts of chapters at various points along the way: Lewis Ayres, Paul Blowers, Patout Burns, Michael Cameron, John Cavadini, Catherine Conybeare, Brian Daley, Marianne Djuth, Daniel Doyle, Allan Fitzgerald, Carol Harrison, John Peter Kenney,

---

17. James J. O'Donnell, *Augustine: Confessions*, Volume 1: *Introduction and Text* (Oxford: Clarendon, 1992). See his remarks on pp. lx–lxi.

Michael Legaspi, Michael McCarthy, Jane Merdinger, Richard Miller, John O'Keefe, Russell Reno, Stanley Rosenberg, Brian Sholl, Eileen Burke Sullivan, Roland Teske, Maureen Tilley, and James Wetzel. Their assistance, corrections, and suggestions have been invaluable on many scores. They helped me thread my way through certain subtleties in Augustine's thought and have pointed me to overlooked texts and scholarly studies. I must also thank Sandra Chavez, who worked as a research assistant in the book's final stages. I need to take this occasion to give thanks for the life and work of Thomas Martin, OSA, who served as Director of the Augustinian Institute at Villanova University. Tom offered help and advice on several chapters and various questions. As I was putting the last touches on the manuscript of this book, I received word that he had passed away after a quiet struggle with cancer. He will be much missed.

ABBREVIATIONS

WORKS OF AUGUSTINE

The standard abbreviations for the complete works of Augustine are found in Allan D. Fitzgerald's *Augustine Through the Ages*, pp. xxv–xlii, and Cornelius Mayer's *Augustinus-Lexikon*, pp. XI–XXIV. Those used in this work are as follows:

c. Acad.	Contra Academicos [Against the Skeptics]
c. Jul. imp.	Contra Julianum opus imperfectum [Against Julian, an Unfinished Work]
conf.	Confessiones [Confessions]
civ. Dei	De civitate Dei [On the City of God]
doc. Chr.	De doctrina christiana [On Christian Teaching]
en. Ps.	Enarrationes in Psalmos [Expositions of the Psalms]
ep.	Epistulae [Letters]
ep. Jo.	In epistulam Johannis ad Parthos tractatus [Tractates on the First Letter of John]
Gn. litt.	De Genesi ad litteram [On the Literal Interpretation of Genesis]
gr. et pecc. or.	De gratia Christi et de peccato originali [On the Grace of Christ and Original Sin]
Jo. ev. tr.	In Johannis evangelium tractatus [Tractates on the Gospel of John]
nat. et gr.	De natura et gratia [On Nature and Grace]
pecc. mer.	De peccatorum meritis et remissione et de baptismo parvulorum [On the Merits and Forgiveness of Sins and On Infant Baptism]
retr.	Retractationes [Reconsiderations]
s.	Sermones ad populum [Sermons to the People]
Simpl.	Ad Simplicianum de diversis quaestionibus [To Simplicianus, on Various Questions]
Trin.	De Trinitate [On the Trinity]
Vita	Possidius, Vita s. Augustini [Life of St. Augustine]

SERIES, TRANSLATIONS, AND REFERENCE WORKS

ACW   Ancient Christian Writers (New York: Newman Press / Paulist
             Press, 1946–)

AOW   Augustinus Opera-Werke, ed. Wilhelm Geerlings (Paderborn:
             Ferdinand Schöningh, 2002–)

AugEncy   Allan D. Fitzgerald, ed., *Augustine Through the Ages: An Encyclopedia*
             (Grand Rapids: Wm. B. Eerdmans, 1999)

Aug-Lex   Cornelius Mayer, ed., *Augustinus-Lexikon* (Basel: Schwabe, 1986–)

BA   *Bibliothèque Augustinienne*, Oeuvres de saint Augustin (Paris: Desclée
             de Brouwer/Institut d'Études Augustiniennes, 1933–)

CCL   Corpus Christianorum, Series Latina (Turnholt: Brepols, 1953–)

CEASA   Collection des Études Augustiniennes, Série Antiquité (Paris:
             Institut d'Études Augustiniennes, 1955–)

CSEL   Corpus Scriptorum Ecclesiasticorum Latinorum (Vienna: Tempsky,
             1865–)

CWS   Classics of Western Spirituality (New York: Paulist Press, 1979–)

Dolbeau, VSS François Dolbeau, ed., *Vingt-six sermons au peuple d'Afrique, Retrouvé à
             Mayence*, CEASA 147 (Paris: Institut d'Études Augustiniennes, 1996)

FOTC   The Fathers of the Church (Washington, DC: The Catholic
             University of America Press, 1947–)

Geerlings   Wilhelm Geerlings, ed. and trans., *Possidius: Vita Augustini*,
             Augustinus Opera-Werke (Paderborn: Ferdinand Schöningh, 2005)

Green   R. P. H. Green, ed., *Augustine: De doctrina christiana*, Oxford Early
             Christian Texts (New York: Oxford University Press, 1995)

LCC   Library of Christian Classics (Philadelphia: Westminster Press,
             1953–1966)

LXX   *Septuaginta*, ed. A. Rahlfs (Stuttgart: Deutsche Bibelgesellschaft,
             2006)

MA   *Miscellanea Agostiniana*, 2 vols. (Rome: Tipografia Poliglotta
             Vaticana, 1930–1931)

NBA   Nuova Biblioteca Agostiniana, Opere de S. Agostino, edizione
             latino-italiano (Rome: Città Nuova, 1965-)

NPNF   Nicene and Post-Nicene Fathers, 1st series (Oxford: 1887; reprint:
             Peabody, MA: Hendrickson, 1995)

O'Donnell   James J. O'Donnell, ed., *Augustine: Confessions*, 3 vols. (Oxford:
             Clarendon Press, 1992)

OECS   Oxford Early Christian Studies, ed. Gillian Clark and Andrew
             Louth (New York and Oxford: Oxford University Press, 1993–)

PL   Patrologia Latina, ed. J.-P. Migne (Paris: 1844–1864)

PLS   Patrologiae Cursus Completus, Series Latina, Supplementum, 3 vols., ed. A. Hamman (Paris: Éditions Garnier Frères, 1958–1963)

SC   Sources chrétiennes (Paris: Éditions du Cerf, 1942–)

WSA   The Works of St. Augustine: A Translation for the 21st Century, ed. John Rotelle and Boniface Ramsey (Hyde Park, NY: New City Press, 1990–)

THE WORKS OF AUGUSTINE
Texts and Translations

LATIN TEXTS: Nearly all of Augustine's works can be found in J.- P. Migne, Patrologia Latina, vol. 32–47. Migne reproduced the excellent 17th-century edition of the Benedictines of St. Maur. This includes almost everything except certain letters (notably the 31 letters discovered by Johannes Divjak in 1980) and several hundred sermons (notably the 26 sermons discovered by François Dolbeau in 1990). The Italian publishers of Augustine's works, the Nuova Biblioteca Agostiniana (NBA), have provided a valuable service to students of Augustine by posting this classic Maurist edition on the Internet:http://www.augustinus.it/latino/index.htm. This older Patrologia Latina (PL) edition is slowly being replaced by modern critical editions in the Corpus Scriptorum Ecclesiasticorum Latinorum (CSEL) and the Corpus Christianorum, Series Latina (CCL). The excellent, but still incomplete, Bibliothèque Augustinienne (BA) has the Latin text with a French translation on facing pages, and includes lengthy introductions and notes.

ENGLISH TRANSLATIONS: 30 volumes of the Fathers of the Church (FOTC) series (Washington, DC: The Catholic University of America Press) are devoted to the works of Augustine, and these have formed a core for this anthology. An older translation, done in the 19th century, is the large 8-volume collection from the 1st series of the Nicene and Post-Nicene Fathers (NPNF) (1887; reprint: Peabody, MA: Hendrickson, 1995); these volumes are also available online at various Internet websites. Other volumes are in other series such as Ancient Christian Writers (ACW) and Library of Christian Classics (LCC). The entire Augustinian corpus is gradually being translated into English; see John E. Rotelle and Boniface Ramsey, eds., The Works of Saint Augustine: A Translation for the 21st Century (WSA).

Below is a listing of the complete works of Augustine arranged by Latin title. In each case, I have listed the major editions of the Latin text, as well as major English translations. I have done so using the standard abbreviations

(PL, CSEL, etc.); for the Latin critical editions and for the English translations, I have listed the date of publication within the parentheses. I have listed the English translations from the FOTC series first, then those from the WSA, then other major ones.

Acta contra Fortunatum Manichaeum [Debate with Fortunatus, a Manichee].

LATIN TEXT: PL 42:111–30. CSEL 25.1 (1891):83–112. BA 17 (1961):132–93.

ENGLISH TRANS.: Roland J. Teske, trans., *The Manichean Debate*, WSA I/19 (2006):145–62. A. H. Newman, trans., *The Writings Against the Manichaeans and the Donatists*, NPNF 4 (1887):113–24.

Ad Catholicos fratres / De unitate ecclesiae [To the Catholic Members of the Church/On the Unity of the Church].

LATIN TEXT: PL 43:391–446. CSEL 52 (1909):231–322. BA 28 (1963):502–707.

Ad inquisitiones Januarii [Responses to Januarius] = Letters 54–55.[1]

LATIN TEXT: PL 33:199–223. CSEL 34.2 (1898):158–213. CCL 31 (2004):226–65.

ENGLISH TRANS.: Wilfrid Parsons, trans., *Letters 1–82*, FOTC 12 (1951):252–93. Roland J. Teske, trans., *Letters 1–99*, WSA II/1 (2001):209–36.

Ad Simplicianum de diversis quaestionibus [To Simplicianus, on Various Questions].

LATIN TEXT: PL 40:101–48. CCL 44 (1970):7–91. BA 10 (1952):410–579.

ENGLISH TRANS.: Boniface Ramsey, trans., *Responses to Miscellaneous Questions*, WSA I/12 (2008):175–231. John H. S. Burleigh, trans., *Augustine: Earlier Writings*, LCC 6 (1953):376–406 [Bk. I].

Adnotationes in Job [Comments on Job].

LATIN TEXT: PL 34:825–86. CSEL 28.2 (1895):509–628.

Adversus Judeaos [Against the Jews].

LATIN TEXT: PL 42:51–64.

ENGLISH TRANS.: Marie Liguori, trans., *Treatises on Marriage and Other Subjects*, FOTC 27 (1955):391–414.

Breviliculus conlationis cum Donatistis [A Summary of the Meeting with the Donatists].

LATIN TEXT: PL 43:613–50. CSEL 53 (1910):39–92. CCL 149A (1974):261–306. BA 32 (1965):94–243.

Confessiones [Confessions].

LATIN TEXT: PL 32:659–868. CSEL 33 (1896):1–388. CCL 27 (1981):1–273. BA 13–14 (1962; rev. ed.: 1992). James J. O'Donnell, ed., *Augustine: Confessions* (Oxford: Clarendon Press, 1992), 1:3–205.

ENGLISH TRANS.: Vernon J. Bourke, trans., *Confessions*, FOTC 21 (1953):3–456. Maria Boulding, trans., *Confessions*, WSA I/1 (1997):39–380. Henry Chadwick, trans.,

---

1. This and several other works, such as *De praesentia Dei* (= *ep.* 187), were listed by Augustine or Possidius as independent treatises, but these are now generally included as part of Augustine's correspondence.

Saint Augustine: Confessions, Oxford World's Classics (New York: Oxford University Press, 1992). Garry Wills, trans., Saint Augustine: Confessions (New York: Penguin, 2006). F. J. Sheed, trans., Augustine: Confessions, 2nd ed. (Indianapolis: Hackett, 2006).

Conlatio cum Maximino Arianorum episcopo [Debate with Maximinus, an Arian Bishop].
LATIN TEXT: PL 42:709–42.
ENGLISH TRANS.: Roland J. Teske, trans., Arianism and Other Heresies, WSA I/18 (1995):188–227.

Contra Academicos [Against the Skeptics].
LATIN TEXT: PL 32:905–58. CSEL 63 (1922):3–81. CCL 29 (1970):3–61. BA 4 (1948):14–203.
ENGLISH TRANS.: Denis J. Kavanagh, trans., Answer to Skeptics, FOTC 5 (1948):103–225. John J. O'Meara, trans., Against the Academics, ACW 12 (1951):35–151.

Contra Adimantum Manichaei discipulum [Against Adimantus, a Disciple of Mani].
LATIN TEXT: PL 42:129–72. CSEL 25.1 (1891):115–90. BA 17 (1961):218–375.
ENGLISH TRANS.: Roland J. Teske, trans., The Manichean Debate, WSA I/19 (2006):176–223.

Contra adversarium legis et prophetarum [Against Adversaries of the Law and the Prophets].
LATIN TEXT: PL 42:603–66. CCL 49 (1985):35–131.
ENGLISH TRANS.: Roland J. Teske, trans., Arianism and Other Heresies, WSA I/18 (1995):357–449.

Contra Cresconium grammaticum partis Donati [Against Cresconius, a Donatist Grammarian].
LATIN TEXT: PL 43:445–594. CSEL 52 (1909):325–582. BA 31 (1968):70–643.

Contra Donatistas post conlationem [Against the Donatists, After the Conference].
LATIN TEXT: PL 43:651–90. CSEL 53 (1910):97–162. BA 32 (1965):248–393.

Contra duas epistulas Pelagianorum [Against Two Letters of the Pelagians].
LATIN TEXT: PL 44:549–638. CSEL 60 (1913):423–570. BA 23 (1974):312–657.
ENGLISH TRANS.: Roland J. Teske, trans., Answer to the Pelagians II, WSA I/24 (1998):116–219. R. E. Wallis, trans., Anti-Pelagian Writings, NPNF 5 (1887):377–434.

Contra epistulam Manichaei quam vocant fundamenti [Against the "Foundation Letter" of Mani].
LATIN TEXT: PL 42:173–206. CSEL 25.1 (1891):193–248. BA 17 (1961):390–507.
ENGLISH TRANS.: Roland J. Teske, trans., The Manichean Debate, WSA I/19 (2006):234–67. R. Stothert, trans., The Writings Against the Manichaeans and the Donatists, NPNF 4 (1887):129–50.

Contra epistulam Parmeniani [Against the Letter of Parmenian].
LATIN TEXT: PL 43:33–108. CSEL 51 (1908):19–141. BA 28 (1963):208–481.

Contra Faustum Manichaeum [Against Faustus, a Manichee].

LATIN TEXT: PL 42:207–518. CSEL 25.1 (1891):251–797.

ENGLISH TRANS.: Roland J. Teske, trans., *Answer to Faustus, a Manichean*, WSA I/20 (2007):69–431. R. Stothert, trans., *The Writings Against the Manichaeans and the Donatists*, NPNF 4 (1887):155–345.

Contra Felicem Manichaeum [Against Felix, a Manichee].

LATIN TEXT: PL 42:519–52. CSEL 25.2 (1892):801–52. BA 17 (1961):644–757.

ENGLISH TRANS.: Roland J. Teske, trans., *The Manichean Debate*, WSA I/19 (2006):280–316.

Contra Gaudentium Donatistarum episcopum [Against Gaudentius, a Donatist Bishop].

LATIN TEXT: PL 43:707–52. CSEL 53 (1910):201–74. BA 32 (1965):510–685.

Contra Julianum [Against Julian].

LATIN TEXT: PL 44:641–874.

ENGLISH TRANS.: Matthew A. Schumacher, trans., *Against Julian*, FOTC 35 (1957):3–396. Roland J. Teske, trans., *Answer to the Pelagians II*, WSA I/24 (1998):268–536.

Contra Julianum opus imperfectum [Against Julian, an Unfinished Work].

LATIN TEXT: PL 45:1049–608. CSEL 85.1 (1974) [Bks. 1–3]; CSEL 85.2 (2004) [Bks. 4–6].

ENGLISH TRANS.: Roland J. Teske, trans., *Answer to the Pelagians III*, WSA I/25 (1999):55–726.

Contra litteras Petiliani [Against the Letters of Petilian].

LATIN TEXT: PL 43:245–388. CSEL 52 (1909):3–227. BA 30 (1967):132–745.

ENGLISH TRANS.: J. R. King, trans., *The Writings Against the Manichaeans and the Donatists*, NPNF 4 (1887):519–628.

Contra Maximinum Arianum [Against Maximinus, an Arian].

LATIN TEXT: PL 42:743–814.

ENGLISH TRANS.: Roland J. Teske, trans., *Arianism and Other Heresies*, WSA I/18 (1995):246–336.

Contra mendacium [Against Lying].

LATIN TEXT: PL 40:517–48. CSEL 41 (1900):469–528. BA 2 (1948):350–453.

ENGLISH TRANS.: Harold B. Jaffee, trans., *Treatises on Various Subjects*, FOTC 16 (1952):125–79. H. Browne, trans., *On the Holy Trinity, Doctrinal Treatises, Moral Treatises*, NPNF 3 (1887):481–500.

Contra Priscillianistas et Origenistas [Against the Priscillians and the Origenists].

LATIN TEXT: PL 42:669–78. CCL 49 (1985):165–78.

ENGLISH TRANS.: Roland J. Teske, trans., *Arianism and Other Heresies*, WSA I/18 (1995):104–15.

Contra Secundinum Manichaeum. [*Against Secundinus, a Manichee*].

LATIN TEXT: PL 42:577–602. CSEL 25.2 (1892):905–47. BA 17 (1961):538–633.

ENGLISH TRANS.: Roland J. Teske, trans., *The Manichean Debate*, WSA I/19 (2006):363–90.

Contra sermonem Arianorum [*Against an Arian Sermon*].

LATIN TEXT: PL 42:683–708. CSEL 92 (2000):47–113.

ENGLISH TRANS.: Roland J. Teske, trans., *Arianism and Other Heresies*, WSA I/18 (1995):141–71.

De adulterinis conjugiis [*On Adulterous Marriages*].

LATIN TEXT: PL 40:451–86. CSEL 41 (1900):347–410. BA 2 (1948):108–233.

ENGLISH TRANS.: Charles T. Huegelmeyer, trans., *Treatises on Marriage and Other Subjects*, FOTC 27 (1955):61–132. Ray Kearney, trans., *Marriage and Virginity*, WSA I/9 (1999):142–85.

De agone christiano [*On the Christian Struggle*].

LATIN TEXT: PL 40:289–310. CSEL 41 (1900):101–38. BA 1 (1949):372–435.

ENGLISH TRANS.: Robert P. Russell, trans., *The Christian Combat*, FOTC 2 (1947):315–53.

De anima et eius origine [*On the Soul and Its Origin*].

LATIN TEXT: PL 44:475–548. CSEL 60 (1913):303–419. BA 22 (1975):376–667.

ENGLISH TRANS.: Roland J. Teske, trans., *Answer to the Pelagians* [*I*], WSA I/23 (1997):473–561. P. Holmes, trans., *Anti-Pelagian Writings*, NPNF 5 (1887):315–71.

De animae quantitate [*On the Greatness of the Soul*].

LATIN TEXT: PL 32:1035–80. CSEL 89 (1986):131–231. BA 5 (1948):226–397.

ENGLISH TRANS.: John J. McMahon, trans., *The Magnitude of the Soul*, FOTC 4 (1947):59–149. Joseph M. Colleran, trans., *The Greatness of the Soul*, ACW 9 (1950):13–112.

De baptismo [*On Baptism*].

LATIN TEXT: PL 43:107–244. CSEL 51 (1908):145–375. BA 29 (1964):56–575.

ENGLISH TRANS.: J. R. King, trans., *The Writings Against the Manichaeans and the Donatists*, NPNF 4 (1887):411–514.

De beata vita [*On the Happy Life*].

LATIN TEXT: PL 32:959–76. CSEL 63 (1922):89–116. CCL 29 (1970):65–85. BA 4.1 (1986):48–129.

ENGLISH TRANS.: Ludwig Schopp, trans., *The Happy Life*, FOTC 5 (1948):43–84.
Mary T. Clark, trans., *Augustine of Hippo: Selected Writings*, CWS (New York: Paulist
Press, 1984), 167–93.

De bono conjugali [On the Good of Marriage].

LATIN TEXT: PL 40:373–96. CSEL 41 (1900):187–231. BA 2 (1948):22–99.

ENGLISH TRANS.: Charles T. Wilcox, trans., *Treatises on Marriage and Other Subjects*,
FOTC 27 (1955):9–51. Ray Kearney, trans., *Marriage and Virginity*, WSA I/9 (1999):33–61.
C. L. Cornish, trans., *On the Holy Trinity, Doctrinal Treatises, Moral Treatises*, NPNF 3
(1887):399–413.

De bono viduitatis [On the Good of Widowhood].

LATIN TEXT: PL 40:431–50. CSEL 41 (1900):305–43. BA 3 (1949):234–305.

ENGLISH TRANS.: M. C. Eagan, trans., *Treatises on Various Subjects*, FOTC 16
(1952):279–319. Ray Kearney, trans., *Marriage and Virginity*, WSA I/9 (1999):113–36.
C. L. Cornish, trans., *On the Holy Trinity, Doctrinal Treatises, Moral Treatises*, NPNF 3
(1887):441–54.

De catechizandis rudibus [On Catechizing Beginners].

LATIN TEXT: PL 40:309–48. CCL 46 (1969):121–78. BA 11.1 (1991):44–231.

ENGLISH TRANS.: Raymond Canning, trans., *Instructing Beginners in Faith*, Augustine
Series, vol. 5 (Hyde Park, NY: New City Press, 2006), 53–173. Joseph P. Christopher,
trans., *The First Catechetical Instruction*, ACW 2 (1946):13–87. S. D. F. Salmond, trans., *On
the Holy Trinity, Doctrinal Treatises, Moral Treatises*, NPNF 3 (1887):283–314.

De civitate Dei [On the City of God].

LATIN TEXT: PL 41:13–804. CSEL 40.1–2 (1899–1900). CCL 47–48 (1955):1–866. BA
33–37 (1959–1960).

ENGLISH TRANS.: D. B. Zema and G. G. Walsh, trans., *The City of God*, FOTC 8
(1950) [Bks. 1–7]; G. G. Walsh and G. Monahan, trans., FOTC 14 (1952) [Bks. 8–16];
G. G. Walsh and D. J. Honan, FOTC 24 (1954) [Bks. 17–22]. R. W. Dyson, trans., *The
City of God Against the Pagans*, Cambridge Texts in the History of Political Thought
(Cambridge: Cambridge University Press, 1998). Henry Bettenson, trans., *City of God*,
Penguin Classics (New York: Penguin Books, 1972). Marcus Dods, trans., *City of God*,
NPNF 2 (1887):1–511.

De consensu evangelistarum [On the Agreement among the Evangelists].

LATIN TEXT: PL 34:1041–230. CSEL 43 (1904):1–418.

ENGLISH TRANS.: S. D. F. Salmond, trans., *Sermon on the Mount, Harmony of the
Gospels, Homilies on the Gospels*, NPNF 6 (1888):77–236.

De continentia [On Continence].

LATIN TEXT: PL 40:349–72. CSEL 41 (1900):141–83. BA 3 (1949):22–101.

ENGLISH TRANS.: Mary Francis McDonald, trans., *Treatises on Various Subjects*, FOTC
16 (1952):189–231. Ray Kearney, trans., *Marriage and Virginity*, WSA I/9 (1999):192–216.
C. L. Cornish, trans., *On the Holy Trinity, Doctrinal Treatises, Moral Treatises*, NPNF 3
(1887):379–93.

De correctione Donatistarum [*On the Correction of the Donatists*] = Letter 185.

LATIN TEXT: PL 33:792–815. CSEL 57 (1911):1–44.

ENGLISH TRANS.: Wilfrid Parsons, trans., *Letters 165–203*, FOTC 30 (1955):141–90. Roland J. Teske, trans., *Letters 156–210*, WSA II/3 (2004):178–206. J. R. King, trans., *The Writings Against the Manichaeans and the Donatists*, NPNF 4 (1887):633–51.

De correptione et gratia [*On Admonition and Grace*].

LATIN TEXT: PL 44:915–46. CSEL 92 (2000):219–80. BA 24 (1962):268–381.

ENGLISH TRANS.: John Courtney Murray, trans., *Admonition and Grace*, FOTC 2 (1947):245–305. Roland J. Teske, trans., *Answer to the Pelagians IV*, WSA I/26 (1999):109–45. R. E. Wallis, trans., *Anti-Pelagian Writings*, NPNF 5 (1887):471–91.

De cura pro mortuis gerenda [*On the Care of the Dead*].

LATIN TEXT: PL 40:591–610. CSEL 41 (1900):621–60. BA 2 (1948):462–523.

ENGLISH TRANS.: John Lacy, trans., *Treatises on Marriage and Other Subjects*, FOTC 27 (1955):351–84. H. Browne, trans., *On the Holy Trinity, Doctrinal Treatises, Moral Treatises*, NPNF 3 (1887):539–51.

De dialectica [*On Dialectic*].

LATIN TEXT: PL 32:1409–20.

ENGLISH TRANS.: B. Darrell Jackson, ed. and trans.; Jan Pinborg, ed., *Augustine: De Dialectica* (Boston/Dordrecht: D. Reidel Publishing Co., 1975), 82–121.

De disciplina christiana [*On Christian Discipline*] = Sermon 399.[2]

LATIN TEXT: PL 40:669–78. CCL 46 (1969):207–24.

ENGLISH TRANS.: Edmund Hill, trans., *Sermons (341–400) on Various Subjects*, WSA III/10 (1995):458–70.

De diversis quaestionibus octoginta tribus [*Eighty-Three Different Questions*].

LATIN TEXT: PL 40:11–100. CCL 44A (1975):11–249. BA 10 (1952):52–379.

ENGLISH TRANS.: David L. Mosher, trans., *Eighty-Three Different Questions*, FOTC 70 (1982):37–220. Boniface Ramsey, trans., *Responses to Miscellaneous Questions*, WSA I/12 (2008):31–157.

De divinatione daemonum [*On the Divination of Demons*].

LATIN TEXT: PL 40:581–92. CSEL 41 (1900):599–618. BA 10 (1952):654–93.

ENGLISH TRANS.: Ruth W. Brown, trans., *Treatises on Marriage and Other Subjects*, FOTC 27 (1955):421–40. Edmund Hill, trans., *On Christian Belief*, WSA I/8 (2005):204–17.

---

2. This and several other sermons (e.g., *De excidio urbis Romae*, *De symbolo ad catechumenos*, *De utilitate ieiunii*) circulated independently of Augustine's *Sermones ad populum*. Hill and others have recently renumbered these and integrated them into that larger collection. Following the *Aug-Lex* and the *AugEncy*, I have given each a separate listing.

De doctrina christiana [*On Christian Teaching*].

LATIN TEXT: PL 34:15–122. CSEL 80 (1963):3–169. CCL 32 (1962):1–167. BA 11.2 (1997):64–427. R. P. H. Green, ed., *Augustine: De doctrina christiana*, Oxford Early Christian Texts (Oxford/New York: Oxford University Press, 1995), 2–285.

ENGLISH TRANS.: John J. Gavigan, trans., *Christian Instruction*, FOTC 2 (1947):19– 235. Edmund Hill, trans., *Teaching Christianity*, WSA I/11 (1996):101–244. R. P. H. Green, trans., *Saint Augustine: On Christian Teaching*, Oxford World Classics (New York: Oxford University Press, 1997).

De dono perseverantiae [*On the Gift of Perseverance*].

LATIN TEXT: PL 45:993–1034. BA 24 (1962):600–765.

ENGLISH TRANS.: John A. Mourant and William J. Collinge, trans., *Four Anti-Pelagian Writings*, FOTC 86 (1992):271–337. Roland J. Teske, trans., *Answer to the Pelagians IV*, WSA I/26 (1999):191–240. P. Holmes, trans., *Anti-Pelagian Writings*, NPNF 5 (1887):525–52.

De duabus animabus [*On the Two Souls*].

LATIN TEXT: PL 42:93–112. CSEL 25.1 (1891):51–80. BA 17 (1961):52–115.

ENGLISH TRANS.: Roland J. Teske, trans., *The Manichean Debate*, WSA I/19 (2006):117– 34. A. H. Newman, trans., *The Writings Against the Manichaeans and the Donatists*, NPNF 4 (1887):95–107.

De excidio urbis Romae [*On the Sack of the City of Rome*] = Sermon 397.

LATIN TEXT: PL 40:715–24. CCL 46 (1969):249–62.

ENGLISH TRANS.: Edmund Hill, trans., *Sermons (341–400) on Various Subjects*, WSA III/10 (1995):435–44.

De fide et operibus [*On Faith and Works*].

LATIN TEXT: PL 40:197–230. CSEL 41 (1900):35–97. BA 8 (1951):354–461.

ENGLISH TRANS.: Marie Liguori, trans., *Treatises on Marriage and Other Subjects*, FOTC 27 (1955):221–82. Ray Kearney, trans., *On Christian Belief*, WSA I/8 (2005):226–61. Gregory J. Lombardo, trans., *On Faith and Works*, ACW 48 (1988):7–56.

De fide et symbolo [*On Faith and the Creed*].

LATIN TEXT: PL 40:181–96. CSEL 41 (1900):3–32. BA 9 (1947):18–75.

ENGLISH TRANS.: Robert P. Russell, trans., *Treatises on Marriage and Other Subjects*, FOTC 27 (1955):315–45. Michael G. Campbell, trans., *On Christian Belief*, WSA I/8 (2005):155–74. John H. S. Burleigh, trans., *Augustine: Earlier Writings*, LCC 6 (1953):353– 69. S. D. F. Salmond, trans., *On the Holy Trinity, Doctrinal Treatises, Moral Treatises*, NPNF 3 (1887):321–33.

De fide rerum invisibilium [*On Faith in the Unseen*].

LATIN TEXT: PL 40:171–80. CCL 46 (1969):1–19. BA 8 (1951):310–41.

ENGLISH TRANS.: Roy J. Deferrari and Mary Francis McDonald, trans., *On Faith in Things Unseen*, FOTC 4 (1947):451–69. Michael G. Campbell, trans., *On Christian Belief*,

WSA I/8 (2005):183–94. C. L. Cornish, trans., *On the Holy Trinity, Doctrinal Treatises, Moral Treatises*, NPNF 3 (1887):337–43.

De Genesi ad litteram [On the Literal Interpretation of Genesis].

LATIN TEXT: PL 34:245–486. CSEL 28.1 (1894):3–435. BA 48–49 (1972).

ENGLISH TRANS.: Edmund Hill, trans., *On Genesis*, WSA I/13 (2002):168–506. John Hammond Taylor, trans., *The Literal Meaning of Genesis*, ACW 41–42 (1982).

De Genesi ad litteram liber imperfectus [On the Literal Interpretation of Genesis, an Unfinished Book].

LATIN TEXT: PL 34:219–46. CSEL 28.1 (1894):459–503. BA 50 (2004):396–505.

ENGLISH TRANS.: Roland J. Teske, trans., *On Genesis*, FOTC 84 (1991):145–88. Edmund Hill, trans., *On Genesis*, WSA I/13 (2002):114–51.

De Genesi adversus Manichaeos [On Genesis, Against the Manichees].

LATIN TEXT: PL 34:173–220. CSEL 91 (1998):67–172. BA 50 (2004):156–383.

ENGLISH TRANS.: Roland J. Teske, trans., *On Genesis*, FOTC 84 (1991):47–141. Edmund Hill, trans., *On Genesis*, WSA I/13 (2002):39–102.

De gestis Pelagii [On the Deeds of Pelagius].

LATIN TEXT: PL 44:319–60. CSEL 42 (1902):51–122. BA 21 (1966):432–579.

ENGLISH TRANS.: John Mourant and William J. Collinge, trans., *Four Anti-Pelagian Writings*, FOTC 86 (1992):111–77. Roland J. Teske, trans., *Answer to the Pelagians [I]*, WSA I/23 (1997):336–81. P. Holmes, trans., *Anti-Pelagian Writings*, NPNF 5 (1887):183–212.

De gratia Christi et de peccato originali [On the Grace of Christ and Original Sin].

LATIN TEXT: PL 44:359–410. CSEL 42 (1902):125–206. BA 22 (1975):52–269.

ENGLISH TRANS.: Roland J. Teske, trans., *Answer to the Pelagians [I]*, WSA I/23 (1997):403–63. P. Holmes, trans., *Anti-Pelagian Writings*, NPNF 5 (1887):217–55.

De gratia et libero arbitrio [On Grace and Free Will].

LATIN TEXT: PL 44:881–912. BA 24 (1962):90–207.

ENGLISH TRANS.: Robert P. Russell, trans., *Grace and Free Will*, FOTC 59 (1968):250–308. Roland J. Teske, trans., *Answer to the Pelagians IV*, WSA I/26 (1999):71–106. P. Holmes, trans., *Anti-Pelagian Writings*, NPNF 5 (1887):443–65.

De gratia Testamenti Novi [On the Grace of the New Testament] = Letter 140.

LATIN TEXT: PL 33:538–77. CSEL 44 (1904):155–234.

ENGLISH TRANS.: Wilfrid Parsons, trans., *Letters 131–164*, FOTC 20 (1953):58–136. Roland J. Teske, trans., *Letters 100–155*, WSA II/2 (2003):242–89.

De haeresibus. [On Heresies].

LATIN TEXT: PL 42:21–50. CCL 46 (1969):286–345.

ENGLISH TRANS.: Roland J. Teske, trans., *Arianism and Other Heresies*, WSA I/18

(1995):31–77. L. G. Müller, trans., *The De Haeresibus of Saint Augustine*, Patristic Studies 90 (Washington, DC: The Catholic University of America, 1956), 54–129.

De immortalitate animae [*On the Immortality of the Soul*].

LATIN TEXT: PL 32:1021–34. CSEL 89 (1986):101–28. BA 5 (1948):170–219.

ENGLISH TRANS.: Ludwig Schopp, trans., *The Immortality of the Soul*, FOTC 4 (1947):15–47.

De libero arbitrio [*On Free Will or On Free Choice*].

LATIN TEXT: PL 32:1221–310. CSEL 74 (1956):3–154. CCL 29 (1970):211–321. BA 6 (1952):136–471.

ENGLISH TRANS.: Robert P. Russell, trans., *The Free Choice of the Will*, FOTC 59 (1968):72–241. John H. S. Burleigh, trans., *Augustine: Earlier Writings*, LCC 6 (1953):113–217. Mark Pontifex, trans., *The Problem of Free Choice*, ACW 22 (1955):35–220.

De magistro [*On the Teacher*].

LATIN TEXT: PL 32:1193–220. CSEL 77.1 (1961):3–55. CCL 29 (1970):157–203. BA 6 (1952):14–121.

ENGLISH TRANS.: Robert P. Russell, trans., *The Teacher*, FOTC 59 (1968):7–61. John H. S. Burleigh, trans., *Augustine: Earlier Writings*, LCC 6 (1953):69–101. Joseph M. Colleran, trans., *The Teacher*, ACW 9 (1950):129–86.

De mendacio [*On Lying*].

LATIN TEXT: PL 40:487–518. CSEL 41 (1900):413–66. BA 2 (1948):240–343.

ENGLISH TRANS.: Mary Sarah Muldowney, trans., *Treatises on Various Subjects*, FOTC 16 (1952):53–110. H. Browne, trans., *On the Holy Trinity, Doctrinal Treatises, Moral Treatises*, NPNF 3 (1887):457–77.

De moribus ecclesiae Catholicae et de moribus Manichaeorum [*On the Catholic and the Manichean Ways of Life*].

LATIN TEXT: PL 32:1309–78. CSEL 90 (1992):3–156. BA 1 (1949):136–367.

ENGLISH TRANS.: D. A. and I. J. Gallagher, trans., *The Catholic and Manichaean Ways of Life*, FOTC 56 (1966):3–117. Roland J. Teske, trans., *The Manichean Debate*, WSA I/19 (2006):31–103. R. Stothert, trans., *Writings Against the Manichaeans and the Donatists*, NPNF 4 (1887):41–89.

De musica [*On Music*].

LATIN TEXT: PL 32:1081–194. BA 7 (1947):20–479.

ENGLISH TRANS.: Robert C. Taliaferro, trans., *On Music*, FOTC 4 (1947):169–379.

De natura boni [*On the Nature of the Good*].

LATIN TEXT: PL 42:551–72. CSEL 25.2 (1892):855–89. BA 1 (1949):440–509.

ENGLISH TRANS.: Roland J. Teske, trans., *The Manichean Debate*, WSA I/19 (2006):325–45. John H. S. Burleigh, trans., *Augustine: Earlier Writings*, LCC 6 (1953):326–48. A. H. Newman, trans., *Writings Against the Manichaeans and the Donatists*, NPNF 4 (1887):351–65.

De natura et gratia [*On Nature and Grace*].

LATIN TEXT: PL 44:247–90. CSEL 60 (1913):233–99. BA 21 (1966):244–413.

ENGLISH TRANS.: John A. Mourant and William J. Collinge, trans., *Four Anti-Pelagian Writings*, FOTC 86 (1992):22–90. Roland J. Teske, trans., *Answer to the Pelagians* [I], WSA I/23 (1997):225–75. P. Holmes, trans., *Anti-Pelagian Writings*, NPNF 5 (1887):121–51.

De nuptiis et concupiscentia [*On Marriage and Concupiscence*].

LATIN TEXT: PL 44:413–74. CSEL 42 (1909):211–319. BA 23 (1974):52–289.

ENGLISH TRANS.: Roland J. Teske, trans., *Answer to the Pelagians II*, WSA I/24 (1998):28–96. P. Holmes, trans., *Anti-Pelagian Writings*, NPNF 5 (1887):263–308.

De octo Dulcitii quaestionibus [*On Eight Questions from Dulcitius*].

LATIN TEXT: PL 40:147–70. CCL 44A (1975):253–97. BA 10 (1952):588–643.

ENGLISH TRANS.: Mary E. Deferrari, trans., *Treatises on Various Subjects*, FOTC 16 (1952):427–66. Boniface Ramsey, trans., *Responses to Miscellaneous Questions*, WSA I/12 (2008):241–69.

De octo quaestionibus ex Veteri Testamento [*On Eight Questions from the Old Testament*].

LATIN TEXT: PL 35:1374–76 [quaes. 1–3]; PLS 2 (1960):386–89 [quaes. 4–8]. MA 2 (1931):333–37. CCL 33 (1958):469–72.

De opere monachorum [*On the Work of Monks*].

LATIN TEXT: PL 40:547–82. CSEL 41 (1900):531–96. BA 3 (1949):316–431.

ENGLISH TRANS.: Mary Sarah Muldowney, trans., *Treatises on Various Subjects*, FOTC 16 (1952):331–94. H. Browne, trans., *On the Holy Trinity, Doctrinal Treatises, Moral Treatises*, NPNF 3 (1887):503–24.

De ordine [*On Order*].

LATIN TEXT: PL 32:977–1020. CSEL 63 (1922):121–85. CCL 29 (1970):89–137. BA 4.2 (1997):68–329.

ENGLISH TRANS.: Robert P. Russell, trans. *Divine Providence and the Problem of Evil*, FOTC 5 (1948):239–332.

De origine animae et de sententia Jacobi [*On the Origin of the Soul and On a Verse in James*] = Letters 166–67.

LATIN TEXT: PL 33:720–41. CSEL 44 (1904):545–609.

ENGLISH TRANS.: Wilfrid Parsons, trans., *Letters 165–203*, FOTC 30 (1955):6–49. Roland J. Teske, trans., *Letters 156–210*, WSA II/3 (2004):77–104.

De patientia [*On Patience*].

LATIN TEXT: PL 40:611–26. CSEL 41 (1900):663–91. BA 2 (1948):530–77.

ENGLISH TRANS.: Luanne Meagher, trans., *Treatises on Various Subjects*, FOTC 16 (1952):237–64. H. Browne, trans., *On the Holy Trinity, Doctrinal Treatises, Moral Treatises*, NPNF 3 (1887):527–36.

De peccatorum meritis et remissione et de baptismo parvulorum [*On the Merits and Forgiveness of Sins and On Infant Baptism*].

LATIN TEXT: PL 44:109–200. CSEL 60 (1913):3–151.

ENGLISH TRANS.: Roland J. Teske, trans., *Answer to the Pelagians [I]*, WSA I/23 (1997):34–137. P. Holmes, trans., *Anti-Pelagian Writings*, NPNF 5 (1887):15–78.

De perfectione justitiae hominis [*On the Perfection of Human Righteousness*].

LATIN TEXT: PL 44:291–318. CSEL 42 (1902):3–48. BA 21 (1966):126–219.

ENGLISH TRANS.: Roland J. Teske, trans., *Answer to the Pelagians [I]*, WSA I/23 (1997):289–316. P. Holmes, trans., *Anti-Pelagian Writings*, NPNF 5 (1887):159–76.

De praedestinatione sanctorum [*On the Predestination of the Saints*].

LATIN TEXT: PL 44:959–92. BA 24 (1962):464–597.

ENGLISH TRANS.: John A. Mourant and William J. Collinge, trans., *Four Anti-Pelagian Writings*, FOTC 86 (1992):218–70. Roland J. Teske, trans., *Answer to the Pelagians IV*, WSA I/26 (1999):149–87. R. E. Wallis, trans., *Anti-Pelagian Writings*, NPNF 5 (1887):497–519.

De praesentia Dei [*On the Presence of God*] = Letter 187.

LATIN TEXT: PL 33:832–48. CSEL 57 (1911):81–119.

ENGLISH TRANS.: Wilfrid Parsons, trans., *Letters 165–203*, FOTC 30 (1955):221–55. Roland J. Teske, trans., *Letters 156–210*, WSA II/3 (2004):230–50. Mary T. Clark, trans., *Augustine of Hippo: Selected Writings*, CWS (New York: Paulist Press, 1984), 403–25.

De sancta virginitate [*On Holy Virginity*].

LATIN TEXT: PL 40:397–428. CSEL 41 (1900):235–302. BA 3 (1949):110–227.

ENGLISH TRANS.: John McQuade, trans., *Treatises on Marriage and Other Subjects*, FOTC 27 (1955):143–212. Ray Kearney, trans., *Marriage and Virginity*, WSA I/9 (1999):68–107. C. L. Cornish, trans., *On the Holy Trinity, Doctrinal Treatises, Moral Treatises*, NPNF 3 (1887):417–38.

De sermone Domini in monte [*On the Lord's Sermon on the Mount*].

LATIN TEXT: PL 34:1229–308. CCL 35 (1967):1–188.

ENGLISH TRANS.: Denis J. Kavanagh, trans., *Commentary on the Lord's Sermon on the Mount*, FOTC 11 (1951):19–199. J. J. Jepson, trans., *The Lord's Sermon on the Mount*, ACW 5 (1948):11–174. W. Findlay, trans., *Sermon on the Mount, Harmony of the Gospels, Homilies on the Gospels*, NPNF 6 (1888):3–63.

De spiritu et littera [*On the Spirit and the Letter*].

LATIN TEXT: PL 44:201–46. CSEL 60 (1913):155–229.

ENGLISH TRANS.: Roland J. Teske, trans., *Answer to the Pelagians [I]*, WSA I/23 (1997):150–202. John Burnaby, trans., *Augustine: Later Works*, LCC 8 (1955):195–250. P. Holmes, trans., *Anti-Pelagian Writings*, NPNF 5 (1887):83–114.

De symbolo ad catechumenos [*On the Creed to Catechumens*] = Sermon 398.

LATIN TEXT: PL 40:627–36. CCL 46 (1969):185–99.

ENGLISH TRANS.: Marie Liguori, trans., *Treatises on Marriage and Other Subjects*, FOTC 27 (1955):289–307. Edmund Hill, trans., *Sermons (341–400) on Various Subjects*, WSA III/10 (1995):445–57. H. Browne, trans., *On the Holy Trinity, Doctrinal Treatises, Moral Treatises*, NPNF 3 (1887):369–75.

De Trinitate [*On the Trinity*].

LATIN TEXT: PL 42:819–1098. CCL 50–50A (1968):25–535. BA 15–16 (1955).

ENGLISH TRANS.: Stephen McKenna, trans., *The Trinity*, FOTC 45 (1963):3–525. Edmund Hill, trans., *The Trinity*, WSA I/5 (1991):63–443. John Burnaby, trans., *Augustine: Later Works*, LCC 8 (1955):37–181 [Bks. 8–15]. Arthur W. Haddan, trans., *On the Holy Trinity, Doctrinal Treatises, Moral Treatises*, NPNF 3 (1887):17–228.

De unico baptismo contra Petilianum [*On the One Baptism in Answer to Petilian*].

LATIN TEXT: PL 43:595–614. CSEL 53 (1910):3–34. BA 31 (1968):664–737.

De utilitate credendi [*On the Advantage of Believing*].

LATIN TEXT: PL 42:65–92. CSEL 25.1 (1891):3–48. BA 8 (1951):208–301.

ENGLISH TRANS.: Luanne Meagher, trans., *The Advantage of Believing*, FOTC 4 (1947):391–442. Ray Kearney, trans., *On Christian Belief*, WSA I/8 (2005):116–48. John H. S. Burleigh, trans., *Augustine: Earlier Writings*, LCC 6 (1953):291–323. C. L. Cornish, trans., *On the Holy Trinity, Doctrinal Treatises, Moral Treatises*, NPNF 3 (1887):347–66.

De utilitate ieiunii [*On the Value of Fasting*] = Sermon 400.

LATIN TEXT: PL 40:707–16. CCL 46 (1969):231–41. BA 2 (1948):584–617.

ENGLISH TRANS.: Mary Sarah Muldowney, trans., *Treatises on Various Subjects*, FOTC 16 (1952):403–22. Edmund Hill, trans., *Sermons (341–400) on Various Subjects*, WSA III/10 (1995):471–83.

De vera religione [*On True Religion*].

LATIN TEXT: PL 34:121–72. CSEL 77.2 (1961):3–81. CCL 32 (1962):187–260. BA 8 (1951):22–191.

ENGLISH TRANS.: Edmund Hill, trans., *On Christian Belief*, WSA I/8 (2005):29–104. John H. S. Burleigh, trans., *Augustine: Earlier Writings*, LCC 6 (1953):225–83.

De videndo Dei [*On Seeing God*] = Letter 147.

LATIN TEXT: PL 33:596–622. CSEL 44 (1904):274–331.

ENGLISH TRANS.: Wilfrid Parsons, trans., *Letters 131–164*, FOTC 20 (1953):170–224. Roland J. Teske, trans., *Letters 100–155*, WSA II/2 (2003):317–49. Mary T. Clark, trans., *Augustine of Hippo: Selected Writings*, CWS (New York: Paulist Press, 1984), 365–402.

Enarrationes in Psalmos [*Expositions of the Psalms*].

LATIN TEXT: PL 36:67–1028 [*en. Ps.* 1–79] and 37:1033–966 [*en. Ps.* 80–150]. CSEL 93.1A (2003) [*en. Ps.* 1–32], CSEL 94.1 (2004) [*en. Ps.* 51–60], CSEL 95.3–5 (2001–2004) [*en. Ps.* 119–50]. CCL 38–40 (1956):1–2196. BA 57A (2009):116–549 [*en. Ps.* 1–16].

ENGLISH TRANS.: Maria Boulding, trans., *Expositions of the Psalms*, 6 vol., WSA III/15–20 (2000–2004). Charles Marriot and Edward Pusey, eds., *Expositions on the Book of Psalms*, Library of the Fathers (Oxford: J. H. Parker, 1847–1857).

Enchiridion (De fide, spe, et caritate) [*Enchiridion (On Faith, Hope, and Love)*].

LATIN TEXT: PL 40:231–90. CCL 46 (1969):49–114. BA 9 (1947):102–327.

ENGLISH TRANS.: B. M. Peebles, trans., *Faith, Hope, and Charity*, FOTC 2 (1947):369–472. Bruce Harbert, trans., *On Christian Belief*, WSA I/8 (2005):273–343. Louis A. Arand, trans., *Faith, Hope, and Charity*, ACW 3 (1947):11–112. Albert C. Outler, trans., *Augustine: Confessions and Enchiridion*, LCC 7 (1955):337–412. J. F. Shaw, trans., *On the Trinity, Doctrinal Treatises, Moral Treatises*, NPNF 3 (1887):237–76.

Epistulae ad Romanos inchoata expositio [*Unfinished Commentary on the Letter to the Romans*].

LATIN TEXT: PL 35:2087–106. CSEL 84 (1971):145–81.

ENGLISH TRANS.: Paula Fredriksen Landes, trans., *Augustine on Romans*, SBL Texts and Translations 23/Early Christian Literature series 6 (Chico, CA: Scholars Press, 1982), 52–89.

Epistulae (1–270) [*Letters (1–270)*].

LATIN TEXT: PL 33:61–1094. CSEL 34.1–2, 44, 57 (1895–1911). CCL 31–31A (2004–2005) [ep. 1–100].

ENGLISH TRANS.: Wilfrid Parsons, trans., *Letters*, FOTC 12, 18, 20, 30, 32 (1951–1956). Roland J. Teske, trans., *Letters*, 4 vols., WSA II/1–4 (2001–2005).

Epistulae 1*–29* [*Letters 1*–29* (Divjak)*].

LATIN TEXT: CSEL 88 (1981):3–138. BA 46B (1987):42–417.

ENGLISH TRANS.: Robert B. Eno, trans., *Letters 1*–29**, FOTC 81 (1989):9–195. Roland J. Teske, trans., *Letters 211–270, 1*–29**, WSA II/4 (2005):227–334.

Expositio epistulae ad Galatas [*Commentary on the Letter to the Galatians*].

LATIN TEXT: PL 35:2105–48. CSEL 84 (1971):55–141.

ENGLISH TRANS.: Eric Plumer, trans., *Augustine's Commentary on Galatians*, Oxford Early Christian Studies (New York: Oxford University Press, 2003), 124–235.

Expositio quarundam propositionum ex epistula apostoli ad Romanos [*Commentary on Statements in the Letter of Paul to the Romans*].

LATIN TEXT: PL 35:2063–88. CSEL 84 (1971):3–52.

ENGLISH TRANS.: Paula Fredriksen Landes, trans., *Augustine on Romans*, SBL Texts and Translations 23/Early Christian Literature series 6 (Chico, CA: Scholars Press, 1982), 2–49.

Gesta cum Emerito [*Proceedings with Emeritus*].

LATIN TEXT: PL 43:697–706. CSEL 53 (1910):181–96. BA 32 (1965):450–87.

In epistulam Johannis ad Parthos tractatus [*Tractates on the First Letter of John*].

LATIN TEXT: PL 35:1977–2062. SC 75 (1961):104–439. BA 76 (2008):62–431.

ENGLISH TRANS.: John W. Rettig, trans., *Tractates on the First Epistle of John*, FOTC 92 (1995):121–277. Boniface Ramsey, trans., *Homilies on the First Epistle of John*, WSA III/14 (2008):19–158. John Burnaby, trans., *Augustine: Later Works*, LCC 8 (1955):259–348. H. Browne, trans., *Homilies on the First Epistle of John*, NPNF 7 (1887):459–526.

In Johannis evangelium tractatus [*Tractates on the Gospel of John*].

LATIN TEXT: PL 35:1379–976. CCL 36 (1954):1–688. BA 71–75 (1969–2003).

ENGLISH TRANS.: John W. Rettig, trans., *Tractates on the Gospel of John*, FOTC 78, 79, 88, 90, 92 (1988–1995). John Gibb and James Innes, trans., *Homilies on the Gospel of John*, NPNF 7 (1888):7–452.

Locutionum in Heptateuchum [*Sayings in the Heptateuch*].

LATIN TEXT: PL 34:485–546. CSEL 28.1 (1894):507–629. CCL 33 (1958):381–465.

Psalmus contra partem Donati [*Psalm Against the Donatists*].

LATIN TEXT: PL 43:23–32. CSEL 51 (1908):3–15. BA 28 (1963):150–91.

Quaestiones evangeliorum [*Questions on the Gospels*].

LATIN TEXT: PL 35:1321–64. CCL 44B (1980):1–118.

Quaestiones expositae contra paganos numero sex [*Six Questions Against Pagans*] = Letter 102.

LATIN TEXT: PL 33:370–86. CSEL 34.2 (1898):544–78.

ENGLISH TRANS.: Wilfrid Parsons, trans., *Letters 83–130*, FOTC 18 (1953):148–77. Roland J. Teske, trans., *Letters 100–155*, WSA II/2 (2003):20–39.

Quaestiones XVI in Matthaeum [*Sixteen Questions on Matthew*].

LATIN TEXT: PL 35:1365–74. CCL 44B (1980):119–40.

Quaestiones in Heptateuchum [*Questions on the Heptateuch*].

LATIN TEXT: PL 34:547–824. CSEL 28.2 (1895):3–506. CCL 33 (1958):1–377.

Regula [*The Rule*].

LATIN TEXT: PL 32:1377–84. Luc Verheijen, ed., *La Règle de saint Augustin*, vol. 1 (Paris: Institut d'Études Augustiniennes, 1967), 105–7, 148–52, 417–37.

ENGLISH TRANS.: George Lawless, trans., *Augustine of Hippo and His Monastic Rule* (Oxford: Clarendon Press, 1987), 74–118.

Retractationes [*Reconsiderations*].

LATIN TEXT: PL 32:583–656. CSEL 36 (1902):7–204. CCL 57 (1984):5–143. BA 12 (1950):266–559.

ENGLISH TRANS.: M. I. Bogan, trans., *The Retractations*, FOTC 60 (1968):3–272.

Sermo ad Caesariensis ecclesiae plebem [*A Sermon to the People of the Church of Caesarea*].

LATIN TEXT: PL 43:689–98. CSEL 53 (1910):167–78. BA 32(1965):416–45.

Sermones ad populum (1–396) [*Sermons to the People*].

LATIN TEXT: PL 38:23–1484 [*s.* 1–340]; PL 39:1493–736 [*s.* 341–96]. CCL 41 (1961) [*s.* 1–50]; CCL 41Aa (2008) [*s.* 51–70A]; CCL 41 Ba (2008) [*s.* 151–56].

ENGLISH TRANS.: Edmund Hill, trans., *Sermons*, 10 vols., WSA III/1–10 (1990–1995).

Sermones (Caillau, Denis, Etaix, Guelferbytanus, Morin, Wilmart, etc.) [*Miscellaneous Sermons*].[3]

LATIN TEXT: G. Morin, ed., *Miscellanea Agostiniana*, vol. 1: *Sancti Augustini Sermones post Maurinos reperti* (Rome: 1930):11–719. PLS 2 (1960):417–748; PLS 2B (1961):749–840.

ENGLISH TRANS.: Edmund Hill, trans., *Sermons*, WSA III/1–10 (1990–1995).

Sermones (Dolbeau) [*Dolbeau Sermons*].

LATIN TEXT: François Dolbeau, ed., *Vingt-six sermons au peuple d'Afrique, Retrouvé à Mayence*, CEASA 147 (Paris: Institut d'Études Augustiniennes, 1996). François Dolbeau, *Augustin et la prédication en Afrique: Recherches sur divers sermons authentiques, apocryphes ou anonymes*, CEASA 179 (Paris: Institut d'Études Augustiniennes, 2005).

ENGLISH TRANS.: Edmund Hill, trans., *Newly Discovered Sermons*, WSA III/11 (1997):25–410.

Soliloquia [*Soliloquies*].

LATIN TEXT: PL 32:869–904. CSEL 89 (1986):3–98. BA 5 (1948):24–163.

ENGLISH TRANS.: T. F. Gilligan, trans., *Soliloquies*, FOTC 5 (1948):343–426. John H. S. Burleigh, trans., *Augustine: Earlier Writings*, LCC 6 (1953):23–63. Charles C. Starbuck, trans., *Soliloquies*, NPNF 7 (1887):537–60.

Speculum [*The Mirror*].

LATIN TEXT: PL 34:887–1040. CSEL 12 (1887):3–285.

Possidius, *Indiculum* [*The Index*].

LATIN TEXT: MA 2 (1931):161–208. Wilhelm Geerlings, ed., *Possidius: Vita Augustini*, AOW (2005):114–37.

Possidius, *Vita s. Augustini* [*Life of Saint Augustine*].

LATIN TEXT: PL 32:33–66. Wilhelm Geerlings, ed., *Possidius: Vita Augustini*, AOW (2005):26–107.

ENGLISH TRANS.: Mary Magdeleine Muller and Roy J. Deferrari, trans., *Early Christian Biographies*, FOTC 15 (1952):73–124.

---

3. On the recent renumbering of these "post-Maurist" sermons, see Chapter 4.

AUGUSTINE

IN HIS OWN WORDS

Fourth-Century Italy and Roman North Africa

CHAPTER 1

CONFESSIONS

❧

Confessions is one of the uncontested classics of world literature. Even if Augustine had written no other work, this alone would have insured his lasting fame. *Confessions* is sometimes described as autobiography.[1] Calling it autobiography is at once true and untrue. It is true inasmuch as it narrates pivotal episodes from his life, from childhood through his dramatic conversion and baptism and ending with his mother's death in 387. But it is untrue in other ways. Augustine records only a handful of events within each of its first nine books, and few facts are given. Even attentive readers lose track of how old Augustine might be at different points or where certain scenes take place. There are also puzzling silences. In Book Four Augustine meditates on his deep sorrow over a friend's death, but he never bothers to give us the friend's name.

Confessions may be thin on facts, but it is long on meditation. Augustine offers detailed psychological self-analyses, and these often intrigue modern readers. *Confessions* is a history of Augustine's heart, a story told from the inside: how things felt to him, what they mean to him as he writes. We as readers get drawn in by the way Augustine reveals himself, by the way he invites us into his inner circle, making us his confidants as he explores the deep recesses of his memory. Psychological analysis, however, forms but one thread. Augustine's deepest concern is theological. *Confessions* is Augustine's attempt to read his life through biblical lenses, to trace out the way God's under-the-surface promptings subtly shaped the twisting and twisted coursings of his life. In *Confessions*, Augustine charts his personal salvation history.

---

1. The scholarly literature on *Confessions* is vast. See especially Brown, *Augustine of Hippo*, 7–124, 151–75; also Serge Lancel, *Saint Augustine*, trans. Antonia Nevill (London: SCM Press, 2002), 204–20; A. Solignac, *Les Confessions*, BA 13, 2nd ed. (1992). Essential is the paragraph-by-paragraph commentary by James O'Donnell, *Augustine: Confessions*, vol. 2–3 (Oxford: Clarendon Press, 1992). Other sources are listed in the "Suggestions for Further Reading."

Augustine composed *Confessions* between 397 and 401, beginning it soon after he became bishop of Hippo Regius.[2] The backward gaze of the bishop governs everything. It is a book only someone at mid-life might write. He sees God's subtle touches in unexpected places and in chance moments. He is alert to ambiguities and to mysteries. And while he repeatedly confesses wrongdoings and wrong thinkings, he also—often subtly—defends himself. *Confessions* can also be read as a document of grief, a chance to mourn life's losses: the death of friends like Nebridius, of his mother Monnica, and of his teenage son Adeodatus.

Be alert to Augustine's voice.[3] He asks more questions than he answers. He knows how tentative claims to truth are, whether psychological or historical, philosophical or theological. Especially striking is the way he speaks not to us, his readers, but to God. Properly speaking, *Confessions* is prayer, not autobiography. And so we readers come to the text as over-hearers, standing behind Augustine, listening in as he prays aloud to the God of his heart. Biblical texts swirl and wind their way through every paragraph. The Book of Psalms, the Bible's own prayer book, is the most quoted and provides a repertoire of melodic themes for Augustine's own deeply musical prose.

Confessions may be Augustine's most precisely titled work. It is what it says it is—a confession—and one with many sides, at once a confession of praise, a confession of sin, and a confession of faith. I have singled out a sampling of the most famous scenes and best known passages, unfortunately but necessarily pruned of much of their profound psychological and theological analysis.

◆◆

THE RESTLESS HEART

Augustine opens Confessions *with an overture of praise, exploring who God is and who we are. Here appears his best known one-liner: that our hearts are restless until they*

2. Pierre-Marie Hombert, *Nouvelles recherches de chronologie augustinienne*, CEASA 163 (Paris: Institut d'Études Augustiniennes, 2000), 9–23, has challenged this traditional dating in light of newly discovered texts and new perspectives. He argues that Books 1–9 were most likely composed between 397 and 400, while Books 10–13 were composed later, in 403.

3. Goulven Madec, "Augustin évêque," in *Augustin prédicateur (395–411): Actes du Colloque International de Chantilly (5–7 septembre 1996)*, CEASA 159 (Paris: Institut d'Études Augustiniennes, 1998), 27, has argued that Augustine did *not*, with pen in hand, write *Confessions*; rather, "after having profoundly and for a long while meditated on his experience, appropriating biblical language, identifying himself with the biblical person, Augustine dictated *Confessions* '*ex abundantia cordis*' ["with an overflow of heart"], in a virtuosity of word; the work must be read aloud, in full voice. It comes under [the category of] 'oral literature,' as do his sermons" (my trans.). I find this bold assessment quite plausible.

rest in God. This names one of his deepest convictions: God alone can satisfy the ever-thirsting human heart. Augustine then invokes God, calling for help as he embarks on this writing project. This leads to a meditation, puzzling at first sight to English speakers. The Latin for "invoke" is invocare, whose root meaning is "to call into" (vocare + in). Playing on this root meaning, Augustine meditates on how an infinite and omnipresent God can be called into somewhere or into some person, as though God were not already present everywhere and within everything. This overture gives a good first taste of the way wordplay and theological meditation combine. Following the example of Augustine's French translators, I have set out the highly poetic prose of this passage in a free-verse format. From Confessions, Book 1:

> (1.1) "You are great, Lord,
>   and greatly to be praised" (Ps 47:2, 95:4, 144:3).
> "Great, Your power,
>   and Your wisdom knows no number" (Ps 146:5).
>
> To praise You is what humanity desires,
>   we, this small portion of Your creation,
>   "carrying our mortality around" (2 Cor 4:10),
>   carrying around the testimony of our sin
>   and the testimony "that You resist the proud" (1 Pt 5:5).
> And yet to praise You is what humanity desires,
>   we, this small portion of Your creation.
>
> You stir us that we take delight
>   in praising You,
> for You have made us for Yourself,
>   and our hearts are restless 'til they rest in You.
>
> "Grant me, O Lord, to know and to understand" (Ps 118:34)
>   what to do first:
>   whether to invoke You or to praise You,
>   whether to know You or to invoke You.
> But who invokes You without knowing You?
>   For the one who does not know You
>   might invoke another in Your stead.
> Or, rather, are You invoked
>   that You may be known?
> Indeed, "how are they to invoke Him in whom they have not believed?
>   Or how are they to believe, if no one preaches" (Rom 10:14)?
> "And they shall praise the Lord who seek Him" (Ps 21:27).

For they who seek Him shall find Him,
and they who find Him shall praise Him.

May I seek You, O Lord, by invoking You,
  and may I invoke You by believing in You,
  for You have been preached to us.
My faith invokes You, O Lord,
  that faith which You have given me,
which You have breathed into me
  through the humanity of Your Son,
  through the ministry of your preacher.[4]

(2.2) How shall I invoke my God,
  my God and my Lord,
since when I invoke Him,
  I call Him into my very self?
What place is in me
  into which my God may come?
Where can God come into me,
  the God who "made heaven and earth" (Gn 1:1)?
Is there anything in me, O Lord my God,
  which can encompass You?
Indeed, can heaven and earth, which You have made
  and in which You have made me, encompass You?
Or since without You nothing that is can be,
  is it that whatever is contains You?
Since, in fact, I am, why do I ask that You should come into me,
  I who would not be unless You were in me?
For I am not now in hell, and yet You are even there.
  Because "even if I descend into hell You are there" (Ps 138:8).
Hence, I would not be, my God,
  not be at all, unless You were in me.
Rather, is it not that I would not be
  unless I were in You, "from whom,
  through whom, and in whom
  are all things" (Rom 11:36)?
It is so, O Lord, it is so.

---

4. "Through the ministry of your preacher": This is ambiguous; it could refer either to Ambrose (*conf.* 5.13.23–14.24; *ep.* 147.52) or to St. Paul (*conf.* 8.12.29). See O'Donnell, 2:17.

Into what can I invoke You since I am in You?
  Or from where can You come into me?
Where may I go beyond heaven and earth
  in order that my God may then come into me,
  He who has said, "I fill heaven and earth" (Jer 23:24)?[5]

INNOCENT INFANTS?

Augustine was a shrewd watcher of babies. He noted how they sleep and nurse, how they cry and smile. At one point, he seems to dabble with the idea that infants are capable of sin, telling the story of two infant brothers, one jealous of the other. This observation foreshadows—but in the end differs from—his eventual teaching on original sin. From Confessions, Book 1:

(6.7) And so the consolations of human milk supported me, for neither my mother nor my nurses filled their own breasts, but You gave me the food of infancy through them, according to Your planning, and riches which are arranged even for the lowest order of things. . . . At that time, I knew only to suckle and to be satisfied with enjoyable things and to cry at injuries to my flesh—nothing more. (6.8) Later, I began to smile: first, while sleeping; then, while waking. This was told me about myself, and I believe it since we so observe it in other babies. Of course, I do not remember those things about myself. . . .

(7.11) The weakness of infant limbs is innocent, but not the mind of infants. I myself have seen and have had experience with a jealous child: he could not yet speak but, growing pale, would stare with a bitter look at his brother who was nursing as well. Who does not know this? Mothers and nurses claim that they exorcise those things by all sorts of devices. Indeed, is this innocence not to permit another child, who is in greatest need and depends for his life on this one sort of food, to share in a source of milk which is flowing freely and abundantly? These things are borne with equanimity, not that they are nothing or are slight, but because they will disappear with increasing age. And it is right to suffer them, though such things cannot be borne with equanimity when they are observed in a person of more advanced years.[6]

---

5. *Conf.* 1.1.1–2.2 (CCL 27:1–2); my trans., based on Bourke, FOTC 21:4–5.
6. *Conf.* 1.6.7–7.11 (CCL 27:4–6); trans. Bourke, FOTC 21:8–9, 12–13. Augustine would later argue that "infants . . . have committed nothing evil by means of their own will" (*pecc. mer.* 1.35.65; CSEL 60:65); see *pecc. mer.* 1.19.24, 3.4.7; *Enchiridion* 13.42–43. On this issue, see Chapter 10.

6 Augustine

LEARNING TO SPEAK

In early adulthood Augustine pursued a career as a professional orator. He was therefore very conscious of words, how we learn them and make them our own. In a famous passage, he meditates on how children acquire language. In the early twentieth century, philosopher Ludwig Wittgenstein quoted this passage at the outset of his Philosophical Investigations, *challenging it as an accurate account of language acquisition.[7] From* Confessions, *Book 1:*

(8.13) Is it not true that, advancing from infancy toward the present, I came to boyhood? Or did it come into me, succeeding infancy? The latter did not go away. Where, indeed, could it go? Nevertheless, it did not now exist. For I was not an infant, one who could not speak, but was now a boy able to talk. This I do remember, and I observed afterwards how I learned to speak. The older people did not teach me by suggesting the words to me according to any definite method of instruction, as was the case a little later with the alphabet; rather, with my own mind which You gave me, O Lord, I wished to make known with diverse grunts and sounds and with diverse gestures the meanings within my heart so that my will would be obeyed. But I did not succeed with all things which I desired nor with all the people from whom I desired them. I would fasten it in memory when these people called something by name and when, at this sound, they made a bodily movement toward it. I would observe and keep in mind that this thing was named by this sound which they uttered when they wanted to indicate the thing. Their desires became evident from their bodily gestures (the natural speech of all humankind), which reveal the disposition of the mind in regard to things sought, possessed, rejected, or avoided, by a facial expression, by a nod, by a movement of the eyes or some other part of the body, and by the tone of voice. As to these words that were used in their own place in different sentences and which I frequently heard, I gradually learned what things they were the signs of, and when my lips became accustomed to these expressions, I now expressed my desires by means of them. In this way I exchanged with the people among whom I lived the signs which were the expressions of my wishes.[8]

7. On this, see Christopher Kirwan, "Augustine's Philosophy of Language," in *The Cambridge Companion to Augustine*, ed. Eleonore Stump and Norman Kretzmann (Cambridge: Cambridge University Press, 2001), 186–204.

8. *Conf.* 1.8.13 (CCL 27:7–8); trans. Bourke, FOTC 21:14–15 (modified).

STEALING PEARS

Augustine recounts how, at age 16, he and some friends stole pears from a neighbor's orchard. Some readers have wondered why Augustine reads this youthful prank in such dark terms. For Augustine, the darkness comes not from the gravity of the deed itself, but from its psychology: it was doing evil for evil's sake—and delighting in it. Augustine is attuned to its symbolic resonances: that it was his personal re-enacting the sin of Adam. From Confessions, Book 2:

(4.9) There was a pear tree near our vineyard which was laden with fruit that was attractive neither in appearance nor in taste. In the dead of night—for we had prolonged our playing in the vacant lots, according to our usual unhealthy custom, until then—we crept up to it, a gang of youthful good-for-nothings, to shake it down and despoil it. We carried away huge loads not as a treat for ourselves, but just to throw to the pigs. Of course, we did eat a few, but we did so only to be doing something which would be pleasant because forbidden. Look at my heart, O God, look at my heart, which You have pitied in the depths of the abyss. Look at my heart; may it tell You now what it sought in this—that I might be evil without any compensation and that there might be no reason for my evil except evil. It was filthy, and I loved it. I loved my own destruction. I loved my own fault; not the object to which I directed my faulty action, but my fault itself, was what I loved, my vile soul leaping down from Your support into extinction (Sir 39:36), not disgracefully eager for anything but disgrace itself. . . .

(8.16) "What fruit did" I the miserable derive "from these things, which it shames me now to recall" (Rom 6:21), particularly that act of theft, in which I loved the theft itself and nothing else, since it was itself nothing and I became more miserable because of it? Yet I would not have done it by myself—that is my recollection of my mind at this time—I certainly would not have done it alone. Therefore, I also loved in it the companionship of those I did it with. So I did love something other than the theft—or rather, I did not in a real sense, for that companionship was itself nothing. What was it really? Who is there who may teach me except the One who "enlightens my heart" (Sir 2:10) and sees through its shadows? What is it that incites my mind to seek and to discuss and to ponder it? For if I loved those pears that I stole and desired to enjoy them, I could also, if that were enough, have done that evil act by myself that I might achieve my pleasure. I would not have needed to inflame the itch of my lusts by scratching together with other guilty souls. But since there was no pleasure for me in those pears, the pleasure was in the evil act itself. It arose from the companionship of those who sinned together with me. . . .

(9.17) O most unfriendly friendship, inscrutable seduction of the mind, this craving to do harm as a game and a joke, this taste to deprive others of things spurred not for personal gain or revenge. Someone just says: "Let's go; let's do it!" and one is ashamed not to be unashamed.[9]

CARTHAGE

Book 3 opens with a portrait of the 18-year-old Augustine arriving in Carthage, the college town of North Africa. The opening line has a famous wordplay, "Carthage" (Cartago) punning with "cauldron" (sartago). From Confessions, Book 3:

(1.1) To Carthage I came, and a hissing cauldron of shameful loves seethed around me on all sides. I was not in love, yet I loved to love and, in the hidden depths of unsated desire, I hated myself for my partial lack of desire. I sought some object that I might love, loving the very act of love. I hated peace of mind and a "path unbeset by pitfalls" (Wis 14:11). For though I was hungry within me, lacking that inner food which You are, my God, I experienced the desire for incorruptible nourishment not because I was filled with it, but the more empty I was, the greater my loathing became. And that is why my soul was unhealthy and, in its ulcerated condition, projected itself into the open, wretchedly desirous of being scraped in rubbing up against sensible things. Yet if they had no soul, they would certainly not have been loved. To love and to be loved was far sweeter to me if I also succeeded in enjoying my beloved in the flesh. Thus I muddied the waters of friendship with the filth of concupiscence, and I clouded its brightness with the scum of lust. Yet, though filthy and unsightly, I strove in excessive vanity to appear refined and polished. So I plunged headlong into love and desired to be taken over by it, O my God, my Mercy (Ps 58:18), though with how much bitterness You in Your goodness sprinkled that which was sweet to me! For I was loved and I both achieved in secret the bond of enjoyment and was joyfully tied down by the entwinements of calamity to be beaten with iron rods, burning with jealousy, suspicions, and fears, with fits of anger and quarrels.[10]

9. *Conf.* 2.4.9–9.17 (CCL 27:22–26); trans. Bourke, FOTC 21:40–41, 46–47 (modified). On this, see John C. Cavadini, "Book Two: Augustine's Book of Shadows," in *A Reader's Companion to Augustine's Confessions*, ed. Kim Paffenroth and Robert P. Kennedy (Louisville: Westminster John Knox, 2003), 25–34.

10. *Conf.* 3.1.1 (CCL 27:27); trans. Bourke, FOTC 21:49. "Beaten with iron rods": This was part of the standard practice of torture used in the Roman justice system to obtain information on criminal activity. For an analysis of Augustine's wordplay in this paragraph, see Gillian Clark, *Saint Augustine: The Confessions*, Landmarks of World Literature (Cambridge: Cambridge University Press, 1993), 83–91.

CICERO AND THE OLD LATIN BIBLE

In Carthage, Augustine studied rhetoric, that is, the art of public speaking. Ancient education relied on a "great books" curriculum, and so students of rhetoric were expected to master the writings of Marcus Tullius Cicero (106–43 B.C.E.), the great statesman of the Roman Republic whose eloquence was esteemed as the pinnacle of Latin oratory. In his studies, Augustine came across Cicero's Hortensius.[11] This led him to commit himself to a life of wisdom. But Augustine was raised Christian and therefore sought out wisdom as Christians understood it. He turned naturally to the Bible, but it proved, especially in its crude Old Latin translation, deeply disappointing. From Confessions, Book 3:

(4.7) In the regular course of study, I came upon the book of a certain Cicero whose tongue nearly all admire, but not his heart.[12] But that book of his contained an exhortation to philosophy. It was called *Hortensius*. In fact, that book changed my way of feeling and changed the character of my prayers to You, O Lord. It altered my wishes and my desires. Suddenly every vain hope became worthless to me, and I yearned with an unbelievable burning fire within my heart for the immortality of wisdom. I began to rise up so that I might return to You. For it was not to sharpen my tongue (this was the apparent object being bought at my mother's expense, for I was in my nineteenth year, and my father had died two years before)—it was not, I say, to sharpen my tongue that I used that book. It was not its style of speech which influenced me, but rather what it spoke about.

(4.8) How burning was my desire, O my God, how burning my desire to fly back to You from earthly things! I was unaware of what You were doing with me. For "wisdom dwells with You" (Jb 12:13, 16). The love of wisdom bears the Greek name "philosophy," and it was this love that that book enkindled in me. . . . What brought me relish in this exhortation [of Cicero] was that I was excited and aroused and inflamed to love, seek after, attain, and strongly embrace not this or that philosophic school, but wisdom itself, whatever it is. The only thing to dim my blaze was the fact that the name of Christ was not there, for this name, by Your mercy, O Lord (Ps 24:7), this name of my Savior, Your Son, my youthful heart had drunk in piously with my mother's milk and until that time had retained it in its depths. Whatever lacked this name could not completely win me over, howsoever well expressed and polished and true appearing.

---

11. Only fragments of Cicero's *Hortensius* survive. See Maurice Testard, *Saint Augustin et Cicéron*, CEASA 5–6 (Paris: Institut d'Études Augustiniennes, 1958), 19–48; Karin Schlapbach, *Aug-Lex* 3 (2006): 425–36.

12. "A certain Cicero": The phrase "a certain" (*cuiusdam*) may sound dismissive, but it simply seems to have been a rhetorical convention. Augustine uses the same of St. Paul: *conf.* 12.15.20. On this, see O'Donnell, 2:164.

(5.9) So I decided to direct my attention to the Holy Scriptures, to see what they were like. I see it now as something not open to the proud nor laid bare to mere children, something lowly on first being approached but exalted on further reading, something veiled in mysteries. But I was not such that I could lower my head to go through its doorway and up its steps. I did not feel the same about turning to Scripture as I now do in speaking of it. Rather, it seemed to me unworthy of being compared with the Ciceronian standard of worth. My unhealthy pride shunned its style, and my intellectual vision failed to penetrate its interiority. True, this vision is such that it grows along with children, but I disdained to be a child and, inflated with arrogance, I thought myself grown-up.[13]

"THE SON OF THESE TEARS"

At this decisive moment Augustine embraced Manicheism, a gnostic religion founded in third-century Persia. Manichees portrayed themselves as a sort of elite Christianity and attacked orthodox Christianity, its teaching, its lifestyle, and its Bible, especially the Old Testament. Much of the drama and the philosophical meditation of Confessions *centers on how Augustine probes his former Manichean self, not only asking why he joined the Manichees but also denouncing his old ways of thinking and sounding out his current and quite pointed objections to the Manichean worldview. We will explore Manicheism and Augustine's arguments against it at length in Chapter 6. Here our focus is on biography. The following is a famous scene of Augustine's mother Monnica begging the local bishop to intervene and convince her son to leave what she saw as a dark heretical cult. From* Confessions, *Book 3:*

(11.20) Almost nine years went by during which I "wallowed in the deep mire" (Ps 68:3) and darkness of error, while I frequently tried to rise above it, only to sink down more heavily. Yet that chaste, holy, and sober widow (such as you love), already more cheerful in her hopes but no more sparing in her tears and lamentations, ceased not to weep for me before You in all the hours of her prayers. And her "prayers entered into Your sight" (Ps 87:3), but You permitted me still to roll about and flounder in that dark fog.

(12.21) You gave me, in the meantime, another answer which I remember. For I pass over many things because I am hurrying on to those things which more urgently demand that I confess to You, and many things I do not remember. Yes, You gave another answer through Your priest, a certain bishop who was educated in the Church and well trained in Your books. When that

13. *Conf.* 3.4.7–5.9 (CCL 27:29–31); trans. Bourke, FOTC 21:56 (modified). See Chapter 5 for Augustine's view of the Bible and its interpretation.

woman begged him to be good enough to talk with me and refute my errors, to teach me to unlearn evil things and to learn good things (he would do this whenever he happened to find any suitable listeners), he refused, prudently of course, as I later realized. He replied that I was not yet teachable due to the fact that I was puffed up with pride at the novelty of that heresy and that I had disturbed many unlearned people with all sorts of trifling questions, as she had pointed out to him. "But," he said, "let him stay where he is. Just pray to the Lord for him. He will find himself, by reading, what the error is and how great an impiety." At the same time he also told her how he, as a little boy, was given over to the Manichees by his mother, who had been led astray, and that he had not only read nearly all their writings but had even copied them often; and without anyone arguing in opposition or convincing him, it became clear to him how much this sect was to be avoided. And so he had left it. When he said this and she refused to be satisfied but began to beg him all the more (and with copious tears) that he would see me and have a discussion with me, he then became irritated and said impatiently: "Leave me now. As you so live, it cannot be that the son of these tears will perish." And she often recalled in her conversations with me that she took this as a message from heaven.[14]

DEATH OF A FRIEND

The Confessions are, in part, a vehicle for Augustine, now a middle-aged bishop, to mourn those he had lost over the years. Here Augustine gives a famous account of the death of a close but unnamed friend. From Confessions, Book 4:

(4.7) During those years, when I first began to teach in the town of my birth,[15] I had made, due to common interests, a close friend of a young man my own age, like myself, budding into the bloom of manhood. He had grown up with me as a boy. We had gone to school together and played together. But he was not such a close friend in the beginning, and even at that time it was not like true friendship—for friendship is not true unless You cement it between those who cleave to You with "the love which has been poured forth into our hearts through the Holy Spirit which has been given to us" (Rom 5:5). Yet it was exceedingly sweet, being heated by the fervor of similar interests. I had turned him away from the true faith, which he held not from his family but just from his adolescence, to the superstitious and pernicious fables for which

---

14. *Conf.* 3.11.20–12.21 (CCL 27:38–39); trans. Bourke, FOTC 21:69–71 (slightly modified).

15. "Town of my birth": Thagaste, now Souk Ahras in Algeria. This year of teaching in Thagaste was 375–376, when Augustine was 21 years old.

my mother wept for me.[16] That man went astray in his mind, along with me, and my soul could do nothing without him. And, behold, You were close upon the backs of Your fugitives, "O God of vengeance" (Ps 93:1) and (at the same time) Fount of mercies, who turn us to You (Ps 50:15) in wondrous ways. Behold, You took the man from this life when he had scarcely completed a year of friendship with me, sweeter to me than all the sweetnesses of this life.

(4.8) What can one person do to "enumerate Your praises" (Ps 105:2) for the things he has experienced within his solitary self? What did you do at that time, my God, and "how impenetrable is the depth of Your judgments" (Ps 35:7)? For when he was struggling with his fever, for a long time he lay senseless in the sweat of death, and when hope was abandoned, he was baptized while unconscious. It was no concern of mine, for I presumed that his soul would retain what it had received from me rather than what was done to the body of the unconscious man. But it was quite otherwise. He rallied and became well. Immediately, as soon as I was able to speak to him (and I could as soon as he was able, for I did not leave him since we were too dependent on each other), I tried to make a joke with him, as if he too would laugh along with me at the baptism which he had received when completely out of his mind and senses. However, he had already learned that he had received it. And he was as much in horror of me as of an enemy, and he warned me, with amazing and sudden independence of mind, that I had to stop saying such things to him if I desired to remain his friend. Dumbfounded and disturbed, I repressed all my feelings so that he might first grow well and be in such condition of health that I could deal with him as I wished. But he was torn away from my folly to be kept with You for my consolation. After a few days, during my absence the fevers returned, and he died.

(4.9) "With this sorrow my heart was clouded over" (Lam 5:17), and whatever I looked upon was death. The place of my birth was a torment to me, and my father's house a strange unhappiness. Whatever I had shared with him was, without him, transformed into a horrible torture. My eyes looked everywhere for him without satisfaction. I hated all places for not possessing him, nor could they now tell me: "See, he is coming," as when he was alive but absent. I became a great problem to myself, continually asking my soul why it was sad and why it disturbed me so much, and it knew no answer to give me. If I said, "Hope in God" (Ps 41:6), it rightly refused obedience, for this man who had been lost as a dear friend was truer and better than the image to which hope was directed. Tears alone were sweet to me. They took the place of my friend in the delights of my mind. . . .

16. "Turned him . . . to the superstitious and pernicious fables": That is, Augustine had converted his friend (and others) to Manicheism.

(6.11) I marveled that other mortals were still alive when he, whom I had loved as if he would never die, was dead. And I marveled all the more that I, who was his other self, should still live when he was dead. . . .

(8.13) Time takes no holiday. It is never idle as it glides through our senses. It works wonders within one's mind. See how it came and went "from day to day" (Ps 60:9), and in coming and going it subtly introduced into me other hopes and other memories. Gradually it restored me to the kinds of pleasures which I formerly enjoyed, and my sorrow gave way to these.[17]

AMBROSE OF MILAN

By age 30, Augustine had reached the pinnacle of his profession. He won the prestigious post of orator for the city of Milan. At the time, Milan was the emperor's residence, and Augustine knew that he would rub shoulders with the most powerful men in the Roman Empire, that if he played his politics right, he could win some high government post. Milan changed Augustine indelibly. His conversion took place there. The one who prompted his turn to orthodox Christianity was Ambrose, bishop of Milan (d. 397).[18] Ambrose had come from a senatorial family, was highly educated, and could do what Augustine could not: read Greek. He was attuned to theological advances in the Greek East and passed these on to his congregation. These included a way of reading the Bible allegorically ("spiritually"). Ambrose drew inspiration especially from the commentaries of Origen (d. 254), the Alexandrian biblical scholar. Ambrose's sermons were a revelation to Augustine, who had been raised with what we today would call a fundamentalist view of the Bible. Ambrose's symbolic readings of Old Testament texts subtly debunked Manichean objections and provoked Augustine's intellectual conversion. From Confessions, Books 5–6:

([Book 5] 13.23) So I came to Milan, to Ambrose the bishop, known throughout the world as among the best of men, reverent in his worship of You. At that time his eloquent words were busy distributing to Your people "the fat of Your wheat" (Ps 80:17, 147:14) and "the gladness of Your oil" (Ps 4:8) and the "sober intoxication" of Your wine.[19] Unknowingly I was led by

---

17. *Conf.* 4.4.7–8.13 (CCL 27:43–46); trans. Bourke, FOTC 21:78–84. For an analysis, see James Wetzel, "Book Four: The Trappings of Woe and Confession of Grief," in Paffenroth and Kennedy, *Reader's Companion to Augustine's Confessions*, 53–69.

18. See Boniface Ramsey, *Ambrose*, Early Church Fathers (New York: Routledge, 1997); Goulven Madec, *Saint Ambroise et la philosophie*, CEASA 61 (Paris: Institut d'Études Augustiniennes, 1974); J. Patout Burns, "Ambrose Preaching to Augustine: The Shaping of Faith," in *Augustine: Second Founder of the Faith*, ed. Joseph C. Schnaubelt and Frederick van Fleteren (New York: Peter Lang, 1990), 373–86.

19. "Sober intoxication": The phrase is from Ambrose, *Hymn* 1.7.23–24 (*Splendor paternae gloriae*). For a translation, see Carolinne White, *Early Christian Latin Poets*, Early Church Fathers (New York: Routledge, 2000), 47–48.

You to him so that through him I might knowingly be led to You. This "man of God" (2 Kgs 1:9) received me in a fatherly way and welcomed my visit with episcopal dignity. I began to like him, though not at first as a teacher of the truth, for I had definitely given up hope of finding the truth in Your Church, but rather as a man who was kind to me. I carefully listened to his public discourses not with the intention that I should have had but, as it were, to test out his eloquence, to see whether it was in keeping with his fame, whether he was more or less fluent than rumor had it. Upon his words I hung all my attention, but as for the things he spoke about, I was indifferent and contemptuous. I was delighted by the sweetness of his language, which, though more learned, was less entertaining and charming than that of Faustus[20]—but as regards content, I mean, the subject matter, there was no comparison between them, for Faustus was carried away by Manichean fallacies, while this man taught the soundest way of salvation. But salvation is far removed from sinners (Ps 118:155) such as I was at that time. Yet I was drawing closer, gradually and without knowing it.

(14.24) Although I was not interested in learning about the things he spoke of but only in listening to the way that he spoke (indeed, that empty interest was all that remained with me now that I was without hope that a way to You lay open for human beings), the meanings that I was not concerned about came into my mind along with the words that I loved hearing. Nor could I keep these distinct. As I opened my heart to catch his eloquence, the truth that he spoke entered in at the same time, though only gradually. What first happened was that I began to see that his teachings were capable of defense. The Catholic faith, which I presumed could not say anything against Manichean attacks, I now began to regard as defensible. This was especially so when I heard one after another of the obscure passages from the Old Testament being explained, passages which I, by taking them literally, had found to kill (2 Cor 3:6). Thus, when many texts from these books had been explained in a spiritual sense, I now came to censure my despair, which had led me to believe that the haters and mockers of the Law and the Prophets were completely incapable of being resisted. I did not yet feel, however, that I should embrace the Catholic way simply because it could have its learned exponents who refuted criticisms fully and without absurd claims. Nor was the view which I then held on to proved wrong just because one side of the defense could hold its own. Just as the Catholic side did not appear to me to

---

20. "Faustus": Faustus of Milevis (d. ca. 390) was a Manichean bishop. In *conf.* 5.6.10, Augustine says that local Manichees had promised that Faustus would be capable of answering Augustine's growing list of scientific and philosophic conundrums that challenged Manichean doctrine. Faustus proved disappointing, and that disappointment fueled Augustine's departure from the Manichees. For excerpts from Faustus's writings, see Chapter 6.

have been conquered, so too it did not yet seem to be the conqueror. Thus, adopting the approach of the Academics[21] (as they are commonly thought of), I was in doubt about everything and took no definite position, but I decided that the Manichees were to be abandoned. I did not think that I should remain in that sect during this period of doubt, for I now preferred some of the philosophers to it. But I refused to completely commit the care of my sickly soul to those philosophers because they were without the health-giving name of Christ. Therefore, I resolved, for the time being, to be a catechumen in the Catholic Church[22] which had been recommended to me by my parents until some light of certainty might appear to which I could direct my course. . . .

([Book 6] 3.3) In my sighing I had not yet begun to pray for You to come to my assistance. But my mind was intent upon the quest and was anxious for discussion. I regarded Ambrose himself as a man who was fortunate in the view of the world, greatly honored, as he was, by so many men of importance. Only his celibate life seemed a burden to me. As to the hope he bore within him, the struggles he had with temptations associated with his lofty position, his consolation in adversities, the sweet joy with which the hidden mouth of his heart partook of Your bread, I had no inkling or experience. Nor did he know my anxieties, nor the pitfall which threatened me. I was unable to seek what I wanted from him, in the way I wanted, since there were throngs of busy people who cut me off from his ear and mouth, people to whose weaknesses he ministered. And when he was not with them, which was a very small bit of time, he was either refreshing his body with necessary sustenance or his mind with reading. As he read, his eyes scanned the pages and his heart searched out the meaning, but his voice and tongue were silent. Often, when we were present (and he never forbade entry to anyone nor was it the custom for a visitor to be announced), we saw him reading quietly in that way and never in any other. After sitting silently for a long time (for who would dare to impose a burden on one so engrossed?) we would depart, thinking that in the small time that he had to himself to refresh his mind, free from the noise of other people's troubles, he preferred not to be distracted by something else; that perhaps he was afraid lest some listener, follow-

21. "Academics": The skeptical successors of Plato and his Academy. The leading figures were Archesilaus (d. 242 B.C.E.) and Carneades (d. 137 B.C.E.) who came to embrace a wide-ranging skepticism. Cicero, while best known for his oratory, embraced the philosophy of the Academics. Augustine's earliest extant work is a refutation entitled *Against the Skeptics* (*Contra Academicos*); see Chapter 2.

22. "A catechumen in the Catholic Church": Augustine was not baptized as a child, but instead made a catechumen (or "hearer") (*conf.* 1.11.17). Adult baptism was still the norm, and the baptism of children tended to be limited to cases of emergency baptism. Catechumens attended only the Liturgy of the Word and were dismissed prior to the Liturgy of Eucharist, which was secret. See William Harmless, *Augustine and the Catechumenate* (Collegeville, MN: The Liturgical Press, 1995), esp. 80–82, 150–51; also "Catechumen, Catechumenate," *AugEncy*, 145–49. Augustine here emphasizes that because of Ambrose's preaching, he left the Manichees and returned to being a catechumen.

ing it with great interest, might ask him about some more obscure passage he was reading, and then it would be necessary to explain it or to lecture on the more difficult problems and, having given time to this task, he would read fewer volumes than he desired. However, it was quite possible that the more likely reason for his silent reading was for the sake of preserving his voice, which, in his case, was easily made hoarse. Anyhow, whatever his purpose was in doing this, this man had a good reason for doing it.

(3.4) But the truth is that no opportunity presented itself for me to ask the questions I desired of Your holy oracle in his breast, except when he would give brief attention to something. My mental anxieties needed considerable free time on his part, so that they could be poured forth to him, but they never found it. I did indeed hear him "rightly preaching the word of truth" (2 Tm 2:15) to the people every Sunday, and I grew more and more certain that all the knots of deceitful calumny, which those deceivers of ours[23] had tied around the divine books, could be undone. Indeed, when I learned that the passage about human beings made by You to Your image (Gn 1:26) was not understood by Your spiritual children, whom You had regenerated from Mother Church through grace, as if they believed and thought in terms of a limitation by the shape of a human body (though I had not even a vague and obscure suspicion of how a spiritual substance is constituted), I was glad to blush at the fact that I had barked for so many years, not against the Catholic faith, but against the pure fictions of fleshly thoughts. What had made my actions even more rash and irreverent was that I had spoken out in accusation about things I ought to have been probing into. You, however, who are very exalted and yet near, who are very much hidden and yet most intimately present, who do not have bodily limbs, some greater and some smaller, you who are entirely in every place and yet belong to no place, certainly You are not this corporeal shape, even though You have made the human person to Your image and see how he is fixed in place from his head down to his feet.

(4.5) . . . So I was confounded, I was converted, I was overjoyed, O my God, that the only Church, the Body of Your only Son, in which the name of Christ had been impressed upon me as infant, did not savor infantile trifles, and did not maintain, as a part of its sound doctrine, that through giving You the shape of human limbs it could press You, the Creator of all things, into the space of a definite location, which, however large and vast, was still bounded on all sides.

(4.6) I rejoiced, too, that the ancient writings of the Law and the Prophets were no longer put before me to be read with that vision which had here-

---

23. "Those deceivers of ours": the Manichees.

tofore made them seem absurd, when I used to charge Your holy people with thinking in a certain way, though they did not actually hold such opinions. And I listened with joy to Ambrose, saying often in his sermons to the people, as though he were most carefully commending it as a rule: "The letter kills but the Spirit gives life" (2 Cor 3:6). When, having lifted the mystic veil (2 Cor 3:14), he laid bare the spiritual meaning of those things which seemed to teach error when taken literally, he said nothing that offended me, though I still did not know whether his statements were true. I was keeping my heart from all assent, fearing a sudden fall, yet by this suspension [of an assent to faith] I was, instead, being killed. . . .

(5.7) Still, as a result of this, I now preferred the Catholic teaching, feeling that it was more moderate and less open to error in the fact that it ordered belief in what was not demonstrated . . . rather than to make a mockery of belief by a rash promise of scientific knowledge, and then to command [as the Manichees did] that so many fabulous and absurd things be believed because they could not be demonstrated.[24]

AUGUSTINE'S CONCUBINE

One common but inaccurate view of Augustine was that, as a young man, he was highly promiscuous. That is hardly the case. In Confessions 4.2.2, he mentions having a live-in girlfriend ("concubine" is the technical term). The woman was likely of a much lower social status, and marriage between them may have been legally impossible. They had a child, a son named Adeodatus (the name means "gift from God"), and Augustine says that he was faithful to her during the nearly 14 years they lived together. In Roman law, concubinage did have certain legal protections but was not recognized as genuine marriage. As he pursued his career in Milan, his mother set about playing matchmaker, trying to arrange a socially acceptable marriage partner appropriate to her son's rising career status. The fiancée came from a wealthy family in Milan but was two years under the marriage age. This meant Augustine had to wait and had to break off his years-long relationship. That upper-class men had concubines was commonplace, that they abandoned them for a socially respectable marriage was also presumed, but that Augustine actually talked about it and let his genuine feelings for his concubine become public is striking. From Confessions, Book 6:

(13.23) I was unceasingly urged to take a wife. I had already proposed marriage and was now engaged, chiefly through the efforts of my mother, for, once married, the saving waters of baptism might cleanse me. . . . A girl

24. *Conf.* 5.13.23–6.5.7 (CCL 27:70–78); trans. Bourke FOTC 21:124–37.

was spoken for who was almost two years younger than the age suitable for marriage; since she was pleasing, we waited. . . .[25]

(15.25) In the meantime, my sins were multiplied (Sir 23:3). When the woman with whom I had lived for so long was torn from my side because she was a hindrance to my marriage, my heart, to which she clung, was cut and wounded, and the wound drew blood. She returned to Africa, vowing to You that she would never know another man and leaving with me the natural son whose mother she was. But I, unfortunate, unable even to emulate a woman and impatient at the delay attendant upon waiting two years for the girl to whom I had proposed, because I was not a lover of marriage but a slave of lust, procured another woman—but not as a wife. Thus, it was as if the whole (or increased) illness of my soul was sustained and continued, under the escort of a persisting custom, into the very realm of matrimony. Nor was that wound of mine healed, which had been made by cutting off the first woman. Rather, after the fever and most severe pain, it began to fester and, though the pain seemed cooler, it was more desperate.[26]

"Books of the Platonists"

In Milan, Augustine came across certain Platonist books. Which Platonists and which books have been much disputed, but they almost certainly included the Enneads of Plotinus (202–270) and/or essays by his disciple Porphyry (c. 232–c. 303).[27] These sparked an intellectual revolution in Augustine, providing him new ways of thinking about God, the soul, evil, beauty, and much else. They also recommended a spirituality and method of meditation by which one turns inward in order to turn upward towards God, passing from the visible to the invisible, from the temporal to the eternal. In the following passage, Augustine speaks of a pivotal experience. This account, while indebted to Neoplatonic terminology, in fact marks out how Christian mysticism differs from Neoplatonic: Augustine experienced not a mystical union with the One but an encounter with God that revealed the reality of his sinful fallen state and his (and all humanity's) need for grace and for an incarnate mediator, Jesus Christ. By the time he wrote

25. "Two years younger than the age suitable for marriage": According to Roman law, girls were permitted to marry at the age of twelve (Justinian, *Institutiones* 1.10.22). Roman practice of marrying such young girls, however appalling to us, was commonplace. On concubinage and marriage in the ancient world, see Paul Veyne, ed., *The History of Private Life*, Vol. 1: *From Pagan Rome to Byzantium* (Cambridge, MA: Harvard University Press, 1987); Gillian Clark, *Women in Late Antiquity: Pagan and Christian Lifestyles* (New York: Oxford University Press, 1994); Charles Munier, "Concubinatus," *Aug-Lex*, 1:1112–13.
26. *Conf.* 6.13.23–15.25 (CCL 27:89–90); trans. Bourke, FOTC 21:155–58.
27. Over the last century, scholars have debated this question at length and in detail. For an overview, see Goulven Madec, "Le néoplatonisme dans la conversion d'Augustin: État d'une question centenaire," in *Petites Études Augustiniennes*, CEASA 142 (Paris: Institut d'Études Augustiniennes, 1994), 51–69; also O'Donnell, 2:421–24. On Augustine's Platonism, see the texts and notes in Chapter 2.

Confessions, *Augustine came to believe that, while contemplation may be mystical, it is an experience that starkly reveals our distance from God and calls forth confession.*[28] From Confessions, Book 7:

(9.13) First of all, desiring to show me how You "resist the proud but give grace to the humble" (1 Pt 5:5) and by what great mercy You have shown the way of humility to humanity in the fact that Your "Word was made flesh and dwelt among us" (Jn 1:14), You provided me, by means of a man who was puffed up with the most monstrous pride,[29] certain books of the Platonists, which were translated from the Greek tongue into Latin. . . .

(10.16) Admonished [by these Platonist books] to return to myself, I entered into my innermost parts under Your guidance. I was able because You became my helper (Ps 29:11). I entered in and saw with the eye of my soul (whatever its condition) the immutable Light above this same eye of my soul and above my mind—not this everyday light which is visible to all flesh, nor was it a brighter light of somewhat the same kind, as it were, which shines out much more clearly and fills the whole of space with its magnitude. It was not this, but something different, quite different from all these. Nor was it above my mind in the way that oil is above water, nor as the heavens are above the earth, but superior in the sense that It had made me, and I was inferior in the sense that I had been made by It. The one who knows the truth knows It, and the one who knows It knows eternity. Love knows It. O eternal Truth and true Love and beloved Eternity, You are my God. For You I sigh day and night (Ps 41:4). When I first knew You, You took me up to You so that I might see that there was something to see, but that I was not yet ready for vision. Shining Your light upon me so strongly, You struck down my feeble gaze, and I trembled with love and with awe. I discovered that I was far from You in this land of unlikeness, as if I heard Your voice from on high: "I am the food of the great. Grow great and you shall eat of me. Nor will you change Me into you, as is done with the food of your flesh, rather will you change into Me." I recognized that "for his iniquity You have corrected man" and "You made my soul shrivel up like a spider web" (Ps 38:12). So I said: "Is truth then nothing because it is not diffused through space, either finite or infinite?" And You cried out from afar: "Yes, truly, I am Who am!" (Ex 3:14). I heard it, as one hears something in one's heart. There was no reason for me to doubt. I could more

---

28. For a careful analysis of these ascent texts, see John Peter Kenney, *The Mysticism of Saint Augustine: Rereading the Confessions* (New York: Routledge, 2005), esp. 49–72. Kenney helpfully demonstrates that while Augustine draws heavily on Plotinus's terminology, his perspectives on the mystical encounter differ radically from those of Plotinus.

29. "Man . . . puffed up with the most monstrous pride": Scholars have speculated on who this might have been. Pierre Courcelle has argued that it was Manlius Theodorus, a prominent Neoplatonist in Milan. For a discussion, see O'Donnell, 2:419–20.

easily have doubted that I was alive than that there is no truth "which is clearly seen, being understood through the things that are made" (Rom 1:20). . . .

(17.23) I marveled that I now loved You, and not a phantasm in place of You. Yet I did not stand still in the enjoyment of my God. Rather, I was snatched up to You by Your glory, but was soon snatched away from You by the natural weight of my will, and I fell back on these lower things with a groan. This was the weight of carnal custom. However, memory of you remained with me.[30]

CONVERSION OF VICTORINUS

Here and there within Confessions, Augustine offers mini-portraits of other converts that circle round the larger central portrait of his own conversion. Here Augustine describes the conversion of Marius Victorinus (d. c. 364).[31] Like Augustine, Victorinus was a North African and a rhetor who had made his way to Italy to win fame and fortune. Victorinus was the one responsible for translating those Platonist books that were so revolutionizing Augustine's thinking. Augustine heard that Victorinus, at the end of his life, had converted to Christianity. In the following passage, he hears the full story from Simplicianus (d. 400), a presbyter of the church of Milan and Ambrose's mentor and eventual successor.[32] From Confessions, Book 8:

(2.3) So I went to Simplicianus, the spiritual father of (then) bishop Ambrose in his reception into grace and loved by Ambrose like a father. I told him the winding course of my error. When I mentioned that I had read some books of the Platonists, which Victorinus (at one time a rhetorician in the city of Rome who had, I heard, died a Christian) had translated into Latin, he congratulated me that I had not happened on the writings of other philosophers filled with errors and deceptions "according to the elements of this world" (Col 2:8), while in the writings of the Platonists God and His Word are indirectly introduced at every turn. Then, in order to exhort me to the humility of Christ, which is hidden from the wise but revealed to the little ones (Mt 11:25), he recalled Victorinus himself whom he had known as a very close friend when he was in Rome. And he told me a story about him concerning which I shall not keep silent. It offers ample opportunity to praise Your grace, which

---

30. *Conf.* 7.9.13–13.23 (CCL 27:101–7); trans. Bourke, FOTC 21:176–86.

31. See Pierre Hadot, *Marius Victorinus: Recherches sur sa vie et ses oeuvres*, CEASA 44 (Paris: Institut d'Études Augustiniennes, 1971); Stephen A. Cooper, *Marius Victorinus' Commentary on Galatians*, OECS (New York: Oxford University Press, 2005); Nello Cipriani, "Marius Victorinus," *AugEncy*, 533–35.

32. Simplicianus would play a key role not only in Augustine's conversion, but also in his later work as a theologian. Augustine's *Ad Simplicianum* in 396 would prove a watershed in his evolving theology of grace and his interpretation of Paul's letters; for a discussion and excerpts, see Chapter 10.

must be confessed to You. This very learned old man, skilled in all the liberal teachings, who had read and criticized so many works of the philosophers, the teacher of so many senators, a man who, as a mark of his distinguished career as a teacher, had deserved and received a statue in the Roman Forum (which the citizens of this world regard as an outstanding honor), up to that time a worshiper of idols and a participant in the sacrilegious mysteries. . . .

(2.4) He read, as Simplicianus said, the Holy Scriptures and studied all the Christian writings with greatest care, examining them in detail. He used to say to Simplicianus, not openly, but in a private and friendly way: "Do you know that I am already a Christian?" The latter would reply: "I will not believe it nor count you among the Christians unless I see you inside the Church of Christ." But he would smile and say: "So, do the walls [of the church] make people Christians?" He said this often, that he was already a Christian, and Simplicianus often gave the same reply, and the bantering remark about the walls was often repeated. For he was afraid of offending his friends, proud worshipers of demons.[33] . . . But afterwards, by reading and longing, he gained firmness of mind and became afraid that he would be denied by Christ before the holy angels because he had been fearful of confessing Him before people. By being ashamed of the mysteries of the humility of Your Word and not being ashamed of the sacrilegious mysteries of proud demons which he had accepted as their proud follower, he appeared to himself to be guilty of a great crime. He put aside the shame arising from vanity and took on the shame arising from truth. Suddenly and unexpectedly, he said to Simplicianus (as the latter told the story): "Let us go to church. I wish to become a Christian." The latter, overcome with joy, went along with him. He was introduced into the first mysteries of instruction and, shortly afterwards, he also turned in his name to be reborn through baptism, to the amazement of Rome and the joy of the Church.[34] The proud saw and grew angry; they gnashed their teeth and pined away (Ps 111:10). But the Lord God was the hope of Your servant, and he regarded not "vanities and lying follies" (Ps 39:5).

(2.5) At last, as the hour approached for the profession of faith (which at Rome was customarily uttered by those who are about to enter into Your grace in set words learned and kept in memory,[35] and from a prominent place

33. "Proud worshipers of demons": For Augustine, paganism of any sort was inherently demonic; the point is that Victorinus was an ex-pagan and his aristocratic friends remained deeply committed to traditional Roman religion.

34. "Turned in his name" (*nomen dedit*): a technical term referring to the formal application for baptism, done usually just before Lent. Those accepted for baptism (*competentes*, "co-petitioners") spent Lent going through a complex set of rites and rigorous ascetical practices. See Harmless, *Augustine and the Catechumenate*, 61–69, 93–98.

35. "In set words learned and kept in memory": During Lent, *competentes* memorized the then-secret Creed. On Holy Saturday, just before baptism, they recited it back in a secret ceremony, known as the

in full view of the crowd of believers), an offer was made by the presbyters to Victorinus—Simplicianus said—to do it privately. It was customary to make this concession to such people as seemed likely to be frightened by embarrassment. However, he preferred to profess his salvation in the sight of the holy congregation. For what he taught as a rhetorician was not productive of salvation, yet he had professed that in public. How much less, then, had he to fear Your meek flock when he uttered Your word since he was not afraid of crowds of madmen when uttering his own words? Thus, when he got up to make his profession, everyone who knew him and all the people whispered his name among themselves with murmurs of thanksgiving. Who was there who did not know him? From the mouths of those gathered rejoicing together, there resounded the sound of a suppressed shout: "Victorinus! Victorinus!" Quickly they applauded in exultation at seeing him, and quickly they fell into an intense silence in order to hear him. He proclaimed the true faith with admirable confidence, and all experienced the desire to snatch him to their hearts. This they did with love and joy, for these were the hands by which they caught him up.[36]

ANTONY AND EARLY MONASTICISM

Augustine's decisive conversion was catalyzed by the story of the Egyptian hermit Antony (d. 356), one of the pioneers of Christian monasticism. The Life of Antony, authored by Athanasius (d. 373), the much-exiled bishop of Alexandria, is one of the classics of Western spirituality and did much to popularize monasticism in both the Greek East and the Latin West.[37] Augustine recounts how in August 386 he and his close friend Alypius spent the summer break at a villa outside Milan. There they heard Antony's story from a fellow African, Ponticianus, who worked in the government. Ponticianus went on to tell them how several members of the imperial intelligence service were converted to monasticism from reading Antony's story. From Confessions, Book 8:

(6.14) So on a certain day (I do not recall the reason why Nebridius was away), a man named Ponticianus came to visit me and Alypius at our house. He was a compatriot of ours in the sense that he was from Africa, and the holder of an important position at court. I do not remember what he de-

---

redditio symboli ("handing back of the Creed"). That ceremony is what Augustine alludes to here. On this, see Harmless, *Augustine and the Catechumenate*, 274–86.

36. *Conf.* 8.2.3–2.5 (CCL 27:114–16); trans. Bourke, FOTC 21:198–202.

37. On the *Life of Antony* and early Egyptian monasticism, see William Harmless, *Desert Christians: An Introduction to the Literature of Early Monasticism* (New York: Oxford University Press, 2004), esp. 57–104; Columba Stewart, "Anthony of the Desert," in *The Early Christian World*, ed. Philip F. Esler (New York: Routledge, 2000) 2:1088–101.

sired of us. We sat down together to have a talk. Just by chance, he noticed a book on the games table before us. He picked it up, opened it, and to his surprise, no doubt, discovered that it was [the letters of] the Apostle Paul. He had thought it one of the books that I was wearing myself out with in teaching. He looked at me with a smile and expressed his congratulations and surprise at unexpectedly finding this work, and only this work, before my eyes. In fact, he was a Christian and a faithful one, accustomed to go on his knees before You, our God, in frequent and lengthy prayers in church. When I pointed out to him that I was devoting much attention to these writings, he began to tell the story of Antony the Egyptian monk whose name shone very brilliantly among Your servants but was unknown to us up to that time. When he discovered this, he dwelt upon this point in his conversation, giving much information to us, who were ignorant, about this man and expressing surprise at this ignorance of ours. We were amazed, of course, to hear of Your miracles, of such recent memory and almost in our own times, which were well supported by testimony—miracles performed in the right faith and in the Catholic Church. We were all in a condition of wonder: we two, because these things were so important, and he, because we had not heard of them.

(6.15) From this, his conversation turned to the flocks [of monks] in monasteries, to their manner of living, sweet with Your scent, and to their fruitful populating of desert wastes: of all this, we knew nothing. There was even a monastery at Milan, outside the city walls, filled with good brothers under the patronage of Ambrose, and we did not know of it. He went right on speaking of his subject, while we remained silent and engrossed. Then he happened to tell how he and three companions (I do not know at what time, but certainly it was at Trier), during the time of the afternoon that the emperor was attending the show in the circus, went out for a walk in the gardens beside the city walls. There they happened to pair off, he taking one companion with him, and the other two wandering off likewise, but in another direction. This second pair, strolling along, happened upon a hut where were dwelling some of Your servants who are "poor in spirit, for of such is the Kingdom of Heaven" (Mt 5:3). There they found a book in which the life of Antony had been written. One of them began to read it, and to wonder, and to catch the spark. As he read, he thought of embracing such a life and of giving up secular affairs to serve You. (They belonged to the group of officials called "special agents.")[38] Then suddenly filled with a holy love and angry at him-

---

38. "Special agents" (*agentes in rebus*): Officers who, at the lower levels, served as couriers of imperial dispatches and, at higher levels, managed the public postal system; they eventually earned a (perhaps exaggerated) reputation as a sort of secret police. See Jean-Michel Carrié, "Agens in rebus," in G. W. Bowersock, Peter Brown, and Oleg Grabar, eds., *Late Antiquity: A Guide to the Postclassical World* (Cambridge, MA: Belknap/Harvard University Press, 1999), 278–79.

self with virtuous shame, he turned his eyes to his friend and said to him: "Tell me, I beg of you, what goal do we hope to achieve with all these efforts of ours? What are we looking for? What reason have we for engaging in public service? Could our aspiration at the court be anything greater than to become 'friends of Caesar'?[39] And what is not unstable and full of danger in that position? Through how many dangers must one go to reach a greater danger? And when will one reach it? Now, if I wish, I can be a friend of God immediately."

He said this and, in the throes of giving birth to a new life, he looked again at the text. As he read, he was changed within, in the part which You saw. His mind withdrew from the world, as soon became evident. For while he read and his heart surged up and down, he groaned at times as he made his decision. He decided in favor of the better, being now Yours, and said to his friend: "I have just divorced myself from that ambition of ours and have determined to serve God. I shall begin this service from this hour and in this place. If you do not care to do likewise, do not speak in opposition." The other man replied that he would join his companion for so great a reward and so important a service. The two men then began building their tower for You (Lk 14:28), making the necessary outlay, leaving all their possessions and following You. . . . Both men were engaged to be married. When their fiancées heard about this, they also dedicated their virginity to You.[40]

AUGUSTINE'S CONVERSION

Few scenes in Western literature are more famous than the following account of Augustine's conversion. After hearing the stories of Antony and of the government agents, Augustine was shaken to the core. He tells how he wandered out of the house to a nearby garden and there heard a child's voice instructing him to read. The account is highly stylized, full of self-conscious literary echoes and laced with numerous Psalm texts.[41] From Confessions, *Book 8:*

---

39. "Friends of Caesar" (*amici imperatoris*): A circle of elite office holders around the emperor. While these "friends" enjoyed great power and other amenities, there were also great dangers, given the intrigues at court and the periodic coups d'état in the late Roman Empire.

40. *Conf.* 8.6.14–6.15 (CCL 27:121–23); trans. Bourke, FOTC 21:209–12.

41. The classic study is by Pierre Courcelle, *Recherches sur les Confessions de saint Augustin*, 2nd ed. (Paris: E. de Boccard, 1968). Courcelle's analysis revolutionized our understanding of the literary threads and sources for this scene. For a balanced assessment of its historicity, see Aimé Solignac, "Historicité des Confessions," *Les Confessions*, BA 13 (1992): 55–84; John J. O'Meara, "Augustine's *Confessions*: Elements of Fiction," in Joanne McWilliam, ed., *Augustine: From Rhetor to Theologian* (Waterloo, ON: Wilfrid Laurier University Press, 1992), 77–96; and Henry Chadwick, "History and Symbolism in the Garden at Milan," in *From Augustine to Eriugena: Essays on Neoplatonism and Christianity in Honor of John O'Meara*, ed. F. X. Martin and J. A. Richmond (Washington, DC: The Catholic University of America Press, 1991), 42–55.

(7.17) Many years of my life had flowed by—about twelve—since that period in my nineteenth year when, having read the Hortensius of Cicero, I was stirred by the love of wisdom. I continued to put off rejecting worldly happiness so that I might be free to search for that wisdom, whose "mere quest—not to speak of its attainment—should have been preferred to finding treasures and ruling kingdoms and to being surrounded by bodily pleasures at my beck and call."[42] Yet as a youth, I was very unhappy, unhappy at the beginnings of adolescence. I even begged You for chastity, saying: "Give me chastity and self-restraint, but not just yet."[43] I was afraid that You would quickly hear my prayer, that You would quickly cure me of the disease of lust, something I preferred to have satisfied rather than abolished. And I had walked along crooked ways in sacrilegious superstition, not exactly certain in it, but preferring it in a way to other teaching which I did not search out with sincerity but which I fought against with enmity.

(7.18) I maintained that the reason I was deferring "from day to day" (Sir 5:8) any rejecting of worldly ambition so as to follow You alone was because nothing seemed certain to me, nothing by which I could direct my course. But the day had come for me to be laid bare before myself. . . . When [Ponticianus] finished his conversation and the business which he had come for, he went his way—and I to myself. What did I not say within me? With what lashes of judgment did I not whip my soul that it would follow me, who yearned to follow You? Yet it balked, it refused and made no effort to be excused. . . .

(8.19) Then, in the middle of a huge argument within my inner house, a quarrel I had strongly provoked against my own soul in our bedroom, that is, my heart,[44] I rush in upon Alypius—I was wild in looks as much as troubled in mind—and cry out: "What's wrong with us? What does this mean, this story you heard? Unlearned men are rising up and storming heaven (Mt 11:12), while we, we with all our learning without any heart—here we are rolling around in flesh and blood! Is it because they have led the way that we are ashamed to follow, yet are not ashamed of the fact that we are not following?" I said some such words, and then this firestorm of feeling tore me away from him, while he kept silent, terrified as he looked upon me. Not even my voice sounded normal. My forehead, my cheeks, my eyes, my color, the tone

42. "Mere quest . . . beck and call": A quote (or paraphrase) of Cicero, Hortensius, frag. 101.

43. On Augustine's struggles with sexuality and his choice of celibacy in the wake of his conversion, see Peter Brown, The Body and Society: Men, Women, and Sexual Renunciation in Early Christianity (New York: Columbia University Press, 1988), esp. 387–95.

44. "Bedroom" (cubiculum): The image Augustine plays on here is that of a married couple having a noisy argument in the inner room of their house. Augustine is having a marital spat with his "soul" (anima). See De magistro 1.2 (CCL 29:158–59) in which he quotes Ps 4:4 ("repent on your beds") and speaks of praying "in the secrecy of our 'bedroom' (cubiculum), a term that means 'the inner recesses of the mind.'" See also s. 155.15, where he compares the internal struggle between spirit and flesh to a marital spat (rixa).

of my voice—these gave more indication of my mental condition than did the words I uttered.

A little garden belonged to our residence, and we used it as we did the rest of the house, for our host, the landlord, did not live there. The uproar in my breast carried me out there where no one could hinder the burning struggle which I had entered upon against myself—and to what outcome, You knew, but I did not. Yet my madness was health-restoring and my dying was life-giving. I was aware of my evil, but I was unaware of the good I would soon come to. So I withdrew to the garden, and Alypius followed my footsteps. There was no lack of privacy for me when he was present. Moreover, how could he leave me alone in such a frame of mind? We sat down as far away from the buildings as possible. I was deeply disturbed in spirit, angered by indignation, distressed at the fact that I had not entered into an agreement and covenant with You, O my God, for all my bones cried out (Ps 34:10) that I should take this step, extolling it to the heavens with praises. . . .

(12.28) Now when a profound self-examination had pulled out from the hidden depths and heaped together the whole of my wretchedness before the gaze of my heart (Ps 18:15), a huge storm arose, bringing a huge downpour of tears. And in order to shed the whole of it, with its accompanying groans, I stood up, away from Alypius (to me solitude seemed more fitting for the business of weeping), and I withdrew to a greater distance so that his presence could be no inhibition to me. That is the way I felt then, and he perceived it. I suppose I said something or other, and the sound of my voice was already weighed down with tears, and so I got up. He stayed where he had been sitting and was much astonished. I threw myself down under a certain fig tree, and let go the reins holding back my tears. They burst forth in rivers from my eyes, an acceptable sacrifice to You (Ps 50:19). Not in these words, but with this meaning, I said many things to You: "And You, O Lord, how long?" (Ps 6:4) "How long, O Lord? Will You be angry to the end?" (Ps 78:5) "Remember not our past iniquities" (Ps 78:8). For I still felt that I was held by them and I uttered these wretched words: "How long, how long this 'tomorrow,' 'tomorrow'? Why not right now? Why not end my shame this very hour?"

(12.29) I kept saying these things and weeping with the bitterest sorrow in this heart of mine. Then suddenly I heard from a nearby house the voice of someone—whether a boy or a girl, I do not know—this sort of sing-song phrase, repeating over and over: "Pick it up, read it! Pick it up, read it!" And immediately, my face, my expression, changed, and I began trying very intensely to think back whether children ever used to chant words like this in some sort of game, and it occurred to me that I had never heard anything like it. Having stemmed the flow of my tears, I got up, taking the words to mean nothing else but a divine command that I should open a book and read the first passage I should find. For I had heard about Antony, that he had been admonished from a reading of the Gospel that he had come upon by chance, as if what was read was said for him: "Go, sell what you have, and give to the poor, and you shall have treasure in heaven; and come, follow me" (Mt 19:21)—and by such a revelation he was immediately "converted to You" (Ps 50:15).[45] And so I hurried back to the place where Alypius was sitting. I had put there the volume of [the letters of] the Apostle [Paul] when I had gotten up. Snatching it up, I opened it and read in silence the first passage my eyes fell upon: "Not in revelries and drunkenness, not in eroticism and indecencies, not in rivalries and jealousies, but put on the Lord Jesus Christ, and as for the flesh, make no provision for its lusts" (Rom 13:13–14). No further did I desire to read, nor was there any need. Immediately by sentence's end, all darkness of doubt was dispersed, and a light of peace flooded into my heart.[46]

CASSICIACUM

In the aftermath of this conversion, Augustine resigned from his post as orator and took a sabbatical during the fall of 386. His resignation was prompted as much by a respiratory illness as by any conversion. He spent this time in Cassiciacum with friends, family, and a few students. There he composed his earliest extant works, a set of four philosophical dialogues. From Confessions, Book 9:

(4.7) The day came on which I was actually to be released from the profession of rhetoric, though I had already been released from it in my thinking. And the deed was done. You delivered my tongue, as You had already delivered my heart from it. I blessed You in my joy and departed for a country house [in Cassiciacum] with all my associates. What I did there, by way of writing, my books of discussions with others present and with myself alone in Your presence[47] are a witness of; those writings, though indeed dedicated to Your service, still breathe forth, as in a rest period, the school of pride. My letters also give evidence of what things were discussed with Nebridius while he was away. When shall I have enough time to bring back the memory of all Your great benefits towards us during that period, especially when I must hasten

---

45. Athanasius, *Vita Antonii* 2 (SC 400:136).

46. *Conf.* 8.7.17–12.29 (CCL 27:124–31); my trans., based on Bourke, FOTC 21:215–25. This "putting on" Christ was symbolized by the newly baptized wearing white robes for the week after their baptism. Augustine thus reads Rom 13:13–14 as a call to baptism. See O'Donnell, 3:61.

47. "Books of discussions with others . . . and with myself alone": At Cassiciacum Augustine composed three philosophical dialogues, using his students, friends, and family as dialogue partners; he also composed *Soliloquies* (*Soliloquia*), a dialogue between himself and his "Reason." For excerpts see Chapter 2.

on to other incidents greater still? My inner recollection recalls them, and it becomes sweet to me, O Lord, to confess to You by what inner spurs You completely subdued me, and how You leveled me down, "having made low the mountains and hills" of my thoughts, and how You "made straight my crookedness and made smooth my rough ways" (Is 40:4).

(4.8) What cries did I give forth to You, O my God, when I read the Psalms of David, those canticles of the faith, those songs of piety which admit of no pride of spirit! As one uninitiated in Your true love, I spent my vacation in the country with Alypius, a catechumen like myself, and with my mother, who in that close association with us, was womanly in her dress but manly in her faith, mature in her serenity, motherly in her love, Christian in her piety. What cries I used to utter while saying those Psalms, and how I was fired by them with love for You! I burned to recite them, if I could, throughout the whole world against the pride of humankind![48]

AUGUSTINE'S BAPTISM

In Milan and elsewhere in the early Church, baptism took place but once a year, at the Easter Vigil. Preparation took years, and some candidates delayed years more, content to remain catechumens. Any who finally decided to seek baptism had to make a formal application, "turning in one's name" before Lent; and the local bishop could, if he chose, deny those he judged unworthy. Through Lent's forty days, one then passed through a rigorous complex of rituals and daily instruction. Finally, at the Easter Vigil, one was baptized in rites whose secrecy was carefully guarded. Here is Augustine's account. He preserves the secrecy of the rites themselves, mentioning only those who joined him and his own emotional response. He uses this occasion to offer a tender memorial for his son, Adeodatus, who would die a few years later. From Confessions, Book 9:

(5.13) When the days of the vintage vacation were at an end, I sent an announcement to the citizens of Milan that they should provide another vendor of verbosity for their students, because I had chosen to serve You and also because I could not meet the demands of that calling on account of my difficulty in breathing and the pain in my chest. I also informed Your bishop, the saintly Ambrose, by letter, concerning my former errors and my present resolution so that he might advise me which of Your books would be best for me to read in order that I might be better prepared and in more suitable condition for the reception of so great a grace. He prescribed Isaiah the prophet, because, I be-

---

48. *Conf.* 9.4.7–4.8 (CCL 27:136–37); trans. Bourke, FOTC 21:233–35 (modified). On Cassiciacum, see Gerard J. P. O'Daly, *Aug-Lex*, 1:771–81.

lieve, Isaiah is more plainly a foreteller of the Gospel and of the calling of the Gentiles than are the others. But since I did not understand the opening passage of this book and thought it all as difficult, I put it aside in order to take it up later, after I became more practiced in the Lord's way of speaking.

(6.14) Then when the time came at which it was required that I turn in my name, we left the countryside and returned to Milan.[49] Alypius also decided to be reborn in You, along with me, for he had already taken on the humility appropriate to Your sacraments and had even gone so far in his very forceful mastery of his body to tread the ice-covered soil of Italy with bare feet, a daring and unusual venture. We also included with us the boy, Adeodatus, born of me in the flesh as a result of my sin. You had fashioned him well. He was almost fifteen years old and surpassed many serious and learned men in his intellectual endowments. I am but confessing to You Your gifts, O Lord my God, Creator of all, who has great power to reform our deformities, for I was responsible for nothing but the sin in that boy. You, and no other, had inspired us to have us nourish him in Your teaching. To You I confess Your gifts. There is a book of mine written under the title, *On the Teacher*.[50] In it, he converses with me. You know that all the views included in it as coming from my dialogue partner are his, when he was sixteen years old. I found many other more amazing qualities in him. His talent was a matter of awe. Who but You is the doer of such wonders? You took his life quickly from this earth, and my memory of him is free of concern, since I have nothing to fear for his boyhood or adolescence or anything for him as a man. We associated him with us as our contemporary in Your grace to be trained in Your studies.

So we were baptized, and the anxiety for our past life fled from us. Nor was I sated during those days with the wonderful sweetness in considering the depth of Your counsels concerning the salvation of humankind. How many tears did I shed, as I was deeply stirred by the voices of Your Church sweetly swelling in the singing of Your hymns and canticles (Eph 5:19)! Those voices flowed into my ears, and truth was distilled into my heart, and a feeling of piety welled up from it. The tears poured forth, and I was happy with them.[51]

---

49. "Turn in my name": That is, applying for baptism. See note 34 above.

50. "*On the Teacher*" (*De magistro*): One of Augustine's early philosophical dialogues, portraying a discussion between him and his son Adeodatus on epistemology. On this, see Goulven Madec, "Augustine et son fils: Le Christ Maître intérieur," *Lectures Augustiniennes*, CEASA 168 (Paris: Institut d'Études Augustiniennes, 2001), 43–58. For excerpts see Chapter 2.

51. *Conf.* 9.5.13–6.14 (CCL 27:140–41); trans. Bourke, FOTC 21:239–41.

VISION AT OSTIA

After baptism, Augustine, his family, and friends decided to return to Africa. They planned to set sail from the Roman seaport of Ostia. There his mother Monnica died. Here Augustine tells the story of a shared mystical moment he and she experienced a few days before her death. It both parallels and differs from the earlier ascent account in Book 7. Again Augustine draws on Neoplatonic turns-of-phrases, but this was no Platonic ascent of "the alone to the Alone." It was shared, not solitary; it was not the rediscovery and recovery of some unfallen self, but the experience of two Christians on the far side of baptism tasting the "first fruits of the Spirit," an ever-so-fleeting glimpse and foretaste of resurrected life. From Confessions, Book 9:

(10.23) When the day on which she was to depart from this life was near at hand—a day You knew but we did not—it happened, I believe, by Your arrangement, in Your hidden ways, that she and I were standing alone, leaning out a window from which the garden inside the house we occupied could be viewed. It was at Ostia on the Tiber where, far removed from the crowds after the hardship of a long journey, we were resting in preparation for the sea voyage. We were talking to each other alone very sweetly, "forgetting what is behind, straining forward to what is before" (Phil 3:13). Between us, in the presence of the Truth, which You are, we tried to find what the eternal life of the saints would be, what "eye has not seen nor ear heard nor has it entered into the human heart" (1 Cor 2:9). But with the mouth of our heart open we also yearned for the flood on high from "Your fountain, the fountain of life which is with You" (Ps 35:10) so that, having been sprinkled from it as much as our capacity would permit, we might meditate in some way about so great a matter.

(10.24) When our conversation had reached its endpoint, recognizing that the greatest delight of the bodily senses in the brightest corporeal light is not capable of comparison with the joy of that life and did not even seem worthy of mention, then rising up, feelings all aflame, toward the Selfsame,[52] we advanced step by step through all visible things up to the sky itself, from which the sun, moon, and stars shine out over the earth, and we ascended still farther in our interior meditation, conversation, and marveling at Your works, came to our own minds. Then we transcended them so that we might touch that region of unending overflowing richness with which You fed Israel (Ps 79:2) eternally on the food of truth. There life is wisdom, through which all these things

---

52. "Selfsame" (*Idipsum*). Kenny, *Mysticism of Saint Augustine*, 77: "'*Idipsum*' or the 'self-same' is a term that recalls both '*ego sum qui sum*' ('I am who am') of Exodus 3:14 and *auto kath'auto*, 'self-sameness,' the classical epithet for the Platonic forms. The Augustinian soul seeks the complete stability of the intelligible and eternal world. This is what the soul had tasted before, in the Book Seven ascension: the 'simplicity of eternity' and freedom from multiplicity, change, and time. And this is God—immediately present and intensely close within the inner recesses of the soul."

come into being, both those that have been and those that will be. Yet it is not made, but is as it was, and thus will be forever; or, rather, to have been in the past or to be in the future does not belong to it. It simply is, for it is eternal. "Having been" or "going to be" is not to be eternal. And while we were speaking of it and panting for it, we did touch it a little with this sudden upsurge of our hearts. We then sighed and left behind "the first fruits of the Spirit" (Rom 8:23) bound to it and came back to the clattering of our mouths, where spoken words have their beginnings and their endings. How is it like Your Word, our Lord, "remaining ageless in Itself and renewing all things" (Wis 7:27)?

(10.25) We were talking then: "Suppose that for someone the tumult of the flesh were silenced; silenced too, any images of earth and water and air; silenced as well, the heavens; if the soul itself grew silent and, not thinking of itself, passed beyond itself; if dreams and visions within the imagination grew silent, and every tongue and every sign and whatever is transient (for if one listens to them, all these things are saying: 'We did not make ourselves, but the One who endures forever made us' [Ps 99:3, 32:11, 116:2])— and if, having said this, these things too became quiet after having lifted up our ears to the One who made them, and He alone spoke not through them but through Himself so that we might hear His Word not through a tongue of flesh nor through the voice of angel nor through the crash of thunder or through the obscurity of parable, but heard the One Himself whom we love in these things—and if we heard Him without these things—that is how it was when at that moment we reached out and in a flash of mind touched eternal Wisdom abiding above all things, and if this could have continued and other visions of a much lower type were taken away, and if this one vision were to enrapture, absorb, and enclose its beholder in inner joys so that life might forever be like that one instant of understanding for which we had sighed, then surely this is the meaning of 'Enter into the joy of Your Lord' (Mt 25:21). And when will this be? When else but when 'we shall all rise but shall not all be changed' (1 Cor 15:51)?" (10.26) Such things I was saying, though not in this way nor in these words.[53]

MEMORY

Book 9 ends with the death of Monnica in 387. Book 10 shifts from autobiography to a book-length meditation on memory and the mysterious depths of human consciousness. Augustine himself had a prodigious memory. He knew much of the Bible and many of the Latin classics by heart. Such feats of memory were essential to ancient oratory, which

53. *Conf.* 9.10.23–10.25 (CCL 27:147–48); my trans., based on Bourke, FOTC 21:250–53.

required that one memorize hour-long speeches by heart (much as modern concert pianists can play hour-long concertos from memory). The following passage, one of the most famous in Western literature, powerfully influenced Petrarch, the founder of Renaissance humanism. From Confessions, *Book 10:*

(8.12) So I shall pass above this power of my nature, ascending by steps toward the One who made me, and I come into the fields and broad palaces of memory where there are treasures of innumerable images of all sorts of objects brought in by the senses. There is stored away whatever we ponder over, too, either by adding to or taking away from or changing in any way the things which sense perception has contacted, and anything else kept or put back there, which forgetfulness has not yet engrossed and buried. When I am in this storehouse, I can request whatever I want be brought forward. Some things come forth immediately. Others are hunted for a longer time, yet they are dug out, as it were, from some more concealed containers. Still others rush out in a mob when something else is sought and looked for, jumping out into the middle as if to say: "Would we do, perhaps?" These I drive away from the face of my memory with the hand of my heart until what I want emerges and enters into view from the secret places. Other things come up as they are required in easy and uninterrupted sequence. The first ones give way to those which follow and, in leaving, are stored up to come forth again whenever I desire it. All of this goes on when I recite something memorized.

(8.13) In [the memory] all things are kept distinct and classified. They are carried in, each by its own channel—light, for instance, and all colors and shapes of bodies through the eyes; all kinds of sounds through the ears; all smells through the channel of the nostrils; all flavors through the channel of the mouth; and then by the sensitivity of the whole body, whatever is hard or soft, hot or cold, smooth or rough, heavy or light, whether outside or inside the body. All these the great recesses of memory and its indescribably hidden and mysterious chasms take in to be called up to mind and reviewed when need arises. All these things go in, each by its own gateway and are there stored away. The things themselves do not go in, of course, but the images of sensory things are ready there for the understanding which calls them up. Just how they are fashioned, who can say?—though it is evident by which senses they are caught up and stored away within. For even while I dwell in darkness and silence, I can, if I wish, produce colors in my memory and distinguish between white and black and between any others as I wish. Nor do sounds rush in and disturb the object drawn in through the eyes when I am considering it. Yet they are there, also, and lie hidden in separation, as it were. I can summon these too if it pleases me, and they are present at once. With tongue at rest and the throat silent, I can sing as much as I want. The images of colors, despite the fact that they are present, do not intervene or break in when that other storeroom, which has flowed in through the ears, is reviewed. Thus, I can remember at will the other things which have been taken in and piled up through the other senses. I can distinguish the fragrance of lilies from that of violets while smelling nothing, and I can prefer honey to musk, smooth to rough, and not by tasting or touching anything at the time, but by recollecting.

(8.14) I do this inside, in the immense palace of my memory. In it sky, earth, and sea are present before me, together with the things I can perceive in them, except for those which I have forgotten. In it I even encounter myself and I bring myself to mind: what, when, and where I did something, and how I felt when I did it. In it are all the things which I remember, either those personally experienced or those told me by others. . . .

(8.15) Great is this power of memory, exceedingly great, O my God; it is a vast and unlimited inner chamber. Who has plumbed its depths? Yet this is a power of my mind, and it belongs to my nature. I myself do not grasp all that I am. Is then the mind too narrow to grasp itself? So then a question arises: Where is this part of myself which it cannot grasp? Is it outside it and not inside it? How then does it not grasp it? This question brings up something really astonishing to me. It leaves me awestruck: People go out to admire mountain peaks, giant waves in the sea, the broad courses of rivers, the vast sweep of the ocean, and the circuits of the stars—and yet [the immense depths of] their own self they ignore and leave aside.[54]

"LATE HAVE I LOVED YOU"

One of the most famous passages in Confessions *is a brief poetic prayer in Book 10. I have tried here to capture the poetic feel of Augustine's elegant Latin. Following his French translators, I set the passage in free verse and with the Latin in parallel. From* Confessions, *Book 10:*

(27.38) *Sero te amaui,*	Late have I loved You,
pulchritudo tam antiqua	beauty so ancient,
et tam noua,	so new,
sero te amaui.	late have I loved You.

---

54. *Conf.* 10.8.12–8.15 (CCL 27:161–63); trans. Bourke, FOTC 21: 273–76 (modified). See Roland Teske, "Augustine's Philosophy of Memory," in Stump and Kretzmann, *Cambridge Companion to Augustine*, 148–58; O'Donnell, 3:174–78.

Et ecce intus eras	And see; You were within, inside me,
et ego foris	and I was outside,
et ibi quaerebam	and out there I sought You,
et in ista formosa, quae fecisti	and I—misshapen—chased after
deformis inruebam.	the beautiful shapes You had made.
Mecum eras,	You were with me,
et tecum non eram.	but I was not with You.
Ea me tenebant longe a te,	Beautiful things kept me far off from You—
quae si in te non essent,	things which, if not in You, would not be,
non essent.	not be at all.
Vocasti et clamasti	You called and shouted out
et rupisti surditatem meam,	and shattered my deafness.
coruscasti, splenduisti,	You flashed, You blazed,
et fugasti caecitatem meam,	and my blindness fled.
fragrasti, et duxi spiritum	You were fragrant, and I drew in my breath
et anhelo tibi,	and panted for You.
gustaui et esurio	I tasted You, and hunger
et sitio,	and thirst for more.
tetigisti me,	You touched me,
et exarsi in pacem tuam.	and I burned for your peace.[55]

THE ART OF CONFESSION

The architecture of Confessions is far from obvious. It is far from clear how autobiography (Books 1–9), psychological meditation (Book 10), and a commentary on the opening verses of Genesis (Books 11–13) fit together. This apparent lack of unity has provoked a vast scholarly industry that, year after year, produces one theory after another attempting to explain why Confessions is a unified work. Some scholars have simply thrown up their hands. The great Augustinian scholar Henri Marrou once wondered aloud whether "Augustin compose mal"—whether Augustine is a poor constructor of books.[56]

55. Conf. 10.27.38 (CCL 27:175); my trans. See O'Donnell, 3:196–98.
56. Henri Marrou, Saint Augustin et la fin de la culture antique, 4th ed. (Paris: Boccard, 1958), 61. In his later "Retractio," 665–72, Marrou recanted this objection, noting that Augustine's organizational style was more like that of a composer of music than of a constructor of scholastic treatises, that Augustine often introduced key themes subtly mezza voce before bringing them symphonically front and center.

One reason why the effort continues is that, despite the odd architecture, Confessions does feel unified and Augustine himself always considered it a unified work. If one reads the entire text, one comes away with the sense that it does somehow fit together. Partly this is because many hidden threads crisscross the text. But one central thread, one that subtly unites the work, is the idea of confession, a three-fold confession of sin, of praise, and of faith.[57] *John O'Meara once remarked that "it is a mistake . . . to seek to separate these three elements, for though the emphasis varies from place to place the confession of sin nearly always implies faith and praise, and likewise each of the other two implies the others."*[58] *Here are a few passages that illustrate the theme. Note they typically appear at the opening of individual books:*

(i) Confession of Sin

From Confessions, Book 2:

(1.1) I want to recall to mind the foul deeds of my past and the carnal corruptions of my soul, not because I love them but that I may love You, O my God. I do this for love of Your love, bringing again to mind my wicked ways in a bitter-tasting remembrance that You may bring sweetness to me, O undeceiving Sweetness, Sweetness both happy and secure. You gathered me together from a dispersion in which I was divided and torn asunder when I turned away from the Oneness of You and frittered myself away on the many.[59]

(ii) Confession of Praise

From Confessions, Book 5:

(1.1) Accept the sacrifice of my confession as the offering of "the hand of my tongue" (Prv 18:21), which You formed and stirred up to confess Your Name. "Heal all my bones" (Ps 6:3) and "let them say: Lord, who is like You?" (Ps 34:10) Not that one who confesses to You teaches You anything about what goes on within him, for the heart that is closed is not shut to Your eye nor does the hardness of humanity stay Your hand. Rather, You soften it whenever You desire, either in compassion or in punishment. "There is no one who

---

57. Augustine discusses the various meanings of "confession" (*confessio*) in his sermons: s. 67.1–2; en. Ps. 29.2.22, 141.19. He does so at length in one of the newly discovered Dolbeau sermons: s. 29B.1–6 (= Dolbeau 8). On this theme in *Confessiones*, see O'Donnell, 2:3–7.

58. John O'Meara, *The Young Augustine: The Growth of St. Augustine's Mind Up to His Conversion*, rev. ed. (New York: Alba House, 2001), 2.

59. *Conf.* 2.1.1 (CCL 27:18); my trans., based on Bourke, FOTC 21:33.

can hide himself from Your heat" (Ps 18:7). Rather, let my soul praise You so that it may love You, let it confess to You Your mercies so that it may praise You. Your whole creation never stops or grows silent in praising You—every spirit praises You through the mouth that is turned to You, and all animals and bodily things through the mouth of those who look upon them so that our soul springs up to You from its weakness, supported by those things which You have made, and passing over to You who have made these things so wonderfully (Ps 71:18). There, there is refreshment and true strength.[60]

(iii) Confession in Writing before Witnesses

From Confessions, Book 10:

(1.1) May I know You who know me. "Let me know You even as I am known" (1 Cor 13:12). O strength of my soul, go deep into it and make it fit for You that You may have it and possess it "without spot or wrinkle" (Eph 5:27). This is my hope and that is why I speak . . . "For behold You have loved truth" (Ps 50:8) since "the one who does the truth comes to the light" (Jn 3:21). I desire to do this in my heart before You in confession and in my writing before many witnesses.

(2.2) . . . Before You, then, O Lord, I stand open, whatever I may be. Of the fruit of confessing to You, I have already spoken. Nor am I doing it with fleshly words and speech, but with the words of the soul and the cry of my mind, words Your ear recognizes. For when I am bad, to confess to You is nothing but to be displeased with myself; when I am good, to confess to You is simply not to attribute this good to myself. For You, O Lord, bless the just, but then You first make the impious just. And so my confession, O my God, is made in silence to You in Your sight, yet not in silence. It may be silent in terms of audible sound, but it cries out loud in inner feeling. Nor do I say anything right to people that You have not first heard from me, nor do You hear any such things which You have not said to me first. [61]

(iv) Confession of Faith by Interpreting Scripture

From Confessions, Book 11:

(1.1) Since eternity is Yours, O Lord, . . . why then do I tell You the detailed story of so many things? Certainly, not so that you can learn them through me. Rather, it is to stir up my feeling of love toward You and the feelings of

60. Conf. 5.1.1 (CCL 27:57); trans. Bourke, FOTC 21:101–2.
61. Conf. 10.1.1–2.2 (CCL 27:155); trans. Bourke, FOTC 21:263–64.

those who read these pages so that we may all say, "You are great, O Lord, and greatly to be praised" (Ps 95:4).[62] I have already said it, and I shall say it again: I do this for the love of Your love.[63] For while we do pray, Truth says: "Your Father knows what you need before you ask Him" (Mt 6:8). So we lay open our feeling of love by confessing to You our own miseries and Your mercies upon us so that You may deliver us completely, that we may cease to be wretched in ourselves and may become happy in You. You have called us that we may be poor in spirit, meek, mournful, hungry, and thirsty for justice, merciful, pure of heart, and peacemakers (Mt 5:3–9). See, I have told You many things [about my life], to the extent that I could and should, because You first willed that I should confess to You, my Lord God, "for You are good, and Your mercy endures forever" (Ps 117:1).

(2.2) But when can "the tongue of my pen" (Ps 44:2) be adequate to the task of proclaiming all Your encouragements and all Your terrors, Your consolations and the guidance by which You have brought me to be a preacher of Your Word and minister of Your sacrament to Your people? Even if I am up to the task of setting them forth in orderly detail, then time's drops are precious to me. Now I have for a long time burned with a desire to meditate upon Your law and to confess to You both my knowledge of it and my ignorance of it— the beginnings of Your illumination and what remains in darkness for me— until my weakness may be engulfed in Your strength. I do not want the hours to flow away, those I find free from the necessary tasks of refreshing the body and of intellectual labor and of the service I owe people and that which we give even though we do not owe it.

(2.3) O Lord my God, "be attentive to my prayer" (Ps 60:2), and let Your mercy hear my desire, because it burns with concern not only for myself, but it also longs to serve others in fraternal charity. You see in my heart that it is so. May I offer up to You this service of my thought and tongue, and may You grant what I may offer to You. "For I am needy and poor" (Ps 85:1), while "You are rich towards all who call upon You" (Rom 10:12), You who, being without cares, take care of us. Circumcise my lips, inwardly and outwardly, from all recklessness and all lying. Let Your Scriptures be my chaste delights to the end that I not be deceived in them and that I not deceive others through them . . . "Yours is the day, and Yours is the night" (Ps 73:16). At Your nod, the moments fly away. Grant space for our meditations on the secrets of Your Law and do not close it against those who knock (Mt 7:7). Not for nothing did you will so many pages of dark secrets be written; not for nothing do those forests have their stags (Ps 28:9), taking refuge in them, recovering, walking

62. "'You are great . . . '": Augustine echoes here the opening words of *conf.* 1.1.1.
63. "I do this for the love of Your love": Augustine refers here to *conf.* 2.1.1.

about and feeding, lying down and ruminating. O Lord, complete your work in me, and reveal those pages to me. Behold, Your voice is my joy, Your voice is greater than an abundance of pleasures. Grant what I love, for I do love it. And this love is also Your gift. Abandon not Your gifts nor spurn Your grass when we are thirsty. Let me confess to You whatever I discover in Your books, and "may I hear the voice of Your praise" (Ps 25:7), and drink You in and "consider the wondrous things of Your law" (Ps 118:18), from the very beginning when You made heaven and earth until the perpetual reign of Your holy city with You.[64]

THE ELDERLY AUGUSTINE'S VIEW OF CONFESSIONS

At the end of his career, Augustine reviewed his books, offering brief reflections and occasional emendations. The following are the laconic but poignant comments of the elderly Augustine after rereading Confessions. *From* Reconsiderations (Retractationes), *Book 2:*

(6.1) The thirteen books of my *Confessions* praise the just and good God for my evil and good acts and lift up the understanding and affection of people to Him. At least . . . they had this effect on me while I was writing them and they continue to have it when I read them. What others think about them is a matter for them to decide. Yet I know that they have given and continue to give pleasure to many of my brethren. The first ten books were written about myself; the last three about Holy Scripture, from the words: "In the beginning God created heaven and earth" (Gn 1:1) as far as the Sabbath rest (Gn 2:2).[65]

64. *Conf.* 11.1.1–2.3 (CCL 27:194–95); my trans., based on Bourke, FOTC 21:328–30. This final sentence spells out the content of *conf.* 11–13, an allegorical commentary on the six days of creation and the sabbath rest of the seventh day, which foreshadows the eternal peace of the City of God.

65. *Retr.* 2.6.1 (CCL 57:94); trans. Bogan, FOTC 60:130. On *Retractationes*, see Goulven Madec, *Introduction aux 'Revisions' et à la Lecture des Œuvres de saint Augustin*, CEASA 150 (Paris: Institut d'Études Augustiniennes, 1996).

CHAPTER 2

AUGUSTINE THE PHILOSOPHER

⁂

In his earliest publication, Augustine noted: "What is philosophy? A love of wisdom."[1] The word's etymology, he believed, defined the endeavor: philosophy is life shaped by a love-spurred search for wisdom. In late antiquity, philosophy was never a mere academic enterprise.[2] It required more than well-honed skills in dialectic, a fondness for abstraction, or an unflinching confidence in reason. It demanded a change of life, indeed, a conversion. It presumed renunciation of wealth and fame. It required ongoing ascetical purification, strict controls of diet and sexuality and the passions. It encouraged deep introspection, honest self-examination, a cleansing of mind and heart. Philosophy in late antiquity was inevitably religious since the search for wisdom implied a search for wisdom's source, the One who is true Wisdom. Thus Augustine, like his educated contemporaries, spoke of Christianity itself as a philosophy. Christians, he once noted, "believe and teach that, as for salvation, there is not one thing called philosophy, that is, the search for wisdom, and another thing called religion."[3]

Augustine began grappling with philosophers and with philosophy from an early date. In his training in rhetoric, he had been required to study Cicero, the Latin orator *par excellence*. But what captured the young Augustine's imagination was Cicero's other side, Cicero the philosopher, the epitomist and interpreter of Greek philosophy.[4] Reading the *Hortensius* at age 18 led Augustine

---

1. *C. Acad.* 2.3.7 (CCL 29:21); my trans. See *De ordine* 1.11.32; *conf.* 3.4.7. On this, see Goulven Madec, *Saint Augustin et la philosophie*, CEASA 149 (Paris: Institut d'Études Augustiniennes, 1996), 15–24.

2. See Pierre Hadot, *What Is Ancient Philosophy?* trans. Michael Chase (Cambridge, MA: Harvard University Press, 2002); also Hadot, *Exercices spirituels et philosophie antique*, CEASA 88 (Paris: Institut d'Études Augustiniennes, 1981).

3. *De vera religione* 5.8 (BA 8:38); my trans.

4. See J. G. F. Powell, ed., *Cicero the Philosopher* (Oxford: Clarendon Press, 1995); Testard, *Saint Augustin et*

to commit himself to philosophy's rigors. Joining the Manichees seemed, at the time, to flow naturally from such a commitment to reason and wisdom. Only later and only gradually did he judge it, in dark terms, as a gravely mistaken false start. This disillusionment led him by his early 30s to revert to his philosophical starting point, to the skepticism of Cicero and the Academics (as the skeptical successors of Plato were then known). In Milan, Augustine momentously encountered another Platonism, the Platonism of Plotinus or Porphyry (or both). This Neoplatonism, as we now call it, offered fresh new ways of conceiving God, the soul, eternity, beauty, and much else. Augustine found these writings all the more intriguing because what he heard in Ambrose's preaching was a brand of Christianity clearly conversant with and, in key ways, harmonious with such sophisticated Neoplatonism.

In this chapter, we focus on Augustine's earliest writings, those composed from 386 to 391, that is, between his dramatic conversion in Milan and his ordination in Hippo Regius. These works hover around topics we associate with philosophy, both ancient and modern: the existence and nature of God, the mind-body problem, the freedom of the will, the nature of evil, the role of language, the quest for truth, the character of time and eternity, and the search for happiness. These works include four philosophic dialogues composed at Cassiciacum in the months after his conversion but before his baptism: *Against the Skeptics* (*Contra Academicos*), *On the Happy Life* (*De beata vita*), *On Order* (*De ordine*), and *Soliloquies* (*Soliloquia*). There are, as well, two later philosophic dialogues: *On the Magnitude of the Soul* (*De animae quantitate*), composed in Rome; and *On the Teacher* (*De magistro*), composed in Thagaste. Some philosophic works were left incomplete, such as his *On the Immortality of the Soul* (*De immortalitate animae*), or left aside after sketching out some rough drafts, such as his planned series on the liberal arts (one of these, *On Music* (*De musica*), was completed and preserved). He also carried on a philosophically-oriented correspondence with his friend Nebridius (*epp.* 3–4, 9–14) and wrote a magisterial apology for Christianity, *On True Religion* (*De vera religione*).

These writings offer glimpses into Augustine's career-altering transitions. The first was his sabbatical at Cassiciacum in the fall of 386, an agitated respite between his conversion and his baptism. He spoke of it as a "pause," and was alert to its dizzy and sometimes confusing liminality.[5] At the time, he alluded obliquely to his own situation: "many persons are suddenly converted to a good and edifying life, but until they become notable by

Cicéron; Harald Hagendahl, *Augustine and the Latin Classics*, Studia Graeca et Latina XX (Guteborg: Acta Universitatis Cothoburgensis, 1967).

5. *Conf.* 9.4.7 (BA 14:82). See Catherine Conybeare, "The Duty of a Teacher: Liminality and *disciplina* in Augustine's *De ordine*," in *Augustine and the Disciplines: From Cassiciacum to Confessions*, ed. Karla Pollmann and Mark Vessey (New York: Oxford University Press, 2005), 49–65.

some outstanding deeds, they are still believed to be what they used to be."[6] We see him still as what he used to be in some respects, yet on the cusp of a new life. By mid-387, after his baptism, Augustine and his circle left Milan for good. They got only as far as Rome—stuck for a full year, unable to set sail for Africa, because a rebel Roman general and his navy had blockaded the seaport of Ostia. During this interim, Augustine's mother would die. In 388, he, his friends, and family finally returned to Africa, first to Carthage and then to Thagaste, where they embarked on a grand experiment in Christian community. This phase, too, was liminal in its own way, a pause between baptism and ordination. His newly formed community could be seen as either something old or something new. To some, like his friend Nebridius, it seemed an old-fashioned gesture, the embrace of a life of philosophic retirement. But it also hinted at something new. The new fashion then sweeping Christianity was organized asceticism. Augustine's community appears as one ephemeral instance of the wide-ranging experiments in monasticism springing up around the late fourth-century Empire.[7] Settled in Thagaste, Augustine and his companions consciously styled themselves "servants of God" (servi Dei). He had grand hopes for them: to "grow godlike in retirement."[8] Such dreams proved short-lived. Within the year, his son Adeodatus and his friend Nebridius would die.

These early works are Augustine's least reader-friendly. Partly it is the subtlety of the topics. Augustine admitted, years later, that even he found one of them, On the Immortality of the Soul, challenging: "Because of the intricacy and brevity of its reasoning, it is so obscure that even my attention flags as I read it and I myself can scarcely understand it."[9] Mostly these seem, from our vantage point, stiff or artificial. The dialogues may adopt the guise of being verbatim transcripts of actual conversations, but they are, in fact, highly self-conscious literary works, composed for an educated elite, at ease with and attuned to the conventions of the philosophic dialogue—and Augustine's subtle disruptions of these.[10] In these works, he still thinks and speaks as a cultivated intellectual addressing other cultivated intellectuals. At the end of his life, he looked back on the Cassiciacum works with mixed feelings: "Even though I had given up the earthly prospects that I had once cherished," these

---

6. De ordine 2.10.29 (CCL 29:123–24); trans. Russell, FOTC 5:307.

7. See William Harmless, "Monasticism," in Oxford Handbook of Early Christian Studies, ed. Susan Ashbrook Harvey and David Hunter (New York: Oxford University Press, 2008), 493–517.

8. Ep. 10.2 (CCL 31:25): deificari . . . in otio.

9. Retr. 1.5.1 (CCL 57:16); trans. Bogan, FOTC 60:20.

10. On the literary aspect of the dialogues, see especially the study of Catherine Conybeare, The Irrational Augustine, OECS (New York: Oxford University Press, 2006). See also Joanne McWilliam, "The Cassiciacum Autobiography," Studia Patristica 18.4 (1990): 14–43; John J. O'Meara, "The Historicity of Augustine's Early Dialogues," Vigiliae Christianae 5 (1951): 150–78.

early "things I wrote while still a catechumen . . . were puffed up with the us-ages of secular literature."[11] He had yet to hone either the poetic immediacy of *Confessions* or the more populist style of his sermons. However quaint or mannered these early works seem to us, they remained popular in elite circles throughout his lifetime.

These writings pre-date *Confessions*, of course; they also overlap with its time-frame. For more than a century, scholars have probed and debated how the Augustine of the dialogues differs from the Augustine of the *Confessions*. In 1918, Prosper Alfaric famously appealed to these early works to argue that "morally as well as intellectually, it was Neoplatonism Augustine converted to rather than to the Gospel."[12] That assessment has been roundly refuted, dismantled as a false antithesis, thanks to the researches of Pierre Courcelle, who argued that "Neoplatonism and Christianity were, for the thinking lead-ers of the Milanese church, intimately tied together and not, as some mod-erns have believed, opposed. This synthesis, already elaborated, was one to which Augustine gave his entire adherence."[13] In Milan, Augustine convert-ed not simply to Catholic Christianity, but to an intellectually sophisticated brand of it, one that had drawn on Neoplatonist perspectives, but selectively and critically. And that selective and discerning appropriation was one Au-gustine continued. No pagan Neoplatonist worth his salt would have been happy with Augustine's synthesis. At this juncture, Augustine felt optimistic that there were legitimate and commendable theological convergences be-tween thinking Christians and sophisticated pagan monotheists like Ploti-nus and Porphyry. His rhetoric at this early date would be irenic.

We see here the beginnings of his dialogue not only with others, but also with himself. Augustine's thinking was no fixity; it was always probing, shift-ing, moving. This chapter gives the earliest freeze-frame we have of that move-ment. Some ideas here are the first enunciations of abiding concerns (e.g., interiority, the search for happiness); others would go through rapid develop-ments and new applications (e.g., words as signs, the inner teacher); still oth-ers would undergo serious modification (e.g., the disparaging of the body, the optimistic estimate of Neoplatonism), even reversal (e.g., freedom of the will). During this same period, especially once he moved to Thagaste, Augustine be-gan directly confronting Manicheism. His earliest anti-Manichean writings (e.g., *On the Catholic and Manichean Ways of Life, On Genesis Against the Manichees*) overlap with this period. For purposes of clarity, I have postponed treating

11. *Retr.* prol. 3 (CCL 57:6); trans. Bogan, FOTC 60:5.

12. Prosper Alfaric, *L'évolution intellectuelle de saint Augustin: I. Du manichéisme au néoplatonisme* (Paris: Nourry, 1918), 380–81 (my trans.).

13. Courcelle, *Recherches sur les Confessions*, 252–53 (my trans.).

these works until Chapter 6.[14] Even so, we need to remind ourselves that even in Augustine's strictly philosophical works, there is often a subtle, under-the-surface wrestling with issues raised by or raised against Manicheism: e.g., the origin of evil, the freedom of the will, the nature of the soul.

※

VOYAGE TO THE PORT OF PHILOSOPHY

In Reconsiderations, *Augustine lists* On the Happy Life *as his second work, but it was the first he actually completed. Composed at Cassiciacum on his birthday in November 386, this brief dialogue explores a theme that stands at the heart of the ancient philosophic quest: What is happiness? He opens the work with a dedication to Manlius Theodorus, a Platonist philosopher he met in Milan, and here gives the earliest account of his spiritual journey, a sort of* Confessions *in miniature. He articulates this more in philosophic terms than in overtly Christian phraseology. From* On the Happy Life:

(1.1) If the sea-voyage to the port of philosophy—a port-city from which one heads out on firm footing into the land of the happy life—were to be conducted via reason and the will itself, I do not think it rash, great and most noble Theodorus,[15] if I said that far fewer are likely to arrive in port than those few, rare individuals whom we actually see launching out for it. For since in this world either God or nature or necessity or our own will or a combination of some or all of these has tossed us around, here and there, blindly as in the billowing waves of a stormy sea (the matter is very obscure, but you have already set out to shed light on it), how very few would perceive where best to exert oneself or where best to return to unless, at some time, some sort of tempest should send us in a direction that to fools would appear wrong-turned, and thrust us, without our realizing it and against our off-course wanderings, onto that most excellent land. . . .

(1.4) At age nineteen, when I read in the school of rhetoric that book of Cicero's called *Hortensius*,[16] I became inflamed by such a great love of philosophy that I considered devoting myself to it at once. Yet I was not free of those foggy mists which confused the course of my journey, and I confess that for

14. I debated with myself whether to place selections from *On Free Will* (*De libero arbitrio*) in this chapter, since its genre and its concerns are philosophical. Because Books 2 and 3 were composed after 391 and because its concerns are anti-Manichean, I decided to place them in Chapter 6 rather than here.

15. "Most noble Theodorus": In *De ordine* 1.11.31, Augustine lavishes praise on Theodorus "as a man standing in very high esteem, excelling others by his ingenuity, eloquence, and preeminently by his spirit." In *retr.* 1.2, he says that he regrets the high praise.

16. "That book of Cicero's called *Hortensius*": Augustine cites it most famously in *conf.* 3.4.7 (as we saw in Chapter 1); it is also cited in *c. Acad.* 1.1.4; *Trin.* 13.4.7, 14.9.12, and 14.19.26.

quite a while I was led astray, with my eyes fixed on stars that sink into the ocean. A childish superstition frightened me from thorough investigation,[17] but as soon as I was made more upright, I threw off the darkness and learned to trust more in those who taught than in those who ordered belief, having myself encountered those to whom the very light, seen by their eyes, apparently was an object of the highest and even divine veneration.[18] I did not agree with them but thought they were concealing under these veils some important secret which they would later divulge. After I shook them off and abandoned them, especially after I crossed the sea, the Academics for a long while steered my course amid the waves as my helm ran up against every sort of wind. And now I have come to this land. Here I have learned to know the North Star to whom I ought to entrust myself. For I have noticed frequently in the sermons of our priest,[19] and sometimes in yours, that the notion of God absolutely excludes any sort of thinking in terms of body and even of soul—though soul is the one of all things nearest to God.

I acknowledge that I did not fly quickly to the bosom of philosophy because I was detained by a woman's charm and the lure of honors so that only after attaining them I finally, as occurs only to a few of the most fortunate, sprinted with sails fully unfurled and all oars bent to that bosom where I found rest. For after I had read only a few books of Plotinus,[20] of whom, as I learned, you are particularly fond, I compared them as best I could with the authority of those who have handed down to us the divine mysteries, and I was so inflamed that I would have broken away from all anchors, had not the counsel of certain people stayed me. What else was left, then, except that a tempest, what seemed an adversity, came to the rescue from the uncertainties that were holding me back? I therefore was seized by such chest pains[21] that, being unable to keep up my onerous profession, through which I might have sailed to the Sirens, I threw off the ballast and brought my ship, shattered and leaking though it was, to that desired resting place.

(1.5) You see, therefore, the philosophy into which, as into a harbor, I am now sailing. But this port also is wide open, and though its breadth offers less danger, it still does not rule out all error. For I simply do not know

17. "A childish superstition": Manicheism.

18. "Light . . . object of the highest and even divine veneration": The Manichees venerated the sun as a site where the light of souls is distilled and purified. See Chapter 6.

19. "Our priest": Ambrose of Milan.

20. W. Green, CCL 29:67, opts for "Plotinus" (Plotini) as the preferred reading; other translators have followed other manuscripts which, instead, have "Plato" (Platonis) here.

21. "Chest pains" (pectoris dolor): Augustine suffered at the time an acute respiratory ailment (asthma?). Some scholars interpret it as psychosomatic, as some sort of stress or anxiety disorder. Augustine refers to it repeatedly: c. Acad. 3.7.15; De ordine 1.2.5; conf. 9.2.4. He told the city fathers of Milan that this—and not his conversion—was the reason for his resignation as orator. See O'Donnell, 3:78–79.

what segment of the land—what alone offers happiness—I should move towards and how I should chance to reach it. What solid ground do I hold onto? Even now, for me, the question of the soul sways back and forth and surges in great waves.[22]

CONVERSION TO PHILOSOPHY

Augustine's earliest extant work is a philosophical dialogue entitled Against the Skeptics. *He dedicated it to his longtime patron and friend, Romanianus, who had helped finance his higher education. At the time of its writing, in fall 386, he served as tutor for Romanianus's teenage son, Licentius, who plays a major role in the dialogue. Augustine here gives the earliest account of his conversion to philosophic Christianity. From* Against the Skeptics, *Book 2:*

(2.4) Whatever I now enjoy in this leisure of retreat—the fact that I have escaped from the chains of excessive desires; that I have laid aside the burdens of deadly cares and am beginning to breathe again, to recover, to return to myself; that I am searching with great focus on a quest for the truth and have already begun to find it; and that I am confident of reaching even the supreme Measure:[23] you encouraged me, you pushed me on, you made it possible. The One whose minister you have been has been, thus far, more conceived by faith than understood by reason. For when I had opened up to you, face-to-face, the deep inner stirrings of my mind, and when I repeatedly and fiercely asserted that to me no fortune seemed favorable if it did not afford the leisure to apply oneself to philosophy, that no life could be happy unless it was lived in philosophy, but that I was held back by so great a burden regarding my family and relatives, whose very life depended on my profession, and by various expenses that were occasioned either by my own empty shame or by the anguishing distress of my relatives—on such occasions you used to be so elated with gladness and so inflamed with a sacred enthusiasm for this kind of life that you used to say that you would break all my chains by sharing even your own inheritance with me if you were in some way freed from the shackles of those troublesome lawsuits.

(2.5) When the fire had just been kindled in us and you had to leave, we did not cease yearning for philosophy and for that way of life which had won favor among us, and we agreed to make no other plans. We aimed at it steadi-

22. *De beata vita* 1.1–1.5 (CCL 29:65–68); my trans., based on Schopp, FOTC 5:43–49. See Robert J. O'Connell, "Augustine's First Conversion: *Factus erectior* (*De beata vita* 4)," *Augustinian Studies* 17 (1986): 15–29.

23. "Supreme Measure": a circumlocution for God the Father. See *De beata vita* 4.33–34 (quoted below) in which Augustine expands on the term.

ly but less intensely—we thought we were doing enough. Because we had not yet been touched by that blaze that was to sweep in upon us, we thought that the low slow flame we burned with was as great as it gets. But suddenly, as soon as certain books brimming [with ideas] exhaled this sweet Arabian fragrance over us (as Celsinus[24] puts it), no sooner had they sprinkled a very few tiny drops of a most precious perfume on that flickering flame than they suddenly sparked in me this wildfire—incredible, Romanianus, it was incredible—maybe, even beyond what you would believe of me—what else can I say?—beyond even what I can believe of myself. What could honors, what could human accolades, what could craving for empty fame, what, in the end, could the poultice and tether of this mortal life move me to? Steadily, I started turning inward, quickly, totally, towards myself. And I looked back— I confess it—as though from a journey's end, back to that religion which had been implanted in us in our childhood, and which had been, as it were, woven into our bone's marrow. That religion was drawing me to herself, although I did not know it. Staggering, hurrying, hesitating, I seized the Apostle Paul. For truly those men, I have to say, could never have accomplished such great things and could never have lived the way they clearly did if their writings and their principles were opposed to so great a good as this. I read the whole book with the greatest care and attention. (2.6) Then philosophy's face, however dim its rays of light before then, revealed itself to me so greatly.[25]

THE CHALLENGE OF RADICAL SKEPTICISM

In his earliest work, Augustine grapples with radical skepticism as argued for by Cicero and the Academics.[26] He knew of this school of philosophy largely through Cicero's dialogue Academica, *and associates its classic views with the Greek philosopher Carneades (214–129 B.C.E.).[27] In the following passage, he summarizes, at the request of his friend Alypius, the Academic position as he knew it. From* Against the Skeptics, *Book 2:*

24. "Celsinus": In *Soliloquia* 1.12.21, Augustine mentions Cornelius Celsus, "who says that wisdom is the supreme good"; in *De haeresibus* pref., he refers to Celsus, "who had compiled, in six books, the tenets of all the founders of distinct philosophic schools." There was also Celsinus of Castabala, who authored an encyclopedia of philosophy, which may have been translated into Latin; see Pierre Courcelle, *Les lettres grecques en Occident* (Paris: de Boccard, 1948), 178–81.

25. *C. Acad.* 2.2.4–2.6 (CCL 29:20–21); my trans. On this passage, see John J. O'Meara, "Plotinus and Augustine: Exegesis of *Contra Academicos* II,5," *Studies in Augustine and Eriugena*, ed. Thomas Halton (Washington, DC: The Catholic University of America Press, 1992), 195–208.

26. John M. Rist, *Augustine: Ancient Thought Baptized* (New York: Cambridge University Press, 1994), 42, notes that "unlike almost every other thinker of late antiquity, Augustine took radical skepticism seriously and was driven by his own experience to attempt to find answers to it." See *retr.* 1.1.

27. This global skepticism did not precisely match what we know of Carneades' own position, but reflects a later "dogmatic skepticism" and Cicero's own position. See Rist, *Augustine*, 41–48.

(5.11) The Academics held, first, that a person could not have certain knowledge concerning things which had to do with philosophy (indeed, Carneades used to say that he did not care about anything else); and, second, that a person can nevertheless be wise and that the role of the wise (as was minutely discussed by you, [Alypius], as well as by Licentius, in our earlier discussion) consists entirely in a diligent search for truth. As a result, the wise give assent to nothing at all, for if one were to give assent to things uncertain, one would inevitably fall into error—something seen as criminal for the wise. The Academics not only claimed that all things are uncertain, but they also reinforced that claim by a huge supply of arguments. Now, as for their view that truth cannot be comprehended, they seemed to have seized on the definition of Zeno the Stoic,[28] who said that truth could be perceived as that which so impressed itself on the mind from what it came from that it could not be impressed from anything other than what it came from. This can be said more clearly and briefly: truth can be perceived by those signs which cannot be present in what is false. The Academics made strenuous efforts to establish the conviction that such a truth could not be found. Thus, in defense of their contention, the dissensions of philosophers, the illusions of the senses, [the experience of] dreams and delirium, pseudo-arguments and sophistries were vigorously set out. And because they had it from the same Zeno that nothing is more disgraceful than to indulge in opinions, they very cleverly concluded that if nothing can be known and if mere opinion is really disgraceful, then the wise ought never to accept anything as certain.

(5.12) For this reason, a great deal of animosity was aroused against them. It seemed to follow as a logical consequence that the one who would accept nothing as certain would thus do nothing. Because the Academics believed that their wise man accepted nothing as certain, they seemed to describe him as sleeping all the time and shirking all his duties. So they brought forward the idea of a certain "probability," what they termed "truth-like," and maintained that the wise never neglect duties since they have something to guide them. The truth, however, lies hidden, buried, or confused either by some sort of darkness within nature or by the misleading similarity of things. Moreover, they claimed that the very act of withholding or, as it were, curbing assent was a great exploit on the part of the wise. Now, I believe, I have expounded their whole system briefly, as you wished, and I have not fallen short of your injunction, Alypius—that is, I have acted with good faith, as they say.[29]

28. "Zeno the Stoic": Zeno of Citium (c. 334–262 B.C.E.), founder of the Stoic school of philosophy. See Brad Inwood, ed., *The Cambridge Companion to the Stoics* (Cambridge: Cambridge University Press, 2003); N. Joseph Torchia, "Stoics, Stoicism," *AugEncy*, 816–20.

29. *C. Acad.* 2.5.11–5.12 (CCL 29:24–25); my trans., based on Kavanagh, FOTC 5:145–47. This passage draws on and summarizes Cicero, *Academica*, 2.6.16–34.111.

AUGUSTINE'S REBUTTAL:
TRUTHS OF LOGIC AND MATHEMATICS

Given the global nature of Academic skepticism, Augustine argues that all he needs to prove is that there are at least a few certainties. Here he points to certain indisputable principles of logic and certain indisputable truths of mathematics. He also touches on the Academics' claim that we can never know with certainty whether we may be living in a dream world or trapped in some insane self-delusion. From Against the Skeptics, Book 3:

(9.21) Let us discuss what Zeno defined . . . I shall now use a very sound dilemma: that definition of his is *either* true *or* false. If true, then I really grasp something. If false, then there is something which can be perceived, even if it has signs in common with something that is false. . . . In any case, even if we are uncertain about that definition, we are not entirely without knowledge regarding it: we do know that the proposition is *either* true *or* false. Therefore, we do know *something*. . . .

(10.23) I myself am still far from being wise. Nevertheless, I know something about physics, for I am certain that *either* there is one world *or* not one; if there is not one world, then the number is either finite or infinite. . . . Furthermore, I know for certain that this world of ours has its present arrangement *either* from the nature of bodies *or* from providence; *either* that it always was and always will be, *or* that, having had a beginning it will never end, *or* that it did not have a beginning but will have an end, *or* that it began to exist but will not exist always. And I have the same kind of knowledge with regard to countless physics problems, for all these disjunctives are *true*—and no one can confuse them with "likeness" or falsity. "Now," says the Academic, "assume the truth of either member of the disjunction." No. I will not. That is the same as saying: "Abandon what you know; assert what you don't know." "But," he says, "your assertion is left hanging." Very well, better to hang in suspense than crash to the ground. While it is hanging, it is at least in plain view, and it can be pronounced *either* true *or* false. I can say that I *know* it as a proposition. . . .

(11.25) But you will ask me: "Is it the very same world that you are seeing, even if you were asleep?" . . . If there were one world and six worlds, then it would be clear that there would be seven worlds, no matter how I may be affected [by sleep or insanity]. And with all due modesty, I maintain that I know this. Show me that either this dilemma or the earlier disjunctives can be false by reason or sleep or mental derangement or the unreality of sense perception . . . It would still be necessarily true that $3 \times 3 = 9$, and that this is the square of rational numbers even if the whole human race were snoring![30]

30. C. Acad. 3.9.21–11.25 (CCL 29:46–49); my trans., based on Kavanagh, FOTC 5:190–97.

AUGUSTINE'S REBUTTAL:
SKEPTICISM SELF-CONTRADICTORY

Augustine goes on to argue that if the Academics are truly wise as they claim, then they must at least know, however obliquely, what wisdom itself is, and that, therefore, they know something. Radical skepticism is thus inherently self-contradictory. From Against the Skeptics, *Book 3:*

(14.30) First of all, Alypius, let us carefully explore what impresses you with such acuity and makes you so cautious. You have said that the Academics' theory—the theory that a wise man knows nothing—is strengthened by many cogent arguments. . . . We are discussing things here not for the sake of gaining glory, but for the purpose of finding the truth. I am satisfied if I can cross over that towering ridgeline that confronts those who would enter philosophy—it towers up darkly from some dark hidden reservoirs and threatens to cast the entirety of philosophy into obscurity, precluding any hope of finding any light within its borders. But I have nothing further to desire now if it is already probable that the wise know something. Our only reason for believing that it was "truth-like" for the wise to withhold assent was the fact that it seemed "truth-like" that nothing could be understood. That assumption must now be abandoned, for it must be conceded that the wise at least understand wisdom. Therefore, there is no reason why the wise should not give assent at least to wisdom. For, without a doubt, it is more monstrous for the wise not to approve of wisdom than not to know wisdom.

(14.31) Now if you will, let us try and visualize for a moment this great spectacle of a quarrel of sorts between a wise man and Wisdom. The only claim Wisdom makes is that she is wisdom. But her opponent says: "I do not believe it." Now who is it that says to Wisdom: "I do not believe there to be wisdom"? Who but one with whom Wisdom could converse and with whom she has deigned to live—in a word, a wise man? Now go and seek me out as someone who is battling against the Academics. Now you have a new squabble here: a wise man and Wisdom battling one another. The wise man does not want to agree with Wisdom. And I, like yourself, am calmly awaiting the outcome, for who would not believe that Wisdom is invincible? Nevertheless, let us strengthen our own position with a dilemma of sorts: In this debate, either the Academic will conquer Wisdom, or he will be conquered by her. In the first case, he will then be conquered by me because he will not be a wise man. In the other case, we shall conclude that a wise man assents to wisdom. Therefore, either the Academic is not a wise man, or a wise man will assent to something—unless, of course, the one who was ashamed to say that a wise man did not know wisdom will not be ashamed to say that a wise man does not assent to wisdom. But if it now seems true that a wise man can reach an understanding of wisdom, it must also seem true that he will give assent to wisdom, for surely there is no reason why we ought to refuse assent to what can be understood. So I see that my contention seems true—the contention that a wise man will assent to wisdom. And if you ask me where he can find Wisdom herself, I shall answer: Within his very self. If you say that he does not know what is in himself, you are going back to that same absurdity, namely, that a wise man does not know wisdom.[31]

Parable of the Two Travelers

Plato's Dialogues not only used arguments, but also the occasional parable; so too, Augustine in his debate against the Academics. Here he tells a parable of two travelers. The credulous one who follows a shepherd's directions is symbolic of simple Christians who follow the shepherding authority of bishops; the skeptical one, who follows the well-dressed trickster, is symbolic of the hyper-cautious Academic. From Against the Skeptics, Book 3:

(15.34) I have for a long while pondered here in the leisure of this countryside how the "probable" and the "truth-like" could defend our actions from going astray. At first it seemed to me to be neatly protected and fortified, just as it used to seem when I used to sell these arguments [in my job as rhetor]. But when I had inspected the matter more carefully, I came to believe that I had discovered an entryway where error might rush in upon the unwary. For I now regard that one errs not only when one follows the wrong path, but also when one does not follow the right one.

Let us suppose that two travelers are journeying to the same place; that one of them has resolved not to believe anybody while the other is overly credulous. They arrive at a crossroad. The credulous man says to a shepherd (or rustic of some kind) who happens to be there: "Hello, tell me, good sir, which is the right road to such-and-such a place?" The answer he gets: "If you travel by this road, you will not go wrong." So the credulous says to his companion: "This man is telling the truth: let's go this way." The hyper-cautious man laughs, and ridicules his companion with a biting wit for giving his assent so quickly. So while the credulous continues on his journey, the other one stands there at the crossroad until his long-prolonged delay begins to make him feel embarrassed. Now, look! From the other branch of the highway, an elegantly dressed and urbane gentleman on horseback comes into view. The traveler re-

---

31. C. Acad. 3.14.30–14.31 (CCL 29:52–54); my trans., based on Kavanagh, FOTC 5:203–6.

joices. As the stranger approaches, the traveler greets him, indicates his purpose, seeks advice about the road. What's more, he tells him the reason for his delay, and by stressing his preference for him over the shepherd, he tries to render him good-willed.[32] But the horseman happened to be one of those who are commonly called *Samardacs*,[33] and the rascal spontaneously followed his usual practice—and did it for free. "Go this way," he said, "for I've just come from there." So he deceived him and went on his way. But how could the hyper-cautious traveler be deceived? "I do not," he says, "accept that information as true. I accept it as 'truth-like.' And since this leisure is neither appropriate nor useful, I shall take to the road." Meanwhile, the first traveler, who had erred by assenting when he so quickly believed that the shepherd's words were true, had already rested and refreshed himself at the place they had set out for. But the one who had avoided error by following the "probable" ended up wandering around a forest of some kind. In fact, he still has not yet found anyone who even knows the place he had proposed going to.

Let me tell you that, when I thought about those arguments of the Academics, I could not keep from laughing. According to the Academics' own words, it ends up somehow or other that one is seen to be in error when one follows the right path by mere chance, but that the one who is led by the "probable" is seen as free from error even though he was led on through trackless mountains and never ends up finding the place he was seeking. While I would censure the practice of assenting rashly, it is more appropriate to say that both of these two were in error than to say that only the latter avoided it. Because of this, I became much more wary with regard to the assertions of the Academics, and I began to reflect on people's deeds and lifestyle. Then I discovered so many and such fundamental arguments against the Academics that I could no longer laugh at them. I began to loathe them and mourn the fact that such sharp-witted and learned men had fallen headlong into such scandalous and shameful opinions.[34]

---

32. "Render him good-willed" (*benevolentiorem reddat*): Augustine's educated audience would immediately recognize that this phrase refers to the orator's first task in any speech: to win over the audience's good will. Augustine portrays the skeptical traveler as a good Ciceronian orator who tries to win over the elegant gentleman; the gentleman is not won over but ironically ends up duping the traveler.

33. "*Samardacs*": an African word of unknown origin. John Chrysostom, *Homilies on the Epistle to the Ephesians* 17, uses it in the sense of "comedian" or "clown."

34. *C. Acad.* 3.15.34 (CCL 29:54–55); my trans., based on Kavanagh, FOTC 5:207–9.

PLOTINUS, PLATONISM, AND THE
AUTHORITY OF CHRIST

The following passage touches on Augustine's early optimistic assessment of Plotinus and Platonism.[35] *Note his crucial distinction between reason and authority.* From Against the Skeptics, Book 3:

(18.41) Not long after [Cicero], when all the obstinacy and all the sophistry had died down and when the clouds of error had been dispelled, then Plato's doctrine—which is the purest and brightest in philosophy—shined forth, especially in Plotinus. Indeed, this Platonist philosopher has been regarded as so like Plato that the two seemed to have lived at the same time, but there is such a long interval of time between them that Plato might be seen as having come back to life in Plotinus.

(19.42) Today we see hardly any philosophers except for Cynics or Peripatetics or Platonists. We have Cynics just because a certain "liberty" and license in life delights them. But as regards erudition and doctrine, as well as morality, by which the soul is ruled, a system of philosophy—the truest philosophy, in my opinion—has crystallized over many centuries and after many disputes because there has been no lack of men with the greatest acuity of insight and quickness of mind who, in their disputations, continued to teach that Aristotle and Plato concur with one another even though to the inattentive and the unskilled the two seem to be out of harmony. Now this is not a this-worldly philosophy, a philosophy which our sacred mysteries would rightly detest. It is a philosophy of the other world, the intelligible world, a world to which even the most acute reasoning would never call back souls blinded by errors' many-sided darkness and smeared deeply by the body's grime. That reasoning could not do so had not the most high God—through a gentle mercy towards all humanity—bent down and submitted the authority of the divine intellect even to a human body, and caused it to dwell therein so that souls would be awakened not only by divine precepts but also by divine deeds, and thus would be enabled to turn back within themselves and to gaze upon their homeland, without any disputatious wranglings.

(20. 43) . . . So, then, that you may have, briefly, my whole position: Whatever may be the mode of human wisdom, I see that I have not yet perceived it. But though I am now in the thirty-third year of my life, I do not think that I should despair of reaching it some day, for I have resolved to disregard all

35. On Plotinus, see Dominic J. O'Meara, *Plotinus: An Introduction to the Enneads* (New York: Oxford University Press, 1995); Pierre Hadot, *Plotinus or the Simplicity of Vision*, trans. Michael Chase (Chicago: University of Chicago Press, 1993); Lloyd P. Gerson, ed., *The Cambridge Companion to Plotinus* (Cambridge: Cambridge University Press, 1996).

other things which mortals consider good and to devote myself to an investigation [of wisdom]. And whereas the arguments of the Academics seriously held me back from such an undertaking, I now believe that through this disputation I am sufficiently protected against them. No one doubts that we are driven towards knowledge by a twofold force: the force of authority and the force of reason. I am, therefore, resolved never ever to deviate from the authority of Christ, for I find none more powerful. But as to what the most subtle reasoning can pursue—for I am so stirred up that I yearn impatiently to apprehend what the truth is, not only by believing but also by understanding—I am confident at the moment that what I will find among the Platonists will not be opposed to our sacred mysteries.[36]

GOD AS HAPPINESS AND WISDOM

For Augustine, the philosophic search for wisdom was inseparable from the religious search for God. Here he cites his classic definition of happiness, mentions experiences of inner illumination, and alludes to the doctrine of the Trinity. The latter prompts his mother Monnica—who functions in these dialogues as a symbol of Mother Church—to quote Ambrose's hymn. From On the Happy Life:

(4.33) [Augustine:] "We said at the beginning of our discussion today that, should we find that the unhappy are nothing other than those suffering some lack, then we would agree that the happy are those who lack nothing. This is exactly what we have now found. Therefore, to be happy means nothing other than to lack nothing, that is, to be wise. If you now seek out what wisdom is—our reasoning analyzed and developed this as far as possible here—the answer is that wisdom is nothing other than the 'measure' of the soul, that is, than the measure through which the soul keeps its equilibrium so that it neither runs over into too much nor comes up short of fullness. 'Running over' refers to luxuries, ambitions, pride, and other things of this kind through which the souls of the immoderate and the unhappy believe they get joy and power. 'Coming up short' refers to filth, fears, griefs, lusts, and many other things through which the unhappy acknowledge their unhappiness. . . .

(4.34) "But what, properly speaking, is wisdom other than the wisdom of God? We have also heard through divine authority that the Son of God is nothing other than the Wisdom of God, and the Son of God is truly God. Thus, whoever has God is happy—a statement already acclaimed by everyone at the beginning of our symposium. But do you believe that wisdom is dif-

36. *C. Acad.* 3.18.41–20.43 (CCL 29:59–61); my trans., based on Kavanagh, FOTC 5:218–20.

ferent from truth? For it has also been said: 'I am the Truth' (Jn 14:6). Truth receives its being through the Supreme Measure from which it proceeds and with which it coincides when perfected. But no other measure is imposed on the Supreme Measure. For if the Supreme Measure is the measure for the Supreme Measure, it therefore is itself what the measure is. Of course, the Supreme Measure also must be a true measure.[37] But just as the truth is engendered through measure, so measure is recognized by truth. Thus neither has truth ever been without measure nor measure without truth. Who is the Son of God? It has been said: 'The Truth.' Who is it that has no father? Who other than the Supreme Measure? Whoever attains the Supreme Measure through the Truth is happy. To have God within the soul is this: it is to enjoy God.

(4.35) "A certain admonition, flowing from that very fountain of Truth, urges us to remember God, to seek Him, and to thirst after Him tirelessly. This mysterious sun pours out its blazing light illuminating our interior lights. From Him is every truth that we speak, even though in our anxiety, we hesitate to turn courageously towards this light and to behold it in its totality, because our eyes, only recently opened, are not yet strong enough. This light appears to be nothing other than God, that perfection which no imperfection can diminish. For in Him all is absolutely perfect, and He is at the same time the omnipotent-est God.[38] But as long as we are still seeking, our thirst not yet satiated by the 'fountain' itself—the 'fullness,' to use our normal word— we must confess that we have not reached our measure; and that is why, even though God has helped us, we are not yet wise or happy. This, then, is the full satiety of souls—this is the happy life: To recognize piously and completely the One by whom you are led into Truth, the One whose Truth you have full enjoyment of, and the One by whom you are linked to the Supreme Measure. For those who have understanding and who exclude all various illusory superstitions, these three are the one God and the one Substance."

My mother, recalling here words that deeply adhered within her memory, woke up, so to speak, in her faith and with joy let flow this verse of our priest: "Protect, O Trinity, those praying."[39] Then she added: "This is, without doubt, the happy life, that is, the perfect life which we must assume that we can attain soon by a well-founded faith, a joyful hope, and a burning love."[40]

37. "Supreme Measure": In the background is Wis 11:20: "You have arranged all things in measure and number and weight." See his longer discussion in *Gen. litt.* 4.3.7–6.12.

38. "Omnipotent-est God" (*omnipotentissimus Deus*): Augustine coins a neologism here, a superlative of a superlative; I have coined one to match it. Cf. *conf.* 1.4.4. See O'Donnell, 2:23.

39. "Protect, O Trinity . . .": Monnica is quoting Ambrose's hymn *Deus creator omnium* ("God, Creator of all"). Augustine himself famously quotes from it in *conf.* 9.12.32; see O'Donnell 3:142–43.

40. *De beata vita* 4.33–35 (CCL 29:83–85); my trans., based on Schopp, FOTC 5:82–84. On this issue, see the classic study of Regnar Holte, *Béatitude et sagesse: Saint Augustin et le problème de la fin de l'homme dans la philosophie ancienne*, CEASA 14 (Paris: Institut d'Études Augustiniennes, 1962).

THE PROBLEM OF EVIL

The presence of evil in a universe overseen by an all-good and all-powerful God was a philosophic problem that deeply haunted Augustine. When he was younger, Manichean dualism had offered him an early and easy answer: the good God had not created the material universe and was thus not responsible for evil within it. Once Augustine converted to orthodox Christianity, he had to rethink the whole question. In On Order, the third of his Cassiciacum dialogues, he confronts the issue in writing for the first time. Here he articulates the classic philosophical dilemma. From On Order, Book 1:

(1.1) To perceive and to grasp the order of reality proper to each thing, and then to see or to explain the order of the entire universe by which this world is truly held together and governed—that, Zenobius, is a very difficult and rare achievement for human beings.[41] Moreover, even if one had this ability, one might not be able to find an audience well-suited by the merits of their life or by the habit of a certain erudition to listening to such divine and obscure matters. And yet there is nothing that the most gifted minds search out more eagerly, nothing that those who, with heads uplifted as much as they may be, still see the rocks and tempests of this life below—there is nothing that these desire to hear and learn about more than how it is that God has a care for human affairs, and nevertheless perversity is so serious and widespread that it must seem possible not to attribute it to God's governance nor even to a slave's management, if indeed such management could be entrusted to a slave. Moreover, those who ponder these matters are seemingly forced to believe *either* that Divine Providence does not reach to these outer limits of things *or* that all evils are committed by the will of God. Both views are impious, but particularly the latter. For although it is unsound and the greatest danger to the soul to hold that anything is beyond God's control, yet even among human beings no one is blamed for what one could not do or prevent. Imputing negligence to God is much more pardonable than the charge of ill will or cruelty. Reason, therefore, is not unmindful of piety and is, in some sense, forced to hold that the things of earth cannot be governed by powers divine or that they are neglected and unnoticed rather than to hold that they are governed in such a way that all complaining about God is inoffensive and blameless.[42]

41. "Zenobius": A friend and patron of Augustine. Their friendship is evident from Augustine's warm remarks to him in *ep.* 2. The dialogue later touches on themes from a poem Zenobius had written (*De ordine* 1.7.20). See Conybeare, *Irrational Augustine*, 22–23.
42. *De ordine* 1.1.1 (CCL 29:89); trans. Russell, FOTC 5:239–40 (modified).

EVIL WITHIN THE AESTHETICS
OF THE UNIVERSE

In this early work, Augustine suggests a preliminary and partial answer for the problem of evil: that we do not see the big picture, we do not see how the dark things of this world fit in with the large-scale beauty of God's creation and providence. This is an aesthetic answer, in a sense. It is also an insufficient one, as Augustine knew, but it would remain one thread of his broader response to the question of evil. In later chapters, we will see others: evil as "nothing" (drawn from reading the Neoplatonists); evil as misused human freedom (in his debate with the Manichees); evil as narcissistic selfishness, a self-willed turning away from God (from his meditation on the book of Genesis); suffering and death as the legacy of original sin (in his debate with the Pelagians). From On Order, *Book 1:*

(1.2) But who is so blind in their mind that they will hesitate to attribute to divine power and divine arrangement whatever rationality there is in bodily movements, that is, any beyond human organization and human will? Unless, perhaps, we have to listen to empty opinions, for instance, that the minutely measured and subtly fitted organic parts of every animal, especially the tiniest, are the result of mere chance? or that what one admits not to be the work of chance cannot in any way be the effect of design? or that what we find marvelous in each and every thing throughout the natural universe arranged in an artistry surpassing the utmost capability of human power does not belong to the hidden control of divine majesty? Yet this point is suggestive of a further line of questioning: that parts of a tiny flea are marvelously framed and fitted together, while human life, meanwhile, gets spun round, utterly unstable, and surges up and down amid waves of innumerable troubles. But given this, if one had such a near-sighted view of an inlaid mosaic that one's eye was not able to take in anything bigger than a single tessera, one might accuse the artisan of lacking any sense of artistic order or composition. What [from very close range] one presumes to be a haphazard scatter of various tiny colored stones can hinder one from discerning and contemplating in a lucid light how this mosaic emblem comes together as a single integral face of beauty. Something very similar to this is found in the case of people poorly instructed, who are unable, because of a weakness of their spirit, to grasp and to examine the universal coherence and universal harmony of things. They think that the whole universe is disarranged when something displeases them and that one thing becomes magnified by their perception.[43]

---

43. *De ordine* 1.1.2 (CCL 29:89–90); my trans., based on Russell, FOTC 5:240. On this and other sides of Augustine's theory, see G. R. Evans, *Augustine on Evil* (Cambridge: Cambridge University Press, 1982).

THE ART OF SOLILOQUY

Augustine, following Plotinus, argued that the way to the divine and to truth lies within, that the way upward to God is via the inward. In an utterly unique (though incomplete) project, Augustine turned the philosophic dialogue inward, creating a new literary genre: a dialogue with one's inner self, or "soliloquy." The word was his own coinage, as he notes here. From Soliloquies, *Book 2:*

(7.14) Because we are speaking to ourselves alone, I have chosen to entitle this *Soliloquies*, a name which is, to be sure, a new one and perhaps an awkward one, but one which is quite suitable to indicate its purpose. Since, on the one hand, truth cannot be better pursued than by question-and-answer and since, on the other hand, hardly anyone can be found who is not ashamed to be defeated in argument, with the result that it almost always happens that a subject for discussion which is well begun is driven out of mind by the unruly noise of self-opinion, accompanied also by wounded feelings which are usually concealed but at times evident—for these reasons, it was my pleasure to seek the truth with God's help in peace and propriety by questioning and answering myself.[44]

TO KNOW GOD AND THE SOUL

Augustine says that he composed Soliloquies *late at night after his students had gone to bed, and he lay awake wrestling interiorly. The following is the opening section where he first enters into dialogue with Reason. As in the opening of* Confessions, *Augustine takes on the problem of how we can say that we love God when we do not clearly know God. From* Soliloquies, *Book 1:*

(1.1) For a long time I was turning over in my mind many different matters, searching for days with all my heart, probing my own inner self, and seeking the good (and what evil needed to be avoided), when all at once a voice spoke to me—whether it was myself or another inside me or outside of me, I do not know. This was the very thing I tried to find out. Reason thus spoke to me:

Reason. Now then, suppose you had found something; to whom would you entrust your discoveries in order to move on to other matters?

Augustine. To my memory, of course.

---

44. *Soliloquia* 2.7.14 (BA 5:112); trans. Gilligan, FOTC 5:397.

R. Is it so sharp that it retains everything you've been thinking out?

A. That would be hard—in fact, impossible.

R. It must be written down then. But what are you going to do now that your poor health shirks the task of writing? These things should not be dictated, for they demand real solitude. . . . (2.7) Now what do you want to know? . . .

A. I desire to know God and the soul.

R. Nothing more?

A. Absolutely nothing else.

R. Begin, then, to search for them. But first explain how, if God is demonstrated to you, you will be able to say: "That is enough."

A. I do not know how God would have to be demonstrated to me so that I could say, "That is enough," for I do not think I know anything the way I want to know God.

R. So what are we to do? Don't you think you ought to know, first, how you can have sufficient knowledge of God so that when you arrive at it you will not have to search further?

A. I believe so, but I do not see how this can be done. For what thing can I ever know to be like God so that I might say that I wish to know God as I know such-and-such?

R. How do you, who do not yet know God, know that you know nothing like God?

A. Because, if I knew something like God, I would, without a doubt, love it. But so far, I love nothing except God and the soul—and I know neither.[45]

THE PHILOSOPHER'S PRAYER

Soliloquies may be read as a sort of rough draft for Confessions. Both works are sustained inner meditations that concern God and the soul. In the middle of the passage quoted above, I skipped over a long-winded prayer that, at Reason's encouragement, "Augustine" (the character in the dialogue) prays. Let us look at that prayer now. It is indebted to Plotinian language and sentiments. Beautiful in some ways, it is also wordy. Its florid repetitiveness highlights how the prayers in Confessions are, by contrast, more skillfully crafted, more economical, more able to advance an ongoing philosophical

---

45. *Soliloquia* 1.1.1–2.7 (BA 5:24–36); my trans., based on Gilligan, FOTC 5:343–51. Cf. *De ordine* 2.18.47: "As for philosophy, it has a two-sided question: one concerns the soul; the other, God. The first works so that we may know ourselves; the second, that we know our origin" (my trans.).

meditation. I have translated here only about 1/3 of the Soliloquies prayer, which continues on in the same vein for some pages. Augustine was, at the time, still unbaptized, still a catechumen, and poured out, he admits, long prayers with great tears.[46] *From Soliloquies, Book 1:*

(1.2) O God, founder of the universe, grant me, first, that I may pray well to you; next, that I may act worthily that you hear my plea; finally, that you may set me free. O God, through whom all things, which would not be in and of themselves, come into being; O God, who does not permit to perish even what is itself self-destructive; O God, who has created out of nothing this world, a world that every eye sees to be extraordinarily beautiful; O God, who does not do evil and does not let evil become the worst sort; O God, who, to those few who make their refuge in what truly is, shows that evil is nothing; O God, through whom the universe, even with its sinister side, is perfect; O God, by whose command the farthest discord is as nothing, since less perfect things harmonize with more perfect ones; O God, whom every being capable of loving, whether knowingly or unknowingly, loves; O God, in whom exist all things, yet the baseness of creatures does not debase You, nor does their wickedness harm You, nor their error deceive You; O God, who has willed that no one but the pure may know the truth; O God, Father of truth, Father of wisdom, Father of the true and highest life, Father of blessed happiness, Father of the good and the beautiful, Father of intelligible light, Father of our wakeful vigil and of our illumination, Father of the pledge by which we are admonished to return to You;

(1.3) You I invoke, O God the Truth in whom and by whom and through whom things that are true are true; O God the Wisdom in whom and by whom and through whom all those who are wise are wise; O God the True and Highest Life in whom and by whom and through whom all things that live truly and loftily live; O God the Blessed Happiness in whom and by whom and through whom all things that are blessedly happy are blessedly happy; O God the Good and Beautiful in whom and by whom and through whom all things that are good and beautiful are good and beautiful; O God, Intelligible Light in whom and by whom and through whom all those things that have intelligible light have intelligible light; O God, whose kingdom is a whole world unknown to sense; O God, from whose kingdom law is promulgated even into these [earthly] realms; O God, from whom to turn away is to fall, to whom to turn is to rise back up, in whom to abide is to stand firm; O God, from whom to depart is to die, to whom to return is to be revived, in whom to dwell is to live; O God, whom no one loses unless deceived,

---

46. *De ordine* 1.10.29 (CCL 29:104).

whom no one seeks unless admonished, whom no one finds unless purified; O God, whom to abandon is to perish, whom to heed is to love, whom to see is to have; O God, to whom faith rouses us, hope lifts us, charity unites us; O God, through whom we overcome the enemy, to you I pray; O God, whom we receive lest we perish altogether; O God, by whom we are admonished to be ever watchful; O God, through whom we distinguish good from evil; O God, through whom we flee evil and follow the good; O God, through whom we overcome yielding to adversities; O God, whom we rightly serve and by whom we are rightly ruled. O God, through whom we learn that so many things once ours are foreign to us, and discover so many things once foreign to us are ours; O God, through whom we learn not to cling to the charms and lures of evil; O God, through whom trivial things lessen their lessening of us; O God, through whom what is better in us is not made subject to our lower self; O God, through whom death is swallowed up in victory; O God, who converts us; O God, who strips us of what is not and clothes us with what is; O God, who makes us worthy to be heard; O God, who strengthens us; O God, who leads us into all truth; O God, who speaks to us of all that is good, who does not lead to senseless things nor permit us to be made so; O God, who calls us back to the road; O God, who brings us to the doorway; O God, who causes it to be opened to those who knock; O God, who gives the bread of life; O God, through whom we thirst for the cup, from which, once drunk, we never more thirst; O God, who "convicts the world in regard to sin, to justice, and to judgment" (Jn 16:8); O God, through whom those who believe minimally do not upset us; O God, through whom we denounce the error of those who think that souls have no merits before you; O God, through whom we do not serve "weak and destitute elemental powers" (Gal 4:9); O God, who purges us, who prepares us for divine rewards, be well-disposed and come to my aid.[47]

The Vision of God

One thing Augustine drew from his reading of those "books of the Platonists"[48] was a method of mystical contemplation that led one to seek to pierce through the ephemeral world visible to the senses and to rise inwardly and upwardly, elevating the mind, however briefly, to the eternity of God. Earlier we saw two accounts of such ascents in

47. *Soliloquia* 1.1.2-1.3 (BA 5:26–30); my trans., based on Gilligan, FOTC 5:344–47. See *retr.* 1.4.2 (BA 12:290). On this prayer, as well as the Trinitarian references in *De beata vita* 4.33–35 (quoted above), see Lewis Ayres, "'Giving Wings to Nicaea': Reconceiving Augustine's Earliest Trinitarian Theology," *Augustinian Studies* 38 (2007): 21–40.
48. See p. 18 in Chap. 1, above.

Confessions. In this dialogue with himself, Augustine meditates on what the vision of God requires. He stresses the distinctly Christian (and very un-Platonic) virtues of faith, hope, and love, a triad drawn from St. Paul and a mainstay of his thinking over the course of his career. From Soliloquies, *Book 1:*

(6.12) *Reason.* It follows, then, that without these three [virtues of faith, hope, and love] no soul can be healed such that it can see (that is, know) God. (6.13) But once the soul has healthy eyes, what more is needed?

Augustine. That it contemplate.

R. Reason is the soul's contemplative gaze. But it does not follow that everyone who contemplates sees. Rightful and perfect contemplation, from which vision follows, is called virtue. For virtue is rightful and perfect reason. But even though the soul may have healthy eyes, the contemplative gaze itself cannot turn toward the light unless these three [virtues] have become permanent: *faith* by which it believes the reality which it gazes upon can, when seen, make us blessedly happy; *hope* by which it trusts that it will see if only it contemplates intently; *love*, by which it yearns to see and to enjoy. Then the vision of God flows from the contemplative gaze. This vision is the true goal of our contemplation, not because the contemplative gaze no longer exists, but because it has nothing further to strive toward. And this is truly perfect virtue: reason arriving at its endpoint, from which comes the happy life. This vision itself, however, is that understanding which is in the soul, brought forth by the one who understands and by the One understood—just as what is called "eyesight" consists of the senses themselves and the reality sensed, such that if either were withdrawn, nothing would be seen.

(7.14) Therefore, let us reflect on whether these three are still necessary once the soul succeeds in seeing (that is, knowing) God. Why should faith be needed since now it sees? Why hope, since it already grasps its hope? But as for love, not only will nothing be taken away, but rather much will be added. For when the soul sees that unique and true Beauty, it will love all the more deeply. But unless it fixes its eye upon it with surpassing love and never withdraws its gaze, it will not be able to continue in that most blessed vision. Now as long as the soul is in this body, even though it may fully see (that is, know) God, the senses of the body still perform their proper function. Even though they may not have the power to lead one astray, they can still cause a wavering unsteadiness. So there still must be faith by which we resist the senses and believe something other [than them] to be true. So too, since in this life the soul labors under the body's many hardships, even though it is already happy in its knowledge of God, it still needs hope that all these trials will not endure beyond death. So as long as it is in this life, hope does not depart the soul. But when, after this life, it unites itself totally with God, love will remain to keep it there. One will no longer have faith since things can no longer be mixed with falsity and be wrongly interpreted; nor does anything remain to be hoped for, since the soul rests in secure possession of everything. There are, then, three things the soul needs: that it be healthy; that it gaze; that it see. For these, three others—faith, hope, and love—are needed. For healing and gazing, faith and hope are necessary; for seeing, all three are necessary in this life; but in the life to come, only love.[49]

AUGUSTINE CONVERSING
WITH AUGUSTINE

Few texts illustrate the range of Augustine's early philosophical and religious concerns as briefly (and playfully) as the following letter to Nebridius, one of Augustine's closest friends. Augustine had sent him the Cassiciacum dialogues, and Nebridius sent back a letter expressing how delighted he was that Augustine had arrived at wisdom and happiness. Here Augustine replies, touching on core concerns and revealing glimpses of his deeper moods. The letter illustrates how Platonic perspectives then shaped his outlook (for example, the sense of this world as a shadowlands; a sharp body-soul dualism). Through much of the letter, he re-enacts for Nebridius the same inner question-and-answer style of Soliloquies. From Letter 3:

(1) You almost convinced me, not, of course, that I am happy, for that is the reward of the wise alone, but that I am comparatively happy—as we say that a person is, comparatively, a person when measured against that [ideal] person Plato knew, or that things are, comparatively, round or square as we look at them, even though they are far from these qualities as the mind of the expert perceives them. I read your letter by lamplight after dinner. It was almost time for bed, but not quite time for sleep. So I reflected for a long time, sitting on my bed, and Augustine held this conversation with Augustine:

"Is it not true that I am happy, as Nebridius claims?"

"Not really, for even he does not dare to deny that there are still fools, and how could happiness be the portion of fools?"

"That's tough! As if happiness were an insignificant thing or as if there were any other misery than folly? How, then, did he reach this conclusion? Was it by reading those treatises that he came to believe me wise?"

"But joy is not premature, especially in a person whose weighty reasoning power I know how to estimate. This, then, must be it: He wrote what he thought would give me the most pleasure, because what I had set down in

49. *Soliloquia* 1.6.12–7.14 (BA 5:50–54); my trans., based on Gilligan, FOTC 5:359. See *retr.* 1.4.3.

those works had given him pleasure, and he wrote with joy, without a thought of what should be allowed a joyous pen."

"But what if he had read the *Soliloquies*?"

"He would have been much more enthusiastic, and yet he would not have found anything else to call me but happy. So he bestowed this supreme title on me, and reserved to himself no other term to use in case he should be feeling even more enthusiastic. See what joy does!"

(2) "But where is the life of happiness to be found? Where? Where is it? Oh, if only it were to consist in rejecting the atomism of Epicurus![50] Oh, if only it were to consist in knowing that there is nothing below but the material world! Oh, if only it were to consist in knowing that the outer edge of a sphere revolves more slowly than its center—and other such things we know [for certain]! But, now, how or in what sense I am happy, that I do not know. . . .

(3) "But wait—let us see what this thought brings to mind. Surely the world of the senses is said to be a reflection of a certain intelligible one. It is a matter of wonder that in the case of images we see what mirrors reflect, for, however large the mirrors, they do not reflect larger images even of the tiniest objects. But in small mirrors (such as the pupils of the eyes), a very small image is formed in proportion to the reflecting surface even if a larger object is presented. Therefore, it is possible for the images of objects to be made smaller if the mirror is smaller, but they cannot be enlarged if the mirror is enlarged. There is certainly some mystery hidden here. But now it is time to go to sleep. For I appear happy to Nebridius not by searching for something but by finding it. But what is this something? Is it this power of reasoning which I cherish as my most beloved and in which I find my greatest joy?"

(4) "Of what do we consist?"

"Of soul and body."

"Which of these is better?"

"The soul, of course."

"What is to be praised in the body?"

"Nothing else than beauty."

"What is beauty of the body?"

"A harmony of its parts along with a certain pleasing color."

"Is this form better when it is true or when it is false?"

"Who could doubt that it is better when it is true?"

"But where is it true?"

50. "Epicurus": The Greek philosopher Epicurus of Samos (341–270 B.C.E.). His views were best known to the Latin-speaking world through Lucretius's poem *On the Nature of Things* (*De natura rerum*). For an overview, A. A. Long, *Hellenistic Philosophy: Stoics, Epicureans, Sceptics*, 2nd ed. (Berkeley: University of California Press, 1986), 14–74. Augustine and other Christian thinkers tended to caricature Epicureanism as a philosophy of hedonism; see s. 150; *civ. Dei* 5.20; 8.5; 11.5; 14.2; 18.41.

"In the soul, of course. Therefore, the soul is to be loved more than the body."

"But in what part of the soul is that truth?"

"In the mind and in the understanding."

"What is opposed to these?"

"The senses. Therefore, it is clear that the senses are to be resisted with the whole force of the mind."

"But what if things of the senses give us too much pleasure?"

"They must be prevented from giving pleasure."

"How?"

"By the practice of renouncing them, and aiming at higher things."

"What if the soul dies?"

"Then truth dies, or truth is not in the understanding, or the understanding is not in the soul, or something in which there is something immortal can die. My *Soliloquies* set forth and prove conclusively that none of these things can be so. In spite of this I am frightened and I stumble because of my acquaintance with evil. Finally, even if the soul dies (which I admit is completely impossible), I have demonstrated in this retreat that happiness does not consist in sensible pleasures. For these and similar reasons, I perhaps seem to my Nebridius, if not happy, at least happy to some degree. May I seem so to myself! For what do I lose from this, or why should I forfeit his good opinion?"

This was the conversation I held with myself. Then I prayed, according to my custom, and fell asleep.[51]

LIBERAL ARTS PROJECT

During these same months, Augustine began sketching out a series of books on the liberal arts. This is one of several grand projects prior to Confessions that ended up as intellectual dead ends and were left incomplete. From Reconsiderations, Book 1:

(6) During that very same time when I was about to receive baptism in Milan, I also tried to write books on the liberal arts, dialoguing with those who were with me and who were not opposed to studies of this sort. I did so, desiring both to reach up, as if by well-defined steps, from the corporeal to the incorporeal, and also to lead others along. But I was able to complete only the book *On Grammar*—which I later lost from my library bookcase—and six books *On Music*, focusing on that element which is called "rhythm." I wrote

---

51. Ep. 3.1–4 (CCL 31:6–8); trans. Parsons, FOTC 12: 7–10 (modified).

these six books, however, only after I was baptized and had returned to Africa from Italy, since at Milan I had only begun to explore this art. Of the other five arts also begun there—dialectic, rhetoric, geometry, arithmetic, and philosophy—I just had first drafts, and I myself have lost even these. But I think that other people have some of them.[52]

The Hierarchy of Being

As he remarked in Soliloquies, he was concerned to "know God and the soul." In this and the next passage, we will see two brief examples of his early meditation on God and the soul. Around 390, Augustine wrote a very brief note to a friend named Caelestinus, asking him for comments on some of his early anti-Manichean writings. Augustine then sketched a dense, schematic outline of his metaphysical worldview. From Letter 18:

(2) Since I know you so well, here is something both great and brief. There is a nature changeable in both time and space, namely, the body. And there is a nature changeable not in space but in time, namely, the soul. And there is a nature which is changeable neither in space nor in time, and that is God. What I have spoken of here as changeable refers to the creature; what is unchangeable, to the Creator. But since we speak of all that exists as existing insofar as it endures and is unified, and since every form of beauty is a form of unity, and you see at once in this classification of natures what is highest, what is lowest (yet still exists), what is in the middle (being greater than the lowest and less than the highest). The highest is Beatitude itself, the lowest can be neither happy nor wretched, but the middle lives wretchedly by inclination, blessedly by conversion. One who believes in Christ does not love the lowest, is not proud in the middle, but thus becomes fit to cling to the highest. And this is the whole of what we are commanded, urged, and set aflame to do.[53]

---

52. *Retr.* 1.6 (CCL 57:17); my trans., based on Bogan, FOTC 60:21–22. A sketch of his views on the liberal arts of grammar, dialectic, rhetoric, music, geometry, as well as philosophy, appears in *De ordine* 2.12.35–18.47. For an exploration of this unfinished project, see the essays in Pollmann and Vessey, *Augustine and the Disciplines*. Augustine says here that he had lost the first drafts, but that others may have them. One, it seems, did survive: his *De dialectica*. The Maurists rejected the authenticity of the text that has come down to us by that title, but most scholars now accept it. For the text and a translation, see B. Darrell Jackson and Jan Pinborg, eds., *Augustine: De Dialectica* (Boston: Reidel, 1975).

53. *Ep.* 18.2 (CCL 31:44); my trans., based on Parsons, FOTC 12:44.

BODY-SOUL RELATIONSHIP

In Augustine's day, most intellectuals—and this includes most Christian ones—thought of the soul in corporeal terms: that the soul was a sort of highly refined "stuff." Neoplatonism revolutionized Augustine's view. He came to think of both God and the soul as utterly incorporeal. Roland Teske has argued that this idea is one of Augustine's two seminal contributions to Western metaphysical thought.[54] In the following passage, Augustine explores the relationship between the immaterial soul and the material body. Augustine saw the soul as a sort of lightning-fast intelligent life-force enlivening the body. From On the Immortality of the Soul:

(16.25) In the natural order, more powerful beings hand down to lower ones the form they have received from the Supreme Beauty. And surely, what they give, they do not take away. Lower things, insofar as they exist, exist for the very reason that more powerful beings hand down to them the form by which they exist. These greater ones are, by reason of their power, more excellent. To these natures it is given that they have greater power. . . . The soul is more powerful and excellent than the body. Therefore, since the body subsists by the soul, . . . the soul itself can in no way be transformed into a body. . . . But the soul is present at the same time wholly, entirely, not only in the entire mass of the body, but also in each of its individual parts. For it is the entire soul that feels pain in any part of the body, yet it does not feel it in the entire body. For when there is an ache in the foot, the eyes take a look at it, the mouth talks about it, and the hand reaches for it. This, of course, would be impossible if whatever of the soul that was in these parts did not also experience a sensation in the foot; if the soul were not present, it would be unable to feel what has happened there. For it would be incredible for a messenger to announce a fact he had not experienced. The sensation of pain that occurs does not run through the mass of the body by continuing in such a way as not to remain unnoticed by other parts of the soul which are elsewhere. Rather, the entire soul feels what is going on in a particular part of the foot and feels it only there where it occurs. Therefore, the entire soul is present at one and the same time in individual parts of the body, and it experiences sensation as a whole, at one and the same time, in the individual parts.[55]

54. Roland Teske, "Augustine as Philosopher: The Birth of Christian Metaphysics," *Augustinian Studies* 23 (1992): 7–32; reprinted in *To Know God and the Soul: Essays on the Thought of Saint Augustine* (Washington, DC: The Catholic University of America Press, 2008), 3–25.

55. *De immortalitate animae* 16.25 (BA 5:216–18); my trans., based on Schopp, FOTC 4:45–47. See Rist, *Augustine*, 92–104; Teske, "Soul," *AugEncy*, 807–12.

A PHILOSOPHY OF LANGUAGE

Augustine composed On the Teacher *around 389, while he, his son, and his friends were living together as "servants of God" on his family property in Thagaste. Augustine alluded to this dialogue in* Confessions *(see Chapter 1, above). The following is the dialogue's opening and touches on a nest of Augustinian concerns: the purpose of language; the nature of memory; signs vs. realities; inner self vs. outer world; the function of prayer. From* On the Teacher:

(1.1) *Augustine.* What would you say we are trying to do when we speak?

Adeodatus. It occurs to me that we want either to teach or to learn.

Aug. I see. I agree with the first of these. But how does this hold true for learning?

Ad. How in the world do you suppose that we can learn anything except by asking questions?

Aug. I hold that even in that case we simply want to teach somebody something. Now I would like you to explore whether you might ask a question for some reason other than teaching the person you asked what you want to know.

Ad. What you say is right.

Aug. So you see that our aim in speaking is simply to teach.

Ad. I don't see that clearly. If speaking is nothing more than uttering words, we do that, as I see it, whenever we sing. And we often sing when we're alone, when no one else is present. I don't think we're trying to teach anything by singing.

Aug. I think there is a form of teaching—a really important one—that involves reminding people of something. This will become clear as we discuss this topic. But if you don't think that we learn by remembering or that when we teach we bring up something to one's mind, I will not debate it with you [right now]. Now I will take the position that there are two reasons for speaking: either to teach something or to remind others—or ourselves—of something. And we do this even when we are singing. Wouldn't you agree?

Ad. Not entirely, for I very rarely sing to remind myself of something. I do it only for pleasure.

Aug. I see what you mean. But you notice, don't you, that what pleases you in singing is a certain melodious ordering of sound? Since melody can be added to the words or removed from them, isn't singing one thing and speaking something else? Flutes and harps make melodies. Birds, too, can sing. And there are times when we hum a musical piece without words. Humming can be called singing, but not speech. Do you disagree?

Ad. No, not really.

(1.2) *Aug.* Do you think then that the language was established for any reason other than these two, either teaching or reminding?

Ad. I would agree, were it not for the difficulty that, when we pray, we use words. And yet it is not right to believe that God is actually being taught anything by us or that we remind Him of something.

Aug. You don't realize, I think, that the command to pray in the secrecy of our "bedroom"—a term that means "the inner recesses of the mind"—was given only for this reason: that God does not need to be reminded or to be taught by us in order to give us what we desire. When one speaks, one gives an outward sign of what one wants through some articulated sound. But we must seek and pray to God in a secret place within the rational soul—what is called the "inner person." This [inner person] He wants to be His temple. Haven't you read in the Apostle: "Do you not know that you are the temple of God and that the Spirit of God dwells in you" (1 Cor 3:16) and that "Christ dwells in the inner person" (Eph 3:17)? And haven't you noticed what is in the Prophet: "Speak in your hearts, and repent on your beds: Sacrifice the sacrifice of justice, and hope in the Lord" (Ps 4:5–6)? Where do you think the "sacrifice of justice" is to be sacrificed, if not in the "temple" of the mind and on the "beds" of the heart? Where sacrifice is offered, that is where prayer is made. That is why, when we pray, there is no need for speech, that is, for the sounding-out of words, except perhaps as priests do, using words as signs to express one's thoughts, not so that God may hear, but that people may hear and, by this verbal reminder, fix their thoughts upon God. But do you have another view?

Ad. No, I agree completely.

Aug. Aren't you concerned, therefore, by the fact that the greatest Teacher of all taught us certain words to say when He taught His disciples how to pray so that He seemed to do nothing else but teach them what they should say when praying?

Ad. That does not bother me at all, for He did not simply teach the disciples words but taught realities using words. In this way they were reminded to whom to pray and for what to pray when, as you said, they pray in the inner recesses of the mind.

Aug. You have the right idea. I believe you notice at the same time that even when someone is trying hard to think, although we utter no sound, yet because we are thinking in words themselves, we are speaking inwardly in our minds. So, too, by speaking, we simply call something to mind since, in turning over the words stored there, memory brings to mind the realities themselves which have words as their signs.

Ad. I understand, and I follow you.

(2.3) *Aug.* So we agree then that words are signs?

Ad. We do.

Aug. What then? Can something be a sign unless it signifies something?
Ad. No.

[*They then analyze at some length a single line from Vergil's Aeneid, proceeding word by word to explore and draw out the sign-based character of human speech*].

Aug. Granted that this is true, . . . still you will at least notice this one point: namely, that you have been explaining words by words, that is, signs by signs, and what is familiar by what is equally familiar. But I would like you to point out to me, if you can, the realities themselves of which these are signs.

(3.5) *Ad.* I am surprised that you do not know—or rather, that you pretend not to know—that what you ask cannot be done in conversation where we cannot answer except by words. But you are looking for those realities that, whatever else they are, are certainly not words, and yet you too are using words to ask me about them. So you will first have to ask a question without words so that I can reply in the same way.[56]

CHRIST THE INNER TEACHER

On the Teacher *is concerned not only with the nature of language but also with the broader question of epistemology, that is, how we know what we know, and it explores this by probing in what sense teachers actually teach anything. Augustine argues that we do not really learn realities outside us, but are reminded interiorly of forgotten truths. This theory of knowledge as "remembrance," while akin in some ways to Plato's, is also quite different. Augustine came to deny Plato's hypothesis that learning is remembering something from a past life.[57] For Augustine, knowing is a matter of inner illumination; Christ is the true teacher teaching truth deep within us. Augustine later, as a preacher, will play on this idea, comparing and contrasting his outer words with Christ's inner teaching. From* On the Teacher:

(11.36) So far, the most I can say for words is that they merely intimate that we should look for realities; they do not present them to us for our knowledge. But the one who teaches me is the one who presents to my eyes or to any bodily senses or even to the mind itself something that I want to know.

56. *De magistro* 1.1–3.5 (CCL 29:157–62); my trans., based on Russell, FOTC 59:7–10. On this, see Rist, *Augustine*, 23–40; Madec, *Saint Augustin et la philosophie*, 53–60.

57. In *Soliloquia* 2.20.35, Augustine hints at holding such an idea. Étienne Gilson, *The Christian Philosophy of Saint Augustine* (New York: Random House, 1960), 70–71, suggested that it was "possible that during the early days of his conversion Augustine combined the theory of the soul's pre-existence with its natural complement, the doctrine of Platonic reminiscence." Gerald J. P. O'Daly, "Did St. Augustine Ever Believe in the Soul's Pre-Existence?" *Augustinian Studies* 5 (1974): 227–54, has argued against this. Late in his career, Augustine explicitly repudiated this Platonic doctrine, noting that the uneducated know things "not because they knew things at some time or other and have forgotten them, as it seemed to Plato or men like him," but rather that "when they have the capacity to grasp it, the light of eternal reason by which they perceive those unchangeable truths is present in them" (*retr.* 1.4.4; trans. Bogan, FOTC 60:18).

So from words we learn only words, or better, the sound and noise of words. For a word, unless it be a sign, cannot be a word; but I still cannot recognize it as a word until I know what it means, what it signifies, even though I have heard the word. Therefore, it is by knowing the realities that we also come to a knowledge of words whereas, by the sound of words, we do not even learn the words. For we do not learn words we already know, and, as for those which we do not know, we cannot profess to have learned them until we have seen their meaning. And this comes about not by hearing the sounds they make, but from a knowledge of the realities they signify. It is perfectly logical and true to conclude that whenever words are spoken, we either know or do not know what they mean. If we do know, they remind us rather than teach something to us. If we do not know, they cannot even remind us of something though they may lead us to inquire. . . .

(11.38) But as for all those things we understand, it is not the outward sound of a speaker's words that we consult, but the truth that presides over the mind itself within us, though we may have been led to consult it because of the words. Now, the One who is consulted and who is said to "dwell in the inner person" (Eph 3:14–17), He is the One who teaches us, namely, Christ, that is, "the unchangeable Power of God and everlasting wisdom" (1 Cor 1:23–24). This is the Wisdom that every rational soul does indeed consult, but Wisdom reveals itself to each one according to one's capacity to grasp it by reason of the good or evil dispositions of one's will. And if one is sometimes mistaken, this does not come about because of some defect on the part of the Truth that one consulted, just as it is not because of a defect in the light outside us that our bodily eyes are often deceived. We acknowledge that it is this light that we consult with regard to visible objects so that it may show them to us as far as we are able.

(12.40) When it is a question of things which we behold with the mind, namely, our intellect and reason, we give verbal expression to realities which we directly perceive as present in that inner light of truth which enlightens and delights the so-called "inner person." But, here again, if the one who hears my words sees those things oneself with that clear and inner eye of the soul, one knows the things I speak of by contemplating them oneself and not by my words. Therefore, even when I speak what is true and one sees what is true, it is not I who teach you. For one is being taught not by my words but by the realities themselves made manifest by the enlightening action of God from within.[58]

---

58. *De magistro* 11.36–12.40 (CCL 29:194–98); trans. Russell, FOTC 59:49–54. On this, see Gareth B. Matthews, "Knowledge and Illumination," in *Cambridge Companion to Augustine*, 171–85. The idea of Christ "the inner teacher" appears routinely in Augustine's preaching; for example, *s.* 134.1.1; *s.* 293A.6 (= Dolbeau 3); *Jo. ev. tr.* 3.15; *ep.* 2*.7 (Divjak).

IF PLATO WERE LIVING TODAY . . .

In 390, Augustine composed a brilliant early synthesis, On True Religion. If Soliloquies anticipates Confessions, then On True Religion anticipates City of God.[59] Like it, On True Religion is an apologia, a defense of Christianity. In the following passage, Augustine describes Christianity as the fulfillment of philosophy's deepest aspirations. This passage illustrates his grandest style of rhetoric, with paragraph-long sentences, with phrase piled upon phrase, steadily ramping up the emotional pitch. From On True Religion:

(3.3) In these Christian times there can be no doubt about which religion should be held onto and which offers the road to truth and to happiness. If Plato were living today and would not spurn my questioning him—or perhaps, suppose one of his own disciples who lived at the same time had questioned him, having been already convinced by him [of these principles]: that truth cannot be seen by the body's eyes, but rather by the pure mind, and that any soul that clings to truth is made happy and perfect; that nothing hinders perceiving the truth more than a life devoted to lusts and the false images of sensory objects, which impress themselves on our minds from the body and which generate various sorts of opinions and errors; that, therefore, the self has to be healed so that it may look upon the unchangeable form of things that always remains the same, preserving its same beauty always and everywhere within itself, not distended in space nor varied in time, but preserving its unity in every aspect; that people do not believe in its very existence while [this form] itself is what truly and supremely exists; that other things are born, die, flow down, dissolve, but insofar as they exist, they exist having been fashioned by the eternal God through His Truth; that it is given to the rational and intellectual soul to enjoy the contemplation of His eternity and [the soul] is influenced by that contemplation and can be rewarded with eternal life; that as long as the soul is wounded both by love of and by grief for things that come to birth and pass away and as long as it is devoted to the customary things of this life and of the bodily senses, it dissipates itself among empty images and mocks those who say there is something that can neither be seen by the eyes nor grasped as some imaginative phantasm, but discerned by the mind and the intellect alone.

So suppose that this disciple had been persuaded about all this by his teacher and asked Plato this question: "What if some great and divine man were to arise, one who would persuade ordinary people that such things

---

59. Goulven Madec, "Le De civitate Dei comme De vera religione," in Petites Études Augustiniennes, CEASA 142 (Paris: Institut d'Études Augustiniennes, 1994), 189–213.

should at least be believed if they are not strong enough to grasp them; or, if they really were able to grasp them, would persuade them not to smother them in vulgar errors by getting entangled in the misguided opinions of the multitude: Would not such a man be worthy of divine honors?"

Plato, I believe, would have answered: "That could not be done by a human being unless God's Power and Wisdom itself were to exempt him from the ordinary course of nature and from human teaching and instead, by enlightening him from his cradle with some secret inner illumination, were to clothe him with such grace, strengthen him with such steadiness, such stability, and, in the end, lift him up with such majesty that he would despise *all* that crooked humanity longs for and endure *all* that horrifies them and do *all* that they are amazed by, and so with consummate love and authority would convert the human race to such a health-giving faith. As for honors due such a person, it is pointless to consult me since it is easy enough to calculate how great the honors are that are due to the Wisdom of God, with whose bearing and with whose governance such a person, working for the genuine salvation of the human race, would have merited a place all his own, a place above all humanity."

(3.4) *What if* this has all happened now; *if* it is being celebrated in books and in monuments; *if* from one small region of the earth where the one God has been worshiped and where it was appropriate for such a man to be born, where chosen men were sent forth throughout the entire world, and by their virtues and by their words flames of divine love have been enkindled; *if* the health-instilling teaching of salvation they established has illumined whole countries; and (not to go on speaking just about the past, which someone may feel free to disbelieve) *if* today there is preached to the nations and to the peoples: "In the beginning was the Word, and the Word was with God, and the Word was God. This was in the beginning with God. All things were made by Him, and without Him was nothing made" (Jn 1:1–3); *if*, for grasping, loving, enjoying this Word that the soul be healed and the mind's eye convalesce and grow strong to drink in its fill of such brilliant light, the greedy *are told*: "Do not store up for yourselves treasures on earth, where moth and decay destroy and where thieves break in and steal, but store up treasures in heaven, where neither moth nor decay destroy nor thieves break in and steal; for where your treasure is, there also is your heart" (Mt 6:19–21); and the luxury-loving *are told*: "The one who sows in his flesh will, from the flesh, reap corruption; the one who sows in the spirit will, from the spirit, reap eternal life" (Gal 6:8); and the proud *are told*: "The one who exalts himself will be humbled, and the one who humbles himself will be exalted" (Lk 14:11); and the hot-tempered *are told*: "You received a slap; offer the other cheek" (Mt 5:39); and the quarrelers *are told*: "Love your enemies" (Mt 5:44); and the superstitious *are told*: "The Kingdom of God is within you" (Lk 17:21); and the curious *are told*: "Do not seek what is seen, but what is unseen; for what is seen is temporal, but what is unseen is eternal" (2 Cor 4:18); and finally, all *are told*: "Do not love the world or the things of the world, for all that is in the world is lust of the flesh and lust of the eyes and worldly ambition" (1 Jn 2:15–16);

(3.5) *what if* these things are now being read to peoples throughout the whole world and are being listened to with such enjoyment and with veneration; *if* after so much martyrs' blood, so many burnings, so many crucifixions, churches have sprouted up with such a fertile harvest, with such abundance, as far afield as the barbarian nations; *if* so many thousands of young men and virgins have turned away from marriage and live in chastity, no one is even surprised (when Plato did this, he was so afraid of the perverse public opinion of his era that he is said to have sacrificed to nature and abolished [celibacy] as a sin); *if* something [like celibacy] is now so accepted that what before used to be so disputed is now monstrous even to dispute; *if* throughout all parts of the earth the sacred rites of Christians are handed down to people willing to undertake such commitments and solemn promises; *if* every day all this is read in churches and expounded by priests; *if* those who try to fulfill these commitments beat their breasts [in contrition]; *if* so countless are the numbers undertaking this pathway, abandoning riches and honors of this world, wishing to dedicate their whole life to the one most high God, that islands once deserted and many lands once left in solitude are being filled by people of every kind; *if*, finally, throughout cities and towns, in castles, villages and the countryside, and even in private estates, there is openly proclaimed and practiced such a renunciation of earthly things and there is such a conversion to the one and true God that daily throughout the whole wide world the human race responds as if with one voice: "We have lifted up our hearts to the Lord,"[60] *then* why would we still gape, hung over from yesterday's drunken bout, and scrutinize the entrails of dead cattle for divine oracles? why, if when it comes to disputation, would we so much more eagerly want to have Plato's name rattling in our mouths than have our chests fill with truth?

(4.6) . . . Let them yield to the One by whom this has taken place, let them not be prevented by empty curiosity and empty boastfulness from acknowledging the gaps between their few timid conjectures and the obvious salvation and reform of whole peoples. For if Plato and these others, whose names these people glory in, were to come to life again and find the churches

---

60. "'We have lifted up our hearts . . . '": Augustine is citing the dialogue that opens the eucharistic prayer. The phrase is central to his spirituality of eucharist: *s.* 227 (see Chapter 4).

crammed and the temples deserted, and the human race being called away from desiring temporal and fleeting goods and running towards desiring hope of eternal life and spiritual and intelligible goods, they would perhaps have said (at least if they were really the men they are remembered to be): "These things are what we did not dare to persuade people of, and we gave in to what people were used to rather than bringing them over to our faith and our outlook."

(4.7) So if these men could live their lives over again with us, they would see to whose authority people could easily turn for advice, and with a change of just a few words and sentiments, they would become Christians as many Platonists of recent times have done.[61]

THE OLD MAN AND THE NEW MAN

In City of God, begun more than two decades later, Augustine would read world history as a winding epic tale of two cities, the City of God and the human city, bound together here and now, but separated finally at the Last Judgment. In On True Religion, Augustine sketches an early formulation using Paul's terminology of "the old man" and "the new man." From On True Religion:

(26.48) After the labors of youth, peace in some measure is granted to old age. But from old age health deteriorates and fades, as one becomes more and more subject to weaknesses and diseases, leading to death. This is human life lived in the body, bound up with lusts for time-bound things. This is called "the old man" (Rom 6:6), or "the exterior" and "the earthly" (1 Cor 15:47), even if he obtains what the crowd calls "happiness," in a well-ordered earthly city, ruled either by kings or emperors or laws or all of them together. . . .

(26.49) A certain number live this way from this life's sunrise to its sunset. But a certain number begin this way, as is necessary, but are reborn interiorly and, with their spiritual strength and with an increase of wisdom, destroy and put to death other parts of "the old man" and bind him to the celestial laws, until after this visible death all will be restored. This is called "the new man" (Eph 4:24), or "the inner" and "the heavenly" (1 Cor 15:48–49), who is proportioned not by years, but by progress in a sort of spiritual equiva-

---

61. *De vera religione* 3.3–4.7 (BA 8:24–34); my trans. Augustine continued to commend Platonism, but became more critical, e.g., in *civ. Dei*, Books 8 and 10. See Frederick Van Fleteren, "Plato, Platonism," *AugEncy*, 651–54. On shifts in the scholarly assessment, see Robert Crouse, "*Pacis Mutatis Verbis*: St. Augustine's Platonism," in *Augustine and His Critics*, ed. Robert Dodaro and George Lawless (New York: Routledge, 2000), 37–50.

lent of ages. . . . Just as death marks the endpoint of "the old man," so eternal life marks the goal of "the new man." The first is a person of sin; the second, a person of justice.

(27.50) Both of these lives are, no doubt, interrelated. One can live the entirety of one's life as the first of these—that is, the "old" or the "earthly"—but no one can live out this life as the "new" and "heavenly" except alongside the "old." It is necessary to begin from the "old," and one must continue until this visible death, though the "old" weakens as the "new" progresses. It is the same way for the whole human race, whose life, like that of a single individual, unfolds from Adam until the end of the ages and is arranged by the laws of divine providence so that it appears divided into two categories. One of these is constituted by the mob of impious who bear the image of "earthly men" from the beginning to the end of the ages. The other is the generations of people dedicated to the one God, from Adam until John the Baptist, and they live out the life of the "earthly man" in servitude to a certain righteousness. Their history is called the Old Testament, as though promising simply an earthly kingdom, but also holding the image of a new people and a New Testament, promising the kingdom of heaven. Meanwhile, the life of this people in its temporal phase begins with the coming of the Lord in humility and goes on until the Day of Judgment, when He will return in brightness. After this judgment, with the "old man" having been extinguished, there will be that change which promises us an angelic life: "All of us will be raised, but not all will be changed" (1 Cor 15:51).[62] The people of holiness will be raised so that the remnants of the "old man" in them may be transformed into the new. The people of impiety who bore this "old man" from the beginning to the end will also be raised so as to be tossed headlong into a second death.[63]

TIME AND ETERNITY

For Augustine, eternity does not mean endless time; it is rather a timeless present utterly beyond past or future. Roland Teske has argued that this is the second of Augustine's two great contributions to Western metaphysical thought.[64] The following passage anticipates the much, much lengthier and better-known formulation found in Book 11 of Confessions. *This dense and rather subtle passage may require some mulling over.*

62. Here Augustine is following the Vetus Latina, which has: "Omnes enim resurgemus, sed non omnes immutabimur." Some editions of the Vulgate have: "Non omnes quidem dormiemus, sed omnes immutabimur" (with the "non" omitted in some manuscripts), and this Vulgate reading is mirrored in the NAB: "We shall not all fall asleep, but we shall all be changed."

63. *De vera religione* 26.48–27.50 (BA 8:90–94); my trans.

64. Teske, "Augustine as Philosopher," esp. 24–25.

Many readers know of Descartes' famous "I think, therefore I am" (cogito ergo sum); note that there is an Augustinian version here. From On True Religion:

(49.97) All that I have said about the light of the mind has been manifested to me by nothing other than this very same light. For by this light I understand that what I have said is true and, in turn, by this, I understand that I understand. . . . I understand that I cannot understand unless I am alive, and I understand with greater certitude that by understanding I come to be more alive, more vivacious. Eternal life, after all, surpasses life within time by its very vivaciousness. Nor do I catch a glimpse of what eternity is except by understanding. Naturally, by gazing into the mind, I separate out all changeability from eternity, and discern within eternity itself no period or space of time, because a period of time consists of movements, whether past or future, of things. In eternity there is nothing past and nothing future, because what is past has ceased to be and what is future has not yet begun to be. Eternity, however, simply is. Neither did it use to be, as if it no longer is, nor will it be, as if it is not yet. That is why Eternity alone was able to say to the human mind in the truest sense: "I am who am" (Ex 3:14), and of Eternity it can be said in the truest sense: "The One who is has sent me" (Ex 3:14).[65]

THE ONENESS OF THE TRINITY

In the closing words of On True Religion, *Augustine sets out an early (and rhetorically intricate) formulation of his understanding of the Trinity. From* On True Religion:

(55.112) Look: I worship one God: the one Principle of all things, and His Wisdom, by whom every wise soul is wise, and His Gift, by whom everyone blessed is blessed. . . . (55.113) Therefore, let our religion (religio) bind (religet) us to the one all-powerful God, because no created thing comes between our minds, by which we understand Him to be Father, and the Truth, that is, the interior light through whom we understand Him. That is why in Him and with Him we venerate the Truth, who is in no way unlike Him and who is the Form of all beings whom the One has made and who, in turn, strive to return to the One. From this it appears to spirit-filled minds that all things have been made by this Form, who alone fills up what all yearn for. But all things would not have been made by the Father through the Son, nor would they be healed and brought to their endpoint unless God were the highest goodness, the One who has no jealousy for any nature whose goodness comes to

---

65. *De vera religione* 49.97 (BA 8:166–68); my trans.

be from Him, and who has given the power to all to remain in this goodness, some as much as they wish, others as much as they can. That is why it is fitting for us to worship and hold to, along with the Father and the Son, this Gift of God, equally unchangeable. [Thus,] a Trinity of one substance, the one God from whom we exist, through whom we exist, in whom we exist; the one God whom we fell away from, whom we have made ourselves unlike, but who has not allowed us to perish; the Source to whom we are running back and the Form after whom we are following and the Grace by whom we are reconciled; the One by whose authority we are founded, and His Likeness through whom we are formed into unity, and His Peace in whom we cling to unity; the God who said, "Let there be" (Gn 1:3), and the Word through whom everything that was made was naturally and substantially made, and the Gift of His kindness by whom whatever was made by Him through the Word not be left to perish but prove pleasing and be reconciled to its Author; one God by whose creating we live, by whose reforming we live wisely, by whose loving and enjoyment we live happily and blessedly; the one God from whom are all things, through whom are all things, in whom are all things, to Him be glory forever and ever. Amen.[66]

66. *De vera religione* 55.112–13 (BA 8:186–90); my trans.

CHAPTER 3

AUGUSTINE THE BISHOP

✣

We think of Augustine as a writer and a theologian. He was both, certainly, but his writing and his theologizing sprang from and were shaped by his very demanding day job. For more than 35 years, Augustine spent his waking hours working as a bishop and pastor of a bustling North African seaport, Hippo Regius (now Annaba, on Algeria's eastern border).[1] That Augustine was a bishop may seem a simple biographical fact, but outside of scholarly circles, its massive implications remain underappreciated. It is, in fact, a fact that puts every other side of Augustine into its rightful perspective.[2]

Getting ordained had never been Augustine's intention. From 387 to 391, he enjoyed retirement from the very public life he had known in Milan. All that changed overnight. In early 391, he traveled north from Thagaste to Hippo to recruit a new member for his monastic community. Standing innocently among the congregation, Augustine was caught off guard when Hippo's bishop, a Greek named Valerius, called on his people to nominate a new presbyter. Augustine was grabbed and ordained on the spot (see the two accounts below). He found a new public life thrust upon him, a life very different from the one he had known as orator in Milan. For the next five years, Augustine served as a presbyter, assisting Bishop Valerius, who encouraged him to relocate his monastic community to Hippo and gave him land to house it, a garden precinct attached to the episcopal residence. In 395, Augustine was consecrated as coadjutor bishop and, after Valerius's death in 396, assumed control of the church.

1. On Hippo and coastal North Africa, see Brown, *Augustine of Hippo*, 183–97; also Serge Lancel, "Hippo Regius," *Aug-Lex* 3: 351–66.

2. Augustinian scholars have appreciated this for decades, ever since Frederic Van der Meer's seminal work, *Augustine the Bishop*, trans. B. Battershaw and G. R. Lamb (London: Sheed and Ward, 1961). Originally published in Dutch in 1948, it is now dated in many respects.

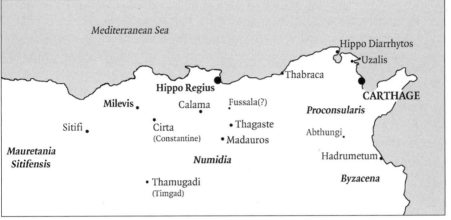

Augustine's North Africa

The episcopacy now defined his life. He spoke of it as a "heavy load" (*sarcina*). Once, in a sermon on the anniversary of his ordination, he remarked: "To preach, to rebuke, to correct, to build up, to feel responsible for every one of you—it's a terrible burden, a huge weight, an enormous task."[3] Why so burdensome? Because Augustine saw his office—and much else—in light of Christ's second coming. Christ's final judgment meant that accounts would be audited and debt payments come due. As he explained to his hearers, "The difference between each of you and me is this: that you are going to have to render an accounting only for yourself, while I am going to have to do it for myself *and* for you."[4]

As bishop, Augustine had sacramental duties, notably, preaching at daily and Sunday liturgies of the Word and presiding at daily and Sunday Eucharists. He also oversaw the years-long training of catechumens and presided over their baptism each Easter. Such duties were but one facet of his work. He also had to supervise his clergy, who sometimes caused him real headaches. He had to make sure that the finances of the church were in order and that church properties were properly managed. He was expected to ensure that the poor, especially widows and orphans, received the church's aid. Augustine's world had nothing like a welfare system or social security. Churches around the Empire clothed and fed, on a daily basis, large numbers of dependents.

---

3. S. 339.1 (PL 38:1480); my trans. The term *sarcina* appears in his letter to Paulinus of Nola right after his ordination (*ep.* 31.4). It becomes a commonplace: see *s.* 339.1, *ep.* 85.2; cf. *s.* 340.1.

4. S. 339.1 (PL 38:1480); my trans. See also *s.* 46.2.

One time-consuming task was serving as a judge or legal arbiter. He spent long hours, much to his chagrin, listening to lawsuits between members of his congregation, typically over disputed wills. When his congregation ran afoul of the law, he was expected to lobby city officials or beg for mercy from imperial judges. As head of the Catholic community, he was automatically a civic notable. He was expected to play the patron and required to stake out his community's claims in the routine rough-and-tumble of city politics, rubbing shoulders with aristocratic landowners who oversaw vast estates in the nearby countryside and transported their harvests to Hippo's markets, or with shipping magnates whose fleets sailed goods into and out of Hippo's harbor and to ports around the Mediterranean and beyond, or with military officers whose legions guarded the Empire's porous frontiers and whose personal ambitions could spark uprisings and bloody civil wars. Paganism was alive and well in certain locales, and rivalry with Christians could, on occasion, turn violent. Augustine put his vast oratorical energies into combating local groups he regarded as heretics or schismatics. He publicly faced off with both Manichees and Arians. He was such a formidable controversialist that local Donatists (wisely) refused to debate him face to face. So he skewered them in sermons and bombarded them with pamphlets. Later chapters will detail these individual controversies, but we need to bear in mind that these disputes sprang from Augustine's pastoral work as a bishop.

Not all tasks were local. North African bishops had, since the time of Cyprian of Carthage (d. 258), worked intensely through regional councils. This meant that Augustine had to travel extensively, especially between Hippo and Carthage, but on occasion west along the coast or inland.[5] His ecclesiastical superior was a good friend, Aurelius, bishop of Carthage and primate of Africa Proconsularis and, for all intents and purposes, head of the North African church. Augustine, in both regional and international disputes, often served as both theoretician and spokesman for the policies of the North African bishops. Augustine often partnered with Alypius, who was an old friend and who had been baptized with him in Milan. Alypius officially served as bishop of Augustine's hometown of Thagaste but spent extended stints in Italy, lobbying on behalf of the North African bishops in their dealings with the imperial court at Ravenna.[6]

In this chapter, I draw on three main sources. First is the brief *Life of*

---

5. See the classic study by Othmar Perler, *Les voyages de saint Augustin*, CEASA 36 (Paris: Institut d'Études Augustiniennes, 1969); this needs to be updated in light of recent discoveries of new letters and sermons.

6. On this, see Serge Lancel, "Africa: Organisation ecclésiastique," *Aug-Lex* 1:205–19; Jan Michael Joncas, "Clergy, North African," *AugEncy*, 213–17. On Aurelius of Carthage, see Anne-Marie LaBonnardière, "Aurelius episcopus," *Aug-Lex* 1: 550–66. On Alypius of Thagaste, see Erich Feldmann, Alfred Schindler, and Otto Wermelinger, "Alypius," *Aug-Lex* 1:245–67.

St. *Augustine* (*Vita s. Augustini*), authored by his friend and editor Possidius of Calama.[7] Possidius's account provides a frame for the chapter as a whole and punctuates the flow. Second, I draw on a handful of sermons, not to illustrate his preaching (for that, see Chapter Four), but rather to highlight aspects of his social world. Let me encourage readers to read these sermons aloud. They were originally delivered orally, of course, and their oral character comes through, even in translation. Finally, I draw selections from Augustine's more than 300 surviving letters to illustrate various pastoral quandaries and crises. Of special interest are 31 letters, lost for centuries but rediscovered and published in 1981 by Johannes Divjak.[8] The excerpts in this chapter do not, for the most part, provide a continuous narrative. Think of them, instead, as snapshots in a photo album. They offer vivid, though disconnected, glimpses into his life and world. Some illustrate the humdrum ordinary; others, headline-making events.

❧

POSSIDIUS ON AUGUSTINE'S ORDINATION

In 391, Augustine traveled to Hippo Regius to convince a friend to join his monastic community in Thagaste. He happened to attend liturgy just as Bishop Valerius asked the congregation to nominate a new presbyter. Augustine found himself dragged to the front of the church and ordained on the spot. From Possidius of Calama, Life of St. Augustine:

(4) Now, at this time, holy Valerius was bishop of the Catholic Church at Hippo. Because of the pressing duties of his ecclesiastical office, this man addressed the people of God, encouraging them to provide and ordain a presbyter for the city.[9] Consequent-

7. On Possidius and the *Vita*, see Erika T. Hermanowicz, *Possidius of Calama: A Study of the North African Episcopate*, OECS (New York: Oxford University Press, 2008).

8. The Benedictines of St. Maur, who edited the classic edition of Augustine's Latin works between 1679 and 1700, numbered his letters between 1 and 270. These include not only letters that Augustine wrote but also ones he received (e.g., *ep.* 135 from Marcellinus, *ep.* 136 from Volusianus). In the 200 years after the Benedictine edition, six others were discovered and inserted into this numbering scheme (e.g., *ep.* 173A to Deogratias, *ep.* 250A to Classicianus). The recently discovered Divjak letters have not been inserted into this numbering; instead, an asterisk has been added (e.g., *ep.* 10* and *ep.* 22*, cited in this chapter). For an overview, see Henry Chadwick, "The New Letters of St. Augustine." *Journal of Theological Studies* 34 (1983): 425–52. See also works in the bibliography.

9. "Presbyter" (*presbyter*, "elder"): While the Latin term is translated by many as "priest," that is somewhat inaccurate for this period. The local church in Christianity's early centuries had a threefold hierarchy: the bishop (*episkopos*, "overseer") was the leader; presbyters were next in rank; below them were deacons (*diakonoi*, "servants"). The epithet "priest" (*sacerdos*) was initially applied only to the bishop. Only in Augustine's time does one begin to see a shift in application, so that here and there one finds the term "priest" applied to presbyters. My translation here and throughout reflects this terminology.

ly the Catholics, who already knew about the life and teaching of holy Augustine, laid hands on him. He was standing among the crowd, in security and ignorant of what was about to happen, for it was his custom as a layman, he has told us, to withhold his presence only from those churches which had no bishops. Therefore, they seized him and, as is customary in such cases, brought him to the bishop for ordination, since this was what all wished. Augustine wept freely as they eagerly presented their request with loud shouting. The cause of his tears, as he himself told us later, was interpreted by some of the people to be the result of wounded pride, and therefore by way of consolation they told him that, though he was worthy of a greater honor, the office of presbyter was close to the bishopric in rank. The man of God, however, as his own words affirm, had a greater understanding of the matter. He grieved because he anticipated the many imminent dangers that would threaten his life in the rule and government of the Church. This was the cause of his tears. Everything, however, was accomplished in accordance with the will of the people.[10]

AUGUSTINE ON AUGUSTINE'S ORDINATION

In a sermon delivered at the end of his career, Augustine recounts these same events. He recalls them within an embarrassing context, namely, that a presbyter of his had not distributed his holdings upon ordination and, in the end, died leaving a will that was bitterly contested between two surviving children. Augustine used this opportunity to set out his personal ideal of a community of shared goods. From Sermon 355:

(2) You all know, or almost all of you do, that we live in a house, known as the bishop's house, living in such a way that we might imitate, as best we can, the holy ones about whom the book of the Acts of the Apostles speaks: "No one claimed anything as their own, but everything of theirs was held in common" (Acts 4:32). . . . I, whom by God's grace you see as your bishop, came to this city as a young man. Many of you know that. I was searching for somewhere to set up a monastery, and there to live with my brethren. I had left behind all hopes of this world. What I could have been, I did not wish to be; nor did I seek to be what I am now. "I chose to be lowly in the house of my God rather than live in tents of sinners" (Ps 83:11). I separated myself from those who love the world, but I did not put myself on equal standing with those who preside over the people [of God]. Nor at the Lord's banquet did I pick a higher place, but rather a lower, lowly one. And it pleased the Lord to say to

10. Vita 4 (Geerlings, 32–34); trans. Muller and Deferrari, FOTC 15:77–78. On such forced ordinations, see Yves Congar, "Ordinations invictus, coactus, de l'église antique au canon 214," *Revue des sciences philosophiques et théologiques* 50 (1966): 169–97; reprinted in *Droit ancien et structures ecclésiales* (London: Variorum, 1982).

me: "Move up higher" (Lk 14:10). So much did I fear the office of bishop that, since I had begun already to get a certain weighty reputation among the servants of God, I would not go near any spot where I knew there was no bishop. I kept up my guard against this. I did whatever I could to find salvation in a humble position rather than in the risky hazards of a high one. But, as I said, a slave ought not to contradict the Lord. I came to this city in order to see a friend, whom I was thinking I could gain for God, that he might come to be with us in the monastery. It seemed as though it were safe, because the place had a bishop. I was grabbed and made a presbyter. And from that rank, I came to the office of bishop.

I brought nothing with me. I came to this church only with the clothes I happened to be wearing. And because I was working on setting up a monastery with the brethren, old Valerius of blessed memory, learning of what I wanted and planned, gave me this garden where the monastery is now. I began to bring together good brothers, my partners in poverty, having nothing just as I had nothing, and imitating me. In the same way that I sold my poor little piece of land and handed out the proceeds to the poor, so did those who wished to live with me, that we might live from what was held in common. The great and highly productive estate we held in common was God Himself.[11]

LEAVE OF ABSENCE

No sooner had Augustine been ordained than he begged for a leave of absence. Why? To study Scripture. He had been baptized only four years earlier, and there was, as yet, nothing like a seminary or divinity school for the training of clergy. Everything was learned on the job. In requesting a leave, Augustine offers perspectives on how he had once viewed clergy and how he viewed them now. He suggests that his ordination was God's just revenge for his earlier outspoken critiques. From Letter 21:

(1) First of all, I beg your religious Prudence to consider that there is nothing in this life, and especially at this time, easier or more agreeable or more acceptable to people than the office of bishop or presbyter or deacon, if it is performed carelessly or in a manner to win flattery; but in God's sight there is nothing more wretched, more melancholy, or more worthy of punishment. On the other hand, there is nothing in this life more difficult, more laborious, or more dangerous than the office of bishop or presbyter or deacon, but noth-

---

11. S. 355.2 (PL 39:1569–70); my trans. Note the citation of Acts 4, a hallmark of Augustinian monastic spirituality. See below for excerpts from Augustine's monastic rule.

ing more blessed in the sight of God, if he carries on the campaign in the way prescribed by our Commander. Neither in childhood nor in youth did I learn what that way was, but just as I was beginning to learn, I was constrained as a punishment for my sins—I can think of no other reason—to accept the post next to the helmsman before I had even learned to handle an oar.

(2) I think my Lord wanted to correct me because, without adequate virtue and experience, I had dared to reprimand what was there being done before I had experienced the misdeeds of many sailors. But after I had been plunged into the midst of things, I began to realize the rashness of my reprimands—although even then I had considered it a most dangerous duty. That was the cause of those tears that some of the brethren noticed me shedding when I was newly ordained; and knowing the cause of my grief, they tried to comfort me, with good intentions, no doubt, but with words that left my inner wound untouched. I have since learned much, very much, more than I expected, not because I have seen any new waves or storms which I had not previously seen or heard or read or thought of, but because I had not known the extent of my skill and strength in avoiding or overcoming them, thinking I was of some use. Then the Lord laughed at me and willed to show me myself in action.

(3) If He did this, not as a punishment, but out of mercy—which I earnestly hope, now that I know my weakness—then I ought to study all His remedies in the Scriptures and, by praying and reading, so act such that strength sufficient for such perilous duties may be granted to my soul. I did not do this before, because I did not have time, but as soon as I was ordained, I planned to use all my leisure time in studying the Sacred Scriptures, and I tried to arrange to have leisure for this duty. Truly, I did not know what I needed for such a task, but now I am tormented and weighed down by it. If I have learned by experience what someone who administers the Sacrament and the Word of God to people needs—and I do not lay claim to what I do not possess—do you, Father Valerius, give me a command which will be my destruction? Where is your charity? Do you truly love me? Do you truly love the Church itself, what you wish me to minister to? I am sure you love both the Church and me, but you consider me fit, while I know myself better. And I should not have known myself if I had not learned by experience.

(4) Perhaps your Holiness may say: "I should like to know what is lacking in your training." So much is lacking that I could more easily tell what I lack than what I have. I venture to say that I know and hold with firm faith all that is necessary for my own salvation. But how am I to make use of this for the salvation of others? "Not seeking that which is profitable to myself, but to the many, that they may be saved" (1 Cor 10:33). Perhaps there are—I should say there undoubtedly are—some instructions in the Sacred Books which

a man of God may learn and hold so as to act with authority in ecclesiastical matters, or, if not that, at least to live with safer conscience in the midst of sinners or to die without losing that life which meek and humble Christian hearts alone aspire to. How can this be done, except as the Lord Himself says, by asking, seeking, knocking: that is, by praying, reading, weeping? For this purpose, I wanted the brethren to secure for me from your most sincere and venerable Charity a little time, at least until Easter, and this I myself now ask. . . .

(6) Therefore, I beg you, by that charity and affection, to take pity on me and grant me as much time as I have asked, for the reason I have asked. Help also with your prayers, that my desire may not be in vain nor my absence unprofitable to the Church of Christ and the service of my brethren and fellow servants. I know that the Lord does not despise the charity of prayers for such a case, but perhaps He will accept them as a sacrifice of sweetness and will restore me in a shorter time than I have asked, armed with saving knowledge from the Scriptures.[12]

PRESBYTER AS PREACHER

Augustine's leave of absence did not last long. By Lent 391, he had returned, and gave his first sermons to catechumens preparing for baptism. In the Latin West, unlike the Greek East, presbyters were not allowed to preach whenever the bishop was present. But Valerius was a Greek and appealed to Eastern customs to allow Augustine, with all his enormous skills as an orator, a platform to preach from. In the following passage, Possidius notes Augustine's growing reputation as a preacher and writer. He also notes that the wealthy used to bring along personal stenographers to transcribe Augustine's sermons. From Possidius of Calama, Life of St. Augustine:

(5) The holy Valerius, who had ordained [Augustine], being a good, God-fearing man, rejoiced and gave thanks to God. He said that the Lord had heard his repeated prayers imploring Divine Providence to send a man of such a character as could edify the Church of the Lord by the salutary teaching of His word. Since Valerius was a Greek by birth and less versed in the Latin language and literature, he realized his limitations in that respect. Therefore, he gave his presbyter the right to preach the Gospel in his presence in church and to hold frequent public discussions, a procedure contrary to that usually practiced in African churches. As a consequence, the criticism of some bishops was incurred. The venerable and prudent Valerius, however, fully cognizant of the fact that such was the custom in Eastern churches, and in consideration

12. Ep. 21.1–6 (CCL 31:48–51); trans. Parsons, FOTC 12:47–51.

of the Church's welfare, paid no attention to the tongues of detractors. He was satisfied in knowing that his presbyter was doing what he himself as bishop could not accomplish. Thus this burning and shining light was placed upon a candlestick to enlighten all who were in the house. News of this practice spread quickly, and because of Augustine's good example, other presbyters with episcopal authorization began to preach to the people in the presence of their bishops. . . .

(7) Publicly and privately, at home and in church, Augustine confidently taught and preached the word of salvation. Both his finished books and his extemporaneous sermons opposed the African heresies, especially Donatism, Manicheism, and paganism; at the same time, the Christians with unspeakable admiration and praise were not silent about the matter, but published it wherever possible. So by the grace of God, the Catholic Church in Africa began to raise its head. . . . Through the wondrous grace of God these writings came forth and flowed out with an abundance of instruction based on reason and with the authority of the Holy Scriptures. At these gatherings, whoever wished and was able to do so brought stenographers to take down what was said. In this way the glorious doctrine and sweet savor of Christ was manifested and spread throughout all Africa.[13]

Appointment as Coadjutor

Valerius was afraid that his talented presbyter would be recruited away to serve as bishop elsewhere. So in a move calculated to hold on to Augustine, he had him ordained as a coadjutor bishop—a move contrary, it turns out, to canonical practice. From Possidius of Calama, Life of St. Augustine:

(8) The venerable old man, Valerius, rejoiced more than others and gave thanks to God for the special blessings his church had received. He began to fear, however, for such is human nature, that some other church which lacked a bishop might seek Augustine for the episcopal office and so take him away. Indeed, that would have happened if the bishop himself, upon discovering the plan, had not taken precautions. He arranged that Augustine should go to a secret place and be hidden so that he could not be found by those who were seeking him. Nevertheless, the old man continued to fear, realizing his age and extreme infirmity. Consequently, he wrote a secret letter to the Bishop of Carthage, the episcopal primate, stressing the weakness of his body and the burden of his years, and for this reason he petitioned the appointment of Augustine as bishop of the church at Hippo. As such, Augustine would not [simply] be his successor, but would [also] be associated with him as coadjutor. Valerius's desire and request were answered by a satisfactory reply. Accordingly, to the astonishment

13. Vita 5–7 (Geerlings, 34–38); trans. Muller and Deferrari, FOTC 15:78–81 (modified).

of all, he revealed his plan when Megalius, Bishop of Calama and primate of Numidia, upon request visited the church at Hippo. Those bishops who happened to be present at that time, as well as the clergy of Hippo, and all the people, rejoiced upon hearing this and eagerly shouted for its fulfillment. The presbyter, however, refused to accept the episcopacy, as being contrary to ecclesiastical practice, since his bishop was still alive. Then everyone tried to convince him that this was common usage by citing examples of its existence in churches across the sea and in Africa, and although Augustine had not heard of it before, he yielded under compulsion and constraint, consenting to ordination to the higher office. Later he said and wrote that his ordination to the episcopacy during the lifetime of his bishop should not have taken place according to the prohibition of the Ecumenical Council.[14] He was unaware of this regulation, however, until after his ordination, but he did not want others to experience what regretfully had happened to him. For that reason he made it his business to have the councils of bishops decree that consecrating prelates should inform those about to be ordained or already ordained concerning the regulations that govern all priests. Accordingly, this was done.[15]

BISHOP AS OVERSEER

Augustine was installed as Hippo's presiding bishop in 396, after Valerius's death. The word episkopos ("bishop") was originally a secular Greek term that meant "overseer." In ancient churches, the bishop sat in a chair on a raised platform at the far end of the church. From there, he could literally oversee his congregation. Augustine used to play on this arrangement both to highlight his distinctive role and to stress his and his congregation's common vocation. From Expositions of the Psalms 126:

(3) Jerusalem had watchmen who stood guard. . . . And this is what bishops do. Now, bishops are assigned this higher place [in the basilica] so that they themselves may oversee and, as it were, keep watch over the people. For they are called *episkopos* in Greek. In Latin, that means "overseer"—because a bishop oversees, because he looks down from above. For just as there's a vineyard worker assigned a higher place to keep watch over a vineyard, so too bishops are given a higher position. And on account of this high place, a perilous accounting will have to be rendered—unless we stand here with a heart such that we place ourselves beneath your feet in humility, and that we pray for you so that the One who knows your minds may Himself stand guard

14. "Prohibition of the Ecumenical Council": Possidius is referring to *Canon* 8 of the Council of Nicaea (325) which forbade having two bishops in a city. For the text, see Norman P. Tanner, *Decrees of the Ecumenical Councils* (Washington, DC: Georgetown University Press, 1990), 1:10.

15. Vita 8 (Geerlings, 38–40); trans. Muller and Deferrari, FOTC 15:81–82.

over them. While we can watch your comings-in and goings-out, we cannot, however, see what you do in your homes, much less what you ponder in your hearts. . . . We stand guard over you in virtue of our office as stewards, but we wish to be guarded along with you. We are, so to speak, shepherds for you, but under that one Shepherd, we are sheep along with you. We are, so to speak, teachers from this [elevated] place, but under that one Teacher we are, in this school, fellow students along with you.[16]

"When in Rome . . . "

Around 401, a man named Januarius sent Augustine a long list of questions on liturgy. Augustine answered in two letters, one a virtual treatise.[17] Medieval theologians would later appeal to these letters as they sought to work out a comprehensive theory of sacrament. The passage below is illuminating especially for what it says of Augustine's pastoral attitude on liturgical diversity. He recounts a famous anecdote about Ambrose, whom Augustine, as a bishop, now saw as an "oracle" and model for episcopal conduct. From Letter 54:

(1.1) In the first place, I want you to hold as the basic truth of this discussion that our Lord Jesus Christ, as He Himself said in the Gospel, has subjected us to His yoke and His burden, which are light. Therefore He has laid on the society of His new people the obligation of sacraments, very few in number, very easy of observance, most sublime in their meaning, as for example, baptism hallowed by the name of the Trinity, communion of His Body and His Blood, and whatever else is commended in the canonical writings—with the exception of those burdens found in the five books of Moses, which imposed on the ancient people [of God] a servitude in accord with their character and the prophetic times in which they lived. But regarding those other observances which we keep and all the world keeps, and which do not derive from scripture but from tradition, we are given to understand that they have been ordained or recommended to be kept by the Apostles themselves, or by

16. En. Ps. 126.3 (CCL 40:1858–59); my trans. Augustine discusses the role of bishop at length, but more diffusely in other sermons: on the anniversary of his ordination (s. 339), at the ordination of a new bishop (s. 340A), and in a sermon on Ezekiel (s. 46). On the bishop as preacher, see s. 95.1–2 and s. 301A.1–2 (cited in Chapters 4 and 5). Vatican II's *Lumen Gentium* 32 famously quotes a sermon preserved in Augustine's corpus, s. 340.2 (PL 38:1483): "What I am for you terrifies me; what I am with you consoles me. For you I am a bishop; but with you I am a Christian. The former is a duty; the latter, a grace. The former is a danger; the latter, salvation." This sermon, as it has come down to us, is actually from Caesarius of Arles (d. 543), who apparently reworked an earlier sermon of Augustine (s. 232; CCL 104:919).

17. In *retr.* 2.20 (CCL 57:106), Augustine catalogued *ep.* 54–55 not as letters (as they are now) but rather as "two books whose title is In Answer to the Inquiries of Januarius." Hombert, *Nouvelles recherches*, 95–100, has argued that the date for these should be pushed back to 403.

plenary councils whose authority is well founded in the Church. Examples are the annual commemorations of the Lord's Passion, Resurrection, and Ascension into heaven, the descent of the Holy Spirit from heaven, and other such observances as are kept by the universal Church wherever it is found.

(2.2) Other customs, however, differ according to country and locale. For example, some fast on Saturday, others do not; some receive the Body and Blood of the Lord daily, others receive it on certain days; in some places no day is omitted in the offering of the Holy Sacrifice; in others it is offered only on Saturday and Sunday, or even only on Sunday; and other such differences may be noted. There is freedom in all these matters, and there is no better rule for the earnest and prudent Christian than to act as he sees the Church act wherever he is staying. What is proved to be against neither faith nor morals is to be considered optional and is to be observed with due regard for the group in which one lives.

(2.3) I believe you heard this [anecdote] some time ago, but let me nevertheless repeat it here: My mother, who had followed me to Milan, found that the church there did not fast on Saturday. She began to be anxious and uncertain as to what she should do. I was not concerned then with such things, but for her sake I consulted on this matter that man of most blessed memory, Ambrose. He answered that he could teach me nothing except what he himself did, because, if he knew anything better, he would do it. When I thought that he wished to impose his views on us, solely on his own authority, without giving any reason, he followed up and said to me: "When I go to Rome, I fast on Saturday, but here I do not. You should follow the custom of whatever church you attend if you do not want to give or receive scandal." When I told this to my mother, she willingly accepted it. And recalling this advice over and over again, I have always esteemed it as something given by a heavenly oracle. For I have often experienced with grief and dismay that the weak are deeply disturbed by the aggressive obstinacy or superstitious fears of certain brethren who stir up such controversial questions that they think nothing is right except what they themselves do. And these are things of such sort that they are not prescribed by the authority of Holy Scripture nor by the tradition of the universal Church, and they serve no good purpose of amending one's life, but they are insisted on simply because somebody thinks up a reason for them, or because someone was accustomed to do so in his own country, or because he saw things done somewhere on a pilgrimage, and he esteemed them to be more correct because they were further from his own usage.[18]

18. Ep. 54.1.1–2.3 (CCL 31:226–28); trans. Parsons, FOTC 12:252–54 (modified). Augustine mentions this incident also in ep. 36.14.32 (CCL 31:153).

Church as Corpus Permixtum

The Church, as Augustine often remarked, was a hodge-podge of good and bad, what he called a corpus permixtum ("mixed-up body"). In the following passage, he gives a glimpse of the varied ways outsiders viewed the Christian Church. From Expositions of the Psalms 99:

(12) Generally speaking, the Church of God is praised: "Christians are really great people." Christians alone get praised this way: "The Catholic Church is great. They all love each other; each and every one of them does all they can for one another. They pray, fast, sing hymns; they do this around the whole world. God is praised in peace, in unanimity." A person may hear this, and nothing gets said about the wicked who are mixed in. He doesn't know about them. He comes, drawn by this high praise. He then runs into these scoundrels mixed up with the others, ones he hadn't been told about before he came. He gets offended by all these false Christians and flees true Christians. On the other side, there are hate-filled people, slanderers—they rush in to condemn: "What sort of people are Christians? Who are Christians? Money-grubbers, loan-sharks. Aren't the very people who pack the theaters or the amphitheaters for the games or for the other big-time entertainments the same people who pack the churches on festival days? They're drunks, gluttons; they're jealous of each other, they tear each other down." Sure, there are Christians like that, but not every one's like that. The slanderer in his blindness says nothing about the good; the praiser in his exaggeration says nothing of the bad.[19]

Suspicious Conversions

In late fourth-century North Africa, Christians were a decided majority. Remaining pagans faced strong social pressures to convert. On one occasion, Augustine was called upon to defend the conversion of a banker named Faustinus who, locals suspected, had his eye on the job of mayor and who certainly realized he would never get it unless he became a Christian. This sermon was delivered not in Hippo, but in Carthage, where Bishop Aurelius routinely invited Augustine to take the podium as guest preacher. Here we see Augustine's willingness to give the benefit of the doubt to what appeared as a less-than-sincere conversion. Note the way Augustine quotes people's gossip and slangy quips; note also his playful use of imagery of sheep and shepherds and of banking and investments. From Sermon 279:

19. En. Ps. 99.12 (CCL 39:1400); my trans.

(10) Because my lord and father [Aurelius] orders that I speak to you, please listen intently just a little longer. Let me announce to your ears what you discern with your eyes: Prey has been snatched and rescued from the wolf's jaws by our great Shepherd's doing and mercy. The Shepherd has brought back the one that [God's] flock used to shout about. The one they shouted about, one who used to be an enemy of the Christian faith, has now taken up the Christian faith. . . . Some may say: "Who? That guy, a Christian? That guy, he has come to believe?" We cannot see into the human heart nor bring it out into the open. . . . The Apostle Paul says: "Brothers and sisters, do not make any judgment before the appointed time, until the Lord comes, for He will bring to light what is hidden in darkness, and will manifest the heart's motives, and then everyone will receive praise from God" (1 Cor 4:5). You cannot peer into the heart of new Christians. Why not? Well, can you do so with the hearts of veteran Christians? You're going to say: "But Faustinus believed because he had to." The same could be said of the one I talked about a little earlier. St. Paul, too, at one point was "a blasphemer and a persecutor and a scoffer" (1 Tm 1:13). He also got forced, a certain necessity imposed on him. A heavenly voice laid him flat. . . . [People say:] "Faustinus believed because he had to." What was he scared of? Tell me: What was he scared of? Sheep crying out "baa"? Sheep may "baa," but they can't bite. Now he could have noticed the glory of God in sheep baa-ing, and he could have gotten scared of God's judgment. . . .

(11) In the meantime, brothers and sisters, let us stay with what's been conceded to us, to what we as human beings can do, and not lay claim to what's beyond us. The Apostle says: "Welcome the one weak in faith, not in judgments on thoughts" (Rom 14:1). Let us not lay claim to judging others' thoughts, but let us set before God our prayers, even for those about whom we maybe have doubts. Maybe this new one himself has certain doubts. Love him abundantly in all his doubting. By your love, remove doubts from the heart of one less-than-firm. . . . [People used to say:] "Who did such-and-such?" "Faustinus." "Who did such-and-such?" "Faustinus." "Who used to be against Christ?" "Faustinus." Who now fears Christ? "Faustinus."[20] . . . And so, brothers and sisters, we commend him to your prayers, and to your love, and to a most faithful friendship, and to holding him up when he's less-than-firm. As you move along, teach him the good pathway. Let him find that good pathway in you. Now that he's been made a Christian, let him discern the difference between what he has dismissed and what he has found. The future

20. Augustine's audience was often noisy and responded to him with both applause and shouts. For more on this, see Chapter 4. I suspect that here the name "Faustinus" might have been called out not by Augustine himself, but by the audience who responded noisily to his rapid-fire questions.

will tell whether his life and his zeal for the faith of Christ prove worthy. . . .

(12) To judge the heart's hiddenness and to refuse to accept a voice's clarity: that's not for us to make recommendations on or decisions about. We recognize, you see, our Lord's merciful greed, everywhere seeking a lucrative return on his money. . . . Christ will be the one who exacts profits not only from this man here, but from all of us. Let us fulfill, therefore, our task as investors and not lay claim to the role of exacting profits. . . . You know what got shouted here, you know it: that "pagans should not be mayors," that "pagans should not rule over Christians." That's what was shouted. . . . Human beings were doing what they could, but Faustinus got minted by Christ as a brand-new banker. Therefore, brothers and sisters, keep the work of God in mind. . . . We all heard Faustinus's voice, out loud and with devotion: "I do not wish to be mayor, I want to be a Christian." Rejoice, exult, love him—more than you ever despised him. Recommend his work to Christ by your prayers. Show a faithful, pious, friendly spirit to an old man's first lessons in school. What difference is it that, as you see, he's already reached an elderly age? He may have come into the vineyard at the ninth hour, but he will receive equal pay (Mt 20:12–15).[21]

DELAYING BAPTISM

Fourth and fifth-century bishops across the Empire used to complain about catechumens delaying baptism. In one of the Divjak letters, Augustine writes to a catechumen named Firmus. Firmus had asked Augustine to send him a copy of On the City of God *after attending a public reading of Book 18. Augustine forwarded the massive text but demanded repayment, namely, that Firmus put in his name for baptism. Firmus offered various excuses, for example, that he had not received the grace yet (exactly the sort of excuse that Pelagius used to complain bitterly about and one reason that Pelagius would attack Augustine's theology of grace). Augustine, even with his radical theology of God's graced initiatives and of predestination, would hear nothing of Firmus's delays and argued that his outer exhortation was an external grace that echoed the grace of God's interior call. From Letter 2* (Divjak):*

(3) I see that in one of your other letters you make excuses about why you have been putting off accepting the sacrament of rebirth and thus, in effect, throwing away the fruits of all those books [of *On the City of God*] you love.

---

21. S. 279.10–12 (MA 1:589–93); my trans. The text here is from s. Morin 1, not the Maurist edition of s. 279. Another time, Augustine brought up an ex-astrologer before the congregation and made a similar public appeal (*en. Ps.* 61.23); however, the man was not a pagan, but a one-time Christian who sought to be restored to communion and committed to doing public penance.

What fruits? Not that someone may have interesting reading nor that he may learn a lot of things he did not know before, but that the reader may be convinced of the City of God so that he enter it without delay and that he become even more determined to stay in it. The first of these two things is conferred by rebirth, the second by a love of justice. If those who read these books and praise them do not actually take action and do these things, what good are the books? As far as you yourself are concerned, when these books have not been able to get you to take even the first step, however much you may praise them, they have thus far failed completely.

(4) [You say:] "The burden of such a great weight cannot be borne by the weak so far without additional strength." That is the first excuse you give. You men who dread this burden, you do not seem to notice how easily you are surpassed in bearing it by women, by the religious multitude of those faithful and chaste women whom Mother Church produces so fruitfully. For if you would pay attention, you would get rid of this needless fear by the shame you should surely feel. One of this multitude (for I must believe that she is one of them, and this makes me very happy) is your wife. I am not afraid of offending you with the example of a woman when I exhort you to enter the City of God. For if the matter is so difficult, the weaker sex is already there. If easy, there is no reason why you cannot be stronger there as well. . . . For I realize that while you, though still a catechumen, can explain to your wife, a baptized Christian, some things regarding religion that you have read about and she has not, still, she knows things that you do not yet know, and she cannot tell you about them. For the mysteries of rebirth are rightly and properly made known only to those who accept them.[22] So while you may be more learned in doctrine, she is more secure in the mystery. . . .

(6) You also say: "This reluctance is commendable when it concerns religion. For a person, in order to attain the august secrets of the sacred mystery, approaches the more distant things hesitantly and so gives assurance of greater reverence for the faith." You state that this is another reason for your procrastination. . . . The following divine words, written in the Gospel, come to mind: "Unless one is born again of water and the Spirit, he will not enter the Kingdom of Heaven" (Jn 3:5). . . . These frightening words of the divine Scriptures [also] strike like a thunderbolt: "Do not delay to turn to the Lord nor postpone it from day to day, for suddenly the wrath of the Lord will go

22. "The mysteries . . . known only to those who accept them": The ancient rites of baptism, chrismation, and eucharist were cloaked under the *disciplina arcani* ("discipline of secrecy"). An unbaptized catechumen such as Firmus would not have known what precisely Augustine was referring to here. Augustine deliberately used this tactic to pique the curiosity of catechumens to induce them to put in their names for baptism. See Harmless, *Augustine and the Catechumenate*, 170–72, 232–33.

forth, and at the time of punishment you will perish" (Sir 5:8-9). Do not, I beg you, let this happen to you.

(7) You go on and put forward a third excuse: that "in these matters we must above all await the good pleasure of Him by whose will we are compelled toward all desires." And you have added . . . that "without him nothing has been done or can be done." You should not think of all this in such a way that you may appear, in your own eyes, to be doing God's will, when in fact you do not want to fulfill his commandments. One of these, in particular, I just quoted: "Do not delay to turn to the Lord, nor postpone it from day to day" (Sir 5:8). You should think of these matters this way: that you must trust that you will accomplish what He has commanded for your eternal salvation not through your own resources but with His help. Therefore, you must commit yourself, without further delay, not to yourself, O infirm Firmus, but to Him who can do all things; and change your life for the better and receive the grace of rebirth. Do not wait "until He wills it" as if you would offend Him if you willed it first, for when you actually do will it, you will be willing it with his help and by his working. In fact, his mercy has gone before you so that you may will it.[23] But when you do will it, it will indeed be you willing it. For if we do not will it when we will, then He does not confer something on us when He brings it about that we will. What on earth am I doing when I say such things to you except that you should will it? Of course I am doing it in one way; and God, in another: I, externally; He, internally; I, when you hear or read; He, when you think or in order that you may think; I, by speaking; He, in an ineffable way; I, only through his gift; He, through Himself; I, as His minister, having this ministry from Him; He, though needing no minister, fashioning such ministers and using faithful ministers for this in order that He may grant, even to them, the benefit of this work; finally, I as a human being who most of the time cannot accomplish much; He as God, to whom the power of persuasion submits whenever He so wills it.[24]

INDULGENT PIETY

Ancient Christians were expected to fast rigorously during Lent. In the following passage, Augustine satirizes how some in his congregation used Lenten rules on abstinence as an excuse to indulge in exotic alternatives. From Sermon 210:

23. "His mercy has gone before you": Augustine echoes Ps 58:11 ("His mercy shall come before [*praeveniet*] me") and alludes here to his theology of prevenient grace. On this, Chapter 10.

24. Ep. 2*.3–7 (BA 46B:62–74); trans. Eno, FOTC 81:19–28 (modified). This letter touches on Augustine's paradoxical views on the human will and the preacher's duty to exhort hearers to virtue. See James Wetzel, *Augustine and the Limits of Virtue* (Cambridge: Cambridge University Press, 1992), 195, 209–10.

(10) Certain people observe Lent more like gourmets than religious, seeking out new flavors instead of curbing old passions. They compete in topping the varieties and flavors of tasty dishes with lavish and expensively prepared fruits. They may shun as unclean the platters which meat has been cooked on, but they do not shun luxurious excess in their flesh's belly and gut. They may fast not to cut down their usual overeating by tempering things, but to bloat their immoderate desires by holding off a while, for when the time for eating comes, they stampede to well-stocked tables like cattle to troughs, overstuffing their bellies and getting heartburn from too many courses. And lest they become jaded by this abundance, they indulge their palates with lots of imported spices, artfully prepared. In the end, they eat so much that even by fasting they can't digest it all.

(11) Then there are those who give up drinking wine, only to go out searching for liquors fermented from other fruits—and not for their health's sake but for the sheer pleasure of it. It's as though Lent were not for the observance of a genuinely humble piety, but an occasion for new types of self-indulgence. If your stomach can't tolerate drinking water, stick with moderate table wine. That would be better than seeking out rare liquors which neither wine dealers nor winepress have ever seen. What could be more absurd? That a time when the flesh should be reined in more strictly is used to procure tasty delights for the flesh so that one's lusty palate doesn't want Lent to come to an end?[25]

VENGEFUL PIETY

Augustine's parishioners could hold bitter grudges and pray bitter prayers for divine vengeance. From Sermon 211:

(1) It is human to get angry. Would that we did not have this power! It is human to get angry; but your anger ought not, like a tender young twig, to be watered by suspicions and finally grow into a tree of hatred. . . . (7) I know that each day people come, bend their knees, touch the earth with their foreheads, sometimes moisten their faces with tears, and in all this humility and distress say: "Lord, avenge me! Kill my enemy!"[26]

---

25. S. 210.10–11 (PL 38:1052–53); my trans.
26. S. 211.1–7 (PL 38:1054–58); trans. Muldowney, FOTC 38:109, 115.

AUGUSTINE THE JUDGE

A time-consuming part of Augustine's day-to-day work involved serving as a judge and hearing lawsuits of his congregation and other locals. This is not what we imagine bishops spent their time doing, but it was a central part of the ancient job description. The roots lay in the New Testament, in St. Paul's injunctions in 1 Cor 6. In the early fourth century, the Emperor Constantine granted clergy the right to function as arbiters in civil cases. Augustine complained repeatedly about the burden of this, but it was a duty he exercised with care. From Possidius of Calama, Life of St. Augustine:

(19) According to the teaching of the Apostle, who said: "How can any one of you with a case against another dare to bring it to the unjust for judgment instead of to the holy ones? . . . If, therefore, you have courts for everyday matters, do you seat as judges people of no standing in the church? I say this to shame you. Can it be that there is not one among you wise enough to be able to settle a case between brethren?" (1 Cor 6:1–5). Accordingly, Augustine, when called upon by Christians or by people of any sect, carefully and dutifully heard their cases, having constantly before his eyes the remark of someone who said he preferred to hear cases between strangers rather than between friends, for he could win a friend in the stranger in whose favor the case was justly decided, whereas he would lose the friend against whom the judgment was passed. Although he was sometimes detained until mealtime and sometimes even had to fast all day, he always examined and judged these cases with particular attention to the value of Christian souls, noting especially the degree of increase or decrease in faith and in good works. Whenever the opportunity was favorable, he taught both parties the truth of divine law. He stressed its importance and suggested means of obtaining eternal life. No recompense was asked of those to whom he thus devoted his time, except Christian obedience and devotion, which are due to God and to human beings.[27]

PAGAN VIOLENCE

Augustine lived in a violent world. This and the next few passages illustrate how Augustine and his congregation dealt with various violent episodes. In 399, Christians in the town of Sufes destroyed a statue of Hercules.[28] The pagans retaliated by killing some sixty

27. Vita 19 (Geerlings, 64); trans. Muller and Deferrari, FOTC 15:96–97. On this issue, Kauko K. Raikai, "St. Augustine on Juridical Duties: Some Aspects of the Episcopal Office in Late Antiquity," in Augustine: Second Founder of the Faith, Collectanea Augustiniana, ed. Joseph C. Schnaubelt and Frederick Van Fleteren (New York: Peter Lang, 1990), 467–83; John C. Lamoreaux, "Episcopal Courts in Late Antiquity," Journal of Early Christian Studies 3 (1995): 142–67.

28. This event was likely sparked by a law promulgated by the Emperor Honorius, which forbade the public practice of paganism. The Christian mob here may have taken the law into its own hands, and ripped

Christians. *The town council ignored the bloodshed and wrote Augustine demanding that the Christian community pay damages. Augustine, who was generally diplomatic even to hostile correspondents, wrote a decidedly sarcastic reply. This is the complete text of Letter 50, to the city elders of Sufes:*

The infamous crime and unspeakable cruelty of your savagery shakes the earth and strikes the heavens, when blood flows and murder cries aloud in your streets and shrines. By you Roman law is buried, respect for upright judges is trampled underfoot; and among you there is surely neither respect nor fear for the emperors. The innocent blood of sixty brothers has been shed among you, and if anyone killed more, he enjoyed praise and held high position in your government. Let us come, now, to the chief cause. If you say Hercules is your god, we will restore him. There is bronze, there is no lack of stone, there are several kinds of marble, and a supply of artisans is at hand. So then your god is carved carefully, he is smoothed off, and adorned. We will add red clay to paint him red so that your prayers may have the true ring of sacredness.[29] For if you say that Hercules is your god, we can take up a collection from everybody and buy you a god from the stone-cutter. You, on the other hand, need to give us back the lives which your fierce hand wrested from us, and your Hercules will be restored to you exactly as the lives of so many are given back by you.[30]

STAYING AN EXECUTION

In 412, two Donatists brutally attacked two Catholic clergy, killing one, mutilating the other. Such violence was not uncommon (see Chapter 7). The following letter is relevant here because it illustrates what Augustine saw as his required episcopal duty vis-à-vis civil authorities. He wrote to an imperial judge named Apringius and asked him to commute the death sentence against the convicted Donatists. Note his passing mention of judicial torture, something we find appalling; but such practice was a routine element of the Roman legal system. From Letter 134, to Apringius:

(1) In exercising the power which God has given you, a human being over other human beings, I am sure you call to mind the divine judgment at which judges, too, will have to give an account of their judgments. I know, of course,

---

down the statue. The law was put into effect inconsistently and may have been widely resisted in some locales, as Augustine indicates here.

29. "Red clay": Ancient statuary was usually painted. Red was associated with very ancient statuary, and so new statues were painted red to give them the allure of antiquity. Augustine is being ironic, associating red paint with the bloody results of pagan religion.

30. Ep. 50 (CCL 31:214); trans. Parsons, FOTC 18:237.

that you are steeped in the Christian faith, and this gives me greater confidence in addressing your Excellency not only with a request, but even with a warning, because of the Lord, in whose heavenly household you are enrolled along with us, in whom we have the same hope of eternal life, and to whom we pray for you during the holy Mysteries. Therefore, noble lord, deservedly exalted and distinguished son, I ask first of all that I may not seem unmannerly in thus intruding upon your field of action with the anxiety which I must needs feel deeply for the Church entrusted to me, whose interests I am bound to serve, and which I desire to benefit rather than to rule. Secondly, I beg that you do not refuse to hear nor delay to agree to what I urge or request.

(2) An indictment, dispatched in advance through the vigilance of the guardians of public order, has brought certain Circumcellions[31] and Donatists under the authority of the courts and the law. These were examined by your brother, my son Marcellinus,[32] a distinguished man and estimable tribune and legate, and without the use of hooks or fire, but solely under the constraint of the rod, they confessed that they had committed revolting crimes against my brothers and fellow presbyters, as, for example, that they had waylaid one of these and killed him, and that they had abducted another from his house and mutilated him by putting out his eye and cutting off his finger. When I heard that they had confessed to these crimes, I had not the slightest doubt that they would be subject to capital punishment at your hands. So I have made haste to write this letter to your Nobility, begging and praying you, by the mercy of Christ, as we rejoice in your great and certain happiness, not to allow similar tortures to be inflicted on them, although, to be sure, the law cannot punish them by stoning or by cutting off a finger or plucking out an eye, acts which their cruelty made possible for them. Therefore, I am at ease about the men who have confessed, that they will not suffer reciprocal treatment, but what I fear is that either they or the others who have been convicted of murder may be sentenced according to the full weight of your authority. As a bishop I warn a Christian, and as a Christian I appeal to a judge, not to let this happen.

(3) It is of you that the Apostle spoke, as we read it, that you "do not bear the sword in vain," and that you be "God's ministers, avengers against those who do evil" (Rom 13:4). But ruling a province is different from rul-

---

31. "Circumcellions": Augustine portrays them as the violent wing of the Donatist party; for a broader discussion of this, see Chapter 7.

32. "My son Marcellinus": Flavius Marcellinus (d. 413) was the imperial commissioner sent to North Africa to resolve the bitter, century-long schism between Catholics and Donatists (see Chapter 7). Marcellinus decided in favor of the Catholics, and he and Augustine became close friends. Augustine ended up dedicating City of God to him (see Chapter 9). Marcellinus was also instrumental in drawing Augustine into the Pelagian controversy (see Chapter 10). Marcellinus and his brother Apringius would be summarily executed in 413, innocent victims, it seems, of a bloody purge.

ing a Church. The former must be governed by instilling fear; the latter is to be made lovable by the use of mildness. If I were making my pleas to a non-Christian judge, I should deal differently with him, but even so I should not fail to present the case of the Church and, as far as he would allow, I should insist that the sufferings of the servants of God, which ought to serve as a pattern of patience, should not be sullied with the blood of their enemies. If, however, he would not agree to this, I should suspect that his opposition came from a hostile source. But now, since the matter is being brought before you, I follow another method, another argument. We see in you a governor of exalted power, but we also recognize you as a son with a Christian idea of duty. Leaving out of consideration your exalted position and your faith, I am treating a matter of common interest with you; you can act in it as I cannot; consult with us about it and lend us a helping hand.

(4) As a result of prudent action, the enemies of the Church have confessed the revolting crimes that they have committed against Catholic clerics, and they have incriminated themselves by their own words, whereas they usually ensnare inexperienced souls with their false and seductive talk, boasting of the persecution that they claim to suffer. The court records should be read in order to heal the souls that they have envenomed with their deadly enticement. Surely it would not please you that we should fear to read to the end of these records, if they should include the bloodthirsty punishment of these culprits, supposing we laid aside our conscientious fear that those who have suffered should seem to have rendered evil for evil. Therefore, if there were no other punishment decreed for curbing the wickedness of desperate men, extreme necessity might require that such men be put to death, although, as far as we are concerned, if no lesser punishment were possible for them, we should prefer to let them go free, rather than avenge the martyrdom of our brothers by shedding their blood. But now that there is another possible punishment by which the mildness of the Church can be made evident, and the violent excess of savage men be restrained, why do you not commute your sentence to a more prudent and more lenient one, as judges have the liberty of doing even in non-ecclesiastical cases? Share, then, our fear of the judgment of God the Father, and show forth the mildness of our Mother Church. For when you act, the Church acts, for whose sake and as whose son you act. Strive to outdo the wicked in goodness. By a monstrous crime they tore limbs from a living body; you can, by a work of mercy, make them apply to some useful work the wholly intact limbs that they exercised in their unspeakable deeds. They did not spare the servants of God who were preaching repentance to them. Spare them now that you have arrested, summoned, and convicted them. They shed Christian blood with impious sword. Withhold,

for Christ's sake, even the sword of the law for their blood. They cut short the lifespan of a minister of the Church by killing him. Lengthen the years for these living enemies of the Church that they may repent. It befits you, a Christian judge, in a case involving the Church, to be such as this; for this we beg, we urge, we intervene. People tend to appeal against sentences deemed too light, but we so love our enemies that we would appeal this severe sentence to you—if we did not rely on your Christian obedience. May the almighty God preserve your Excellency to a richer and happier life, illustrious lord, justly exalted and most excellent son.[33]

MOB VIOLENCE

An angry mob in Hippo once lynched a corrupt government official. The details are not clear, but he seems to have been a military officer, apparently connected with the customs office. In a sermon given very soon after the incident, Augustine demands that his congregation examine their collective conscience. He argues that Christians must endure governmental injustices and never take the law into their own hands. Note the way he mentions in passing that Christians in Hippo are a decided majority. Note also his account of the way city and imperial officials make him sit and wait in their waiting rooms. From Sermon 302:

(10) Why do you rage against the bad? You say, "Because they're bad." By raging against them, you add yourself to them. I'm going to give you some advice: Does someone who's evil bother you? Don't let there be two of you. You condemn him, and you get added on, you increase the number of what you're condemning. You want to conquer the bad with the bad? Conquer evil with evil? That's two evils, both to be overcome. Didn't you hear the Lord's advice through the Apostle: "Do not be conquered by evil, but conquer evil with good" (Rom 12:21)? Maybe the other guy is worse; but when you're bad, that's still two bad ones. I, at least, would like there to be one good one. You raged, in the end, until death. What about after death, where your punishment no longer reaches that evil man? Only the malice of the remaining evil one rages on. That's insanity, not vindication.

(11) What am I to say to you, my brothers and sisters, what am I to say to you? Don't let such [violent] people [who committed this act] get your approval. But do I think of you that way, that you approve such people? Far be it from me that I think of you that way. But it's not enough that such people don't get

---

33. Ep. 134.1–4 (CSEL 44:84–88); trans. Parsons, FOTC 20:9–11. On the issue of judicial torture, see Aline Rosselle, "Torture," in Bowersock, *Late Antiquity: A Guide*, 729–30. It deeply troubled him; see s. 355.5 (cited later in this chapter); also *civ. Dei* 19.6 (cited in Chapter 9).

your approval. That's not good enough. Something more is expected of you. Don't just say: "Now God knows that I didn't do it, God knows that I didn't do it, and God knows that I didn't want it done." See, you said two things: "I didn't do it" and "I didn't want it done." Now that's not good enough. It's really not good enough that you didn't want it done—because you also didn't stop it from being done. . . .

(13) [You say:] "But that bad man did so many things, oppressed so many people, turned so many into beggars and destitute." He had his judges; he had the powers-that-be [to hold him accountable]. The state is ordered, "for those authorities that exist have been established by God" (Rom 13:1). You wish to rage? What official power were you given? Because this was not about public punishments, but open banditry. . . . Now I am not defending evil people [like this official], nor am I saying the evil aren't evil. Those who serve as judges will have to render an account [to God]. Why do you want to render a very difficult accounting for someone else's death, you who don't carry the heavy load of public power? God has liberated you; you don't have to be a judge. Why lay claim to someone else's [authority] as yours? Render an account of yourself! . . .

(16) [You say:] "He oppressed me when I was doing business." And you: Did you do business properly? Did you never commit fraud in your business? Did you never swear to a false contract in your business? Did you never say: "By the One who brought me across the sea, I bought this item for this much," when you did not buy it for that much? . . .

(17) To sum up, brothers and sisters, why am I keeping you so long? We are all Christians, but I carry a heavy load—a danger all the greater. It's often said about me: "Why does he go to that official?" And "what's the bishop wanting with that official?" And yet all of you know because your necessities force me to go to those I don't wish to go to: To pay respects; to stand at the door; to wait while the worthy and the unworthy are let in; finally to get announced; sometimes hardly even to get admitted; to put up with slights; to beg, sometimes succeeding, sometimes going away sad. Why would I want to endure such things unless I was forced to? . . . People say: "[The bishop] should admonish officials to do good." Am I to admonish them in your presence? Do you know if I've admonished them? You don't know whether I did it or I didn't. . . . It can be said to me about those in power: "If he admonished them, they would do good." And I answer: "I did admonish him, but he did not listen to me." . . .

(19) One thing I do know, and all of you know it along with me: In this city there are many homes in which there is not a single pagan. There are no homes where there are no Christians to be found. And if one were to inves-

tigate it carefully, no home would be found where there are not more Christians than pagans. It's true. You agree. You see, therefore, that these bad things would not have happened if Christians weren't willing. No easy answer for that. Bad things might be done on the sly, but they couldn't be done in public—not if Christians were opposed and didn't want it to happen, because each one of you would hold back his slave; each one of you would hold back his son. Young people would be tamed by a father's strictness, an uncle's strictness, a teacher's strictness, a good neighbor's strictness, strictness from greater correction—physically. If this had been done, these bad things would not have so saddened us. . . .

(21) My brothers and sisters, I exhort you, I beg you by the Lord and by his gentleness that you live gently, that you live peacefully. Let the authorities do what belongs to them—for they will have to render an account to God and to their superiors.[34]

LIBERATING CAPTIVES FROM SLAVERY

Augustine retails his congregation's vices more vividly than their virtues. Here we get a different view. In the following account from one of the Divjak letters, we see his congregation's courage of conviction as well as patterns of institutional violence in the late Roman world. Augustine writes his friend and fellow bishop Alypius, recounting the activities of a ring of slave traders from Galatia who made their living by kidnapping free people and selling them into slavery. Augustine's congregation got wind that one of these slave ships was anchored in Hippo's harbor, and broke in and liberated 120 captives, some from the ship, others from a local prison. The slavers had friends in high places and were demanding back their "merchandise." Augustine writes Alypius about a brutal imperial law against those who enslaved free persons. Augustine did not want the legislation to be enforced (since it stipulated whipping with lead-tipped thongs) but simply to keep the slavers from pressing their case, to make sure authorities neither returned the liberated captives to their kidnappers nor harassed those of his congregation who had engineered the escape.[35] From Letter 10* (Divjak):

(2) Another matter: There are so many of those in Africa who are commonly called "slavers"[36] that they seem to be draining Africa of much of its human population and transferring their "merchandise" to the provinces across the sea. Almost all these are free persons. Only a few are bound to

34. S. 302.10–21 (PL 38:1389–92); my trans.

35. On this case, see Claude Lepelley, "Liberté, colonat et esclavage d'après le Lettre 24*: la jurisdiction épiscopale 'de liberali causa,'" in *Les Lettres de saint Augustin découvertes par Johannes Divjak*, CEASA 98, ed. Claude Lepelley (Paris: Institut d'Études Augustiniennes, 1983), 329–42.

36. "Slave dealers": Augustine uses the slang term *mangones*.

have been sold by their parents, and these people buy them, not as Roman law permits, as indentured servants for a period of twenty-five years, but in fact they buy them as slaves and sell them across the sea as slaves.[37] True slaves are sold by their masters only rarely. Now from this bunch of merchants has grown up a multitude of pillaging and corrupting "dealers" so that in herds, shouting, in frightening military or barbarian attire, they invade sparsely populated and remote rural areas and they violently carry off to these merchants those they seek. . . .

(7) Even if I wished to list all the crimes—just the ones we have had contact with—it would not be possible to do so. Listen to this one case, from which you can get some idea of what is going on all over Africa, and especially in the coastal areas, but especially from Numidia; people were being brought by Galatian merchants—these are especially avid and throw themselves into this type of business—for transportation from the shores of Hippo. There are not lacking faithful Christians who, knowing our custom in missions of mercy of this kind, made this known to the church. Immediately, partially from the ship in which they had already been loaded, partially from the spot where they had been hidden prior to boarding, about 120 were freed by our people, though I myself was absent. Scarcely five or six were found to have been sold by their parents.

(8) Your Holy Prudence can imagine how much similar trafficking in unfortunate souls goes on in other coastal areas, if at Hippo Regius, where in God's mercy the great vigilance of the church is on the watch so that poor people can be freed from captivity of this sort, and these people who carry on such a trade, though far from suffering from the severity of this law, are nevertheless punished, at least by the loss of the money they originally spent; so great is the greed of these people, so bold the barbarism of these Galatians. I beseech you, through your Christian charity, that these words have not been written to your Charity in vain. For these Galatians do not lack advocates, with whose support they demand back from us those whom the Lord has freed, restored through the action of the church, even those already restored to their own families who had been seeking them and who came to us with letters from bishops. Even as I dictate these lines, they are beginning to upset several of the faithful, our sons, with whom some of those entrusted to them have been staying—for the church could not feed all those whom it freed. Despite the fact that a letter has come from an authority they could fear, they have not in any way halted their efforts to get their captives back.[38]

37. "Indentured servants": We may find it appalling, but it was legal for parents to "rent" their children as servants, a sort of temporary slavery. On this, Michel Humbert, "Enfants à louer ou à vendre: Augustin et l'authorité parentale (Epist. 10* et 24*)," in Leppelley, Les Lettres découvertes, 189–204.

38. Ep. 10*.2–8 (BA 46B:168–82); trans. Eno, FOTC 81:76–80.

EATING DINNER WITH AUGUSTINE

Possidius lived in Augustine's monastery for years and observed him at close range. In this passage, he describes Augustine's lifestyle and dinner habits. From Possidius of Calama, Life of Saint Augustine:

(22) His clothing and footwear, and even Augustine's house furnishings, were modest yet adequate, neither luxurious nor too plain. In such matters, men have the habit either of arrogantly displaying or degrading themselves; in either case "seeking their own interests, not those of Jesus Christ" (Phil 2:21). Augustine, however, as I have said, held the middle course, deviating neither to the right nor to the left. His table was frugal and sparing, although, indeed, it sometimes included meats, herbs, and vegetables, out of consideration for guests or the sick. Moreover, he always had wine, because he knew and taught, as the Apostle says, "everything God created is good, and nothing is to be rejected when received with thanksgiving; for it is sanctified by the word of God and prayer" (1 Tm 4:4–5). . . . Only his spoons were of silver, but the vessels in which food was served were earthen, wooden, or marble; this was not by force of necessity, but from Augustine's own choice. Moreover, he always showed hospitality. At the table itself he preferred reading and discussion to mere eating and drinking, and against the pestilence of human nature he had the following inscription carved on his table: "Whoever slanders the name of an absent friend/May not as guest at this table attend." Thus he warned every guest to refrain from unnecessary and harmful tales. When, on one occasion, some of his closest fellow bishops forgot that warning and spoke carelessly, Augustine became exasperated and sharply rebuked them, declaring that either those verses should be removed from the table or that he would leave in the middle of the meal and go to his room. Both I and others who were at the table experienced this.[39]

A POOR MAN OF POOR PARENTS

In the passage above, Possidius mentions that Augustine dressed simply. In the following sermon, Augustine talks to his congregation about what happened when people donated expensive clothes to him. From Sermon 356:

(13) Whatever you willingly want to donate, donate it to us all. What's held in common will be distributed to each as each has need. Put it in the collection box, and we will all have it. It pleases me very, very much to think of that box as a sort of feeding trough for us, that we may be God's beasts of bur-

---

39. *Vita* 22 (Geerlings, 68–70); trans. Muller and Deferrari, FC 15:99–100.

den and you be God's fields [where we graze]. No one should give a cloak or linen tunic, unless it be for common use. Whatever we get, we get from the common room. As for me, I want to have whatever I have from what's held in common, and so I don't want your Graces to donate such things that only I, as it were, might make proper use of. An expensive cloak, for example, might be donated to me. It might be well suited for a bishop, but it is really not suited to Augustine, that is, a poor man born of poor parents. Otherwise, people will say that I wear expensive clothes, things I could not have had either in my father's house or in that secular profession of mine. It's not right that I should have clothes that I can't pass along to my brother if he doesn't have something. Clothes such as a presbyter can have, things a deacon or a subdeacon might suitably wear—that's the sort of thing that I wish to accept because I accept what's for common use. If someone gives something better, I sell it . . . I sell it, and I give the money to the poor.[40]

CHURCH FINANCES AND CARE OF THE POOR

Augustine largely delegated to others the financial administration of the church. In the following passage, Possidius offers an overview of Augustine's policies. From Possidius of Calama, Life of Saint Augustine:

(24) The care of the church buildings and all its property Augustine assigned and entrusted, in turn, to more capable clerics, for he never held the key nor wore a ring, but all receipts and expenditures were recorded by these household overseers. At the end of the year, the accounts were read to him so that he might know how much was received and how much was spent, and also what balance remained. In many cases, he took the word of the overseer rather than investigate its veracity by actual proof. He never wished to buy a house, land, or a farm; however, if anything of the kind was donated, perchance, or left as a legacy, he did not refuse it, but insisted that the gift be accepted. Still, we know that he did refuse some legacies, not because they could not be used for the poor, but because it seemed right and just that the children, parents, or relatives of the deceased should own them, even though that was not the will of the deceased. . . . New buildings Augustine never desired, avoiding entanglements of his soul in them, because he wanted it always free from all temporal annoyance. Nevertheless, he did not prohibit those who wanted to build them, unless their plans were too extravagant. Meanwhile, if his church needed money, he told the Christian people that he had nothing to give to the poor. For the benefit of captives and the

40. S. 356.13 (PL 39:1579–80); my trans.

large number of needy he ordered the holy vessels to be broken and melted down for distribution among the poor.[41]

THE HAZARDS OF BEQUESTS

Possidius mentions that Augustine occasionally turned down bequests. Here is an instance. In a late sermon, given in the wake of a financial scandal involving one of his clergy, he offers a public accounting of financial matters and explains why he turned down a bequest from a local shipping magnate. From Sermon 355:

(5) I did not want to accept the bequest from Boniface (also known as Fatus). It was not a matter of generosity, but of fear. I did not want the Church of Christ to be in the shipping business. There are a lot of people who earn a lot from ships. If, however, there is just one accident, if a ship goes down and is wrecked, are we going to hand over the crew to torturers? After all, there would be an inquest inquiring why the ship sank, and those men who just escaped drowning in the waves would now be tortured by a judge. But would we hand them over? It's not right for the Church to agree to that. How, therefore, would this enormous financial burden be paid off? Where would it get paid off from? It's not right for us to have a special reserve fund. It is not for bishops to set aside gold and then walk away from the beggar's hand. Every day so many are asking for help, so many groaning, so many needy pleading that we have to leave many, many sad people behind because we do not have enough to give to all of them. Yet should we be required to set up a special fund to deal with shipwrecks? Therefore, I made this decision to avoid problems like this. No one should praise it, but no one should gripe either.[42]

AUGUSTINE AS A NUMIDIAN BISHOP

Augustine spent lots of time in meetings with fellow bishops. The conciliar tradition was exceptionally vibrant in the North African church. The senior bishop in each province was known as the primate. Aurelius, as bishop of Carthage, automatically held the primacy in the province of Africa Proconsularis, but in the province of Numidia, where Augustine worked, the primacy rotated from see to see, to whoever was the senior bishop. Primates had certain carefully guarded privileges, such as the right to preside over ordinations of the province's new bishops and the right to summon province-wide councils. In a letter,

41. *Vita* 24 (Geerlings, 70–74); trans. Muller and Deferrari, FOTC 15:101–3.
42. S. 355.5 (PL 39:1572); my trans.

dating around 402, Augustine deals with a touchy dispute. Two senior colleagues both laid claim to the primacy, and one of them, Victorinus, formally summoned a regional council. Augustine did not want to be caught in the crossfire and diplomatically bowed out of coming. He noted subtle irregularities in the names and order of addressees (likely evidence of behind-the-scenes power plays). Such squabbling caused dangerous tensions among Catholics who needed to act as a united front against their formidable Donatist rivals. Here he counsels Victorinus to find a peaceful solution. From Letter 59:

(1) The synodal summons reached me on November 9, at the end of the day, and it found me altogether unprepared, so that I was not able to go. But whether it disturbed me because of my inexperience, or whether I was disturbed with good reason, it is for your Holiness and Dignity to decide. I read in the same summons that it had been addressed even to the Mauretanias, although we know that those provinces have their own primates. And if any of them were summoned to a council held in Numidia, then it was certainly proper to put in the summons the names of other Maurish bishops who have precedence there, and I was much surprised at not finding them there. In the second place, even the notice to the Numidians was in so mixed and disorderly an arrangement that I found my name in the third place, and I know how much more recently I became bishop than many others. This is unjust to others and unfair to me. Moreover, our venerable brother and colleague, Xanthippius of Tago, says that the primacy belongs to him, that he is recognized as such by many, and he sends out letters in this capacity. No doubt, this mistake can easily be recognized and settled between your Holinesses; still, his name should not have been passed over in the summons which your Reverence sent out. I should have been much surprised if he had been listed halfway down and not at the head of the list, but it is much more surprising that no mention is made of him at all, since he had the best claim to come to the council, so that the question of his rank as primate might be treated first of all before the bishops of all the Numidian churches.

(2) For these reasons I would have hesitated to come, fearing that the summons in which such mistakes occur might have been forged, although the emergencies of the time and other pressing necessities would doubly prevent me. Consequently, I ask your Beatitude to pardon me and to deign to insist first of all on harmonious agreement between your Holiness and the aged Xanthippius, on the question of which one of you should summon a council; or at least—which I think would be better—that you both convoke your colleagues, especially those that are near in age in the episcopacy, who would easily distinguish which one of you speaks the truth. Let the controversy be settled among the few of you, and when the mistake is rectified, let the younger ones be summoned by the others, since they neither can nor ought

to trust anyone in this matter but you, their elders, and at present they do not know which one of you they are to believe unquestionably. I have sent this letter sealed with a ring which has a head of a man looking to one side.[43]

AUGUSTINE AS MONASTIC LEGISLATOR

Augustine was a monk. This fact is too often overlooked. The idea of a monk-bishop may not seem striking now, but it was avant-garde at the time. Such a dual vocation began appearing more often in the Greek East, among contemporaries such as Basil of Caesarea (d.379) and John Chrysostom (d. 407).[44] Like Basil, Augustine was not only a monk-bishop, but also one of the earliest monastic legislators. Around 397, soon after taking office as bishop, he authored his Rule (Praeceptum), one of several legislative documents used by monastic communities under his authority. The Rule's opening, quoted below, captures the spirit of Augustinian monasticism. His model was the Jerusalem community of Acts 4. The lifestyle, while austere, did not embrace the ascetical athleticism found in monastic communities in Egypt and Syria. Centuries later, Augustine's Rule would be resurrected as the constitutional basis for medieval orders such as the Augustinians and Dominicans. From Rule 1:

(1) These are the rules we set down that you are to observe when admitted to the monastery. (2) First, the basis on which you are gathered into one community is that you live in a single-minded unity in the house and that you be of "one soul and one heart in God" (Acts 4:32). (3) And do not call anything your own, but you are to have all things in common. Your Superior should distribute food and clothing to each of you, not equally to all, because you do not all have the same health, but to each one according to his need. For you read in the Acts of the Apostles: "They held everything in common," and "distribution was made to each according to each one's need" (Acts 4:32, 35).

(4) Those who owned anything in the world before they entered the monastery should will freely that it become common property. (5) But those who had nothing should not seek in the monastery what they could not have had on the outside. But what they require, because of any infirmities of theirs, should be provided for even if their poverty would not have allowed them those necessities when they were outside. Let them not consider themselves fortunate because they now have found food and clothing of the sort they

---

43. Ep. 59.1–2 (CCL 31A:9–10); trans. Parsons, FOTC 12:298–300. On this issue, see Jane Merdinger, "Augustine and Church Authority: The Developing Role of the Provincial Primate," *Studia Patristica* 33 (1997): 183–89.

44. On this, see Andrea Sterk, *Renouncing the World Yet Leading the Church: The Monk-Bishop in Late Antiquity* (Cambridge, MA: Harvard University Press, 2004); Augustine Holmes, *A Life Pleasing to God: The Spirituality of the Rules of St. Basil* (Kalamazoo, MI: Cistercian Publications, 2000).

could not have found on the outside. (6) Nor should they be stiff-necked or haughty because they associate with those they would not have dared approach on the outside, but let them lift up their hearts, not seeking empty earthly goods. Otherwise, monasteries might begin to be useful for the rich but not for the poor if the rich are humbled there but the poor become puffed up there with pride.

(7) But, on the other hand, those who were seen to have been something in the world should not look down on their brothers who come to that holy community from poverty. Instead, they should strive to boast not about the social status of their wealthy relatives, but about the community of their poor brothers. Let them not hold a high estimate of themselves if they have contributed their wealth to the common life, lest they become more proud over their wealth, because they shared it with the monastery, than they would have been if they had simply enjoyed it in the world. Every other vice leads to evil deeds, but pride disguises itself among good deeds in order to spoil them. What good does it do to distribute one's goods by giving them to the poor and to become poor oneself if the unhappy soul then becomes prouder by despising wealth than it had been by possessing it? (8) Therefore, all of you, live in single-minded unity and in harmony; and honor in one another the God whose temple you have become (2 Cor 6:16).[45]

MONASTERY AS SEMINARY

There was no such thing as a seminary or divinity school in the early Church. But Augustine's monastery came to function as a training center for episcopal openings around North Africa. From Possidius of Calama, Life of Saint Augustine:

(11) As the divine teaching prospered, the clerics of the church at Hippo, who had served God in the monastery of holy Augustine, began to be ordained. Consequently, the truths taught by the Catholic Church, as well as the manner of life practiced by the holy servants of God, especially their continence and extreme poverty, became more celebrated day by day. To insure peace and unity, the Church eagerly began to

---

45. Regula: Praeceptum 1.1–8 (George Lawless, ed., *Augustine of Hippo and His Monastic Rule* [Oxford: Clarendon Press, 1987], 80–82); my trans. Two other documents included among Augustinian monastic legislation are: *Regulations for a Monastery* (Ordo monasterii), authored perhaps by Alypius; and *Reprimand* (Obiurgatio), with a feminine version of the Rule (Praeceptum), preserved among Augustine's letters as *ep.* 211. The research of Luc Verheijen, *La Règle de saint Augustin*, 2 vols. (Paris: 1967) overturned the earlier view that the feminine version of the Praeceptum was the earliest, and showed that the masculine version dates to Augustine's early years as bishop. See George Lawless, "Regula," *AugEncy*, 707–9; Kevin Madigan, "Regula, Use after Augustine," *AugEncy*, 709–10. On the Rule's spirituality, see Luc Verheijen, *Saint Augustine's Monasticism in the Light of Acts 4:32–35* (Villanova: Villanova University Press, 1979).

demand bishops and clerics from the monastery that had been founded and strength-ened by the zealous Augustine. Later, the request was fulfilled. The most blessed founder gave ten men, holy and venerable, chaste and learned, to various churches, some of them being quite prominent. Like him, those holy men who came from that community increased the churches of the Lord and established monasteries. As their zeal for spreading God's word increased, they in turn supplied other churches with brethren who had been elevated to the priesthood. And thus, because of their num-ber, the teaching of the Church's salutary faith, hope, and charity became known to many people. This was true not only throughout all parts of Africa but even across the sea, by means of Greek editions and translations.[46]

MISCONDUCT OF ANTONINUS OF FUSSALA

Possidius acclaimed Augustine's successes and passed over in silence certain disastrous personnel decisions. None is more vivid or more embarrassing than the case of Antoninus, one-time bishop of Fussala. We can see the case in all its anguishing detail in one of the Divjak letters.[47] Around 423, Augustine wrote to a wealthy Roman matron, Fabiola, warning her not to be taken in by Antoninus, who had been raised in Augustine's monastery and whom Augustine later nominated as bishop of Fussala. Antoninus used his office to create a sort of criminal organization that carried out all manner of illicit gain—crimes of theft, extortion, and intimidation. At a tribunal in Hippo, Augustine and Alypius handed down a verdict depriving Antoninus of his see, but allowing him to retain nominal status as a bishop. This decision left them with a legal quandary, since the Council of Nicaea had, in its canons, forbidden moving bishops from one see to another. They, therefore, granted Antoninus a sort of quiet exile to a few small rural parishes. On the eve of the ordination of a replacement for Fussala, Antoninus appealed his case to Pope Boniface, who ended up ordering an appellate investigation. The story at this point becomes extremely complex, with dramatic courtroom shenanigans. Antoninus proved a ruthless and skilled manipulator with an eye for loopholes in both canon and civil law. I have abridged this lengthy account considerably, excising the legal complexities and machinations of the case. Perhaps nowhere else in Augustine's surviving writings does one see him so powerless and so frustrated. At this same time, Augustine wrote Pope Celestine, noting that he was so disheartened by the embarrassment that he was ready to resign his bishopric.[48] From Letter 20* (Divjak):

46. Vita 11 (Geerlings, 44–46); trans. Muller and Deferrari, FOTC 15:85.

47. On this, see J. E. Merdinger, Rome and the African Church in the Time of Augustine (New Haven: Yale Uni-versity Press, 1997), 154–82; also Serge Lancel, "L'affaire d'Antonius de Fussala: pays, choses et gens de la Numidie d'Hippone saisis dans la durée procédure d'enquête épiscopale," in Lepelley, Les Lettres de saint Augustin découvertes par Johannes Divjak, 267–85; and (also in Lepelley) W. H. C. Frend, "Fussala, Augustine's Crisis of Credibility," 251–65.

48. See ep. 209 to Pope Celestine (c. 423).

(2) I have found out that with great kindness you have taken in my beloved son and fellow bishop Antoninus in his need, and with your usual hospitality you have been most Christian to him. Let me tell you then who I am to Antoninus and who Antoninus is to me and what I owe him and what I am going to ask of you. He came to Hippo as a small boy with his mother and stepfather. They were very poor, not knowing where their next meal would come from. Then when they came to the church for help, I discovered that Antoninus's real father was still living and that his mother, after separating from her husband, had united herself to this other man. I was able to convince both to embrace continence. And so it came about that the man went with the boy to the monastery, while the mother was on the rolls of the poor supported by the church. So in God's mercy, they all came to be part of our pastoral responsibility. Time passed—to make a long story short—the man died, the mother grew old, the boy grew up. Among his colleagues, he filled the post of reader and soon began to appear to be a good prospect so that our brother, Urbanus, then a presbyter here and prior of the monastery, now the bishop of Sicca, while I was away, wanted to have him become a presbyter in some nearby rural area in our diocese. . . .

(3) Then there came a time when I could no longer cope in the way that was required with a diocese suddenly made so much larger by the influx of converted Donatists not only in the town itself but also in the surrounding rural districts. Talking this over with the clergy, it seemed to me that in the area of the village of Fussala, which came under the see of Hippo, someone should be ordained bishop to whose care this charge could be entrusted. I contacted the primate; he agreed to come. At the last minute, the presbyter I thought I had ready ran out on us. What was I to do to avoid postponing so important a matter? I was afraid that the elderly gentleman who had come such a long distance to us would be coming on a fruitless mission and that all those who were to be the beneficiaries would be crushed. There they would find those whom the enemies of the Church would deceive, by jeering at our frustrated endeavor. So I decided that it would be best to put forward for ordination one who was available, especially since I had heard that he knew Punic, and so, when I did put him forward, the responsibility was mine. [The people of Fussala] did not ask for him on their own initiative, but they did not dare refuse someone from my own community whom I liked.

(4) Thus did I thrust such a burden on this young man, hardly more than twenty years of age, one not tested previously in other ranks of the clergy. The things I should have known about him earlier, I did not. So you see my great sin; now consider the consequences. At first the young man was frightened, rising so suddenly to the honor of the episcopate but without deserving such

promotion by his previous work. Then, seeing both clergy and laity subject to him, he quickly learned the lesson and became puffed up with the arrogance of power. Rather than teaching by example, he gave orders, forcing people to do his will. He was happy to see himself feared when he did not see himself loved.

(5) As if to fill out the role completely, he sought out others like himself. There was in our monastery a copyist from my staff who, to my sorrow, had not turned out very well. Because he was once found by the prior of the monastery alone at an unreasonable hour talking with certain nuns, he was punished with a beating and was generally thereafter held in low esteem. This is the one who, taking off from the monastery, betook himself as quickly as possible to this same bishop about whom we have been talking and was ordained presbyter by the same, though I knew nothing about it and my views were not sought. Before I had heard what was done, how could I have believed what was going to happen, even if someone worthy of credence had pointed it out to me? Then, when I began to dread the coming desolation of that church because of him, I ask you to understand the grief that flooded into my heart though I cannot fully explain it to myself. . . . He also made another deacon, one sent to him in correct fashion from the monastery, though the man in question did not appear to be unsettled before he became a deacon.

(6) Through these two clerics, presbyter and deacon, and through the defender of the Church,[49] and through whomever else, whether former soldier or deserter, to whom he habitually gave orders, and through those men of the same village whom he made guards for the night watches, and those he used when there was need for some slightly greater force—what evils that village and the surrounding territory endured because of these men, anyone can learn who can stomach reading the record which was drawn up in sadness from the testimony of many given in the presence of the bishops gathered in Hippo, among whom I also sat. There the reader will find the sorrowful grievances of poor men and women and, worse still, of widows whom neither the very name which Holy Scripture commends to us as in special need of protection nor even old age was able to shelter to some degree from the thefts and pillaging and unspeakable injuries which were done by them. Anyone who fell into their clutches lost money, furnishings, clothing, farm animals, fruits, wood, finally even stones. The homes of some people were taken over, the houses of others were even demolished, to provide materials necessary for new buildings; some things were "purchased," but payment was nev-

---

49. "Defender of the Church" (*Defensor ecclesiae*): a lay official charged with protecting the welfare and legal rights of the local church. The Council of Carthage in 407 asked for the establishment of this position. The bishop nominated the candidate, and the emperor approved the choice.

er made; some people had their fields occupied; they were handed back but only after all the produce from several years had been carried off. . . .

(8) [At a tribunal held in Hippo] we ordered that all the spoils be restored, but we allowed the bishop to keep his episcopal rank safe and intact. But in order that those evil deeds not remain completely unpunished, lest they be perpetuated by him, or imitated by others, we permitted him only this much: that he sit as a bishop on one of his *cathedrae*, lest it be said that he had been transferred to another, that we were acting against the canons, and that he might no longer remain in control at Fussala since the people there would tolerate him no longer.[50] I think that this type of penalty should be seen as a blessing, for if he stayed there where they did not want him, his presence might inflame dangerously their already bitter hatred. We did not imagine it possible to enter into communion with him again until the stolen goods were first restored. This decision of ours he also embraced to the extent that he did not appeal, and after a very few days he was able to make restitution for the pillaged goods with borrowed money so that communion would not be withheld from him any longer. And many of the brethren and my sons consequently felt sorry for him, as I did, because of the serious capital offenses of four counts of sexual assault which some people (though not the inhabitants of Fussala, but others whom he had injured in some way) either had charged him with or intended to do so. He was cleared of these charges by the best evidence available so that they in fraternal joy congratulated him on the outcome.[51] . . . [*Initially Antoninus accepted the verdict but then appealed to Pope Boniface, who demanded a fresh investigation and a retrial. The long middle section of the letter details negotiations, fact-finding missions, the gathering of witnesses and collecting of formal depositions, as well as Antoninus's often clever diversionary legal maneuvers. The affair came to a head once Antoninus realized he would never regain his seat of power in Fussala.*]

(25) Then when he found himself being urged by the words of the bishops to whom he could not respond, at last what was hidden in his heart came out, and, with frightful countenance and words, he said he would never accept the proposition that there was no possibility of bringing about his return to the see of Fussala. When we heard this, I began to press the primate that something should be done with him in line with the decisions at Tegulata for the digest of proceedings that could be sent to the apostolic see. "I am not going to say anything for the record," he declared, and he got up and stormed out. He immediately came back in and, disturbed mentally and physically, threat-

---

50. "The canons": Canon 15 of Nicaea forbade the translation of a bishop from one see to another.

51. "Counts of sexual assault" (*stuprum*): If Antoninus had been found guilty of this, he could have been given the death penalty; that is why his being cleared was such a relief to Augustine and his colleagues.

ened to go to the apostolic see, as if we had been going to send whatever had been done with him in the acts to some other place.

(26) It remained therefore for the apostolic see to be informed with letter and the official digest. To accomplish this, we acted as quickly as we could. See what a spectacle we had become to Jews, pagans, and heretics and all the enemies within, if only without the death of those freed from heresy and now breathing in the light of unity for whom we have made the catholic name hateful, if their weakness will not at least be consoled by the fact that they no longer have a bishop whom they exclaim with just sorrow that they cannot tolerate.

(27) Therefore I thought that I should write these things to your Excellency so that, if he sees you, you will not be unaware of what you should advise him. . . . Let him stop lusting to dominate the members of Christ gathered by the blood of others. There where he began to be a bishop, neither he nor any presbyter or cleric nor anyone at all under his regime suffered any losses or wounds from the Donatists. But that he might find such peace there, what evils these our people bore is a horror to say. . . . (28) Do not be afraid to give counsel based on faith to a bishop who seeks the things of earth. You who are in the world seek God, but he who is in the Church seeks the world. . . .

(31) To this day, this poverty-bound monk-become-bishop tells the people of Fussala, "Give me back the house I built in your village." This house he seemed to be building for the Church, not for himself; would that it had been built from good and honest offerings, not from spoils! . . .

(32) But this is all beside the point. I simply wanted to make known to you my unhappiness that a young man trained by us in the monastery who, when we took him in, left nothing of his own behind, gave nothing to the poor, brought nothing to the community, the very same now glories, as it were, in his estates and homes and wishes to make his own not only these things but also the very flock of Christ, while he wants to be of the number of those of whom the apostle said: "They seek what is their own, not the things of Jesus Christ" (Phil 2:21). How much all this wounds my heart, He knows, the One who can heal me.[52]

WORK BY DAY, DICTATE BY NIGHT

We think of Augustine as a writer of numerous and voluminous theological works. That was not his day job. Much of his writing was done after hours, often late into the night.

---

52. Ep. 20*.2–32 (BA 46B:292–340); trans. Eno, FOTC 81:134–49.

As Augustine makes clear here in this letter, which dates from either late 411 or early 412, he did not so much write as dictate. From Letter 139 to Flavius Marcellinus:

(3) I have forgotten why I received back the copy of the book on the baptism of children[53] which I had sent to your Excellency, unless, perhaps, it was because I found it faulty when I had looked it over, and I wanted to correct it, but I have been so unbelievably busy that I have not done so. There was also a letter to be written and added to the manuscript, and I began to dictate it while I was there, and you must know that I have added a little to it and it is still unfinished. If I could give you an account of my days and of the labor I expend at night on other pressing duties, you would be surprised and very sorry at the great burdens which weigh me down, which cannot be put off, and which prevent me from doing those things which you ask and urge me to do, willing though I am and more grieved than I can say at not being able to do them. When I get a little time, free from my obligations to those men who put such pressure upon me that I cannot in any way avoid them—and I ought not to show them contempt—there are plenty of details having a priority on the scraps of time devoted to dictation, and they are such as will not bear delay. . . . Charity, like a nurse caring for her children, gives the weak preference over the strong, not that they are more worthy of love, but more needy of help, and she wishes them to be like the others whom she passes over for a time as a mark of trust, not of contempt. Such necessities cannot be lacking for dictating something, and they prevent me from dictating what I ardently long to do, when a small bit of time is left me between my piled-up duties, which keep me weighed down with other people's ambitions and necessities, and I do not know what else I can do.[54]

THREE MONTHS OF WRITING

In one of the Divjak letters, we get a further glimpse into Augustine's work habits. On December 1, 419, Augustine wrote Possidius, listing what he had written over the previous three months. It totaled 6,000 lines (= 60,000 words)! The picture here reminds one of a chess master playing multiple games simultaneously. From Letter 23*A (Divjak):

53. "Book on the baptism of children": Augustine is referring to *On the Merits and Forgiveness of Sins and On the Baptism of Infants* (*De peccatorum meritis et remissione et de baptismo parvulorum*), which he wrote in late 411 or early 412 in response to Marcellinus's request. Augustine looked back on this as his first anti-Pelagian treatise (*retr.* 2.37); for excerpts, see Chapter 10.

54. Ep. 139.3 (CSEL 44:152–53); trans. Parsons, FOTC 20:56–57.

(3) I do not know which of our shorter works we were dictating when you left us. Therefore, I will recall all that I dictated, from the time we came back from Carthage: I wrote back to the Spanish bishop Optatus once again concerning the question of the origin of the soul;[55] I replied to Gaudentius of Timgad, bishop of the Donatists, as he answered the things I had earlier written to him;[56] I dictated something against the Arians (replying) to what our Dionysius had sent me from Vicus Juliani and three sermons to be sent to Carthage; among other things, as I was getting ready to go back to the books *On the City of God*, all of a sudden, I received a letter from the holy Renatus, sending me from Caesarea two books of someone named Victor, an ex-Donatist or ex-Rogatist, a former disciple of that Vincent to whom I once wrote, who has become a Catholic.[57] And he wanted something about the soul, rebuking my hesitations because I did not dare define whether the soul came from generation or was breathed into each person anew as he was being born, and he stated that he was attracted to the idea that the soul did not come from begetting but was given to us. In those two books of his, he said very many false and absurd things as well as things against the Catholic faith. Because our friend mentioned above asked me strongly to refute them, because with his smooth speech they are perverting many, I did write one book on this to the very same dear friend of ours, and I want to write to Victor himself, since it is quite necessary. And that I may do what remains to be done with the Gospel of John, I have now begun to dictate some sermons for the people, not too long, to be sent on to Carthage on the condition that if the same elderly gentleman[58] wants more in the future, he says so and, when he so says, to stop putting off their publication. So far I have dictated six. I have set aside Saturday and Sunday nights for them. Therefore, I have dictated from the time of my arrival, that is, from September 11 to December 1, about 6,000 lines.

(4) . . . But I am annoyed because of the demands which are thrust on me to write, arriving unannounced from here, there, and everywhere. They interrupt and hold up all the other things we have so neatly lined up in order. They never seem to stop and can't be put aside.[59]

55. "Optatus": Optatus was bishop of Mauretania Tingitana in what is now western Morocco; though in Africa, it was under civil administration from Spain. The reference here is to *ep.* 190.

56. "Gaudentius of Timgad": Gaudentius was a leading Donatist bishop who, after the forced unification of Donatist and Catholic congregations in 411, had threatened to burn himself and his flock alive in his church. Augustine refers here to *Contra Gaudentium*, book 2.

57. "Victor, . . . ex-Rogatist": Vincentius Victor converted to Catholicism from the Rogatists, an offshoot of the Donatists who rejected the violence of the Circumcellions. Vincentius came across Augustine's *ep.* 192 and, upset by Augustine's unwillingness to take a stand on the origin of the soul, composed a two-volume attack. Augustine eventually responded with *On the Soul and Its Origin* (*De anima et eius origine*).

58. "The elderly gentleman": Aurelius of Carthage. The reference is to Augustine's *Tractates on the Gospel of John*, likely, Tractates 55–60.

59. *Ep.* 23*A.3–4 (BA 46B:372–78); trans. Eno, FOTC 81:166–69. A similar listing of his writing projects appears at the beginning and end of *ep.* 169 to Evodius, dating from 415; also *ep.* 224 to Quodvultdeus.

Nominating a Successor

In 426, Augustine announced his retirement and nominated a successor, a presbyter named Eraclius (or Heraclius). What follows is the official transcript of an event scrupulously recorded and preserved by the church's stenographers. Augustine refers, in passing, to his career and to the controversy that arose when he had first been consecrated coadjutor bishop by Valerius. It also offers a fascinating glimpse of Augustine's congregation. It may remind readers of modern political rallies with their sometimes carefully scripted applause. Preserved as Letter 213:

(1) On the 26th day of September, in the 12th consulship of the most glorious Theodosius and the 2nd of Valentinian Augustus, after Bishop Augustine had seated himself on his throne in the Basilica of Peace, attended by his brother bishops, Religianus and Martinianus, in the presence of the presbyters Saturninus, Leporius, Barnabas, Fortunatianus, Rusticus, Lazarus, and Eraclius, as well as of the accompanying clerics and a large crowd of people, Bishop Augustine spoke thus:

"Yesterday I made a promise to your Charity because I wished you to be here in large numbers, so we must now forgo all delay and proceed to business, for if I were to speak of anything else you would not listen because your attention is on the proceedings. In this life we are all mortals, and the last day of this life is always uncertain for everyone. In infancy our hopes are fixed on childhood, in childhood we look to adolescence, in adolescence we look forward to adulthood, in adulthood to middle age, and in middle age to old age. Whether this will be our lot we do not know, but it is what we hope for. Old age, however, has no other period to expect. How long old age itself will last is hidden from us, but it is certain that there is no other age to follow old age. God willed that I should come to this city in the vigor of manhood, but I have now passed through middle age and have reached old age. I know that after the decease of bishops churches are regularly thrown into confusion by ambitious or restless men, a fact which I have often observed and grieved over, and I consider it my duty, as far as it depends on me, to take measures that it may not happen to this city. . . . Therefore, that no one may complain of me, I make known to all of you my choice which I believe is the choice of God: I want the presbyter Eraclius for my successor."

The people raised a shout: "Thanks be to God! Praise to Christ!"—this was said twenty-three times; "Hear us, O Christ! Long life to Augustine!"—this was said sixteen times; "You are our father, you our bishop!"—this was said eight times.

(2) When silence was restored, Bishop Augustine said: "I have no need to speak in his praise; I am silent about his wisdom; I yield to his modesty; it is enough that you know him, and I say that I wish what I know is your wish; if I had not known it before, I should have proof of it today. Therefore, I wish this, I ask it of the Lord our God with prayers that are ardent even in the chill of age, and I exhort, advise, and entreat that you join with me in praying that, while the minds of all are transformed and welded

together in the peace of Christ, God may confirm what He has wrought in us. May He who sent this man to me keep him, may He keep him safe, may He keep him blameless, so that as he is my joy in life, he may take my place at my death.

"What I am saying is being taken down, as you see, by the stenographers of the Church; what you say is being taken down as well. [Because of this] neither my words nor your shouts of approval fall uselessly to the ground. To speak more openly, we are putting together an official ecclesiastical record, for I wish this act to be ratified as far as it is humanly possible."

A shout was raised by the people: "Thanks be to God! Praise to Christ!"—said thirty-six times; "Hear us, O Christ! Long life to Augustine!"—said thirteen times; "You are our father, you our bishop!"—eight times; "It is right and just!"—said twenty times; "He is well-deserving, he is truly worthy!"—said five times; "It is right and just!"—said six times.

(3) When silence was restored, Bishop Augustine said: "Therefore, as I was saying, I wish the ratification of my choice and your choice, as far as it rests with human beings, to be recorded in the annals of the Church; but as to what belongs to the hidden will of almighty God, let us pray, as I said, that He may confirm what He works in us."

A shout was raised by the people: "We give thanks for your decision!"—said sixteen times; "May it be so, may it be so!"—said twelve times; "You are our father, Bishop Eraclius!"—said six times.

(4) When silence was restored, Bishop Augustine said: "I know what you also know, but I do not want what happened to me to happen to him. Many of you know what happened; the only ones who do not know are those who were either not yet born or had not yet attained the age of knowledge. While my father and bishop, the elder Valerius of blessed memory, was still alive, I was ordained bishop and I sat with him; something which I did not know had been forbidden by the Council of Nicaea, nor did he know it.[60] Therefore, I do not wish my son to be blamed for what was blamed in me."

A shout was raised by the people: "Thanks be to God, praise to Christ!"—said thirteen times.

(5) When silence was restored, Bishop Augustine said: "He will be a presbyter as he is, and when God wills he will be a bishop. But now at least I shall do, with the help of God's mercy, what up to now I have not done. You know what I wanted to do a few years ago, and you did not let me. It was agreed between you and me that no one should disturb me for five days so that I might devote myself to the study of the Scriptures which my brothers and fathers, my fellow bishops, were pleased to lay upon me at the two Councils of Numidia and Carthage. It was entered in the acts, it was voted, you acclaimed it, your vote and your acclaim were read out to you. It was kept in my

60. "Forbidden by the Council of Nicaea": Augustine refers here to *Canon* 8; see note 14 above.

regard for a short time, then it was rudely broken, and I am not allowed time for the work I wish to do. Both morning and afternoon I am enmeshed in people's affairs. I beg you and I enjoin you by Christ to allow me to lay some of the burdens of my duties on this young man, that is, the presbyter Eraclius, whom I designate today in the name of Christ to succeed me as bishop."

A shout was raised by the people: "We give thanks for your decision!"—said twenty-six times.

(6) When silence was restored, Bishop Augustine said: "I give thanks before the Lord our God to your charity and kindness; I give thanks for it. Therefore, my brethren, whatever is now referred to me, let it be referred to him. When my advice is needed, I will not refuse it. God forbid that I should withdraw my help. However, what has been referred to me up to now, let it be referred to him. Let him either consult me if he does not discover what he ought to do or call on the help of one whom he knows as a father, so that you may suffer no loss and, if God gives me even a little time, that I may at length busy myself with the holy Scriptures, and, as far as He permits and grants it, that I may not spend the little remnant of my life in idleness or give myself over to laziness. This will be advantageous to Eraclius, and through him to you. Let no one, then, begrudge me my leisure, because my leisure implies great labor.[61] I see that I have paid my debt in full by transacting with you the matter for which I invited you to be here. I ask this one last favor: that those of you who are able would please sign these official records. I need your assent to this, show me some agreement by your acclaim."

A shout was raised by the people: "So be it, so be it!"—said twenty-five times; "It is right and just!"—said twenty-eight times; "So be it, so be it!"—said fourteen times; "Long worthy, long deserving!"—said twenty-five times; "We give thanks for your decision!"—said thirteen times; "Hear us, O Christ! Protect Eraclius!"—said eighteen times.

(7) When silence was restored, Bishop Augustine said: "It is well that we are able to transact the affairs of God about the time of His sacrifice. In that hour of our prayer I especially recommend your Charity to lay aside all your interests and occupations and pour forth prayer to the Lord for this church, for me, and for the presbyter Eraclius."[62]

VANDAL INVASION

In his last days, Augustine watched the wholesale collapse of his world. Possidius here recounts the brutal Vandal invasion of North Africa and the siege of Hippo. From Possidius of Calama, Life of St. Augustine:

61. Note the wordplay, both an oxymoron (leisure as labor) and a rhyme: "leisure" (*otium*) rhyming with "labor" (*negotium*).

62. Ep. 213.1–7 (CSEL 57:372–79); trans. Parsons, FOTC 32:52–57.

(28) It happened soon after, in accordance with the divine will and power, that a great host of men, armed and trained for war, came in ships from the land of Spain across the sea and rushed into Africa. They were a mixed group of savage Vandals and Alans, together with a Gothic tribe and people of different races. Everywhere throughout the regions of Mauretania, and even crossing to other provinces and lands, they gave vent to their rage by every kind of atrocity and cruelty, devastating everything they possibly could by pillage, murder, various tortures, fires, and other countless indescribable evil deeds. No sex or age was spared, not even God's priests and ministers, neither church ornaments and vessels nor the very buildings. Now, the man of God did not feel and think as others did concerning the enemy's fierce assault and devastation, but he considered them more deeply and profoundly. Most of all, he perceived in them the dangers and even death of souls, so that more than ever—since, as we read, "He that adds knowledge, adds also sorrow" (Eccl 1:18) and, "an understanding heart is a worm in the bones" (Prv 14:30)—tears were his bread both day and night (Ps 41:4). Thus he spent those days, almost the last of his life, and endured them as most bitter and sad in comparison with the rest of his old age. He saw cities completely destroyed, and farmers together with their buildings either annihilated by the enemy's slaughter or put to flight and scattered. Churches were deprived of their priests and ministers; consecrated virgins and monks, dispersed in all directions. In one place some died from torture; others were killed by the sword; still others, in captivity, lost their chastity and faith in soul and body, serving the enemy under vile, harsh treatment. Hymns and praises of God disappeared from churches, church buildings in many places were burned down, while the regular offerings due to God in their usual places were cut off. The divine sacraments were no longer sought, or if they were, it was difficult to find someone to administer them. Moreover, when the people fled together to mountain forests or rocky caves and caverns or any kind of shelter, some were captured and killed while others were robbed and deprived of necessary nourishment to such an extent that they perished from hunger. Augustine likewise saw bishops of the churches and clergy who, by chance, through God's kindness, did not meet the enemy or who escaped if they did, despoiled and stripped of everything, forced to beg in dire poverty, and they could not all be supplied with enough to live. Of the countless churches scarcely three survive—at Carthage, Hippo, and Cirta. It was through God's kindness that these were not destroyed. These cities likewise remain, supported by divine and human protection, although after Augustine's death the enemy burned the city of Hippo, which had been abandoned by its inhabitants. Amid these disasters Augustine was consoled by the sentiment of a certain wise man who said: "He is not great who thinks it wonderful that wood and stones fall and mortals die."

Because of his profound wisdom, Augustine daily and copiously lamented all these occurrences. His grief and sorrow were intensified by the fact that the enemy came also to besiege the city of the Hippo-Regians, which so far had maintained its position. At this time the defense of the city was in the charge of the former Count Boniface[63] and an army of allied Goths. For almost fourteen months the enemy blockaded and besieged the city, cutting off even its seacoast with their blockade. We and other fellow bishops from the neighborhood had taken refuge there, and were present during the entire siege. Therefore, we frequently conversed with each other and considered the dreadful judgments of God, which were placed before our eyes, saying: "You are just, O Lord, and Your judgment is right" (Ps 118:137). In our common grief, with groans and tears we prayed to the Father of mercies and the Lord of all consolation to deign to help us in this tribulation.[64]

63. "Count Boniface": Boniface was, in Augustine's final years, the top military commander in North Africa. He had contemplated, after the death of his first wife, retiring from the military and becoming a monk, but both Augustine and Alypius dissuaded him, arguing that he better served the Church by protecting the Empire's borders against barbarian incursions. Boniface rose through the ranks as the years went on, but his morals, in Augustine's view, went downhill. In *ep.* 220, Augustine confronted him on violating his marriage vows by sleeping with concubines and on neglecting military duties. His soldiers were so busy extorting valuables from villagers that they failed in their military mission of halting barbarian incursions. Later, Boniface used his army to wage a successful civil war against imperial authorities, but failed against the invading Vandal armies.

64. *Vita* 28 (Geerlings, 82–84); trans. Muller and Deferrari, FOTC 15:108–10.

CHAPTER 4

AUGUSTINE THE PREACHER

✣

Augustine's friend, Possidius of Calama, once remarked that "those who read
what Augustine has written in his works on divine subjects profit greatly, but
I believe that the ones who really profited were those who actually heard him
and saw him speak in church."[1] Augustine was, by all accounts, a virtuoso orator, a fact that even enemies acknowledged.[2] In this chapter, we take a look
at the Augustine his North African congregation knew best, Augustine the
preacher.

The main church in Hippo was known as the Basilica Major (also called
the *Basilica Pacis*, "Basilica of Peace"). Its ruins were excavated in the 1950s,
and its floor plan—41 yards long, 20 yards wide—makes it one of the largest
churches uncovered in Roman North Africa.[3] It lay on the outskirts of town,
away from the central marketplace with its old pagan temples. The first thing
one would have noticed upon entering Augustine's church was the flicker of
flames from small oil lamps, filling the interior with a golden glow. The basilica's floor, like that of many ancient Christian churches, was inlaid with
bright-colored mosaics. There were no pews. The congregation stood, men
on one side, women on the other. Services could draw packed audiences. "The
great numbers," Augustine once noted, "crowd right up to the walls; they an-
noy each other by the pressure and almost choke each other by their over-

1. *Vita* 31 (Geerlings, 104); my trans.
2. Secundinus, a Manichean opponent, once called Augustine "a consummate orator and a god of eloquence" (*Ep. ad Augustinum* 3 [BA 17:514]).
3. Erwan Marec oversaw the archeological excavation of Hippo for two decades. His research appears
in *Monuments chrétiens d'Hippone: Ville épiscopale de saint Augustin* (Paris: Arts et Métiers Graphiques, 1958).
Most scholars now accept that the ruins uncovered are those of Augustine's main church. For an overview,
see Serge Lancel, *Saint Augustine*, 235–44; George Radan, "The Basilica Pacis of Hippo," in Schnaubelt and
Van Fleteren, *Augustine in Iconography*, 147–88. Other church properties in Hippo include the older Basilica
Leontiana and a chapel (*memoria*) that housed the relics of St. Stephen.

The Ruins of Augustine's *Basilica Pacis*: Hippo Regius (Annaba, Algeria).
Photo: Michael Flecky, S.J. Used with permission.

flowing numbers."[4] The altar, unlike that found in medieval and many modern churches, stood in the center of the nave and was surrounded by wood railings. At the basilica's far end was a semi-circular apse, lined with stone benches where the presbyters sat. At the apse's center, slightly elevated, was the bishop's seat (*cathedra*). From here Augustine presided and preached.

No sacramentary from North Africa has survived, but scholars have been able to reconstruct the outlines of the Sunday liturgy from passing references in Augustine's sermons, treatises, and letters.[5] The service began with the bishop greeting the congregation: "The Lord be you." "And with your spirit," they would answer. Then a reader—typically, a teenage boy—read an excerpt

4. En. Ps. 39.10 (CCL 38:433); my trans.

5. On the ancient Eucharistic rites, see Paul F. Bradshaw, *Eucharistic Origins* (New York: Oxford University Press, 2004); Geoffrey Wainwright and Karen B. Westerfield Tucker, eds., *The Oxford History of Christian Worship* (New York: Oxford University Press, 2006). For a reconstruction of the liturgy in Hippo, see Harmless, *Augustine and the Catechumenate*, 161–64, 312–13; Robin M. Jensen and J. Patout Burns, "The Eucharistic Liturgy in Hippo's Basilica Major at the Time of Augustine," *AugEncy*, 335–38.

from the Old Testament or from one of St. Paul's letters.[6] Augustine then sent word to the cantor which Psalm he wanted sung. The Psalm was sung in responsorial style, the cantor intoning the verses with the congregation joining in the refrain. After this, a deacon stepped up and read an excerpt from one of the Gospels. Each Gospel was likely bound as a separate codex. When finished, the deacon handed the Gospel book over to Augustine. Augustine then preached. He normally remained seated, preaching with the Gospel book in hand. The earliest known portrait of Augustine, a rather crude sixth-century fresco found in the Lateran Basilica in Rome, captures him in this classic pose, seated at a bishop's chair, the Scriptures under his gaze, his hand extended in the gesture of a teacher. In Augustine's day, sermons were expected to last an hour, and while some were shorter, others went much longer.

When we today meet Augustine the preacher, we encounter printed words, not a living voice. Reading Augustine's sermons simply as printed texts, as words fixed in black-and-white on a page, gives the wrong impression. Augustine worked neither from notes nor from a text first written out, then memorized. He prepared, as he tells us, only by prayer and study. The written texts we now possess record his on-the-spot improvisations, recorded in shorthand by stenographers known as *notarii*.[7] We need to read these surviving texts with a vibrant historical imagination, remembering that Augustine was a performing artist of enormous skill, charm, and vigor. The texts preserve only a faint residue of his living speech. What has been lost is the very thing that gave his speech its dynamism: the cadence of delivery, the accents and pauses, the gestures and facial expressions. We need only compare the written transcript of Dr. Martin Luther King's "I Have a Dream" with the film to appreciate how striking this gap is between written text and oral performance.

The surviving corpus of Augustine's sermons is staggering, yet it likely represents only a small proportion of what he actually delivered.[8] It includes the 124 sermons of his *Tractates on the Gospel of John (In Johannis evangelium trac-*

6. On the feast day (*natalis*, "birthday") of martyrs, such as Perpetua or Cyprian, the *acta* of their martyrdom was inserted into the service of readings; see *s.* 275.1; 276.1; 280.1; 302.1; 313D.1–2.

7. On the extemporaneous character of the sermons, the classic studies are those of Roy J. Deferrari, "St. Augustine's Method of Composing and Delivering Sermons," *American Journal of Philology* 43 (1922): 97–123, 193–219; "Verbatim Reports of Augustine's Unwritten Sermons," *Transactions and Proceedings of the American Philological Association* 46 (1915): 35–45.

8. Pierre-Patrick Verbraken, "Lire aujourd'hui les Sermons de saint Augustin," *Nouvelle Revue Théologique* 109 (1987): 830, estimates that Augustine, over his career, would have preached "around 8000 times" and thus we still possess only about 1 in 14 that he delivered. Verbraken, "Forward," in *Sermons I (1–19)* on the Old Testament, WSA III/1 (1990): 11, gives a total of 548 authentic sermons. This number does not include the *Tractates on John* or the *Expositions of the Psalms*, nor does it include discoveries since 1990 by Dolbeau and others. For a chart listing Augustine's complete sermons, see Éric Rebillard, "Sermones," *AugEncy*, 774–89; see also Verbraken's chart, WSA III/1 (1990): 138–63. Readers should be cautious about dates cited in both charts; on this issue, see Hubertus R. Drobner, "The Chronology of St. Augustine's *Sermones ad populum*," *Augustinian Studies* 31 (2000): 211–18; 34 (2003): 49–66; 35 (2004): 43–53.

tatus) and the 10 sermons of his *Tractates on the First Epistle of John* (*In epistulam Johannis ad Parthos tractatus*) It includes his massive *Expositions of the Psalms* (*Enarrationes in Psalmos*), which preserves at least one sermon on each of the 150 psalms. But the largest collection is his *Sermons to the People* (*Sermones ad populum*). Hundreds of individual sermons were passed down in the Middle Ages under Augustine's name, but not all were authentic. When Augustine's seventeenth-century editors, the Benedictines of St. Maur, published their remarkable edition of his complete Latin works, they concluded that some 363 sermons had good claim to authenticity, with another 33 classified as "doubtful."[9] Later nineteenth- and early twentieth-century researchers continued the effort, authenticating (by a rough count) over 170 additional sermons, some complete, some fragments.[10] The hard work of recovering lost sermons continues. In 1990, François Dolbeau made a momentous discovery, unearthing 26 long-lost sermons from a fifteenth-century Carthusian manuscript, now preserved in the Mainz Stadtbibliothek. Dolbeau's discovery, published in a scatter of remarkable articles in the 1990s, has sparked international scholarly conferences and a host of reassessments.[11] The discovery of six more sermons was announced in 2008.[12]

Augustine was not only an accomplished orator but also an ex-teacher of oratory. Scattered through his sermons and treatises, one finds seasoned reflections on both the art and the experience of preaching. Especially striking is his influential treatise on Christian oratory, *De doctrina christiana*. The title is best translated not as *On Christian Doctrine* but rather as *On Christian Teaching*, or even *On Teaching Christianity*. Its first three books were written around 397, soon after Augustine became bishop of Hippo. These first three explore prin-

9. The Maurists' edition of Augustine's sermons is reprinted in PL 38–39. On the authenticity of individual sermons, see Pierre-Patrick Verbraken, *Études critiques sur les sermons authentiques de saint Augustin*, Instrumenta Patristica 12 (Steenbrugis: In abbatia S. Petri, 1976); Hubertus R. Drobner, *Augustinus von Hippo: Sermones ad Populum; Überlieferung und Bestand Bibliographie-Indices*, Supplements to Vigiliae Christianae 49 (Leiden: Brill, 2000).

10. For most of these texts, see Germain Morin, ed., *Sermones post Maurinos reperti*, vol. 1 of *Miscellanea Agostiniana* (Rome: Tipografia Poliglotta Vaticana, 1930–31); and A. Hamman, ed., *Patrologia Latina Supplementum*, vol. 2. In older scholarly studies, one sees this miscellany listed under the names of individual discoverers (e.g., Michel Denis, Cyrille Lambot, Germain Morin) or the manuscript collection (e.g., Guelferbytanus). Verbraken, in *Études critiques*, renumbered these more recent finds and integrated them into the Maurists' numbering system by adding a letter to the number; for example, *s.* Guelferbytanus 7 is listed as *s.* 229A. Verbraken's proposal has recently become the standard numbering system.

11. François Dolbeau, ed., *Augustin d'Hippone: Vingt-six sermons au peuple d'Afrique*, CEASA 147 (Paris: Institut d'Études Augustiniennes, 1996). For an overview, see Henry Chadwick, "The New Sermons of St. Augustine," *Journal of Theological Studies* 47 (1996): 69–91. For studies of these newly discovered sermons, see Madec, ed., *Augustin Prédicateur (395–411)*. Dolbeau has discovered four others since then.

12. In May 2008, it was announced at the annual conference of the North American Patristics Society that four new sermons and two partly known sermons had just been discovered by I. Schiller, D. Weber, and C. Weidmann. The new texts are preserved in a 12th-century manuscript in the Bibliotheca Amploniana in Erfurt, Germany. They will be published in a forthcoming publication of the CSEL.

ciples of biblical interpretation and will be discussed in the next chapter. Augustine left the work incomplete for decades, but around the year 426 or 427, he brought it to a close, adding a fourth book on the art of preaching. This final book, while brief, has special poignancy because it comes at the very end of his career, after more than three decades as a preacher.[13]

In this chapter, I assemble excerpts from Augustine's sermons and intersperse with these his reflections on preaching, drawing especially on Book 4 of *On Christian Teaching*. This back-and-forth movement between theory and practice will give readers a sense of the way Augustine's reflections intersect with his actual practice. Once again, I recommend that texts be read aloud. This is particularly true of the sermons, which were, of course, delivered orally. You may meet them only in translation, but you can still hear something of their wordplay, their balanced parallelisms and antitheses, their spontaneous, sometimes conversational, tone. Of course, preaching includes—indeed, requires—the interpretation of Scripture. But we will defer looking at the specifics of his exegesis (both in theory and in practice) until the next chapter.

PREPARING TO PREACH

Augustine recognized that preaching differed both from teaching in an academic sense and from public speaking, whether in a political or in a legal forum. He presumed preachers had thorough command of the Scriptures and solid oratorical aptitude. Here he advises that preachers follow his lead, preparing not by reading or writing but by praying. From On Christian Teaching, *Book 4:*

(15.32) In praying for himself and for those he is about to address, the preacher should be a person of prayer before he is a speaker of words. As the hour when he is to speak approaches, before he uses his tongue, he should raise his parched soul to God that he may gush forth what he has drunk in and pour out what has filled him up. For on any subject that needs to be discussed with regard to faith and love, there are many things to be said and many ways in which they may be said by those who know about them. But who knows what is appropriate for us to say or for our audience to hear at the present moment except the One who sees "the hearts of all" (Acts 1:14)? And

13. On this, see especially Duane W. H. Arnold and Pamela Bright, eds., *De Doctrina Christiana: A Classic of Western Culture* (Notre Dame: University of Notre Dame Press, 1995); Karla Pollmann, *Doctrina Christiana: Untersuchungen zu den Anfängen der christlichen Hermeneutik unter besonderer Berücksichtigung von Augustinus, De doctrina christiana* (Freiburg: Universitätverlag, 1996).

who can make sure that we say what we should say and in a way we should say it except the One in whose "hands are both we and our words" (Wis 7:16)? Therefore, anyone who wants both to be knowledgeable and to teach should certainly learn everything necessary for teaching and acquire speaking skills appropriate for a man of the Church. Yet as the hour for speaking nears, he should consider what the Lord says as well suited for a good frame of mind: "Do not be anxious about what to say or how to say it; for what you are to say will be given to you in that hour. For it is not you who are speaking, but the Spirit of your Father who speaks in you" (Mt 10:19–20). Therefore, if the Holy Spirit speaks in those who are delivered to their persecutors for the sake of Christ, why will He not speak in those who deliver Christ to those intent on learning?[14]

THE BREAD OF THE WORD

Augustine sometimes spoke of his task as preacher as feeding hearers with the bread of God's word. He opens the following sermon on Jesus' multiplying the seven loaves (Mk 8:1–9) by discussing his own role as God's table-servant. From Sermon 95:

(1) When I set out the holy Scriptures for you, it's as though I were breaking open bread for you. You the hungry, come, get it. Belch forth praises from your well-fed hearts. And you who are wealthy and have fine tables, don't be cheap in your good deeds and works. What I spend on you is not mine. What you eat, I eat. What you live on, I live on. We have in heaven a common store-house, for from it comes the Word of God.

(2) [*After explaining how the seven loaves in the Gospel story symbolize the seven gifts of the Holy Spirit, Augustine adds:*] When I explain these things to you, I am waiting table on Christ. You, when you listen quietly, are reclining at table. I may be seated here physically [in the bishop's chair], but in my heart, I am standing and waiting table on you, anxious not about the food, but worried that the dishes it's served on not offend any of you. You know God's fine feast, you hear it often. Our minds, not our stomachs, yearn for it.[15]

14. *Doc. Chr.* 4.15.32 (Green, 234–36); my trans.
15. S. 95.1–2 (PL 38:581); my trans. Cf. *doc. Chr.* 1.1; s. 339.4.

PREACHING GOD INCARNATE

Let us turn now to Augustine's practice as a preacher by examining one complete sermon. The centerpiece of Augustine's preaching was Christ, of course. He believed that Christ's identity had been succinctly encapsulated in the prologue to John's Gospel: Christ is, on the one hand, the divine Word (Jn 1:1–3), and, on the other, the Word-made-flesh (Jn 1:14). So fond was Augustine of John's prologue that he quoted it more than any other single biblical text. Brian Daley has noted that Augustine, unlike his contemporaries in the Greek East, did not generally embark on "technical speculation on the unity and inner constitution of Jesus' person"; Augustine preferred "to speak of the mystery of Christ in concrete, rhetorically challenging phrases that let the believer savor the inherent paradox of preaching an incarnate God."[16] One sees this played out in his Christmas sermons. This is the complete text of Sermon 188:

(1) The Son of God: Now if we set about the great task of praising Him as He exists with the Father—equal to and co-eternal with the Father, the One in whom all things, visible and invisible, in heaven and on earth, were established, God and Word of God, Life and Light of humanity—it is no wonder that no human thinking, no words, can suffice. For how can our tongues rightly praise the One whom our hearts do not yet have the health and vigor to see? For it is in our hearts that He put the eyes He can be seen with—if wrongdoing be purged, if weakness be healed—and so we may come to be those blessed clean-of-heart, "for they shall see God" (Mt 5:8). It's no wonder, I say, we cannot find words that we might speak about the one Word [of God] who spoke us into being and about whom we seek to say something. For our minds may form words like these, pondered over and uttered forth, but our minds were themselves formed by the Word. Nor does a human being make words in the same way human beings are made by the Word, because the Father did not beget His one and only Word in the same way He made all things through the Word. For God begot God, but the Begetter and the Begotten are together one God. God certainly made the world; the world, however, passes away while God endures. And so these things that were made did not make themselves, but by no one was God made, the One by whom all things were made. It is no wonder, then, that a human being [like me], a creature in the midst of it all, cannot explain the Word through Whom all things were made.

(2) Let us direct our ears and minds to this issue for a little while, to see if we, by chance, can say something suitable and worthy not about [the truth that] "In the beginning was the Word, and the Word was with God; and the

16. Brian E. Daley, "A Humble Mediator: The Distinctive Elements in St. Augustine's Christology," *Word and Spirit* 9 (1987): 101; also Daley, "Christology," *AugEncy*, 164–69.

Word was God" (Jn 1:1), but about [the truth that] "the Word was made flesh"
(Jn 1:14); to see if, by chance, we can speak about why He "dwelt among us"
(Jn 1:14), or if, by chance, there is something say-able about why he wished to
be visible. It's for this reason that we celebrate this day on which He deigned
to be born of a virgin, a begetting which He Himself caused people to narrate the story of. In that eternity, however, "who shall declare his generation"
(Is 53:8) in which God is born of God? There, there is no such day for annual
solemn celebration. For [in eternity] a day does not pass away and then return
with the revolving year, but endures without a sunset because it began without a sunrise. Therefore, the one and only Word of God, the Light and Life
of humanity, is, in fact, the Eternal Day. This [Christmas] day, however, on
which He was joined to human flesh and became, as it were, a "bridegroom
coming out of his bride-chamber" (Ps 18:6)—this day is our today and will
pass away as tomorrow becomes yesterday. Nevertheless, today commemo-
rates that Eternal Day who was born of the Virgin because the Eternal Day
born of the Virgin consecrated this day.

What praises for God's love should we be voicing, what thanks should we
be giving? After all, He loved us so much that He, through whom all times
were made, became human within time for our sake; that He, more ancient
in eternity than the world itself, became younger in age than many of His servants in the world; that He, who made humankind, became human. He loved
us so much that He was created from a mother whom He had created, was
carried in hands He had made, was nourished at breasts He had filled; that
He, the Word without whom all human eloquence is mute, wailed in a man-
ger in mute infancy.

(3) See, O humankind, what God became for your sake. Acknowledge this
teaching of enormous humility from a Teacher who, as yet, cannot even speak
a word. Once, back in paradise, you were so fluent [in speaking] that you
named every living thing (Gn 2:19–20). For your sake, however, your Creator
lay speechless and could not even call His mother by her name. You lost yourself in the trackless groves of fruit trees by neglecting obedience. He obediently came into the narrow confines of mortality so that, by dying, He might
search for you who were dead. You, though you were human, wished to be
God and so got lost (Gn 3:5). He, though He was God, wished to be human
that He might find what had gotten lost. Human pride brought you to such a
depth that only divine humility could raise you up again.

(4) Therefore, let us celebrate with joy the day on which Mary brought
forth the Savior; a day when a married woman brought forth the Creator of
marriage, a day when a virgin brought forth the Prince of virgins; when a virgin, though given to a husband, was a mother not by her husband, a virgin

before marriage, a virgin in marriage, a virgin while pregnant, a virgin while nursing. Her all-powerful Son in no way deprived His holy mother of her virginity by being born, she whom He had chosen to be born from. Fruitfulness in marriage is certainly a good thing, but integrity in holiness is better. Therefore, the human Christ, who was able to furnish her both—for the same One was God as well as human—would never have granted His mother the good thing which married people care about in such a way as to deprive her of the better gift for which virgins forgo motherhood.

And so the virgin holy Church celebrates today a virgin's child-bearing. For to the Church the Apostle says: "I have betrothed you to one husband to present you a chaste virgin to Christ" (2 Cor 11:2). How "a chaste virgin" when there are in so many communities persons of both sexes, including not only children and virgins, but also married people, fathers and mothers? Why, I ask, "a chaste virgin" unless [the phrase refer to] the integrity of faith, hope, and charity? And so Christ, intending to establish virginity in the heart of the Church, first preserved Mary's in the body. In human marriage, naturally, a woman is given to her spouse so that she is no longer a virgin. The Church, on the other hand, could not be a virgin unless she had found that the Spouse to whom she had been given was the Son of a virgin.[17]

Rhetoric as a Tool for the Gospel

The intricate paradoxes of this sermon illustrate Augustine's consummate skills as an orator. He knew rhetoric inside and out, as both a practitioner and a theoretician. He knew its power and its perils, that language is a tool—and, potentially, a weapon—that can be used for good or for ill. He begged that Christian preachers start learning how to use it. From On Christian Teaching, Book 4:

(2.3) Since the art of rhetoric is about persuading people to things, whether true ones or false ones, who would dare to say that the defenders of truth should stand their ground unarmed against falsehood? That those who try to convince people of falsehoods should know how to use their opening remarks to win over the audience's goodwill, to grab their attention, to make them receptive, while defenders of truth do not know how to do this? That those who argue falsehoods know how to do so cogently, clearly, and plausibly, while defenders of truth make their case in ways too boring to listen to, too convoluted to understand, and, in the end, too distasteful to believe? That

---

17. S. 188.1–4 (PL 38:1003–5); my trans. On this linking of Mary and the Church, see David G. Hunter, "The Virgin, the Bride, and the Church: Reading Psalm 45 in Ambrose, Jerome, and Augustine," *Church History* 69 (2000): 281–303.

those others be able to attack truth with fallacious arguments, while truth-tellers are not strong enough either to defend truth or to refute falsehood? That those others, in order to move or force their hearers' minds into error by their speaking, know how to inspire fear, to move hearers to tears, to get them laughing or burning with enthusiasm, while truth-tellers seem slow and tepid and end up putting people to sleep? Who's so insane as to think that's right? Look, the capacity for eloquence—so very effective in persuading people to either wrong or right—is available to both sides. Why, then, do the good not acquire the skill to battle for truth, if the wicked, in order to win unjustifiable and baseless cases, usurp it on behalf of injustice and error?[18]

SPICY SPEECH

Augustine, while trained to speak in elegant, high-brow Latin, was quite willing to violate canons of proper Latinity to get his point across. Clarity was his bottom-line. He also knew that just as many people enjoy spicy food, so many in his audience enjoyed spicy speech as the favored medium for instruction. From On Christian Teaching, *Book 4:*

(11.26) Eloquence in teaching does not consist in speaking in such a way that we prompt a person to like what was distasteful or to do what he was reluctant to do, but in making what was obscure come clear. Yet if this is done without elegance, its benefit reaches only a few very zealous students who are anxious to know what they should learn no matter how low-brow or unpolished things are said. Once they have grasped it, they feast upon truth itself with delight. It is an outstanding quality of noble minds to love not the words themselves, but the truth within the words. Of what use is a golden key if it is unable to open what we desire? Or what objection is there to a wooden one if it can? We are asking only that what is closed be opened. But since eating and learning have some similarity to each other, food, without which we cannot live, must be spiced to satisfy the tastes of the majority.[19]

RAP LATIN

Augustine peppered his speech with rhetorical seasonings of various sorts. Rhyme was one favorite. It pervades all his works but appears especially in his sermons. Remember that since he delivered sermons extemporaneously, his rhymes flowed extemporaneously.

18. Doc. Chr. 4.2.3 (Green, 196–98); my trans. See John C. Cavadini, "The Sweetness of the Word: Salvation and Rhetoric in Augustine's De doctrina christiana," in Arnold and Bright, De doctrina, 164–81.

19. Doc. Chr. 4.11.26 (Green, 226–28); my trans., based on Gavigan, FOTC 2:192.

Such a skill may remind contemporary audiences of rap artists. Augustine used rhyming not only for its verbal musicality; he also knew that his largely illiterate audience could absorb and learn to repeat such phrases. In a sermon delivered during the Easter Vigil, he opened with a barrage of rhymes. I have put the Latin and English in parallel so that readers can see the wordplay. From Sermon 220:

Scimus fratres,	We know, brothers and sisters,
et fide firmissima retinemus	and we hold with firmest faith,
semel Christum mortuum esse pro nobis	that Christ died for us but once:
pro peccatoribus iustum,	the Righteous for sinners,
pro servis Dominum,	the Master for slaves,
pro captivis liberum,	the Free for captives,
pro aegrotis medicum,	the Doctor for the sick,
pro miseris beatum,	the Happy for the miserable,
pro egenis opulentum,	the Rich for the needy,
pro perditis quaesitorem,	the Seeker for the lost,
pro uenditis redemptorem,	the Redeemer for the sold,
pro grege pastorem,	the Shepherd for the sheep,
et quod est omnibus mirabilius,	and what's most awe-inspiring of all,
pro creatura creatorem.	the Creator for the created,
servantem tamen quod semper est,	holding on to what He always is,
tradentem quod factus est;	handing over what He was made;
Deum latentem,	hidden from sight, the Godhead,
hominem apparentem;	appearing to sight, the human,
uirtute uiuificantem,	by his power, life-giving,
infirmitate morientem,	by his weakness, dying,
diuinitate immutabilem,	in his divinity, unchanging,
carne passibilem.	in his flesh, capable of suffering.[20]

A Tongue Twister

Augustine had a wide repertoire of verbal tricks at his fingertips. The following sermon shows Augustine using what we would call a tongue-twister. Here he contrasts Jesus with John the Baptist. Once again, I have put the Latin and the English in columns so that readers can see his wordplay. From Tractates on the Gospel of John 5:

(1) Verax Iohannes,	John is truthful,
ueritas Christus;	Christ is truth.
uerax Iohannes,	John is truthful,

20. S. 220 (PL 38:1089); my trans.

sed omnis uerax a ueritate	but every truthful person is truthful
uerax est;	from the Truth,
si ergo uerax est Iohannes,	If, therefore, John is truthful,
et uerax esse homo non potest,	and a person cannot be truthful
nisi a ueritate;	except from the Truth,
a quo erat uerax,	from whom was he truthful
nisi ab eo qui dixit:	except from the one who said,
"Ego sum ueritas"?	"I am the Truth" (Jn 14:6)?
Non ergo possit dicere	Thus neither could
aut ueritas contra ueracem,	the Truth speak against the truthful,
aut uerax contra ueritatem. . . .	nor the truthful against the Truth. . . .
Si ueritas Iohannem miserat,	If the Truth had sent John,
Christus eum miserat.	Christ had sent him.[21]

A Noisy Audience

Augustine's audiences were noisy. They routinely applauded. On occasion, they might even boo him or shout in protest.[22] Augustine always kept a close eye on his hearers, extending things if they were silent, breaking things off if they applauded. Here the audience reacts to the elegance of Augustine's parallel phrases with applause. Their applause catches him off-guard. From Sermon 96:

(4) Loved is the world, but let your love prefer the One by whom the world was made. Vast is the world, but more vast is the One by whom the world was made. Beautiful is the world, but more beautiful is the One by whom the world was made. Alluring is the world, but more alluring is the One by whom the world was made. [The congregation here begins cheering.] What did I say? What is there to start cheering about? Look, the problem [in the biblical text] has only just been laid out, and you've already started cheering.[23]

Being Attuned to the Audience

Augustine valued spontaneity. He was critical of preachers who wrote sermons out in advance and then read them or performed them from memory. He thought this ignored

21. Jo. ev. tr. 5.1 (BA 71:292); trans. Rettig, FOTC 78:108–9.
22. In one of the recently discovered Dolbeau sermons, Augustine was actually jeered out of the pulpit. Augustine details the events in s. 359B (= Dolbeau 2) (Dolbeau, VSS, 328–44). See S. A. H. Kennell, "Vt adhuc habeat fides nostra reprobatores: Augustine's Hostile Hearers," in Madec, Augustin Prédicateur, 343–52.
23. S. 96.4 (PL 38:586–87); my trans.

the fundamentals of good communication, namely, that the speaker be attuned to spontaneous reactions from his audience and respond accordingly. From On Christian Teaching, Book 4:

(10.25) In ordinary friendly conversations everyone has the chance to ask questions, whereas during a sermon everyone quiets down and turns their faces in rapt attention in order to listen to the one speaking. And so it is neither customary nor appropriate for someone to interrupt and ask a question about what he does not understand. The speaker should, therefore, be especially attentive to come to the aid of the silent. Now an enthusiastic crowd, eager to learn, usually shows by its behavior whether it has understood things, and, until it does, the speaker needs to keep going over and over whatever he is discussing in a whole variety of different ways. Now those who get up and deliver what they have previously prepared and memorized word-for-word cannot do this. However, once a speaker makes himself understood, he should either bring his sermon to an end or move on to other matters. For just as a speaker who sheds light on what needs to be known is appreciated, so one who pounds away on what is already known is annoying—at least to those whose whole expectation depends on his dissolving those [knotty scriptural problems] that are unraveled only with difficulty.[24]

BEATING BREASTS

Augustine's crowd-watching eye can be seen in action in the following sermon. During liturgy, North Africans sometimes beat their breasts as a sign of repentance. Augustine notes here how they had misinterpreted the biblical text. He uses their miscue to explore the dual meaning of the word "confession." From Sermon 67:

(1) When the holy Gospel was read, we heard how the Lord Jesus exulted in the Spirit and said: "I confess to you, Father, Lord of heaven and earth, because you have hidden things from the wise and the prudent and have revealed them to the little ones" (Mt 11:25). To begin with, let's consider the Lord's words, taking them with great seriousness, with real care, and, above all, with great piety. And at the outset, we find that whenever we read the word "confession" in the Scriptures, we ought not always to understand it as the voice of sinners. Now this especially needs to be said, to alert your Charitableness[25] from now on about this. Because no sooner did this word come

---

24. Doc. Chr. 4.10.25 (Green, 226–28); my trans.

25. In Augustine's day, it was part of etiquette to address noble individuals using certain abstract adjectives: "Your Excellency," "Your Illustriousness." There are remnants of this today in the way we address

rolling out of the reader's mouth, than there followed the sound of the beating of your breasts, naturally, because you heard what the Lord said: "I confess to you, Father." The moment the word "I confess" (Confiteor) rang out,
you all beat breasts. To beat one's breast: What is it other than accusing what
lies hidden within the breast and punishing it by thumping the hidden sin
out into the open? Why did you do this? Because you heard: "I confess to you,
Father." You did hear "I confess," but you didn't pay attention to the One who
was doing the confessing. Now, come and get turned around the right way
on this. If Christ says, "I confess"—Christ, from whom every sin is far, far
removed—then confessing is not only for sinners but is sometimes also for
praisers. We, therefore, confess either by praising or by accusing ourselves.
Both confessions are good piety, either when you, who are not without sin,
blame yourself or when you praise the One who can have no sin.[26]

THE THREE AIMS OF ELOQUENCE

*Augustine, the ex-teacher of rhetoric, remained convinced, even at the end of his career,
that the pagan Cicero had insights that could aid Christian orators. Following Cicero,
he argues that eloquence has three aims: teaching, delighting, and persuading. From On
Christian Teaching, Book 4:*

(12.27) A certain man of eloquence[27] has said—and said rightly—that an
eloquent person should speak in such a way that he "teaches, delights, and
persuades," adding: "To teach is a necessity, to delight makes it enjoyable, but
to persuade is a triumph."[28] Of these three aims, the one mentioned first, that
is, the necessity of teaching, shapes *what* we say; the other two shape *how* we
say it. So the one who speaks with the aim of teaching should not think he
has spoken to the person he wishes to teach so long as he has not been understood. Although he has verbalized what he himself understands, he should
not consider that he has really spoken—really communicated—if the one listening to him has not really understood. But if the speaker has really been
understood, then he has truly spoken, no matter how he happens to speak.

royalty ("Your Highness") and clergy ("Your Holiness"). Augustine and his contemporaries, such as John
Chrysostom, played on this custom and invented various polite titles in addressing their congregations. So
here Augustine speaks to his congregation as "Your Charitableness."

26. S. 67.1 (PL 38:433); my trans. On this theme of "confession," see also *en. Ps.* 29.22, 78.17, 94.4, 141.19;
s. 29B.1–6 (= Dolbeau 8).

27. "A certain man of eloquence": Cicero.

28. "'To teach . . . triumph'": Quoting Cicero, *Orator* 69; however, Cicero has "prove" (ut *probet*) rather
than "teach" (ut *doceat*). Augustine, in other words, is adapting Cicero to an ecclesial setting: lawyers prove,
preachers teach.

But if he is also trying to entertain the one he is speaking to, or persuade him, he will not succeed by speaking in just any way. For the way a speaker speaks is important to produce the right outcome. For the listener needs to be entertained to keep a firm grip on him as a listener and needs to be persuaded to move him to doing what needs doing. And just as the listener is entertained if you sweeten what you say, so he will be persuaded if he loves what you promise, fears what you threaten, hates what you condemn, embraces what you commend, grieves over what you lambaste as deplorable, rejoices in what your preaching sets out as joyous, pities those whom you set before his eyes as objects of pity, flees those whom you, by awakening his fear, single out to be avoided—or whatever else can be done through a grandeur of eloquence to influence the hearts of listeners. They must thus be persuaded, not only that they may know what should be done, but also that they may do what they already know they should do. . . .

(13.29) When what we teach must be acted on, and the very reason we teach is that it be acted on, it is useless simply to persuade people about the truth of what we are talking about, and useless simply to entertain them by the way we speak, if what is said is not acted on. Therefore, the eloquent churchman, when he is trying to persuade people that something be done, must not only teach in order to instruct and entertain in order to hold their attention, but he must also persuade them in order that he may be victorious.[29]

THE THREE STYLES OF SPEAKING

To the three aims, Cicero had linked three distinct styles of speaking: "subdued," "moderate," and "grand." Augustine thought this linkage, however apt for the law courts where Cicero worked, did not do justice to the situation of Christian preaching. Much of Book 4 of On Christian Teaching is devoted to Augustine's analysis of the three styles. He claims that one can find exemplars of the three in certain biblical texts (e.g., Gal 4:21–26, Rom 12, 2 Cor 6:2–11) and in the writings of certain theologians, such as Cyprian and Ambrose. Here I excerpt Augustine's comments on the three styles themselves: how they differ, how they intersect, and to what end. He tells of one striking instance when he used the "grand" style to reduce his audience to tears. Note also how he speaks of the unusual power of his "subdued" style. If one surveys Augustine's sermons, one finds that this subdued style was his preference, and he used it especially to unfurl the riddles of Scripture. From On Christian Teaching Book 4:

---

29. Doc. Chr. 4.12.27–13.29 (Green, 228–32); my trans.

(17.34) The authority on Roman eloquence[30] himself wanted, it seems, to tie these three aims—that is, teaching, delighting, and persuading—to the three styles when he said in a similar way: "One will therefore be eloquent who can speak about minor matters in a subdued style, ordinary matters in a moderate style, and noble matters in a grand style"[31]—as though to add together those three [aims] and so explain it all in one single sentence, saying, as it were: One will therefore be eloquent, who, in order to teach, is able to speak about minor matters in a subdued style; who, in order to delight, is able to speak of ordinary matters in a moderate style; and who, in order to persuade, is able to speak of noble matters in a grand style.

(18.35) Now he was able to illustrate those three styles, as defined by him, in terms of courtroom cases, but not in terms of ecclesiastical questions, investigations which engage the sort of speaker whom I would like to inform and shape. In courtrooms, things are considered minor when the case involves financial matters; they are considered major when people's health or life is at stake. But in cases where neither of these is involved and where the task is not to get the hearer to act or make a decision but simply to delight him, then the subject matter is midway between the two, as it were, and for this reason is called "middling," that is, moderate. For *modus* gives us the word "moderate," and we would not be speaking correctly if we confused "moderate" with "small." However, in our situation, we should refer everything (especially what we say to people from our raised spot)[32] not to people's temporal, but to their eternal, welfare. Since we have to warn them as well about eternal damnation, everything we say is of great importance. So true is this that whatever an ecclesiastical teacher says about financial matters, whether about gain or loss, or whether the amount be large or small, should not be seen as unimportant. For justice is not small, and we should certainly protect it even in regard to small amounts of money, because the Lord says: "The person who is faithful in very small matters is also faithful in great ones" (Lk 16:10). . . .

(20.42) Now as for the grand style of speaking: it differs from the moderate not so much by the way it is embellished with verbal ornaments as by the way it gives vent to the spirit's passionate feelings. It may latch onto nearly all those ornaments of the [moderate] style, but it does not search around for them if it does not have them at hand. In fact, it is driven on by its own fervor, and, if it chances upon any beauty of style, it seizes upon it and claims it, not

30. "The authority on Roman eloquence": Cicero.

31. "'One will . . . grand style'": Quoting Cicero, *Orator* 101.

32. "Raised spot": Augustine is referring here to the *cathedra*, the bishop's elevated chair in the apse of the church from which he did his preaching.

because of any concern for beauty, but because of the sheer force of the subject matter. It is good enough for its purpose that words are fitted to pursuing the fire in the speaker's chest; they need not be chosen by some laborious word search. . . .

(22.51) No one should think that it is against the rules to blend these styles. On the contrary, a speech should be varied and draw on all [three] styles insofar as this can be accomplished gracefully. When a speech is long and drawn out in just one style, it does not hold listeners' attention. But when a [well-timed] transition from one style to another is done, the speech proceeds more effectively, even if it continues on longer. Yet in the mouth of eloquent speakers, each style has its own varieties, which do not permit listeners' feelings to cool off or grow lukewarm. Even so, the subdued style by itself can be more easily tolerated for a good length of time than the grand style by itself. Indeed, the more profoundly listeners' spirits need to be stirred up that we may win their assent, the less time they can be held at that [high] pitch, once they have been sufficiently aroused. For this reason, we must be careful when we are trying to arouse to a higher pitch what is already high, that it not fall from the emotional heights to which it has been carried. But after inserting things said in a more subdued style, we can effectively return to what has to be spoken in the grand style so that the vehemence of our speech ebbs and flows like the waves of the sea. As a result, if the grand style of eloquence must be maintained for a rather long time, it should be varied by introducing the other styles. . . .

(24.53) If a speaker is applauded repeatedly and eagerly, we should not, for that reason, believe that he is speaking in the grand style. Keenness of intellect in the subdued style and the rhetorical embellishments of the moderate style also have this effect. The grand style, by its weight, is able not only to make voices hush, but also to make tears gush.[33] Once, I was at Caesarea in Mauretania, trying to dissuade people from civil war, or worse than civil war—something they called *caterva*—for not only fellow-citizens, but even relatives, brothers, yes, parents and children, divided into two factions, and, according to custom, fought one another with stones for several successive days at a certain time of the year, and they each killed whomever they could.[34] I pleaded in the grand style as powerfully as I could that I might root out and banish by my speech such a barbarous and deep-rooted evil from their hearts

33. "Voices hush . . . tears gush" (*voces premit, sed lacrimas exprimit*). I have drawn this felicitous rhyme from Edmund Hill's translation (WSA I/11:234).

34. *Caterva*: literally "a mob" or "band." This sounds as though it was some sort of ritual combat or ritual gang-war. Odd behavior, perhaps, but think of cities today that have venerable, long-standing traditions that allow raucous or violent behavior (e.g., Mardi Gras in New Orleans; the running of the bulls in Pamplona). On this incident, see Lancel, *Saint Augustine*, 350–51.

and customs. It was not when I heard them applauding, but when I saw them weeping, that I realized I had accomplished anything. Their applause showed that they were being taught and being entertained. It was by their tears they showed they were being persuaded. When I saw these, I believed (even before they demonstrated it in fact) that the frightful custom handed down from their fathers and grandfathers and from their far-off ancestors—something which had been besieging their hearts like an enemy, or rather had taken possession of them—had been completely conquered. As soon as my speech was finished, I directed their hearts and lips to thank God. And, look, thanks to Christ's good favor, for nearly eight years or more, nothing like that has been attempted there. There are many other experiences as well which have taught me the effects of a wise speaker's grand style: It is not the roar of applause, but rather people's groans, and sometimes even their tears, and ultimately a change in their lives. . . .

(25.55) The moderate style with its aim—that is, to give pleasure by its very eloquence—must not be exercised for its own sake, but rather it is to be used either to draw in listeners, because of the pleasure it offers, to agree a little more readily, or it is to be used to help make things that are discussed usefully and properly stick [in the memory] a little more firmly. This presumes, of course, that listeners are both informed and sympathetic and do not need a style that instructs or persuades. For it is the universal task of eloquence, in whichever of the three styles, to speak in a way geared to persuading, and, since the end you are aiming at is to persuade by your eloquence, the eloquent speaker certainly speaks in a way geared to persuading in any of these three styles. For unless the speaker persuades, he does not achieve the goal of eloquence. Now in the subdued style, he persuades us that what he says is true; in the grand style, he persuades us to do what we know should be done but are not doing. But in the moderate style, he persuades us that he is speaking beautifully and elegantly. What use is this aim for us? Let those who glory in their tongues aim for it, those who pride themselves on panegyrics and other such things, where the audience does not need to be taught or moved to action. Let us refer this aim to another purpose: . . . that we use even the rhetorical embellishments of the moderate style, not for mere show, but discreetly, not satisfied with merely entertaining listeners, but working instead for this goal: that by reason of their being delighted, listeners may be helped even to doing the good which we are anxious to persuade them of. . . .

(26.56) It often happens that a speech in the subdued style, when it solves very difficult questions and demonstrates things with unexpected clarity, or when it elicits and displays highly acute insights from sources from

which nothing was expected, or when it clearly refutes the error of its opponent and demonstrates what seemed irrefutable to be false—especially when
one's words have a certain beauty, unsought-for but somehow natural, and
use rhythmic sentence endings, put in not for show, but as though essential,
drawn from the subject itself—this subdued style often occasions such thun-
derous applause that it is hardly even recognized as subdued. It advances into
battle neither well-dressed nor well-armed, but goes in, as it were, naked, and
yet that fact does not prevent it from crushing its opponent with its sinewy
and muscular biceps, overthrowing any resistance, and demolishing falsehoods with its enormous arm-strength. Why are those who speak in this way
applauded so often and so enthusiastically? Only because it is a pleasure to
see truth thus demonstrated, thus defended, thus unconquered. Therefore, in
this subdued style this teacher and speaker of ours should strive to make his
words not only understandable, but also enjoyable and persuasive.[35]

CHRIST THE DOCTOR

*It is no surprise that Augustine had favorite themes and images that he returned to again
and again in his sermons. What is surprising is his inventiveness, the way he gives
well-worn themes unexpected turns. Augustine's favorite—or at least, most frequent—
image of Christ was as a medical doctor. He adapts the image now this way, now that,
depending, in part, on the biblical text in his hand and, in part, on the liturgical season
in which he was preaching. What follows are snippets from various sermons, gathered to
illustrate the richness of Augustine's poetic creativity.*

(i) Ignoring Doctor's Orders

*Augustine drew the image of Christ the Doctor not only from the fact of Jesus' healing
miracles, but also from Jesus' remark that "the doctor is not needed by the healthy, but by
the sick" (Mt 9:12). From Sermon 88:*

(1) Your Holinesses[36] know as well as I that our Lord Jesus Christ is the
physician of our eternal health and well-being. And for this He took upon
Himself the weakness of our nature: that our weakness not be everlasting. He
took up a mortal body by which He would kill death. . . .

(7) My brothers and sisters, from [Adam] we too were born, and, as the

---

35. *Doc. Chr.* 4.17.34–26.56 (Green, 238–74); my trans., based on Gavigan, FOTC 2:201–28.
36. "Your Holinesses": This is another of those polite titles Augustine bestows on his congregation.
On this, see note 25 above.

Apostle says, "In Adam all die" (1 Cor 15:22). Back then we were just two human beings, back when we were unwilling to comply with the Doctor's orders
so as not to get sick. Let us comply now so that we can get free of the disease.
When we were healthy, the Doctor gave us orders. The Doctor gave us orders
so that we would not need a Doctor. "The doctor is not needed by the healthy,
but by the sick" (Mt 9:12). While healthy, we disregarded His orders, and we
tasted from experience how deadly an injury it was to disregard His orders.
We began to get sick, we were in pain, we lay in our sickbed, but we must not
get discouraged. So because we were not able to go to the Doctor, He Himself
deigned to come to us. Though he was disregarded by the healthy, He did not
disregard the wounded.[37]

(ii) Human Doctors vs. Christ the Doctor

*Augustine contrasted the medical know-how of human doctors with Christ the Doctor.
From Expositions of the Psalms 102:*

(5) The Lord "heals all your diseases" (Ps 102:3). All your sluggishness
and weaknesses will be healed. There's no need to fear. "They are great,"
you say—but the Doctor is greater. For this all-powerful Doctor, no disease
is incurable. . . . A human doctor sometimes makes mistakes and promises
health for the human body. Why is he wrong? Because he's not taking care of
something he himself made. God made your body. God made your soul. God
knows how to re-create whatever He created. He knows how to re-form what
He Himself formed.[38]

(iii) Christ's Diagnostic Skills

*In a sermon on Peter's triple denial, Augustine compares Jesus to a doctor whose diagnostic
abilities allow him to read the inner workings of the human heart. From Sermon 229O:*

(1) The Lord, like a highly skilled doctor, knew what was going on in the
sick man, knew it better than the sick man himself. Doctors do for the health
and well-being of bodies what the Lord does for the health and well-being
of souls. So does it seem to you—I ask you—that the patient should expect
to hear from the doctor what's going on inside him? The patient is certainly
able to know what pains he's suffering, but whether they are dangerous, and
what the underlying causes are, whether he can or cannot get past it—well, a
doctor listens to the pulse and tells the patient what is happening inside the

37. S. 88.1–7 (PL 38:539–43); my trans.
38. En. Ps. 102.5 (CCL 40:1454–55); my trans.

patient. So when the Lord said to the blessed Peter, "You will deny me three times" (Mk 14:30), He was taking the pulse of Peter's heart.[39]

(iv) The Pathology Beneath the Symptoms

Augustine also played on the difference between doctors who treat only the symptoms of diseases versus those who see the root cause. For Augustine, the root cause of our diseased humanity is pride. From Tractates on the Gospel of John 25:

(16) The source of all diseases is pride because the source of all sins is pride. When a physician clears up an illness, if he should heal what occurred through some cause and not heal the cause itself through which it occurred, the disease may seem to be cured for a time, but since the cause remains, it strikes again. For example—let me express this more clearly—a fluid in the body produces mange or sores; a high fever and no small pain develop in the body. Some medicines are employed which curb the mange and ease the burning of the sores; they are applied and bring results. You see a man who was covered with sores and mange healed, but because that fluid was not eliminated, the sores come back again. The physician, knowing this, gets rid of the fluid, removes the cause, and there will be no sores. From what source does wickedness abound? From pride. Heal pride, and there will be no wickedness. Therefore, in order that the cause of all diseases, that is, pride, might be healed, He came down and the Son of God became humble.[40]

(v) Christ the Surgeon

Until the twentieth century, surgery was performed without anesthetic. Augustine plays on this grim aspect of ancient medical practice, routinely speaking of Christ as a surgeon who performs painful but life-saving surgery to remove gangrene from our hearts. From Tractates on the First Letter of John 9:

(4) Fear of God wounds in the same way as a physician's scalpel does. It removes the purulence and yet seems, as it were, to increase the wound's size. Look, when the purulence was in the body, the wound was smaller but dangerous. The physician's scalpel comes into use. That wound may have hurt less then than it hurts now when it is being cut. It hurts more when it is being cured than when it is being cut. It hurts more when it is being cured than if it were not cured, but with this medical treatment it hurts more for the very purpose that it may never hurt again once good health follows. Therefore, let

---

39. S. 229O.1 (MA 1:495–96); my trans. See also s. 299A.5 (= Dolbeau 4).
40. Jo. ev. tr. 25.16 (CCL 36:256–57); trans. Rettig, FOTC 79:253.

fear occupy your heart that it may lead in love. Let the scar follow upon the physician's scalpel. Such is this Physician that not even scars appear. Just submit yourself to His hand. . . . Fear is the medication, love is health.[41]

(vi) Christ the Eye Doctor and Pharmacist

Augustine often compared Christ to an eye doctor who cures the spiritual cataracts that block the human heart from seeing God. Here he speaks of Christ as an eye doctor who uses his own flesh to create the medicine to heal our spiritual blindness. From Tractates on the Gospel of John 2:

(16) Indeed, because "the Word was made flesh, and dwelt among us" (Jn 1:14), by the Nativity itself He made a salve by which the eyes of our heart may be wiped clean and we may be able to see His majesty through His lowliness. Thus "the Word was made flesh, and dwelt among us." He healed our eyes. And what follows? "And we saw His glory" (Jn 1:14). His glory no one could see unless one were healed by the lowliness of His flesh. Why could we not see? Concentrate, my beloved people, and see what I am saying. Dust, so to speak, had forcibly entered humanity's eye; earth had entered it, had injured the eye, and it could not see the light. That injured eye is anointed; it was [once] injured by earth, and earth is put there that it may be healed. For all salves and medicines are nothing but [compounds] of earth. You have been blinded by dust, you are healed by dust; thus the flesh had blinded you, flesh heals you. For the soul had become carnal by assenting to carnal passions; from that, the eye of the heart had been blinded. "The Word became flesh" (Jn 1:14). That Physician made a salve for you. And because He came in such a way that by His flesh He might extinguish the faults of the flesh and by His death He might kill death, it was therefore effected in you that, because "the Word became flesh," you could say, "And we saw His glory."[42]

(vii) Doctor's Scars as Medicine

The image of Christ the Doctor appears especially in the Lenten and Easter sermons because Augustine sees Christ's Passion and Resurrection as the climax of our healing. In this Easter Week sermon, Augustine describes Christ as both the doctor and the medicine. From Sermon 237:

(1) Today the story of the Lord's Resurrection according to Luke's Gospel was brought to a close, and we heard of the Lord's appearance in the midst of

41. Ep. Jo. 9.4 (SC 75:386); trans. Rettig, FOTC 92:252. See also s. 278.4–5.
42. Jo. ev. tr. 2.16 (BA 71:204–6); trans. Rettig, FOTC 78:73–74.

His disciples, who, in their unbelief, were arguing about the Resurrection. In fact, His appearance was so unexpected and unbelievable that, seeing, they did not see. For they saw Him alive and well, the One they had thought dead and had beaten their breasts over. They saw Him standing in their midst, the One they had grieved over as He hung on the cross. They saw, therefore, and because they did not believe their own eyes, that what they saw was real, they thought they were deceived. For, as you heard, they "thought they saw a spirit" (Lk 24:37). The wavering Apostles anticipated what the worst heretics later believed about Christ.[43] For there are people today who do not believe that Christ had a body. . . .

(3) The Lord said to them: "What is troubling you? And why do thoughts rise up in your hearts? See my hands and my feet, rub and see" (Lk 24:38–39). It's not enough for you just to look. Reach out your hands. If it's not enough to reach out your hands, if it's not good enough just to touch, rub him. He did not only say "touch" but also "rub" and "handle." Let your hands prove it to you if your eyes are lying. Rub and see. You have eyes in your hands. Why? Because "a spirit does not have flesh and bones as you see I have" (Lk 24:37–40). You were mistaken, just as the disciples were. Be corrected along with them. I admit, it's human. You suppose Christ is a ghost. Peter did too. The others did too. They thought they saw a ghost, but they did not remain in their mistake. To show that they earlier had a wrong idea in their hearts, the Doctor did not leave them in this condition. He approached. He applied a cure. He saw the wound in their hearts. He bore in His body the scars from which their wounded hearts would be healed.[44]

(viii) Church as Hospital

Augustine linked the image of Christ the Doctor with the image of the Church as a hospital. Playing on Jesus' parable of the Good Samaritan, he interpreted Christ himself as the Good Samaritan, who carries fallen humanity back for healing to an inn called Church. The innkeeper is St. Paul, who nurses us back to health with the twofold medicine of the love of God and of neighbor. From Tractates on the Gospel of John 41:

(13) Let us, the wounded, beg the Doctor, let us be carried to the inn to be healed. For it is He who promises health, He who pitied the man left half-dead on the road by the robbers. He poured oil and wine, He healed the

---

43. "Worst heretics": Augustine goes on to specify that he is speaking of the Manichees, who denied the bodily resurrection because they denied the Incarnation. See Chapter 6.

44. S. 237.1–3 (PL 38:1122–24); my trans. See also s. 80.2; 159B.12 (= Dolbeau 12); 242.3. In s. 374.23 (= Dolbeau 23), Augustine puts it tersely: "He Himself is the Doctor; He Himself, the Medicine; the Doctor, because the Word; the Medicine, because the Word-made-flesh" (Dolbeau, VSS, 614–15; my trans.).

wounds, He lifted him onto His beast, He brought him to an inn, He entrusted him to the innkeeper (Lk 10:30–35). To what innkeeper? Perhaps to [Paul] who said, "We are ambassadors for Christ" (2 Cor 5:20). The Doctor also gave two coins to pay for healing the wounded man; perhaps these are the two precepts on which the whole Law and the prophets are based. Therefore, brothers and sisters, in this time the Church, too, in which the wounded man is healed, is the inn of the traveler; but for the Church itself the possessor's inheritance is on high.[45]

PREACHER AS TOUR GUIDE

Around 403, Deogratias, a deacon from the church in Carthage, requested that Augustine "write something on catechizing inquirers."[46] Deogratias was in charge of evangelizing new converts, and while he had theological acumen, the routine of teaching had begun to wear thin. Augustine answered with On Catechizing Beginners (De catechizandis rudibus). This brief treatise is a gem in many ways. Augustine recognized that the bearing of the messenger affects the bearing of the message and insisted that a good teacher needs more than pedagogical tricks and techniques. Teaching is about loving. From On Catechizing Beginners:

(12.17) Now if we feel disgusted because we are so often repeating things geared to the little ones, familiar things, let us equip ourselves with a brother's or a father's or a mother's love, and by linking our hearts to theirs, those things will again seem new to us. For so great is this feeling of compassion that when people are touched by us as we speak, and we by them as they learn, we each dwell in the other, and so it is as if they speak in us what they hear while we, in some way, learn in them what it is we teach. Isn't it quite common that when we show certain beautiful, spacious locales, whether in town or out in the countryside, to those who have never seen them before, we who have been in the habit of passing them by without any enjoyment find our own delight renewed by their delight at the novelty of it all? And how much more enjoyable the closer our friendship, because as we come together more and more through this bond of love, what had gotten old becomes new to us all over again. But if we have made some progress in contemplative matters, we do not wish those who are learning from us simply to enjoy and be amazed when they gaze upon human handiwork, but we want them to en-

45. Jo. ev. tr. 41.13 (BA 73A:376–78); trans. Rettig, FOTC 88:148–49 (modified). Augustine would develop this imagery at length in the Pelagian controversy: e.g., nat. et gr. 43.50, 52.60. See Chapter 10.

46. This has been traditionally dated to either 399 or 400. Hombert, Nouvelles recherches de chronologie augustinienne, 41–44, has argued for shifting this work to 403.

joy and be amazed by the deeper design and underlying purpose of the Artist himself and, from there, to soar up in admiration and in praise of the All-creating God, where the richest fruitfulness of love finds its endpoint. How much more then ought we to rejoice when people now approach to learn of God Himself, for whatever things we learn, we learn to learn of God; and how much more ought we to be renewed in their newness, so that if our preaching, now a routine, has cooled off, it may again catch fire because of our hearers.[47]

A PASSWORD CALLED CREED

Augustine brought great enthusiasm to teaching beginners. That enthusiasm is evident in the way that he taught, year after year, the most basic matters to catechumens. From here to the end of the chapter, we will explore several examples. First, a sermon on the Creed. Each year, catechumens who wished to be baptized at Easter turned in their names and, if approved, were officially enrolled as competentes *("co-petitioners"). These advanced catechumens spent the forty days prior to Easter—what we now call Lent—practicing an ascetic regimen and passing through a series of special initiation rituals.[48] One was the "handing over of the Creed"* (traditio symboli)*. In this ceremony, the bishop recited the Creed and then explained it phrase-by-phrase.* Competentes *memorized it and, a week later, recited it publicly at a second ritual known as the "handing back of the Creed"* (redditio symboli).[49] *The wording of the creeds that can be reconstructed from these sermons is similar to, but ever so slightly different from, the later "Apostle's Creed."[50] Note the way Augustine repeats the Creed's phrases again and again, as though a refrain, as though he wanted to pound them into his hearer's memory. The Latin word for "creed" was* symbolum, *and, as he notes, it meant "password." Like any password, it was kept secret and used to distinguish allies from enemies. Note also the imagery he uses at one point, in portraying God's justice as topsy-turvy: that Christ is like a lawyer whom we have hired to work on our case and then who strangely gets assigned to act as our judge, implying that our court-case before God has been rigged in our favor. From Sermon 213:*

(1) The Apostle says, "Everyone who invokes the name of the Lord will be saved" (Rom 10:13). You who have given in your names for baptism, you are running to this salvation, a salvation not for the short-term but for eternity. . . . The Apostle himself then added, "But how can they invoke Him in

47. *De catechizandis rudibus* 12.17 (CCL 46:141); my trans.

48. For an overview of the ritual, ascetical, and catechetical path followed by catechumens, see Harmless, "Catechumens, Catechumenate," *AugEncy*, 145–49; "Baptism," *AugEncy*, 84–87.

49. Augustine described this ceremony in his account of Victorinus's conversion: *conf.* 8.2.5 (quoted in Chapter 1).

50. On this issue, see Harmless, *Augustine and the Catechumenate*, 274–86, 299; Joseph T. Lienhard, "Creed, Symbolum," *AugEncy*, 254–55; J. N. D. Kelly, *Early Christian Creeds*, 3rd ed. (London: Longman, 1972).

whom they have not believed? And how can they believe in Him of whom they have not heard? And how can they hear without someone to preach? And how can people preach unless they are sent? As it is written, 'How beautiful are the feet of those who bring the good news of peace, the good gospel!'" (Rom 10:14–15; Is 52:7)[51] So no one can be saved who does not invoke Him; and no one can invoke Him unless one first believes.[52] Because of this, this is the order of things: first, *what* you are to believe; then, *whom* you are to call upon. Today you are to receive the Symbol of faith, the Creed, in which you express your belief. Eight days from now, you will then receive the [Lord's] Prayer, with which you are to call upon Him.[53]

(2) The Creed is the rule of faith, succinctly worded so as to instruct the mind without overburdening the memory. It is expressed in just a few words, but much instruction may be drawn from it. It is spoken of as a "symbol," a sort of password by which Christians can recognize one another. This, then, is what I will first briefly proclaim to you. Then, inasmuch as the Lord deems worthy to grant me to give, I will open it up for you in order that you come to understand what I want you to hold onto. Here now is the Creed: [*Since the Creed was a carefully guarded secret, the stenographer who recorded this sermon did not transcribe Augustine's words as he recited the Creed out loud. Instead, he waited until Augustine had finished and then inserted into the manuscript the words: "And after the Creed:"*]. It's not a lot—yet it is a lot. It's not a matter of you counting words, but weighing them.[54]

"I believe in God the Father Almighty." See how quickly it is said and how much it means! God exists and He is the Father: God, by His power; Father, by His goodness. How fortunate we are who have discovered that God is our Father! Let us, therefore, believe in Him, and let us promise ourselves all things from His mercy because He is all-powerful. That's the reason we believe in God the Father Almighty. Let no one say: "He is not able to forgive me my sins." How can the All-Powerful lack that power? But you say: "I have sinned much." I answer: But He is all-powerful. You insist: "I have committed sins of such a serious nature that I cannot be freed or cleansed from them." I reply: But He is all-powerful. Look at what you sang in the Psalm: "Bless the Lord, O my soul, and never forget all He has done for you. Who forgives all your iniquities? Who heals all your diseases?" (Ps 102:2–3). . . .

---

51. "Good news of peace, the good gospel!" (*evangelizantium pacem, evangelizantium bona*): Augustine has added to Paul's own quotation of Is 52:7, adding Second Isaiah's phrase about "peace."

52. "Invoke . . . believes": This opening echoes *conf.* 1.1 (see Chapter 1).

53. "Eight days from now . . . receive the Prayer": A similar ceremony of "handing down the Prayer" (*traditio orationis*) was held a week later. See s. 56 (below) for a sample of this.

54. This opening paragraph is missing from the Maurist version of s. 213; the translation here is based on s. Guelferbytanus 1 (MA 1:441–50); my trans.

(3) What comes next? "And in Jesus Christ." You say: "I believe in God the Father Almighty, and in Jesus Christ His only Son, our Lord." If only Son, then equal to the Father. If only Son, then of the same substance as the Father. If only Son, then all-powerful, just as the Father is. If only Son, then co-eternal with the Father. All this He is in Himself, and with Himself, and with the Father. What is He for our sake? What is He to us? "Who was born of the Holy Spirit and the Virgin Mary." Look, see who comes, to whom He comes, and how. Through the Virgin Mary—in whom not her husband but the Holy Spirit acted, making the chaste one fruitful and preserving her chastity intact. Thus the Lord Jesus Christ was clothed with human flesh. Thus He who made humanity was made human by taking upon Himself something He wasn't without losing what He was. For "the Word was made flesh and dwelt among us" (Jn 1:14). The Word was not changed into human flesh, but, remaining as Word, He assumed flesh. He who had always been invisible became visible when He wished it, and He "dwelt among us." What does "among us" mean? Among human beings. He became one of the multitude of humanity, the One who was the one and only-begotten of the Father. How is He an "only" for us? He is our only Savior. No one except Him is our Savior. And He is our only Redeemer. No one except Him has redeemed us, doing so not with gold or silver, but with His blood.

(4) Therefore, let us look at this transaction of His by which we were bought. These words were said in the Creed: "Born of the Holy Spirit and the Virgin Mary." What then did he undergo for us? These words follow: "Under Pontius Pilate, was crucified and buried." What? The only Son of God our Lord crucified? The only Son of God our Lord buried? The Man was crucified; God was not changed; God was not killed, and yet, in terms of His humanity, was killed. "For if they had known it," says the Apostle, "they would never have crucified the Lord of glory" (1 Cor 2:8). Paul both showed that Christ was the Lord of glory and confessed that He was crucified. Now if anyone should tear your tunic without harming your flesh, you wouldn't yell about your clothes: "You've torn my tunic." You'd say: "You've torn me up, ripped me to pieces, left me in shreds." You're still together, and yet you speak the truth, even though the one who harmed you tore away none of your flesh. So too was the Lord Jesus Christ crucified. He is the Lord. He is the only Son of the Father. He is our Savior. He is the Lord of glory. Yet He was crucified, but in the flesh, and buried in flesh alone. For there where He was buried and while He was buried, there was no soul there then. Flesh alone lay in the tomb. Still you confess: "Jesus Christ, the only Son of God, our Lord, born of the Holy Spirit and the Virgin Mary." Who? Jesus Christ, the only Son of God, our Lord. "Under Pontius Pilate crucified." Who? Jesus Christ, the only Son of God, our

Lord. "And buried." Who? Jesus Christ, the only Son of God, our Lord. Flesh alone lies there, and you say: "Our Lord"? Yes, I say so, I say so emphatically. Because I look at the clothing, and I adore the One clothed. That flesh was his clothing, because "though He was in the form of God, He did not think being equal to God something to be clung to, but emptied himself, taking the form of a servant," not losing the form of God, "being made in the likeness of humanity, and found in the garb of a human being" (Phil 2:6–7).

(5) Let us not despise flesh, for when it lay buried there, then He purchased us. How did He purchase us? Because His flesh did not always lie there: "He rose from the dead on the third day." That [phrase] follows in the Creed. When we acknowledge His Passion, we also confess His Resurrection. What did He do in the Passion? He taught us what we must endure. What did He do in the Resurrection? He showed us what we hope for. Here, it's work; there, it's reward; work in the Passion, reward in the Resurrection. . . .

(6) What then? "He will come to judge the living and the dead." Let us confess Him as Savior; let us not fear Him as Judge. The one who believes in Him now and who does His commands and who loves Him will not be afraid when He comes to judge the living and the dead. Not only are we unafraid, but we hope that He does come. What, after all, is more joyful for us than that someone whom we yearn for, whom we love, is coming? But we might be afraid because He's going to be our judge. Look, He will then be our judge; right now he's our advocate. Listen to John: "If we say we have no sin, we deceive ourselves, and the truth is not in us; if, however, we confess our sins," he says, "[God] is faithful and just; He forgives our sins and cleanses us of every wrongdoing. I write this to you that you not sin; and if anyone does sin, we have an advocate with the Father, Jesus Christ the righteous one; and He Himself is the expiation for our sins" (1 Jn 1:8–9, 2:1–2). If you were to have a case scheduled before some judge and you contacted a lawyer, you would be upheld, supported by the lawyer, and he would act on your case as best he could. And if, before he finished [preparing your case], you hear that he's going to come as the judge, how you would rejoice! For the very one who just a little while ago was your lawyer is now going to be your judge! Now [Christ] Himself pleads for us; He Himself intervenes on our behalf. We have Him as our lawyer, our advocate. Why should we fear Him as judge? No, because we have sent Him on ahead as our lawyer, we rest in the secure hope He will be our judge. . . .

(9) "In the forgiveness of sins." If this [forgiveness] were not in the Church, there would be no hope. If there were no remission of sins within the Church, there would be no hope of future life and of eternal liberation. We give thanks to God who gave this gift to His Church. Look, you are about to

come to the sacred font; you will be washed in baptism; you will be renewed in the "bath of rebirth" (Ti 3:5); rising up from that washing, you will be without any sin. All the sins that, in the past, haunted you will be wiped out there. Your sins will be like the Egyptians following the Israelites, pursuing them, but only up to the Red Sea. What does "up to the Red Sea" mean? Up to the font consecrated by the cross and blood of Christ. Of course, what's red reddens [things?]. Don't you see how being part of Christ reddens [you?].[55] Ask the eyes of faith. If you see the cross, then you should see the blood. If you see what hangs on the cross, then you should see what drips down from it. A lance pierced Christ's side, and our purchase price flowed forth. That's the reason baptism is signed with the sign of Christ, that is, the water where you are immersed and dyed and you pass through as though through the Red Sea. Your sins are your enemies. They follow you, but only up to the Red Sea. Once you plunge in, you will escape. But those sins will be obliterated, just as the waters engulfed the Egyptians while the Israelites escaped on dry land.[56]

THE LORD'S PRAYER AS BILGE-PUMP

Eight days after receiving the Creed, competentes went through another rite, the "handing over the Prayer" (traditio orationis). Augustine explained the Lord's Prayer phrase-by-phrase much as he had done with the Creed. Early Christians believed that only the baptized were God's true sons and daughters, and so only they had the right to call God "Father" and, therefore, only they had rightful claim to pray the Lord's Prayer. Augustine plays on this and compares competentes to unborn children in the Church's womb who enjoy in advance the privileges and inheritance rights of sons and daughters. Below are two excerpts from a lengthy sermon. Note in speaking of "daily bread," he emphasizes the "bread of the Word" and alludes obliquely to the Eucharist, still secret to his as-yet-unbaptized audience. The Creed that competentes had memorized spoke of "one baptism for the forgiveness of sins." Augustine raises the question of sins on the far side of baptism: How are they forgiven if there is only one baptism? Augustine argues that the Lord's Prayer serves as a daily baptism and compares it to a pump that pumps bilge-water out of a ship. From Sermon 56:

55. "What's red reddens . . ." (*Quod enim rubrum est, rubet. Non vides, quomodo rubeat pars Christi?*): This phrase is terse and ambiguous. Augustine seems to play on the metaphor of dyeing clothes: the font is like a dyer's vat in which one is plunged and dyed red by Christ's blood; its indelible blood-red dye thus "tints" the baptized and "signifies" that one has become a member of Christ's body. Could the font in Hippo have been lined with red mosaic tiles, giving the water in the font something of a red tinge?
56. S. 213.1–9 (PL 38:1060–65); my trans. This is one of several sermons delivered on the Creed; see also s. 212, 214, 215, and *De symbolo ad catechumenos.* Augustine, as a presbyter, also published an address on the Creed that he delivered to a council of the North African bishops meeting in Hippo in 393: *On Faith and the Creed (De fide et symbolo).* For excerpts, see Chapter 8.

(4) First of all, our Lord chopped back on long-windedness so that you not pour out many, many words to God, as though you could teach God by many, many words. Piety, not wordiness, is what you need when you pray, "for your Father knows what you need before you ask Him" (Mt 6:8). Therefore, don't talk a lot, for He knows what you need. It might happen that someone will say: "If He knows what we need, why should we use even a few words, or why should we pray at all? He knows. Let Him give us what He knows we need." Even so, He wants you to pray so that His gift may be yearned for, lest it be unappreciated. After all, He Himself has implanted this very yearning. So the words that our Lord Jesus Christ taught in the Prayer are to shape our yearnings. You are not allowed to ask for anything other than what's written there.

(5) Our Lord says: "You are to say therefore: 'Our Father who art in heaven'" (Mt 6:9). You have begun, you see, to have God as your Father, but you'll really have Him so when you're born [in baptism]. But even now, before you're born, you have been conceived by His seed, and you are to come to birth from the font, as though from the Church's womb. "Our Father who art in heaven." Remember that from your father Adam you have been born for death, but from God the Father you will be born for life. Whatever you say [in prayer], say it in your hearts. Let there be feeling in the one praying so that there'll be results from the One hearing it.

"Hallowed be thy name." Why should you have to ask that the name of God be hallowed? It is holy. Why then are you to ask for the hallowing of what's already holy? What's more, when you ask that His name be hallowed, doesn't it sound as if you were asking Him for His sake and not for yours? Think about it, for you are to pray for your own sake. What you're asking for is this: that what's always holy in itself may be hallowed in you. . . .

(9) "Give us this day our daily bread" (Mt 6:11). It's very clear that in this petition we are praying for ourselves. When you said, "Hallowed be thy name," it had to be explained that you were praying for yourself, not for God. . . . But from this point on to the Prayer's end, it's clear that we are begging God for our own sake. When you say: "Give us this day our daily bread," you publicly profess that you come before God as a beggar. But don't be ashamed of that. No matter how rich someone may be here on earth, one comes before God as a beggar. A beggar stands in front of a rich person's house; the rich themselves stand before the house of the truly Rich and Powerful. . . .

(10) But, dearest ones, this bread by which the stomach is filled, by which the flesh is remade every day, this sort of bread you see God giving not only to His praisers but also to His blasphemers—a God who "makes his sun to rise on the good and the evil and sends rain on the just and the unjust" (Mt 5:45). You praise God; He feeds you. You blaspheme God; He feeds you. He waits for

you to do penance, but if you don't change, He will condemn you. Now just because both the good and the evil receive bread of this sort from God, don't you think that there's bread of some kind which His children seek, bread about which the Lord said in the Gospel: "It is not fair to take the children's bread and to cast it to the dogs" (Mt 15:16)? Clearly, there is—but what sort of bread is it? And why is it called "daily bread"? It too is necessary. Without it we could not live; without this bread, we could not live. It's shameless to ask God for wealth; it's not shameless, however, to ask for daily bread. From wealth comes arrogance; from bread comes living. Still, since bread of that visible and tangible sort is given both to the good and to the evil, there is a daily bread which [God's] children ask for: the word of God. It's doled out to us every day. That's our daily bread. On it live not our stomachs, but our minds. It's necessary even now for us workers in the vineyard. It's food, not pay. The manager who hires a worker for the vineyard owes him two things: food (otherwise he'll drop); and pay (which he enjoys). Our everyday food on this earth is God's word, what's always being doled out in churches. Our pay after this work: that's called eternal life. Then again, in terms of that daily bread, if you understand what the faithful receive (and what you as baptized will receive), we do well when we ask for it and say, "Give us this day our daily bread," that we may live so as not to be excluded from this altar.

(11) "And forgive us our debts, as we also forgive our debtors" (Mt 6:12). This petition needs no explanation since we ask it for our own sake. We ask that our debts be remitted, for we are debtors not in money but in sins. Now perhaps you say: "You too?" I answer, Yes, me too. "What! Even you holy bishops are debtors?" Yes, we too are debtors. "Even you! Far be it from you, my lord. Do not wrong yourself." I do not wrong myself. I speak the truth. We [bishops] are debtors. "If we say that we have no sin, we deceive ourselves, and the truth is not in us" (1 Jn 1:8). We are baptized, and we are sinners. That's not because anything was left over after what was remitted us in baptism. It's because living means contracting [debts] that need daily remission. Those who are baptized and depart rise up without any debt, go forth without any debt. Those, however, who are baptized and hold on to this life contract things due to human frailty. Even if from these they're not shipwrecked, the bilge-pumps must be used, for if the pumps are not used, there's a gradual leaking that can sink the whole ship. By this prayer, the bilge gets pumped out. What's more, we should not only pray, but give alms as well. For when we use bilge-pumps to stop the ship from sinking, we work with both voices and hands.[57] We work our voices when we say: "Forgive us our debts as we also forgive our debtors."

57. "Voices and hands": Augustine saw the Lord's Prayer as something not just to be prayed, but also enacted, interpreting it in light of Luke 6:37–38: "Forgive, and it will be forgiven you; give, and it will be given

We work our hands when we do this: "Deal your bread to the hungry, and bring the needy into your house" (Is 58:7); "Enclose alms in the heart of the poor, and it shall intercede for you before the Lord" (Sir 29:12).[58]

EUCHARIST AND MYSTAGOGY

The Liturgy of the Word, that is, the first half of the Sunday service, was open to all: to baptized, to catechumens, even to pagans. But the second half, the Liturgy of the Eucharist, was secret. Only baptized were permitted to attend. Catechumens were dismissed after the sermon, and the church doors were closed and locked. At the Easter Vigil, the competentes were baptized and chrismated (or, as we say today in the Western Church, "confirmed"). They then joined the assembled faithful behind closed doors and witnessed and received the Eucharist for the first time. Fourth-century bishops took this opportunity, beginning on Easter morning and continuing through Easter Week, to instruct the newly baptized on the secret ceremonies of baptism, chrismation, and eucharist, a form of preaching known as "mystagogy" ("teaching of the mysteries"). Mystagogical sermons survive from Augustine's contemporaries, such as Cyril of Jerusalem, John Chrysostom, Theodore of Mopsuestia, and Ambrose. Here is an example of Augustine's mystagogy, delivered to the newly baptized (he calls them infantes, "newborns"). It touches on Augustine's influential (and sometimes misunderstood) theology of sacrament. This is Sermon 227, given in its entirety:

I remember my promise. I promised you who have just been baptized a sermon to explain the sacrament of the Lord's table, something which you now see and which you were made participants in last night. You need to know what you have received, what you are going to receive, and what you ought to receive daily. That bread, which you see on the altar, sanctified by the word of God, is the Body of Christ. That cup (or rather what the cup holds), sanctified by the word of God, is the Blood of Christ. Through these the Lord wished to commemorate for us His Body and Blood, which He poured out for the remission of sins. If you receive them properly, you are what you have received,[59] for the Apostle says: "We the many are one bread, one body"

---

you." He thus insisted that a twofold action of forgiveness and almsgiving was to accompany the prayer. Thus he spoke of these as the Prayer's "two wings," enabling it to fly to God (s. 58.10). See Harmless, *Augustine and the Catechumenate*, 286–93; also Louis Swift, "Giving and Forgiving: Augustine on *Eleemosyna* and *Misericordia*," *Augustinian Studies* 32 (2001): 25–36.

58. S. 56.4–11 (PL 38:387–82); my trans. This is one of several surviving sermons on the Lord's Prayer delivered at the *traditio orationis*; see also s. 57, 58, 59. Augustine's exegesis of the Lord's Prayer owes much to his North African predecessor, Cyprian of Carthage. See Alistair Stewart-Sykes, ed., *Tertullian, Cyprian, Origen: On the Lord's Prayer*, Popular Patristic Series (Crestwood, NY: St. Vladimir's Seminary Press, 2004).

59. "You are what you have received": This echoes Augustine's famous one-liner from s. 272: "Be what you see, receive what you are" (*Estote quod uidetis, accipite quod estis*).

(1 Cor 10:17). Thus he explained the sacrament of the Lord's table: "We the many are one bread, one body."

So this bread serves as a reminder to you how much you should love unity. After all, was that bread made up of just one grain? Weren't there many grains of wheat? Before they all came together as bread, they were separate. They were joined together, after a certain amount of pounding, through water. For unless wheat is ground down and sprinkled with water, it can't come together to form what we call bread. In the same way, you too were ground down, so to speak, by the humiliation of fasting and the sacrament of exorcism.[60] Then came baptism, and you were, so to speak, moistened with water so as to form bread. But without fire, it's not bread yet. So what symbolizes the fire? That's the chrism, the oil. That's the sacrament of the Holy Spirit, the fueler of the fire. Notice this when the Acts of the Apostles is read. (The reading of the book itself begins soon; today we start the book called "Acts of the Apostles.") Whoever wants to make progress has a way to do it. When you come together in church, put aside empty talk. Concentrate on the Scriptures. We are your books.[61] So pay attention, and you'll see. The Holy Spirit will come on Pentecost. And this is how He will come: He will show Himself in tongues of fire. For He breathes charity into us. We are set on fire for God, and we spurn the world, and the straw in us is burned up, and our hearts are, so to speak, refined into gold. Therefore, the Holy Spirit draws near, the fire after the water, and you become bread, what is the Body of Christ.[62] That's the way in which unity is symbolized.

You now grasp the sacraments in order. First, after the Prayer [of the Faithful], you are admonished to lift up your heart. This befits members of Christ. For if you have become members of Christ, where is your Head?[63] A body's members have a head. If the Head had not gone on ahead, the members would not follow along. Where has our Head gone? What did you say when you handed back the Creed? "On the third day He rose again from the dead; He ascended into heaven; He is seated at the right hand of the Father." Therefore, our Head is in heaven. That's why after the "Lift up your heart" is said, you

60. "Sacrament of exorcism": Augustine, one of the pioneers of Western sacramental theology, used the term "sacrament" much more broadly than is done today. Here and elsewhere, he uses it to mean any "sacred sign," and thus can apply it to ceremonies such as exorcisms, or, as he does later in this sermon, to particular moments within the broader Sunday liturgy. For helpful perspectives, see Emmanuel Cutrone, "Sacrament," *AugEncy*, 741–47.

61. "We are your books" (*Codices vestri nos sumus*): The phrase is deeply evocative, but also ambiguous. The "we" may refer either to the readers who read the Scriptures or to Augustine (or any other clergy) who interpret the Scriptures.

62. On this extended metaphor of "becoming bread" and its relation to baptismal training and rites, see Harmless, *Augustine and the Catechumenate*, 316–22.

63. "Members . . . Head": Augustine here is playing on the Pauline theme of the Church as Christ's Body and the risen Christ as the Head (Col 1:18; Eph 4:11–16). This is a major theme in his *Expositions of the Psalms*; see Chapter 5.

answer: "We have lifted it up to the Lord."[64] And you should not attribute this lifting-up of the heart to the Lord to your own strength, to your own merits, to your own hard work—for this lifting-up of your hearts to God is a gift of God. That is why the bishop or the presbyter who is offering [the Eucharist], after people answer, "We have lifted them to the Lord," goes on to say, "Let us give thanks to the Lord our God," because we have lifted up our hearts. Let us give thanks, because unless he did give [this grace] we would still have our hearts on earth. And you bear witness to this, saying, "It is right and just," for we give thanks to Him who caused us to lift up our hearts to our Head.

Then after the sanctification[65] of God's sacrifice—for He wanted our very selves to be His sacrifice, which is demonstrated by where that sacrifice first took place and that's the sign of the thing itself, what we ourselves are. See, that's where, once the sanctification is finished, we say the Lord's Prayer, which you received and which you handed back. After this, the "Peace be with you" is said, and Christians kiss one another with a holy kiss. This is a sign of peace. As the lips indicate, make peace in your conscience; that is, when your lips draw near to those of your brothers or sisters, do not let your heart draw back from their hearts.

Great, therefore, are these sacraments, extraordinarily great. Do you want to know how they are to be commemorated? The Apostle says: "Whoever eats the body of Christ or drinks the cup of the Lord unworthily is guilty of the body and blood of the Lord" (1 Cor 11:27). What is "receiving unworthily"? To receive in contempt, to receive in mockery. Do not let [the sacrament] seem of little value to you just because you can see it. What you see passes away, but the invisible reality it is a sign of does not pass away, but endures. Look: it is received, it is eaten, it is consumed. Is the body of Christ really consumed? Is the Church of Christ really consumed? Are the members of Christ really consumed? Hardly! Here they are cleansed; there they will be crowned. The "what" that it is a sign of will endure even though the sign seems to pass away. Receive, then, that you may understand, that you may hold unity in your hearts, that your heart be lifted up, fixed always on high. Let your hope not be on earth, but in heaven. Let your faith be firm in God. Let it be acceptable to God. Because what you do not see now, but believe, that you will see there, where you will rejoice without end.[66]

---

64. "Lift up your heart" (Sursum cor): Augustine quotes here and elsewhere in this paragraph from the traditional opening dialogue of the eucharistic prayer. See Enrico Mazza, The Origins of the Eucharistic Prayer, trans. Ronald E. Lane (Collegeville, MN: Liturgical Press, 1995).

65. "Sanctification" (sanctificatio): Augustine uses this term rather than "consecration" to refer to the change of the eucharistic elements.

66. S. 227 (PL 38:1099–101); my trans., based on Muldowney, FOTC 38:195–98. On this within Augustine's broader theology, see J. Patout Burns, "The Eucharist as the Foundation of Christian Unity in North African Theology," 2000 St. Augustine Lecture, Augustinian Studies 32 (2001): 1–23.

CHAPTER 5

AUGUSTINE THE EXEGETE

❧

First-time readers of Augustine are struck by his deep biblicism. Every page, every paragraph, is threaded with biblical quotations, biblical allusions, biblical images. Augustine did more than comment on the Bible: he *spoke* Bible, making its words his words. Once, on the anniversary of his ordination, he explained why: "From what I feast on, from that I feed you. I am a table servant, not the master of the house. From what I set before you, from that I too draw my life."[1] For Augustine, the Bible's words were food, were life itself. In this chapter, we turn to the Bible Augustine gazed upon as he preached, exploring how he read it and how he opened up its words to feed his hearers.

Augustine's culture held books in deep esteem. In the ancient world, books were valuable commodities, made of expensive materials and preserved with great care.[2] To be educated in the ancient world was to be a reader. Ancient education focused almost obsessively on mastering "the great books." Educated Latins like Augustine had spent long years not only reading their Vergil, Cicero, Horace, and Ovid; they memorized them and could quote and analyze them word-for-word, line-by-line.[3] Educated Christians brought such skills to reading the Bible. But for Augustine, the Bible was not just another classic to be memorized, quoted, and analyzed. Addressing pagan readers in his *City of God*, he noted that the Scriptures' "divine authority puts them above the literature of all other peoples and brings under their sway every type of human genius."[4] This is his view in a nutshell: that the Bible is no

---

1. S. 339.3 (PL 38:1481); my trans. Cf. *s.* 101.4; 179A.8; and 260D.2.
2. See Harry Y. Gamble, *Books and Readers in the Early Church: A History of Early Christian Texts* (New Haven: Yale University Press, 1995).
3. See Henri I. Marrou, *A History of Education in Antiquity*, trans. George Lamb (1956; reprint: Madison: University of Wisconsin Press, 1982); R. A. Kaster, *Guardians of Language: The Grammarian and Society in Late Antiquity* (Berkeley: University of California Press, 1988).
4. *Civ. Dei* 11.1 (CCL 48:321); trans. Walsh and Monahan, FOTC 14:187.

mere classic of world literature; that its words hold a wisdom and a power, a density and a mystery, befitting divine speech; that of its very nature, the Bible draws in the restless, searching human mind, orders it, and elevates it.

Augustine normally read the Bible in Latin translation, the so-called Ve- tus Latina ("Old Latin").[5] Its various versions—and there seem to have been several—used a clumsy, clunky Latin. When the teenage Augustine first read them, he thought them laughably bad literature compared to the elegant prose stylings of a Cicero. But on the far side of his conversion, he saw things differently. He came not only to love the broader biblical message and the epic biblical narratives; he even came to savor the Vetus Latina's often odd and ungainly turns-of-phrase.

Meanwhile, Jerome (d. ca. 420), the greatest biblical scholar of the day, had settled in a monastery in far-off Bethlehem and had set himself to the task of replacing the Vetus Latina with an elegant new translation.[6] Jerome had linguistic skills as had few before him (and as no one would again un- til the Renaissance), combining a solid command of both Greek and biblical Hebrew with the gifts of a Latin stylist. Jerome's translation, the Vulgate, be- came the Bible for Western Christianity during the Middle Ages. Around 394 or 395, Augustine embarked on a long-running and, initially, quite conten- tious correspondence with Jerome. The exchange bore fruit, prompting Au- gustine to articulate some deeply held convictions about the Bible and the task of interpretation. In one letter, Augustine touched on the difference be- tween their respective talents and respective ministries: "For I neither have nor can have as much knowledge of the divine Scriptures as I see abounds in you. If I do gain any stock of knowledge, I pay it out immediately to the peo- ple of God."[7]

The young Augustine had found the Bible, especially its Old Testament, a serious stumbling block. Only in his 30s, listening week after week to Am- brose's "spiritual" interpretations, did he slowly come to consider that Chris- tianity might have some intellectual plausibility. In *Confessions*, he noted how Ambrose used to quote 2 Cor 3:6 ("The letter kills, but the spirit gives life") as though an exegetical principle. On the far side of ordination, Augustine passed on to his North African congregation this Ambrosian fondness for "spiritual" interpretation. Readers today tend to describe Augustine's meth- od as "allegorical." That is inexact. "Figurative" was Augustine's usual term

5. See Philip Burton, *The Old Latin Gospels: A Study of Their Texts and Language*, OECS (New York: Oxford University Press, 2001).

6. On Jerome, see J. N. D. Kelly, *Jerome: His Life, Writings and Controversies* (New York: Harper & Row, 1975); Megan Hale Williams, *The Monk and the Book: Jerome and the Making of Christian Scholarship* (Chicago: Univer- sity of Chicago Press, 2006); Mark Vessey, "Jerome," *AugEncy*, 460–62.

7. Ep. 73.2.5 (CCL 31A:47); trans. Parsons, FOTC 12:332.

for it. He not only practiced figurative methods, but also justified their place within a broader theory of interpretation, sketching core principles in his *On Christian Teaching*. As we saw, this work's fourth book focused on the art of preaching and was composed only at the very end of his career, around 427. But the work's first three books had been written 30 years earlier, around 397, and were among the first projects Augustine took on after becoming bishop.[8] In their pages, he meditates on many matters: the canon of Scripture, the vagaries of the Vetus Latina, the need to know biblical languages, biblical geography, and much else. He also argues a basic thesis: that the Bible, however simple its surface, masks deeper mysteries; that for those who wrestle with it, its wording reveals a vast network of hidden meanings and a subtle, under-the-surface pedagogy that exercises both mind and heart for the ascent to God. Augustine's practice of figurative interpretation would influence how Western Christians read the Bible for the next thousand years.

The inspiration for writing such a handbook probably came from Tyconius (d. ca. 400), a lay Donatist theologian who, in the late 380s, had written the so-called *Book of Rules* (*Liber regularum*). Tyconius claimed to offer seven "mystic keys" that unlocked the Bible's "closed doors" and enabled one to walk sure-footedly through the Bible's "vast forest of prophecy . . . as by pathways of light."[9] From Tyconius, Augustine drew the idea of the Church as a "mixed-up body" (*corpus permixtum*) of good and evil persons, an idea he later turned against the Donatists. From Tyconius, he also drew the idea of the *totus Christus*, "the whole Christ." This theme became the gravitational center of his exegesis of the Psalms. Augustine came to commend Tyconius's work as a "great help in penetrating the hidden meanings of the Scripture."[10] Many are aware that reading Plotinus and Porphyry revolutionized Augustine's philosophic outlook; fewer appreciated how Tyconius revolutionized his reading of Scripture and, indeed, of world history.[11]

Over his career, Augustine focused his vast literary energies on four biblical sources. The first was Genesis, for which he wrote three commentaries: *On Genesis Against the Manichees* (*De Genesi adversus Manichaeos*); *On the Literal Interpretation of Genesis, An Unfinished Book* (*De Genesi ad litteram liber imperfectus*); and the massive *On the Literal Interpretation of Genesis* (*De Genesi ad litteram*). To

8. *Retr.* 2.4.1 (CCL 57:92–93). He completed two-thirds of Book III, breaking off at 3.25.35. On the context, the issues, and a possible reason for this break-off, see Charles Kannengiesser, "The Interrupted *De doctrina christiana*," in Arnold and Bright, *De doctrina: A Classic*, 3–13. The first two books circulated independently, as evidenced by a remarkable early manuscript; see Kenneth B. Steinhauser, "Codex Leningradensis Q.v.13: Some Unresolved Problems," in *De doctrina: A Classic*, 33–43.

9. Tyconius, *Liber regularum*, praef., in *De doctrina christiana* 3.30.43 (Green, 174); my trans.

10. *Doc. Chr.* 3.30.42 (Green, 172); my trans.

11. Paula Fredriksen, "Tyconius," *AugEncy*, 855. While Augustine appropriated Tyconius's ideas, he also transfigured them, taking them places where Tyconius would have never dreamed of going.

these should be added *Confessions*, Books 11–13, and *City of God*, Books 11–16, which offer lengthy analyses of and meditations on Genesis' first three chapters, its stories of creation and fall. Exegesis of Genesis was an apt vehicle for Augustine the ex-Manichee to affirm in depth and detail his faith in a God who, unlike the God of the Manichees, was understood to have created the earth and the visible cosmos and declared them "good." Genesis also helped Augustine focus his search for and meditation upon the origin and nature of evil. His investigations would crystallize around a distinctive understanding of original sin and its massive consequences for world history. We will defer examining his Genesis commentaries until later chapters on the Manichees, on the *City of God*, and on the Pelagians.

The second was the Psalms. At Augustine's baptism, the "sweet singing" of the Psalms had left him drenched in tears. Their music continued to cast a spell over him. Nearly every page of *Confessions* quotes or echoes the Psalms. The Psalms, he came to believe, touched the "ears of the heart," drawing in hearers with the "sweet sound of someone softly strumming an instrument."[12] Augustine read the book more as a sort of fifth Gospel than as Old Testament. Its lyrics, he believed, were sung by the voice of Christ—by turns, the voice of the Risen Lord and the voice of His body, the Church on earth: "It is His voice in all the psalms: now strumming gently, now moaning, now rejoicing in hope for what will come, now sighing about things as they are."[13] Augustine became convinced of the Psalms' therapeutic power and called on his congregation to lay claim to the Psalms' emotional repertoire as a way to repair and renew their own damaged hearts. By career's end, he had commented on all 150 psalms, mostly in sermons delivered before a live audience.[14] These were collected in his *Expositions of the Psalms* (*Enarrationes in Psalmos*), a massive work twice the length of *City of God*.

The third was the Gospel of John. Augustine commented on the entire Gospel via 124 sermons ("tractates"), many delivered before a live audience, others dictated to stenographers. Augustine loved John's Gospel for its sublimity.[15] "The evangelist John," he once told his congregation, "soars to greater heights like an eagle; he transcends the murky darkness of earth; he looks upon the light of truth with a steadier gaze."[16] What John the apostle gazed

---

12. En. Ps. 41.9 (CCL 38:467); my trans.

13. En. Ps. 42.1 (CCL 38:474); my trans. Cf. en. Ps. 96.2

14. One exception was his commentary on Psalm 118 [119], which, because of its length, Augustine dictated to scribes. Much of his commentary on Psalms 1–32, among his earliest exegeses, are notes prepared for a sermon rather than a transcription of the actual live performance—and thus unlike the bulk of the *Enarrationes*.

15. On this, see Marie-François Berrouard, *Introduction aux Homélies de saint Augustin sur l'Évangile de saint Jean*, CEASA 170 (Paris: Institut d'Études Augustiniennes, 2004), esp. 39–44.

16. Jo. ev. tr. 15.1 (BA 71:756); trans. Rettig, FOTC 78:78.

on was the Word, at once the divine Word (Jn 1:1) and the Word-made-Flesh (Jn 1:14), and the unfathomable paradox of this captivated Augustine. Where the Synoptic Gospels focused on Jesus' concrete words and deeds, John's Gospel probed their inner meanings. This appealed to Augustine's taste, for he was fascinated less by history's facts and more by its deeper rhythms and undercurrents.

The fourth was not a book, but an author, St. Paul. Reading Paul's Letter to the Romans had catalyzed Augustine's conversion back in the garden in Milan. After ordination, he hoped to write at length on Paul. He did author a modest commentary on Galatians and a miscellany of reflections on Romans based on a question-and-answer session held in Carthage. But his grand plans for a full-scale commentary on Romans fizzled out after examining only its opening verses.[17] Paul's letters shaped Augustine's biblical exegesis rather differently. One finds him citing Paul repeatedly, in virtually every sermon, commentary, and treatise, but most often, he commented not so much on Paul himself; rather, he used Paul to comment on the Bible as a whole. Paul's letters were his window on the Bible, his lenses for reading it, and he invoked Paul not only to resolve exegetical problems, but at least as often to articulate them.

That said, one work of Pauline exegesis does stand out. In 396, Augustine, newly installed as bishop of Hippo, received a letter from his old mentor in Milan, Simplicianus, asking him to address two troublesome texts from Romans. Augustine's reply, *To Simplicianus on Various Questions* (Ad Simplicianum de diversis quaestionibus), records startling new insights on grace, free will, and divine election. These, in turn, opened up fresh new perspectives on his life's journey, which he would record, soon after, in *Confessions*. Augustine came to see this early exegetical work as an anticipation of his debate with Pelagius. We will, therefore, explore this text not here, but in Chapter 10 on the Pelagian controversy.

These were his major, but hardly his only, biblical projects. He meditated on Jesus' most famous words in *On the Lord's Sermon on the Mount* (De sermone Domini in monte); he probed overlaps and contradictions among the Synoptic Gospels in *On the Agreement Among the Evangelists* (De consensu evangelistarum) and *Questions on the Gospels* (Quaestiones evangeliorum); he addressed conundrums in the historical books of the Old Testament in his *Questions on the Heptateuch* (Quaestiones in Heptateuchum) and *Sayings on the Heptateuch* (Locutiones in Hepta-

---

17. Eric Plumer, ed. and trans., *Augustine's Commentary on Galatians*, OECS (New York: Oxford University Press, 2003); Paula Fredriksen Landes, ed. and trans., *Augustine on Romans: Propositions from the Epistle to the Romans and Unfinished Commentary on the Epistle to the Romans*, Texts & Translations, vol. 23 (Chico, CA: Scholars Press, 1982).

teuchum). Of course, his exegesis was hardly limited to sermons or commentaries. Virtually everything he wrote, whether an ordinary letter or an erudite treatise, cites and discusses scriptural texts and scriptural issues in one way or another.

In this chapter, Books 1–3 of *On Christian Teaching* will provide the organizing framework and will serve as a springboard to explore issues. We will also see how its broad theoretical principles take flesh in his routine exegetical practice by focusing on sermons from the *Tractates on the Gospel of John* and *Expositions of the Psalms*. While Augustine's exegetical theories and exegetical practices do cohere closely, there is nothing either wooden or predictable about Augustine the exegete sitting down to the nitty-gritty task of interpreting specific texts. His theoretical statements do little to prepare one for how, in exegetical practice, the unexpected is routine: abrupt turns, sudden syntheses, surprising conjunctions, bold poetic flights, and memorable turns-of-phrase.

⁊⸹

GOSPEL AS MIRROR, CHRIST AS TEACHER, AUGUSTINE AS STUDENT

Augustine was acutely conscious that as bishop he sat, quite literally, above the heads of his congregation, elevated on the cathedra in the apse of the church. This visual prominence could be read—or misread—as symbolic of a spiritual superiority and thus a contradiction of the servant-leadership Jesus demanded in the Gospel. In the opening of one sermon, Augustine sets out what he sees as the relationship between Christ, the Scriptures, himself, and the gathered congregation. From Sermon 301A:

(1) The Gospel and living Word of God, what penetrates into the soul's marrow and probes the heart's axis: This is offered to all of us for the sake of our health. Its soothing touch does not comfort whoever does not give comfort to another. Look, the Gospel is put here in front of us as a mirror in which we are able to look at ourselves, and if, in our glimpsing into it, we happen to see dirt on our faces, we may wipe them clean so that the next time we glimpse into its mirror we won't have to blush.

And so the crowd was following the Lord, as we heard when the Gospel was read, and He turned and spoke to those who were following Him.[18] Now if those things which He spoke were spoken only to His twelve apostles, each one of us could say: "He's talking to them, not us. That's something relevant

---

18. "He . . . spoke to those who were following": This sermon focuses on Lk 14: 25–35. Augustine is alluding here to Lk 14:25, noting that Jesus addresses "the great crowd."

for shepherds; something else is relevant for us sheep." But He was speaking to the crowds following Him. And so He said it to all, all of them and all of us. No, just because we weren't there, that doesn't mean it wasn't said to us. We, too, believe in the One whom they were able to see. We hold on in faith to the One whom they gazed upon with their eyes. . . .

(2) Let's go, therefore, and let's listen to what He said, and, as I said, let us take a hard look at ourselves, and, whatever we find missing in ourselves, let us refine things with great diligence to the standard of beauty which is pleasing in His eyes. And because we are not self-sufficient, let us call upon Him for help. May the One who formed us re-form us. May the One who created us re-create us. May the One who constructed us re-construct us, that we may come to integrity. . . .

If it were only those people back then who could be called disciples, then the Gospel would not be spoken to us. But because, as the Scriptures bear witness, all Christians are disciples of Christ ("for," as it says, "One alone is your teacher: Christ" [Mt 23:10]), let those who claim Christ as teacher not deny that they're Christ's followers. Now just because I speak to you from this elevated place [in the basilica], that does not mean that I am your teacher. That One—Christ—is the teacher of us all, the One whose professorial chair sits above all the heavens. Under that One we come together, convening as a single school. And you and I—we are fellow students. But I'm here to advise you, just the way older students tend to do.[19]

SCRIPTURES' MYSTERIES

Around 411, Augustine was encouraged by Flavius Marcellinus,[20] a high-ranking imperial official, to write to a circle of pagan aristocrats who strongly objected to Christianity. Augustine was conscious that such a highly educated group looked down on the Bible's inelegant prose, much as he had done as a young man. In a letter to the circle's leader, Volusianus, Augustine makes some poignant remarks about how he now viewed the Bible's surface style and its hidden depths. From Letter 137:

(1.3) The depth, the profundity, of Christian literature is so great that I might have made some day-to-day progress in it if I had tried to apply myself to it exclusively from my earliest childhood to extreme old age, spending all my free time on it, all my effort, and if I had had a better gift of mind. I

19. S. 301A.1–2 = Denis 17 (MA 1:81–82); my trans.
20. On Flavius Marcellinus, see Chapter 3, note 32.

am not saying that it is too difficult to attain to the knowledge necessary for salvation. But whoever remains firm in the faith (without which one cannot live religiously and uprightly) finds so many truths shrouded in the manifold darkness of mystery, and one finds such a depth of wisdom lying hidden, not only in the words in which the truths are expressed, but also in the truths themselves, which are to be known, that even the most advanced in years, the most penetrating in mind, the most ardent in zeal for learning, might find himself described by what the same Scripture says elsewhere: "When a person has reached the end, then shall he begin" (Sir 18:6). . . .

(5.18) The very language in which Holy Scripture is woven is accessible to all, though very, very few penetrate it. In its easily understood parts it speaks to the heart of the unlearned and the learned like a familiar friend who uses no guile, but in those truths that it veils in mystery, it does not raise itself aloft with proud speech. Hence, the backward and untutored mind dares to draw near to it as a poor man to a rich one, because it invites all in simple language and feeds their minds with its teachings in plain words, while training them in the truth by its hidden message, having the same effect in both the obvious and the obscure. But lest the obvious should cause disgust, the hidden truths arouse longing; longing brings on certain renewal; renewal brings sweet inner knowledge. By these means depraved minds are set right, small ones are nourished, great ones are filled with delight.[21]

Exegetical ABCs

Augustine composed On Christian Teaching as a way to reflect on and articulate principles of biblical interpretation. He thought of the task as teaching exegetical literacy. From On Christian Teaching, preface and Book 1:

(1) There are certain norms for interpreting the Scriptures, which, I am convinced, can be profitably presented to those devoted to its study. Such people may benefit not only personally by acquiring knowledge from those who have unveiled the mysteries of the sacred writings, but may also learn how to disclose these mysteries to others. I intend to hand on these principles to those who are able and are willing to grasp them, provided, of course, that our Lord and God not refuse to supply me, as I write, with the same help which he usually grants me whenever I reflect upon the subject. . . .

(9) Now one who reads a text out loud to listeners simply articulates what

21. Ep. 137.1.3–5.18 (CSEL 44:99–123); trans. Parson, FOTC 20:19–34 (modified).

he sees, while one who teaches literacy does so in such a way that others, too, learn how to read. Both instill the know-how they have received. In a similar way, [a preacher] who explains to hearers what he understands in the Scriptures acts a bit like one in the office of reader, articulating things he gazes upon, while one who teaches others how to understand the underlying principles of Scripture is like a person teaching literacy. Someone who knows how to read has no need of another reader whenever he comes upon a book, no need to have someone tell him what is written in it. In a similar way, someone who has learned the principles that I am proposing here, whenever he comes upon some obscurity in the Scriptures, learns to observe certain rules, as he did in reading, and does not require another interpreter to lay open for him whatever is obscure. Instead, by following certain clues, he may arrive at the hidden meaning on his own, without any false step, or, at least, without falling into some absurdly misguided view.

([Book 1] 1.1) There are two things that the whole treatment of the Scriptures depends on: a method of discovering what we need to understand and a method of presenting what we have understood.[22]

The Biblical Canon

The first step is obvious: The exegete needs to read the entire Bible. But that is only the beginning. Like other early Christian exegetes, Augustine was convinced that the best way to interpret the Bible is with the Bible. This method presumed that one had the entire Bible at one's fingertips, that one had, for all practical purposes, memorized it. But which Bible? The Bible, Augustine recognized, is a library, not a book. The question, therefore, is which books make up its canon (that is, the list of books Christians officially regard as the word of God).[23] The canon of the Hebrew Bible—what Christians came to think of and speak of as "the Old Testament"—only began to be settled in the late first century. Early Christians embraced the longer canon of Greek-speaking Jews embodied in the Septuagint (more on this below). The canon of the New Testament was largely settled by the late second century, in part, because of a pitched debate with gnostic Christians

---

22. *Doc. Chr.* praef. 1–9; 1.1.1 (Green, 2–12); my trans. "Method of discovering . . . method of presenting": This is the basic outline of *De doctrina christiana*: Bks. 1–3 focus on "discovery," that is, his exegetical principles; Bk. 4, as we saw, focuses on "presentation," that is, his rhetorical principles and reflections. "Discovery" (*inventio*) refers to the subject matter of the address. On this, George A. Kennedy, *A New History of Classical Rhetoric* (Princeton: Princeton University Press, 1994).

23. See Bruce Metzger, *The Canon of the New Testament: Its Origin, Development, and Significance* (Oxford: Clarendon Press, 1987); Joseph T. Lienhard, *The Bible, the Church, and Authority: The Canon of the Christian Bible in History and Theology* (Collegeville, MN: Liturgical Press, 1995).

*who had authored and appealed to a bevy of apocryphal gospels.*²⁴ *In the fourth century, the canon, while no longer a highly contested issue, does resurface as a concern. In 393, at a council in Hippo, the North African bishops set out an official list of books they considered authentic.*²⁵ *Augustine passes on this North African canon and the principle of catholicity. From* On Christian Teaching, Book 2:

(8.12) The most expert investigator of the divine Scriptures will be a person who has in the first place read them all and has a good working knowledge of them—if not an in-depth understanding, at least a basic familiarity from reading them, especially those books which are called "canonical." . . . In terms of canonical Scriptures, [the investigator] should follow the authority of the majority of Catholic churches, which, of course, includes those found worthy to have been apostolic sees and to have received apostolic letters.²⁶ He should hold on to the following principle regarding the canon: to prefer those books which are recognized by all Catholic churches over those books which certain churches do not accept. In regard to those books not accepted by all, let him favor those which the greater number of churches and the more eminent churches accept rather than those upheld by a minority of churches or by churches with lesser authority. . . .

(8.13) The complete canon of the scriptures that we are talking about turning our attention to consists of the following books: the five of Moses, that is, Genesis, Exodus, Leviticus, Numbers, and Deuteronomy; the one book of Joshua, son of Nun, and the one of Judges; a little book which is called Ruth, which seems to belong instead to the beginning of Kings; then four books of Kings²⁷ and the two of Chronicles (these do not follow in sequence after [Kings], but, as it were, run alongside them, parallel to them). These are the historical books, which contain a connected narrative of the times and have an orderly arrangement. There are others, histories of a different order, which are not united to this order nor to one another, such as the books of Job and Tobit and Esther and Judith, and the two books of the Maccabees, and the two of Ezra.²⁸ These last two follow the basic historical order which

---

24. With the discovery of the gnostic Nag Hammadi library in 1945 and with the publication of the gnostic *Gospel of Judas* in 2006, we can better appreciate the high stakes of this debate within early Christian communities. See Kurt Rudolph, *Gnosis: The Nature and History of Gnosticism* (San Francisco: Harper San Francisco, 1987); Bart D. Ehrman, *Lost Christianities: The Battles for Scripture and the Faiths We Never Knew* (New York: Oxford University Press, 2003); Madeleine Scopello, ed., *The Gospel of Judas in Context*, Nag Hammadi and Manichaean Studies 62 (Leiden and Boston: Brill, 2008).

25. Council of Hippo (393), *Canon* 38; reaffirmed at the Council of Carthage (397), *Canon* 47.

26. "Apostolic sees": cities such as Jerusalem, Antioch, Alexandria, and Rome. "Received apostolic letters": towns that were recipients of Pauline letters, such as Corinth, Ephesus, and Thessalonica.

27. "Four books of Kings": 1 and 2 Samuel, 1 and 2 Kings.

28. "Two of Ezra": Ezra and Nehemiah.

had left off with the books of Kings and Chronicles. Then come the Prophets, which include David's one book, the Psalms, and Solomon's three books: Proverbs, Canticle of Canticles, and Ecclesiastes. The [next] two books, the one entitled Wisdom and the other, Ecclesiasticus, are said to be Solomon's, because of a certain similarity of style, but Jesus, son of Sirach, has been the one most consistently regarded as their composer.[29] Because they have been found worthy to be included as authoritative, they are to be numbered among the prophetic books. The rest are books of those who are called prophets in the proper sense of the term. There are the individual books of the twelve prophets, which are connected with one another (since they have never been separated) and are counted as one; these are their names: Hosea, Joel, Amos, Obadiah, Jonah, Micah, Nahum, Habakkuk, Zephaniah, Haggai, Zechariah, and Malachi. Then there are the four prophets, each with his own volume: Isaiah, Jeremiah, Daniel, and Ezekiel. These forty-four books contain the authoritative Old Testament.

As for the authoritative New Testament, there are the four Gospel books: according to Matthew, according to Mark, according to Luke, according to John; fourteen epistles of the Apostle Paul: to the Romans, two to the Corinthians, to the Galatians, to the Ephesians, to the Philippians, two to the Thessalonians, to the Colossians, two to Timothy, to Titus, to Philemon, to the Hebrews; two epistles of Peter, three of John, one of Jude, and one of James; one book of the Acts of the Apostles and one of the Apocalypse of John.

(9.14) From all these books, those who fear God and have a docile piety seek out the will of God. The first step in this laborious task is, as I have said, to know these books. And even if we may not yet understand them, nevertheless, by reading them we can either memorize them or become somewhat acquainted with them. Then those things asserted clearly in them, whether guidelines about how to live or rules about what to believe, should be studied with greater care and diligence. The greater one's intellectual capacity, the more of these one finds. In texts where the Scriptures put things plainly and openly, we discover all the things which concern faith and moral living, namely, hope and love. . . . Then only after acquiring a certain familiarity with the language of the divine Scriptures should one try to uncover and analyze thoroughly the obscure passages, selecting examples from clearer texts to explain those that are more obscure, and allowing the testimony of indisputable texts to remove the uncertainties from doubtful passages. In this

---

29. "Jesus, son of Sirach": In *retr.* 2.4.2 (CCL 57:93), Augustine corrected himself, noting that Sirach was the author *not* of the Book of Wisdom, but only of Ecclesiasticus.

matter, one's memory is of very great value. Without a good one, these principles cannot be of much help.[30]

EXILES SEEKING HOME

Augustine believed that one has to see the big picture first. So he devotes the entire first book of On Christian Teaching *to setting out certain broad, philosophical perspectives. He begins by defining terms and making a series of philosophical distinctions whose relevance emerges only slowly. One initial and famous distinction is between "things to be enjoyed" and "things to be used."[31] For Augustine, God is the "thing to be enjoyed" since God alone provides genuine happiness. All other "things" need to be read as signs of God's presence and used as goods that spur us back to God. This lengthy discussion seems, at first sight, oblique to the practical task of interpreting the Bible, but its relevance is teased out slowly. In the passage below, I highlight a key thread in his argument. As Augustine sees it, the human condition is one of exile. We, like Odysseus, may yearn to get back to our homeland, but somehow along the way we have become distracted, seduced by other beauties. Augustine here lays the foundation for his view that the Bible is a collection of road signs that helps us to read the world right and so orients us to use the world as a roadway to get back to God, our true home. From* On Christian Teaching, *Book 1:*

(3.3) There are, then, some things that are to be enjoyed, others that are to be used, still others that are to be enjoyed and used. Those that are to be enjoyed make us happy. Those that are to be used help us as we strive for happiness and, in a certain sense, sustain us so that we are able to arrive at and cling to those realities that make us happy. But if we, who both use and enjoy things, strive to enjoy things we are supposed to use, we find our progress impeded and sometimes even turned aside. Because we are fettered by affection for lesser goods, we are either delayed from gaining those that we are to enjoy or are even drawn away from them altogether.

(4.4) To enjoy something means to cling to it with affection for its own sake. To use a thing is to employ what we have received for our use to obtain what we want, provided that it is right for us to want it. (An unlawfully applied use ought rather to be termed "abuse.") Suppose, then, that we were

---

30. *Doc. Chr.* 2.8.12–9.14 (Green, 66–70); my trans. On this, see Anne-Marie LaBonnardière, "The Canon of Sacred Scripture," in Pamela Bright, ed. and trans., *Augustine and the Bible* (Notre Dame: University of Notre Dame Press, 1999), 26–41.

31. On this famous distinction, Raymond Canning, "Uti/frui," *AugEncy*, 859–61. For a valuable, but rather technical study, see Oliver O'Donovan, "Usus and Fruitio in Augustine, *De doctrina christiana* I," *Journal of Theological Studies*, n.s. 33 (1982): 361–97.

wandering pilgrims who could not live happily except in our native land, and that we, feeling miserable from wandering and yearning to end this home-sickness, decided to go back home: we would need vehicles of some sort, to go either by land or by sea, that we would use to reach our homeland, where we could find true enjoyment.[32] But suppose we ended up enjoying the plea-sures of the journey, even the delights of the vehicles themselves, getting side-tracked, enjoying what we should be using, and unwilling to finish our jour-ney home quickly, having become ensnared in wrong-turned pleasures, and so alienating ourselves from a homeland whose savory sweetness could make us truly happy. So it is that we are "wanderers from the Lord" (2 Cor 5:6) on the road of this mortal life. If we wish to return to our homeland, where we can be truly happy, we must use this world, not enjoy it, in a such way that the "invisible attributes of God may be clearly seen, being understood through the things that were made" (Rom 1:20), in other words, so that we may grasp what is eternal and spiritual through what is bodily and temporal.

(5.5) The thing to be enjoyed is the Father and the Son and the Holy Spir-it—at once, Trinity and the one highest reality shared and enjoyed in com-mon by all. . . . (10.10) Since we are to enjoy fully Truth itself, who lives un-changeably, and since that Truth—God the Trinity, the Author and Founder of the universe—takes good care of those things that He has created, the self must be purified that it may be able to look upon that light and cling to it. Let us consider this process of cleansing as a sort of journeying or sailing to our homeland. We are not brought any closer to the One who is ever present by moving from place to place, but by good desire and a good lifestyle.

(11.11) This we would not be able to do unless Wisdom Himself deigned to share such a great weakness as ours and to put forward for us a paradigm for living, not being anything other than completely human, since we ourselves are human. Now when we come to Him, we act wisely; but when He came to us, he was thought to have acted foolishly by people full of pride. But "the foolishness of God is wiser than the wisdom of human beings, and the weak-ness of God is stronger than the strength of human beings" (1 Cor 1:25). So though He Himself is our homeland, He made Himself the highway to that homeland.[33]

---

32. "Our homeland": This whole passage echoes Plotinus, *Enneads* 1.6.8.

33. *Doc. Chr.* 1.3.3–11.11 (Green, 14-22); my trans. "Highway . . . homeland" (*viam . . . patriam*): This theme is central to Augustine's Christology: see s. 123.3; *en. Ps.* 123.2. For a survey, see Goulven Madec, *La patrie et la voie: Le Christ dans la vie et la pensée de saint Augustin*, Collection 'Jésus et Jésus-Christ' 36 (Paris: Desclée, 1989).

THE LOVE COMMAND

As the argument of Book 1 unfolds, Augustine edges toward the problem of biblical interpretation. This distinction between enjoyment and use, as well as this journey analogy, are meant to situate how we should understand human life and, by implication, how we understand the Bible's function within Christian living. As we journey the road of life, we need to get oriented, get turned the right way. The Bible makes that possible. It is like a compass whose needle points in one direction: to love. The entire meaning of the Bible, Augustine insists, lies in Christ's double commandment of love of God and love of neighbor. This core message orients not only Christian life, but also orients how any specific biblical text is interpreted. If one's interpretation contradicts this, then, according to Augustine, one has not understood the text. From On Christian Teaching, *Book 1:*

(26.27) There is no need to command us to love ourselves and our own bodies, because we love who we are—and also what is below us, yet belongs to us—by an unshakeable law of nature. (It extends even to brute beasts, for even animals love themselves and their own bodies.) It remained only to impose commandments upon us concerning God, who is above us, and our neighbor, who is beside us. "You shall love the Lord your God," He said, "with your whole heart, and with your whole soul, and with your whole mind, and you shall love your neighbor as yourself. On these two commandments depend the whole Law and the Prophets" (Mt 22:37–40). Now the aim of this commandment is a twofold love of God and neighbor. . . . (28.29) Of all who can enjoy God with us, we love some whom we help and some by whom we are helped; some whose assistance we stand in need of and some whose wants we relieve; some on whom we neither bestow any benefit nor expect that they bestow any upon us. Nevertheless, we ought to desire that they all love God with us, and all the help that we either give them or receive from them must be directed to that one purpose. . . .

(35.39) Therefore, the summary of all that has been said since we began our discussion of things[34] is to understand that the fulfillment and the end of the law and of all divine Scriptures is the love of the Thing to be enjoyed [that is, God] and the love of the one who can enjoy that First Thing with us [that is, the neighbor] (since there is no need for a commandment that one love oneself) (Rom 13:9–10). In order that we might know this and might be able to do it, divine Providence created for our salvation the whole temporal dispensation. This we ought to use, but not with any permanent love or enjoyment. Our loves should be like transitory pleasures felt towards being on the

---

34. "Summary of . . . discussion of things": Augustine is referring to his outline of *Doc. Chr.*: Bk. 1 focuses on "things," "realities"; Bks. 2 and 3 (cited below) focus on "signs."

road or felt about the vehicles or other sorts of tools (it may be possible to express this more appropriately) so that we love the means that carry us along for the sake of the end towards which we are being carried.

(36.40). So whoever, in his own view, thinks he has understood the divine Scriptures, or some part of them, and yet does not, by his interpretation, build up the twofold love of God and neighbor, then that person has not yet understood the text.[35]

Later Augustine refers back to this discussion and pinpoints its application to biblical interpretation in a series of definitions and aphorisms. From On Christian Teaching, *Book 3:*

(10.14) I must first point out the method of discovering whether a passage is literal or figurative. Generally, the method is this: anything in the divine words which cannot be referred either to moral integrity or to true faith you should understand as figurative. Moral integrity refers to our loving God and neighbor; true faith, to our understanding of God and neighbor. . . .

(10.15) Now Scripture commands nothing but love (*caritas*) and censures nothing but lust (*cupiditas*), and in that manner moulds people's morals. . . .

(10.16) I define "love" as any movement of the soul to enjoy God for God's own sake, and to enjoy one's self and one's neighbor for God's sake. "Lust," on the other hand, is any movement of the soul to enjoy one's self or one's neighbor or any bodily thing, not for God's sake. . . .

(15.23) So when dealing with figurative expressions, follow this as a basic rule: that the text being read should be turned over and over, considered diligently for a long while, until your interpretation can be led over into the kingdom of love. If the text already rings true in the literal, then no figurative meaning needs to be probed for.[36]

THEORY OF SIGNS

One focus of contemporary philosophy (and linguistics) is semiotics, that is, the theory of signs. Augustine was one of its pioneers. Book 1 of On Christian Teaching *focused on "things"; Books 2 and 3 focus on "signs." Signs, by their very nature, are things that point to other things; they show us which direction to look and to go toward. Augustine's concern is the Bible. The Bible is made up of words, and words are "things that signify": they point to and reveal deeper or unseen realities. From* On Christian Teaching, *Book 2:*

35. *Doc. Chr.* 1.26.27–36.40 (Green, 36–48); my trans., based on Gavigan, FOTC 2:41–60.
36. *Doc. Chr.* 3.10.14–15.23 (Green, 146–56); my trans. Cf. *De catechizandis rudibus* 3.6. See William S. Babcock, "Caritas and Signification in *De doctrina christiana* 1–3," in Arnold and Bright, *De doctrina: A Classic,* 145–63.

(1.1) A sign is a thing which, besides the impression that it presents to our senses, causes some other thing to enter our thoughts. For example, at the sight of a footprint, we think of the animal who passed this way and left its track; at the sight of smoke, we recognize that there is a fire beneath it; on hearing a human voice, we turn our attention to the feeling that animates the voice's spirit; at the sound of the trumpet, soldiers know whether to advance or retreat, or whatever else the fight requires them to do.

(1.2) Some signs are natural; others are conventional. Natural signs are those that, independent of any purpose or any desire of being a sign of anything except themselves, cause something else to be recognized. Such is the case when smoke indicates fire. It is not that the smoke has a will to signify that causes this [signifying]. Rather, through observation and attention to our experiences, we learn that fire is near at hand even though only the smoke is visible. The footprint of a passing animal belongs to this same category. The face of an angry or a sad person signals his or her feeling, even if that is not the wish of the one who is angry or sad. And so too any other movement of one's spirit that gets revealed by a facial expression, even when we are not working to bring it out. . . .

(2.3) Conventional signs are those which living creatures give to one another. They thus indicate, as far as possible, either the inner movements of their spirit or anything they have sensed or understood. The only reason we have for displaying things by signs is that we may call forth and transfer to another's mind what we who give the sign have in mind. I intend, therefore, to examine and treat this type of signs insofar as it applies to human beings. This I do because even the God-given signs found in the Holy Scriptures were communicated to us through human beings who wrote them down. Animals too have certain signs among themselves by which they reveal the desires they feel. After a cock finds food, he gives a vocal sign to the hen to hurry over to him; and the dove calls his mate, or is called by her, by cooing. We are used to observing many such signs. Whether some signs, such as the anguished face or the vocal cry of one in pain, simply follow from the spirit's inner movement, or whether they are given for the specific purpose of signifying, is another issue. It has no relevance to the matter under discussion, and so I will set it aside from this work as unnecessary.

(3.4) Some signs by which people communicate to one another involve the sense of sight; most involve the sense of hearing; and a very few involve other senses. When we nod, we give a sign to the eyes alone, to someone whom we want, through this sign, to engage as a participant in our will. Hand gestures can signal a lot of things. Actors, by the way they move every limb, give off signals to those in the know and, in a way, tell stories to viewers' eyes.[37] Flags and military standards announce to the eyes, in their winding way, the commander's will. All these signs are, so to speak, visible words. But, as I said, there are many more signs that belong to the ears, notably words. The trumpet, the flute, and the lyre often produce not only a pleasing sound, but also one full of meaning. But all these meanings, when compared to words, are few in number. Words have gained by far a preeminence among human beings for expressing whatever ideas in the mind we might want to make public. The Lord, it is true, gave a sign via the perfume of the ointment that His feet were anointed with (Jn 12:3–7); He made known through taste what He intended in the sacrament of His body and blood; and when the woman was healed by touching "the tassel of His cloak" (Mt 9:21), the act signified something. But words constitute an incalculable number of signs by which people convey their ideas. Now I have been able to enunciate via words a brief discussion of all other categories of signs, but I could in no way have been able to enunciate via those other signs a discussion of words.

(4.5) But because words reverberate through the air, then pass away, lasting no longer than the sounds they make, letters were invented as signs of words. Thus voices are presented to the eyes—not in themselves, but through certain unique signs. Those signs could not be the same for all nations because of the sin of human dissension, when each one sought to seize political control for itself. A sign of this pride is that tower raised up towards heaven where impious humanity merited the just verdict of having not only their minds, but also their voices in dissonant discord (Gn 11:1–9).

(5.6) As a result of this, even divine Scripture—which heals such serious diseases of the human will—began from one language, and from it was able to be spread at an opportune moment across the entire globe, diffused far and wide through the various languages of its translators, and thus became known to the nations for their salvation. Readers, in reading it, seek only to discover the thoughts and will of those who wrote it down and, through them, the will of God, which, we believe, such authors spoke. . . .

(10.15) Now there are two reasons why written texts are not understood: Either they are veiled in unknown signs or in ambiguous ones. Now signs are either literal or metaphorical. They are said to be literal when they are used as signs for those things they were originally intended to point to. For example,

37. "Those in the know": It is not clear who these theater *cognoscenti* are. In *conf.* 3.2.2–2.4, Augustine says that soon after arriving in Carthage, he became an enthusiast for theater shows. Had he, at that time, crossed paths with groups of theater critics and connoisseurs? Early Christian moralists were highly critical of ancient theater both for its celebrating of pagan myths and for its frank eroticism. The early third-century North African theologian Tertullian once asserted: "By this they know a man to be Christian: that he has repudiated the shows" (*De spectaculis* 24.3). Augustine, as bishop, was sharply critical of theater (e.g., *De catechizandis rudibus* 11.48). Here, however, the reference is neutral: The gestures of the actors are an example of a visual sign-language.

when we Latins say *bos*, we mean an ox, because that is the name by which we and all Latin speakers call it. Signs are metaphorical when the very things we signify by the literal term are used to signify something else. So when we say *bos*, we recognize by this syllable the animal to which we typically give that name; but we also understand by that farm animal "evangelist" because Scripture, as the Apostle interpreted it, applied this meaning to it, saying: "You shall not muzzle the ox that treads the grain" (1 Cor 9:9; cf. Dt 25:4).[38]

THE PLEASURES AND PEDAGOGY OF OBSCURITY

Augustine was convinced that the Bible's "obscure signs," that is, its hard-to-grasp texts, were part of God's conscious pedagogy. God placed some signs to block the proud from entering. God also built in certain obscurities to evoke delight in the discoverer. From On Christian Teaching, *Book 2:*

(6.7) Casual readers are misled by the [Scriptures'] many and multiple sorts of obscurities and ambiguities, misjudging one meaning for another. In some passages they do not find anything to think about, even wrongly, so thoroughly do certain texts wrap themselves in the densest fog. I am convinced that divine foresight anticipated this so that hard work would tame pride and would reinvigorate our intellects, which tend to disdain things investigated and resolved too quickly and easily. Why is it, I wonder, that there are those saintly, perfect people whose lives and morals the Church of Christ puts forward to those who come to her from all manner of superstitions, that she incorporates these [converts] into herself by having them imitate these good men and women, that these [converts] become good and truly faithful servants of God, ridding themselves of worldly burdens, coming to the holy washing of baptism, and rising up from the font having been conceived by the Holy Spirit to give forth as fruit the twin loves, that is, of God and neighbor? Why is it, I ask, that when one simply asserts all this to an audience, it affords less delight than when one explains exactly the same ideas using that text from the Canticle of Canticles where the Church is spoken of as though she were a beautiful woman deserving praise: "Your teeth are as flocks of shorn sheep, which come up from the washing, all of which give birth to twins, and there is none barren among them" (Sg 4:2)? Does one learn anything more than when one hears that same set of ideas phrased in plain words without

---

38. *Doc. Chr.* 2.1.1–10.15 (Green, 56–70); my trans. See Robert A. Markus, "St. Augustine on Signs," and B. Darrell Jackson, "The Theory of Signs in St. Augustine's *De doctrina christiana*," in *Augustine: A Collection of Critical Essays*, ed. Robert A. Markus (Garden City: Anchor Books, 1972), 61–91 and 92–147.

the aid of this extended metaphor? And yet somehow I find it tastes sweeter to imagine the saints, picturing them as the teeth of the Church biting converts off from their errors and ingesting them into the body of the Church, breaking down and softening up their hardness [of heart] as if by chomping down and chewing. Also it is with great, great joy that I look upon these new converts as shorn sheep who have put aside worldly cares as if shedding fleece, and ascended up from the washing, that is, the baptismal font, and I see every one of them giving birth to twins, that is, the dual commandments of love, that there is not one of them barren of that holy fruit.[39]

(6.8) But why all this tastes sweeter to me than if no analogies were drawn from the Sacred Books, even though the content and the understanding are exactly the same—why that is is hard to say and is another question. No one, however, is uncertain now that all sorts of things are learned more willingly through the use of analogies, and that we discover meaning with much more delight when we have experienced some trouble in searching for it. Those who do not find what they are searching for suffer from starvation, while those who do not bother even to search because they think they have it in easy reach often wither away from disdain. In both cases, we must be on guard against a dangerous drowsiness. The Holy Spirit has thus wonderfully—and for our good health—planned the Holy Scriptures in such a way that in the more open passages He relieves our hunger and that in the more obscure ones He drives away our distaste. Practically nothing is dug out from those obscurities which is not found plainly said somewhere else.[40]

NUMBER SYMBOLISM

Book 2 discusses various "obscure literal signs." Augustine notes, for example, the need to know the etymological meaning of names, both of people (Adam, Eve, Abraham, Moses) and of places (Jerusalem, Zion, Jericho, etc.). In his sermons, he often elucidates what he took to be the hidden meanings of such names. One other "obscure literal sign" that drew his attention (and that of other ancient interpreters) was the Bible's number symbolism. From On Christian Teaching, *Book 2:*

(16.25) Unfamiliarity with numbers is the reason why many things expressed metaphorically and mystically in the Scriptures are not understood.

---

39. See *en. Ps.* 3.7 (CCL 38:10–11).

40. *Doc. Chr.* 2.6.7–6.8 (Green, 60–62); my trans. Cf. *en. Ps.* 10.8 (CCL 38:80), where he grapples with the very odd locution in the Vetus Latina's rendering of Ps 10 ("His eyelids question the sons of men"). On the broader issue, see Roland J. Teske, "Criteria for Figurative Interpretation in St. Augustine," and J. Patout Burns, "Delighting the Spirit: Augustine's Practice of Figurative Interpretation," in Arnold and Bright, *De doctrina: A Classic,* 109–22, 182–90.

Certainly a mind with an innate genius for ingenuity[41]—if I can put it that way—cannot help but be intrigued that Moses and Elijah and the Lord Himself fasted forty days. The knotty mystery this act symbolizes cannot be unraveled except by thinking about and pondering this number. It holds four times ten—symbolizing the knowledge of all existence as intertwined with times and seasons. Now it is by the number four that the cycles of both day and year run their course: the day is spaced out over morning, afternoon, evening, and nighttime hours; the year, over seasons of spring, summer, autumn, and winter. In the times we live in, we need to fast and abstain from enjoying times' delights for the sake of the eternity we want to live in, but in a roundabout way it is in time's very cycling that disdaining the temporal and grasping the eternal are brought home to us. . . . In similar ways, certain analogies lie buried secretly in many other places and other numbers in the Sacred Books, which are closed to readers lacking knowledge of numbers.[42]

JOHN'S GOSPEL VS. THE SYNOPTICS

I wish to illustrate how all these principles come together to shape Augustine's practical exegesis. For this, we will examine a lengthy sermon from the Tractates on the Gospel of John. First, a brief word on how Augustine viewed John and his Gospel. He used to speak of John as an eagle who flew above the misty earth; he also often noted that John had leaned on Jesus' breast at the Last Supper, symbolic of him nursing at the breast of the Word of God.[43] In the following passage, Augustine alludes to both images and spells out the difference between John's Gospel and the Synoptics. From Tractates on the Gospel of John 36:

(1) In the four gospels, or rather the four books of the one Gospel, the holy Apostle John, not unjustly compared to an eagle because of his spiritual understanding, has elevated his preaching more highly and much more sublimely than the other three. And in this elevation of his, he also wanted our hearts to be elevated. The three other evangelists, as though they were walking on earth with the Lord in his humanity, said few things about his divinity, but this [evangelist], as if he loathed to walk upon the earth, thundered from the very prologue of his discourse, elevating himself not only above the earth and above all the circuit of air and sky, but also above even the whole host of angels and above the whole hierarchy of invisible powers, and he came

---

41. "Innate genius for ingenuity" (ingenium quippe . . . ingenuum): an effort to capture Augustine's wordplay.

42. Doc. Chr. 2.16.25 (Green, 84–86); my trans.

43. On the eagle theme, see Jo. ev. tr. 15.1 (BA 71:756); on the nursing theme, see Jo. ev. tr. 1.7 (BA 71:140).

to [Christ,] through whom all things were made, saying: "In the beginning was the Word, and the Word was God. He was in the beginning with God. All things were made through Him, and without Him was nothing made" (Jn 1:1–3). Harmonious with such a sublime meaning as this, he also preached the rest, and he spoke about the divinity of the Lord as no other had. He belched out what he had drunk in. For not without reason is it told about him in this very Gospel that at the [Last] Supper he reclined upon the Lord's breast. From that breast he drank in secretly; but what he drank in secretly he has uttered openly so that to all nations may come [the proclamation of] not only the Incarnation of the Son of God and His Passion and Resurrection, but also [of] what was before the Incarnation, the only One of the Father, the Word of the Father, coeternal with the Begetter, equal to Him by whom He was sent, but in the sending itself, He became the lesser that the Father might be the greater.[44]

THE MYSTERY OF THE 38 YEARS

Let us see now how principles enunciated in On Christian Teaching *shaped Augustine's practical exegesis. The following sermon interprets the healing of the paralytic at the pool of Siloam (Jn 5:1–18). Augustine opens with a favorite device: pinpointing some obscurity, some "mystery," in the text that requires elucidation. He knew that hearers were intrigued by such mysteries, much as we today enjoy a good detective story. Like Sherlock Holmes, Augustine tends to zero in on some minute, overlooked clue. Here the textual clue is that the man whom Christ healed had suffered for 38 years. To unravel the hidden significance of the number, Augustine ranges around the whole Bible for evidence, linking Old and New Testaments; he reads what he finds in terms of the twofold love of God and neighbor; he appeals to St. Paul repeatedly to name broader issues or to look for clues to decipher conundrums; he alludes to his theory of signs and their soul-strengthening power; and, at the end, he refers to his highway analogy. Rarely does one find an instance where so many concerns and principles enunciated in* On Christian Teaching *come together in a single sermon. From Tractates on the Gospel of John 17:*

(1) The performance of an amazing deed by God ought not to be a source of amazement. It would be an amazing thing only if a human being had performed it. We ought to rejoice more than be amazed, rejoice more that our Lord and Savior Jesus Christ became human than be amazed that God performed divine acts among human beings. For what He became *for* human beings is more valuable for our salvation than what He did *among* human beings. That He healed the vices of souls is more valuable than that He healed

44. *Jo. ev. tr.* 36.1 (BA 73A:174–76); trans. Rettig, FOTC 88:81–82.

the maladies of bodies destined to die. But because the soul itself did not know the One by whom it had to be healed, and because it had eyes of flesh with which it might see physical acts but did not yet have healthy eyes in the heart with which it might recognize God lying hidden, He did something that the soul could see so that it might be healed by what it could not see. He entered a place where there lay a great multitude of sick, blind, lame, and shriveled-limbed. And since He was the physician of both souls and bodies, He who had come to heal all those souls who would come to believe, He chose one of the sick whom he might heal in order to signify unity. If we were to reflect on this with an ordinary heart, as though with a human grasp and insight, then [we would judge that] in regard to power, He performed nothing great, while in regard to kindness, He did too little. So many were lying there, and only one was cured, when with one word He could have made all of them rise up. What, then, ought we to understand except that that power and that goodness were doing what souls might understand in His deeds for their eternal salvation rather than what bodies might gain for their temporal health? For the true health of bodies—what in the end we wait for from the Lord—will come at the resurrection of the dead. Only then what will live will die no more. Only then what will be healed will not become ill. Only then what will be filled will not hunger or thirst. Only then what will be renewed will not grow old. But here, even with those deeds of our Lord and Savior Jesus Christ, the opened eyes of the blind would [eventually] be closed by death, and whatever was healed temporarily in mortal limbs would succumb in the end, but the person who believed would make the passageway to eternal life. Therefore, from the healing of this sick man, Christ gave a great sign to any soul who would believe, to any soul whose sins He had come to forgive, whose maladies He had humbled himself to heal. As far as God deigns to bestow, if you give your attention and assist my weakness by your prayer, I shall discuss as best I can the profound mystery of this event and this sign. But whatever I cannot do, that One with whose help I do what I can do will supply you. . . .

(4) Let us, therefore, see what He intended to signal in that one who alone of so many sick He . . . deigned to heal. He found in the years of the man a number, so to speak, of the sickness: "He was thirty-eight years under his infirmity" (Jn 5:5). How this number refers more to the sickness than to the cure must be explained a little more carefully. I want you to be attentive. The Lord will help that I may speak aptly and you may hear sufficiently. The number forty has been recommended to us as sacred and refers to a certain perfection. I think, my beloved people, you know this well. The divine Scriptures very often attest it. Fasting was consecrated by this number, as you well

know. For Moses fasted for forty days (Ex 34:28); and Elijah, too, the same number (1 Kgs 19:8). And our Lord and Savior Jesus Christ Himself brought this number to fulfillment in His fasting (Mt 4:2). Through Moses, the Law is symbolized; through Elijah, the Prophets are symbolized; through the Lord, the Gospel is symbolized. And so the three appeared on that mountain, there where He showed Himself to His disciples in the brightness of His face and garments (Mt 17:1–3). For He appeared between Moses and Elijah, in other words, so that the Gospel give witness to the Law and the Prophets. Therefore, whether in the Law or in the Prophets or in the Gospel, in terms of fasting, the number forty is recommended to us.

But there is a great and broader sort of fast: to abstain from iniquities and the illicit pleasures of the world. This is the perfect fast: "that denying ungodliness and worldly desires, we may live soberly and justly and godly in this world" (Ti 2:12). What reward, according to the Apostle, comes with this fast? He goes on to say: "looking for that blessed hope and the manifestation of the glory of the blessed God and our Savior, Jesus Christ" (Ti 2:13). Therefore, in this world we celebrate, so to speak, a Lent of abstinence when we live well, when we abstain from iniquities and illicit pleasures. In order that this abstinence not come without reward, we look for "that blessed hope and revelation of the glory of the great God and our Savior, Jesus Christ" (Ti 2:13).[45] In that hope, when hope shall pass over into reality, we shall receive a *denarius* as our pay, for this salary was paid to the workers laboring in the vineyard, according to the Gospel (Mt 20:2, 9–10), which I believe you remember (for not everything has to be rehashed as if for the unlearned and the inexperienced). A *denarius*, which gets its name from the number "ten," was paid. When joined to forty, it becomes fifty. We, therefore, celebrate with hard labor the forty-day period before Easter; we celebrate with joy, as if having received our pay, the fifty-day period after Easter.[46] For, as it were, to this health-giving labor of good deeds, which belongs to the number forty, there is added a *denarius* of rest and happiness that it may become fifty.

(5) The Lord Jesus Himself also signified this much more clearly when He spent forty days after His Resurrection on earth with His disciples. What's more, when He had ascended into heaven on the fortieth day and ten days had passed, He sent the Holy Spirit as pay (Acts 2:1–4). These things were sym-

---

45. Note that Augustine gives Ti 2:13 in two different wordings here: "that blessed hope and the manifestation of the glory of the blessed God" (*illam beatam spem, et manifestationem gloriae beati Dei*) and "that blessed hope and revelation of the glory of the great God" (*beatam illam spem, et revelationem gloriae magni Dei*). The reason is not clear. It may be that he is paraphrasing; it may also be that he is drawing on two different versions of the Vetus Latina, simply setting them side-by-side.

46. We know that *Jo. ev. tr.* 11 and 12 on John were delivered during Lent, and *Jo. ev. tr.* 13 was given during the Easter season. This sermon too seems to have been delivered between Easter and Pentecost.

bolic, and by certain signs the realities themselves were anticipated. We are nourished by signs that we may be able to come to the enduring realities themselves. For we are workmen, and we still labor in the vineyard. When the day ends, when the work ends, wages will be paid. But what workman endures to get his wages if he isn't nourished while he works? For even you don't just give your workman wages, do you? Don't you also bring him something that he may restore his strength with during his hard labor? Of course, you feed those you'll give wages to later. So too the Lord feeds us, while we work hard with these signs of the Scriptures. For if this joy of understanding mysteries were taken away from us, we would faint from our hard labor, and there would be no one to come and get paid.

(6) How, therefore, is this deed brought to perfection in the number forty? Perhaps for this reason: Because the Law was given in the Ten Commandments, and the Law had to be preached through the whole world, and this whole world is known in its four parts—east and west, south and north. From this, a *denarius* multiplied by four gives forty. Or maybe: Because through the Gospel—which has four books—the Law is fulfilled, because it was said in the Gospel: "I have not come to destroy the Law but to fulfill it" (Mt 5:17). Therefore, whether it's the first reason or the second, or some other more likely one (which escapes me but doesn't escape the more learned), still it is clear that a certain perfection in good works is symbolized by the number forty. And these good works are especially practiced in our abstaining from illicit desires for the world, that is, by this broader sort of fasting. Listen also to the Apostle speaking: "Love is the fulfillment of the Law" (Rom 13:10). Where does love come from? From the grace of God, from the Holy Spirit. For we would not come up with it ourselves as if it were of our own making. It is a gift of God—and a great gift. "Because the love of God," he says, "is poured forth in our hearts by the Holy Spirit who has been given to us" (Rom 5:5). Love, therefore, fulfills the Law, and it was very truly said: "Love is the fulfillment of the Law." Let us seek out this love in the way the Lord made it known. Remember what I have proposed: I intend to explain the number of thirty-eight years in that sick man, why that number thirty-eight belongs to the sickness rather than the cure. Therefore, as I was saying, love fulfills the Law. The number forty refers to the fulfillment of the Law in all deeds. But in love two commandments are recommended to us. Look, I beg you, and fix what I am saying in your memory. Be not despisers of the word [of God] so that your soul not become the wayside where tossed grains cannot germinate: "And the birds of the sky," it says, "will come and gather it" (Mt 13:4). Collect it, and lay it up in your hearts. Two commandments of love were recommended by the Lord: "You shall love the Lord, your God, with your whole heart, and with

your whole soul, and with your whole mind," and "You shall love your neighbor as yourself. On these two commandments depend the whole Law and the Prophets" (Mt 22:37–40). Rightly, too, did the widow place all her means, two mites, among the gifts of God (Mk 12:42–44). Rightly, too, did that innkeeper receive two pieces of money for that ailing man wounded by the robbers that he might be healed (Lk 10:30–35). Rightly did Jesus spend two days among the Samaritans that he might strengthen them in love (Jn 4:40).⁴⁷ Therefore, in cases when the number two symbolizes something good, this twofold love is being especially recommended. If, therefore, the number forty holds the perfection of the Law, and if the Law is not fulfilled except in the double commandment of love, why should you wonder that he was sick who had two less than forty?

(7) Let us, for this reason, now see with what mystery the Lord cures this sick man. For the Lord came, the teacher of love, himself full of love, "making short," as it was predicted about him, "his word upon the earth" (Rom 9:28), and he showed that the Law and the Prophets depend upon the two commandments of love. Therefore, Moses depended on them in his forty; Elijah [depended] on them with his; and the Lord brought this number in his witness. This Lord, when He is present, cures the sick man, but what does He say to him first? "Do you want to be healed?" (Jn 5:6) The man answered that he had no one who might put him into the pool. Truly a human being was necessary for his healing, but that [necessary] human being was also God: "For there is one God, and one mediator between God and humanity, the man Jesus Christ" (1 Tm 2:5). Therefore, the human being who was necessary came. Why should the healing be put off? "Arise," He says, "take up your bed and walk" (Jn 5:8). He said three things: "Arise," "Take up your bed," and "Walk." But "Arise" was not a command to work, but the working of a cure. But He commanded the cured man [to do] two things: "Take up your bed and walk." I ask you, why would not "Walk" have sufficed? Or at any rate, why would not "Arise" have sufficed? For when that man arose healed, he would not have stayed on in that place. Would he not have arisen and gone away? Therefore, it also strikes me that Christ, who found the man lying there, found him lacking two things and so ordered him to do two things so that, by doing the two, the cured man fulfilled what he was lacking.

(8) How, then, may we find signified in these two commands of the Lord those two commands of love? He said, "Take up your bed and walk." Remember along with me, my brothers and sisters, what those two commandments are. For they ought to be very well known, and they ought not to come into

47. "Two days . . . love": See Jo. ev. tr. 15.33, 16.3 (BA 71:810–12, 818).

your mind only when they are mentioned by me. Rather, they ought never to be erased from your hearts. Indeed, always consider that God and neighbor must be loved: "God with all one's heart, with all one's soul, with all one's mind," and "the neighbor as one's self" (Mt 22:37–39). These must always be reflected upon. These must be pondered. These must be adhered to. These must be acted upon. These must be fulfilled. The love of God is first in the order of commandments, but the love of neighbor is first in the order of action. For the One who would enjoin this love on you in two commandments would not recommend to you the neighbor first and God afterwards, but God first and the neighbor afterwards. But because you do not yet see God, by loving your neighbor you merit seeing Him. By loving your neighbor you cleanse your eye for seeing God, as John clearly says: "If you do not love your brother whom you see, how will you be able to love God whom you do not see?" (1 Jn 4:20) Look, it is said to you, "Love God." If you should say to me, "Show me the one whom I am to love," what shall I answer except what John himself says: "No one has seen God at any time" (Jn 1:18)? And that you may not suppose that you are altogether unworthy of seeing God, he says: "God is love, and the one who abides in love abides in God" (1 Jn 4:16). Therefore, love your neighbor, and look upon the source within you from which you love your neighbor. There you will see, as far as you can, God. Therefore, begin to love your neighbor. "Break your bread with the hungry; bring the needy without shelter into your house; if you see a naked man, clothe him, and despise not the household of your seed" (Is 58:7). But doing this, what will you achieve? "Then your light shall break forth as the morning" (Is 58:8). Your light is your God; he is "the morning" to you because He will come to you after the night of this world, for He neither rises nor sets because He remains forever. The One who had set for you when you were lost will be "the morning" for you when you return. Therefore, it seems to me that "Take up your bed" was a way of saying "Love your neighbor."

(9) But it is still closed [to us] and requires explanation, I think, why the love of neighbor is represented through the taking up of the bed—it should not upset us that a neighbor is represented by a bed, an inert and insensate thing. Let the neighbor not get angry if he is represented to us by something that is without soul or sensation. Our Lord and Savior Jesus Christ Himself was called a "cornerstone" in that he brought and held together two peoples in himself (Eph 2:19–22).[48] He was also called a "rock" from which water flowed forth: "And the rock was Christ" (1 Cor 10:4). Why is it surprising, then, that if Christ is a rock, a neighbor might be wood? Yet not just any kind

---

48. "'Cornerstone' . . . two peoples": See Jo. ev. tr. 9.17, 15.26 (BA 71:542–44, 800).

of wood, just as that was not just any kind of rock, but a rock from which water flowed forth for the thirsty. Nor was that just any kind of stone, but a cornerstone which joined in itself two walls coming from different directions. So neither should you understand the neighbor to be just any kind of wood but a bed. What symbol, what sign, is there, then, in a bed, I ask you? What except that a sick man was carried on a bed but, when healed, is now to carry a bed? What did the Apostle say? "Bear your burdens, each for the other, and so you will fulfill the law of Christ" (Gal 6:2). Now the law of Christ is love, and love is not fulfilled unless we bear one another's burdens, each for the other. "Bearing with one another," he says, "in love, eager to preserve the unity of the Spirit in the bond of peace" (Eph 4:2–3). When you were sick, your neighbor was carrying you. You have been healed. Now carry your neighbor. "Bear your burdens, each for the other, and so you will fulfill the law of Christ." So you will fulfill what was lacking to you. "Take up," therefore, "your bed." But when you have taken it up, do not stay put. Walk! In loving your neighbor, in being concerned about your neighbor, you are making a journey. Where are you journeying to, except to the Lord God, to the One whom we ought to love with all our heart, with all our soul, with all our mind? For we have not yet reached the Lord, but we have our neighbor with us. Therefore, carry the one you are walking with so that you may reach the One you long to stay with. Therefore, take up your bed and walk.[49]

All Truth Is God's Truth

Medieval and Renaissance thinkers justified their studies of the humanities by appealing to the following passage in Augustine's On Christian Teaching. *Here he stresses the value of the liberal arts, arguing that all truth is God's truth, even truths found in pagan literature. He adds that such knowledge can be usefully adapted by Christians to the study of Scripture, and appeals to a famous allegorical exegesis of Exodus that dates back to Philo and Origen.[50] From* On Christian Teaching, *Book 2:*

(18.28) We should not avoid music just because of pagan superstition if we can take from it anything useful for comprehending the Sacred Scriptures. . . . We should not ignore literature just because Mercury is reputed to

49. Jo. ev. tr. 17.1–9 (CCL 36:169–75); trans. Rettig, FOTC 79:108–18 (modified).

50. The best known version of this interpretation appears in Origen, *Letter to Gregory* 2; for a translation, see Michael Slusser, St. Gregory Thaumaturgus: Life and Works, FOTC 98 (Washington, DC: The Catholic University of America Press, 1998), 190–91. On the long tradition of this, see Joel Stevens Allen, The Despoliation of Egypt in Pre-Rabbinic, Rabbinic, and Patristic Traditions, Supplements to Vigiliae Christianae 92 (Leiden/Boston: Brill, 2008).

be its presiding deity. Nor just because [pagans] have consecrated temples to Justice and Virtue and have chosen to adore in stone what should be carried in the heart must we, therefore, shun justice and virtue. On the contrary, every good and true Christian should understand that wherever one discovers truth, it is the Lord's. . . .

(40.60) Furthermore, if those who are called philosophers, especially the Platonists, have perhaps said things that are truthful and can be conformed to our faith, we must not only have no fear of them, but even appropriate whatever we find useful from those who are, in a sense, their illegal possessors. The Egyptians not only had idols and crushing burdens, which the people of Israel detested and from which they fled, but they also had vessels and ornaments of gold and silver and clothing, which the Israelites, as they left Egypt, secretly claimed for themselves as though for a better use (Ex 11:2–3, 12:35–36). Not on their own authority did they make this appropriation, but by the command of God, while the Egyptians themselves, without realizing it, were supplying the things that they were not using properly. In the same way, all the teachings of the pagans have counterfeit and superstitious notions and oppressive burdens of useless labor, which any one of us, leaving the association of pagans with Christ as our leader, ought to abominate and shun. They also, however, contain liberal instruction more adapted to the service of truth and also very useful principles about morals; even some truths about the service of the one God Himself are discovered among them. These are, in a sense, their "gold" and "silver." They themselves did not create these things, but excavated them, as it were, from the mines of divine Providence, which is everywhere present, but they wickedly and unjustly misuse this treasure for the service of demons. When a Christian severs himself in spirit from a wretched association with these people, he ought to take these truths from them for the lawful service of preaching the Gospel. It is also right for us to receive and possess, in order to convert it to Christian use, their "clothing," that is, those human institutions appropriate to human society which we cannot do without in this life.[51]

THE LEGEND OF THE SEPTUAGINT

The Septuagint was a translation of the Hebrew Bible into Greek, done during the third century B.C.E. According to legend, it was commissioned by Pharaoh Ptolemy II Philadelphius (283–246 B.C.E.) for his great library at Alexandria. Supposedly seventy

---

51. *Doc. Chr.* 2.18.28–40.60 (Green, 88–126); trans. Gavigan, FOTC 2:87–113 (modified).

translators (thus "septuagint"), each working independently, translated the Hebrew original and miraculously produced the exact same Greek translation.[52] *This translation became the Bible for Greek-speaking Jews and, therefore, for the earliest Christian communities. Contemporary scholars are alert to many differences, large and small, between the Hebrew original and this ancient Greek translation. They differ in respect to canon; for instance, the Hebrew lacks books such as Maccabees and Sirach. They also differ in many, many places in word choice. The Old Testament that Augustine commented on was the Septuagint as translated (often awkwardly) into Latin. He recounts here the famous legend of its creation and expresses his deep veneration of its authority. From* On Christian Teaching, *Book 2:*

(15.22) In emending any Latin translations, we must consult the Greek texts. Of these, the reputation of the seventy (*septuaginta*) translators is the most distinguished in regard to the Old Testament. These translators are now considered by the more learned churches to have translated under such a sublime inspiration of the Holy Spirit that, even with so many, they spoke with one voice. According to tradition and to many deserving of our trust, these, while translating, were isolated from one another in separate cells. Nothing was discovered in the codex of any one of them that was not discovered [also] in the others, expressed in the same words and the same word order. Who, then, would venture to put anything on a level with this authority; still less, esteem anything better? But even if they had consulted one another so that that one version was produced as a result of working together and a common agreement among them all, even then it is certainly not reasonable or proper for any one person, however expert, to presume to reform the common judgment of these more senior and more learned scholars.[53] Therefore, even if we discover something in the Hebrew original different from what they have interpreted, it is my opinion that we should yield to the divine direction. This guidance was accomplished through them so that the books that the Jewish people were not willing to transmit to other nations, either because of reverence or jealousy, were revealed so far ahead of time, with the aid of the authority of King Ptolemy, to those nations who would later believe through our Lord. It may be that they translated according to the manner in which the Holy Spirit—who directed them and caused them to speak the same words—judged how best to adapt things to the Gentiles. But, as I said earlier, a comparison of translators who have adhered quite closely to the actual words is often useful in interpreting a passage. So, as I began to say, the Latin texts

52. See Abraham Wasserstein and David J. Wasserstein, *The Legend of the Septuagint: From Classical Antiquity to Today* (New York: Cambridge University Press, 2006).

53. "Any one person, however expert": Augustine's target here seems to be Jerome. See below.

of the Old Testament should be corrected, if need be, by authoritative Greek ones, and especially the version of those who, though seventy in number, are held to have translated in unanimous agreement.[54]

CORRESPONDENCE WITH JEROME

Translating the Old Testament

Around 394 or 395, Augustine embarked on a long-running correspondence with Jerome, the greatest biblical scholar of his day.[55] Their correspondence got off to a rough start. Augustine's first letter never reached Jerome, while the second did so only by a roundabout route, and both letters stoked Rome's gossip-mill. Jerome was a notoriously prickly and cantankerous personality and was deeply offended by Augustine's challenges. Two issues came to the fore. The first was whether one should use the Septuagint as the basis for any translation of the Old Testament (Augustine's view) or the Hebrew original (Jerome's preference as of the early 390s).[56] In the following letter, written around 403, Augustine apologizes about earlier letters going astray and commends Jerome's scholarly work. He then recounts a humorous incident: a colleague of his faced a near-riot in his congregation after using Jerome's Vulgate. From Letter 71:

(2.3) I have learned that you have translated the Book of Job from the Hebrew, although we have had for some time your translation of that Prophet, rendered into Latin from the Greek tongue, in which you marked by asterisks what is found in the Hebrew version but not in the Greek, and by obelisks what is found in the Greek but not in the Hebrew, with such extraordinary care that in some places we see stars appended to single words, indicating that these words are in the Hebrew but not in the Greek version.[57] But in your later translation, which was made directly from the Hebrew, there is not the same fidelity to the words, and it rouses no little disquiet when one wonders why in the earlier translation the asterisks were placed with such care as to show even the most insignificant parts of speech that are lacking in the Greek texts but are found in the Hebrew, [but] less care [in the new translation] is

54. *Doc. Chr.* 2.15.22 (Green, 80–82); my trans., based on Gavigan, FOTC 2:80–81.

55. For an overview and analysis of the correspondence, see Kelly, *Jerome*, 263–72.

56. Jerome, in the Preface to his *Hebrew Questions*, began speaking of "Hebrew verity" (*Hebraica veritas*) as opposed to what he came to see as mistakes in the Septuagint. On Jerome's growing conviction on this issue, see Kelly, *Jerome*, 153–67.

57. "Asterisks . . . obelisks": Symbols used by ancient text critics to mark discrepancies in texts. Origen famously applied these symbols in his massive 6-column compilations of versions of the Old Testament, known as the *Hexpla*. Jerome apparently had access to Origen's volume for this work. Augustine, himself well-trained in literary critical scholarship, was impressed with such careful textual scholarship. On Origen's *Hexpla* and his work as a grammarian, see Joseph W. Trigg, *Origen*, Early Church Fathers (New York: Routledge, 1998).

shown in assigning these particles to their places. I should like to give you an example of this, but at the moment I have no texts from the Hebrew. As you surpass me, however, in quickness of mind, I think you understand not only what I say, but even what I want to say, and you can clear up what troubles me as if the case had been presented.

(2.4) For my part, I would rather you translated the Greek Scriptures for us as they are presented in the Septuagint. It will be very difficult if people begin to read your translation more commonly in many churches, because the Latin churches will differ from the Greek, and especially because anyone who objects is easily refuted by producing the book in Greek, as that is a well-known language. But if anyone is disturbed by an unusual passage translated from the Hebrew and claims that it is wrong, seldom or never is there a way to appeal to the Hebrew to sustain the passage challenged. Even if there were, who would allow so many Latin and Greek authorities to be overruled? In addition to this, Hebrew experts could conceivably give different answers, and you would then seem to be the sole indispensable critic to convince them. Who will be able to be the judge? It would be surprising if one could find one.

(3.5) There was a certain bishop of ours who decided to read your translation in the church over which he presided, and he caused a sensation by some passage from the Prophet Jonah, which was very different from the version enshrined in the memory and hearing of all and sung for so many generations. There was such a disturbance made among the people, with the Greeks arguing and stirring up passions with the charge of falsification, that the bishop—it was in the city of Oea[58]—was forced to call on the testimony of the Jews. Whether it was through ignorance or malice, they answered that what the Greek and Latin texts said and maintained was found in the Hebrew texts. To make a long story short, the man was forced to correct an apparently wrong statement, not wishing to run the great risk of remaining without a flock. So it seems to us that you, like others, can be mistaken as well. You see the sort of thing that can happen when a text cannot be corrected by comparison with the familiar languages.

(4.6) . . . I wish you would be so kind as to explain what you think about the difference of authority in many places between the Hebrew texts and the Greek version known as the Septuagint. Surely that version has no little weight, which was duly published abroad and which experience shows was used by the Apostles—a fact which you asserted, as I recall. In this you would perform a great service if you would put into correct Latin the Greek translation which the Seventy made, for our Latin Scriptures vary so much from text

---

58. "Oea": modern Tripoli, Libya.

to text that it is almost unbearable, and they are of such dubious authority that we hesitate to quote them or prove anything by them, lest it be different in Greek. I intended this letter to be short, but somehow or other I find great sweetness in going along as if I were talking to you. But I beg you by the Lord not to disdain to answer all this and to lend me your presence so far as that may be [possible].[59]

Interpreting Paul

The second issue between Jerome and Augustine was the exegesis of Paul. Jerome had published a commentary on the Epistle to the Galatians, drawing heavily on Origen and other Greek exegetes. Augustine was alarmed by Jerome's interpretation of Gal 2:11–14, which recounts how Paul confronted Peter. Jerome, following Origen, claimed that the dispute between the two apostles was feigned, a "useful lie." Augustine found this interpretation potentially disastrous. In his first letter to Jerome, Augustine sets out the problem. From Letter 28:

(3.3) I have read certain writings, said to be yours, on the Epistles of the Apostle Paul, in which you were attempting to explain some difficulties in Galatians, and I came upon that passage where the Apostle Peter is called back from a dangerous dissimulation. That lying should be defended by such a fine man as you (or by someone else if someone else wrote it) causes me, I confess, no small sorrow; and I shall go on feeling this way until it is refuted—if what disturbs me can be refuted. I think it extremely dangerous to admit that anything in the Sacred Books should be a lie; that is, that those who have composed and written the Scriptures for us should have lied in their books. Of course, one might raise the question whether a good person should ever lie. But it is another question altogether whether a writer of the Holy Scriptures might have lied—but, no, this is not another question: It is no question at all! If we once admit even one "politically useful" lie in that supreme authority, there will be nothing left of those books, because whenever anyone finds something difficult to practice or hard to believe, one will follow this most dangerous precedent and explain it as the idea or practice of a lying author.[60]

---

59. *Ep.* 71.2.3–4.6 (CCL 31A:36–39); trans. Parsons, FOTC 12:325–28 (modified). Later, in *ep.* 82.5.34–5.35, Augustine concedes the value of Jerome's translations in debating with Jews, but he continues to worry about the Vulgate's use in churches. Augustine's last word appears years later in *civ. Dei* 18.43, where he insists on the canonical value and inspiration of the Septuagint, while acknowledging Jerome's contribution. He there nuances his theory of inspiration to include all versions of the Old Testament.

60. *Ep.* 28.3.3 (CCL 31:94); trans. Parsons, FOTC 12:95–96 (modified). This was initially not delivered. A man named Profuturus, who was to be the original mail-carrier, was elected as bishop of Cirta and died not long after. Another letter, *ep.* 40, made its way to Rome, and Jerome got wind of Augustine's accusa-

The Truth of the Scriptures

These two issues remained the ongoing focus of their correspondence, though at least as much space is devoted, on the one hand, to Jerome venting his anger that Augustine was waging a behind-the-scenes campaign against him, and, on the other, to Augustine playing the diplomat, soothing hurt feelings, apologizing profusely for misunderstandings. Jerome finally changes moods and concludes Letter 81 with the comment: "Let us, if you will, play together in the field of the Scriptures without hurting each other."[61] *For Augustine, biblical interpretation was no light-hearted sport, but tough mountain-climbing. In the following passage, excerpted from a treatise-length letter, Augustine uses their dispute over Galatians as a springboard to explain his broader understanding of the truth of the Scriptures. From Letter 82:*

(1.2) You ask, or rather, with the boldness of charity you command, that we play together in the field of the Scriptures without hurting one another. As far as I am concerned, I would rather deal with these matters seriously and not as if some game. But if it pleased you to use that wording because of your facility in that field, I confess that I ask something greater of your kind ability, of your learned, exact, experienced, expert, and gifted prudence and care: that in these great and involved questions, by the gift, or rather under the guidance, of the Holy Spirit, you would help me. For it is not as though I am playing on some [level] field, but rather am gasping for air in the [high altitude of] Scriptures' mountains. . . .

(1.3) I admit to Your Charity that only to those books of the Scriptures that are now called canonical have I learned to pay such honor and respect as to believe most firmly that not one of Scriptures' authors has erred in writing anything. If I do find anything in those books that seems contrary to truth, I decide either that the text is corrupt, or that the translator did not follow what was really said, or that I have failed to understand it. But when I read other authors, no matter how eminent they may be in sanctity and learning, I do not necessarily believe a thing is true just because they think so, but because they have been able to convince me, either on the authority of the canonical writers or by a plausible reason that is not inconsistent with the truth. And I think that you, my brother, feel the same way. Moreover, I have to say, I do not believe that you want your books to be read as if they were those of Prophets or Apostles, about whose error-free writings it is unlawful to doubt. Far be it from you to think [your books infallible], given your pious humility and your truthful self-understanding, for if you were not so endowed, you would cer-

---

tions. Augustine worked hard to patch up the misunderstanding and sent a copy of these letters in the same large packet of materials that accompanied *ep.* 71, quoted above.

61. *Ep.* 81 (CCL 31A:96); trans. Parsons, FOTC 12:390.

tainly not have said: "How I wish I might deserve to embrace you, and that we might teach or learn something by mutual conversation."[62]

(2.4) But if, as I believe, you said this as an expression of your own life and character and not as a pretense or deception, how much more reasonable is it for me to believe that the Apostle Paul thought nothing other than what he wrote, when he said to Barnabas about Peter: "When I saw that they were not living rightly according to the truth of the Gospel, I said to Peter in the presence of all: If you, while a Jew, live as a Gentile and not as a Jew, why do you force Gentiles to live like Jews?" (Gal 2:14) For how can I be certain that the Apostle does not deceive me in writing or speaking, if he was deceiving his own children? He was in labor bringing them to birth until Christ, that is, the Truth, should be formed in them. And given that he began by saying to them, "As to what I am writing to you, behold, before God, I am not lying" (Gal 1:20), was he not writing the truth? Or was he [as you think] making use of some sort of diplomatic pretense when he said that he had seen Peter and Barnabas walking not rightly according to the truth of the Gospel, and when he said that he had stood up to Peter face-to-face for no other reason than that Peter was forcing Gentiles to live like Jews?

(2.5) Is it really better to believe that the Apostle Paul wrote something untrue than that the Apostle Peter did something unrighteous?[63] If it were, then we could (God forbid!) go on and say that it is better to believe that the Gospel lies than that Christ was denied by Peter; and that the Book of Kings lies [in saying] that a great prophet [like King David], so eminently chosen by the Lord God, committed adultery by coveting and seducing another man's wife, and was guilty of a revolting murder by killing her husband. On the contrary, I will read Sacred Scripture with complete certainty and confidence in its truth, founded as it is on the highest summit of divine authority; and I would rather learn from it that human beings were truly approved or corrected or condemned than allow my trust in the divine word to be everywhere undermined just because I am afraid to believe that the all-too-human conduct of certain excellent and praiseworthy persons is sometimes worthy of blame. . . .

(2.7) One should not believe, you say, that Paul blamed Peter for what Paul himself had done. I am not now asking what he did; I am asking what he wrote. The fact that the truth of the Divine Scriptures, so necessary for

62. "'How I wish . . . mutual conversation'": Quoting Jerome, *ep.* 68.2 (CCL 31A:30).
63. Parsons, following the CSEL edition of Augustine's letters, translates this as: "Surely, it is better to believe that the Apostle Paul wrote something untruthful than that the Apostle Peter acted not uprightly." This, however, plainly contradicts the view that Augustine is so strongly arguing for here. I have modified the translation so as to follow the new CCL critical edition of Augustine's letters, which gives this sentence as a question, not a statement.

building up our faith, has been handed down to our memory not on the authority of any chance writers, but on that of the Apostles themselves, and has been received with the sanction of the highest canonical authority, and that it remains true in every part and not subject to doubt—this fact has the greatest bearing on the question that I have raised. If what Peter did was what he ought to have done, then Paul lied when he said that he had seen Peter not walking rightly according to the truth of the Gospel. Surely, when anyone does what he ought to do, he acts rightly, and therefore whoever says that the accused has not done rightly what he knew he ought to do, that accuser accuses him falsely. If, however, Paul wrote the truth, then it is true that Peter was not then walking rightly according to the truth of the Gospel; therefore, Peter was doing what he ought not to have done. And if Paul had done the same thing himself, I prefer to believe that, having been himself corrected, he could not pass over the correction of his fellow Apostle rather than that he put some lying statement in his Epistle or in any Epistle, much less in the one Epistle which he prefaced with the words: "As to what I am writing to you, behold, before God, I am not lying" (Gal 1:20).

(2.8) For my part, I believe that Peter did act so as to compel the Gentiles to live like the Jews. For I read that Paul wrote this, and I do not believe he lied.[64]

BIBLICAL POLYSEMY

Augustine argued that Scripture's obscurity may lead to the possibility of multiple orthodox interpretations. He was convinced, in other words, of the Bible's polysemy. "Polysemy" is a term post-modern literary critics use to speak of the way a text contains, or gives birth to, multiple meanings. In Augustine's view, biblical texts contained a treasure trove of hidden meanings that exceeded the explicit intention of their human author. For him, the Bible was divine speech compressed into human speech. It thus possessed a density and a multivalence that providentially anticipated the abilities of multiple interpreters and the needs of multiple audiences. From On Christian Teaching, Book 3:

(27.38) Not just one but sometimes two or more interpretations are understood from the same words of Scripture. And even if the writer's meaning lies hidden, there is no danger, provided that one can show from other passages of the Holy Scriptures that each of these interpretations is consistent with

---

64. Ep. 82.1.2–2.8 (CCL 31A:98–101); trans. Parsons, FOTC 12:391–419 (modified). In one of the new Dolbeau sermons, Augustine alludes to this dispute with Jerome on the interpretation of Galatians; see s. 162C.3–4 (= Dolbeau 10). This offers an interesting example of the way Augustine popularized his more erudite disputes.

the truth. The person who thoroughly examines the divine utterances must try and chase down the intent of the author through whom the Holy Spirit brought that segment of the Holy Scriptures into being. [The interpreter] may end up arriving at this intention, or he may chisel out from the words some other meaning which draws its evidence from some other passage within the divine utterances and which does not run counter to right faith. The biblical author maybe saw that very meaning in the same words which we are trying to interpret. Certainly, the Spirit of God—who worked through the author to produce these words—foresaw that this very meaning would, without any doubt, occur to the reader or listener, or rather the Spirit took care that it should occur to the reader or listener because it too is based on the truth. What could God have possibly built into divine eloquence more generously and more exuberantly than that the very same words might be understood in multiple ways, each deriving support from other no-less-divinely-inspired passages?[65]

TYCONIUS'S BOOK OF RULES

Augustine was intrigued by and learned much from Tyconius, the Donatist theologian, whose Book of Rules sets out seven principles or "keys" for unlocking the mysteries of the Scriptures.[66] Scholars have speculated that Tyconius's little book may have inspired Augustine to create his own, namely, On Christian Teaching. When, at the end of his career, Augustine sat down to complete the incomplete On Christian Teaching, he discussed Tyconius's book, quoting its preface and offering a précis of its rules. From On Christian Teaching, Book 3:

(30.42) A man named Tyconius, although he himself was a Donatist, wrote very convincingly against the Donatists and appears, on this issue, absurdly divided in heart, since he was unwilling to leave them altogether.[67] He wrote what he called The Book of Rules, because in it he outlines seven rules which, like keys, one can use to unlock the obscurities of the Holy Scriptures. The first of these rules is Concerning the Lord and His Body; the second, Concerning the Lord's Twofold Body; the third, Concerning the Promises and the Law; the fourth, Concerning Species and Genus; the fifth, Concerning Times; the sixth, Con-

65. Doc. Chr. 3.27.38 (Green, 168–70); my trans.
66. For the Latin text with a parallel English translation, see William S. Babcock, trans., Tyconius: The Book of Rules, Texts and Translations 31 (Atlanta, GA: Scholars Press, 1989). For studies on the influence of Tyconius, see the bibliography for this chapter.
67. "Unwilling to leave them": In the 380s, Tyconius was excommunicated by Parmenian, the Donatist bishop of Carthage, because of his overly Catholic views on the Church; see Contra epistulam Parmeniani 1.1.1 (BA 28:208–210).

cerning *Recapitulation*; and the seventh, *Concerning the Devil and His Body*. When these rules, in the way he opens them up, have been carefully examined, they help greatly in penetrating hidden meanings within the [Bible's] divine eloquence. Even so, not every hard-to-understand passage can be deciphered by these rules; we must employ several other methods as well. . . .

(30.43) Yet when Tyconius recommended these as rules, he assigned a little too much importance to them, arguing that if we know and apply them fully, we will be capable of understanding everything we find stated obscurely in the Law, that is, in the divine books. He began his book by saying:

> I considered it necessary above all, as it seemed to me, to write a little book of rules and, as it were, to forge keys and lamps for the hidden places of the Law. For there are certain mystic rules which give access to the secret recesses of the whole Law and make visible those treasures of truth invisible to many. If the theory of these rules is received without ill will, in the spirit I offer them, every closed door will be opened, and every obscurity will be illuminated, so that anyone strolling through the vast forest of prophecy will be prevented from going astray, guided by these rules as if by pathways of light.

If he had said here: "For there are certain mystic rules which give access to *some* secret recesses of the Law"; or even: "which give access to *great* secret recesses of the Law"; and not what he did say: "the secret recesses of the *whole* Law"; and if he had not said: "*every* closed place will be opened," but said instead: "*many* closed places will be opened," he would have spoken accurately, without raising false hopes in his readers by attributing more than the facts warrant for this otherwise painstaking and very beneficial work. I thought that I ought to say this in order that the book may be read by students because, on the one hand, it is a very helpful aid for understanding the Scriptures, and, on the other, one should not hope for more than it has to offer. Certainly, we need to read it with some caution not only because of certain human mistakes he has made in it, but especially because of the things he says as a Donatist heretic. Let me now explain briefly what those seven rules teach or suggest.

(31.44) The first rule is *Concerning the Lord and His Body*. We know that we get hints sometimes of the Head and the Body—that is, Christ and the Church—that are presented to us as of one person, for it was said to the faithful, not without good reason: "then you are the seed of Abraham" (Gal 3:29), although there is only one seed of Abraham, namely, Christ. We should not be puzzled when a text shifts from Head to Body or from Body to Head, yet the subject does not change, but is one and same person. For example, a single person speaks here: "He placed a garland on me as on a bridegroom, and He adorned me with ornaments as on a bride" (Is 61:10). Yet we have to understand which of these two phrases refers to the Head and which to the Body, that is, which to Christ and which to the Church.[68]

THE *TOTUS CHRISTUS*

Augustine's précis of Tyconius's first rule gives one little hint of the frequency, richness, and depth with which he himself used this optic of Christ, Head and Body, to interpret the Bible. This theme is pivotal to his exegesis, especially his Expositions of the Psalms. It is also key to appreciating how he inextricably intertwines his views on Christ and on the Church. From here to the end of this chapter, we will explore variations he gives to this theme in his exegesis of the Psalms. As one scans the Expositions, one finds him asking again and again: "Who is speaking?" This would have been an obvious question for readers in the ancient world as they read poems or plays or philosophic dialogues since their texts lacked quotation marks. It is, therefore, no surprise that Augustine asks it as he walks his congregation through the poetry of the Psalms. Scholars refer to this ancient technique of exploring the identity and intention of the speaker as "prosopological exegesis." The term "prosopological" comes from the Greek prosopon, meaning "person," especially a "character" in a play. As Augustine saw it, the speaker of the Psalms is not— or at least, not simply—King David, the Psalms' purported author; the speaker is "the whole Christ" (totus Christus), sometimes the risen Christ, other times His Body, the Church. In the following passage, Augustine sets out his basic scheme. From Expositions of the Psalms 56:

(1) Let us listen to Christ in this Psalm. Opportunely, and by His foresight, it so happens that the Gospel echoes the Psalm, commending to us the love of Christ, who laid down His life for us that we might lay down ours for our brothers and sisters. This [theme] rings out and sings along with the Psalm in order that we may see in what way Our Lord Himself laid down His life for our sake. The Psalm sings about the Passion itself. After all, the whole Christ (totus Christus) is both Head and Body, as you know quite well. The Head is Christ our Savior Himself, who, having suffered under Pontius Pilate, rose from the dead and now sits at the right hand of the Father. His Body is the Church, not simply this or that church, but the Church scattered across the entire globe—and not only people who live at the present moment, but also those who have gone before us, belong to it, and so too do those who will come after us, even to the end of the ages. Because all the faithful are members of Christ, the whole Church, firm and secure among all believers, is this Head established in the heavens from where He governs His Body. Even if

68. Doc. Chr. 3.30.42–31.44 (Green, 172–76); my trans., based on Gavigan, FOTC 2:150–52.

separated from us in sight, He is connected to us in love. Now because the whole Christ is the Head and His Body, let us hear in all the Psalms the voice of the Head in such a way that we also hear the voices of the Body. He does not want to speak separately from us just as He does not want to be separated from us, for He said: "Behold, I am with you until the end of ages" (Mt 28:20). If He is with us, He speaks in us, He speaks about us, He speaks through us, for we too speak in Him. And because we speak in Him, for that reason do we speak the truth.[69]

Two in One Voice

In his earliest commentaries on the Psalms, Augustine tended to follow Tyconius's distinction more woodenly, carefully and sharply distinguishing the different voices of Christ and of Church.[70] But as Michael Cameron has pointed out, Augustine gradually came to "telescope" these voices, hearing them not as separate, but as the single voice of the whole Christ.[71] This is illustrated in the following passage. This "single voice" perspective had major consequences for both his Christology and his ecclesiology. Here he uses the Head/Body scheme to stress how the Church's feelings of anguish become Christ's feelings of anguish, implying that the work of Christ's redemptive suffering continues and is experienced even now, even though the risen humanity of Christ is in heaven. From Expositions of the Psalms *142:*

(3) Our Lord Jesus Christ is both Head and Body. He who deigned to die for us also wanted to speak in us. He made us His members. Sometimes, therefore, He speaks in the person of His members; other times, in His own person as our Head. He has some things which He says without us; we can say nothing without Him. The Apostle says: "that I may fill up what was lacking in the afflictions of Christ in my flesh" (Col 1:24). Note what Paul says: "that I may fill up what was lacking," not in my "afflictions," but in "Christ's"; and not in Christ's "flesh," but in "mine." Christ is still suffering, he says, not in His own flesh, that He ascended into heaven with, but in my flesh, which still labors hard on earth. Christ, as Paul says, is still suffering in my flesh: "I live, no longer I, but Christ lives in me" (Gal 2:20). If Christ were not suffering real affliction in His members, that is, His faithful, Saul on earth would not have been able to persecute Christ seated in heaven. In fact, Paul openly explains

69. En. Ps. 56.1 (CCL 39:693–95); my trans. Cf. en. Ps. 62.2 (CCL 39:794–95). For an overview of Augustine's hermeneutics of the Psalms, see Michael Fiedrowicz, "General Introduction," Exposition of the Psalms (1–32), WSA III/15 (2000): 13–66; on prosopological exegesis, see pp. 50–60.

70. For example, en. Ps. 3.1–10 (CCL 38:7–13).

71. On the totus Christus, see Michael Cameron, "Enarrationes in Psalmos," AugEncy, 292–93.

in a certain place: "Just as a body is one and has many members, and still all the members of the body, though many, are one body, so also Christ" (1 Cor 12:12). He does not say: "So also Christ *and His Body*," but "one body, many members, so also Christ." All, therefore, is Christ; and because the whole Christ is one, for that reason, the Head from heaven spoke: "Saul, Saul, why are you persecuting me?" (Acts 9:4)

Hold onto this. I recommend it be fixed indelibly in your memory as sons and daughters, erudite in ecclesiastical matters and the Catholic faith. That way, you will recognize that Christ, Head and Body, is one and the same Christ, Word of God, only-begotten, equal to the Father. And from this you will see with how much grace you stretch out to God such that He Himself wants to be one with you, He who is one with the Father. How one with the Father? "I and the Father are one" (Jn 10:30). How one with us? "Scripture does not say, 'To his descendants,' as though indicating many, but as to one only, 'To your seed,' who is Christ" (Gal 3:16). . . . This is a great mystery: "The two will be in one flesh" (Gn 2:24). The Apostle says: "This is a great mystery; I am speaking of Christ and the Church" (Eph 5:32). Christ and Church—two in one flesh. Take account of the distance between the two's majesty. Two, clearly. Not that we are the Word, not that we were God in the beginning, not that through us all things were made. But when it comes to flesh, there's Christ, both Him and us. So don't be amazed by this in the Psalms. He says many things in the person of the Head; many others in the person of His members; and this all as being just one person, and so He speaks as one. Don't be surprised that there are two in one voice if there are two in one flesh.[72]

THE STAIRWAY IN THE HEART

Psalms 119–133 (in the Septuagint numbering) are known as the "Psalms of Ascent"— or as Augustine's Old Latin Bible entitled them, the "Songs of Steps." Originally Jewish pilgrims used to sing these songs as they traveled up the steep road to Jerusalem on pilgrimage to the Temple. Augustine devoted his sermons on these Psalms to encouraging hearers to embark on an interior pilgrimage to the City of God. He argued that God had placed a ladder within the human heart, giving us the aptitude and wherewithal to make such an ascent. In the following passage, Augustine plays on the Head/Body theme in the inverse of what we saw above. He stressed above how the union of Head and Body made it possible for Christ still to suffer in the suffering members of His Church. Here he stresses the inverse: how Christ's joys become the Church's joys such that we experience foretastes

72. En. Ps. 142.3 (CCL 40:2061–62); my trans.

of heaven even though the Church continues to labor on earth. Augustine saw the Psalms as the feelings of the whole Christ. They thus offered a therapeutic program for repairing the diseased human heart, a sort of spiritual cardiological rehab. The Psalms provided a paradigm and pedagogy for the affections, offering a path both of purgation and of delight that instilled in the faithful the graced courage to make the often grueling journey to God.[73] Christ's ascent made possible believers', and one savors this in both Christ and the Church's forerunners, the martyrs. Both dwell in the City of God, and because of the union of our hearts with theirs, we glimpse the endpoint and see ourselves in their mirror. From Expositions of the Psalms *123:*

(1) Dearest brothers and sisters, you already know quite well that a Song of Steps is a song of our ascent, and that this ascent is done not by the body's feet, but the heart's feelings. And this song you have just heard sung to you: It has "Song of Steps" written on its top line. That's its title. Sing it, therefore, as people ascending upwards. Sometimes it seems as though one person is singing, sometimes as though many are. Since we many are one because Christ is one, thus in Christ the members of Christ become one with Christ. And the Head of all these members is in heaven. The Body, even if it labors on earth, is not cut off from its Head. For the Head looks down from above and takes care of the Body. For if He had not been taking care of it, He would not have said to His persecutor, Saul (not yet Paul): "Saul, Saul, why are you persecuting me?" (Acts 9:4) You know all this really well. These things are old hat to you. . . . Well then, either one sings or many sing, and many people are one person because there is unity; and Christ, as we have said, is one, and all Christians are members of Christ.

(2) What then do they sing, these members of Christ? What do they sing? For they are in love, and loving, they sing; yearning, they sing. Sometimes, when troubled, they sing, and sometimes exulting, they sing; when in hope, they sing. Trouble is our lot in this present age; hope is ours in the future age. And unless the hope of that future age console us in our present-age troubles, we will perish. Thus joy is not yet ours, brothers and sisters, in reality, but it is already ours in hope. Hope is certainly ours, as if the reality has already come to fulfillment. For that reason, we don't get anxious about what Truth promises us. Truth, you see, cannot be deceived nor deceive us. It is good that we cling to Truth. It frees us, but only if we remain in His word. So now we believe; later we will see. When we believe, it's in the hope of that future age; when we actually see, it shall be in the reality of that age. We shall then see

---

73. Michael Cameron has adopted that neologism "psychagogy" (that is, "soul-leading" or "soul-education") to describe what Augustine is doing here; see his "*Totus Christus* and the Psychagogy of Augustine's Sermons," *Augustinian Studies* 36 (2005): 59–70.

[God] face to face. But we shall see face-to-face only when we have a cleansed heart. For "blessed are the clean of heart, for they shall see God" (Mt 5:8). By what are hearts cleansed if not by faith, just as Peter said in the Acts of the Apostles: God "cleansed their hearts by faith" (Acts 15:9). Faith cleanses our hearts as well, that we be able to be fit enough to seize the sight. So we walk now by faith and not yet by sight, for just as the Apostle says, "While we are in the body, we are on pilgrimage to the Lord" (2 Cor 5:6). So what's "being on pilgrimage"? "We walk," he says, "by faith, not by sight" (2 Cor 5:7).

So one who is on pilgrimage and walks by faith is not yet home, but is already on the road. One who does not believe, however, is neither home nor on the road. So let us walk as if we're already on the road. Because the King Himself has made Himself the road. The King—that's the Lord Jesus Christ. There He's the Truth, but here He's the road. To whom are we going? To Truth. How are we going? By faith. To whom are we going? To Christ. How are we going? Through Christ. That's the reason He Himself said: "I am the Way, the Truth, and the Life" (Jn 14:6). He had said sometime earlier to those who believed in Him: "If you remain in my word, truly you will be my disciples; and you will know the truth, and the truth will set you free" (Jn 8:31–32). Now He did say, "and you will know the truth," but added: "if you remain in my word." In what word? It's just as the Apostle says: "This is the word of faith that we preach" (Rom 10:8). First, therefore, the word is a word of faith. In that word of faith, if we remain in it, we will know the truth, and the truth will set us free. Truth is immortal, Truth is unchangeable. Truth is that Word of whom it is spoken: "In the beginning was the Word, and the Word was with God, and the Word was God" (Jn 1:1). Who can see this unless the heart be cleansed? How's the heart cleansed? "And the Word became flesh, and dwelt among us" (Jn 1:14). The Word—what He remains in Himself—is the Truth to whom we are coming and the One who sets us free. What is preached is the word of faith, in whom the Lord wishes us to continue to remain so that we understand the Truth; that is, "The Word became flesh, and dwelt among us." You believe in Christ born in the flesh, and you are journeying to Christ born of God, God with God.

(3) In what we read, the singers are jubilant, exulting. It is the members of Christ exulting—they're singing this Psalm. Now, who can exult here, as I said, unless it be in hope. Let this hope hold steady in us, and let us sing exulting for joy. It's not that those singers are foreign to us. And it's not as if the voice in this Psalm wasn't also our voice. So listen as though listening to yourselves. Yes, listen as if you were gazing at yourselves in the mirror of the Scriptures. So when you gaze into the scriptural mirror, your own cheerful face looks back at you. When you find that image of yourself exulting in hope, you

will see your likeness to the members of Christ, the members who first sang this. Then you too will be within His membership, and you will sing this.

Now why are these singers singing this and exulting? Because they have escaped. Therefore, hope is what they are singing in. For when we are here and on pilgrimage, we have not yet escaped. But some members of this Body, which we are also part of, have gone on ahead, and they can sing of it there in truth. The martyrs sing it this way, for they have already escaped and are with Christ in exultation, already sure of receiving back their bodies free from corruption, the very bodies which once were corrupted, in which they suffered terrible torments. There, these [once tormented bodies] will be made emblems of justice. Therefore, let us all sing the Psalm together—both those already rejoicing in reality and we who live in hope and are joined in affection together with them, celebrating their victory garlands and yearning for such a life, one which we do not have here and which we will not be able to have unless we yearn for it here. So let us all sing together and say: "Except because the Lord was in us" (Ps 123:1). For the martyrs have looked down on whatever troubles which they once suffered, and they have considered them from their vantage point, well-established in blessing and in security, and have reflected on the road they went along and on the place where they have come to; and because it would have been difficult to be liberated from here, had not the liberator's hand helped, and so in joy they have said: "Except because the Lord was in us." So have they begun singing. Not yet have they said what they escaped from, so much is their joy, their exultation: "Except because the Lord was in us."

(4) "Let Israel now say: 'Except because the Lord was in us'" (Ps 123:1). Now let [Israel] say it because it has already escaped. The escapees, that is, those who have already escaped—this Psalm sets them up for us to look upon. Let us also set them up in our hearts, those who are already triumphant, and rejoice as though we ourselves are also there, just as in a previous Psalm it was said: "Our feet were standing in the outer courts of Jerusalem" (Ps 121:2). Not even there yet, but still on the road, yet so much was their joy hurrying them along, and so much was their hope of arriving, that even here, laboring along on the road, they saw themselves already set up there in Jerusalem. Yes, we too may now place ourselves in that triumph which will be ours in the future age, when we will trample upon Death already ended, already swallowed up, where we will say: "Where, O Death, is your struggle?[74] Where, O Death, is your sting?" (1 Cor 15:55)[75]

---

74. "Where, O Death, is your struggle?" (*Ubi est, Mors, contentio tua?*): This reflects the Vetus Latina that Augustine used. The Vulgate has "victory" (*victoria*) rather than "struggle."

75. *En. Ps.* 123.1–4 (CCL 40:1825–27); my trans. This sermon is part of a larger sequence. M. LeLandais, in his "Deux années de prédication de saint Augustin: Introduction à la lecture de l'*In Joannem*," in *Études Augustiniennes*, Théologie 28, ed. Henri Rondet (Paris: Aubier, 1953), 1–95, demonstrated that Augustine gave

FROM JUBILANT WORDS TO
WORDLESS JUBILATION

At the climax of the journey to God, one enters into a joyousness beyond words. To describe this joy, Augustine alludes to the songs sung by harvest workers who labored in the searing heat amid the verdant olive orchards of North Africa. Here we catch a glimpse of what one might call Augustine's ecclesial mysticism. From Expositions of the Psalms *32, sermon 2:*

(8) "Sing to Him a new song" (Ps 32:3). Strip off your old self! You know a new song. A new person, a New Covenant, a new song. A new song doesn't belong with oldness. Only new persons can speak of it, new selves renewed by grace out of their oldness, ones belonging already to the New Covenant—what is the Kingdom of Heaven. All our love breathes this newness and sings this new song. Let us sing this new song not with our tongues, but with our lives. "Sing to him a new song, beautifully sing to him" (Ps 32:3). Each and every one of us is searching out some way to sing to God. Sing to Him—but you don't want it to be off-key. Brothers, sisters, sing beautifully. Now if someone had to perform before some audience well trained in music, and you're told, "Sing so you please them," you'd be nervous without some sort of formal training in the art of music and singing, afraid that real artists would critique your performance. A casual audience might not spot your lack of expertise, but a real artist would be highly critical. Now who would offer to get up and try to sing beautifully before God, since He's so good at judging a singer, so careful to examine everything, so attuned to hearing everything? When will you, in your singing, be able to put forward a performance of such artistry, such elegance, that not a single note of yours would grate on such finely tuned ears? Look, it's as though he is giving you a new style of singing. Don't go searching for words and lyrics, as if you could talk about what God would delight hearing about. "Sing in jubilation" (Ps 32:3). This, you see, is what singing beautifully to God is: it's to sing in jubilation. What is it "to sing in jubilation"? To understand that what's sung in the heart cannot be spelled out in words. Think of those who sing at harvest or in vineyards or at some other rugged work, the way they express their rapture by beginning with songs set to words, and then, as if bursting with a joy so full that they cannot give vent to it in set syllables, they drop the words and break into this improvised mel-

a series of sermons that intertwined En. Ps. 119–133 with Jo. ev. tr. 1–13. Anne-Marie LaBonnardière, in her *Recherches de chronologie augustinienne,* CEASA 23 (Paris: Institut d'Études Augustiniennes, 1965), 21–39, argued that this sequence took place not in the mid-410s, as was previously thought, but earlier, during the Donatist crisis, specifically, from December 406 through June 407. She also showed that his Ep. Jo. 1–10 were given during the Easter season of this same period. On this, see Berrouard, *Introduction aux Homélies,* 22–27.

ody of pure jubilation. This is the sound of pure joy. It signals the heart bringing to birth what cannot be spoken. And to whom does that jubilation rightly ascend, if not to God, who is ineffable? Truly God is ineffable. You cannot give voice to Him in words. And if you cannot give voice to Him in words—and you ought not stay silent—what else can you do but break into jubilation? In this way the heart rejoices without words, and the boundless expanse of rapture is not bound in by set syllables. "Sing beautifully to Him in jubilation" (Ps 32:3).[76]

76. En. Ps. 32.2.8 (CCL 38:253–54); my trans. This analogy of workers singing during harvest is applied in en. Ps. 99.4 (CCL 39:1394) in reference to the joy that comes from contemplating God within the glories of creation.

CHAPTER 6

CONTROVERSIES (I)
Against the Manichees

✣

Augustine has often been thought of as a systematic theologian. That is not accurate. He was, by training and by temperament, a controversialist, a debater. Four great debates shaped his career and have come to define his theological legacy. The earliest of these was his debate against his onetime coreligionists, the Manichees.

Mani (216–277), Manicheism's founder, was a Persian prophet and visionary who believed himself called to preach a final definitive revelation, to complete what previous religious founders—Buddha, Zoroaster, Jesus—had left incomplete.[1] He was born in southern Babylonia, then part of the Persian Empire. His family seems to have belonged to the Elchasaites, a Jewish-Christian baptismal sect. At age 24, he experienced a series of visions and began proclaiming his "Religion of Life." He spoke of himself as "the apostle of Jesus Christ," while followers went further, calling him "the Paraclete," the "Spirit of Truth" prophesied by Jesus. He eventually converted members of the Persian royal court and won the favor of the king, Shapur I, who supported his missionary efforts for some 30 years. When Shapur died in 273, Mani fell from favor and in 277 was arrested, tortured, and died in prison.

The religion of Mani owed much to gnosticism. Mani claimed to reveal a secret mystical knowledge of God and of the universe, its origin and its des-

---

1. On Mani and Manicheism, see Iain Gardner and Samuel N. C. Lieu, "Introduction," *Manichaean Texts from the Roman Empire* (Cambridge: Cambridge University Press, 2004), 1–45; Samuel N. C. Lieu, "Manichaeism," in Harvey and Hunter, *Oxford Handbook of Early Christian Studies*, 221–36. On Manicheism as Augustine knew it, see François Decret, *L'Afrique manichéenne (IVe–Ve siècles): Étude historique et doctrinale*, CEASA 74–75 (Paris: Études Augustiniennes, 1978); Johannes Van Oort, Otto Wermelinger, and Gregor Wurst, eds., *Augustine and Manicheism in the Latin West*, Nag Hammadi and Manichaean Studies 49 (Leiden: Brill, 2001).

tiny. His starting point was a cosmic dualism. As one Manichean psalm proclaims it:

Let us worship the Spirit of the Paraclete [= Mani]. . . . He came, He separated us from
the error of the world. He brought us a mirror. We looked; [we] saw this universe in it.
When the Holy Spirit came, he revealed to us the way of truth. He taught us that there
are two natures, that of the Light and that of the Darkness, [separate] from one another from the beginning.[2]

The visible universe, reflected in the "mirror" of Mani's revelation, is a tumultuous war-torn frontier land, the front lines of a cosmos-wide struggle between the Kingdom of Light and the Kingdom of Darkness. The anguish of
our world is traceable back to a great battle that took place before the creation
of the present material universe. Long ago, long before our present world,
light and darkness, good and evil, were once originally separate realms. How
then did this terrible mixed-up world of ours come into being? According to
Mani, border forces within the Kingdom of Darkness, instinctively drawn to
the beauty of light across the frontier, plotted and succeeded in invading a
segment of the Kingdom of Light. In response, God (or "the Father of Greatness") evoked emanations of his own light-substance and sent one of them,
Primal Man, to turn back this invasion from the Kingdom of Darkness. In the
great battle that followed, the forces of darkness succeeded in capturing and
imprisoning this Primal Man. He himself was eventually rescued, but what
got left behind was the current muddled material world, with its painful mixture of divine brightness and dark evil matter. This primeval battle is but the
opening episode in Mani's intricate mythological account of how the world
came about and how it will slowly come to be redeemed. Something about
Manichean myth resonated deeply with ancient audiences. Its appeal is not
unlike that of modern films such as Lord of the Rings or Star Wars. Both film series tell entertaining epic tales of a many-sided, universe-wide clash between
long-suffering goodness and a seemingly invincible evil empire. Manicheism,
in its own day and in its own way, offered just such a cosmic tale. Its story
helped explain why our world is so dark and yet why there exists hope of salvation, at least for some.

　　According to Mani, every person carries this cosmic battle of the Kingdom of Light and the Kingdom of Darkness within himself or herself. He
claimed that we do not really know ourselves; we do not realize that, in our
deepest core, we are sparks of divine light trapped in material bodies. We

2. Coptic Manichean Psalm 223.2–3. For the Coptic text, see C. R. C. Allberry, A Manichaean Psalm-Book, part
2 (Stuttgart: W. Kohlhammer, 1938). The translation here is from Jason D. BeDuhn, "Manichean Theology,"
in Religions of Late Antiquity in Practice, ed. Richard Valantasis (Princeton: Princeton University Press, 2000),
482. This psalm offers one of the best summaries of Manichean myth.

have forgotten who we are because we have become drunk from long years trapped in the dark delusions of the material world. Mani's teaching opens us to the truth of ourselves. As another Manichean psalm proclaims:

> I have known my soul and the body that lies upon it,
> that they are enemies to each other before the creations.[3]

Manichees saw the task of redemption as a slow, painstaking recovery of the tiny tidbits of divine light trapped in matter. They viewed the visible universe as a vast light-processing plant, a place where the dross of dark matter can gradually and painstakingly be distilled away and shirked off and where tiny fragments of divine light can be recovered like precious diamonds from a subterranean mine. In the Manichean scheme of things, the sun and moon are two celestial refineries in this cosmic purification process:

The sun and moon were established; they were placed on high [to] purify [the] soul. Daily they take up the purified part to the height; this sediment, however, they scrape [off and cast it below; and the] mixed [portion] they rotate, now above and now below.[4]

Manichees thus deeply venerated the sun and the moon, and enemies like Augustine would accuse them of being sun-worshipers and moon-worshipers. When Manichees looked up at the night sky and saw the Milky Way (what they called the "Pillar of Glory"), they saw it as visible evidence of distilled light-souls gathering together and making their way back to the Kingdom of Light.

Mani consciously sought to create a world religion. He authored a body of writings that, together, formed an official canon of scriptures. He even put together a picture book for illiterate followers. Only fragments of these texts have been preserved. In fact, Augustine is the major preserver of one, a letter known as The Foundation.[5] Mani also commissioned missionaries to go out and spread his teachings in all directions. Some went east into China; others, west into the Roman Empire. Manicheism tended to blend in with its local religious surroundings. Manichees in China adopted a Buddhist guise and spoke of Mani as "the Buddha of Light." In the West, Manichean missionaries portrayed themselves as elite Christians and wrote off ordinary believers as ignorant semi-Christians. They fiercely rejected Judaism and the Old Testament but routinely appealed to the New Testament, especially the letters of

---

3. Coptic Manichean Psalm 248.26–27; trans. Allberry, 56.

4. Coptic Manichean Psalm 223.14; trans. BeDuhn, 483.

5. For a reconstruction of the Foundation Letter, see Gardner and Lieu, Manichaean Texts, 168–72; see also Madeleine Scopello, "L'Epistula fundamenti à la lumière des sources manichéennes de saint Augustin," in Van Oort, et al., Augustine and Manicheism, 161–73.

Paul. Still, they denied that Jesus had truly become human (and thus rejected the Incarnation) and interpreted Jesus' death as purely symbolic. Manichean congregations had two levels or ranks: Elect and Hearers.[6] The Elect were the evangelists. They committed themselves to a life of wandering and spreading the Manichean message of salvation. They were austere ascetics, and practiced disciplines of celibacy and vegetarianism. Hearers, by contrast, were allowed to marry and hold jobs but were expected to provide hospitality for wandering Elect.

For centuries, much of what was known of Manicheism came from what could be reconstructed from Augustine's polemic. That changed in the early twentieth century. Archeologists discovered the ruins of Manichean monasteries and remnants of Manichean manuscripts in Turfan in central Asia, where eighth-century Uighur Turks had adopted Manicheism as the state religion. This was the first of a series of key discoveries. In 1929, workmen stumbled upon a cache of papyri in Medimet Madi in Egypt. These included a remarkable Manichean *Psalm Book* and a theological tract called the *Kephalaia of the Teacher*. In 1969, there was another remarkable discovery, a manuscript known as the *Cologne Mani Codex*. This pocket-size booklet contained Mani's purported autobiography, *Concerning the Origin of His Body*.[7] Archeologists have recently uncovered remains of a thriving Manichean community in Kellis in Egypt.

Augustine converted to Manicheism during his student days in Carthage and remained a Hearer for some years (he says nine).[8] In *Confessions*, he says that he became increasingly dissatisfied with Manicheism intellectually but continued to rely on Manichean contacts for his career, including when he moved to Rome in 383 and again when he sought the position of orator for Milan in 384. Only after arriving in Milan and after hearing the preaching of Ambrose and reading the books of the Platonists did he make his decisive break. Some of Augustine's earliest works, written in the aftermath of his baptism, confront Manicheism. He continued to compose anti-Manichean treatises after his ordination as a presbyter in Hippo and during his early years as bishop. Debate with Manicheism forms a central thread running through his *Confessions*.

Manicheism may seem a rather arcane religion, of little interest to any except historians of antiquity. One might presume, therefore, that Augustine's polemic against it would be of little long-term theological significance. The

---

6. See Jason D. BeDuhn, *The Manichaean Body in Discipline and Ritual* (Baltimore: Johns Hopkins University Press, 2000).

7. For a translation of the *Cologne Mani Codex*, see Gardner and Lieu, *Manichaean Texts*, 46–84.

8. *De utilitate credendi* 1.2 (CSEL 25.1:4); *conf.* 3.11.20 (CCL 27:38). See O'Donnell, 2:297–98.

opposite is the case.[9] His anti-Manichean writings were a crucible where he forged fundamental elements of his theology, and these would prove no less fundamental for later Christian theology. Six themes stand out: (1) the relationship between faith and reason, (2) the origin and nature of evil, (3) the freedom of the will, (4) the goodness of creation, (5) the relationship between the Old and New Testaments, and (6) the reality of the Incarnation.

᪥

MANICHEES IN THEIR OWN VOICE

Augustine, on occasion, debated Manichees face-to-face. He has left behind the record of two such debates, one with a Manichean priest named Fortunatus, another with a Manichean teacher named Felix.[10] But Augustine's most extensive debate was a literary one against a Manichean bishop named Faustus of Milevis (d. ca. 390).[11] Augustine had first met Faustus around 382 in Carthage. According to Confessions, Book 5, Faustus's inability to answer Augustine's questions about philosophic and scientific weaknesses in Manichean thought was a decisive factor in his abandoning the sect. Sometime between 386 and 390, Faustus composed a question-and-answer treatise called Chapters (Capitula). Augustine preserved and rebutted this work in his Against Faustus the Manichee. These preserved fragments allow us to hear an eloquent Manichee in his own voice and in his own terms.

(i) Living the Beatitudes

Augustine says that Manichean missionary successes came, in part, from the attractive asceticism practiced by the Elect.[12] One gets a glimpse of this as Faustus describes his commitment to living out Jesus' Beatitudes. From Faustus, Chapters, quoted by Augustine, Against Faustus the Manichee, Book 5:

(5.1) Faustus said: "Do I accept the Gospel? You ask me even when it's obvious that I do because I do what it commands. Maybe I ought to ask you whether you accept it, since one sees in you no evidence of accepting it. I—I have left father and mother, wife

---

9. A point stressed by Gerald Bonner, *St Augustine of Hippo: Life and Controversies*, 3rd ed. (Norwich: Canterbury, 2002), 193. See also J. Kevin Coyle, "Saint Augustine's Manichaean Legacy," 2002 St. Augustine Lecture, *Augustinian Studies* 34 (2003): 1–22.

10. *Acta contra Fortunatum Manichaeum*, and *Contra Felicem Manichaeum*; see Roland J. Teske, trans. *The Manichean Debate*, WSA I/19 (2006): 145–62 and 280–316.

11. Scholars typically speak of him as Faustus of "Milevis." Henry Chadwick has noted that ancient inscriptions give the town's name as "Mileu" or "MILEV"; see Eric Plumer, *Augustine's Commentary on Galatians*, 69 n. 53.

12. See *De moribus* 1.2 (CSEL 90:4).

and children, other things which the Gospel commands. And you question whether I accept the Gospel? Maybe it's just that you don't know what committing to the Gospel means. The Gospel is nothing other than the preaching and the commands of Christ. I've rejected silver and gold. I've given up having money in my wallet. I'm content with each day's food. I don't worry about tomorrow. Nor am I anxious about whether my stomach's going to get filled or my body clothed. And you want to know whether I accept the Gospel? You see in me Christ's Beatitudes—those things that make up the Gospel. And you ask me whether I accept this Gospel? You see a poor man. You see someone meek. You see a peacemaker, one pure in heart, one mourning, hungering, thirsting, one persecuted and hated for righteousness' sake. And you doubt whether I accept the Gospel!"[13]

(ii) Manichean Rejection of the Incarnation

Manicheism had three different Christ figures. One was "Jesus the Splendor," a mythical being who served as messenger from the Kingdom of Light. Another was the "suffering Jesus" whose light remained trapped in the material world (especially within vegetation). A third was the Jesus of the Gospels, though Manichees denied that this Jesus was really born of the Virgin Mary or really died on the cross. From Faustus, Chapters, quoted in Augustine, Against Faustus the Manichee, *Books 2, 3, and 20:*

(2.1) Faustus said: "Do I accept the Gospel? Absolutely! Do I therefore accept that Christ was born? Absolutely not! For it does not follow that, if I accept the Gospel, on account of that I accept that Christ was born. Why? Because the Gospel came into being and gets its name from the preaching of Christ. And He Himself never says that He was born from human beings. Genealogy is so far from being Gospel that even its writers did not dare name the genealogy 'the Gospel' . . .

(3.1) "Do I accept the Incarnation? For my part, I really tried for a long time to persuade myself, somehow or other, that God was born. But I ran up against the discrepancy of two of the evangelists, Luke and Matthew, who wrote down His genealogy, and I hesitated, uncertain which would be better to follow. For I thought it might happen that, since I'm not prescient, the one I figured to be lying was telling the truth and the one I figured to be telling the truth was perhaps lying. So I went on past their unending and, to me, interminable wrangling, and conferred with John and Mark—from those two to these two, from those evangelists to others who go by the same name. The beginnings [of John's and Mark's Gospels] immediately and not undeservedly pleased me, because they brought in neither David nor Mary nor Joseph, but John says: 'In the beginning was the Word, and the Word was with God, and the Word was God' (Jn 1:1)—meaning Christ. Mark says: 'The Gospel of Jesus Christ Son of God'

---

13. *Contra Faustum* 5.1 (CSEL 25.1:271); my trans.

(Mk 1:1), as though correcting Matthew, who calls him 'Son of David.' Maybe the Jesus that Matthew proclaims is not the same Jesus that Mark does. This, therefore, is the reason that I do not accept a Christ who is born. You: Make them agree with one another, if you can; remove this stumbling block for me, and I, somehow or another, will give ground. In any case, it will certainly not be worthy to believe that out of some womb God was born—the God of the Christians. . . .

(20.2) "We believe that the Father dwells in the highest or principal light, which [the Apostle] Paul calls 'inaccessible' (1 Tm 6:16). The Son takes His stand in this second or visible light. The Son is twin-like, as the Apostle knew him, speaking of Christ being God's power and God's wisdom. So we believe that His power dwells in the sun, but His wisdom, in the moon. And, further, we confess that the Holy Spirit, who is third in majesty, takes up residence within the whole ambit of the air, and from His powers or spiritual outpouring, the earth conceives and bears forth the suffering Jesus, who, hanging from every tree, is the life and salvation of humankind. . . . This is our faith."[14]

(iii) Manichean Rejection of the Old Testament

The Manichees rejected the Old Testament. Here Faustus lists stock reasons for that rejection. From Faustus, Chapters, quoted in Augustine, Against Faustus the Manichee, Book 4:

(1) Faustus said: "Do I accept the Old Testament? If it's my inheritance, I accept it; if not, I don't accept it. Now it's the height of unscrupulousness to seize and lay claim to a will that testifies to one's own disinheritance. Or are you oblivious to the fact that the Old Testament promises the land of the Canaanites to the Jews, that is, to the circumcised and to sacrificers and to abstainers from pigs and the rest of the meats which Moses labeled unclean; to observers of Sabbaths and feasts of unleavened breads and the rest of that sort of stuff—which Moses himself as testator mandated them to observe? No Christian has agreed to these things, and not one of us keeps up these practices. It is only right that in refusing the inheritance we should also hand back the legal documents. This, therefore, is the first reason, I believe, why we should reject the Old Testament—unless you can teach me some more prudential way of seeing it. The second reason is that this inheritance is so miserable, so bodily, and so far off from what profits the soul that, after seeing the blessed promise of the New Testament—which promises me the kingdom of heaven and eternal life—I would turn up my nose at it even if the testator foisted it on me free of charge."[15]

14. *Contra Faustum* 2.1–20.2 (CSEL 25.1:253–536); my trans. Augustine discusses these in *Contra Faustum* 20.11 (CSEL 25.1:548–51), cited below. See Julien Ries, "Jésus le Splendeur, Jesus patibilis, Jésus historique dans les textes manichéens occidentaux," in *Gnosisforschung und Religiongeschichte: Festschrift für Kurt Rudolph zum 65. Geburtstag*, ed. H. Preißler and H. Seiwert (Marburg: diagonal-Verlag, 1994), 235–45; Majella Franzmann, *Jesus in the Manichean Writings* (London: T&T Clark, 2003).

15. *Contra Faustum* 4.1 (CSEL 25.1:268); my trans. On Faustus's anti-Jewish rhetoric and Augustine's

MANICHEES IN DISGUISE

We turn now to Augustine's viewpoint. One thing that frightened orthodox Christians was the way that certain Manichees led double lives, cloaking themselves as practicing Christians while carrying on underground as Manichees. Augustine describes the case of a Manichean hearer named Victorinus who posed as a member of the Christian clergy in his day job, but continued to work behind the scenes as a Manichean evangelist. Here Augustine writes Deuterius, bishop of Caesarea in Mauretania Caesariensis, to alert him to Victorinus. In paragraph 2, Augustine offers Deuterius a quick overview of Manichean beliefs and practices. This is the complete Letter 236:

(1) I think the best thing I can do is to write directly to your Holiness, so that my negligence may not allow the Enemy to lay waste to the flock of Jesus Christ in your province, for he never ceases to lay snares to destroy the souls bought at so dear a price. It has come to my knowledge that a certain Victorinus, a subdeacon of Malliana, is a Manichee, and that he hides his sacrilegious error under the name of cleric. He is also a man of advanced age. He was so well known that I questioned him before he could be arraigned by witnesses. He could not deny the accusation, for he knew that there were many to whom he had incautiously given himself away. He would have appeared altogether too bold, not to say out of his mind, if he had tried to deny it. He admitted that he was indeed a Manichean hearer but not an elect.

(2) Those who are called "hearers" among them eat flesh meat, till the soil, and, if they wish, have wives, but those called "elect" do none of these things. The hearers kneel before the elect that these may lay a hand on the suppliant, and this is done not only toward their presbyters or bishops or deacons, but toward any of the elect. Like these, they adore and pray to the sun and moon. Like them, they fast on Sunday; like them, they believe all the blasphemies for which the heresy of the Manichees is to be abominated: denying, for example, that Christ was born of a virgin, claiming that His body was not real but only appeared so, and that there was no resurrection. They revile the patriarchs and prophets. They say that the Law given through Moses, the servant of God, did not come from the true God, but from the Prince of darkness. They think that the souls of human beings as well as of beasts are of the substance of God and are, in fact, pieces of God. Finally, they say that the good and true God fought with the tribe of darkness and let a part of Himself be mingled with the princes of darkness, and they assert that this part, spread over the world, defiled and bound, is purified by the food of the

---

response, see Paula Fredriksen, *Augustine and the Jews: A Christian Defense of Jews and Judaism* (New York: Doubleday, 2008), esp. 213–89.

elect and by the sun and the moon; and whatever is left of that part of God which cannot be purified is bound with an everlasting and penal bond at the end of the world. As a consequence, they believe that God is not only subject to violation, corruption, and contamination, since it was possible for a part of Him to be brought to such an evil outcome, but the whole God cannot even be purified from such foulness and filthiness and misery even at the end of the world.

(3) That subdeacon, posing as a Catholic, not only believed those intolerable blasphemies as the Manichees do, but he taught them as vigorously as he could. He was discovered by his teaching when he trusted himself, so to speak, to his pupils. Indeed, he asked me, after he had confessed that he was a Manichean hearer, to lead him back to the way of truth of Catholic doctrine, but I confess I was horrified at his duplicity under his clerical guise and I took steps to have him confined and driven from the city. And I was not satisfied with that until I had notified your Holiness by letter that he should be known to all as a person to be shunned, having been degraded from his clerical rank with fitting ecclesiastical severity. If he seeks an opportunity for repentance, let him be believed only if he will make known to us the other Manichees whom he knows, not only at Malliana but in the whole province.[16]

AUGUSTINE SNARED

In Confessions *Augustine bitterly denounced his youthful self, how he had been snared by Manichean teaching. In the passage below, he describes how Manichean myth left him intellectually empty, hungry for the food of truth. Running under the surface is Augustine's self-portrait as the starving prodigal son of Jesus' parable. Augustine makes passing mention of Manichean veneration of the sun and moon and of the beauty of Manichean books. From* Confessions, *Book 3:*

(6.10) Thus did I fall among men mad with pride, extremely carnal and talkative, in whose mouths were the snares of the devil, smeared with a sticky mixture of the syllables of Your name and that of our Lord Jesus Christ and of the Paraclete our consoler, the Holy Spirit. These names never left their lips, but were empty sounds and the rattling of the tongue. As for the rest, their heart was void of truth. They kept saying: "Truth, truth," and they said it often to me, yet it was never in them. Rather, they continually spoke false things not only of You, who are truly the Truth, but also of the elements of

16. Ep. 236.1–3 (CSEL 57:523–25); trans. Parsons, FOTC 32:179–81 (slightly modified). A somewhat longer overview is found in *De haeresibus* 46 (CCL 46:312–20).

this world, Your creatures. I should even have passed by, for the sake of Your love, the philosophers who do speak the truth about such things, O my Father, the highest Good, the Beauty of all things beautiful.

O Truth, Truth—how deeply even then did the marrow of my mind long for You, when they spoke the sound of Your Name to me, frequently and many times in mere words and in many huge books! These were the dishes on which were brought to me—who was starving for You—the sun and moon and Your beautiful works instead of You, Your works and not You, not even the first of these. For Your spiritual works are superior to these bodies, no matter how shining and celestial. But I was hungry and thirsty not for these first things, but for You, O Truth, in whom "there is neither change nor shadow of alteration" (Jas 1:17). Still they set these glowing phantasms on these dishes before me. It would have been better to have loved this sun, which is, at least, true to these eyes, than those falsehoods which deceive the mind through the eyes. Yet because I thought them to be You, I ate—not eagerly, indeed, for You did not savor in my mouth as You are (indeed You were not these empty fictions), nor was I nourished by them, but rather exhausted. Food in dreams is very much like food when one is awake, but sleepers are not nourished by it, for they are asleep. . . . On such empty things was I then nourished—and I was not nourished.

But You, O my Love, for whom I faint that I may be strong (2 Cor 11:10), are neither those bodies which we see, even though they are in the heavens, nor those things which we do not see there, for You have established them in creation yet have not included them among the highest works of Your creation. How distant are You, then, from these phantasms of mine, the phantasms of bodies which do not even exist! The images of bodies which exist are more certain than these, and more certain than these images are the bodies themselves—and You are not that. Nor are You a soul. Soul is a body's life-force, and, for that reason, what gives the body life is better and more certain than a body is.[17] But You are the Life of souls, the Life of lives. Living Yourself, You do not change, O Life of my soul.

(6.11) Where were You, then, in relation to me at that time, and how far away? Of course, I was wandering far from You, cut off even from the husks of the swine whom I was feeding on husks.[18]

---

17. "More certain than a body is": Henry Chadwick, *Saint Augustine: Confessions* (New York: Oxford University Press, 1991), 42, has noted: "It is axiomatic for Augustine that what the mind knows by discernment of eternal, metaphysical truth is more certain than its judgment of the perceptions of the five senses, which are unreliable."

18. *Conf.* 3.6.10–6.11 (CCL 27:31–32); trans. Bourke, FOTC 21:57–59 (modified). After this passage, Augustine gives a terse summary of what, in retrospect, he saw as specific points on which he was deceived. He repeats the phrase "I did not know" (*non noveram*) and applies it to three issues: (1) evil as a privation of

THE MANICHEAN CHRIST OF LIGHT

The young Augustine denied the Incarnation, having absorbed Manichean docetism, that is, the claim that Christ is not really human, but only appears so. The young Augustine thought of God as a vast mass of light and of Christ as a light-being emanating out from God's light-being. On the far side of his conversion, Augustine deeply regretted how he had been trapped by this materialist (or more precisely, corporealist) conception of God. From Confessions, Book 5:

(10.19) I had no hope of finding the truth in Your Church, O Lord of heaven and earth, Creator of all things visible and invisible. [The Manichees] had turned me away from it, and it seemed disgraceful to me to believe that You were possessed of the shape of human flesh and limited by the bodily outlines of our corporeal parts. And since, when I wished to think of my God, I knew of no way of thinking except in terms of a corporeal mass (for it seemed to me that nothing whatever existed which was not like that), in that lay the greatest and practically the only reason for my inescapable error. . . .

(10.20) . . . Thus, I was of the opinion that our Savior, Your Only-begotten Son, was, as it were, projected from the main bulk of Your most luminous mass, for our salvation. I believed nothing else about Him but what I could imagine in my vanity. I thought that a nature such as His could not be born of the Virgin Mary without some mingling with the flesh. But how what I pictured to myself could be mingled without defilement: that, I did not see. Hence, I was afraid to believe in the Incarnation lest I be compelled to believe that He was defiled by the flesh. Nowadays Your spiritual-minded people will laugh at me, in a sympathetic and loving way, if they read these confessions of mine. But that is the way I was.[19]

AUGUSTINE'S CONVERSION: A PRE-*CONFESSIONS* ACCOUNT

In 391, right after his ordination as presbyter, Augustine composed the treatise On the Advantage of Believing (De utilitate credendi), *dedicating it to an old friend, Honoratus, whom he had once converted to Manicheism. Augustine wrote it to win him back to orthodox Christianity. In the following passage, he sets out an account of his conversion that predates the more extended and more famous version found in*

---

the good; (2) God as incorporeal spirit; and (3) God's eternal law measured out in ways appropriate to times and places, thus explaining discrepancies between the Old Testament patriarchs and the ethics of his time.

19. *Conf.* 5.10.19–10.20 (CCL 27:68–69); trans. Bourke, FOTC 21:120–22.

Confessions. *This passage highlights one factor which drew the two friends to the Manichees: the Manichean appeal to reason. From* On the Advantage of Believing:

(1.2) I intend to prove to you, if I can, that the Manichees are sacrilegiously and rashly attacking those of us who, following the authority of the Christian faith before we can gaze upon that Truth that pure minds look upon, are, by believing, both fortified in advance and prepared by God, who will enlighten us. And you know, Honoratus, that for no other reason did we fall in with such men than that they kept saying that they would lead willing listeners to God by pure and simple reason, separate from any terror-inspiring authority, and free them from all error. What else forced me for almost nine years, during which time I rejected the religion my parents had implanted in me as a child, to follow these people and listen to them diligently? What other reason than their saying that we had been terrified by superstition, that faith had been demanded of us before reason, while they, on the other hand, imposed faith on no one, but rather first hunted for and disentangled the truth? Who would not be enticed by these promises? And would there not be special enticement for a young mind desiring the truth and yet haughty and talkative in debates within the school of certain learned men? Such a one they then found me, spurning, of course, what seemed to be old wives' tales and desiring to get hold of and drink in the sincere and open truth they promised. But, again, what reason kept me from embracing them completely, so that I remained in that rank they call "hearers" (so as not to lose hope of this world altogether with its affairs), except that I noticed that they themselves were more fluent and eloquent in refuting others than they were strong and sure in proving their own beliefs? . . .

(8.20) Let me outline for you, as best I can, the method I used in seeking true religion. . . . For as I left you and crossed the sea, I was wavering, now delaying, now hesitating, as to what I should hold to and what I should discard. For my vacillation grew greater from day to day from the time I heard that man[20] whose coming, as you know, was promised to be like one sent from heaven to solve all our difficulties, and I found him, except for a certain eloquence, just like the others. I deliberated long and hard, once I settled down in Italy, not as to whether I should remain in that sect that I now regretted having fallen into, but how to find the truth. No one knows better than you how I sighed, longing for that truth. Often it seemed to me that it could not be found, and the surging, agitated waves of my thinking carried me along to favor the Academics.[21] Often, reflecting as best I could, gazing into the hu-

---

20. "That man": Faustus of Milevis. See *conf.* 5.6.10–7.13 (CCL 27:61–64).
21. "Academics": On this philosophical school, see Chapter 2.

man mind—so lively, so wise, so perceptive—I did not think that the truth lay hidden, only that the way to search for it did, and that the approach to it would have to be taken on the basis of some divine authority. It remained to figure out what that authority was, since there was a great cacophony of voices, and every one promised that he could deliver it. I, therefore, ran up against this impenetrable forest, which was frustrating to be stuck in for so long a time. And in the middle of this, without any respite, my mind was driven by a passionate desire once more to find the truth. I kept turning more and more away from those I was determined to get away from. In such serious dangers there remained no other alternative than to beg the help of Divine Providence with tears and anguished cries, and this I did without ceasing. And now some arguments of the Bishop of Milan moved me to wish to explore, not without some hope, into many matters concerning the Old Testament itself, which, as you know, we used to invoke curses on since it had been misrepresented to us. And I also decided to be a catechumen in the Church that my parents had committed me to until I should either find what I wanted or convince myself that the search could not be made. Had there been anyone who at that time could teach me, he would have found me very ready and receptive. In this and similar ways let there be a care for your soul. Long have you also seen yourself moved, and if now you think you have been tormented long enough and you wish to put an end to sufferings of this kind, follow the path of Catholic teaching which has come down to us from the apostles through Christ Himself, and will continue on through the ages.[22]

BELIEVE IN ORDER TO UNDERSTAND

Manichean mockery of Christianity's demand for faith prompted Augustine on the far side of his conversion to meditate on the relationships among faith and reason and authority. To summarize his core position, he appealed to the Septuagint's rendering of Isaiah 7:9: "Unless you believe, you shall not understand." In the following passage, Augustine notes that belief is necessary not only for religious progress but even for secular society. First, he observes that our knowledge of history always depends on faith of sorts: trusting the historical documents we use to reconstruct our past. Here he points to a textbook example of Cicero. Second, he points out that we would not even know if our parents were really our parents without some degree of belief. From On the Advantage of Believing:

22. De utilitate credendi 1.2–8.20 (CSEL 25.1:4–25); my trans., based on Meagher, FOTC 4:392–417. On this, see Isabelle Bochet, "L'unité du De utilitate credendi d'Augustin," in Van Oort et al., *Augustine and Manichaeism*, 24–42.

(9.21) [Manichees] accuse the Catholic Church especially of commanding those who come to her to believe, whereas they boast that they do not impose the yoke of believing on their followers, but open up a fountain of teaching. "What should one say?" you ask. "Is that not more a side of theirs that deserves praise?" No, that's not the point. For they do this not because they are endowed with real strength, but to win over large numbers under the name of "reason." The human soul naturally enjoys such promises, but it fails to consider its powers or well-being and craves for the food of the healthy—food wrongly given to any but the strong—and quickly downs these deceivers' poison. One cannot rightly enter the path of true religion without submitting to a certain weight of authority about things that must first be believed, things that later, once one has performed well and proved worthy, one arrives at and perceives.

(9.22) Now perhaps you ask for some reasonable explanation of this issue that would convince you that you ought to be taught first by faith rather than by reason. This is easy to do, provided you stay fair-minded. But so as to do it in a helpful way, I want you to answer me as though I were questioning you. First of all, tell me why you think one should not believe. "Because," you say, "credulity—from which the credulous get their name—seems to me to be a fault. Otherwise, we would not be in the habit of using this term as a criticism. . . ." (10.23) You [also] say, "Let's see whether we should even believe in matters that have to do with religion. For even if we concede that it is one thing to believe and another thing to be credulous, it does not follow that there is no fault in believing in matters of religion." . . .

(11.25) Now, in other matters, if someone believes something, there is no fault in it provided one does not claim to understand what one does not know [for certain]. For example, I believe that wicked conspirators were once put to death thanks to Cicero's virtue, and yet I not only do not know this [historical fact]; I even know that there is no way in which I can know it. . . . For even if someone thinks he knows that fact that I mentioned about Cicero, although nothing prevents one from learning about it, the matter itself cannot be grasped as a matter of knowledge. Now, if one does not understand that there is a great difference between grasping something with certainty by the mind's reasoning—what we call "understanding"—and believing what has been profitably handed down by oral tradition or by books for later generations, then one certainly errs, and no error lacks some disgrace. Therefore, whatever we understand we owe to reason; whatever we believe we owe to authority; whatever we are opinionated about we owe to error. But everyone who understands also believes, and everyone who is opinionated believes as well. But not everyone who believes understands, and no one who is opinionated understands. . . . Now those people who say that we are to believe nothing except what we know [with certainty] are on their guard against what goes under the name of "opinion"—what, admittedly, is ugly and wretched. But if they would consider carefully the great difference between thinking that one knows something and believing, on the basis of authority, something that one is aware that one does not know [for certain], then they would avoid errors and the charge of pride and lacking humanity.

(12.26) Now if something unknown is deemed unworthy of belief, then I ask: How are children to serve their parents? How are they to love with mutual affection those whom they do not believe to be their real parents? There is no way we can know by reason that [our parents are our parents]. Who one's father is is believed on the authority of one's mother; as for one's mother, she herself has to believe midwives, nurses, and slaves. Now can't she, from whom a son can be stolen and another substituted, having been deceived herself, deceive others? Nevertheless, we believe, and we believe without any hesitation what we admit we cannot know. For who would not see that, unless this were so, filial devotion, the most sacred bond of the human race, would be violated by massive criminal arrogance? Is there anyone so insane as to think that someone is guilty for carrying out filial duties towards those he believed to be his parents even if they were not in reality? Who, on the other hand, would not judge that a person deserves exile, if, for fear that he might possibly love imposters, he did not love those who were his real parents? Many examples can be cited which would show that absolutely nothing would remain intact in human society if we decided not to believe what we cannot grasp with a certainty of perception.[23]

THE PROBLEM OF EVIL

Augustine notes, in a brief autobiographical aside in an early philosophic dialogue (begun around 388), how the problem of evil had haunted him from a young age and how Manichean evangelists had used it to win him over. From On Free Will, Book 1:

(2.4) Evodius. Tell me the reason we do evil.

Augustine. You raise a question which sorely perplexed me while I was still a young man, and one which in my weariness drove me into the company of heretics and resulted in my fall. I was so injured by this fall, so weighed down by the vast accumulation of nonsensical fables that, had not the love of find-

---

23. De utilitate credendi 9.21–12.26 (CSEL 25.1:26–34); my trans., based on Meagher, FOTC 4:417–27.

-ing the truth obtained divine aid for me, I would have been unable to rise from this fall and to breathe again in the former atmosphere of free inquiry. And as I took great pains to extricate myself from this perplexity, so I will follow the same procedure with you that led to my liberation. For God will be at hand and will enable us to understand what we have believed. We know well that we are following the course enjoined by the prophet who says: "Unless you believe, you shall not understand" (Is 7:9 [LXX]). We believe that all things in existence are from the one God, though He is not the author of sin. But this problem confronts the mind: If sins come from souls created by God, while these souls in turn come from God, how is it that sins are not at once chargeable to God?[24]

THE CORRUPTIBLE GOD OF THE MANICHEES

The Manichees offered, at first glance, an easy solution to the problem of evil: evil was a realm opposed to God, something that God neither made nor was responsible for. In Manichean myth, God sent forth an emanation of his own substance which, in turn, was captured by the Kingdom of Darkness, resulting in the world's current mixed-up condition. This cosmological myth implied that the God of the Manichees, while good in and of Himself, was divisible, changeable, and corruptible. It further implied that He is not all-powerful. Augustine credits his friend Nebridius with spotting this web of philosophic problems built into the very heart of Manichean cosmogony. Augustine came to see this as the most formidable argument against Manicheism. From Confessions, Book 7:

(2.3) That argument proposed by Nebridius so long ago back in Carthage—O Lord, that was enough for me to refute those deceived deceivers and voiceless chatterers (for out of them your Word never resonated). All of us who heard it were all struck by it: What would those forces of darkness, which had massed in opposition [to the Kingdom of Light], have done if You had refused to fight them? If one were to answer that You would have been harmed, then that would mean that You would be capable of violation and, thus, corruptible. If, however, one were to say that nothing is able to harm You, then no reason for fighting would arise, no fight such that some portion of You, some segment of Yours, or some offspring of Your very substance could get mixed up with those opposing powers (with natures that You supposedly did not create) and by them become so corrupted and so changed for the worse that blessedness would be turned into misery and need help to be

24. De libero arbitrio 1.2.4 (CCL 29:213); trans. Russell, FOTC 59:75.

plucked up and purged, and this fragment, supposedly, is the soul to whom Your Word comes to the rescue, making the enslaved free, and the contaminated pure, and the corrupted whole. But [in Manichean myth] Your Word is itself corruptible because it comes from the very same substance as the soul. Thus if one says that You—whatever You are, that is, the substance You are—are incorruptible, the whole thing becomes false and execrable; but if corruptible, then from the outset this all would be false and abominable. So this argument should have been enough to refute these people whom I should have vomited out from my bloated stomach, for they had no way of escaping the horrible sacrilege in heart and tongue present in thinking and speaking those things about You.[25]

INSUBSTANTIAL EVIL

In his earliest anti-Manichean treatise, On the Catholic and the Manichean Ways of Life, *begun in Rome around 388, not long after his baptism, Augustine discusses his breakthrough insight about the nature of evil. Where the Manichees spoke of evil as something opposed to God, Augustine came to see evil not as a thing in itself, but as nothing, a privation of being, an unmaking of the good that God had made. This breakthrough came, in part, from his reading of those "books of the Platonists" while in Milan. The following passage on the metaphysics of evil is not an easy one and may need to be read aloud to savor its logic. From* On the Catholic and the Manichean Ways of Life, *Book 2:*

(2.2) You Manichees often, if not always, ask those whom you are working hard to win over to your heresy where evil comes from. Suppose that I had just met you for the first time. And here, if you don't mind, I request a favor: that you lay aside for the time being the impression that you already know the answer, and that you approach this great question as an untrained mind would do. You ask me where evil comes from, and I, in turn, ask you what evil is. Who is asking the right question? Those who ask where evil comes from, although they do not know what it is? Or the person who thinks he must first ask what it is so as not to perpetuate what is absurd, namely, seeking the origin of an unknown thing? You are quite correct in asking who is so blind mentally as not to see that evil for any species is whatever is contrary to its nature. But once this is established, your heresy is turned upside down, for evil is no nature if it is what is contrary to nature. Yet you claim that evil is some sort of nature and substance. Moreover, whatever is contrary to nature

25. *Conf.* 7.2.3 (CCL 27:93–94); my trans.

opposes nature and attempts to destroy it, seeking to make whatever exists cease to exist. For a nature is nothing other than what a thing is understood to be in terms of its species. And just as we call what a being is by the new word "essence" or, more often, "substance," so the ancients who did not have these [terms] used the word "nature." And, therefore, if you are willing to put aside all obstinacy, you will see that evil is that which falls away from essence and tends to non-being.

(2.3) When the Catholic Church declares that God is the author of natures and substances, those who understand what this means understand at the same time that God is not the author of evil. For how can He who is the cause of the being of all things be at the same time the cause of their not being—that is, of their falling away from being and tending to non-being? That is what the most accurate reasoning declares evil to be. But how can that evil kingdom of yours, which you like to call "the supreme evil," be contrary to nature, that is, to substance, when you claim it to be a nature and a substance? For if it acts against itself, it deprives itself of its own being, and if it were even to succeed completely in this, it would then arrive at the supreme evil. But this will not happen, inasmuch as you choose, not only to have it exist, but to exist eternally. Therefore, it is not possible that the supreme evil be considered a substance. . . .

(3.5) Let us, therefore, pursue this question more carefully and, if possible, more clearly. I ask you once again: What is evil? If you say it is what is harmful, you would not be inaccurate. But I ask you to pay attention, to stay alert, to put aside partisan spirit, and seek the truth in order to find it, not fight it. Whatever is harmful deprives what it is harmful to of some good. For if no good is taken away, no harm is done. What, may I ask, could be more obvious than this? What could be plainer or easier to understand by a person of even ordinary intelligence, provided he not be stubborn? Once this is granted, however, it seems to me that the consequences become obvious. Surely, no harm can come to anything in the kingdom you think of as "the supreme evil" since there is nothing good there. If, as you claim, there are two natures, the kingdom of light and the kingdom of darkness, and since, as you admit, the kingdom of light is God—to whom you concede a simple nature with no part inferior to any other—then you must grant something irreconcilably opposed to your position, yet unavoidable: You must grant that this nature [of God], which you do not deny to be the supreme good (and, in fact, vehemently proclaim to be so), is immutable, impenetrable, incorruptible, and inviolable. Otherwise, it would not be the supreme good. The supreme good, after all, is that than which there is nothing better. But such a nature can in no way be harmed. Now, if to harm is to deprive of good, as I have shown, then the kingdom of darkness cannot be harmed because there is nothing good in it, and the kingdom of light cannot be harmed because it is inviolable. To what, then, can the evil you speak of do harm?

(4.6) Since you are unable to extricate yourself from this difficulty, see how easily the problem is solved according to Catholic doctrine. It teaches that there is one good in itself and in the highest sense, that is, by its own nature and essence and not by participation in some other good, and that there is another good that is good by participation, deriving its goodness from the Supreme Good, which, however, continues to be itself and loses nothing. We say that this [derived] good . . . is a creature to whom harm can come by defecting, by unmaking, but God is not the author of such defect, such an unmaking, since God is the author of existence and, so, of being. It becomes clear, then, how "evil" is to be spoken about, for it is properly applied not to essence, but to privation. Now it is apparent that nature can be harmed. The supreme evil cannot itself be a nature from which some good can be stripped away. Nor can it be the supreme good, since it can fall away from the good, not because it is good in its own being, but because it has goodness. And no thing which is spoken of as being made can be good by nature, since to be made means to receive goodness from another. So God is the supreme good, and things He has made are all good, although they are not as good as the One who made them. For it would be madness to demand that works be equal to the workman, that creatures be equal to the Creator. What more do you Manichees want? Do you wish something even clearer than this?

(5.7) Then let me ask you a third time: What is evil? You will perhaps answer, "corruption." And who would deny that this belongs to evil in general since corruption does not exist in itself? It exists in some substance, which it corrupts, for corruption itself is not a substance. Therefore, the thing it corrupts is not corruption, is not evil, for what is corrupted is deprived of integrity and purity. That which has no purity that it can be deprived of cannot be corrupted, while that which has purity is good by participation in purity. Furthermore, what is corrupted is perverted, and what is perverted is deprived of order. But order is good. Therefore, what is corrupted is not devoid of good, and it is for this very reason that it can be deprived of good in being corrupted. Thus, if the kingdom of darkness were devoid of all goodness, as you say it is, it could not be corrupted, for it would not have anything that corruption could take away, and if corruption takes nothing away, it does not corrupt. Now try to say, if you can, that God and the kingdom of God can be corrupted, when you have not even found a way in which the kingdom of the devil, as you describe it, can be corrupted.

(6.8) What is the Catholic light on this issue? What do you suppose it is, other than having the truth? Namely, that what is able to be corrupted is a created substance, for the uncreated (what is the supreme good) is the incorruptible, and that corruption itself (what is the supreme evil) cannot be corrupted since it is not a substance. If, however, you want to know what corruption is, look and see the state to which it tends to bring whatever it corrupts. For it affects things that are corrupted. By corruption, all things cease to be what they were and are brought to non-permanence, to non-being. Being, after all, implies permanence. Therefore, what we call "the supreme and highest being" is so called because it is permanent in its very self. . . . Some things change for the better and in so doing tend toward being. They are not said to be perverted by the change, but rather reverted and converted, turned round and turned right. Perversion, after all, is opposed to setting in order. But those things which tend toward being thus tend toward order, and, in attaining order, they attain being so far as it can be attained by creatures. Order brings about whatever it orders to a certain fittingness. To be, however, is nothing other than to be one. And so, to the extent that a thing acquires unity, to that extent it has being. Unity, you see, brings about the fittingness and harmony by which composite things have their measure of being. Simple things exist in themselves because they are one. But those that are not simple imitate unity through the harmony of their parts and, in the measure that they achieve their harmony, they exist. From all of this, we can conclude that order produces being, and disorder, which is also called perversion or corruption, produces non-being. . . .

(7.9) But the goodness of God does not permit a thing to be brought to this point [of non-being]. Goodness disposes all things that fall away so that they occupy the place most suited to them until, by an ordered movement, they return to that from which they fell away. And even the rational souls that fall away from Him, although they possess that immense power of free choice, are placed in the lower ranks of creatures, where such souls ought to be. And thus, by the divine judgment, they are made to suffer since they are ranked in accordance with their merits.[26]

UNDE MALUM?

In the passage above, Augustine notes how Manichean evangelists used the question "Where does evil come from?" (Unde malum?) to draw in hearers and bring them over

26. De moribus 2.2.2–7.9 (CSEL 90:89–95); my trans. based on Gallagher and Gallagher, FOTC 56:66–71. On this aspect of Augustine's worldview and its difficulties, see Rowan Williams, "Insubstantial Evil," in Dodaro and Lawless, Augustine and His Critics, 105–23.

to Manichean views. In that same passage, Augustine insisted that one must first answer the metaphysical question "What is evil?" He did go on to confront the question where evil comes from in his philosophical dialogue On Free Will (De libero arbitrio). Its opening book dates from the same period as On the Catholic and the Manichean Ways of Life, namely, his stint in Rome (387–388) soon after his baptism. His dialogue partner is presumed to be Evodius, a friend of his who later became bishop of Uzalis (though the key manuscripts lack the name).[27] The following passage from the work's opening sets out key initial distinctions. From On Free Will, Book 1:

(1.1) Evodius. Tell me, is God not [ultimately] the author of evil?

Augustine. I will tell you if you make it clear what kind of evil you are in-quiring about. For we usually speak of evil in two ways: first, when we say that someone has done evil; second, when someone has suffered something evil.

Ev. I am eager to know about both kinds.

Aug. But if you know (or take it on faith) that God is good—and it would be irreligious to think differently—then He does no evil. Again, if we ac-knowledge that God is just—and to deny this would be sacrilegious—then just as He bestows rewards upon the good, so He metes out punishments to the wicked. Such punishments seem, of course, to be evil to those who suffer them. Accordingly, if no one suffers penalties unjustly—and this we must be-lieve since we believe that the universe is ruled by Divine Providence—God is not at all the cause of the first kind of evil, though He is of the second.

Ev. Is there not, therefore, some other author of that evil which we have found cannot be God?

Aug. There certainly is, for without an author, evil could not happen. But if you ask me who that author is, no [one] answer is possible, for it is no one person but rather each evil person who is the author of his or her own mis-deeds. If you have any doubt of this, take note of our earlier remark that evil deeds are punished by God's justice. For unless they were committed volun-tarily, their punishment would not be just.[28]

27. Printed editions ever since the Maurists' 17th-century edition have designated De libero arbitrio's two characters as "Evodius" and "Augustine," even though there is not good evidence in surviving manuscripts. In ep. 162.2, Augustine mentions to Evodius that this work was one that "I composed when you were in con-versation and discussion with me." On that basis, presumably, most scholars accept the Maurist decision to insert Evodius's name. But an examination of surviving manuscripts and a recognition of ancient ways of designating dialogues open up alternative readings. On this issue, see Simon Harrison, Augustine's Way into the Will: The Theological and Philosophical Significance of De Libero Arbitrio, OECS (New York: Oxford Uni-versity Press, 2006), 31–50.

28. De libero arbitrio 1.1.1 (CCL 29:211); trans. Russell, FOTC 59:72–73. The role of the will as the source of evil would become a central point of contention in the later Pelagian controversy. In fact, Pelagius him-self would quote from this treatise of Augustine, and Augustine would feel compelled to defend this work at length; see retr. 1.9 [8]. See Chapter 10.

Defining Free Will

Augustine completed Books 2 and 3 of On Free Will *several years later, after his ordination as a presbyter.*[29] *In these later books, Augustine explores and argues for the freedom of the will. We need to bear in mind how his opponents viewed things. Manichees saw the human person as a battleground in the war between the Kingdom of Light and the Kingdom of Darkness and located evil within the human body. They also presumed that a certain moral determinism came from being embodied. Augustine came to affirm not only the body's goodness, but also freedom of the will. Our wills, not our bodies, are the real (though still mysterious) origin of evil. In the following passage, Augustine stresses both human freedom and responsibility and the necessity of the grace of Christ. From* On Free Will, *Book 2:*

(19.53) Evil consists in the will's turning away from the changeless good [that God is] and in its turning to goods that are changeable. Since this turning from one thing to another is not done from necessity, but freely, the unhappiness that results is justly deserved.

(20.54) Since the will undergoes movement when it turns from the unchangeable good to changeable goods, you may ask how this movement originates. It is really evil, though free will itself must be considered a good, since it is impossible to live rightly without it. If this movement, namely, the turning away of the will from the Lord, is unquestionably sinful, we cannot say that God is the cause of sin. If this movement, therefore, does not come from God, then where does it come from? If I reply to your question by saying that I do not know, you may be distressed all the more. Yet I would be answering you correctly because that which is nothing cannot be known. Only make sure to hold firm to your religious conviction that any good that you know—either by the senses or by the intellect or in any other way—comes from God. . . . All good is from God and, consequently, there is no nature that is not from God. Hence, that movement of the soul's turning away, which we admitted was sinful, is a defective movement, and every defect arises from non-being. Look for the source of this movement and be sure that it does not come from God. Yet since it is voluntary, this defect lies within our power. If you are fearful of it, then your will is against it, and unless you will it, it will not exist. What could be more secure than to live a life where nothing can happen to you which you do not will? But since a human being cannot rise of his own will as he fell of his own will, the right hand of God, namely, our Lord Jesus Christ, is outstretched to us from above. Let us embrace Him

---

29. *Retr.* 1.9.1 (CCL 57:23). Because of the gap between Book 1 and Books 2–3, some scholars have argued for shifts and differences; on this, see Simon Harrison, *Augustine's Way into the Will,* 17–27. Harrison himself has argued persuasively for treating the work as unified (pp. 28–31, 50–54).

with a strong faith, await Him with a sure hope, and love Him with an ardent charity.[30]

ANSWERING OBJECTIONS TO GENESIS

The Manichees attacked Genesis on numerous scores. They especially singled out Gn 1:26, that human beings are made in God's "image and likeness"—which, they argued, implied that the God of Genesis had a body, just as humans do. Here Augustine, to rebut this, alerts his audience to the metaphorical character of the Genesis text. From On Genesis Against the Manichees, *Book 1:*

(17.27) It is this question above all that the Manichees raised with their endless chatter, and they taunt us for believing that the human person was made to the image and likeness of God. They look at the shape of our body and ask so infelicitously whether God has a nose and teeth and a beard and also inner organs and other things we need. It is, however, ridiculous, even wicked, to believe that there are such things in God, and so they deny that we were made to the image and likeness of God.[31] We answer them that the Scriptures generally mention bodily parts in presenting God to an audience of the little ones, and this is true, not only of the books of the Old Testament, but also of the New Testament. For the New Testament mentions God's eyes and ears and lips and feet, and the Gospel proclaims that the Son is seated at the right hand of God the Father. The Lord himself says, "Do not swear by heaven, for it is the throne of God, nor by the earth, for it is his footstool" (Mt 5:34–35). Likewise He says that He was casting out demons by the finger of God (Lk 11:20). All who understand the Scriptures spiritually have learned to understand by those terms, not bodily parts, but spiritual powers, as they do in the case of helmets and shield and sword and many other things (Eph 6:16, 17). Hence, we should first point out to these heretics the impudence with which they attack such words of the Old Testament, since they see these things used in the New Testament as well. Or perhaps they do not see them since they are blinded by their disputes.

(17.28) Let them know, nonetheless, that the spiritual believers in the Catholic teaching do not believe that God is limited by a bodily shape. When a person is said to have been made to the image of God, these words refer to the interior person, where reason and intellect reside. From these the human being also has power over the fish of the sea and the birds of heaven and all cattle

---

30. *De libero arbitrio* 2.19.53–20.54 (CCL 29:273); trans. Russell, FOTC 59:162–63.

31. See *conf.* 6.3.4 (CCL 27:76), where Augustine notes his relief that Christians did not actually hold the anthropomorphic view of God that Manichees accused them of holding.

and wild animals and all the earth and all reptiles which creep upon the earth. For when God said, "Let us make man to our image and likeness," he immediately added, "And let him have power over the fish of the sea and the birds of heaven" (Gn 1:27–28) and the rest, so that we might understand that the human being is said to have been made to the image of God, not on account of his body, but on account of that power by which he surpasses the cattle. For all the other animals are subject to us, not by reason of the body, but by reason of the intellect, which we have and they do not. Even our body has been made so that it reveals that we are better than the beasts and, for that reason, like God. For the bodies of all the animals which live either in the waters or on the earth, or which fly in the air, are turned toward the earth and are not erect as is the human body. This signifies that our mind ought to be raised up toward those things above it, that is, to eternal spiritual things. It is especially by reason of the mind that we understand that the human person was made to the image and likeness of God, as even the erect form of the body testifies.[32]

THE GOODNESS OF CREATION

In the opening chapter of Genesis, God is said to affirm repeatedly that what He had made on each day was "good" and that at the creation's completion, it was all "very good." At the close of Confessions, *Augustine meditates on Genesis and its affirmation of the goodness of creation. This section is important because it alerts us that* Confessions *is not simply autobiography. It is what its title says it is: a confession of faith. Here Augustine the ex-Manichee affirms what he had once denied. From* Confessions, *Book 13:*

(28.43) And You saw, O God, all the things that You had made, and, behold, "they were very good" (Gn 1:31). We too see them, and, behold, they are all very good. For each kind of Your works, when You had said that they were to be made and they were made, You saw that each in turn is good. I have counted seven times where it is written that You did see that what you had made is good; and this is the eighth, that You did see all things that You had made, and, behold, they are not merely good, but very good when taken all together. For the individual things are merely good, but all together they are both good and very much so. All beautiful bodies express the same truth, for a body is far more beautiful in the fact that it is constituted out of parts which are all beautiful than are these parts taken individually; for the whole is perfected by the most orderly gathering of these parts—even though they are also beautiful when considered individually. . . .

---

32. *De Genesi adversus Manichaeos* 1.17.27–17.28 (BA 50:218–22); trans. Teske, FOTC 84:74–76.

(32.47) Thanks be to You, O Lord! We see heaven and earth, either the higher and lower corporeal parts, or spiritual and corporeal creation. And for the adornment of these parts, by which either the whole bulk of the world or the entire created universe is constituted, we see light made and separated from darkness. We see the firmament of heaven, the original body of the world, . . . or this stretch of atmosphere (for it is also called heaven, through which the birds of the heavens fly about aimlessly between the waters which are carried above them in vapor and which even fall in dew on calm nights), and those waters which are heavy and flow upon the earth.

We behold the beautiful form of the waters gathered upon the plains of the sea and the dry land, either bare [of vegetation] or formed so as to be visible and ordered, the mother of plants and trees. We see the luminous bodies shining on high: the sun is adequate for the day, the moon and stars console the night—and periods of time are marked and indicated by all these. We see the moist part of nature, teeming in every portion with fish and animals and birds, because the density of the atmosphere which supports the flight of birds thickens by means of the evaporation of the waters. We see that the face of the earth is adorned by earthly animals and that the human person, in Your image and likeness, is placed above all irrational living things by this image and likeness of Yours, namely, the power of reason and of understanding. And just as there is one thing in his soul which rules by virtue of the act of deliberation and there is another which is made subject so that it may obey, so also there was also made for man, corporeally, woman—who had, indeed, a nature equal in mental capacity of rational intelligence but made subject, by virtue of the sex of her body, to the male sex in the same way that the appetite for action is made subject in order to conceive by the rational mind the skill of acting rightly. We see these things, and they are individually good; but all together, they are very good.[33]

The Unity of the Testaments

In debating the Manichees, Augustine had to work out principles for the unity of the Testaments. He eventually encapsulated his view in a favorite one-liner: "In the Old Testament the New is concealed, and in the New the Old is revealed."[34] Here is an earlier account. From On the Advantage of Believing:

(3.9) These wicked [Manichees], while they try to render the Law null and void, . . . note the saying that those who are under the Law are in servitude,

33. Conf. 13.28.43–32.47 (CCL 27:267–70); trans. Bourke, FOTC 21:447–52.
34. De catechizandis rudibus 4.8 (CCL 46:128); my trans.

and they air widely one final passage in preference to others: "You who are justified in the Law are empty, separated from Christ. You have fallen from grace" (Gal 5:4). We grant all this to be true, and we do not say the Law is necessary except for those for whom its servitude is still profitable. For this reason was the Law well enacted, that people who could not be recalled by reason from sin had to be forced by such a law, that is, by the threats and terrors of those penalties which even fools can understand. And when the grace of Christ frees us from these, it does not condemn the Law, but invites us to be obedient to its love, not to be a slave to a fear of the Law. This itself is a grace, that is, a blessing, that they who still desire to be under the chains of the Law do not realize it has providentially come to them. Paul rightly rebukes these as unbelievers because they do not believe that they have now been set free through Jesus Christ our Lord from the servitude to which, for a fixed period, they had been subjected according to the very just dispensation of God. Hence that statement of the Apostle: "For the Law was our pedagogue in Christ" (Gal 3:24). God thus gave people a pedagogue to fear; later He gave them a teacher to love. And yet in these precepts and commandments of the Law—things that are not now lawful for Christians to use, such as sabbath or circumcision or sacrifices or anything of this kind—such great mysteries are contained that every faithful person realizes that nothing is more dangerous than to take whatever is there literally, that is, according to its wording, while nothing is more health-giving than what is revealed by the spirit. Thus, the saying: "The letter kills, but the spirit gives life" (2 Cor 3:6).[35] And also: "The same veil remains when they read the Old Testament and there is no revealing, yet in Christ it is taken away" (2 Cor 3:14). What is taken away in Christ is not the Old Testament but its veil so that through Christ it may be understood and, as it were, laid bare—what, without Christ, would be obscure and covered over. And so the same Apostle immediately adds: "But whenever you are converted to Christ, the veil will be taken away" (2 Cor 3:16). But he does not say, "The Law will be taken away" or "The Old Testament will be taken away." These, then, have not been taken away through the grace of the Lord as though they concealed useless things. Rather, what was removed was their covering under which useful things were hidden. This is the regimen followed in the case of those who seek the meaning of the Scriptures studiously and faithfully, not wildly or rashly. A painstaking demonstration can be made of the order of things—of the reasons for deeds and words and of the agreement of the Old Testament with the New—so that not a point is left where there is not harmony, where among the figures such secret truths are con-

35. "'The letter kills . . .'" (2 Cor 3:6): See *conf.* 6.4.6 (cited in Chapter 1), where Augustine notes that Ambrose routinely cited this text "as though he were most carefully commending it as a rule" of exegesis.

veyed that, once interpreted, force those who wanted beforehand to condemn rather than learn to confess their own misery.[36]

CHRIST'S REFRESHING PRESENCE IN THE OLD TESTAMENT

Faustus had dismissed the Old Testament as unworthy of and worthless to true Christians. This attitude exasperated Augustine. In his Against Faustus, he spends more energy answering this objection than any other. Why? Because, as time went on, he became deeply convinced that the Old Testament did not simply offer scattered predictions about Christ's coming; it itself contained the story of Christ. To reject the Old Testament was to reject Christ. He tells Faustus at one point: "Everything contained there in the texts [of the Old Testament] is said either of Christ or on account of him."[37] In the following passage, one sees how Augustine sensed Christ's "refreshing" presence everywhere in the pages of the Old Testament. From Against Faustus the Manichee, Book 12:

(25) You say that Christ was not predicted by the Israelite prophets—Christ, the One for whom all those [Old Testament] pages keep vigil, looking out so as to predict him. If only you would just piously scrutinize things rather than superficially rail against them. Who else left his own land and his own kinsmen in the person of Abraham in order to grow rich and prosperous among outsiders (Gn 12:1–3) but the One who, as we see, abandoned the land and kin of the Jews—from which He was born according to the flesh—and flourished and prevailed among the Gentiles? Who else carried wood for sacrifice in the person of Isaac (Gn 22:6) but the One who Himself carried the cross for His own Passion? What other soon-to-be-immolated ram got His horns snagged in a thornbush (Gn 22:13) except the One who got fastened to the cross-beam of the cross as an offering on our behalf?

(26) Who else wrestled with Jacob in the person of the angel when, on the one hand, He blessed—as the weaker to the stronger and the conquered to the conqueror—the one who overcame him and yet, on the other hand, He rendered [Jacob's] thigh bone lame (Gn 32:24–31), but the One who, having allowed the people of Israel to overcome Him, blessed those among them who believed in Him? Jacob's thigh, however, became lame, as it were, in the multitude of the people of His flesh. What other stone was placed at Jacob's head and was even anointed (Gn 28:11) but Christ, the head of the [new] man? (This happened so that, in some way, it would be named and expressed. For

---

36. *De utilitate credendi* 3.9 (CSEL 25.1:12–13); my trans., based on Meagher, FOTC 4:400–402.
37. *Contra Faustum* 12.7 (CSEL 25.1:335); my trans.

who is unaware that "Christ" means "anointed one"?) Christ refers to this very thing in the Gospel and testifies to it openly as a figure of Himself when He said that a certain Nathaniel was a true Israelite, in whom there was no deceit. And when that man (as though having that Stone at his head) confessed that Christ was Son of God and King of Israel (Jn 1:47–50), by this confession in some way anointing the stone, that is, acknowledging that Christ was the Anointed One, then the Lord rightly recalled the matter, what Jacob—who, through the blessing, was called Israel—saw: "Amen I say to you, you will see the heavens open and the angels of God ascending and descending upon the Son of Man" (Jn 1:51). For Israel had seen this when he had the stone at his head: a stairway from earth to heaven on which the angels of God were ascending and descending (Gn 28:11–18).

The angels symbolize the evangelists, the preachers of Christ. The ascending refers to how they, in seeking to understand Christ's super-eminent divinity, transcend the created universe to find, as in the beginning, God with God, the One through whom all things were made. The descending, however, refers to finding Him "born from a woman, born under the Law, in order that He may redeem those who were under the Law" (Gal 4:4–5). For in Him there is a stairway from earth to heaven, from flesh to spirit, because, in progressing in Him, fleshly persons become spiritual ones by ascending. And these spiritual persons themselves descend in a certain way to those being nourished on milk when they cannot speak to them as spiritual ones but only as fleshly (1 Cor 3:1–3). And thus they both ascend and descend upon the Son of Man. For the Son of Man is above as our Head—that is, the Savior Himself—and the Son of Man is below in His body—that is, the Church. We understand that He Himself is the stairway because He Himself said: "I am the Way" (Jn 14:6). To Him, therefore, one ascends in order that He may be understood as He is in heaven's heights; and to Him one descends in order that the little ones may be nourished in His members. And so through Him one ascends and descends. Following His example, those who are preachers not only rise up in order that they may see Him in His sublimity but, humbling themselves, announce Him soberly. Look, see the Apostle ascending: "If we become ecstatic in mind," he says, "it is for God." Look, see him descending: "If we become sober," he says, "it is for you" (2 Cor 5:13). Let the Apostle speak of the One by whom he ascends and descends: "For the love of Christ compels us to the conviction that if one has died for all, then all have died. And He died for all, that those who live live no longer for themselves but for Him who died and rose for them" (2 Cor 5:14–15).

(27) Those who take no delight in these sacred scenes of sacred Scripture turn to [Manichean] fables, unable to sustain themselves on healthy teaching (2 Tm 4:3–4). And, of course, those fables provoke all sorts of delights in the

childish-minded, whatever their bodily age. But we who are the body of Christ recognize in the Psalm our own voice, and so let us say to them: "The unjust have told me of their delights; they are not like your law, Lord" (Ps 118:85). I wander and scour [the Old Testament], winded, sweating from humanity's condemnation, and Christ meets me and refreshes me everywhere in those books, everywhere in those Scriptures, whether out in the open or in hidden ways. He sets me on fire, sparked by the desire that comes from the difficulty in discovering Him, so that I may soak up what I avidly find and, by what's hidden in its marrow, reach journey's end in good health.[38]

THE REALITY OF THE INCARNATION

Augustine challenged inconsistencies in Manichean Christology: its multiple Christs, its fears about the Incarnation, its claims that the "suffering Christ" was trapped in fruits and vegetables and liberated by the Elect, whose vegetarian eating habits free up light fragments. Against this, Augustine insisted on the accuracy, authenticity, and authority of the Gospels and on the reality of the Incarnation. From Against Faustus the Manichee, Books 20 and 26:

(20.11) You say that the earth—conceived by the Holy Spirit—brings forth "the suffering Jesus." This Jesus, you claim, hangs from every tree in the form of fruits and vegetables, and, besides this contamination, is further contaminated by the living bodies of innumerable animals who eat these fruits, and that this Jesus is purified only in a small portion to which your hunger comes to the rescue. We [on the other hand] believe in heart and confess in prayer that Christ, the Son of God, the Word of God, put on flesh without contamination because God's substance—what no thing can contaminate—cannot be contaminated by flesh. . . . Tell us then how many Christs you say that there are. Isn't one of them the suffering Jesus, whom earth conceives and brings forth, hanging not only from every tree but also sprouting up in the grass, and then a second one whom the Jews crucified under Pontius Pilate, and then a third one strung out between the sun and the moon? Or is it one and the same Christ: one part, tied up in the trees; the other, free, coming to the rescue of the tied-up and held-hostage? If this is so, and you concede that Christ suffered under Pontius Pilate, although, as you tell it, he did so without flesh—I'm not yet asking how it's possible he could suffer such a death without flesh, but I am asking to whom he left those ships [of the sun and the moon] so that he might come down from there and suffer the sort of things

---

38. *Contra Faustum* 12.25–27 (CSEL 25.1:353–56); my trans.

that he could not possibly suffer without a body of some sort. In terms of spiritual presence he could not suffer such things. In terms of bodily presence, he could not at the same time be in the sun and in the moon and on the cross. So then, if he did not have a body, he was not crucified. But if he had one, where, I ask, did he get it? After all, you say that all bodies come from the realm of the Kingdom of Darkness since you cannot think of divine substance as anything but bodily. From this, you are forced to say either that he was crucified without a body (nothing more absurd and more demented can be said!) or that he only seemed to be crucified, an apparition, a phantasm rather than reality (here again, can impiety get worse?). Or that not all bodies come from the realm of the Kingdom of Darkness, but that there may be a body of divine substance, which, however, is not immortal but can be nailed to wood and killed (this, no less, is overwhelming madness). Or that Christ got a mortal body from the realm of the Kingdom of Darkness. And so you are afraid to believe that the Virgin Mary was the mother of His body, but you are not afraid that the Kingdom of demons is His body's mother. . . .

(26.7) . . . We do not believe that He was born of the Virgin Mary simply because He could not appear to human beings in any other way but existing in real flesh. We believe it because that is what is written in the Scriptures. And unless we so believe them, we will neither be Christians nor be saved. We believe, therefore, that Christ was born from the Virgin Mary *because* it is written in the Gospel. We believe that Christ was crucified and died *because* it is written in the Gospel. Truly born and truly died *because* the Gospel is truth. But why He willed to suffer all those things in the flesh that He had taken up from the womb of a woman—that most lofty decision-making belongs to Him. Perhaps He judged that taking the form of a male and being born from a female was a way of commending and honoring both sexes—both of which He had created. Perhaps it was some other reason. Whatever it may have been, I will not carelessly speculate. But I can confidently say that it did not happen any other way than what the truth of the Gospel teaches; nor would it have happened in any other way than what the Wisdom of God judged right. We prefer the faith of the Gospel over the wranglings of heretics, and we praise the decision of God's Wisdom over the decision of whatsoever kind of creature.[39]

A PERORATION ON THE CONTROVERSY

In concluding his early commentary on Genesis, Augustine appended a summary of the points where Manichees and Christians differ. Roland Teske has remarked that "this

39. *Contra Faustum* 20.11–26.7 (CSEL 25.1:548–736); my trans.

battery of crisp questions and answers forms a sort of brief catechism for the Catholic believer to use when faced with the standard Manichaean complaints."[40] From On Genesis Against the Manichees, Book 2:

(29.43) Finally, we are discussing with the Manichees the question of religion, and the question of religion is: what does piety demand that we think concerning God? Since they cannot deny that the human race is in the misery of sin, they say that the nature of God is in misery. We deny this and say that the nature that God made from nothing is in misery and that it came to this state, not under compulsion, but by the will to sin.

They say that the nature of God is forced by God Himself to do penance for its sins. We deny this and say that the nature that God made from nothing is forced, after it sinned, to do penance for its sins.

They say that the nature of God receives pardon from God Himself. We deny this and say that the nature that God made from nothing receives pardon for its sins, if it turns from its sins to its God.

They say that the nature of God is by necessity changeable. We deny this and say that the nature that God made from nothing has been changed by its own will.

They say that the sins of others harm the nature of God. We deny this and say that sins harm only the nature of the sinner. We say that God is of such great goodness, of such great justice, and of such great incorruption that He does not sin, that He harms no one who does not will to sin, and that He is harmed by no one who wills to sin.

They say that there exists an evil nature to which God is forced to surrender a part of His own nature to be tortured. We say that there is no natural evil, but that all natures are good and that God is the highest nature. We say that other natures are from God and that all are good insofar as they are, because God made them all very good, but He ordered them in distinct levels so that one is better than another. Thus this universe is filled with every kind of good, and this universe, with some beings perfect and others imperfect, is perfect as a whole, and God its Maker and Creator does not cease to administer it with His just governance. He made all things good by His will. He suffers no evil by necessity, for His will surpasses all things. In no respect does He experience something against His will.

[Manichees] hold the former positions, and we hold the latter ones. Let each person choose which he will follow.[41]

---

40. Teske, FOTC 84:140, n. 196.

41. *De Genesi adversus Manichaeos* 2.29.43 (BA 50:380–82); trans. Teske, FOTC 84:140–41.

CHAPTER 7

CONTROVERSIES (II)
Against the Donatists

The Christians of Hippo who in 391 seized and ordained Augustine called themselves "Catholics." They had good claim to the title. Their church was allied with and recognized by a worldwide communion of Christian churches across the Empire. But in 391 Catholics were a local minority, not only in Hippo, but also across the provinces of Numidia and the Mauretanias. For much of the fourth century, the majority church of North Africa was Donatist. Donatists claimed that they—and they alone—were the one true Church, a Church "without spot or wrinkle" (Eph 5:27), the true descendants of the Church of the martyrs, the Church who alone possessed the Holy Spirit, and the only one whose Spirit-charged waters of baptism could cleanse sinners of their sins. In their view, Catholics, whether locally or worldwide, were not real Christians; Catholics were the "church of Judas," a demonic parody of authentic Christianity.[1] Catholic baptism, far from cleansing one of sin, only polluted one's soul with new layers of filth. This rivalry between Catholic and Donatist was often bitter and, at times, violent. It affected the most ordinary things. As Augustine told his Donatist counterpart in Hippo, "husbands and wives agree about their bed and disagree about the altar of Christ."[2]

The schism dated back nearly a century, to the empire-wide persecution under the Emperor Diocletian in 303. Diocletian had ordered Christians to turn over their sacred books to local officials to be burned. Some clergy refused, of course, and were arrested, jailed, and, in some cases, martyred.

---

1. On Donatist theology, see Serge Lancel and James S. Alexander, "Donatistae," Aug-Lex, 2:606–38; Maureen A. Tilley, The Bible in Christian North Africa: The Donatist World (Minneapolis: Fortress Press, 1997).

2. Ep. 33.5 (CCL 31:122); trans. Parsons, FOTC 12:129. Augustine's relative Severinus was a Donatist: see ep. 52.

Others submitted. These came to be branded by fellow Christians as *traditores*. The word literally means "handers-over"; it is also the origin of the word "traitor." To hand over the Scriptures was, as they saw it, a deed worthy of Judas, a betrayal of one's very Christianity. When Mensurius, bishop of Carthage, received orders to turn over his Bible, he sent local officials books by Christian heretics. This clever but less-than-heroic gesture earned him scorn later.

Things came to a head when some Christians from Abitina, a small town near Carthage, were arrested; one of Mensurius's deacons, Caecilian (d. before 343), set up a security detail that blocked food and support for the jailed Christian confessors. The reason is not clear, but when friends and relatives arrived to comfort the jailed, a violent scuffle broke out. The confessors, prior to their execution, sent out a letter with dire threats: "If anyone communicates with the traitors, that person will not have a share with us in the heavenly kingdom."[3] This separatist ideology would define Donatist self-understanding. Donatists saw themselves as descendants of the martyrs, untouched by the contaminating sin of *traditio*.

It is not uncommon, once persecution ends, for a besieged community to turn in on itself and against itself, with angry finger-pointing and bitter recriminations. In-fighting of this sort plagued North African Christianity once Diocletian's persecution died down around 307. The controversial Caecilian was elected the new bishop of Carthage in 313 and was ordained by the three neighboring bishops. His enemies were outraged and set out to undo the election. They argued that one of the ordaining bishops, Felix of Abthungi, had been a *traditor*, invalidating Caecilian's ordination. The primate of Numidia, Secundus of Tigisis, arrived in Carthage and summoned a council of seventy bishops, who declared Caecilian's ordination null and void and chose a man named Majorinus as the new bishop of Carthage. Majorinus died not long after. His very able successor was Donatus (d. 355), the one for whom the schism was named.

This local squabble surfaced at one of the great turning points in Christian history. In 313, Constantine, the first Christian emperor, issued his edict of toleration, formally ending the persecution and allowing Christians freedom of worship. The two Carthaginian factions soon appealed to Constantine, who passed the case on to Miltiades, bishop of Rome (d. 314). Miltiades settled in Caecilian's favor and officially recognized him as the legitimate bishop of Carthage. The opposition pursued appeals, first to some Gallic

---

3. *Acts of the Abitinian Martyrs* 20. For a translation, see Maureen A. Tilley, *Donatist Martyr Stories: The Church in Conflict in Roman North Africa*, Translated Texts for Historians (Liverpool: Liverpool University Press, 1996), 25–49.

bishops, who met in Arles in 314, and finally to Constantine himself. Each time Caecilian was vindicated.

Undaunted, Donatus and the opposition not only survived, but prospered. In the famous phrase of Optatus of Milevis, "altar was raised against altar."[4] There emerged, in town after town, rival churches and rival clergies. Two bodies of Christians, indistinguishable in worship and creed, faced each other in communities across North Africa. The government moved against the Donatists briefly and inconsistently, but when it did, it was heavy-handed. There were property seizures, onerous fines, brief exiles of leaders, and episodes of police brutality. In 346, Constantine's son, the Emperor Constans, sent two imperial notaries, Macarius and Paul, to address complaints from both sides. They threw their favor to the Catholics and, for a few brutal years, proscribed the Donatists. A government-enforced Catholic unity became the order of the day. Donatus himself was exiled to Gaul and died a few years later. These "Macarian times" became the stuff of legend in Donatist circles.

Catholics, too, suffered violence, notably from roving bands of Circumcellions. The term literally means "around the cells." They arose in the 340s and seem, as best scholars can reconstruct it, to have been loosely organized migrant farm laborers who combined economic grievances, religious fervor, and violence (not unlike certain peasant revolts in the Middle Ages).[5] Attacks were sporadic, some against landowners and tax collectors, some against Catholic clergy or Donatist defectors. The Circumcellions were known for a deep devotion to the cult of the martyrs. Their violence provoked sharp government reprisals, and those who died in these mêlées were heralded by some as "martyrs." Certain Donatist bishops enlisted Circumcellions as bodyguards; others were more wary and kept them at arm's length or disavowed them altogether.

The Donatists emerged in the 360s as the establishment church, a comfortable and prosperous majority. Catholics were strongest in the Romanized cities along the coast. In cities inland, as well as in farming communities, especially in Numidia and the Mauretanias, Donatists held strong sway. From the 360s to the 390s, they enjoyed moderate, stable leadership under Donatus's successor, Parmenian (bp. 361–391). After his death the tide began turning to the Catholic side. Donatists suffered a brief but scandalous schism between Parmenian's successor, Primian, and Maximinus, a relative of Donatus. In 397, Optatus of Thamugadi and other Donatist bishops threw their

---

4. Optatus of Milevis, *De schismate Donatistarum* 1.15, 19 (CSEL 26:18, 21). See Mark Edwards, trans. and ed., *Optatus: Against the Donatists*, Translated Texts for Historians 27 (Liverpool: Liverpool University Press, 1997). Augustine takes up the phrase and uses it as a regular refrain; see, e.g., *Psalmus contra partem Donati* 23, 30, 293; *ep.* 43.4.

5. For recent interpretations, see Claude Lepelley, "Circumcelliones," *Aug-Lex* 1:930–35.

support to a rebellion against imperial authorities led by a local aristocrat, Count Gildo. This imprudent politics rebounded badly on the Donatist cause after the rebellion was crushed.

The tide began to turn in the 390s, in part, because of robust new leadership on the Catholic side. Augustine was part of that new generation. So too was Aurelius of Carthage, whose political savvy did much to challenge Donatist hegemony. Augustine had little patience with the fervent but narrow-minded theology of the Donatists, who had severed all ties with Christians worldwide and who claimed that in Africa alone and among them alone did Christianity exist. Augustine had converted to Christianity overseas and, in Milan, had seen with his own eyes how the Christian Church had spread across the known world. The Christianity he admired and converted to was Ambrose's, an intellectually robust and politically sophisticated brand. Donatists seemed, by comparison, narrow sectarians. Particularly offensive to him and his Catholic colleagues was the Donatist policy of rebaptizing any Christians who joined their ranks.

Confronting Donatism had been on his agenda from his earliest days as a presbyter, but Augustine's campaign moved into full swing around 400 and occupied his best pastoral and literary energies over the next decade. During these years, he authored lengthy polemical treatises, notably, *Against the Letter of Parmenian* (*Contra epistulam Parmeniani*), *On Baptism* (*De baptismo*), and *Against the Letters of Petilian* (*Contra litteras Petiliani*). Donatist issues also took center stage in frequent sermons, most famously, in a series of sermons he gave in 407 on the Gospel of John and on the First Epistle of John. One-fifth of Augustine's voluminous correspondence is devoted to the controversy.[6] His letters from these years offer both vivid glimpses of pastoral realities he faced and cogent expositions of his theology. Augustine's anti-Donatist writings gravitate around two main issues: the theology of Church and the theology of baptism.[7] These two issues will be the focus of much of this chapter. Augustine's views on both would indelibly shape Christian theology for the next millennium, and when kindred controversies surfaced during the Reformation, Reformers and Catholics alike turned to Augustine's writings for guidance and for ammunition.

A third theological issue came to the fore as the decade progressed: religious coercion. In 405, Catholic lobbying, combined with Circumcellion violence, prompted the Emperor Honorius to issue an Edict of Unity, which

---

6. Pierre Monceaux, *Histoire littéraire de l'Afrique chrétienne* (Paris: Leroux, 1923), 7:130. Vol. 7 of Monceaux's work, while dated, offers a detailed overview of Augustine's anti-Donatist corpus.

7. On Augustine's anti-Donatist theology, see especially Yves Congar, "Introduction générale," BA 28:71–124, and R. A. Markus, "*Afer scribens Afris*: The Church in Augustine and the African Tradition," *Saeculum: History and Thought in the Theology of St. Augustine* (Cambridge: Cambridge University Press, 1970), 105–32.

decreed a union of the two churches and attached stiff penalties for non-compliance. While erratically enforced, it took its toll, and a number of Donatist clergy and whole congregations came over to the Catholic side. The climax took place in June 411 at the Conference of Carthage. The government summoned the two sides to meet for one final definitive judgment. It was a momentous affair, with exactly 284 bishops from each side, facing off against one another. The imperial commissioner, Flavius Marcellinus, presided over the sometimes raucous gathering with scrupulous procedural fairness. We have the raw, unedited stenographic minutes, and they offer a remarkable "group photo" of each side.[8] We can listen in on noisy debates, glimpsing Augustine going toe-to-toe with Donatist spokesmen like Petilian of Constantine. We also glimpse rank-and-file bishops on both sides, and the Conference's roll call has enabled scholars to reconstruct the precise geographical spread and strength of each church. On June 26, 411, Marcellinus handed down the verdict that was all but a foregone conclusion from the outset: the Catholics were the one Church of North Africa. In its wake, two churches were forcibly united. There would be holdouts and flamboyant gestures of protest, like Gaudentius of Thamugadi, who threatened to gather his congregation into his basilica and burn it down in a mass suicide. But in the main, Donatist resistance collapsed, and Augustine and his colleagues had to grapple with the messy pastoral consequences of integrating the two congregations.

Over these years, Augustine sketched a theological justification for religious coercion. He openly admitted his own change of heart (see excerpts below), but came to see government coercion as legitimate and theologically defensible. Beneath this sudden *volte face*, there were deeper, long-simmering roots: reflections on suppressing paganism; intricate meditations on a wealth of Scripture texts; philosophic probings on free choice and its limits.[9] Still, his expositions proved an ominous legacy to the medieval Church, leading some twentieth-century scholars to brand him "the first theorist of the Inquisition."[10] Interpretations vary, but as Serge Lancel, a leading scholar of the Donatist controversy, has cautioned: "these texts must be read while keep-

8. See Lancel, *Saint Augustine*, 293–304. Lancel is the expert on this vast material, having edited the critical edition of the *Gesta conlationis carthaginensis* (CCL 149A) and translated it in its entirety, together with abundant notes: *Actes de la Conférence de Carthage en 411*, SC 194, 195, 224, and 373 (Paris: Éditions du Cerf, 1972–1991). About half of the manuscript with the complete *Gesta* is unfortunately missing, preserving the minutes only from the first half; its surviving table of contents does offer a chapter-by-chapter précis of what is missing. Augustine himself took the unwieldy minutes and edited them down to a digestible (though biased) form in his *Breviliculus conlationis cum Donatistis*. In one of the Divjak letters, Augustine notes that some churches had the minutes publicly read aloud during Lent (*ep.* 28*.2–3).

9. Peter Brown, "St. Augustine's Attitude to Religious Coercion," in *Religion and Society in the Age of Saint Augustine* (1972; reprint: Eugene, OR: Wipf & Stock, 2007), 237–59.

10. Markus, "*Coge Intrare*: The Church and Political Power," *Saeculum*, 133–53.

ing in mind the strict demands that dictated them, but, in their time, never caused, either directly or indirectly, any physical attack, still less any death. Augustine was not the father of [medieval] Augustinianism, nor was he responsible for Torquemada."[11]

Since the late nineteenth century, scholars have sought to understand the tenacity of the Donatist movement, the loyalty and violence it inspired. Some have suggested that religion was simply a veneer for what was, in reality, a sort of African nationalism, a native resistance movement to Roman colonialism. Others have applied economic and sociological analyses to Donatism, highlighting reports of clashes between rich and poor, town and country, Latin-speaking and Punic-speaking.[12] These interpretations have faced withering criticism, at least as global explanations.[13] The current consensus acknowledges social, economic, and political factors in the mix, but insists on the centrality of the religious. The Donatists tenaciously clung to an old-fashioned view of Church, famously articulated by the great hero of North African Christianity, Cyprian, the bishop-martyr of Carthage (d. 258), who drew strict lines between Church and world, famously insisting: "there is no salvation outside the Church."[14] It is no accident that Augustine felt compelled to address not only Donatists, but also the venerated grandfather of North African theology. On the far side of Constantine, the Church had grown large and messy, and Cyprian's old-fashioned view of a Church "without wrinkle or spot" did not match reality. The reality was a discomfiting mix of good and bad, of fervent and lukewarm. This *corpus permixtum* Church was one Augustine came to defend. It is not without irony that Augustine took some exegetical cues on this from a maverick Donatist theologian, Tyconius, whose own views on this very point led his Donatist bishop, Parmenian, to excommunicate him.

❧

11. Lancel, *Saint Augustine*, 304.

12. See W. H. C. Frend, *The Donatist Church: A Movement of Protest in Roman North Africa* (Oxford: Clarendon Press, 1952); Jean-Paul Brisson, *Autonomisme et christianisme dans l'Afrique romaine de Septime Sévère à l'invasion vandale* (Paris: Boccard, 1958). For a survey, see Congar, BA 28:25–48.

13. Brown, "Religious Dissent in the Later Roman Empire: The Case of North Africa," in *Religion and Society in the Age of St. Augustine*, 237–59; R. A. Markus, "Christianity and Dissent in Roman Africa: Changing Perspectives in Recent Works," *Studies in Church History* 9 (1972): 21–36.

14. Cyprian, *ep.* 73.21.2. See Brent Allen, trans., *St. Cyprian of Carthage: On the Church: Select Letters*, Popular Patristics Series 33 (Crestwood, NY: St. Vladimir's Seminary Press, 2006).

THE LEGACY OF CYPRIAN

Both Donatists and Catholics lionized the memory of Cyprian, the heroic third-century bishop of Carthage. Both also owed deep debts to his theology. In the wake of the ferocious but short-lived persecution of the Emperor Decius in 250, Cyprian organized North African bishops via councils to deal as a united front with Christians who had lapsed during the persecution. The initial debate was over what to do with the lapsed: reconciliation by public penance? or lifelong excommunication? Cyprian led the bishops to agree on reconciliation and hammered out guidelines for bringing the lapsed back into communion. But he faced hardliners, known as Novatianists, who severed communion with Cyprian and his colleagues. Cyprian responded with one of the most influential treatises in the history of Christianity, On the Unity of the Church (De unitate ecclesiae). He argued that only those in communion with the unified Church, as led by the college of bishops, could be saved; neither schismatics nor anyone they baptized could claim to be within the one Church. Cyprian noted that there were no survivors outside Noah's ark. From Cyprian of Carthage, On the Unity of the Church:

(4) The beginning proceeds from unity, that the Church of Christ may be shown to be one. This one Church, the Holy Spirit in the Canticle of Canticles designates in the person of the Lord and says: "One is my dove, the chosen one of her that bore her" (Sg 6:8). Does he who does not hold this unity think that he holds the faith? Does he who strives against the Church and resists her think that he is in the Church, when too the blessed Apostle Paul teaches this same thing and sets forth the sacrament of unity saying: "One body and one Spirit, one hope of your calling, one Lord, one faith, one baptism, one God" (Eph 4:4–6).

(5) This unity we ought to hold to firmly and defend, especially we bishops who watch over the Church, that we may also prove that the episcopate itself is one and undivided. . . . The Church [is] bathed in the light of the Lord . . . which is diffused everywhere, and the unity of the body is not separated. She extends her branches over the whole earth in fruitful abundance; she extends her richly flowing streams far and wide; yet her Head is one and her source is one, and she is the one mother copious in the results of her fruitfulness. By her womb we are born; by her milk we are nourished; by her spirit we are animated.

(6) The spouse of Christ cannot be defiled; she is uncorrupted and chaste. She knows one home; with chaste modesty she guards the sanctity of one couch. She keeps us for God; she assigns the children whom she has created to the Kingdom. Whoever is separated from the Church and is joined to an adulteress is separated from the promises of the Church, nor will he who has abandoned the Church arrive at the rewards of Christ. He is a stranger; he is profane; he is an enemy. He who does not have the Church as mother cannot have God as Father. If whoever was outside the ark of Noah was able to escape, he too who is outside the Church escapes. The

Lord warns, saying: "He who is not with me is against me, and who does not gather with me, scatters" (Mt 12:30). He who breaks the peace and concord of Christ acts against Christ; he who gathers somewhere outside the Church scatters the Church of Christ. . . . He who does not hold this unity, does not hold the law of God; who does not hold the faith of the Father and the Son, does not hold life and salvation.[15]

Cyprian, a few years later, got into a tense debate with Pope Stephen on how to reconcile those baptized by schismatic Novatianists. Stephen treated returning Novatianists as penitents, reconciling them by the laying-on of hands. Cyprian insisted that they be rebaptized—or rather, receive genuine baptism within the one and only Church. On this policy, he and his North African colleagues formed a united front and strongly defended rebaptism. From Cyprian of Carthage, Letter 70:

(1) When we were together in council, dearly beloved brethren, we read your letter which you wrote concerning those who seem baptized among heretics and schismatics, as to whether they ought to be baptized when they come to the Catholic Church, which is one. Concerning this matter . . . we express our judgment, . . . judging plainly and holding for certain that no one can be baptized outside the Church, since there is one baptism appointed in the Holy Church. And it is written in the words of the Lord, "they have forsaken me, the source of living water; and they have dug themselves broken cisterns that cannot hold water" (Jer 2:13). But the water ought first to be cleansed and sanctified by the bishop that it may be able to wash away in its baptism the sin of the person who is baptized since the Lord says through Ezekiel: "And I will sprinkle clean water upon you, and you shall be cleansed from all your impurities and from all your idols. And I will cleanse you. And I will give you a new heart and place a new spirit within you" (Ezek 36:25–26). But how can he who is himself unclean and who does not have the Holy Spirit cleanse and sanctify water, since the Lord says in Numbers: "Whatever the unclean person touches will be unclean" (Nm 19:22)? Or how can one who baptizes grant to another the remission of sins who, himself outside the Church, cannot put aside his own sins?

(2) . . . Among the heretics where the Church is not, sins are not forgiven. . . . Who can give what he himself does not have, or how can he accomplish spiritual deeds who himself has lost the Holy Spirit? And, therefore, he who comes ignorant to the Church must be baptized and renewed that he may be sanctified within through the holy ones since it is written: "Be holy, for I am also holy, says the Lord" (Lv 19:2). . . .

---

15. Cyprian, *De unitate ecclesiae* 4–6 (CCL 3: 252–54); trans. Deferrari, FOTC 36:99–101. Note that there are two recensions of this text. That both recensions are by Cyprian was demonstrated by Maurice Bévenot; see *Cyprian: De Lapsis and De Ecclesiae Catholicae Unitate*, Oxford Early Christian Texts (Oxford: Clarendon, 1971); see also Stuart G. Hall, "The Versions of Cyprian's *De Unitate* 4–5: Bévenot's Dating Revisited," *Journal of Theological Studies* 55 (2004): 138–46. This translation here is from the *textus receptus*, which reflects Cyprian's more collegial accent. On the broader context, see J. Patout Burns, *Cyprian the Bishop*, Routledge Early Church Monographs (New York: Routledge, 2002), esp. 78–99, 151–65.

(3) . . . If one [outside] could baptize, he could also give the Holy Spirit. But if he cannot give the Holy Spirit because, established outside, he is not with the Holy Spirit, he cannot baptize the one who comes since baptism is also one, and the Holy Spirit is one, and the Church founded by Christ upon Peter in the order and established plan of unity is also one. Thus it happens that, since all things are useless and false among those men, none of those things which they have done ought to be approved by us.[16]

DONATISTS IN THEIR OWN VOICE

Petilian of Constantine (d. ca. 419) was a Donatist contemporary of Augustine and an articulate exponent of Donatist views. He had been raised by Catholic parents, and while still a Catholic catechumen, was forcibly baptized into the Donatist church. Around 393, he was forcibly ordained as bishop of Constantine/Cirta (now Ksantina, Algeria). Around 399 or 400, Augustine stumbled across an excerpt of a pastoral letter by Petilian and dashed off a response. This became Book 1 of his treatise Against the Letters of Petilian.[17] Later Augustine got hold of the entire letter and, for Book 2, composed a line-by-line rebuttal. These piecemeal quotations allow us to reconstruct Petilian's original letter. Petilian's text gives one a good taste of the mud-slinging and inflammatory language some Donatists favored. From his Letter to the Presbyters and Deacons, reconstructed from Augustine, Against the Letters of Petilian, Book 2:

(1.2) Bishop Petilian, to his most beloved brethren, fellow presbyters and deacons, who are ministers with us, appointed in the holy Gospel throughout the diocese: Grace and peace to you from God our Father and the Lord Jesus Christ.

(2.4) We are criticized for baptizing a second time by people who have polluted their souls with an unlawful washing, a baptism in name only. They are people who, because of their perverse cleansing, emerge defiled by the water they dipped in, people so loathsome that the lowest filth is cleaner. (3.6) Now what we look to is for the conscience of the giver, in holiness, to cleanse that of the receiver.[18] (4.8) For the one who knowingly embraces faith from the faithless receives not faith but guilt. (5.10) For everything gets its existence from its origin and its roots; and if it does not have something as its head, it is nothing; nor does something regenerate well unless regenerated from a good seed. (6.10) Since this is so, brethren, what kind of perversity must it be to think that one guilty of crimes can make someone else innocent? For

---

16. Cyprian, *ep.* 70.1–3 (CCL 3: 501–13); trans. Donna, FOTC 51:259–61. See also Cyprian, *ep.* 69 and 71–73. See Burns, *Cyprian the Bishop,* esp. 100–150.

17. This work has traditionally been dated to 400. Hombert, *Nouvelles recherches,* 189–93, argues that Books 1 and 2 date to 400–401, while Book 3 dates sometime between 403 and 405.

18. "In holiness" (*sancte*): In his citation of Petilian's letter, Augustine had dropped this phrase, as well as "knowingly" (*sciens*) from the next sentence. Petilian later chided Augustine for dropping both words: see *Contra litteras Petiliani* 3.23.27 (BA 30:638–40).

the Lord Jesus Christ says: "A good tree produces good fruit; an evil tree produces evil fruit; how does one harvest grapes from thorns?" (Mt 7:17, 16) And again: "A good person brings good things out of the treasury of his heart; an evil person brings evil things out of the treasury of his heart" (Mt 12:35).

(7.14) And again: "As for the one baptized by the dead, his washing is of no benefit to him" (Sir 34:40). By "dead," He does not mean a corpse, a lifeless body, a person's remains ready for burial. He means one who does not have the Spirit of God; this [not having the Spirit of God] He compares to being dead, as He shows to His disciple in another place, according the Gospel's witness. The disciple said: "Lord, permit me to bury my father." Jesus said to him: "Follow me, and let the dead bury the dead" (Mt 8:21–22). The disciple's father was not baptized; so he left a pagan to the pagans. Jesus was [obviously] speaking about unbelievers since dead cannot bury dead. The disciple was dead, therefore, not by a literal sort of death, but by a beaten-down life. Now one who lives in such guilt is tortured by a death-in-life. To be baptized, therefore, by the dead is to take up death, not life. But we must consider and discuss to what extent a *traditor* must be considered the living dead. Dead is the one who does not deserve the rebirth of true baptism. Similarly dead is the one who, though born of a legitimate baptism, has entered into communion with a *traditor*. Neither of these has the life of baptism, neither the one who never had it nor the one who had it and lost it. The Lord Jesus Christ said: "Then there shall come into that man seven spirits more wicked than the earlier one, and the last state of that person shall be worse than the first" (Mt 12:45).

(8.17) We must consider this, as I said, and discuss to what extent the treacherous *traditor* is to be considered the living dead. Judas was an apostle when he handed over Christ. That same one lost the honor of being an apostle, dying spiritually before he died by hanging himself, as it is written: "'I repent for having handed over the blood of the Righteous One,' he said, and he went off and hanged himself" (Mt 27:4–5). The traitor perished by rope, a rope he left for others like himself, of which the Lord Christ cried out to the Father: "Father, all those that you gave me, I have guarded them, and not one of them has perished except the son of perdition in order that Scripture be fulfilled" (Jn 17:12). . . . How do you,[19] as heir of an even worse *traditor*, lay claim to a bishopric for yourself? Judas handed over Christ, betraying him in the flesh; you in your mad rage handed over the holy Gospel to sacrilegious flames, betraying it in spirit. Judas betrayed the Lawgiver to unbelievers; you, in a sense, handed over to men for destruction what He left behind, the Law of God. If you had loved the Law, like the young Maccabees, you would have perished for the Law of God—if one can call it "death," this dying for a Lord who gives immortality. . . . If you were to burn

---

19. "You": Petilian is engaged in a diatribe here against Catholic clergy; the "you" refers not to his original audience of Donatist clergy, but to Catholics (or "Caecilianists," as a Donatist would say).

in flames the last will and testament of someone who had died, would you not be punished for fraud, for falsifying [a legal will]? So what will come of you who burned up the most holy Law of our God and Judge? Judas repented of his deed by his death. You not only do not repent, but you, murderous *traditor*, have shown yourself as our persecutor and a butcher of those of us who keep the Law. (9.21) Locked in by these crimes, you, thus, cannot be a true bishop. . . .

(25.28) You the guilty engage in a fiction [of baptism]. I do not do baptism twice— what you have never done once. . . . (27.62) The Apostle Paul said: "One God, one faith, one baptism" (Eph 4:5). We profess there is only one. For this much is certain: those who judge there to be two are mad. . . . (32.72) But, you, O persecutor, do not even have the baptism of repentance; you hold on to the power not of the murdered John [the Baptist], but of the murderer Herod. Therefore, you, O *traditor*, do not have the Holy Spirit of Christ, for Christ did not betray or hand over others to death, but was himself betrayed and handed over. For you, the spirit's fire is lively and hot—in hell. In its hunger, its dry tongues will lick your limbs forever without ever consuming them. For it is written of those condemned to hell: "Its fire shall not be extinguished" (Is 66:24).

(33.77) . . . How then can you baptize in the name of the Holy Spirit when the Holy Spirit came only on apostles who had not committed betrayal? Seeing that God is not your Father and that you are not born of the true water of baptism, no one among you is born inwardly; you, the impious, have neither father nor mother. Shouldn't I therefore baptize people like you, even after a thousand of your baptisms, which resemble the purely physical baths that Jews do? (34.79) If the apostles were allowed to baptize those whom John [the Baptist] had washed with his baptism of repentance, shall I not be allowed to baptize you, the sacrilegious? (35.81) The Holy Spirit will not be able to descend upon a person by the bishop's imposing hands if the water which produces the pure conscience has not given birth to him first. (36.83) In any case, the Holy Spirit would not be able to descend upon you, whom not even a baptism of repentance has purified; and the truth is this: what needs repenting of is the water of the *traditor* which dirtied you. . . .

(108.246) Come, therefore, to Church, all you people, and flee the *traditores* if you do not wish to perish along with them. For you easily recognize that, while they themselves are guilty, they have judged and hold the highest view of our faith: I baptize the stained, the undone, among them; yet they receive my baptized, which they would not in any way do if they recognized any faults in our baptism. See, therefore, how holy what we give is, when even our sacrilegious enemy fears to destroy it.[20]

20. Petilian's Latin text was reconstructed by Monceaux, *Histoire littéraire*, 5:311–28; my trans. The numbering here follows that of Augustine's *Contra litteras Petiliani* (BA 30:222–560).

DONATISTS AS THE PURE CHURCH

The Donatists saw themselves as the pure Church, but, as Peter Brown has noted, they were not Puritans in the moralistic sense; "the Donatist idea of 'purity' drew its strength from a different source. It was the purity of a group in its relationship to God, that mattered. . . . The anxiety that genuinely haunted the Donatist bishops was that, by tolerating any breach in a narrow and clearly defined order of ritual behavior, they might alienate God from His Church. . . . Anyone who reads a Donatist pamphlet, or indeed, a work of S. Cyprian, will be struck by the power of the idea of ritual purity that stemmed straight from the Old Testament: the fear of a sudden loss of spiritual potency through contact with an 'unclean thing,' and the elemental imagery of the 'good' and the 'bad' water."[21] That sense and worldview is reflected in Petilian's letter above; it is also reflected in Augustine's report below. From To the Catholic Members of the Church (also known as On the Unity of the Church):

(5.9) So one of their bishops, when he was here in Hippo and was giving a sermon to their people, said—according to what we heard—that this ark of Noah had been caulked with pitch both on the inside, so as not to let the water inside out, and on the outside, so as not to let the water outside in. By this, he wanted to stress in this way a definite interpretation: that it must be believed that baptism cannot be given outside the Church nor can one from the outside be received who was given it on the outside. One would guess that when he had said this, there was a lot of applause from those who loved hearing it without reflecting very well on what they had come to understand.[22]

ALPHABETICAL PSALM

Augustine's earliest work against the Donatists was not a learned treatise; it was a pop song, composed around 393, while he was still a presbyter. Its genre is an abecedarian psalm; that is, the first stanza begins with A, the second with B, etc. Augustine wanted to make it easy to memorize. He also wanted it easily intelligible to the unlearned within his congregation, and thus avoided the strict metrics of classical Latin poetry. At the end of his career, he reflected back on its composition and stated what had been his goal at the time. From Reconsiderations, Book 1:

21. Brown, Augustine of Hippo, 218.
22. Ad Catholicos fratres 5.9 (BA 28:542–26); my trans. While generally accepted as an authentic work of Augustine, some scholars have pointed to its less elegant style and attribute its authorship to one of his disciples. Whoever the author, it accurately reflects Donatist self-understanding.

(20) Because I wished to familiarize the most lowly people and especially the ignorant and uneducated with the case of the Donatists and to impress it on their memory to the best of my ability, I composed a psalm to be sung by them, arranged according to the Latin alphabet, and only as far as the letter V, that is, in the so-called abecedarian style. I omitted, however, the last three letters, but in their place at the end, I added an epilogue, so to speak, as though Mother Church were addressing them. Moreover, the refrain, which is repeated again and again, and the prologue to the case which we wanted sung, are not in alphabetical order. Furthermore, I did not want this psalm composed in any form of metrical verse lest the metrical requirements force me [to use] some words which are not familiar to the common people.[23]

While Augustine did not use a fixed meter for the poem's nearly 300 lines, he did make use of musical devices, such as rhyme and alliteration. Each line is divided into two hemistiches, each hemistich averaging eight syllables. The poem sets out the Catholic case against the Donatists, both historically and theologically. I have translated here the first two stanzas and the epilogue. The first introduces Augustine's classic view that the Church here and now is a mix of good and bad, which he illustrates with Jesus' parable of the catch of fish (Mt 13:47–48). The second sets out his central accusation against the Donatists: they have shattered the unity of the Church. The epilogue, as Augustine noted, has Mother Church give a speech lamenting the divisions. From Psalm against the Donatists:

[*Refrain*] You who rejoice in peace,   now judge the truth.

Abundant sin   tends to spin the brethren dizzy.
For this reason, our Lord   wanted to give fair warning,
(10) Comparing Heaven's kingdom   to a net tossed into the sea,
Gathering loads of fish,   all kinds, from here and from there,
and when dragged to shore,   then began the separating:
the good, put into barrels;   the bad, tossed back into the sea.
Any who know the Gospel   recognize it with fear.
They see the Church is the net,   they see this world's the sea,
The many fish, all kinds mixed,   that's the righteous with sinners;
World's end, that's the shore.   Then will be the time of separating
Fish who once split the nets: too much did they love the sea;
The barrels, that's the saints' seats,   to which sinners cannot reach.

(20) You who rejoice in peace   now judge the truth.

---

23. *Retr.* 1.20 (CCL 57:61); trans. Bogan, FOTC 60:86.

But, good hearer, perhaps you're   looking for those who burst the nets,
people of such pride   who claim themselves righteous,
they did a ripping-to-shreds,[24]   pitting altar against altar.
To the devil, themselves they handed over   when they fought over the
    handing-over;
And, of crimes they committed,   they sought to pass along blame to others.
They too handed over the Books,   and it's us they dare accuse
in order to commit worse crime   than that they had committed before,
because, in the Books' case, handers-over could   be excused for fear,
as when Peter denied Christ,   so terrified was he of dying.
(30) But how will they excuse   their deed of setting altar against altar?
The peace of Christ is ripped to shreds   by placing hope in a human being,
so that what persecution could not do   they did themselves in peacetime.

You who rejoice in peace   now judge the truth. . . .

(270) Now what if Mother Church herself   addressed you calmly, in peace,
and said: "O my children,   what complaints have you against your Mother?
Why have you deserted me?   I want to hear it from you now.
You accuse your brethren,   and this lashing-out wounds me deeply.
Many deserted me,   but they did so in fear.
But no one's forcing you   to rebel against me so.
You say you are with me;   you see that to be false.
I'm spoken of as Catholic,   and you are of Donatus's sect. . . .
But what have I done to you,   I, your mother [spread] across the wide world?
I expel the bad ones I can,   but the ones I can't, I'm made to bear with.
Them I bear with until they're cleansed   or separated out at time's end.
(290) Why do you send me away   and leave me tortured by your death?
If there are evil ones you hate,   look instead at those you have.
If you yourself tolerate evil,   then why not in unity,
where no one rebaptizes,   nor pits altar against altar?
Evil ones, so many, do you tolerate   but to no advantage
Because what you owe for Christ   you willingly bear only for Donatus."
Brothers, sisters, we have sung to you   of peace if you'd just be willing
    to listen.
Coming is Our Judge: ourselves, we give; what's due, he exacts.[25]

---

24. "A ripping-to-shreds" (conscissuram): The word is a neologism. See Christine Mohrmann, Die
altchristliche Sondersprache in den Sermones des hl. Augustin (Nijmegen, 1932), 251.

25. Psalmus contra partem Donati 7–297 (BA 28:150–90); my trans.

DIVIDED TOWNS, DIVIDED FAMILIES

Augustine tried initially to engage Donatists using a variety of tactics: friendly con-
versations, exchanges of letters, public debates. He may have thought public debate,
which had been rather effective in dealing with the Manichees, might work against the
Donatists. Around 396, he wrote his cross-town rival, Proculeian, the Donatist bishop
of Hippo (bp. 395–410), asking to meet and discuss and, if need be, formally debate
the issues. In his letter, Augustine alludes to the way the schism divided families. He
also contrasts the daily routine of bishops acting as judges settling their congregation's
lawsuits with the inability of rival bishops to settle disputes with one another. From
Letter 33:

(5) I ask you: What have we to do with those old quarrels such that
wounds, which the antagonism of proud men has inflicted on your members,
should have lasted so long? By the putrefying of those wounds we have lost
all feeling of pain which ordinarily makes one call in a doctor. You see with
what great and what wretched foulness the families of Christian homes are
defiled. Husbands and wives agree about their bed and disagree about the altar of Christ. They swear by Him in order to have mutual peace, but they cannot have it in Him. Sons share one home with their parents, but they do not
share the same house of God. They wish to receive the inheritance of those
with whom they quarrel about the inheritance of Christ; slave and master tear
asunder the common God who "took the form of a servant" (Phil 2:7) that He
might free us all from slavery. Yours honor us, ours honor you; yours swear
to us by our crown, ours swear to you by yours. We take the word of everyone;
we wish to offend none; but what injury has Christ done us that we tear His
members apart? People, wishing to advance their worldly aims through us—
as far as we are useful to them—call us saints indeed and servants of God,
so as to further the interest of their own lands. Let us, then, work at the business of their salvation and of our own. We are daily greeted by people with
suppliant heads, begging us to settle their quarrels, but the disgraceful and
dangerous division between [our congregations] is not a question of gold or
silver, or of land and flocks. It is a dispute about our very Head. Those who sa-
lute us may bow their heads as low as they will, begging us to reconcile them
on earth, but our Head has bowed down from heaven to the cross, and we are
not reconciled in Him.[26]

---

26. Ep. 33.5 (CCL 31:122–23); trans. Parsons, FOTC 12:129–30.

ORIGIN OF THE SCHISM

Augustine may rhetorically have asked, "What have we to do with those old quarrels?" but he certainly knew that to combat Donatist claims he had to study the long, bitter history of the controversy, a task which required mastering various dossiers of documents from both government and church archives. Here, in a letter written in late 396 or early 397 to a group of moderate Donatist laymen, Augustine gives his synopsis of the schism's origins and implications. From Letter 43:

(1.2) If I were writing you about the business of a farm or of quashing a financial lawsuit, probably no one would object. So dear is the world to human beings, and so cheap are they to themselves! This letter, then, will be a witness in my defense at the judgment of God, who knows with what motive I have acted and who has said: "Blessed are the peacemakers, for they shall be called children of God" (Mt 5:9).

(2.3) Therefore, you will kindly call to mind that, when we were in your city [of Carthage] and were treating some questions about the nature of Christian unity, certain public records were produced by your partisans, in which it was related that about seventy bishops had once condemned Caecilian, a bishop of the church of Carthage of our communion, together with his colleagues and consecrators. There the case of Felix of Abthungi also was trumpeted about much more violently and more objectionably than the others.[27] When these records had been read, we answered that it was no wonder if the people who were responsible for that schism (as well as for the correctness of the records) should think that the absent were to be rashly condemned without a hearing, roused as they were against them by envious and wicked persons. But we have other records of the church, in which Secundus of Tigisis, who then held the primacy in Numidia, left proven and avowed *traditores* to the judgment of God and even allowed them to occupy their episcopal thrones. And their names are listed among the accusers of Caecilian.

(2.4) Then we said, sometime after the ordination of Majorinus, whom they wickedly raised up against Caecilian, setting altar against altar, and rending the unity of Christ with frightful divisions, that they had requested Constantine, then emperor, to appoint bishops as judges to arbitrate the differences that had arisen to break the bond of peace in Africa. But when this was granted, in the presence of Caecilian and those who had gone abroad

---

27. "Felix of Abthungi": Abthungi (modern Henchir es-Souar) was a small town south of Carthage. Felix was one of Caecilian's consecrators and was accused of *traditio* by the Donatist party. According to Donatist theology, if Felix had committed *traditio*, he would have lost the Holy Spirit and thus lost the spiritual power to ordain; one cannot give the Holy Spirit if one does not have the Holy Spirit. That is why such a minor character would be such a bitter point of contention.

to appear against him, Miltiades, Bishop of Rome, acting as judge, with his colleagues whom the emperor had sent at the request of the Donatists, had decided that nothing could be proved against Caecilian, that he was thereby confirmed in his bishopric, and that Donatus, who had appeared against him, was censured. After this development, it was noted that, when all of them persisted obstinately in their detestable schism, the emperor made provision for examining the same case more carefully and for concluding it at Arles, but they appealed the ecclesiastical verdict and asked for a hearing by Constantine. After this meeting, with both sides present, Caecilian had been declared innocent, and they had returned defeated, but perversely determined not to give in. Nor was the case of Felix of Abthungi passed over; by order of the same emperor his record was cleared in the proconsular archives. . . .

(5.14) If the proconsular records displease you, turn to the ecclesiastical ones. All the facts are set out in order for you. But perhaps Miltiades, bishop of the church of Rome, with his colleagues, the overseas bishops, should not have taken over the jurisdiction of a case which had been concluded by seventy Africans under the primacy of Tigisis? The emperor, when requested, sent bishop-judges to sit with him and decide what seemed just to them about the whole affair. We prove this by the petition of the Donatists and the emperor's own record. You recall that both were read to you, and you now have the liberty of examining and transcribing them. Read them all and weigh them well. See how carefully all the discussions were carried on with a view to preserving or restoring peace and unity; how the character of the accusers was treated, and, in the case of some of them, how it was degraded when it became clear by the evidence of those present that they had nothing to say against Caecilian.

(5.16) . . . Yet what kind of final verdict was given by blessed Miltiades! How blameless, how upright, how far-seeing and peaceful! By it he did not try to remove from his flock colleagues who had nothing against them, but when he had laid the blame on Donatus alone, whom he found to be the cause of all the trouble, he gave the rest full opportunity to recover spiritual health. He was even ready to send pastoral letters to those who were admittedly ordained by Majorinus, with the provision that, wherever there were two bishops, because dissension had doubled the office, he would confirm the one who had been ordained first. For the other, another flock would be found over whom he could rule. O excellent man! O son of Christian peace and father of Christian people! . . .

(7.19) But when [Caecilian's accusers] had learned by this experience that Caecilian was in union with the rest of the world and that pastoral letters from the overseas churches had recognized him and not the one whom they had wrongfully ordained, they were ashamed of their silence, because they could not answer the objection that a church, unknown in so many countries, was in communion with the condemned, but they had cut themselves off from communion with all the rest of the blameless world. . . .

(7.20) What they did afterward is very plainly shown from the emperor's letter. They presumed to criticize, on the grounds of false verdict, the ecclesiastical judges—bishops of such influence, by whose judgment the innocence of Caecilian and their own malice were published—and this, not to their colleagues but to the emperor. He gave them another trial at Arles, doubtless with other bishops, not because it was necessary, but by way of yielding to their obstinacy and wishing by all means to restrain their excessive boldness. Yet as a Christian emperor, he did not venture to sustain their disorderly and unfounded complaints by giving a judgment on the court of bishops which had sat at Rome, but, as I said, he appointed other bishops. And even from these they chose to appeal to the emperor in person. . . . He ordered that both sides come to him at Rome to try the case. . . . [Shifting the venue to Milan,] when Caecilian also arrived, he had him appear, heard his case, and with the care, precaution, and foresight manifested in his letters, he declared him completely innocent, and his accusers guilty of base injustice.

(8.21) And still they baptize outside the Church, and, if they could, would rebaptize the whole Church. They offer the sacrifice in a state of disunion and schism, and greet people in the name of peace whom they cut off from the peace of salvation. The unity of Christ is blasphemed, the baptism of Christ is scorned, and they refuse to be corrected of those sins by common human authority, through temporal penalties, which would ward off the eternal chastisement due to their great blasphemies. We sharply criticize them for the violence of schism, the madness of rebaptism, the sinful separation from the inheritance of Christ, which [in its true form] is spread abroad among all peoples. Not only from our documents, but even from theirs, we can list [the apostolic] churches whose names they read today, but with which they are not in communion.[28] When these names are read in their places of assembly, they say to their readers: "Peace be to you!" but they do not share peace with the peoples to whom those epistles were written. And they bring against us the false charges of dead men, not realizing that, even if they were true, they would have nothing to do with our complaints against them. . . .

(9.27) Go, then, consult together; discover what [Donatist leaders] can answer to these arguments of ours. If they bring out documents, we bring out documents; if they say ours are spurious, they cannot resent our saying the same of theirs. No one blots out of heaven the ordinance of God; no one

---

28. "Churches whose names they read": New Testament churches of Ephesus, Corinth, etc. Augustine develops this point on catholicity more clearly in *ep.* 87.1–5 (cited below).

blots from the earth the Church of God. He promised the whole earth; [the Church] has filled the whole earth, and she includes both bad and good; but she loses none on earth but the bad, and admits to heaven none but the good. This is our word to you, by the grace of God; and He knows how we have uttered it out of our love of peace and our love for you that it may correct you, if you are willing, but will be a witness against you if you are not.[29]

THEOLOGY OF CHURCH

During the Donatist controversy, Augustine worked out a theology of Church that would shape Christian self-understanding for centuries. He focused on three elements: (i) the Church's oneness; (ii) its catholicity; and (iii) its holiness. Let us look at a classic articulation of each.

Theology of Church: Oneness

Like Cyprian before him, Augustine stressed that there must be one and only one Church, united by charity and opposed to schism. During Easter Week, 407, Augustine embarked on a series of sermons on the First Letter of John. At one point, he had his congregation turn their attention to those who had been baptized a few days earlier at the Easter Vigil and who stood as a group in their white baptismal robes, clustered within the railings around the altar in the center of the basilica. He knew that Donatists denied that Catholics possessed the Holy Spirit because they accused Catholics of inheriting the sin of traditio. Augustine sets out a different understanding of the gift of the Holy Spirit. From the Tractates on the First Epistle of John 6:

(10) In the early days, the Holy Spirit fell upon those who believed, and they spoke with tongues that they had not learned, as the Spirit gave them to utter. These signs were suited to that time. For it was necessary that the Holy Spirit thus be signified in all tongues because the Gospel of God was about to travel via all tongues into the whole world. That was done as a sign and passed away. Now as for those upon whom hands are laid that they may receive the Holy Spirit: Is it expected that they should speak in tongues? Or when we laid our hands upon these newly baptized, each one of you could observe whether or not they spoke in tongues. And when you saw that they did not speak in tongues, was anyone of you of such a perverse heart that you said, "These [newly baptized] did not receive the Holy Spirit, for if they had received the

---

29. Ep. 43.1.2–9.27 (CCL 31:170–86); trans. Parsons, FOTC 12:184–207.

Spirit, they would speak in tongues as happened then"? Therefore, if the testimony of the presence of the Holy Spirit should not now occur by these miracles, by what does it occur? By what sign does anyone recognize that someone has received the Holy Spirit? Let each question his heart. If he loves his brother, then the Spirit of God abides in him. Let him see, let him prove himself before the eyes of God; let him see if there is in him the love of peace and unity, the love of the Church spread throughout the whole world. . . .

(13) Here, right now, let us question all heretics. Has Christ come in the flesh? [A Donatist would say:] "He has come; I believe this, I confess this." No, you don't; you deny this. "How do I deny it? You heard me confess it." No, I accuse you of denying it. You say it in words, you deny it in your heart; you say it with words, you deny it in your acts. "How," you ask, "do I deny it in my acts?" Because Christ came in the flesh precisely that He might die for us. He died for us precisely because He taught much love: "Greater love than this no one has than that he lay down his life for his friends" (Jn 15:13). You do not have love because for your own honor you divide unity. Therefore, from this we understand whether one has the Spirit of God. Knock on earthen pots to see if perhaps they give back their full sound or resound poorly. See if they give off the sound of wholeness; see if there is love there. You take yourself away from the unity of the world; you divide the Church by schisms; you tear to pieces Christ's body. He has come in the flesh to gather together; you cry out precisely so that you may scatter. Therefore, this is the Spirit of God who says that Jesus has come in the flesh, who says it not with the tongue, but with acts, who says it not by making sounds, but by loving.[30]

Theology of Church: Catholicity

For Augustine, the true Church is one, united at the local level by charity; it is also catholic, united with other Christian churches across the globe. Augustine had, of course, become a Christian in Milan, and from the beginning saw Christianity from an internationalist perspective. He therefore badgered Donatists for being out of touch with the worldwide perspective proclaimed in the Scriptures and for being out of communion with the worldwide communion of churches, East and West. Around 405, Augustine wrote Emeritus, Donatist bishop of Caesarea in Mauretania. He notes that he had heard Emeritus was a well-educated man who would, therefore, appreciate this internationalist perspective. From Letter 87:

(1) I grieve that you are severed and separated from the Catholic Church, which is spread through the whole world, as it was foretold by the Holy Spirit.

---

30. Ep. Jo. 6.10–13 (SC 75:298–308); trans. Rettig, FOTC 92:208–14.

I do not know why [you chose this separation]. For it is certain that a large part of the Roman world, not to mention the barbarian tribes to which the Apostle said he was also a debtor, with whose Christian faith our own is intertwined, knows nothing of the sect of Donatus, nor have they any idea when or from what cause that dissension arose. Assuredly, unless you admit that all those Christians [worldwide] are innocent of the charges that you make against the Africans, you are forced to say that all of you are guilty of the evil deeds of all, since there lurk among you, to put it mildly, some misguided characters. You do not expel anyone, or at least you only expel him when he has done something that requires expulsion. Or is it that you do not condemn someone who has been in hiding for some time and is afterward betrayed and convicted? I ask, therefore, whether he contaminated you during the time he was in hiding? You will answer: "Not at all." Then if he remained in hiding the whole time, he would not contaminate you at all, for it often happens that after people die their deeds come to light, but this is no harm for the Christians who lived in contact with them during their lifetime. Why, then, have you, by a rash and accursed schism, cut yourselves off from communion with innumerable Eastern churches, which knew nothing of what happened in Africa according to what you teach or claim?

(2) Whether what you say is true is another question, while we prove your facts to be false by much more authoritative documents, and we hold that this is proved even better by your own documents, in regard to the charges which you make against us. But, as I said, this is another question, one to be taken up and discussed when need arises. Turn the attention of your mind now upon this: that no one can be contaminated by the unknown crimes of unknown people. From this it is clear that you are separated by a sacrilegious schism from communion with the rest of the world, to which the charges, true or false, which you make against the Africans are completely unknown and have always been unknown. . . .

(5) How could the betrayers (traditores) among the Africans, whoever they may have been, have been known to the churches of the Corinthians, the Ephesians, the Colossians, the Philippians, the Thessalonians, the Antiochenes, the Pontians, the Cappadocians, and people of the other parts of the world, evangelized by the apostles and brought to Christ, or how did they deserve to be condemned by you if they could not have been known? Yet you are not in communion with them, and you say that they are not Christians, and you attempt to rebaptize them. What more is to be said? It makes me want to complain and to cry out.[31]

31. Ep. 87.1–5 (CCL 31A:131–35); trans. Parsons, FOTC 18:12–17.

Theology of Church: Holiness

The Donatists stressed that the Church here and now is "without spot or wrinkle" and associated its holiness with the "uncontaminated" purity of its bishops. Augustine's view was very different. He saw the Church here and now as a corpus permixtum, a mix of good and bad. In an open letter to the Donatist churches, Augustine invokes a series of Jesus' parables to articulate his eschatological view of the Church's holiness. From Letter 105:

(5.16) We do not know why you speak of betrayers (traditores) when you have never been able to prove your charges, never even been able to point them out. I do not say this because it was, instead, your people who were found out and who admitted their crime openly. But what have we to do with the burdens of others, except those whom we are able to amend by chastisement or by some discipline applied in the spirit of mildness and the anxious care of love? As for those whom we are not able to amend, even if necessity requires, for the salvation of others, that they share the sacraments of God with us, it does not require us to share in their sins, which we would do by consenting to or condoning them. We tolerate them in this world, in which the Catholic Church is spread abroad among all nations, which the Lord called His field, like weeds among the wheat (Mt 13:24–30); or like chaff mingled with the good grain on this threshing floor of unity; or like the bad fish enclosed with the good in the nets of the word and the sacrament (Mt 13:47–48). We leave them until the time of the harvest, or of the winnowing, or of the arrival on shore. We tolerate them so as not to root up the wheat, or to winnow the good grain away from the threshing floor (Mt 3:12), and before the harvest time throw it out—as opposed to storing it in the granary—to let it be gathered by the birds (Lk 8:5). We tolerate them so that, after our nets are broken by schism, we do not swim out into the sea of destructive freedom to try and avoid the bad fish. For this reason, the Lord strengthened the patience of His servants by these and other parables, to prevent them from thinking that their virtue would be defiled by contact with the wicked, and thus, through vain and human dissensions, they should lose the little ones, or they themselves should perish.[32]

---

32. Ep. 105.5.16 (CSEL 34.2:608–9); trans. Parsons, FOTC 18:209–10.

DONATIST FROGS

Given his internationalist view of the Church, Augustine often poked fun at the Donatists for their sectarianism, referring to them disdainfully as the pars Donati ("sect of Donatus"). He also satirized their provincialism when preaching on the Psalms, which often speak of the whole world praising God. From Expositions of the Psalms 95:

> (11) "Let the entire earth be moved before His face. Say to the nations, 'The Lord reigns from the wood.' For He has corrected the whole world, which is not to be moved" (Ps 95:9–10). What great testimonies for building up the house of God! Heavens' clouds thunder out throughout the whole world where God's house is being built up. Meanwhile the [Donatist] frogs croak from their marsh, "We alone are the Christians!" What testimonies can I bring forward? Psalms. I bring forward what you, the deaf, sing. Open your ears. You sing the words, you sing them with me, but you are out of tune with me. Your tongue sings out what mine sings out, but your heart is out of harmony with my heart. Don't you sing these words? Look at the testimony of the whole world. "Let the whole world be moved before His face."[33]

THEOLOGY OF BAPTISM

Through the dispute, Augustine also forged a theology of baptism that influenced Christianity for centuries. He set out three key principles: (i) the power of baptism vs. the moral purity of its minister; (ii) the character of baptism; and (iii) the validity of baptism vs. its fruitfulness. Let us look at each, one by one.

Theology of Baptism: Power vs. Minister

Whereas Petilian had argued that the giver's conscience cleansed the receiver's, Augustine insisted that the minister's conscience was irrelevant; what mattered was Christ's power. Christ, not the minister, made baptism effective. Augustine found this view confirmed in John's Gospel where it says that Christ baptized more than John the Baptist "although Jesus himself was not baptizing, just his disciples" (Jn 4:2). This distinction allowed Augustine to counter those like Petilian who dismissed Catholic baptism as the baptism of Judas. From Tractates on the Gospel of John 5:

> (6) For it is one thing to baptize in the role of a minister; another to baptize with power. For the quality of baptism is commensurate with the quality

---

33. En. Ps. 95.11 (CCL 39:1350); my trans.

of the person by whose power it is given, not with the quality of the person through whose ministry it is given. . . .

(15) If the minister is just, I rank him with Paul, I rank him with Peter. I rank just ministers with them, because, in fact, just ministers do not seek their own glory, for they are ministers. They do not wish to be considered as judges. They dread that hope be put in them. Therefore, I rank the just minister with Paul. For what does Paul say? "I have planted, Apollos watered, but God gave the increase. Neither he who plants is anything, nor he who waters, but God who gives the increase" (1 Cor 3:6–7). The one who is a proud minister, however, is in a class with the devil, but uncontaminated is the gift of Christ which flows through him undefiled, which passes through him the way perfectly clear water flows into fertile soil. Think of [the proud minister] as made of stone because he cannot produce fruit from the water. But the water passes through the stone conduit, the water flows onto garden plots; in the stone conduit it produces nothing but nevertheless brings forth plentiful fruit in the gardens. For the spiritual power of a sacrament is like light in this way: it is both received pure by those to be enlightened, and, if it passes through the impure, it is not defiled. Let the ministers be just, indeed, and let them not seek their own glory but Christ's, whose ministers they are. Let them not say, "It is my baptism," because it is not theirs.[34]

Theology of Baptism: Character

Few things irritated Catholics more than the Donatist policy of rebaptism. But why was it wrong? Augustine knew (as did his opponents) that the New Testament spoke of one and only one baptism. This led him to speculate on whether there might be a deeper spiritual reality that made rebaptism offensive. He argued that baptism marked one as belonging to the flock of Christ in some indelible way, what he called "the Lord's brand-mark" (dominicus character).[35] The analogy Augustine routinely appealed to was a military one. Roman soldiers received a tattoo, known as a stigma or puncta, on the back of the right hand.[36] Just as soldiers who deserted were not re-tattooed, so those who received baptism outside the Church were not to be rebaptized. Augustine admitted that Donatists possessed a valid baptism, that they bore the "tattoo" of Christ; but since they had broken from the unity of the Church, they were, in effect, deserters from the militia of Christ. If readmitted, they were not to be rebaptized, but simply brought back into communion. From On Baptism (Against the Donatists), Book 1:

34. Jo. ev. tr. 5.6–15 (BA 71:302–28); trans. Rettig, FOTC 78:122–23 (modified). See De baptismo 3.10.15.
35. Ep. 185.23 (CSEL 57:22).
36. On this, see Bradley Mark Peper, "On the Mark: Augustine's Baptismal Analogy of the Nota Militaris," Augustinian Studies 38 (2007): 353–64. He argues that, given military procedures of the time, this nota militaris should be spoken of as a "tattoo," not a "brand."

(3.4) That baptism exists in the Catholic Church, and that it is rightly received in it, and that it is not rightly received among the Donatists—these are things we assert. That baptism is truly found among Donatists—that is something that they assert and that we concede. . . . (4.5) Now if anyone does not really understand how baptism can be done by the Donatists—which we do confess exists there, but which we say is not rightly given there—let the person notice that we say that it cannot exist rightly there, just as they say it cannot be rightly had by one who has marched out of their communion. Let the person consider the analogy of a military tattoo: both deserters can have it and those outside the army can get it [illegally], but nevertheless it should neither be had nor gotten outside the military. When a deserter is escorted back or someone is inducted, that tattoo is neither changed nor redone.[37]

Theology of Baptism: Validity vs. Fruitfulness

Augustine distinguished between the validity of baptism and its fruitfulness. By this distinction, he could claim that Donatists were validly baptized, but they did not enjoy baptism's fruits (forgiveness of sins, eternal life) unless or until they ended their schism and rejoined the Church. He presumed Cyprian's formula that "there is no salvation outside the Church" to be a non-negotiable foundation and concluded that baptism conferred outside the Church, while valid, must be ineffective. From On Baptism (Against the Donatists), *Book 1:*

(12.18) Let them acknowledge that a person can be baptized with the true baptism of Christ, and yet that person's heart, if it perseveres in malice or in sacrilege, can block allowing the abolition of sins to take place; and so let them understand that people are able to be baptized in communions separated from the Church, communions where the baptism of Christ is given and embraced in the very celebration of the sacrament, but that baptism will be of no avail for the remission of sins unless the person, now reconciled to unity, has stripped off the sacrilege of dissension, by which his sins are held onto and their dismissal not allowed. Take the case of one who, through deception, gets access to the sacrament; he is not baptized all over again, but purges himself by pious correction and a truthful confession, so that what was given before then begins to work powerfully for his salvation, once he withdraws that deception by a truthful confession. So too in the case of a person who received the baptism of Christ in some heresy or schism (from those who

37. *De baptismo* 1.3.4–4.5 (CSEL 51:148–50); my trans. This analogy of the military tattoo appears also in *Contra epistulam Parmeniani* 2.13.29; *ep.* 185.23; *s.* 359.5; *De symbolo ad catechumenos* 8.16. The analogy of a sheep-brand is also common: *ep.* 105.1.1; *ep.* 173.3; *s.* 299A.2 (= Dolbeau 4).

had separated themselves but not lost Christ's baptism) and so received it as an enemy of the love and peace of Christ; but when he corrects himself and comes to the community and unity of the Church, he should not be baptized over again because, by his reconciliation to peace, he receives this benefit: that now, in unity, the sacrament begins to produce the remission of his sins, what it could not produce when received in schism.[38]

THE ARK'S COOING DOVE

We have seen Augustine's anti-Donatist theology in a piecemeal fashion; now let us see how the individual elements come together in a single address. In 407, Augustine delivered a sermon-series on John's Gospel, in the course of which he routinely discussed the Donatists, rebutting their behavior and their claims, making these sermons, in the phrase of Marie-François Berrouard, "a combat for the honor of Christ."[39] We see here how biblical exegesis and theological controversy come together. The following sermon focuses on John 1:32–33: "John testified further, saying, 'I saw the Spirit come down like a dove from the sky and remain upon Him. I did not know Him, but the one who sent me to baptize with water told me, "On whomever you see the Spirit come down and remain, He it is who baptizes with the Holy Spirit."'" Here, as elsewhere, Augustine focuses his audience's attention on some clue, some "mystery," buried within the text that he argues is key to its deeper meaning. Here the clue is that the Holy Spirit appears as a dove. Throughout the sermon, Augustine plays on the Latin word gemitus, which generally means "moaning," but, in the case of a dove, means "cooing." From Tractates on the Gospel of John 6:

(1) My holy people, I had feared, I admit it to you, that this cold [weather] might cool your enthusiasm for coming together; but because you show by the great number and crowd of you that you are on fire in the Spirit, I have no doubt that you have also prayed for me that I may pay what is owed to you. For I had promised, in the name of Christ, to discuss today why God wanted to show the Holy Spirit in the form of a dove—something that the shortness of time had prevented me from being able to give an interpretation and explanation of earlier. That this may be explained, this day has dawned for us. And I see that, because of a desire for listening and a holy devotion, you have come together in unusual numbers. May God, through our mouth, fulfill your expectation. For you have loved [so much] that you came. But what have you loved? If us, this too is good, for we want to be loved by you, but we do not

---

38. *De baptismo* 1.12.18 (CSEL 51:162–63); my trans.
39. Berrouard, *Introduction de saint Augustin sur l'Évangile de saint Jean*, 55–78.

want to be loved in ourselves. Therefore, because we love in Christ, love us in return in Christ; and let our love for one another be a moaning to God, for moaning, or cooing, is characteristic of the dove.

(2) If, then, cooing is characteristic of a dove, as we all know, and doves coo in love, hear what the Apostle says, and do not wonder that the Holy Spirit wished to be shown in the form of a dove. He says: "For we do not know what we should pray for as we ought, but the Spirit Himself intercedes for us with unspeakable moanings" (Rom 8:26). . . . And it is no small thing that the Holy Spirit teaches us to moan. For He makes known to us that we are in exile, and He teaches us to sigh for our native land, and we moan with that very longing. One who is well off in this world—or, rather, who thinks he is well off, who revels in the enjoyment of carnal things, and in the abundance of temporal possessions, and in a hollow happiness—has the voice of a raven. For the voice of the raven is full of loud shrieking, not of moaning. . . . But one who knows that he lives in the midst of the affliction of this mortal life, and that he is exiled from the Lord, that he does not yet possess that unending beatitude which has been promised to us, but that he has it in hope, and will have it in fact, when the Lord comes with shining brightness in His manifestation, who before came hidden in His lowliness—he who knows this is the one who moans. And as long as he moans on this account, he moans well. . . . Rightly the raven was sent from the ark, and it did not return; the dove was sent and returned. Noah sent both birds. Noah had the raven there; he also had the dove. That ark contained each kind. If the ark symbolized the Church, you see, of course, that it is necessary for the Church in this flood of the world to contain each kind, both the raven and the dove. Who are the ravens? They who seek the things that are their own. Who are the doves? They who seek the things that are Christ's. (3) Therefore when [Christ] sent the Holy Spirit, He showed [the Spirit] visibly in two ways: as a dove and as fire; as a dove upon the baptized Lord, as fire upon the assembled disciples. . . .

(7) What then did [John the Baptist] learn through the dove? . . . That there would be a certain peculiar characteristic in Christ, such that, although many ministers would baptize, whether [they were] just or unjust, the holiness of baptism would be ascribed only to Him upon whom the dove descended, about whom it was said, "He it is who baptizes with the Holy Spirit" (Jn 1:33).[40] Let Peter baptize; "He it is who baptizes." Let Paul baptize; "He it is who baptizes." Let Judas baptize; "He it is who baptizes."

(8) For if baptism is holy in proportion to the diversity of merits, be-

---

40. "He it is who baptizes" (Hic est qui baptizat): This phrase from John 1:33 becomes a sort of slogan or refrain that punctuates this and other sermons. Augustine's point is that, while others serve as ministers of baptism, the baptism itself is empowered by Christ and claimed by Christ as His own.

cause merits are diverse, baptism will be diverse; and the better the person from whom one seems to have received something, so much the more does one suppose that he is receiving a better thing. But understand this, brothers and sisters, that the saints themselves, the good who are associated with the dove, who are associated with the destiny of that city of Jerusalem, the good themselves in the Church, about whom the Apostle says, "The Lord knows who are His" (2 Tm 2:19), possess different graces; they do not all have equal merits. Some are holier than others; some are better than others. Therefore, if one should be baptized, for instance, by a true saint, while another by one with less merit before God, one of lesser hierarchical rank, with less continence, and of a lesser spiritual life, why, nevertheless, is that baptism they have received one and equal and identical, except that "He it is who baptizes"? Therefore, when a good man baptizes and a better man baptizes, one person does not receive a good baptism while another person gets a better one. Even though, of the ministers, one is good and the other is better, what they received is one and the same, not better in one and inferior in the other. So too when an evil man baptizes, either from some lack of knowledge or from some toleration on the part of the Church (for either the evil are not known or they are tolerated; even chaff is tolerated until the wheat on the threshing-floor has been completely winnowed), what has been given is one, and it is not unequal just because the ministers are unequal, but is equal and identical because "He it is who baptizes."

(9) Therefore, my dearest people, let us see what [the Donatists] do not wish to see, not what they cannot see, but what they would grieve to see, as though it were made inaccessible to them. Where were the disciples sent in the name of the Father and of the Son and of the Holy Spirit, to baptize the ministers? Where were they sent? "Go," he said; "baptize the nations" (Mt 28:19). You have heard, brothers and sisters, how that inheritance came: "Ask of me, and I will give you the nations for your inheritance and the ends of the earth for your possession" (Ps 2:8). You have heard how the Law went forth from Zion and the word of the Lord from Jerusalem. For there the apostles heard, "Go, baptize the nations in the name of the Father and of the Son and of the Holy Spirit" (Mt 28:19). . . .

(10) But, "look," say the disciples to the Lord, "we have heard in what name we are to baptize; you have made us ministers, and you have said to us, 'Go, baptize in the name of the Father and of the Son and of the Holy Spirit' (Mt 28:19). Where shall we go? Where?" "Did you not hear? To my inheritance. You ask, 'Where shall we go?' To that which I bought with my blood. Where then? To the nations," he says. Am I to suppose he said, "Go, baptize the Africans in the name of the Father and of the Son and of the Holy Spirit"?

Thanks be to God! The Lord solved the problem; the dove taught it. Thanks be to God! The apostles were sent to the nations; if to the nations, then to all tongues. The Holy Spirit, parted in tongues, united in the dove, signified this. On this side tongues are parted; on that the dove joins them together. Have the tongues of the nations achieved harmony and only the tongue of Africa become disharmonious? What is clearer, my brothers? In the dove is unity; in the tongues of the nations is community. . . .

(12) On [the Donatists'] side, too, assuredly they say that there are good and evil people; for if they say that they have only good, let their own believe them and assent. Let them say, "There are among us only the holy, the just, the chaste, the sober, no adulterers, no usurers, no defrauders, no perjurers, no wine guzzlers." Let them say it; for I do not pay attention to their tongues, but I touch their hearts. But since they are known to us and to you and to themselves, as you are also known both to yourselves in the Catholic Church and to them, neither let us reprimand them nor let them flatter themselves. We admit there are good and evil in the Church, but as grain and chaff. Sometimes the one baptized by grain is chaff and the one baptized by chaff is grain. If one argued that one baptized by grain has a valid baptism while one baptized by chaff did not have a valid one, then "He it is who baptizes" would be a false statement. If, on the other hand, it is true that "He it is who baptizes," what is given by chaff has validity, and thus chaff baptizes as validly as the dove. Granted, such an evil [minister] is not a dove, nor does he belong to the membership of the doves; nor can he be said to be Catholic or among them (as they say the dove is in their own church). How then do we understand things, brothers and sisters? We understand—and this is clear and known to all, and even if they do not wish to understand it, they stand convicted—that even when evil [ministers] give baptism, a second baptism is not given after it. The dove does not baptize the raven. Why then does the raven want to baptize after the dove does?

(13) Pay attention, my beloved people! Why also was something designated through a dove, so that the dove (that is, the Holy Spirit in the form of a dove) came to the Lord after his baptism and was hovering over Him, in consequence of which in the coming of the dove John should understand that [there was] a certain exclusive power in the Lord for baptizing? For through this exclusive power, as I have said, the peace of the Church was confirmed. And it is possible that someone may have baptism outside the dove; but that any baptism outside the dove benefits him is impossible. Pay attention, my beloved people, and understand what I am saying; for often by that chicanery they mislead those of our brothers who are lazy and frigid. Let us be simpler and more zealous. "Look," they say, "did I receive or didn't I?" I answer: You

received it. [They say:] "Well, if I received it, you have nothing to give me; I am secure, even by your testimony. For I say that I have received it and you admit that I have received it; we both assert that I am secure. What, then, are you promising me? Why do you want to make me a Catholic when you are not going to give me anything more, and you admit that I have already received what you say you have? But when I say, 'Come to me,' I declare that you, who admit that I do have it, do not have it. Why do you say, 'Come to me'?"

(14) The dove teaches us. For he answers from above the Lord's head and says, "You have baptism, but the love with which I coo you do not have." "What does this mean," he says, "that I have baptism but I do not have love? Do I have the sacraments and not love?" Do not shout. Show me how one who divides unity has love. "I," he says, "have baptism." You do, but that baptism profits you nothing, because without love you are nothing. For that baptism, even in him who is nothing, is not nothing. For that baptism is something, and something great on account of Him about whom it was said, "He it is who baptizes." But that you might not think that that which is great could somehow benefit you if you are not in unity, the dove descended upon him baptized, as if saying, "If you have baptism, be in the dove; otherwise, what you have may not benefit you." Come, therefore, to the dove, we say, not that you may begin to have what you did not have, but that what you had may begin to benefit you. For, outside, you had baptism to your ruin; if you have it within, it begins to benefit for salvation.

(15) For it is possible not only for baptism to be beneficial to you; it is also possible for it to be injurious to you. Even holy things can injure; for in good people holy things involve their salvation, but in the evil, they involve their judgment. . . . Consider what you have—what belongs to the dove outside the dove. If you have what belongs to the dove within the dove, you have it securely. Suppose you are a soldier. If you should have the mark of your general within [the army], you serve as a soldier securely. If you have it outside [the army], not only does that mark not benefit you for military service, but you will also be punished as a deserter. . . .

(18) Therefore, do not boast about baptism, as if salvation through it suffices for you. Do not be angry, put aside gall, come to the dove. Here that will benefit you which, outside, not only did not benefit but also injured.

(19) And don't say, "I am not coming because I was baptized outside." Look, begin to have love, begin to bear fruit; let fruit be found in you; the dove will send you inside. We find this in Scripture: "The ark had been built from incorruptible woods" (Gn 6:14). The incorruptible woods are the saints, the faithful who belong to Christ. For just as in a temple faithful people are called the living stones of which the temple is built (1 Pt 2:5), so people persevering

in the faith are the incorruptible woods. In that ark, then, were incorruptible woods; for the ark is the Church. The dove baptizes there; for that ark was borne over the water. The incorruptible woods were baptized within. We find that certain woods were baptized outside, that is, all the trees which were in the world. Nevertheless, the water was the same, and there was no other; it had come from the sky and from the abysses of springs. It was the very water in which the incorruptible woods that were in the ark were baptized and in which the woods outside were baptized. The dove was sent and at first did not find a resting place for its feet, and it returned to the ark. For all places were filled with the waters, and it preferred to return rather than to be rebaptized. But the raven was sent out before the water dried up. Rebaptized, it did not wish to return, and it died in those waters. May God turn away [from us] the death of that raven! For why did it not return, except that it had been cut off by the waters? But the dove, not finding a resting place for its feet, although on all sides the water cried out to it, "Come, come, bathe yourself here," just as these heretics shout out, "Come, come you have [baptism] here," the dove, not finding a resting place for its feet, returned to the ark. And Noah sent it out again, as the ark sends you to speak to them. And what did the dove do after that? Because there were woods that had been baptized outside, it carried back to the ark an olive branch. That branch had both leaves and fruit. Let there not be only words in you. Let there not be only leaves in you. Let there be fruit, and you return to the ark. But not through yourself, for the dove calls you back. Coo on the outside that you may call them back inside. . . .

(23) But what do you [Donatists] say? "Look, we suffer many evils." Would that you suffered them for Christ and not for your own honors. . . . Those martyrs who suffered in the time of persecution acted out of love. They acted out of love. But these men act out of ostentation and out of pride. For since there is no persecutor, they hurl themselves down [to a violent death]. Come then, that you may have love. "But we have martyrs." What martyrs? They are not doves. They tried to fly and fell from the rock.[41]

(24) And so, my brothers and sisters, you see all things shout out against them, all the holy pages, all the prophecy, the whole Gospel, all the apostolic letters, all the moanings and cooings of the dove; and they do not yet awaken, they do not rouse themselves up. But if we are the dove, let us moan and coo,

41. "What martyrs? . . . They tried to fly and fell from the rock": Optatus of Milevis, *De schismate Dona-tistarum* 3.5 (CSEL 26:81–85; Edwards, 69–70), reports that certain Donatists leapt off cliffs, apparently as a sort of ritual suicide, and that other Donatists honored them as martyrs. W. H. C. Frend, *Rise of Christianity* (Philadelphia: Fortress Press, 1984), 574, reports finding Donatist stone monuments at the foot of certain cliffs. Augustine is satirizing this here; see also *ep.* 43.8.24; *Contra epistulam Parmeniani* 3.6.29; *Contra litteras Petiliani* 1.24.26; *Contra Cresconium* 3.49.54. When he says, "They fell from the rock," note the singular; Augustine is consciously echoing Paul (1 Cor 10:4), who says that "the rock is Christ."

let us endure, let us hope. The mercy of God will be at hand that the fire of the Holy Spirit might flame forth in your simplicity, and they will come. We must not despair. Pray, preach, love. The Lord is absolutely powerful. Already they have begun to recognize their impudence. Many have recognized it. Many have blushed. Christ will be present so that the rest, too, may recognize it. And certainly, my brothers, let the chaff alone remain there. Let all the grains be gathered. Whatever has borne fruit there, let it return to the ark through the dove.[42]

DISPUTING CYPRIAN'S LEGACY

By 400, Augustine had come to appreciate how elements of Donatist theology depended on Cyprian's. So he decided to grapple at length and in detail with Cyprian's theological legacy, devoting Books 2–5 of his voluminous On Baptism to a close analysis of key letters. Augustine argued that Cyprian, like St. Peter (Gal 2:14), had made a fundamental theological misjudgment, but that did not diminish his heroic stature as a leader and a martyr. Around 407 or 408, Augustine wrote Vincent of Cartenna, bishop of a Donatist splinter group, known as the Rogatists. In this letter, Augustine cogently summarizes his earlier arguments on and assessment of Cyprian: namely, that the Donatists had faithfully and wrongly followed Cyprian's misguided policy of rebaptism, while at the same time they had betrayed Cyprian's deeper and rightful commitment to unity. From Letter 93:

(10.36) You like the testimony of Cyprian, a holy bishop and illustrious martyr, which, indeed, as I said, we distinguish from the authority of the canonical Scriptures. Why do you not also like the fact that he held with firm affection to the unity of the whole world and of all nations; that he defended it by his arguments; that he considered the self-righteous, who wished to separate from it, as utterly arrogant and proud? He even laughed at them for daring to arrogate to themselves what the Lord did not allow to the Apostles: that they should gather the weeds before the time; that they should separate the chaff from the good grain, as if it had been permitted them to carry off the chaff and clean the threshing-floor. Cyprian also showed that no one can be stained by another's sins, something which all the authors of this accursed revolt [of yours] allege as the sole cause of the separation, and he gave as his opinion that his colleagues who held views different from his in this very matter were not to be judged nor to be deprived of the right of communion with him. In that very letter to Jubaianus which was first read in the council[43]—the one whose au-

42. Jo. ev. tr. 6.1–24 (BA 71:340–96); trans. Rettig, FOTC 78:129–51 (modified).
43. "Letter to Jubaianus": that is, Cyprian's ep. 73. In this letter, he refers Jubaianus back to ep. 70 (quoted above). Augustine examines ep. 73 in De baptismo, Books 3–5, and ep. 70 in Book 5.

thority you cite in the matter of rebaptism—he confesses that in the past some were admitted to the Church who had been baptized elsewhere. These were not baptized again, so that some [bishops] thought these were not baptized at all. In this, did he not hold the peace of the Church so vital and so necessary that for the sake of it he did not believe that they were deprived of its gifts?

(10.37) Thus—as far as I know your mind—you can easily see that your whole case is undermined and destroyed. For if the worldwide Church was destroyed by sharing its sacraments with sinners, as you think—and this is why you separated from it—then it had already been totally destroyed when, as Cyprian says, some were admitted to it without baptism; and if not even Cyprian himself held this view of the Church in which he was reborn, how much less should your later founder and father Donatus hold it! But if at that time when members were admitted to it without baptism, it was still the Church which produced Cyprian, and also produced Donatus, it is clear that the just are not defiled by the sins of others when they partake of the sacraments with them. Thus you can offer no excuse for the separation by which you withdrew from unity, and in you is fulfilled this wise saying of Holy Scripture: "A wicked son calls himself just, but he did not cleanse his going forth" (Prv 24:35, LXX). . . .

(10.40) To sum up, then, Cyprian . . . covered over that blemish [of advocating rebaptism] with the overflowing charity of his most pure heart; since he most eloquently defended the unity of the Church, then spreading over the world; and he held most firmly to the bond of peace, for it is written: "Charity covers a multitude of sins" (1 Pt 4:8). We must add, too, that the Father purged that most fruitful branch—if anything in him needed correcting—with the pruning knife of martyrdom, for the Lord said: "The branch in me that bears fruit, my Father purges that it may bring forth more fruit" (Jn 15:2). And how does He do this except by one clinging [as Cyprian did] to the root of unity in the pruning of the vine? For even if one should deliver one's body to be burned, and not have charity, it profits one nothing (1 Cor 13:3).[44]

THE CIRCUMCELLIONS

Donatists were victims of sporadically enforced but often tough government policies. Catholics too suffered violence, namely, from wandering gangs known as Circumcellions. Their roots and motives and organization are difficult to discern from surviving sources. While surviving sources offer intriguing comments, they are not unbiased. One has to read

---

44. Ep. 93.10.36–10.40 (CCL 31A:193–96); trans. Parsons, FOTC 18:91–94.

surviving accounts with a critical eye, alert to the politics of the reporter. From Possidius of Calama, Life of St. Augustine:

(10) Now these Donatists had in almost all their churches a strange group of men, perverse and violent, who professed continence and were called Circumcellions. They were very numerous and were organized in bands throughout almost all the regions of Africa. Inspired by evil teachers of insolent boldness and lawless temerity, they spared neither their own people nor strangers, but, contrary to right and justice, deprived men of their civil rights. Those who refused to submit to them were visited with the severest losses and injuries, as the Circumcellions, armed with various kinds of weapons, madly overran farms and estates and did not even fear to resort to bloodshed. Moreover, when the word of God was diligently preached and a plan for peace was suggested, they who hated peace freely assailed the person who proposed it. Those Circumcellions who wished and were able broke away or secretly withdrew from their sect, when, in the face of their teachings, the truth became known. They then came back to the peace and unity of the Church with as many of their own group as they could take with them. Consequently, when the remaining Circumcellions saw that the congregations of their sect were growing smaller, they became envious of the Church's growth. Inflamed with intense anger, they carried out intolerable persecutions against the unity of the Church, with the help of confederates. By day as well as by night, Catholic priests and ministers were attacked; they were robbed of all their possessions; many servants of God were even crippled by torture. Some had lime mixed with vinegar thrown in their eyes, and others were killed. As a result, these rebaptizing Donatists came to be hated even by their own people.[45]

EPISODIC VIOLENCE

In the early 400s, the Catholic campaigning was enjoying some successes. With it came an uptick in the level of violence. Sometimes it was Circumcellions, sometimes local ruffians, who committed acts of violence, especially against those who left the Donatists and joined the Catholic cause. Such violence brought reprisals from the government and, in the end, damaged the Donatist cause. In an open letter to Donatist churches, from around 406, Augustine retails a recent wave of violence. From Letter 105:

(2.3) If you are angry with us because you are forced by the decrees of the emperors to rejoin us,[46] you brought this on yourselves by stirring up violence and threats whenever we wished to preach the truth, and you tried to pre-

---

45. Vita 10 (Geerlings, 42–44); trans. Muller and Deferrari, FOTC 15:84.
46. "Decrees of the emperors": Augustine seems to be referring here to the Edict of Unity in 405, which was only erratically enforced.

vent anyone from listening to it in safety or choosing it voluntarily. Do not hiss and stir up your minds; think tolerantly, if you can, over what we say; call to memory the deeds of your Circumcellions and the clerics who have always been their leaders, and you will see what brought this on you. Your complaints are baseless because you forced the enactment of all these decrees. Not to go back over numerous past instances, consider, at least, your recent conduct. Mark, a presbyter of Casphaliana, became a Catholic of his own free will, without compulsion from anybody; thereupon your people pursued him and would almost have killed him, if the hand of God had not restrained their violence by means of some passersby. Restitutus of Victoriana came over to the Catholic faith without any compulsion, and was dragged from his house, beaten, rolled in the water, clothed in reeds, kept in custody I-don't-know-how-long, and would probably not have been restored to liberty if Proculeian had not seen himself threatened with a showdown, largely on his account.[47] Marcian of Urga chose Catholic unity of his own free will, and when he went into hiding, your clerics took his subdeacon, beat him almost to death, and stoned him. For this crime their houses were destroyed.

(2.4) What is the use of saying more? Lately, you sent a herald to proclaim at Sinitus: "If anyone remains in communion with Maximinus, his house will be burned down." Why? Before he had been converted to the Catholic faith, when he had not yet returned from overseas, why else did we send there a presbyter of Sinitus, except to visit our people without troubling anyone, and, from his lawful dwelling, to preach Catholic unity to those who were willing to hear him? But your people expelled him, and did him a great wrong. What other purpose did we have when one of ours, Possidius, bishop of Calama, was traveling to the estate of Figulina to visit our flock, few as they were, and to give an opportunity to any who wished it to hear the word of God and return to the unity of Christ? But while he was on his way, they lay in wait for him like a band of brigands, and, failing to catch him in their toils, they attacked him violently at the farm of Oliveta, left him half-dead, and tried to burn down the house from which he had escaped. They would have done it, too, if the tenants of that same farm had not three times put out the flames that endangered their own safety. Yet when Crispinus was convicted in the proconsular court as a heretic of this very deed, he was let off the fine of ten pounds of gold, at the request of this same Bishop Possidius.[48] Crispinus not only showed no gratitude for this kindly indulgence, but he even went so far as to appeal to the Catholic emperors. This is what has brought down on you

47. Proculeian was the Donatist bishop of Hippo.
48. Crispinus was the Donatist bishop of Calama, and thus Possidius's local rival. The fine of 10 librae of gold, a formidable sum, was a fine associated with the heresy laws. On this and other attacks Possidius faced, see Hermanowicz, *Possidius of Calama*, 108–20, 132–87.

the wrath of God with greater force and persistence, and you complain of it!

(2.5) You see, you are suffering from your own evil deeds, not for Christ, when you stir up violence against the peace of Christ. What kind of madness is it to claim the glory of martyrdom when you are being justly punished for your evil life and your deeds of brigandage? If you, private citizens, so boldly and violently force men either to accept error or to remain in it, how much greater right and duty have we to resist your outrages by means of the lawfully constituted authority, which God has made subject to Christ, according to His prophecy, and so to rescue unfortunate souls from your tyranny, to free them from long-continued false teaching, and to let them breathe the clear air of truth![49]

An Assassination Plot

The Circumcellions once tried to assassinate Augustine during one of his trips outside Hippo. From Possidius of Calama, Life of St. Augustine:

(12) These armed Circumcellions frequently blocked the roads even against the servant of God, Augustine, when, upon request, he chanced to visit the Catholics whom he frequently instructed and exhorted. It once happened that, although the heretics were out in full force, they still failed to capture him. Through his guide's mistake, but actually by the providence of God, the bishop happened to arrive at his destination by a different road. He later learned that, because of this error, he had escaped impious hands. Thereupon, together with his companions, he gave thanks to God, his Deliverer.[50]

Augustine himself refers to the incident on several occasions. Here is one example. From Enchiridion (On Faith, Hope, and Charity):

(5.17) Benefit, likewise, has come to some through mistaking the road—but in traveling, not in morals. For example, it once happened that I took a wrong turn at a crossroads and thus did not pass by a certain place where an armed band of Donatists lay in wait for me, expecting me to come. The result was that I reached my destination, but by a long detour. On learning of the plot, I congratulated myself on my mistake and gave thanks to God. Who would not choose to be a traveler who made a mistake like this rather than the highwayman who made none?[51]

49. Ep. 105.2.3–2.5 (CSEL 34.2:596–98); trans. Parsons, FOTC 18:197–99. See *ep.* 28*.7 (Divjak), which reports that a bishop named Rogatus had his hand chopped off and tongue cut out.

50. Vita 12 (Geerlings, 46); trans. Muller and Deferrari, FOTC 15:86.

51. Enchiridion 5.17 (CCL 46:57); trans. Peebles, FOTC 2:382 (modified). In one of the Dolbeau sermons,

GOVERNMENT INTERVENTION:
AUGUSTINE'S CHANGE OF HEART

We saw one excerpt from the treatise-length letter to Vincent of Cartenna earlier. In the same letter, Augustine traces out his change of mind on government coercion, how he had opposed his Catholic colleagues who wanted to call in governmental authorities to enforce existing (but often ignored) legislation against the Donatists, but how in the aftermath of the Edict of Unity (405) he reversed his view and came to appreciate that government-imposed unity might actually lay the groundwork for genuine conversion. From Letter 93:

(5.16) You see now, I think, that the point to be considered is not whether anyone is being forced to do something, but what sort of thing he is being forced to do, whether it is good or bad. Not that anyone can be good against his will, but by fear of enduring what he does not want, he either gives up the hatred that stands in his way, or he is compelled to recognize the truth he did not know. So through fear he repudiates the false doctrine that he formerly defended, or he seeks the truth which he did not know, and he willingly holds now what he formerly denied. It would perhaps be useless to say this in any number of words if it were not shown by so many examples. We see that not only these or those people, but many cities which were formerly Donatist are now Catholic, now detest the diabolical separation, and now ardently love unity. These became Catholic by the effect of that fear which displeases you, through the laws of the emperors from Constantine, to whom yours first accused Caecilian without cause, to the present emperors. And these with perfect justice order that Constantine's sentence be enforced against you, since you took him for judge and preferred his decision to that of the court of bishops.

(5.17) I have, then, yielded to the facts suggested to me by my colleagues, although my first feeling about it was that no one was to be forced into the unity of Christ, but that we should act by speaking, fight by debating, and prevail by our reasoning, for fear of making fake Catholics out of those whom we knew as open heretics. But this opinion of mine has been set aside, not because of opposing arguments, but by reason of proven facts. First of all, the case of my own city was set before me, which had been wholly Donatist, but was converted to Catholic unity by the fear of imperial laws, and which now holds your ruinous hatred in such disdain that one could believe it had never existed there at all.[52] Similarly, many other cities were recalled to me by

---

Augustine also mentions the incident, noting that the Donatists "hate us, and if they can get the chance, they try to kill us at the hands of the Circumcellions. But because the Lord was at hand to help us, we escaped and for this we give thanks for the Lord's mercy" (s. 198.45).

52. "My own city": Augustine acknowledges here that his hometown of Thagaste had once been a Donatist stronghold, but probably after the forced unity in the late 340s, it shifted to the Catholic camp; so that Augustine grew up in a Catholic enclave.

name, and by these examples I recognized how truly the word of Scripture could be applied to this case: "Give an occasion to a wise man, and he will be wiser" (Prv 9:9). How many there are—as we know for a fact—who have been for a long time wishing to be Catholics, drawn by such manifest truth, but who kept delaying from day to day through fear of offending their families! And how many are held by the heavy bond of inveterate custom rather than by truth—something on which you have never relied—and thus fulfill the divine saying: "A stubborn slave will not be corrected by words, for, even if he shall understand, he will not obey" (Prv 29:19)! How many thought that the sect of Donatus was the true church because security made them too slothful, contemptuous, and unconcerned to acknowledge Catholic truth! How many were debarred from entering the Church by the reports of the evil-minded who kept saying that we place some unnamed thing on the altar of God![53] How many believe that it makes no difference to what section of Christianity a man belongs, and remain in the Donatist sect because they were born there and no one forced them to leave it and come over to the Catholic faith!

(5.18) For all these, the fear of the law promulgated by temporal rulers who serve the Lord in fear has been so beneficial that some now say: "This is what we wanted all along, but *thanks be to God*[54] who has given us an opportunity to act at once, and has cut off all our little delays and postponements!" Others say: "We have known long since that this is true, but we have been held back by some force of habit; *thanks be to the Lord* who has broken our bonds and brought us under the bond of peace!" Others say: "We did not know that truth was here, and we did not want to learn it; but fear has made us alert to recognize it, the fear of being struck with the possible loss of temporal goods without any gain of eternal goods; *thanks be to the Lord* who shook off our sloth with the goad of fear, and made us seek in our anxiety for what we should never have troubled to know if we had been secure." Others say: "We were held back from entering the Church by false rumors which we could not know as false without entering, nor would we enter without being forced; *thanks be to the Lord* who has removed our anxiety by this scourge, who has taught us by experience what vain and baseless stories lying rumor has circulated about His Church; by this we now believe that those charges, too, are false which the originators of this heresy made, since their successors have invented falsehoods which are so much worse." Others say: "We thought

53. "Unnamed thing on the altar": This is not clear, but it seems to refer to something reported by Optatus of Milevis, *De schismate Donatistarum* 3.12: During the persecution under Macarius and Paul, a rumor spread that the two imperial officials used to place an image on the altar during the Eucharist; Donatists claimed that this turned the Eucharist of the Catholics into a pagan rite (and thus demonic).

54. "Thanks be to God" (*Deo gratias*). This was a favorite Catholic slogan, intended to counter the Donatist slogan, "May God be praised" (*Deo laudes*). Augustine may well be echoing this clash of slogans in his refrain of *Gratias Domino* ("Thanks be to the Lord") in this paragraph.

it made no difference where we held the faith of Christ, but thanks be to the Lord who has gathered us out of our separation, and has shown us that it befits one God that men should dwell in unity."

(5.19) Was I to resist or contradict my colleagues and thereby prevent these gains for the Lord, that the sheep of Christ, wandering on your mountains and hills—that is, on the swelling of your pride—should not be gathered into the sheepfold of peace, where there is "one fold and one shepherd" (Jn 10:16)? Ought I to have opposed this arrangement, to keep you from losing the property which you call yours, and thereby leave you to proscribe Christ without danger? Were you to safeguard your wills by Roman law, and break by slanderous accusations the testament safeguarded for the Fathers by divine law, where it is written: "In your seed shall all nations of the earth be blessed" (Gn 22:18)? Were you to have freedom of contract in buying and selling and then dare to divide for yourselves what Christ bought by being sold Himself? Should the gifts which you make to anyone have value, and what the God of gods gave to those called His sons "from the rising of the sun even to the going down thereof" (Ps 49:1) have no value? Should you be saved from being sent into exile from your earthly land, yet attempt to make Christ an exile from the kingdom of His blood, "from sea to sea and from the river unto the ends of the earth" (Ps 71:8)? Rather, let the kings of the earth serve Christ even by making laws in behalf of Christ. Your forefathers exposed Caecilian and his companions to punishment by the kings of the earth on false charges; let the lions turn to break the bones of the calumniators, and let Daniel himself, proved innocent, not intercede for them, for he "that digs a pit for his neighbor, himself shall justly fall into it" (Prv 26:27).[55]

LOVE, AND DO WHAT YOU WILL

One of Augustine's most famous sayings is "Love, and do what you will" (dilige et quod vis fac). Few realize the original context is the Donatist controversy. It appears in a sermon delivered just after Easter, 407. Augustine invokes the principle as a way to justify what hardly looked like or felt like love to Donatist Christians, namely, the tough laws and penalties forcing Donatists into unity with the Catholics. From Tractate on the First Epistle of John 7:

(4) "We are from God" (1 Jn 4:6). Let's see why. . . . Let's see what [John] advises, and let's listen—not to antichrists, not to lovers of the world, not to

---

55. Ep. 93.5.16–5.19 (CCL 31A:178–81); trans. Parsons, FOTC 18:72–75. See Emilien Lamirande, *Church, State, and Toleration: An Intriguing Change of Mind in Augustine* (Villanova: Villanova University Press, 1975); Lamirande, "Coercitio," Aug-Lex 1:1038–46.

the world—let's listen to him—if we are born from God—as he gives advice in the spirit of truth. "Beloved": That follows what came earlier. See what's next: "We are from God. The one who knows God knows us; the one who is not from God does not listen to us. That is how we know the spirit of truth and that of error" (1 Jn 4:6). Now he's got our attention. The one who knows God is the one who listens; however, the one who does not know Him does not listen; and this is how one discerns the spirit of truth and that of error. Let us see what's being advised, what we need to listen to him about: "Beloved, let us love one another" (1 Jn 4:7). Why? Because a human being is advising it? "Because love is from God" (1 Jn 4:7). He has commended love a great deal because it is "from God" (1 Jn 4:7). He's going to say more. Let's listen intently. Now he says: "Love is from God, and everyone who loves has been born of God and knows God. The one who does not love does not know God" (1 Jn 4:7–8). Why? "Because God is love" (1 Jn 4:8). What more could be said, brothers and sisters? If nothing more were said in praise of love in all the pages of his epistle—if nothing else in any other pages of the Scriptures—and if this were the one and only thing we hear from the voice of God's Spirit, that "God is love," then there's nothing more we have to search for. . . .

(7) See, it's because love alone discerns. See, it's because that alone distinguishes [between] human deeds. (8) . . . A father beats his boy; a slave-trader flatters him. If you set out the two things, beatings and flattery, who would not choose flattery and flee a beating? If you pay attention to the person doing it, love beats, iniquity flatters. Look, see what we're recommending: that one cannot discern human deeds apart from the root of charity. . . . Even thorn bushes have flowers. In fact, some things seem harsh, seem savage, but they are done for discipline according to the dictates of charity. Once and for all, therefore, let this brief commandment be given you: Love, and do what you will. Should you be silent, be silent out of love. Should you cry out, cry out out of love. Should you correct someone, correct him out of love. Should you spare someone, spare him out of love. Let the root of love be on the inside. Out of this root, only good can come.[56]

"Compel Them to Come In"

Around 417, Augustine received a letter from Boniface, a rising military commander.[57] As a newcomer to Africa, he was unfamiliar with the Donatist controversy and asked Augustine for advice. Augustine sent back a treatise-length letter tracing the history of

56. Ep. Jo. 7.4–8 (SC 75:320–28); my trans.
57. On Count Boniface, see p. 121, n. 63.

the schism and a detailed survey of disputed issues. Much of the letter revisits what we have already seen. Towards the end, Augustine makes a famous plea to enforce the verdict of unity decreed by Flavius Marcellinus at the Conference of Carthage of 411. Augustine plays on Jesus' parable of the wedding feast to call on Boniface to "compel them to come in" (coge intrare). From Letter 185 (also called On the Correction of the Donatists):

(22) Who can love us more than Christ, who laid down His life for His sheep? Nevertheless, although He called Peter and the other Apostles by word alone, in the case of Paul, previously Saul, a dread destroyer of the Church, and afterward its great builder, He not only compelled him by words, but used His power to strike him prostrate, and, in order to force him to leave off the savagery of his dark unbelief and to desire the light of his heart, He afflicted him with corporeal blindness. If it had not been for that punishment, he would not have been healed of it afterward, and since he saw nothing, though his eyes were open, if he had been able to see, Ananias would not have laid his hands upon him that his sight might be restored, when, as Scripture relates, there fell from his eyes, as it were, scales with which they had been closed. What ground is there for the cry generally raised by schismatics: "There is freedom to believe or not to believe"? See, now they have the Apostle Paul. Let them acknowledge in him Christ first compelling and afterward teaching, first striking and afterward consoling. It is a wonderful thing how he who came to the Gospel under the compulsion of bodily suffering labored more in the Gospel than all the others who were called by word alone, and that in him whom greater fear drove to love, "perfect charity casts out fear" (1 Jn 4:18).

(23) Why, then, should the Church not compel her lost sons to return if the lost sons have compelled others to be lost? And yet, even in the case of those whom they have not compelled but only enticed, if they are called back to the bosom of the Church by stern but salutary laws, their loving mother embraces them more kindly and rejoices much more over them than over those whom she has never lost. Is it no part of the shepherd's care, when he has found those sheep, also, which have not been rudely snatched away but have been gently coaxed and led astray from the flock, and have begun to be claimed by others, to call them back to the Lord's sheepfold by threats or pain of blows if they try to resist? And especially if their numbers are increased by fruitful generation in the midst of runaway slaves and bandits, has he not more authority over them because he recognizes on them the brand mark of the Lord which is not tampered with in those whom we receive back without rebaptism? The wandering of the sheep is to be remedied without destroying in it the mark of the Redeemer. But if anyone is tattooed with the royal mark by a deserter who has himself been branded, and if they both find mer-

cy and the one returns to his service, while the other begins a service which he had not yet undertaken, the mark is not erased in either of them. In fact, is it not rather recognized in both of them and accorded due honor since it is the king's mark? As the Donatists cannot prove that what they are forced to is evil, they claim that they ought not to be forced into good. But we have shown that Paul was forced by Christ; therefore, the Church imitates her Lord in forcing them, although in her early days she did not expect to have to compel anyone in order to fulfill the prophetic utterance.

(24) Indeed, this is not an unreasonable deduction from that statement of the Apostle, where blessed Paul says: "Having in readiness to revenge all disobedience when your obedience shall be fulfilled" (2 Cor 10:6). In the same way, the Lord Himself commands the guest first to be brought in to His great supper, but afterward to be compelled, for, when the servant answered the king: "Lord, it is done as you have commanded, and yet there is room," he said: "Go out into the highways and hedges, and whomsoever you find, compel them to come in" (Lk 14:16–23). Thus, the obedience was first fulfilled in those who were first brought in gently, but the disobedience is put under restraint in those who are compelled. That is the purpose of that: "Compel them to come in," after he had first said: "Bring them in," and had been answered: "It is done as you have commanded, and yet there is room." If He meant us to understand that they are to be compelled by the fear engendered by miracles, many more divine miracles were wrought for those who were invited first, especially the Jews of whom it is said: "The Jews require signs" (1 Cor 1:22). Among the Gentiles, too, in the time of the Apostles, such miracles won faith in the Gospel so that, if the command was given to compel them by such means, it is more reasonable to believe that the first guests were compelled to come. Consequently, if the Church in the era of kings exercises, as she ought, the power which she has received by a divine gift, together with religion and faith, and if those who are found in the highways and hedges, that is, in heresies and schisms, are compelled to come in, she is not to be blamed for compelling them, but they [are to be blamed] for waiting to be compelled. The banquet of the Lord is the unity of the Body of Christ, not only in the sacrament of the altar, but also in "the bond of peace" (Eph 4:3). But of the Donatists we can say with absolute truth that they compel no one to what is good; whomsoever they compel, they compel only to evil.[58]

---

58. Ep. 185.22–24 (CSEL 57:20–23); trans. Parsons, FOTC 30:163–65. Augustine thought of this more as a treatise than a letter, entitling it, De correctione Donatistarum (retr. 2.48 [75]).

CHAPTER 8

AUGUSTINE THE THEOLOGIAN
On the Trinity

❦

Theology literally means "speaking of God." For Augustine and his age, the great theological issue was how to speak rightly about "the Trinity who God is."[1] His classic exposition appears in the fifteen books of On the Trinity (De Trinitate), a work nearly as influential as Confessions. He worked on it, off and on, for two decades, roughly from 400 to 422.[2] As he told Aurelius of Carthage, "I began the work . . . as a young man; I finished it as an old one."[3] He did not imagine that such a demanding work would be widely read. When his old friend Evodius, bishop of Uzalis, asked about the project, Augustine said that other writings were getting his best energies because they seemed "more pressing" and "useful to more people" while his still-incomplete exposition on the Trinity was "too exacting a work" and "comprehensible to few."[4] Only after the unfinished manuscript had been published without his permission did he finally complete, revise, and publish it (for more on this theft, see below).

The issue of Trinity was a tumultuous one and had been so for a century. Controversy began in Alexandria, Egypt, about 318 when Arius (d. 336), a presbyter and popular pastor, clashed with his bishop, Alexander (d. 328).[5] The point of contention touched—and continues to touch—the heart of the

---

1. Trinitate quae Deus est: a favorite Augustinian locution: Trin. 1.4.7; 15.6.10; 15.17.28; cf. 8.5.8 (Trinitate quod Deus est). For a comprehensive study of Augustine's theology of God, see Lewis Ayres, Augustine and the Trinity (Cambridge: Cambridge University Press, 2010). Other key sources are listed in the "Suggestions for Further Reading."

2. On the complexities of the dating of this work, see Hombert, Nouvelles recherches, 45–80.

3. Ep. 174 (CSEL 44:650); my trans.

4. Ep. 169 (CSEL 44:612); trans. Parsons, FOTC 30:51.

5. The scholarly literature on this controversy is vast. For a comprehensive study, see R. P. C. Hanson, The Search for the Christian Doctrine of God: The Arian Controversy, 318–381 AD (Edinburgh: T&T Clark, 1988); see

Christian faith: Is Jesus God or not? The problem, both logically and theologically, is this: How can one call Christ "God" and call the Father "God" and still claim to believe in one God? To pagan ears, Christians sounded not like monotheists, but ditheists.[6] Arius sought to safeguard monotheism and insisted that "the Father alone is God." He added that Christ was no divine offshoot, no fragment of God's substance (for God is not divisible). Thus Christ could not be the same substance as God. Rather, God made the Son out of nothing, much as the universe would be made from nothing. But Arius's Christ was no God-inspired human being; rather, he was the Word who pre-existed and created the visible universe and who bridged a vast cosmic gap between our messy changeable material world and the unchangeable immaterial God. Arius's Christ, even though creator, was not eternal, but had a beginning before the beginning of the universe. Arius thus sidestepped the idea of two "unbeguns," two gods, in effect. Arius's denial of Christ's full divinity led to his excommunication by Alexander and a regional council of Egyptian bishops.

This local dispute quickly internationalized and divided churches around the Greek East. To address the crisis, Constantine, the first Christian emperor, called the Council of Nicaea in 325. The Council brought together some 300 bishops from around the Empire and approved a creed phrased so as to contradict Arius's key views. The bishops formally affirmed Christ's divinity, declaring Him to be "true God from true God, begotten not made, one-in-being (*homoousios*) with the Father."[7] These pivotal phrases have come to define Christian orthodoxy.

But in the aftermath of Nicaea, things were anything but simple. Arius himself was exiled, but the debate continued for decades and reached some degree of resolution only at the Council of Constantinople in 381. Older textbooks have traditionally referred to this debate as the "Arian Controversy" and portray it as a clash between two camps, Nicenes and Arians. That is simply not accurate. There was no clear-cut battle between orthodoxy and heresy, but rather a halting, contentious, and muddled "search for the Christian doctrine of God," to use R. P. C. Hanson's apt phrase.[8]

Immediately after Nicaea, controversy centered not on Arius, but on one

---

also the new perspectives of Lewis Ayres, *Nicaea and Its Legacy: An Approach to Fourth-Century Trinitarian Theology* (New York: Oxford University Press, 2004).

6. See, for example, Celsus, the 2nd-century Platonist philosopher, quoted in Origen, *Contra Celsum* 8.12 (SC 150:198).

7. Council of Nicaea, *Creed*. For the text, see Jaroslav Pelikan and Valerie Hotchkiss, eds., *Creeds and Professions of Faith in the Christian Tradition* (New Haven: Yale University, 2003), 1:155–59. For an analysis, see J. N. D. Kelly, *Early Christian Creeds*, 3rd ed. (London: Longman, 1972), 205–54; Hanson, *Search*, 163–72; Ayres, *Nicaea*, 15–20, 85–104.

8. Hanson chose this phrase as his title for his magisterial study. For a discussion of the issue, see Hanson, *Search*, xvii–xix.

of Nicaea's architects, Marcellus of Ancyra (d. 374), whose unitarian theology seemed to blur any real distinction between Father and Son.[9] The other controversial figure was Athanasius (d. 373), Alexander's successor as bishop of Alexandria.[10] Athanasius's opponents accused him of violence and various criminal misdeeds and had him deposed in 335. Athanasius claimed that the real issue was theological: his opponents were, at heart, "Arians" who denied Christ's divinity.[11] During two exiles in the West (335–337 at Trier and 339–345 at Rome), he won over much of the Latin-speaking world to his interpretations, both politically and theologically. Early on, Athanasius positioned himself as a stalwart defender of Christ's divinity, but he championed Nicaea's Creed and its language late, only in the 350s (a fact often overlooked and variously interpreted).[12] His *Orations Against the Arians* and later treatises laid the groundwork for the eventual orthodox consensus on Christ's divinity. But that consensus arose slowly.

In the 350s, there evolved various competing theologies that were not "Arian" (despite Athanasius's claims), but were anti-Nicene.[13] Some anti-Nicene bishops were willing to speak of Christ as "God," but in some lesser, derived sense, and they envisioned an unequal hierarchy within the Godhead. In 359, a pair of large councils held at Rimini and Seleucia sanctioned and promulgated a creed seen as official and universal, insisting in self-consciously vague terms that Christ was "like" (*homoios*) the Father. Proponents of this tradition would be labeled by Augustine and his pro-Nicene contemporaries as "Arian." Scholars now regard this label as inaccurate (and as polemical sloganeering) and speak of them instead as "Homoians." Augustine would have bumped into Homoian Christians during his days in Milan since Ambrose's immediate predecessor, Auxentius, had been a leading Latin Homoian.[14] Here and there, in sermons and treatises, Augustine denounces "Arians" in passing, but around 419, he got hold of an eloquent Homoian pamphlet. He published it under the title *The Arian Sermon*, and composed a refutation. Here are a few of its propositions:

---

9. See Joseph Lienhard, *Contra Marcellum: Marcellus of Ancyra and Fourth-Century Theology* (Washington, DC: The Catholic University of America Press, 1999); Sara Parvis, *Marcellus of Ancyra and the Lost Years of the Arian Controversy 325–345*, OECS (New York: Oxford University Press, 2006).

10. See Khaled Anatolios, *Athanasius*, Early Church Fathers (New York and London: Routledge, 2005); Thomas G. Weinandy, *Athanasius: A Theological Introduction* (Burlington, VT: Ashgate, 2007).

11. See David M. Gwynn, *The Eusebians: The Polemic of Athanasius of Alexandria and the Construction of the 'Arian Controversy,'* Oxford Theological Monographs (New York: Oxford University Press, 2006).

12. See Lewis Ayres, "Athanasius' Initial Defense of the Term Ὁμοούσιος: Rereading the *De Decretis*," *Journal of Early Christian Studies* 12 (2004): 337–59.

13. See Michel René Barnes and Daniel H. Williams, eds., *Arianism After Arius: Essays on the Development of the Fourth-Century Trinitarian Conflicts* (Edinburgh: T&T Clark, 1993).

14. See Daniel H. Williams, *Ambrose of Milan and the End of the Nicene-Arian Conflicts*, OECS (New York: Oxford University Press, 1995).

17. The Son is subject to the Father; the Holy Spirit is subject to the Son.

18. The Son does what the Father orders; the Holy Spirit speaks what the Son commands.

19. The Son adores and honors the Father; the Holy Spirit adores and honors the Son. . . .

24. The Father is greater than the Son; the Son is incomparably greater and better than the Spirit.

25. The Father is God and Lord for his Son; the Son is God and Lord for the Spirit. . . .

27. The Father alone adores no one, because He has no one greater or equal to adore; He thanks no one, because He has received a benefit from no one. Out of His goodness He has given being to all things; He has received His being from no one. There is, then, a distinction of the three substances: the Father, the Son, and the Holy Spirit; and there is a difference of three realities: the unbegotten God, the only-begotten God, and the advocate Spirit.[15]

Note the emphasis on the stark inequality within the Homoian trinity: the three Persons are "three substances" and "three different realities." Also note the way the Homoian author speaks of the Father as the Son's God and of the Son as an obedient second-in-command. These sorts of claims illustrate what Augustine and other pro-Nicenes feared and opposed. Recent scholarship has uncovered how Augustine, in the early books of On the Trinity, was alert to Homoian arguments and prooftexts and took pains to counter them.[16] A few years after completing On the Trinity, Augustine actually met in a face-to-face debate with a Latin Homoian bishop named Maximinus.[17]

The issue was not simply the status of the Son. Note the way the Homoian author refuses to speak of the Spirit as God even in some derivative sense and strongly subordinates the Spirit to the Son. This reflects a shift in the debate that took place around 360. The new question became: Is the Spirit God, or not? This new question became the focus for the generation of pro-Nicene bishop-theologians after Athanasius. The leaders were the Cappadocian fathers: Basil of Caesarea (c. 330–379); his younger brother, Gregory of Nyssa (c. 335–c. 396); and his friend, Gregory of Nazianzus (c. 329–389).[18] The Cap-

---

15. Arian Sermon 17–27 (CSEL 92:37–40); trans. Roland J. Teske, Arianism and Other Heresies, WSA I/18 (1995): 135.

16. Until recently, scholars have presumed that Augustine grappled with Homoian views only late in his career. Michel R. Barnes, "Exegesis and Polemic in Augustine's De Trinitate I," Augustinian Studies 30 (1999): 43–59, has disputed the stock interpretation that De Trinitate was written in an air free of polemics and has broken new ground by demonstrating that Augustine from an early date engaged theological issues (and biblical texts) raised by Homoians. His speaking of this engagement as "polemical" may overstate things, for De Trinitate is not overtly polemical the way Augustine's treatises against the Donatists or Pelagians are.

17. Debate with Maximinus, an Arian Bishop (Conlatio cum Maximino Arianorum episcopo), in Teske, Arianism and Other Heresies, WSA I/18:188–227.

18. See Stephen M. Hildebrand, The Trinitarian Theology of Basil of Caesarea: A Synthesis of Greek Thought

padocians shared Athanasius's commitment to Christ's divinity (though they typically framed their defense as a rebuttal of the anti-Nicene extremist Eunomius of Cyzicus). The Cappadocians' originality came from the way they defended the Spirit's divinity and formulated the classic doctrine of the Trinity. The Cappadocian formula is that God is "three persons (*hypostaseis*) in one essence (*ousia*)." This, in time, became the ecumenical standard for Christian orthodoxy. Cappadocian views on the Spirit received formal ratification in 381, in the Creed of the Council of Constantinople which acclaimed that "we believe . . . in the Holy Spirit, the Lord and Life-giver, who proceeds from the Father, who with the Father and the Son is together worshiped and together glorified. . . ."[19] Christians today recite these words in liturgy, thinking they are reciting the Nicene Creed. They are not. Nicaea had been silent on the Spirit's status. Today's "Nicene Creed" is, in fact, the Cappadocian-inspired Creed of Constantinople.

Augustine never mastered Greek—at least, not to a level at which he could read Greek theological texts. This meant he did not know the writings of Athanasius or the Cappadocians at first hand. When Augustine converted to orthodox Christianity in the mid-380s, Ambrose symbolized and defined for him what orthodoxy meant. Ambrose, however, did read Greek and passed on insights and formulations from the Cappadocians—obvious in his treatises *On the Faith* and *On the Holy Spirit*. Augustine would, in later years, draw not only on Ambrose's works, but also those of Marius Victorinus and of Hilary of Poitiers (d. c. 368).

This complex background—complex both historically and theologically—serves as the starting point for Augustine's own quite original work as a theologian. In the excerpts that follow, I will draw mostly from his *On the Trinity*. But I open with earlier samplings to give a glimpse of the way that he worked out his views gradually and offered different elements to different audiences.

---

and Biblical Truth (Washington, DC: The Catholic University of America Press, 2007); Christopher A. Beeley, *Gregory of Nazianzus on the Trinity and the Knowledge of God: In Your Light We Shall See Light*, Oxford Studies in Historical Theology (New York: Oxford University Press, 2008).

19. Council of Constantinople, *Creed* (Pelikan and Hotchkiss, *Creeds and Professions*, 1:162–63). For analysis, see Kelly, *Early Christian Creeds*, 296–357; Hanson, *Search*, 812–20; Ayres, *Nicaea*, 253–60.

TRINITY AND INCARNATION:
FIRST EXPLORATIONS

Augustine's friend Nebridius had long been a provocative thinker and questioner. His challenges had helped Augustine see deep philosophic flaws in Manicheism. Around 389, when Augustine was settling into his monastic experiment in Thagaste, Nebridius wrote and asked how it could be that the Trinity always acted as one and yet only God the Son became human. Here we see Augustine trying to sketch a solution from a pro-Nicene perspective for how the three Persons of the Trinity always work inseparably, how they form a single power and a single activity. As in others of his early, philosophically inclined works, the argumentation here can be dense (not unlike a mathematical proof). From Letter 11:

(2) Here, then, is what I think about [God's] mystical assumption of the human being,[20] [a doctrine] that the religion in which we are both steeped proposes to us for the sake of our salvation as something we are to believe and to know. I have selected this question, not as the easiest of all, or the one I am best able to answer, but as the one that seemed to me more worthy than others of thought and attention. For the other questions are matters about this world and seem to me to have no bearing on the achievement of happiness. Even if it gives us pleasure to search into them, we ought to be concerned that the time spent on them should really be devoted to better things. Therefore, in regard to this present question of God assuming [a human being], I am surprised, in the first place, at your finding it hard to understand why the Son—and not the Father or even the Holy Spirit—is said to have become human. For the Catholic faith commends and believes—and even a few holy and blessed ones understand—that the Trinity is so inseparable that whatever action the Trinity performs must be performed at the same time by the Father and by the Son and by the Holy Spirit. The Father does not do anything that the Son and the Holy Spirit do not also do; nor does the Holy Spirit do anything that the Father and the Son do not do; nor does the Son do anything that the Father and the Holy Spirit do not do. From this it would seem to follow that the whole Trinity became human, for if the Son assumed the human being, and the Father and the Holy Spirit did not, They would be acting in some way other than mutually. Why, then, in our mysteries and our sacred rites is the assuming of the human being celebrated as if [only] attributable to the Son? This is a very deep question and so difficult and of such great import that it cannot be solved in a sentence, nor can its proof be wholly satis-

---

20. "Mystical assumption of the human being" (*de susceptione hominis mystica*): Augustine's early locution for speaking of "the mystery of the Incarnation."

fying. Nevertheless, when I write anything to you, I venture to outline rather than to develop what is in my mind, leaving you to work it out for yourself, according to your own gifts of mind.

(3) There is no nature, Nebridius, and certainly no substance, which does not possess and behave with these three characteristics: first, that it exists; second, that it is a "this" or a "that"; third, that it continues to be what it is as far as possible. The first shows us the very cause of nature from which all things exist. The second shows us the species in which all things are fashioned and in some way formed. The third shows a certain permanence [of identity] in which, as one might say, all things exist. But if it were possible: *that* something exists that is not a "this" or a "that," nor that it maintains its genus; *or that* it is a "this" or a "that," but does not exist nor maintain its genus as far as possible; *or that* it maintains its genus according to the strengths of its genus, but still neither exists nor is a "this" or a "that"; if that really were possible, then it could happen that in that Trinity one of the Persons could do something without the others. But if you discern that it necessarily follows that whatever exists must simultaneously be a "this" or a "that" and must maintain its own genus as far as possible, then those Three do nothing outside of what They do mutually. I see that I have thus far treated the part of this question whose solution is difficult. But I wanted to show you briefly (at least, if I did what I wanted to do) what subtlety is needed to deal with the inseparability of the Trinity—and with what depth of truth it is understood in the Catholic world.

(4) Now think about this as a possible way that what troubles your mind might not be so troubling. The characteristic attributed properly to the Son refers to a discipline of life and to a certain "artistry"—if we can legitimately use such vocabulary about these issues—and also to the understanding by which the mind itself is formed in its thinking about things. Therefore, since [God's] assuming a human being has brought it about that a certain discipline of living and example of precept has been conveyed to us under the majesty and clarity of His teachings, it is not without reason that all this is attributed to the Son. For in many issues, which I leave to your thoughtful and prudent consideration, though many truths are implied, one stands out and rightly demands special notice. For in those three types of questions, even if one were to probe whether something exists, there is implied also the question of what it is, for it certainly cannot exist unless it is a something. Likewise, there is implied the question whether we approve or disapprove, for whatever something is, it deserves some estimate of its worth. So when one probes what it is, it necessarily implies both that it exists and that it is weighed by some estimate of its worth. In this way as well, when one probes

what sort of thing it is, then that thing, in some way, exists. Thus, all these arguments are inseparably joined together, but the question does not take its name from all of them, but according to the intention of the questioner. Therefore, a discipline of life was necessary for human beings in which they might be imbued and in whose mode they might be formed. Now, as to what is accomplished in human beings by that discipline of life, are we to say that it does not exist or is not to be desired? But, first, we propose to know on what we may construct an argument and on what grounds we may remain. That is why a certain norm and rule of discipline first had to be demonstrated. This has been done through that dispensation of God's assuming of the human being, which is properly attributed to the Son, so that there follows through the Son both a knowledge of the Father, that is, the one principle from Whom all things come, and a certain interior and ineffable sweetness and delight of remaining in that understanding and of scorning all mortal things—a gift and function rightly attributed to the Holy Spirit. Thus, though all these operations occur with the most complete union and inseparability, they still had to be demonstrated distinctly, on account of our intellectual weakness through which we have lapsed from unity into multiplicity. For no one raises another to the place where he is, without stooping down a little to the place where the other is. You now have a letter that may not solve your difficulty on this point, but will perhaps set your own thoughts on a firm foundation, so that you may complete the argument with that genius, which I know so well, and continue with that devotion to which we must, above all, cling.[21]

THE DIVINE WORD VS. HUMAN WORDS

In 393, while still a presbyter, Augustine was invited to address a council of bishops gathered in Hippo. His address, published as On Faith and the Creed *(De fide et symbolo), is a remarkable work in many respects.[22] That as a presbyter he was even allowed to lecture bishops on the Creed is remarkable. Early in his address, he meditates on the way Christians call Christ the "Word of God" and notes how Christ as the divine Word is generated in a way different from the way human beings generate words in their minds. Remember that Augustine was, by training, an orator and was exceptionally self-conscious about spoken words, their origin, nature, and performance. This comparison and contrast between human words and the divine Word is a commonplace in Augustine's works. From* On Faith and the Creed:

21. Ep. 11.2–4 (CCL 31:26–29); my trans., based on Parsons, FOTC 12:26–29. See Ayres, Nicaea, esp. 366–72.

22. On the wording of the creeds found in Augustine's sermons and works, see the references cited on p. 146, n. 50, in Chapter 4.

(3.3) We also believe in Jesus Christ, the Son of God, the Only-begotten of the Father, that is, His one and only, our Lord. Yet we must not think of this Word as we do our own words, words which, once uttered by the voice and mouth, reverberate through the air and last no longer than their sound. But that Word [of God] remains beyond change. For what was said of Wisdom has been spoken about the Word: "Remaining in herself, she renews all things" (Wis 7:27). He is also called the Word of the Father because it is through Him that the Father is made known. When we speak truly, we act with our words and aim to disclose our mind to the hearer and to bring to the knowledge of another through such signs what we hold hidden away in our heart. Similarly, that Wisdom which God the Father begot is most fittingly called His Word since it is through Him that the great hiddenness of the Father is made known to worthy souls.

(3.4) But there is a great difference between our mind and the words by which we try to express that same mind. We do not, of course, beget the vocal sounds, but we form them, and it is the body that supplies the basic material in their formation. There is a vast difference between mind and body. In begetting the Word, God begot what He Himself is. Neither did He produce the Word from nothing nor from some kind of matter already found and fashioned in creation, but begets from Himself what He Himself is. If we examine carefully our motive for speaking, we shall see that this is also our aim—provided we are not lying but telling the truth. For what other objective do we have but to introduce (if such a thing were possible) our very mind into the mind of our hearer so that it can be known and fully grasped while we really remain within ourselves, not withdrawing from ourselves? Yet we bring into existence a sign by which our knowledge is engendered in another. As a result, another mind is, so to speak, brought forth by the mind through which this self-revelation is made. We try to do this by words and by our very tone of voice and by facial expression and by bodily gestures, being eager to disclose by so many mechanisms, so to speak, what lies within. We are unable to give perfect expression to a reality of this kind, and consequently the speaker's mind cannot be fully disclosed. Because of this, there is room left for telling lies. But God the Father, who has been both willing and able to reveal Himself perfectly to souls destined to know Him, has, for the sake of revealing Himself, begotten what He Himself, the Begetter, is.[23]

---

23. De fide et symbolo 3.3–3.4 (CSEL 41:6–8); my trans., based on Russell, FOTC 27:319–21. This meditation on the similarities and differences between human words and the Divine Word appears often in Augustine's works: e.g., Jo. ev. tr. 1.8–12; Trin. 15.11.20, 15.14.24–15.15.25. It appears especially in his sermons on John the Baptist: e.g., s. 288.3–4; s. 293A.5–13 (= Dolbeau 3).

Unity of Substance
and Distinction of Persons

In this same talk, Augustine sets out principles for thinking about the unity of the divine essence and the distinction of the Three Persons. He opens with a traditional analogy of three forms of water (a spring, a river, drinking water). While acknowledging its usefulness for illustrating unity of substance, he stresses that this and other material analogies are of only limited usefulness. From On Faith and the Creed:

(9.16) The Holy Spirit is not inferior in nature to the Father and the Son, but is, as I would put it, consubstantial and co-eternal, for this Trinity is one God. This does not mean that the Father is the same Person as the Son and the Holy Spirit. It means, rather, that the Father is the Father, and the Son is the Son, and the Holy Spirit is the Holy Spirit, and that this Trinity is one God, as it is written: "Hear, O Israel, the Lord your God is one God" (Dt 6:4). But if we are asked about Each in particular and someone says to us: "Is the Father God?" we will reply that He is God. If asked whether the Son is God, we will answer that He is. And if the same question is raised about the Holy Spirit, we will have to reply that He is none other than God. . . . It is to the Trinity that the Apostle refers when he says: "For from Him and in Him and through Him are all things" (Rom 11:36). Thus, when asked about Each individually—whether the Father, the Son, or the Holy Spirit—we must answer "God," not, however, giving anyone the impression that we are worshiping three gods.

(9.17) It is not surprising that words like this are spoken about a nature that is ineffable. Something akin happens in the case of those objects that we observe with our bodily eyes and discern by sense perception. When we are asked about a spring, we may not say it itself is a river; if asked about a river, we may not call it a spring; again, we may not refer to drinking water that comes from a spring or a river as itself a "spring" or a "river." Yet if we are asked separately about the members in this trinity called water, we answer in each instance that it is water. If I inquire whether that is water in the spring, the answer would be "water"; if I inquire whether that is water in the river, the answer would be no different; and no other reply would be possible in the case of drinking water. Yet we do not say there are "three waters," but "one water."[24] We must, of course, take care that no one represent the ineffable substance of the divine majesty as if one were thinking about that visible and

---

24. "Not . . . 'three waters,' but 'one water'": The analogy was a commonplace. Augustine's episcopal audience would have been familiar with it from Tertullian, *Adversus Praxean* 8 (CCL 2:1167–68). It appears also in Marius Victorinus, *Hymnus* 3 (PL 8:1143); see Mary T. Clark, trans., *Marius Victorinus: Theological Treatises on the Trinity*, FOTC 69 (1968), 324–35.

material spring or river or drinking water. In these instances, the water from the spring now flows out into the river and has no fixed resting place; when it flows from the river or the spring and becomes drinking water, it does not remain in the same place where it is drawn from. In this way it is possible for water to be labeled now as "spring," now as "river," now as "drinking water." But we have stated that in the Trinity it is impossible for the Father to be at any time the Son, or for the Son to be at any time the Father. . . . These material illustrations have been given, not because of a similarity to that divine nature, but because of a oneness that is discernible even in sense objects. In this way we are able to see how three objects can have, not only individually but even simultaneously, one single name. Nor should anyone think it strange or absurd that we call the Father "God," the Son "God," and the Holy Spirit "God," yet say that in this Trinity there are not three gods but one God and one Substance.[25]

EQUALITY OF FATHER AND SON

Here Augustine takes on the question of the equality of the Father and Son. The passage is interesting because it illustrates Augustine's awareness of favorite prooftexts used by Homoians to argue for the inequality of the Father and Son. Augustine, like other pro-Nicenes, insists on the "absolute equality" of Father and Son. Yet he does acknowledge one element of subordination: the Father is the source of the Son's existence and, paradoxically, of the Son's equality with the Father. From On Faith and the Creed:

(9.18) Learned and religious men have dealt with the subject of the Father and the Son in numerous books. As far as humanly possible, they have tried to show in these writings how the Father and the Son are not one Person (unus), but one reality (unum), and tried to work out what is proper to the Father and what is proper to the Son; how the Father is the Begetter, and the Son, the Begotten; how the Father is not from the Son, but the Son is from the Father; how the Father is the origin (principium) of the Son, for which reason He is also called the "Head of Christ" (1 Cor 11:3); but Christ, too, is called the beginning (principium), but not of the Father; the Son is called the Father's Image (Col 1:5), though He differs in no respect and enjoys absolute equality. These matters are treated at greater length by those who do not aim at presenting so brief an exposition of the whole Christian faith as I do.

---

25. *De fide et symbolo* 9.16–9.17 (CSEL 41:18–19); my trans., based on Russell, FOTC 27:331–34. Gregory of Nazianzus, in his fifth Theological Oration (*Oratio* 31.31; SC 250:338), delivered just a little more than a decade earlier, expresses a similar uneasiness with the analogy.

Now insofar as He is the Son, He receives being from the Father, whereas the Father does not receive it from Him. And it was from the Father that the Son, in His ineffable mercy and in His ordering of salvation history, took on becoming a human being, mutable, a created being destined for a more perfect transformation. Many statements are found in the Scriptures concerning the Son, but they have been put in such a way as to occasion error in the ungodly minds of heretics who want to teach before they understand, leading them to believe that the Son is not equal to the Father nor of the same substance. Some examples are these: "For the Father is greater than I" (Jn 14:28); and "The head of the woman is the man, and the head of the man is Christ, but the head of Christ is God" (1 Cor 11:3); and "Then [the Son] Himself will also be made subject to the One who has subjected all things to Him" (1 Cor 15:28); and "I go to my Father and your Father, to my God and your God" (Jn 20:17). There are other similar statements, but not one of them was made to indicate an inequality of nature and substance. Otherwise, these other statements would not be true: "I and the Father are one" (Jn 10:30); and "The one who sees me sees also the Father" (Jn 14:9); and "The Word was God" (for He was not made) "since all things have been made through Him" (Jn 1:1,3); and "He did not consider equality with God a thing to be grasped" (Phil 2:6); and so on. The first texts were composed partly because of the economy of [Christ's] assuming the human, about which it is said that "He emptied Himself" (Phil 2:7). This does not mean that Divine Wisdom, being absolutely unchangeable, has undergone change, but that He chose to reveal Himself to humankind in such a humble manner. So these declarations, which the heretics falsely interpret, were written down partly because of the economy of salvation and partly to show that what the Son Himself is, He owes to the Father; in fact, He also owes it to the Father that He is equal to and like the Father Himself. The Father, on the contrary, owes nothing of what He is to anyone.[26]

THE TRINITY WITHIN: FIRST EXPLORATIONS

Augustine believed that if God is truly Trinity, then human beings, who, according to Genesis 1:26, are made in God's image, should themselves be Trinitarian in some way. In the final book of Confessions, *Augustine suggests that in the depths of human consciousness, a Trinitarian dynamism can be uncovered. This passage offers a first, terse glimpse of a direction that Augustine would explore at length and with great originality in Books 8–15 of* On the Trinity. *From* Confessions, *Book 13:*

26. *De fide et symbolo* 9.18 (CSEL 41:20–22); my trans., based on Russell, FOTC 27:334–36.

(11.12) Who understands the All-powerful Trinity? Yet who does not speak about it, if it is really That that people speak of. It is a rare soul who, saying anything whatever concerning the Trinity, knows what he is talking about. People argue and engage in controversies, yet no one may see this vision without peace. Here are three elements I would suggest that people reflect upon within themselves. These three are far different from that Trinity, but I mention them so that people may think them over carefully, test them, and realize how distant they are from the Trinity. I speak now of these three: being, knowing, willing. For I am and I know and I will. I am a knowing and willing being. I know that I am and that I will. I will to be and to know. Let the one who can, therefore, see how inseparable in life these three are: one life and one mind and one essence—in short, how inseparable is the distinction, and yet there is a distinction. Each one confronts the evidence within himself; let each pay attention to it within himself and see it and tell me about it. But when each one finds and speaks about these three, let him not suppose that he has already found That which exists immutably above these—what is immutably, knows immutably, wills immutably. Is the Trinity on account of these three, or are these three in each [Person] in such a way that each [Person] has all three; or is it both of these, so that God is both wondrously simple and yet multiple, being infinite in God's Self and yet each [Person] the endpoint of and in the other, whereby God is and is known to God's Self and is immutably sufficient to God's Self in the overflowing greatness of the unity? Who can easily meditate upon this? Who can speak of it in any way? Who would be so rash as to voice any sort of judgment on it?[27]

PUBLISHING ON THE TRINITY

On the Trinity was a work that Augustine composed slowly and fitfully. Other projects kept intervening, and the work sat on the shelf for years. His readers grew restless, and someone got hold of the still incomplete manuscript, copying it and publishing it. Augustine was so upset that he nearly refused to finish the work. Finally, he brought the project to completion and sent the following letter to his friend Aurelius, bishop of Carthage, asking that it serve as a preface for the work. This is Letter 174, given in its entirety:

In my youth I began a work on the Trinity, the supreme and true God; I have finished it in my old age. Indeed, I had laid the work aside after discovering that it had been carried off prematurely or stolen from me before I had

27. *Conf.* 13.11.12 (CCL 27:247–48); my trans., based on Bourke, FOTC 21:417–18.

finished it or revised and corrected it as I had planned. I had intended to publish it as a whole, not in separate books, for the reason that the subsequent
books are linked to the preceding ones by a continuous development of the
argument. Since my intention could not be carried out because of the persons
who had secured access to the books before I wished it, I left off my interrupted dictation, thinking to make a formal complaint of this in some of my
other writings, so that those who could might know that the said books had
not been published by me but filched from me before I deemed them worthy
of publication under my name. Now, however, under the insistent demands
of many brethren and the compulsion of your bidding, I have devoted myself, with the Lord's help, to the laborious task of finishing them. They are
not corrected as I should wish, but as best I could, so that the whole work
might not differ too much from the parts which have for some time been cir-
culating surreptitiously. I send it now to your Reverence by my son and very
dear fellow deacon, and I give you my permission for it to be read, heard, and
copied by any who wish. If I had been able to carry out my original plan, it
would have been much smoother and clearer, though the statements would
have been the same; always, of course, as far as my ability and the difficulty
of explaining such matters would allow. There are some persons who have
the first four or, rather, five books without the introduction, and the twelfth
without most of the last part. If they come to know of this edition they will
make the corrections, provided they have the good will and the ability. I ask
earnestly that you order this letter to be used as a preface, separated from but
at the head of those same books. Pray for me.[28]

A Covenant with the Reader

Augustine opens On the Trinity *with a careful statement of what he is trying to do.
He stresses the orthodox formulation: that God is Trinity: three Persons, one Essence. He
also stresses that his quest is a faith seeking understanding—but it is more than that.
Augustine warns of unnecessary polemics, and he sets out his stance vis-à-vis the reader,
namely, a covenant of a mutual correction and of necessary tentativeness. Note the way
he quotes Ps 104:4—"Seek his face always"—a phrase that reappears at key moments in
the work. From* On the Trinity, *Book 1:*

(2.4) With the help of the Lord our God and as far as lies in our power, we
shall try to give an explanation of that very thing [believers] demand, namely,
that the Trinity is the one and only and true God and that one rightly pro-

28. Ep. 174 (CSEL 44:650–51); trans. Parsons, FOTC 30:83–84.

fesses, believes, and understands that the Father and the Son and the Holy Spirit are of one and the same substance or essence so that [believers] may not feel mocked, as it were, by our excuses, but may learn from actual experience that the supreme Good exists, which can be discerned only by minds that are wholly purified, and that they themselves are unable to see it or to comprehend it for this reason: because the weak eye of the human mind cannot be fixed on a light so dazzling unless it has been nourished and become stronger by the justice of faith. But we must first find out by an appeal to the authority of the sacred Scriptures whether faith is in a position to do so. Next, if God is willing and grants us His help, we shall perhaps render such a service to these garrulous disputants—more arrogant than capable, and therefore suffering from a dangerous disease—that they may discover something which they cannot doubt. But if no such certainty can be found, then they will grumble at their own minds rather than at the truth itself or at our explanations. And thus if there is any spark of the love or fear of God in them, they may return to the principles of faith and to the right course, and may at last realize how wholesome is the medicine that has been entrusted to the holy Church for the faithful. By it a carefully-regulated piety heals the weakness of the mind in order that it may perceive the unchangeable truth, lest some disorderly rashness plunge it into beliefs that are harmful and false. As for myself, I shall not be reluctant to make inquiries if I am anywhere in doubt, nor shall I be ashamed to learn if I am anywhere in error.

(3.5) Therefore, let everyone who reads these pages proceed further with me, where he is as equally certain as I am; let him make inquiries with me where he is as equally hesitant as I am; wherever he recognizes the error as his, let him return to me; wherever it is mine, let him call me back. Thus let us enter together on the path of charity in search of Him of whom it is said: "Seek His face always" (Ps 104:4). This is the sacred and the secure agreement into which I, in the presence of the Lord our God, shall enter with those who read what I am writing, in all my writings, and especially the present one, where we are investigating the unity of the Trinity, of the Father and the Son and the Holy Spirit. For nowhere else is the error more dangerous nor the search more laborious nor the discovery more fruitful.[29]

ON THE TRINITY: AUGUSTINE'S OVERVIEW

In his letter to Aurelius, Augustine stressed that individual "books are linked to the preceding ones by a continuous development of the argument." Despite Augustine's stress,

---

29. Trin. 1.2.4–3.5 (CCL 50:31–32); trans. McKenna, FOTC 45:7–8 (modified).

commentators have often divided the work in half, treating it as if it were two separate works: the first half (Books 1–7), often described as a systematic treatise on the dogma of the Trinity; the second half (Books 8–15), described as a speculative exploration of the Trinitarian structures of human consciousness. The second half represents Augustine's most original contribution. Modern philosophers and psychologists have fruitfully explored these later books for insights on Augustine's philosophy of mind. Still, it is vital not to detach the overall work from its historical, literary, and theological contexts. The first half bears little resemblance to later medieval or modern dogmatic treatises on Trinity; nor is the second half merely a personal speculative enterprise. It has been argued recently that the work needs to be read as a unified whole, as a sort of spiritual exercise, an exercitatio mentis, not unlike those Neoplatonic-inspired ascents of mind described in Confessions and elsewhere.[30] The work can thus be read as a progressively deeper and interior probing of what within us makes it possible for us to encounter, and thereby come to know and love, the God who is Trinity. Augustine, at the opening of Book 15, offers an intriguing overview of the first fourteen books. While this is no substitute or shortcut for working through the entire treatise, it helps us see what Augustine saw himself trying to do. From On the Trinity, Book 15:

(3.4) The necessity of our argumentation and reasoning, therefore, compelled us to say many things in the course of these fourteen books which we were unable to view in their entirety at one and the same time. In order that we may, therefore, refer them quickly in thought to what we wish to grasp, I shall, with the help of the Lord, have everything that I have made known and discussed in each of the books brought together briefly and without discussion, and shall place it, as it were, under a single gaze of the mind, not how each thing led to certain convictions, but the convictions themselves, in order that what follows may not be so far away from what precedes that the study of what follows may bring about the forgetfulness of what precedes, or, if this has already happened, then in order that what has escaped from one's memory may be quickly recalled by reading them once again.

(3.5) In the first book the unity and equality of that highest Trinity is shown according to the sacred Scriptures, and the same subject is continued in the second, third, and fourth. But in these three later books, the question about the sending of the Son and the Holy Spirit is carefully studied. And it is shown that He who was sent is not, therefore, less than He who sends just because the latter sends and the former is sent, since the Trinity—which is equal in all things and is also, in its nature, equally unchangeable, invisible, and present everywhere—works inseparably.

30. On this, see John Cavadini, "The Structure and Intention of Augustine's De Trinitate," Augustinian Studies 23 (1992): 103–23.

The fifth is concerned with those to whom it seems, therefore, that the substance of the Father and of the Son is not the same. For they thought everything said of God to be said according to the substance, and, therefore, claimed that, since "to beget" and "to be begotten," or "begotten" and "unbegotten" are different terms, therefore the substances [of the Father and the Son] are different. Consequently, it was shown here that not everything said of God is said according to substance, as according to substance He is said to be good and great, or whatever else is said of Him in respect to Himself; but that some things are also said of Him relatively, that is, not in respect to Himself, but to something that He Himself is not, as He is called "the Father" in relation to the Son, or "the Lord" in relation to the creature who serves Him; and that in the realm of creation, where anything thus predicated, that is, in relation to something which He Himself is not, also includes the idea of time, as when it is said: "O Lord, you have become a refuge for us" (Ps 89:1), nothing takes place in Him whereby He is changed, but He Himself continues altogether unchangeable in His own nature or essence.

In the sixth, how Christ was called by the mouth of the Apostle the "Power of God" and the "Wisdom of God" (1 Cor 1:24) was discussed in such a way that a more careful study of the same question was put off until later: whether He, by whom Christ was begotten, is not Himself wisdom, but only the Father of His own wisdom, or whether wisdom begot wisdom. But whichever of these it might be, the equality of the Trinity (as well as the fact that God is not threefold but a Trinity) also appeared in this book. Nor are the Father and the Son, as it were, something double in relation to the single Holy Spirit, where the three are not something more than one of them. We also discussed how the words of Bishop Hilary[31] can be understood: "Eternity in the Father, the form in the Image, and the use in the Gift."

In the seventh, the question that was deferred is explained in such a way that the God who begot the Son is not only the Father of His own power and wisdom but is Himself also power and wisdom, and so, too, the Holy Spirit; but yet that they are not together three powers or three wisdoms, but one power and one wisdom as one God and one essence. Then we inquired how they may be called "one essence, three persons," or by some Greek au-

---

31. "Bishop Hilary": Hilary of Poitiers (c. 315–c. 367), one of the leading Latin-speaking pro-Nicenes of the 4th century. He unsuccessfully tried to organize resistance to the anti-Nicene drift that took place under the Emperor Constantius in the 350s, an effort which cost him a lengthy exile in the Greek East. Hilary's De Trinitate (SC 443, 448, 462) was one of Augustine's major sources. On this, see Mark Weedman, The Trinitarian Theology of Hilary of Poitiers, Supplements to Vigiliae Christianae 89 (Leiden: Brill, 2007). Augustine's quotation here does not match Hilary's De Trinitate 2.1: "infinite in eternity" (infinitas in aeternitate, PL 10:51); the phrase, "Eternity in the Father" (Aeternitas in Patre), is found in a Pseudo-Ambrosian commentary on the Apostle's Creed (PL 17:538A).

thors, "one essence, three subsistences." And we found that we are compelled by necessity to speak in this manner so that we might be able to answer in one word when anyone asks what the three are, whom we truly confess to be three, namely, the Father, the Son, and the Holy Spirit.

In the eighth, it also became clear, from the reasons which we gave for those capable of understanding, that not only is the Father not greater than the Son in the substance of truth, but neither are both together something greater than the Holy Spirit alone, nor are any two something greater than one in the same Trinity, nor are all three together something greater than each other. After this, I reminded [readers] that the incorporeal and also unchangeable nature that God is might be understood (insofar as it can be understood) by the truth which is beheld by the understanding, by the highest good from which comes every good, by the justice on account of which the just soul is also loved by a soul that is not yet just, and by the love which in the sacred Scriptures is called God—by which those who have understanding also begin to discern, however it may be, the Trinity, namely, the lover, what is loved, and love.

Our discussion in the ninth book brought us to the image of God, which the human being is in terms of mind, and we found a kind of trinity in it, namely, the mind, and the knowledge by which it knows itself, and the love by which it loves itself and its knowledge. And we pointed out that these three are equal among themselves and are of the same essence. We treated this subject more carefully and more precisely in the tenth book, and this brought us to an even more evident trinity in the mind, that is, in the memory, the understanding, and the will. But we also made this discovery: that the mind could never be such that it would not always remember itself, understand itself, and love itself, even though it would not be always thinking of itself, and that even when it did think of itself, it did not always separate itself in the same thought from corporeal things; hence, we put off the discussion about the Trinity of which this is the image, in order that a trinity might also be found in corporeal things themselves, where the reader's mind could be more suitably exercised.

For this reason we chose the sense of sight in the eleventh book, since what we found in it could also be recognized in the other four senses of the body, even though we did not mention them. And so the trinity of the outer person appeared, first of all, in those things that are perceived on the outside, that is, from the body that is seen, from the form imprinted thereby in the gaze of the beholder, and from the attention of the will which combines both. But these three, as is obvious, are not equal among themselves, nor are they of the same substance. Next we discussed another trinity in the mind itself, introduced, as it were, by those things that were perceived on the outside where the three things appeared to be of the one substance, that is, the image of the body which is in the memory, the form which is then impressed when the gaze of thought is turned to it, and the attention of the will which joins both together. But this trinity, therefore, as we discovered, also pertains to the outer person because it was brought in from the corporeal things that are perceived on the outside.

In the twelfth, it was seen that wisdom is to be distinguished from knowledge, and, in that which is properly called knowledge (because it is inferior), a certain trinity of its own kind is first to be sought; and it together already pertains to the inner person. Still it is not yet to be called or to be regarded as the image of God. And this subject is treated in the thirteenth book by the recommendation of the Christian faith. But in the fourteenth, we discussed humanity's true wisdom, namely, the wisdom given by a gift of God in the partaking of God in Himself, which is distinct from knowledge. Our argument has now progressed so far that the Trinity appears in the image of God, which the human being is in terms of the mind. This is being renewed in the knowledge of God according to the image of the One who created the human being according to His own image (Col 3:10), and so one may perceive wisdom which consists in the contemplation of eternal things.

(4.6) Therefore, let us now seek the Trinity, which God is, in the eternal, incorporeal, and unchangeable things themselves, in the perfect contemplation of which the blessed life (which is none other than eternal life) is promised to us. For not only does the authority of the divine Books proclaim that there is a God, but the whole natural universe itself, which surrounds us and to which we also belong, cries aloud that it has the most exalted Creator of all, who has given us a mind as well as a natural reason.[32]

SEEKING THE GOOD

Serge Lancel has remarked that "the De Trinitate is a mighty river which sweeps powerful ideas along a course that is rich in meanders and swelled by unexpected tributaries."[33] Let me highlight a few meanders and tributaries. In the preface of Book 8, Augustine says that he wants "to analyze things in a more inward way" (modo interiore). He begins with an exploration of our experience of the many goods of this life: physical, aesthetic, social, etc. He insists that whenever we know this or that individual good, we at the same time get some sense of the good God who made all these goods. From On the Trinity, Book 8:

32. Trin. 15.3.4–4.6 (CCL 50A:462–67); trans. McKenna, FOTC 45:453–58.
33. Lancel, Saint Augustine, 385.

(3.4) Certainly you love only what is good, for good is the earth with its mountain heights and its modest-sized hills and its level fields; and good is an estate, pleasant and fertile; and good is a house whose architectural layout is well-balanced and spacious and bright; and good are animals with bodies charged with life; and good is mild and healthy air; and good is food that is pleasant and conducive to health; and good is health without pains or weariness; and good is the human face with its fine-proportioned features, cheerful expression, and glowing color; and good is the soul of a friend with the sweetness of concord and fidelity of love; and good is the just man; and good are riches because they expedite and ease matters; and good are the heavens with the sun and the moon and the stars; and good are the angels with their holy obedience; and good is a speech that graciously instructs and suitably admonishes the listener; and good is the poem with its measured rhythm and the seriousness of its reflections. But why go on and on? This is good, and that is good. Take away this and that and see good itself if you can. Thus you will see God, who is good not by another good, but is the Good of every good. For in all these good things, either those I enumerated or any others seen or thought of, we would, if we judged in accord with truth, be unable to call one better than the other if the idea of the good itself had not been impressed upon us by which we approve of something as good and also prefer one good to another. Thus God is to be loved, not as this or that good, but as the Good itself.

(3.5) There would thus be no changeable goods unless there were an unchangeable Good. When you hear then of this good and that good—things one might even call "not good" in other ways—and if it were possible to put aside those particular goods which are good by a participation in the Good and see the Good itself of which those others are good by participation (for when you hear of this good or that good, you also understand the Good itself at the same time); if, therefore, you could put these goods aside and perceive the Good in itself, you would see God. And if by love you cling to Him, you will be at once blest.[34]

PARADOX OF INQUIRY

In Book 8, Augustine raises a philosophical problem known as the "paradox of inquiry": How do we know how to seek out what we do not know? Plato had raised the question when he examined the nature of virtue. Augustine raises it as he examines the human

---

34. Trin. 8.3.4–3.5 (CCL 50:271–73); my trans., based on McKenna, FOTC 45:247–49.

search for God. It had long been a key issue for him. As we saw, he raised it on the very first page of his Confessions. He recognized that this search for God has unique epistemological challenges because God remains an infinite and ineffable mystery. From On the Trinity, *Book 8:*

(4.6) We must remain in this good [that God is] and cling to it by love, that we may enjoy the presence of that from which we are, in the absence of which we would not be at all. For since "we walk by faith, not by sight" (2 Cor 5:7), we certainly do not yet see God, as the same apostle says, "face-to-face" (1 Cor 13:12). Unless we love Him now, we shall never see Him. But who loves what he does not know? For something can be known and not loved, but what I am asking is whether something can be loved that is not known. If that is impossible, then no one loves God before one knows Him. And what does it mean to love God except to see Him and to perceive Him firmly with our mind? For He is not a body to be sought for with bodily eyes. But even before we are capable of seeing and perceiving God as He can be perceived (which is granted to the clean of heart, for "blessed are the clean of heart, for they shall see God" [Mt 5:8]), He must be loved by faith. Otherwise, the heart cannot be cleansed so as to be fit and ready to see Him. For where are those three—faith, hope, and love—for whose building up in the soul all the divine books have been composed and work together, where else other than in the soul who believes what it does not yet see and yet hopes for and loves what it believes? Therefore, even He, who is not known but in whom one believes, is already loved. Care must, of course, be taken lest the mind, in believing what it does not see, picture to itself something that does not exist, and so hope for and love what is false. . . .

(5.8) When we, therefore, speak of and believe in the Trinity, we know what a trinity is, because we know what three are. But this is not what we love. For we can easily have a trinity whenever we wish (to pass over other things) simply by raising three fingers. Or is it that we do not love every trinity, but only what is God the Trinity? What we love in the Trinity, therefore, is that it is God. But we have not seen nor do we know of any other god, since there is only one God, that One whom we have not seen and yet whom we love by believing. But the question here is this: By what likeness or by what comparison with known things can we believe so that we may also love the not-yet-known God?[35]

35. Trin. 8.4.6–5.8 (CCL 50:274–79); trans. McKenna, FOTC 45:250–55 (modified).

IMAGINING JESUS AND PAUL

For centuries, Christian artists have painted scenes from the Gospels, imagining what Jesus and the apostles may have looked like, and in so doing have profoundly shaped Christian imaginations. Augustine plays on this and, in the midst of meditating on what it means to know and love God, discusses the fact that the Gospels do not give any description of what New Testament figures looked like, neither Paul nor Mary nor Jesus Himself. How, Augustine asks, can we truly say that we know them and thus rightfully say that we love them if we have never seen them face-to-face? From On the Trinity, Book 8:

(4.7) Who, upon reading or listening to the writings of Paul the Apostle or what has been written about him, does not draw a picture in his mind of the face of the Apostle himself, and of all those whose names are mentioned there? And since, among the vast number of people whom those writings are known to, one person imagines their physical features and figures in one way, and another in a different way, it is certainly uncertain whose thoughts are closer to and more like the reality. But our faith is not busied there with the physical faces of those men, but only with the lives that they led through the grace of God, and with the deeds that those Scriptures bear witness to. This is what is useful to believe, and this must not be despaired of but must be sought for. For even the face of the Lord Himself in the flesh is represented differently by reason of the diversity of countless imaginations, even though Jesus had only one face, whatever it was. But in terms of our faith in the Lord Jesus Christ, it is not the image that leads to salvation, an image that the mind forms for itself and that may perhaps be far different from what it actually was. What matters is what we think of Him as a human being. For an idea has been impressed upon human nature, as if it were a law, according to which, when we see such-and-such a thing, we at once recognize it as a human being or in the shape of a human being.

(5.7) Neither do we know the face of the Virgin Mary, from whom, without contact with a man and without any detriment in the birth itself, Christ was born in a wondrous manner. Nor have we seen what were the characteristic features of the body of Lazarus, nor Bethany, nor the sepulcher, nor the stone that Christ ordered to be removed when He raised Lazarus from the dead (Jn 11:1–44), nor the new tomb hewn out of the rock from which He Himself rose (Mt 27:60), nor the Mount of Olives, from which He ascended into heaven (Acts 1:9–12). Those of us who have never seen these things do not even know whether they were as we imagine them to be. In fact, I regard it as more probable that they were not as we imagine it.[36]

36. Trin. 8.4.7–5.7 (CCL 50:275–77); trans. McKenna, FOTC 45:251–52 (modified).

TRINITARIAN ANALOGY OF LOVER, BELOVED, AND LOVE

At the end of Book 8, Augustine proposes the first of his interior (or psychological) analogies for the Trinity. Playing on 1 Jn 4:7 ("God is love"), Augustine suggests the structure of human loving—namely, a lover, the beloved, and the love between them—and offers a possible mirror of the Trinity. From On the Trinity, Book 8:

(7.10) In this question concerning the Trinity and the knowledge of God, nothing else is to be considered other than what is true love, or rather, what is love. For only true love may properly be called "love"; otherwise it is lust (*cupiditas*). Therefore, it is a misuse of terms to say about those who lust, that they "love," just as it is a misuse of terms to say about those who love, that they "lust." But this is true love: that while holding fast to the truth, we live justly and, therefore, despise every mortal thing for the sake of the love of humanity by which we wish every person to live justly. For in this way we can be prepared even to die usefully for our brothers and sisters, something that the Lord Jesus Christ has taught us by His example. For since "the whole Law and Prophets depend on these two commandments," the love of God and the love of neighbor (Mt 22:40), it is not without reason that Scripture generally names one of these for both of them. At times it mentions only the love of God, as in this passage: "We know that for those who love God all things work for good" (Rom 8:28), and again: "But if one loves God, one is known by Him" (1 Cor 8:3), and again: "Because the love of God is poured forth into our hearts by the Holy Spirit who has been given to us" (Rom 5:5), and so on in many other texts. It follows logically that the one who loves God must do what God has commanded and love Him in the way He commands; therefore, one must also love one's neighbor since God has commanded this. At other times, Scripture mentions only the love of our neighbor, as in the following text: "Bear one another's burden, and so you will fulfill the law of Christ" (Gal 6:2), and again: "You shall love your neighbor as yourself" (Gal 5:14), and in the Gospel: "All the good that you wish people to do to you, that is what you are to do to them; for this is the Law and the Prophets" (Mt 7:12). And we can discover many other passages in the sacred Scriptures where the love of our neighbor alone seems to be commanded for perfection, and the love of God is passed over in silence, although the Law and the Prophets depend on both commandments. But this also follows logically, for the one who loves his neighbor must also love love itself above everything else, for "God is love, and he who abides in love abides in God" (1 Jn 4:16). Therefore, it follows that one must love God above everything else. . . .

(7.11) Behold, "God is love." Why then, if we want to be with Him, do we set out for and run to heavens' heights or to the earth's depths in search of Him who is within us?

(8.12) Let no one say: "I do not know what I should love." Let him love his brother, and he will love the very same love. For he knows the love by which he loves more than the brother whom he loves. And so now God can become more known to him than his brother, more known because more present, more known because more interior, more known because more certain. Embrace God, who is love, and embrace God by love. It is love itself that unites all the good angels and all the servants of God by the bond of holiness and that unites us and them mutually with ourselves and makes us subject to God Himself. Therefore, the more we are cured of the swelling of pride, the more we are filled with love, and with what, if not with God, is one filled when one is filled with love? But one may object: "I see love, and I conceive it in my mind as best I can, and I believe the Scripture when it says: 'God is love, and he who abides in love abides in God' (1 Jn 4:16), but when I see it I do not see the Trinity in it." But as a matter of fact you do see the Trinity if you see love. But I will give you a proof, if I can, in order that you may see that you see the Trinity. Only let love itself be present that we may be moved by it to something good. For when we love love, then we love that which loves something, precisely because it loves something. What, therefore, does love love, that love itself may also be loved? For in loving, there is nothing that is not love. But if it loves itself, it must love something in order that it may love itself as love. For just as a word both indicates something and also indicates itself (though it does not indicate itself as a word unless it indicates that it is indicating something), so too does love indeed love itself. But unless it loves itself as loving something, then it does not love itself as love. What, therefore, does love love, except what we love with love? . . .

(10.14) But what is love or charity, which the holy Scripture praises and proclaims so highly, but love of the good? Now love includes someone who loves and something loved with love. So then there are three: the lover, the beloved, and the love. What else is love, therefore, but a kind of life which binds and seeks to bind a certain two together, namely, the lover and the beloved? And this is so even in external and carnal love. But that we may draw from a purer and clearer source, let us tread the flesh under foot and rise up to the spirit. What does the spirit love in a friend but spirit? And, therefore, even here there are three: the lover, the beloved, and the love.[37]

---

37. Trin. 8.7.10–10.14 (CCL 50:284–91); my trans., based on McKenna, FOTC 45:260–66.

ANALOGICAL BREAKDOWN

Augustine is never uncritical and recognizes the fragility of the various analogies he proposes. No sooner does he suggest the triad of lover, beloved, and love at the end of Book 8 than at the beginning of Book 9 he demonstrates its inadequacy. From On the Trinity, *Book 9:*

> (2.2) We are not yet speaking of heavenly things, not yet about God the Father and the Son and the Holy Spirit, but of this imperfect image [of God], but still an image, that is, the human person. For the weakness of our mind perhaps gazes upon this image more familiarly and more easily. Look, when I as the one conducting this inquiry love something, then three things are found: I, what I love, and love itself. For I do not love unless I love a lover, for there is no love where nothing is loved. There are, therefore, three: the lover, the beloved, and the love. But what if I love only myself? In that case aren't there only two, what I love and love? For the lover and the beloved are one and the same when one loves oneself, just as to love and to be loved are likewise one and the same when someone loves himself. For the same thing is being said twice when you say "he loves himself," and "he is loved by himself." For love is not loved unless as already loving something, for where nothing is loved, there is no love. So when anyone loves himself there are just two: love and what is loved, for here the lover and the beloved are one. It does not seem to follow, therefore, that wherever there is love, three things are understood.[38]

TRINITARIAN ANALOGY OF MIND, KNOWLEDGE, AND LOVE

In Books 8–14, Augustine proposes various psychological triads. In Book 9, after dismantling the triad of love, he proposes a new interior triad: mind (mens), knowledge (notitia), and love (amor). The first time one reads this (and many similar passages) in On the Trinity, *it can sound as though Augustine's logic is simply an intricate word game. It is not. He is carefully testing analogies using very specific criteria, criteria at the heart of the doctrine of the Trinity. In the following passage, he is testing whether this triad of mind, knowledge, and love is what the Trinity is: namely, if each is (i) the same substance, (ii) equal to each of the others, (iii) distinct (but not different) from one another, (iv) mutually inter-related, (v) mutually indwelling, and (vi) united (but without any mixture). From* On the Trinity, *Book 9:*

---

38. Trin. 9.2.2 (CCL 50:294); trans. McKenna, FOTC 45:271–72.

(5.8) In these three, when the mind knows itself and loves itself, a trinity remains: the mind, love, and knowledge. And there is no confusion through any commingling, though each is a substance in itself, and all are found mutually in all, whether each one in each two or each two in each one; in any case, all are in all. For the mind is certainly in itself, since it is called a mind in respect to itself, though in relation to its knowledge it is spoken of as loving, as being loved, or as lovable. And knowledge, though it is referred to a mind that either knows or is known, yet in respect to itself it is also spoken of both as known and as knowing, for the knowledge by which the mind itself knows itself is not unknown to itself. And love, though it is referred to as the mind that loves, whose love it is, yet it is likewise love in respect to itself so that it also exists in itself. For love is also loved, nor can it be loved with anything else except with love, that is, with itself. And so each exists in itself. But they are mutually in each other in such a way that the mind that loves is in the love, and the love is in the knowledge of the one that loves, and knowledge is in the mind that knows. And so each one is in each two because the mind that knows and loves itself is in its own love and knowledge; and the love of the mind that knows and loves itself is in the mind and in the knowledge; and the knowledge of the mind that knows and loves itself is in the mind and in its love, because it loves itself as knowing and knows itself as loving. And for this reason each two are also in each one because the mind that knows and loves itself is in the love with its knowledge, and in the knowledge with its love, since the love itself and knowledge are also together in the mind that loves and knows itself. But we have shown above how all are in all since the mind loves itself as a whole and knows itself as a whole, knows all in love and loves all in knowledge, when these three are perfect in respect to themselves. These three, therefore, are in a marvelous way inseparable from one another, and yet each of them is a substance, and all together are one substance or essence, while the terms themselves express a mutual relationship.[39]

AUGUSTINE'S COGITO

The French philosopher and mathematician René Descartes (1596–1650) is famous for his terse proof against radical skepticism: "I think, therefore I am" (cogito ergo sum). Augustine had actually proposed a cogito of his own, playing on the fact that the very doubting of existence proves existence. From On the Trinity, Book 10:

39. Trin. 9.5.8 (CCL 50:300–301); trans. McKenna, FOTC 45:277–78. On this issue of self-knowledge and self-love, see Oliver O'Donovan, *The Problem of Self-Love in St. Augustine* (New Haven: Yale University Press, 1980; reprint: Eugene, OR: Wipf & Stock, 2006), 60–92.

(10.14) But since we are investigating the nature of the mind, let us not take into consideration any knowledge that is obtained from the outside, through the senses of the body, but consider more attentively the principle which we have laid down: that every mind knows and is certain concerning itself. For people have doubted whether the powers to live, to remember, to understand, to will, to think, to know, and to judge are due to air or to fire or to the brain or to the blood or to atoms or to a fifth body (I do not know what it is, but it differs from the four customary elements); or whether the combination or the orderly arrangement of the flesh is capable of producing these effects. Some try to maintain this opinion; others, that opinion. On the other hand, who could doubt that one lives and remembers and understands and wills and thinks and judges? For even if one doubts, one lives; if one doubts, one remembers why one doubts, for one wishes to be certain; if one doubts, one thinks; if one doubts, one knows that one does not know; if one doubts, one judges that one ought not to comment rashly. Whoever then doubts about anything else ought never to doubt about all of these; for if they were not, one would be unable to doubt about anything at all.[40]

TRINITARIAN ANALOGY OF MEMORY, UNDERSTANDING, AND WILL

At the end of Book 10, Augustine shifts rather abruptly from his previous triad to a new one: memory (memoria), understanding (intelligentia), and will (voluntas). Here Augustine plays on his experience as an educator. He knows how the young eagerly search for knowledge and delight in discovery. He also notes that education in the best sense involves not only learning new things but also shaping students' morals and character. That seems to Augustine an apt paradigm for believers who, as God's "little ones," search for God. This new analogy is one that he will take up again at the end of On the Trinity. It is also one that medieval thinkers like Bonaventure would appeal to.[41] Note that Augustine does not see these three as "faculties" (as some medievals would), but as distinguishable dynamisms within the united mind: that is, the whole mind remembering; the whole mind understanding; the whole mind willing. From On the Trinity, Book 10:

40. Trin. 10.10.14 (CCL 50:327–28); trans. McKenna, FOTC 45:308. Here doubt becomes a proof of existence. Augustine argues in a similar way, "If I am mistaken, I exist" (*si fallor, sum*) in *civ. Dei* 11.26 (CCL 48:345–46); see also Trin. 15.12.21. On this, see Rist, *Augustine*, 63–67; Gareth B. Matthews, *Thought's Ego in Augustine and Descartes* (Ithaca: Cornell University Press, 1992).

41. For example, Bonaventure, *Itinerarium mentis ad Deum* 3.5. On this, see William Harmless, "Mystic as Cartographer: Bonaventure," *Mystics* (New York: Oxford University Press, 2008), 79–105.

(11.17) Let us, therefore, put aside for the time being the rest of the things which the mind is certain of concerning itself and discuss three that demand special consideration: memory, understanding, will.[42] For it is from these three that we are also wont to gain an insight into the talents and the character of the young. For the more tenaciously and the more easily a boy remembers, the more acutely he understands; and the more eagerly he studies, the more praiseworthy is his talent. But when we inquire into a person's learning, we do not ask about the sureness or the facility of his memory, or the keenness of his understanding, but what he remembers and what he understands. And because a mind (animus) is considered worthy of praise not only for its learning but also for its goodness, we have to consider not only what it remembers and understands but also what it wills—not how passionately it wills, but first what it wills and then how much it wills it. For a mind that loves enthusiastically is only to be praised when that which it loves deserves to be enthusiastically loved. When we speak, therefore, of these three—talent, learning, use—our judgment upon the first of these three depends upon what a person can do in his memory and understanding and will. In the second, we consider what each one has in his memory and understanding and at what point he has arrived by his studious will. But the third one, use, lies in the will which disposes of those things that are contained in the memory and the understanding, whether it refers them to something else or rests satisfied in them as an end. For to use is to take up something into the power of the will, but to enjoy is to use with the joy, not of hope, but of the actual thing. Therefore, everyone who enjoys, uses, for everyone takes up something into the power of the will and finds pleasure in it as an end. But not everyone who uses, enjoys, if they have sought after what they take up into the power of the will, not on account of the thing itself, but on account of something else.

(11.18) Since these three—memory, understanding, will—are, therefore, not three lives, but one life, not three minds, but one mind, it follows that they are certainly not three substances, but one substance. For when we speak of memory as life, mind, and substance, we speak of it in respect to itself. But when we speak of it simply as memory, we speak of it in relation to something else. We may also say the same of the understanding and the will, for they are called "understanding" and "will" in relation to something else, yet each in respect to itself is life, mind, and essence. Therefore, these three are one in that they are one life, one mind, and one essence. And whatever else they are

42. "Memory, understanding, will": Augustine's triad modifies that found in Cicero: "Prudence is the knowledge of things, good, evil, and indifferent. The parts of prudence are memory, understanding, and foresight" (De inventione 2.53.160). Augustine quotes Cicero's passage at length in his early De diversis quaestionibus octoginta tribus 31 (BA 10:88–94; trans. Mosher, FOTC 70:58–61).

called in respect to themselves, they are spoken of together not in the plural, but in the singular. But they are three in that they mutually refer to each other. And if they are not equal, not only each one to each one, but each one to all, they would certainly not comprehend each other. For not only is each one comprehended by each one, but all are also comprehended by each one. For I remember that I have memory and understanding and will; and I understand that I understand and will and remember; and I will that I will and remember and understand; and at the same time I remember my whole memory and understanding and will. For what I do not remember of my memory is not in my memory. But nothing is so much in the memory as the memory itself. Therefore, I remember my whole memory. I likewise know that I understand whatever I understand, and I know that I will whatever I will; but whatever I know, I remember. Therefore, I remember my whole understanding and my whole will. Similarly, when I understand these three, I understand them as a whole at the same time. For there is nothing of intelligible things that I do not understand except what I do not know. But what I do not know, I neither remember nor will. Therefore, whatever of intelligible things I do not understand, it follows that I also do not remember them nor will them. On the other hand, whatever of intelligible things I do remember and will, it follows that I also understand. My will also comprehends my whole understanding and my whole memory, if only I make use of the whole of what I understand and remember. That is why, when all are mutually comprehended by each one and are comprehended as wholes, then each one as a whole is equal to each other one as a whole, and each as a whole is equal to all [three] together as wholes; and these three are one life, one mind, one essence.[43]

WOMEN AS IMAGES OF GOD

In Book 12, Augustine rejects the idea that a trio of persons—husband, wife, and child—can be used as an image of God as trinity, noting that two biblical texts, Gn 1:26–27 and 1 Cor 11:7, refer to the individual person as an image of God. The Corinthians text, however, might be read—and, in fact, was read by some Christians—to imply that women are not truly made in God's image. Augustine disputes this and is committed to the equal human dignity of women, but, in a complex exegesis, accepts also that Scripture sees some subordination in the symbolic function of women, that is, as analogous to the lower realm of human consciousness which deals with the earthly affairs. Feminist

---

43. Trin. 10.11.17–11.18 (CCL 50:329–31); trans. McKenna, FOTC 45:311–12 (modified). Augustine also discussed this with a popular audience in s. 52.19–23; see Lewis Ayres, "'Remember That You Are Catholic' (serm. 52.2): Augustine on the Unity of the Triune God," Journal of Early Christian Studies 8 (2000): 39–82.

scholars have examined this (and other texts) and come to differing assessments—some positive, some negative—of Augustine's theological attitudes on women.[44] From On the Trinity, Book 12:

(7.9) We ought, therefore, not to understand the human being as made in the image of the exalted Trinity (that is, to the image of God) in such a way that the same image is understood to be in three human beings, especially since the Apostle says that the man is the image of God and so should remove the covering from his head, which he warns the woman to use, when he speaks as follows: "A man indeed ought not to cover his head because he is the image and glory of God. But the woman is the glory of the man" (1 Cor 11:7). What, then, is to be said about this? If the woman according to her own person completes the image of the Trinity, why is the man still called that image when she has been taken from his side? Or if even one person rather than three can be called the image of God as each Person in the exalted Trinity is also God, why is the woman not also the image of God? For this is the reason why she is commanded to cover her head, something the man is forbidden to do because he is the image of God.

(7.10) But we must see how what the Apostle says about the man (and not the woman) being the image of God is not contradictory to what is written in Genesis: "God made the human being to the image of God; male and female he made them; he made them and blessed them" (Gn 1:27). For Genesis says that human nature itself, which is complete in both sexes, has been made to the image of God, and it does not exclude the woman from being understood as the image of God. For after it said that God made the human being to the image of God, it goes on to say: "He made them male and female," or, if we in any case punctuate this passage differently, "male and female, he made them." In what sense, therefore, are we to understand the Apostle, that the man is the image of God and so is forbidden to cover his head, but the woman is not and so is commanded to do so? The solution lies, I think, in what I already said when discussing the nature of the human mind, namely, that the woman together with her husband is the image of God so that that whole substance is one image. But when she is assigned her role as helpmate, a function that pertains to her alone, then she is not the image of God, but as far as the man is concerned, he is by himself alone the image of God, just as fully and completely as when he and the woman are joined together into

44. See Kari Elizabeth Børresen, "In Defense of Augustine: How *femina* Is *homo*," in Bernard Bruning, ed., *Collectanea Augustiniana: Mélanges T. J. van Bavel* (Leuven: Leuven University Press, 1990), 1:411–28; Kari Elizabeth Børresen, "La feminologie d'Augustin et les droits humains des femmes," *Augustiniana* 54 (2004): 325–41; E. Ann Matter, "Christ, God, and Woman in the Thought of St. Augustine," in *Augustine and His Critics*, 164–75.

one. As we said of the nature of the human mind: if as a whole it contemplates the truth, it is the image of God; and when its functions are divided and something of it is diverted to handling temporal things, still that part that consults the truth is the image of God, but that other part that is directed to handling inferior things is not the image of God. And since the more it has extended itself towards what is eternal, the more it is formed thereby to the image of God, and so it is not to be restrained to hold itself back and refrain from this direction; therefore, "the man ought not to cover his head" (1 Cor 11:7). . . .

(7.12) Not only true reason, but also the authority of the Apostle himself declares that "the human being is made to the image of God," not according to the form of the body but according to the rational mind. For it is vain and degrading thinking which represents God as circumscribed and limited by the outlines of bodily limbs. Moreover, does not this same blessed Apostle say: "Be renewed in the spirit of your mind, and put on the new man who is created according to God" (Eph 4:23–24), and even more plainly in another place: "Stripping yourselves of the old man with his deeds, put on the new who is renewed to the knowledge of God according to the image of the One who created him" (Col 3:9–10)? If, therefore, we are renewed in the spirit of our mind and if it is precisely the "new man" who is renewed to the knowledge of God according to the image of the One who created him, then no one can doubt that the human being has been made to the image of the One who created him, not according to the body nor according to any part of the mind, but according to the rational mind, where the knowledge of God can reside. But according to this renewal, we are made children of God through the baptism of Christ, and when we put on the "new man," we certainly put on Christ through faith. Who is it, then, who would exclude women from this fellowship since they are, with us, co-heirs of grace and since the same Apostle says in another place: "For you are all children of God through faith in Christ Jesus. For whoever has been baptized in Christ has put on Christ. There is neither Jew nor Greek, there is neither slave nor free, there is neither male nor female. For you are all one in Christ Jesus" (Gal 3:26–28)? But then have believing women, therefore, lost their bodily sex? Because they are renewed to the image of God where there is no sexual identity, the human being is made to the image of God where there is no sexual identity, namely, in the spirit of the mind. Why, then, is "the man on that account not bound to cover his head because he is the image and glory of God," but the woman must cover it because "she is the glory of the man" (1 Cor 11:7), as though a woman were not renewed in the spirit of her mind, which "is renewed to the knowledge of God according to the image of the One who created" her (Col 3:10)? But because she differs from the man in terms of her bodily sexuality, that part of the reason that is turned aside to regulate temporal things could be properly symbolized by her bodily veil so that the image of God does not remain except in that part of the mind of the human being where it clings to the contemplation and consideration of the eternal ideas, an aptitude which, as is evident, not only men but also women possess.

(8.13) Therefore, in our minds a common nature is recognized; but in our bodies the division of this one mind itself is symbolized.[45]

CHRIST AS *SCIENTIA* AND *SAPIENTIA*

At the end of Book 12, Augustine sets out a key distinction between knowledge (scientia) and wisdom (sapientia): "But there is a difference between the contemplation of eternal things and the action by which we use temporal things well; the first is called 'wisdom,' the latter, 'knowledge.'"[46] *In Book 13 he links these two modes of human knowing to the two natures of Christ. Christ as God incarnate unites these two in His one person and thus becomes both the pathway and the endpoint. From* On the Trinity, *Book 13:*

(19.24) According to the distinction we have sought to point out, all these things which the Word-made-flesh did and suffered for us in time and place belong to knowledge and not to wisdom. But because the Word is outside of time and outside of place, He is co-eternal with the Father and is wholly present everywhere. And if anyone is able, insofar as he is able, to utter a truthful word about this, then that word belongs to wisdom. Therefore, the Word-made-flesh, which is Christ Jesus, possesses the treasures of wisdom and of knowledge. For the Apostle says, when writing to the Colossians: "For I wish you to know what great struggle I am having for you and for those at Laodicea and for all who have not seen my face in the flesh, that your hearts may be comforted, being joined together in charity and in all the riches of the fullness of understanding, so as to know the mystery of God, which is Christ Jesus, in whom are hidden all the treasures of wisdom and knowledge" (Col 2:1–3). How well the Apostle knew these treasures, to what depths he had penetrated them, what great things he had come to—who can know? But as for me, according to what is written: "The manifestation of the Spirit is

45. Trin. 12.7.9–8.13 (CCL 50:363–67); my trans., based on McKenna, FOTC 45:351–55. Cf. Ambrose, *hexaemeron* VI.7.4–8.45 (CSEL 32:321–36). See David G. Hunter, "The Paradise of Patriarchy: Ambrosiaster on Woman as (Not) God's Image," *Journal of Theological Studies* n.s. 43 (1992): 447–69.

46. Trin. 12.14.22 (CCL 50:375).

given to everyone for profit; to one is given through the Spirit a word of wisdom; to another, a word of knowledge according to the same Spirit" (1 Cor 12:7–8). If these two so differ between themselves that wisdom has been attributed to divine things and knowledge to human things, I recognize both in Christ, and everyone who believes in Him agrees with me. And when I read: "The Word was made flesh and dwelt among us" (Jn 1:14), I recognize in the Word the true Son of God, and I recognize in the flesh the true Son of man, and both are united together into one person, God and human, by the ineffable liberality of grace. As [John] goes on to say: "And we saw his glory, glory as of the only-begotten of the Father, full of grace and truth" (Jn 1:14). If we refer "grace" to knowledge and "truth" to wisdom, I think that we will not be inconsistent to that distinction between these things that we have commended. For in things that have their origin in time, the supreme grace is that a human being is united with God in the unity of person; but in eternal things the supreme truth is rightly attributed to the Word of God. But that very same one is Himself the only-begotten of the Father, full of grace and truth. This was done that He Himself might also be in things done for us in time; the same one for whom we are cleansed by the same faith in order that we may contemplate Him unwaveringly in eternal things. . . . Christ, therefore, is our knowledge, and the same Christ is also our wisdom. He Himself plants within us the faith concerning temporal things; He Himself manifests the truth concerning eternal things. Through Him we travel to Him. Through knowledge we stretch out for wisdom; but we do not depart from the same Christ, "in whom are hidden all the treasures of wisdom and knowledge" (Col 2:3).[47]

FROM IMAGE TO LIKENESS

In Book 14, Augustine returns to Book 10's triad of memory, understanding, and will. Here he emphasizes that it is not simply the mind remembering, understanding, and loving itself, but the mind remembering, understanding, and loving God, whose image it is. He also stresses that the journey to God is more than introspection or contemplation; it requires moral reform, it is impossible without grace, and it reaches fulfillment not in this life, but only at the resurrection. Here I have pruned out Augustine's various side-arguments so as to highlight his core argument. From On the Trinity, Book 14:

47. Trin. 13.19.24 (CCL 50A:415–17); my trans., based on McKenna, FOTC 45:404–6. On this, see Lewis Ayres, "The Christological Context of Augustine's De trinitate XIII: Toward Relocating Books VIII–XV," Augustinian Studies 29 (1998): 111–39; Goulven Madec, "Christus, scientia et sapientia nostra: Le principe de cohérence de la doctrine augustinienne," Recherches augustiniennes 10 (1975): 77–85.

(8.11) But we have now finally arrived at that point in our discussion where we can begin to consider the principal part of the human mind, that by which it knows, or can know, God so that we may find within it an image of God. Although the human mind is not of the same nature as God, yet the image of His nature, which is better than any other nature, ought to be sought for and found there within us, where there is the best that our nature has. But we must first consider the mind in itself before it is a partaker of God and before His image is to be found in it. For we have said that, even though the image has become impaired and disfigured by the loss of its participation in God, it nonetheless remains an image of God. For it is His image by the very fact that it has the capacity for Him and can be a partaker of Him; and it cannot be so great a good except that it is His image. Look, the mind remembers itself, understands itself, and loves itself. If we perceive this, we perceive a trinity, not yet God, but now finally an image of God. . . .

(12.15) Now this trinity of the mind is not, properly speaking, the image of God just because the mind remembers itself, understands itself, and loves itself, but because it can also remember, understand, and love the God by whom it was made. And when it does so, it becomes wise; but if it does not, even though it remembers itself, knows itself, and loves itself, it is foolish. Let the mind, then, remember the God to whose image it has been made, and let it understand Him and love Him. Or to express this more briefly, let it worship the uncreated God who created it so that it is capable of Him and can be made a partaker of Him. For this reason, it is written: "Behold, the worship of God is wisdom" (Jb 28:28). Not by its own light, but by a participation in that highest light, will the mind be wise, and where the eternal light is, there it will reign in blessedness. This is spoken of as humanity's wisdom, but it is really God's. This then is true wisdom. Now if it were only human, it would be vain. . . .

(12.16) The uncreated nature of the One who has made all natures, both great and small, is undoubtedly more excellent than those which that uncreated nature has made, and, therefore, than this, too, of which we are speaking, namely, the rational and intellectual nature that is the human mind, and that has been made to the image of Him who made it. But the nature more excellent than all the others is God. And, indeed, "He is not far from any one of us," as the Apostle says, adding: "In him we live and move and have our being" (Acts 17:27–28). If this were said with regard to the body, it could also be understood of this corporeal world, for we also live and move and have our being in Him in terms of our body. But the text must be understood in a more excellent and, at the same time, an invisible and intelligible way, namely, with respect to the mind that has been made to His image. For what is not "in Him," about whom it is divinely written: "For from Him and through Him and in Him are all things" (Rom 11:36)? So if all things are in Him, in whom can the living live and the moving move other than Him in whom they are? Yet not everyone is with Him in that way it was said: "I will always be with you" (Ps 72:23). Nor is He Himself with all things in the way that we say [in the Eucharist]: "The Lord be with you." Humanity's great wretchedness, therefore, is not to be with Him, without whom we cannot exist. For undoubtedly we are not without Him in whom we are, and yet if we do not remember Him nor understand Him nor love Him, then we are not with Him. . . .

(14.18) But when the mind loves God and consequently (as we have said) remembers and understands Him, then with respect to one's neighbor, it is rightly commanded to love one's neighbor as oneself. For the mind no longer loves itself perversely but rightly when it loves God, by partaking in the One in whose image it not only exists, but is also renewed so as not to grow old, is reformed so as not to be disfigured, and is beatified so as not to be unhappy. . . .

(17.23) This renewal, of course, is not brought about in a single moment of some conversion, the way baptism brings about a renewal in a single moment through the remission of all sins, for with baptism there does not remain even one sin, however small, that is not forgiven. Just as it is one thing to be free from fevers and another thing to recover from the weakness that results from fevers, and just as it is one thing to remove an arrow that pierced the body and another thing to heal the wound that it inflicted through some treatment that follows, so too the first step in a cure is to remove the cause of the disease, and that is done through the remission of all sins; the second step is to heal the disease itself, and that is done gradually by making progress in the renewal of this image. These two things are pointed out in the Psalm where we read: "Who forgives all your faults"—that takes place in baptism; it continues on: "Who heals all your diseases" (Ps 102:3)—that takes place by daily advances as this image is renewed. The Apostle spoke quite plainly about this subject when he said: "Even though our outer man is decaying, yet our inner man is being renewed day by day" (2 Cor 4:16). But one "is renewed in the knowledge of God," that is, "in justice and holiness of truth," according to the testimonies of the Apostle which I have just cited. Whoever, then, is being renewed in the knowledge of God and in justice and holiness of truth by making progress day by day transfers his love from the temporal to the eternal, from the visible to the invisible, from the carnal to the spiritual, and constantly tries to restrain and to lessen the desire for the first ones and tries to bind himself by love to the latter ones. But one does so in proportion to the divine help that one receives, for the word of God is: "Without me you can do nothing" (Jn 15:5). If the last day of this life finds anyone progressing and growing, holding fast to the faith of the Mediator, then one will be received by the holy angels in order that one may be brought to the God whom one has worshiped and by whom one is to be brought to perfection, and at the end of the world one will receive an incorruptible body not for punishment but for glory. For our likeness to God in this image will be perfect when our vision of God is perfect. The Apostle Paul says of this vision: "We now see through a mirror in an obscure manner, but then face-to-face" (1 Cor 13:2). He likewise says: "But we, beholding the glory of the Lord with face unveiled, are transformed into the same image from glory to glory, as through the Spirit of the Lord" (2 Cor 3:18). This is what takes place in those who are making progress steadily, day by day.[48]

THE TRINITY WHO GOD IS

One finds in textbooks certain glib contrasts between Greek and Latin Trinitarian theologies. The Greek East supposedly begins with the three Persons and struggles to locate God's unity, while the Latin West begins with the divine unity and struggles to locate the distinctiveness of the three Persons. In such textbooks, Augustine is described as the paradigm and source of this Western approach. Recent scholarship has debunked this. As Lewis Ayres has noted, "the charge that Augustine's theology describes the divine essence as prior to the divine persons, or as the source of the persons, is unwarranted. In fact, he consistently and specifically rules out any such account of the divine essence. . . . Using the grammar of divine simplicity, Augustine argues that we should beware of speaking about a substance in which the three persons are 'contained': there is nothing but the three co-eternal and consubstantial persons."[49] For example, Augustine notes in On the Trinity, Book 15:

(7.11) But that Trinity that the mind is an image of is nothing else in its totality than God, nothing else in its totality than Trinity. Nor does anything belong to the nature of God that does not belong to the Trinity; and the three Persons are of one essence, but not as each individual human being is one person.[50]

---

48. Trin. 14.8.11–17.23 (CCL 50A:435–55); my trans., based on McKenna, FOTC 45:417–45.

49. Lewis Ayres, "The Fundamental Grammar of Augustine's Trinitarian Theology," in Dodaro and Lawless, eds., Augustine and His Critics, 68.

50. Trin. 15.7.11 (CCL 50A:475); trans. McKenna, FOTC 45:465.

This grammar of divine simplicity shapes the argument of Book 15. In Books 8 to 14, Augustine explored possible vestiges of the Trinity within human consciousness. Here Augustine deconstructs this quest, insisting that psychological analogies do not, in the end, work because any Trinitarian unities within human consciousness do not accurately mirror the intricate paradox of divine simplicity. From On the Trinity, *Book 15:*

(22.42) This [difference between ourselves and God] can be expressed briefly: I remember, I understand, I love—I who am neither my memory nor my understanding nor my love, but I have these. Such things could be said, therefore, by one person who has these three and is not himself these three. But in the simplicity of that highest nature, which God is, although there is one God, yet there are three Persons: the Father, the Son, and the Holy Spirit.

(23.43) The reality of the Trinity itself is one thing, the image of that Trinity in something other is very different. . . . The inseparability within that highest Trinity, which incomparably surpasses all other realities, is so great that it defies comparison. A trinity of three human beings cannot be called one human being, yet the Trinity is such that it is both called and is the one God; and that Trinity is not in the one God; it is the one God. Once again, this image in the human being who has these three [that is, memory, understanding, love] is just one person; the Trinity, on the other hand, is these three Persons, the Father of the Son, the Son of the Father, and the Spirit of both the Father and the Son. In ourselves as the image of the Trinity, human memory (particularly as distinct from what beasts have, that is, containing intelligible realities not brought into it through the body's senses) has a likeness, yet incomparably inferior, yet nonetheless some kind of likeness to the Father; in the same way, human understanding, which is formed from the memory by the effort of thought when what is known is spoken—it is the tongue of the heart and belongs to no language—has some sort of likeness, in all its great disparity, to the Son; and human love, which proceeds from knowledge and combines memory and understanding as though common to parent and offspring—from which it is understood to be neither parent nor offspring—has in this image some likeness, though a strongly unequal one, to the Holy Spirit. Nonetheless, in terms of an image of the Trinity, these three are not the one person, but belong to one person. But in the highest Trinity itself, whose image we are, those three are not of one God; they are the one God, and there are three Persons, not one.

And what is indeed wonderfully ineffable, or ineffably wonderful, is that, although this image of the Trinity is one person, while there are three Persons in the highest Trinity itself, yet this Trinity of three Persons is more inseparable than that trinity in the one person. For this Trinity by the nature of its divinity—or it may be better to call it the "Godhead"—what it is is mutually unchangeable and always equal. There never was a time when it was not, nor when it was otherwise; neither will there ever be a time when it will not be what it is, nor when it will be otherwise. These three, however, which are in the unequal [human] image, are now separated from one another in this life, not in place since they are not bodies, but in terms of their magnitudes. For though no bulk is present there, we do not, therefore, fail to see that the memory is greater in one person than the understanding, while in another person it is just the opposite; in another person, these two [dynamics] are surpassed by a greatness of love, whether the two themselves are equal to each other or not. And so each two are surpassed by each one, and each one by each two, and each one by each one, and the lesser by the greater. And when these [three inner dynamics] are cured of every weakness and shall be mutually equal, even then that human being, which through grace will not be changed, will not be made equal to the reality [of God] who is unchangeable in nature, because the creature cannot be equal to the Creator and will have to undergo a change when it is cured of every weakness.

(23.44) But when the "face-to-face" vision shall come that is promised to us, we shall see the Trinity—the Trinity that is not only incorporeal, but in the highest degree inseparable and truly unchangeable—much more clearly and with much more certainty than we now see its image in who we are. But those who see "through this mirror" and "in this enigma" (1 Cor 13:12), as it is permitted to see in this life, are not those who see those things which we have explained and commended in their minds, but those who look upon their mind as an image so that they are able, in some way or another, to refer what they see to Him, whose image they are, and also to see by conjecturing that which they now see through the image by beholding, since they cannot yet see face-to-face, for the Apostle did not say that "We now see a mirror," but that "We now see through a mirror" (1 Cor 13:12).

(24.44) Therefore, those who now see the mind as it can be seen, and that trinity in it that I have explained in as many different ways as I could and yet do not believe or understand it to be an image of God, they see a mirror indeed, but see so little of Him through a mirror, who is to be seen now through a mirror, that they do not even know the mirror itself, which they see, to be a mirror, that is, an image. If they did know this and cleansed their hearts by an unfeigned faith (1 Tm 1:5), then they would perhaps perceive that He, whom their mind is this mirror of, is to be sought through this, and in the meantime seen through this, in whatever way He can be seen, and in order that He may be able to be seen "face-to-face" who is now seen "through a mirror" (1 Cor 13:12).[51]

51. Trin. 15.22.42–24.44 (CCL 50A:519–22); my trans., based on McKenna, FOTC 45:509–12.

FILIOQUE

In seventh-century Spain, a key phrase was inserted into the Creed: that the Holy Spirit "proceeds from the Father and the Son." This added phrase, "and the Son" (Filioque), eventually became standard in the Latin West and made its way officially into the Roman rite. After the great schism of Rome and Constantinople in the eleventh century, it became a serious point of doctrinal controversy and remains a source of tension between Orthodox and Catholics to this day. Augustine is often blamed for this. In fact, this teaching on the double procession of the Spirit had been a commonplace in the Latin West and appears in Marius Victorinus, Hilary of Poitiers, and others. But Augustine gave the teaching its classic exposition. It appears in many places in Augustine's works, but the passage below is one that Augustine himself thought was his best version. It comes from Tractates on the Gospel of John 99. Augustine dictated that this passage be added word-for-word into Book 15 of On the Trinity:

(7) Why should we not believe that the Holy Spirit proceeds from the Son as well since He is also the Spirit of the Son? For if He did not proceed from Him, [Jesus], showing Himself anew to His disciples after the Resurrection, would not have breathed upon them, saying, "Receive the Holy Spirit" (Jn 20:22). For what else did that "breathing upon" signify except that the Holy Spirit also proceeds from Him? . . .

(8) If the Holy Spirit proceeds, therefore, both from the Father and from the Son, why did the Son say: "The Spirit proceeds from the Father" (Jn 15:26)? Why do you think, except that He usually refers even what belongs to Himself to the Father, whom He Himself also is from? For this reason, He says: "My teaching is not my own, but is from the One who sent me" (Jn 7:16). If, therefore, the teaching here is understood as His, which He nonetheless said was not His, but the Father's, how much more must it be understood there that the Holy Spirit proceeds from Him of whom He said, "He proceeds from the Father," in such a way that He did not say: "He does not proceed from me"! But He, from whom the Son has that He is God (for He is God from God), has it also that the Holy Spirit also proceeds from Him. And because of this, the Holy Spirit has it from the Father Himself that He proceeds also from the Son, just as He proceeds from the Father.

(9) Here, too, to some extent, it is understood (as far as it can be understood by those such as us) why the Holy Spirit is not said to have been "born," but rather to "proceed." For if He were also called "son," then, of course, he would be called the "son" of both—and this is utterly absurd. For, indeed, no one is the son of two except of a father and a mother. But far be it from us to suspect some such thing between God the Father and God the Son. For neither does the son of human beings proceed at the same time both from the

father and from the mother. When a son proceeds from the father into the mother, he does not proceed from the mother; and when he proceeds into the light of day from the mother, he does not then proceed from the father. But the Holy Spirit does not proceed from the Father into the Son, and from the Son proceed to sanctifying the creature. He proceeds from each at the same time, although the Father has given this to the Son: that the Holy Spirit proceeds from Him just as He does as from Himself. For we cannot say that the Holy Spirit is not life when the Father is life, when the Son is life. And for this reason, just as the Father, who has life in Himself, has given also to the Son to have life in Himself, so too He has given to the Son that life proceed from Him as it also proceeds from Himself.[52]

"SEEK HIS FACE ALWAYS"

In the prologue to Book 15, Augustine returns to Ps 104:4: "Seek his face always." Here Augustine makes clear the deeper intent of On the Trinity. As Robert Wilken has noted, "what Augustine is seeking is not a theological concept or an explanation as such, but the living God who is Father, Son, and Holy Spirit. . . . [This] means more than simply getting things straight or discovering the most appropriate analogy in human experience for the Triune God. There can be no finding without a change in the seeker. Our minds, he says, must be purified, and we must be made fit and capable of receiving what is sought."[53] From On the Trinity, Book 15:

(2.2) The very God we are seeking will, I hope, grant us His help so that our labor may not be without some fruit and that we may understand why it says in the sacred Psalm: "Let the heart of those who seek the Lord rejoice. Seek the Lord, and be strengthened. Seek His face always" (Ps 104:3–4). Now it seems that what is searched for *always* is never found. In that case, how will the heart of those who seek rejoice rather than be saddened if they cannot find what they are searching for? For the Psalm does not say: "Let the heart of those *who find* the Lord rejoice," but rather "those *who seek* the Lord." And yet the Lord God can be found even while He is being searched for, as the Prophet Isaiah testifies when he says: "Seek the Lord, and as soon as you find Him, call upon Him; and when He draws near to you, let the wicked forsake their ways, and the unjust their thoughts" (Is 55:6–7). If, therefore, He who is searched for can be found, why does the Psalm say: "Seek His face *always*"

52. Jo. ev. tr. 99.7–9 (BA 74B:362–68); trans. Rettig, FOTC 90:226–28 (modified). Augustine quotes this passage in De Trinitate 15.27.48 (CCL 50A:529–30). On the Filioque, see Kelly, Early Christian Creeds, 358–67.

53. Wilken, Spirit of Early Christian Thought, 106–7.

(Ps 104:4)? Or is He perhaps still to be searched for, even when found? That is how incomprehensible things have to be searched for. Otherwise, we may not value it as worth the effort once we are able to find out how incomprehensible what we are searching for is. So why search for something when you have comprehended the incomprehensibility of what you are searching for? Only this: because you should not give up the search as long as you are making progress in the search itself for things incomprehensible, and because you are becoming better and better by searching for so great a good, which is both searched for in order to be found and is found in order to be searched for. For it is both searched for in order that it may be found sweeter and is found in order that it may be searched for all the more eagerly.[54]

54. Trin. 15.2.2 (CCL 50A:460–61); my trans.

CHAPTER 9

CONTROVERSIES (III)
On the City of God, Against the Pagans

✦

On the City of God (De civitate Dei) is Augustine's third masterpiece. It is, as he admits in his final words, "a huge work," running nearly 900 pages in the Latin original.[1] Its scope is epic, an ambitious meditation on the contours and meaning of human history, from the genesis of the human race to its final judgment. It received rave reviews from the beginning. In 413, Macedonius, the powerful Vicar of Africa, read the first three books and proclaimed: "I am in doubt what to admire most in them: the lofty state of the priesthood, the teachings of philosophy, the extensive knowledge of history, or the charm of their style, which is such as to bewitch even the unlearned."[2]

Many today treat City of God as a classic in the history of political thought. Such a reading has certain merits. Augustine consciously draws on and positions himself over against a long tradition of classical political thought, from Plato's Republic to Cicero's. He meditates repeatedly and at length on the topics germane to political philosophy: the right ordering of human society and the foundations of government, the duties of citizens and the qualities of good rulers, the quest for civil peace and the demand for social justice, as well as the waging of wars, whether just or unjust. Augustine's penetrating insights into these matters, while far from systematic, would become a touchstone and massively influential resource for later medieval theorists and beyond.

But reading City of God as political philosophy skews things and miscon-

---

1. Civ. Dei 22.30 (CCL 48:866). The critical edition of the Latin is 866 pages; the translation in FOTC, volumes 8, 14, and 24, totals just under 1500 pages.

2. Macedonius, preserved in Augustine's corpus as ep. 154.2 (CSEL 44:429); trans. Parsons, FOTC 20:304.

strues Augustine's fundamental purposes. The work is explicitly (and especially in its first half) a work of controversy. We have seen Augustine the
controversialist in previous chapters on the Manichees and Donatists. Augustine's target in City of God is paganism. Many early manuscripts add a subtitle:
Against the Pagans.³ While this subtitle did not, in all likelihood, come from
Augustine himself, it is accurate as far as it goes. The work was occasioned,
as he himself notes, by Alaric's sack of Rome in 410. The Goths spent three
days wreaking havoc and brutalizing the city's inhabitants. Thousands, both
Christians and pagans, packed city churches, desperately seeking asylum.
However horrific the actual scene, the destruction was, in the end, short-lived
and minor. The deeper impact was psychological. The thousand-year success
story that had been the history of Rome seemed irretrievably damaged. Not
merely Rome, but also the broader Empire now seemed, almost overnight,
vulnerable, fragile. Jerome, in far-off Bethlehem, was shaken to the core:
"Where is salvation if Rome perishes?"⁴ Pagans, especially aristocratic tradi-
tionalists, attributed Rome's sack to the Empire's embrace of Christianity and
its neglect of its traditional gods, who had so long been venerated as Rome's
supernatural protectors and the guarantors of its success and peace. So in the
first 10 of 22 books, Augustine dismantles pagan charges at length and in detail. This massive work thus stands in a centuries-long tradition of Christian
apologetics, pioneered by Justin Martyr and Athenagoras, later broadened
and deepened by Tertullian and Origen. Augustine's work has been called the
finest Christian apology of antiquity.

Its title, as Augustine notes at various points, comes from Ps 86:3: "Glorious things are spoken of you, O city of God."⁵ The choice is ironic since pagans were hardly saying glorious things about Christianity and Christianity's
God. Augustine had tinkered for decades with the idea of human history as
an interweaving and clash between two cities, the earthly city and the City of
God, or, as they appear in their classic biblical guise, between Babylon and
Jerusalem.⁶ In one of the newly discovered Dolbeau sermons, Augustine gives
a thumbnail description:

3. Gerard O'Daly, *Augustine's City of God: A Reader's Guide* (Oxford: Clarendon Press, 1999), 273, argues
that *contra paganos* was an addition from later editors, basing his judgment primarily on Augustine's references to the work in *retr.* 2.69, in his letters (*ep.* 169.1; 184A.5; 1A*.1–2; 2*.1), and in other writings (*Contra adversarium legis et prophetarum* 1.18; *Trin.* 13.9.12).

4. Jerome, *ep.* 123.16, quoted in Lancel, *Saint Augustine*, 392.

5. *Civ. Dei* 2.21, 10.7, 11.1 (CCL 47:55, 47:279, 48:321).

6. On the "two cities" theme, see A. Lauras and H. Rondet, "Le thème des deux cités dans l'oeuvre de
saint Augustin," in H. Rondet, ed., *Études Augustiniennes*, Théologie 28 (Paris: Aubier, 1953), 97–160; also Johannes van Oort, *Jerusalem and Babylon: A Study into Augustine's City of God and the Sources of His Doctrine of the
Two Cities*, Supplements to Vigiliae Christianae 14 (Leiden: Brill, 1991).

So there's a certain godless city, described as likeminded in its human godlessness even though scattered among all the world's lands, and in the Scriptures it is known mystically as Babylon. On the other hand, there's a certain city, on this earth a pilgrim among all the world's peoples, likeminded in its godliness, and this one's called Jerusalem. Both cities are now mixed up together; at the end they will be separated.[7]

An early version of this idea appears in *On True Religion*, written around 390.[8] Around 403, in *On Catechizing*, Augustine recommended it as an organizing motif to explain the Bible to pagans who were considering joining the Church (see below). It also shows up here and there in the routine of his preaching.[9] In his *Literal Interpretation of Genesis*, Augustine notes that the two cities flowed from two loves, "one holy, the other unclean . . . one peaceable, the other seditious," manifested first among the angels and then played out over the course of human history as two cities; he then adds: "Concerning these two cities, I will perhaps discuss the issue much more broadly, if the Lord is willing, in some other venue."[10] This passing comment has led scholars to suggest that Augustine would have written *City of God* even without Rome's fall.[11] But Alaric's sack helped Augustine crystallize his views and provided a newsworthy occasion to "discuss the issue much more broadly."

While Augustine's explicit target is Christianity's pagan detractors, he positions his own stance in marked contrast to two earlier strains of Christian thinking about Rome and the wider political order.[12] One is exemplified by Hippolytus (c. 170–c. 236), who read the Empire in dark apocalyptic terms, as demonic in inspiration, an irredeemable Babylon. The other is exemplified by Eusebius (c. 260–339), the church historian and scholarly bishop of Caesarea. Eusebius saw in the Emperor Constantine's conversion a watershed moment in the history of salvation. Rome, the one-time persecutor of Christians, was now Christianity's God-given ally and vindicator. Under Constantine's beneficence, the Gospel not only had imperial acknowledgment but also was given free rein to spread to the ends of the known world. Eusebius thus forged a pro-imperial theology. Echoes of this appear in others, notably in Augustine's mentor, Ambrose. But few voice it more vibrantly than another contemporary, the poet Prudentius, who celebrated the Emperor Theodosius's official banning of paganism in the 390s and the triumph of Christianity as the official religion of the Empire:

7. S. 299A.8 (= Dolbeau 4) (Dolbeau, VSS, 519); my trans.

8. *De vera religione* 27.50 (BA 8:90–94), cited in Chapter 2.

9. En. Ps. 64.2, 84.10 (CCL 39:823–24, 1170–71).

10. Gn. litt. 11.15.20 (BA 49:260–62); my trans.

11. Brown, *Religion and Society in the Age of Saint Augustine*, 35, n. 1.

12. On this, see R. A. Markus, *Saeculum: History and Society in the Theology of St. Augustine* (Cambridge: Cambridge University Press, 1970), 22–44.

Rome fled from her old errors and shook the dark mist from her wrinkled face; her nobility now ready to enter on the ways of eternity and to follow Christ at the calling of her great leader. . . . The world receives you now, O Christ, the world which is held in bonds of harmony by peace and by Rome. These you have appointed to be the chief and highest powers in the world. Nor does Rome please you without peace; and it is only Roman excellence that ensures a lasting peace. Her supremacy keeps order; awe of her power checks disorder.[13]

Augustine had, for a time, dabbled with such heady optimism, proclaiming in one sermon: "The whole world is now Christ's chorus; from the east to the west, Christ's chorus echoes in harmony."[14] But by 410, he had quietly shucked off the remnants of imperial theology. He no longer counted the Christianization of the Roman Empire as a landmark on the map of salvation history. Aspirations for a Christian empire were a mirage. Rome, he now believed, had become one more empire in a long line of empires to rise and fall. It had no sacred significance.

That was not to deny Rome all value—far from it. But its value remained temporal and temporary. Under Rome's aegis, the inhabitants of the earthly city and the City of God made (or, at least, could make) common cause in searching for earthly peace. The elderly Augustine was never one to shortchange peace. He believed deeply that while the best human realities are fraught with ambiguities and shot through with selfishness, still, earthly peace, however fragile, however shortlived, was worth committing to and working hard for. Peace, he recognized, is the very foundation of human civilization; and civilization, while inevitably tainted by original sin and marred by violence, is nonetheless a very good thing. But for Augustine, everyone and everything must, in the end, be seen and judged in eternity's light, from eternity's vantage point. Only in the mystery of God's judgments can history's empires and the loves that create them be judged aright.

Like On the Trinity, this great work took Augustine long years to complete. He began it around 413 and finished around 426. Scattered in his letters are reports of steady progress: three books by 413, five by 415, fourteen by 418.[15] Augustine never wrote a summa; but this work comes as close as any to being one. All his great ideas appear here, sometimes in passing, but often at length and in their most quotable exposition. Augustine's favored theological method—setting things in crisp antitheses—controls the larger flow. At one point, he remarks that "the antithesis is the most elegant of rhetoric's

---

13. Prudentius, Contra Symmachum I.506–II.641 (CSEL 61:238, 270); trans. Markus, Saeculum, 28.

14. En. Ps. 149.7 (CCL 40:2183); my trans.

15. Macedonius reports having read Books 1–3 in ep. 154. In ep. 169, Augustine writes his friend Evodius (c. 415) and reports finishing Books 1–5. In ep. 184A to two monks, Peter and Abraham (c. 418), he reports finishing Books 1–13 and working on Book 14.

ornaments" and that "just as antithesis lends beauty to literary style, so in the antitheses of history one finds a rhetoric not of words but of facts that give it beauty."[16] The way Augustine pits the earthly city against the heavenly reminds me of those master photographers, like Ansel Adams, who prefer shooting in black-and-white. When such photographers balance light and dark with a discerning eye, they unveil to us the world's subtle shades of gray. Augustine's City of God is a similar study in black-and-white, an effort to capture and lay bare both the fine-grained textures and the broad contours of this world's grayness over against and within the frame of the dazzling light of God.

✥

BACKGROUND TEXTS
CATECHIZING PAGANS

Around 403, Deogratias, a deacon from Carthage, wrote Augustine, seeking advice on what to say to pagans interested in joining the Church. Augustine responded with a minor masterpiece, On Catechizing Beginners (De catechizandis rudibus). He offered Deogratias advice on many matters and appended to the treatise two sample addresses illustrating what a catechist might say to a pagan inquirer. In one address, Augustine suggests that one survey the Bible by describing human history as a winding tale of two cities, Babylon and Jerusalem. From On Catechizing Beginners:

(19.31) And so there are two cities, one of the wicked, the other of the saints, cities that existed from the beginnings of the human race and so on down to the end of the ages. Now they are mixed together physically, in terms of bodies, but are separate in terms of wills, and on Judgment Day, will be separated in body as well. All those human beings who are lovers of pride and of dominating worldly things with empty vanity and flashy arrogance and all those spirits who love such things and strive for glory by subjugating people are bound together as a single society. And even if they often fight one another over these things, still they will be tossed, by the weight of their desires, into the same depths, bound to one another by the similarity of the ways they live and the punishments they deserve. On the other hand, all those human beings and all those spirits, all who humbly search for God's glory, and not their own (Jn 7:18), and follow along after Him in piety, also belong to a single society. Still God is incredibly merciful and patient with

16. *Civ. Dei* 11.18 (CCL 48:337); my trans.

ungodly human beings and gives them opportunity for repentance and correction (Rom 2:4). . . .

(20.36) And so through the many and varied signs of things to come—it
would be too long to spell them out completely, things we now see fulfilled
in the Church—the [Jewish] people were led forth into the Promised Land,
where in the flux of history and flesh, they reigned in accord with their yearnings. Nevertheless, that earthly kingdom was an image of the spiritual kingdom. There Jerusalem was founded, that most famous city of God, which in
its bondage served as a symbol of the free city which is called the heavenly Jerusalem (Heb 12:22)—the word "Jerusalem" is Hebrew and means "vision of
peace." Its citizens comprise all people made holy—all who have lived, who
live now, and who shall in the future—and all spirits made holy, whichever
ones in the highest regions of heaven obey God with deep devotion and do
not imitate the godless pride of the devil and his angels. The King of this City
is the Lord Jesus Christ, the Word of God, who reigns over the highest angels, the Word who became flesh that He might rule as well over human beings, those who will reign together with Him in eternal peace. As a prefigur-
ing of this King in the earthly kingdom of the people of Israel, there stood out
especially King David, of whose seed, according to the flesh (Rom 1:3), our
most true King, the Lord Jesus Christ, was to come, the One "who is above all
things, God blessed through all ages" (Rom 9:5). Many things done in that
Promised Land were symbolic of the future Christ and the Church, and these
you will be able to learn about gradually from the holy books.

(21.37) Then, after several generations, there appeared another figure, another symbol, one very much at the heart of things. For that city [of Jerusa-
lem] was captured, and a large part of it was led off into Babylon. Now just as
Jerusalem is symbolic of the city and society of the saints, so Babylon is symbolic of the city and society of the wicked, because the name is said to mean
"confusion." About these two cities, I spoke a little earlier, of the way they
move down through the ages all mixed together, from the beginnings of the
human race to the end of the ages, separated ultimately at the Last Judgment.
Thus the Lord ordered, through Jeremiah, the prophet of that time, that the
captive city of Jerusalem and its people be led off into Babylon in bondage
(Jer 21:1–10). And there appeared some kings of Babylon, under whom the
[Chosen People] were in bondage, kings who, struck by certain dazzling
events due to the [Jewish] people's presence, came to recognize and worship
(and order others to worship) the one true God, the founder of everything in
creation. Also, the people were ordered both to pray for those who held them
captive and to hope, within these kings' peace, for peace, that they may go
about begetting children and building homes and planting gardens and vine-

yards (Jer 29:5–7). And so they were promised that, after seventy years, they would be liberated from their captivity (Jer 25:12, 29:10).

Now all this has a symbolic meaning and refers figuratively to when Christ's Church, in all its saints who are heavenly Jerusalem's citizens, lives in bondage under the kings of this world. . . . Still, all are directed to remain subject to human and earthly powers until the time foreordained—symbolized by the seventy years—when the Church is liberated from this world's confusion, just as Jerusalem was freed from the Babylonian captivity. . . . This captivity has become an occasion even for earthly kings themselves to abandon idols (on whose behalf they used to persecute Christians) and to come to know and worship the one true God and Christ the Lord. The Apostle Paul commands us to pray for them, even when they persecute the Church (1 Tm 2:1–2). . . . And so through these kings peace was given to the Church—admittedly, a temporary one, a temporary tranquility for building, in a spiritual sense, homes and planting gardens and vineyards. Look, right now, we are, in a way, building you and planting you by these very words. And this is being done across the entire globe as a result of the peace of Christian kings.[17]

THE SACK OF ROME

News of Rome's sack by Alaric and his Gothic army set off anguished reflections. In certain sermons preached around 410–411, we glimpse the complex, even contradictory, feelings of both Augustine and his congregation.[18] We also see something of his change of mind: whereas in the early 400s he was willing to entertain ideas of a Christian empire, by this point he wrote them off as a false hope. In the following sermon, he reflects on Rome's sack, drawing on images from Luke's Gospel, both Jesus' lament over Jerusalem and Jesus' words: "What father among you would hand his son . . . a scorpion when he asks for an egg? If you then, who are wicked, know how to give good gifts to your children, how much more will the Father in heaven give the Holy Spirit to those who ask him?" (Lk 11:12–13) From Sermon 105:

(9) The city that gave birth to us in the flesh still stands. Thanks be to God! If only it could come to birth spiritually and cross over with us into eter-

17. *De catechizandis rudibus* 19.31–21.37 (CCL 46:156–62); my trans. On this passage, see Hombert, *Nouvelles recherches*, 42–43, who notes links between it and the recent Dolbeau sermons, esp. s. 198 (= Dolbeau 26), which confronts pagans at length and in detail, and s. 299A (= Dolbeau 4), which discusses the two cities theme.

18. Others include s. 81, s. 296, and *De excidio urbis Romae* (*On the Sack of the City of Rome*, now numbered as s. 397). On these, see J.-C. Fredouille, "Les sermons sur la chute de Rome," in Madec, *Augustin predicateur*, 349–448.

nity! Even if the city that gave birth to us in the flesh stood no more, then the City that gave birth to us in the spirit still does: "The Lord builds up Jerusalem" (Ps 146:2). Do you think that He fell asleep on the job, losing what He built? Or that He, by failing to keep watch over things, let enemies in? "Unless the Lord guard the city, in vain does the guard keep watch" (Ps 126:1). . . . The holy City, the faithful City, that City—while on earth a pilgrim sojourner—has its foundation in heaven. O faithful ones, don't corrupt your hope, don't dismiss your love. Gird your loins, get up, hold out your oil lamps, "wait for the Lord when he comes to the wedding" (Lk 12:35–36). What are you scared about, just because earthly kingdoms perish? That's the reason that a heavenly one's been promised you, that you won't perish with the earthly. Now this collapse was foretold—and foretold quite expressly. We cannot deny, after all, what's been foretold. Your Lord, the One you're waiting for, has said to you: "Nation shall rise against nation, and kingdom against kingdom" (Mk 13:8). Earthly kingdoms go through changes, but there will be One coming of whom it is said: "And of His kingdom there will be no end" (Lk 1:33).

(10) Those who have promised this sort of thing to earthly kingdoms have not been guided by truth, but have told flattering lies. [Vergil], a poet of theirs, once ushered in Jupiter and got him to say this concerning the Romans:

> For them I set neither boundaries nor term of years,
> Empire without end have I given.[19]

That clearly is not the truth speaking. This endless empire that you [Jupiter] have supposedly given, you, who have given nothing: Is this empire on earth or in heaven? On earth, of course. And if it were in heaven, still "heaven and earth shall pass away" (Lk 21:33). [Heaven and earth] are things God Himself made, and they shall pass away. How much more quickly will something Romulus founded! . . .

(11) Therefore, brothers and sisters, don't get discouraged. An end shall come to all the kingdoms of the earth. If now be the end, God sees it. Maybe, by chance, it's not here yet. Whether it's our weakness or pity or misery—let's hope that it's not here yet. Even so, won't it come sometime? Fix your hope in God, yearn for eternal things, be on the lookout for eternal things. You are Christians, brothers and sisters—*we* are Christians. Christ didn't come down in the flesh for fineries. Let us put up with, rather than love, present realities. Adversity is openly pernicious; prosperity is charmingly deceitful. Fear the sea, even when it's dead calm. Let us never ever listen in vain to the words:

19. Vergil, *Aeneid* 1.278–79.

"Lift up your heart."[20] Why do we place our heart on earth when we can see earth is getting turned upside down? I can do no more than exhort you that you have your heart where you say you do and you answer on behalf of your hope those who taunt and blaspheme the Christian name. Let no one's murmuring turn you away from waiting expectantly for the things to come. All who, because of these disasters, blaspheme our Christ are the scorpion's tail. Let us place our egg under the Gospel's Hen who calls out to that false and lost city: "O Jerusalem, Jerusalem, how often have I wished to gather your children together as a hen does her chicks, but you would not!" (Lk 13:34) Let it not be said to us: "How often would I, but you would not!" That Hen, you see, is divine Wisdom, but She took flesh to be on a par with Her chicks. See the Hen, feathers ruffled, wings drooping, Her voice cracking and quivering and rasping and fainting to be on a par with Her little ones. As for our egg—that is, our hope—let us place it beneath this Hen's wings.

(12) You may have noticed how a hen can rip a scorpion to pieces. If only the Gospel Hen would cut to pieces these blasphemers, scurrying on the ground, poking up out of their dens, stinging in nasty ways! If only She would gobble them up, ingest them into Her body, and turn them into egg! Let them not get angry. I may look excited, but I am not returning curses for curses. We are cursed and we bless; defamed, we plead with God. But people say of me: "Don't let him talk about Rome. O, if only he would just shut up about Rome!" As if I were some scoffer and not, instead, one pleading with the Lord and one encouraging you whatever way I can. Far be it from me to taunt Rome! May God turn such thoughts as these from my heart and from my saddened conscience. Didn't we have many brethren there? Don't we have them there still? Isn't a large segment of the pilgrim city of Jerusalem spending its days there? Has it not endured temporal losses there? But it has not lost eternal things. So what do I talk about when I don't keep quiet about these things? That it's false what they say about our Christ, false that He's the one who lost Rome, false that it had wooden and stone gods watching over it. . . .

See what sort of guardians those learned men have entrusted Rome to—to gods "who have eyes and cannot see" (Ps 113:5). Or if the gods could have preserved Rome, why did they themselves perish first? But those [learned men] say: "Rome perished at the same time." Whatever! The gods perished. "No," they say, "the gods didn't perish; their statues, their look-alikes, did." Well, how could gods that couldn't even take care of their look-alikes take care of your homes? Alexandria once lost such gods. Constantinople, once it

20. "The words: 'Lift up your heart' (sursum cor)": From the opening dialogue of the eucharistic prayer. See Augustine's interpretation of them in s. 227 (cited in Chapter 4).

was founded as a great city, once a Christian emperor founded it, lost its old-time false gods. Yet it grew, and it's still growing, and still stands. As long as God wills, it'll stand. Now, just because I say this, I'm not promising eternity even for that city. Carthage stands in the name of Christ, but in the old days Caelestis was overthrown because she wasn't heavenly, but earthly. . . .

(13) But our people were there [in Rome] too, and they were afflicted. But they knew how to say: "I will bless the Lord at all times" (Ps 33:2). They were afflicted in terms of the earthly kingdom, but they did not lose the king-dom of heaven. Instead, they were made better for it through tribulation's tough exercises. And if they did not blaspheme in their terrible sufferings, they came out of the kiln as fire-hardened jars and filled up with the Lord's blessing. These blasphemers, on the other hand, are following after earth-ly things, longing for earthly things, pinning their hope on earthly things, even though—whether they want or not—they lose all that stuff. What's left? Where will they stay? Nothing on the outside, nothing on the inside, emp-ty coffers, emptier consciences. Where will they find rest? Where salvation? Where hope? Let them come, therefore, and stop blaspheming and learn to adore [God]. Let these stinging scorpions be gobbled up by the Hen. Let them be ingested and converted into her body. Let them, on earth, be trained; let them, in heaven, be crowned.[21]

OBJECTIONS OF PAGAN ARISTOCRATS

Augustine alludes repeatedly to pagan nay-sayers who blamed Rome's sack on Chris-tianity. Who were they? One group was a circle of highly educated aristocrats who gravitated around a senator named Volusianus. This group came to Augustine's attention through his friend Flavius Marcellinus, the imperial commissioner who had overseen the resolution of the Donatist controversy. These pagan aristocrats objected to Christianity on various grounds. They dismissed Jesus' miracles as small stuff compared to celebrated pagan miracle-workers, and they regarded the Incarnation as so much nonsense. One politically sensitive objection was that Christian ethics was not only a bizarre foreign import, but was plainly destructive of the militarism required to maintain an empire. They were wary of voicing objections too publicly and passed on their concerns to Augustine via Marcellinus. In this passage Marcellinus stresses that Augustine's response will make the rounds and should therefore be "a brilliant solution." From Flavius Marcellinus, preserved as Letter 136 in Augustine's corpus:

21. S. 105.9–13 (PL 38:622–25); my trans.

(1) The receipt of your Reverence's letter made such an impression on the man [Volusianus], who was being drawn away from adherence to the faith by the influence of many—and there are plenty of them in this city—that, as he admitted himself, he would not have recoiled from the length of such a letter if he could have confided to your Beatitude every doubting thought he had. And, to the extent that you yourself will deign to agree, he has earnestly asked to have certain difficulties solved for him in that cultured and exact language of yours and that shining splendor of Roman eloquence. The question has become a much-discussed one, and the cleverness of those who defame the dispensation of the Lord's Incarnation is quite well known in this group. Because I trust that whatever you write in answer will be profitable to many in this group, I approach you as a petitioner, asking you to be so kind as to answer that point carefully, in which they falsely maintain that the Lord did no more than other men were able to do, and they bring up for our benefit their Apollonius[22] and Apuleius[23] and other men adept in magic who, according to their claim, worked greater miracles.

(2) But that above-mentioned illustrious man said in the presence of several people that there were many questions which could fitly be added to this one, as I said before, except that he, on his side, had some regard for epistolary brevity. But he did not pass them over in silence, even though he would not write them, for he said that, even if an explanation of the Lord's Incarnation were given him today, it would still be hard to make plain to him why this God, who is established as the God of the Old Testament, should delight in new sacrifices, having rejected ancient ones. He insisted that a thing cannot be corrected unless it was proved to have been wrongly done before, or at least, that what was rightly done once should never be changed. He said it was wrong to change right things, largely because such useless action could ascribe fickleness to God, and he added that His preaching and doctrine were not adaptable to the customs of the state. This, indeed, is said by many, such, for instance, as His teaching that we should not return evil for evil to anyone; that we should turn the other cheek when anyone strikes us (Mt 5:39); that we should let go our cloak when anyone takes our coat (Mt 5:40); and, when anyone forces us to go with him, we should go twice as far (Mt 5:41); all of which he says is contrary to the laws of the state. For who could allow anything to be taken from him by an enemy, or who would not wish to return evil, as the law of war allows, to the ravager of a Roman province? Your Reverence understands what can be said about the rest. Thus, he believes, even if he

---

22. "Apollonius": Apollonius of Tyana (late 1st cent.) was a neo-Pythagorean philosopher; his biographer, Philostratus (late 2nd cent.), portrays him as a sage, miracle worker, and exorcist. See John P. Meier, *A Marginal Jew: Rethinking the Historical Jesus* (New York: Doubleday, 1994), 2:576–81.

23. "Apuleius": Apuleius of Madauros (active, 150s), a North African philosopher and novelist, best known for his *Metamorphoses* (also known as *The Golden Ass* [*Asinus Aureus*]); see Tim Whitmarsh, ed., *The Cambridge Companion to the Greek and Latin Novel* (Cambridge: Cambridge University Press, 2008). Augustine discusses Apuleius's *On the God of Socrates* (*De deo Socratis*) in *civ. Dei* 8.14–22 and 9.8–16 and discusses *Metamorphoses* in *civ. Dei* 18.18. Augustine also contrasts Jesus' miracles with the magic attributed to Apuleius in *ep.* 102.32, 137.13, and 138.18–19.

says nothing on this score, that all those points can be related to this same question, that at least to this extent it is evident that great evils befall the state when Christian rulers generally observe the Christian religion.

(3) Consequently, as your Beatitude is so good as to agree with me in recognizing that, as the much-desired answer of your Holiness to all this will pass through many hands, it should be full in appearance and carefully worked out, a brilliant solution; especially as the excellent landlord and ruler of the countryside of Hippo was present when these questions were raised, and he praised your Holiness with sarcastic flattery, insisting that he had not been at all satisfied when these queries were made. So then in the midst of all this, I do not forget your promise. I insist on it, and I ask for the completion of works which will be unbelievably useful to the Church, especially at this time.[24]

PUBLISHING CITY OF GOD

Firmus, a catechumen in Carthage, had once begged Augustine for a complete copy of City of God *after hearing a public reading of Book 18.[25] Augustine complied, sending him the manuscript not long after finishing it. In one of the Divjak letters, Augustine outlines, in broad terms, the 22 books that make up the completed work.[26] This self-conscious outline is repeated both within* City of God *itself as well as in* Reconsiderations *and in other letters. [27] Here Augustine suggests how this outline should shape the publication, whether it should be bound as a two-volume or a five-volume work. The letter thus offers fascinating clues about the book business in the ancient world, about publishing, copying, binding, and dissemination. Note Augustine's stress that it be made available to pagans, also his stress that it not only be read, but re-read and meditated on. In certain medieval manuscripts, this letter was used as a preface to* City of God. *From Letter 1*A (Divjak):*

(1) As I had promised, I have sent the books On the City of God for which you so earnestly entreated me. Indeed, I re-read them myself. . . . There are twenty-two books which are rather too bulky to be bound together into one volume. If you wish for two volumes, they must be divided up so that one volume has ten books, and the other, twelve. In the first ten, the vanities of the impious have been refuted, and in the other twelve, our religion has been de-

---

24. Ep. 136.1–3 (CSEL 44:93–96); trans. Parsons, FOTC 20:15–17 (modified). In *ep.* 135, Volusianus himself details specific concerns about the Incarnation. Augustine answers Volusianus in *ep.* 137 and Marcellinus in *ep.* 138. This correspondence forms a sort of first draft for the broader, more far-reaching rethinking of religion, history, and government played out in *De civitate Dei*.

25. Ep. 2*.3 (BA 46B:62). For the other letter to Firmus, see Chapter 3.

26. A slightly different version of this letter had been discovered by Cyrille Lambot and published in *Revue Bénédictine* 51 (1939): 109–21.

27. Similar outlines are found in *civ. Dei* 1.35–36, 10.32, and 18.1; they appear also in *ep.* 184A.3.5 and *retr.* 2.69.

scribed and defended although, where it was more opportune, I have undertaken the defense in the first ten, as well as the refutation in the last twelve.

If, however, you would prefer to have more than two volumes, then you
must have five, of which the first will contain the first five books in which I
dispute those who claim that the worship, not of the gods, but of demons,
helps to achieve happiness in this world; the second group of five is aimed
[against those] who think that the many gods such as we have mentioned
above, or of whatever kind of gods, must be worshiped with ceremonies and
sacrifices on account of the life to come after death. Then the next three volumes which follow must have four books each. This section has been so arranged by us that four demonstrate the origins of that city, and an equivalent number, its progress, or as we prefer to say, its development, and the last
four, its appointed ends.

(2) If you are as eager to read these books as you were to get hold of them,
you will know of how much assistance they are from your own experience
rather than from my assurance. Concerning the work On the City of God, which
our brothers in Carthage do not yet have, I ask you kindly to give it to those
who want to copy it—not to many at the same time, but only to one or two,
and they will pass it on to others; you will also arrange how to give it to your
friends, whether they are Christians who want to learn or people still held by
some superstition, from which they will seem to be able to be freed by the
grace of God through this effort of mine.

(3) Accordingly in my letters, if the Lord is willing, I shall frequently take
the trouble to ask you how far you have gotten in your reading; as a learned
man, you are not unaware of how helpful re-reading a section can be in understanding what is read; for the difficulty of understanding is non-existent
or certainly very slight where there is facility in reading and this becomes so
much the greater the more it is repeated; by persistence, as it were, [some-
thing becomes more mature which through lack of attention] had remained
immature.[28]

❧

THEME OF THE TWO CITIES

MAGNUM OPUS ET ARDUUM

Augustine dedicated On the City of God to his friend Marcellinus, who had first
brought the issues so forcefully to his attention. Marcellinus was tragically executed in

---

28. Ep. 1*A.1–3 (BA 46B:54–58); trans. Eno, FOTC 81:14–16.

413 on trumped-up charges of collusion in a failed coup. When Augustine speaks here of this work as a "great and hard task" (magnum opus et arduum), he is referring not to its eventual bulk, but to the complexity of argumentation and depth of learning that such a refutation required. From On the City of God, *preface:*

My dear Marcellinus: This work which I have begun makes good my promise to you. In it I am undertaking nothing less than the task of defending the glorious City of God against those who prefer their own gods to its Founder. I shall consider it both in its temporal stage here below (where it journeys as a pilgrim among sinners and lives by faith) and as solidly established in its eternal abode—that blessed goal for which we patiently hope "until justice be turned into judgment" (Ps 93:15), but which, one day, is to be the reward of excellence in a final victory and a perfect peace. The task, I realize, is a great and hard one, but God will help me. I know, of course, what ingenuity and force of arguments are needed to convince proud men of the power of humility. Its loftiness is above the pinnacles of earthly greatness, which are shaken by the shifting winds of time—not by reason of human arrogance, but only by the grace of God. For in Scripture, the King and Founder of the City that I have undertaken to speak of revealed to His people the judgment of divine law: "God resists the proud and gives grace to the humble" (Jas 4:6). Unfortunately the swollen spirit of human pride claims for itself this high prerogative, which belongs to God alone, and longs and loves to hear repeated in its own praise [Vergil's] line: "To be merciful to the conquered and beat the haughty down."[29] Hence, insofar as the general plan of the treatise demands and my ability permits, I must speak also of the earthly city—of that city which lusts to dominate the world and which, though nations bend to its yoke, is itself dominated by its passion for dominion.[30]

THE TWO CITIES: BIBLICAL BASIS

We saw how Augustine, in the opening paragraph of individual books of his Confessions, *gradually unfurled the motif of confession. In a similar way in* On the City of God, *Augustine gradually unfurls the "two cities" theme, notably in the introductions or conclusions to individual books. Here are several key instances. This first one appears at the opening of Book 11 where, after hundreds of pages, Augustine finally brings the "two cities" theme front-and-center and here notes its biblical basis in the Psalms. From* On the City of God, *Book 11:*

29. Vergil, Aeneid 6.853.
30. *Civ. Dei*, praef. (CCL 47:1–2); trans. Zema and Walsh, FOTC 8:17–18.

(1) The expression "City of God," which I have been using, is justified by that Scripture whose divine authority puts it above the literature of all other people and brings under its sway every type of human genius—and that, not by some casual intellectual reaction, but by a disposition of Divine Providence. For in Scripture we read: "Glorious things are said of you, O city of God" (Ps 86:3); and in another Psalm: "Great is the Lord, and exceedingly to be praised in the city of our God, in His holy mountain, increasing the joy of the whole earth"; and a little later in the same Psalm: "As we have heard, so have we seen, in the city of the Lord of hosts, in the city of our God: God has founded it forever" (Ps 47:2, 3, 9); and in another text: "The stream of the river makes the city of God joyful: the Most High has sanctified his own tabernacle. God is in its midst; it shall not be moved" (Ps 45:5–6). Through these and similar passages too numerous to quote, we learn of the existence of a City of God whose Founder has inspired us with a love and longing to become its citizens. The inhabitants of the earthly city who prefer their own gods to the Founder of the holy City do not realize that He is the God of gods—though not, of course, of those false, wicked, and proud gods who, because they have been deprived of that unchangeable light which was meant for all, are reduced to a pitiful power and, therefore, are eager for some sort of influence and demand divine honors from their deluded subjects. He is the God of those reverent and holy "gods" who prefer to obey and worship the one God rather than to have many others obeying and worshiping them.[31] In the ten preceding books, I have done my best, with the help of our Lord and King, to refute the enemies of this City. Now, however, realizing what is expected of me and recalling what I promised, I shall begin to discuss, as well as I can, the origin, history, and destiny of the respective cities, earthly and heavenly, which, as I have said, are at present inextricably intermingled, one with the other. First, I shall explain how these two cities originated when the angels took opposing sides.[32]

---

31. "Those reverent and holy 'gods' . . .": Augustine is emphasizing that obedience makes souls holy and thus god-like. This may seem an odd locution, but it is crucial both exegetically and theologically. In terms of exegesis, Augustine is conscious of and playing on a network of scripture texts that he discusses more elsewhere. Notable is Ps 81:6 (LXX): "I said, 'You are Gods'" (Dixi, dii estis), which Jesus, in Jn 10:34, cites and interprets favorably to mean: "[Scripture] calls them gods to whom the word of God came . . ." These (and a whole host of other texts) would serve as the theological foundation for the classic Orthodox doctrine of deification. On this, see Norman Russell, The Doctrine of Deification in the Greek Patristic Tradition, OECS (New York: Oxford University Press, 2004). Augustine himself had, over the course of his career, wrestled with these issues and formulated his own distinctive brand. On this, see Gerald Bonner, "Augustine's Concept of Deification," Journal of Theological Studies 87 (1986): 369–86, reprinted in Church and Faith in the Patristic Tradition: Augustine, Pelagianism, and Early Christian Northumbria (London: Variorum, 1996).

32. Civ. Dei 11.1 (CCL 48:321–22); trans. Walsh and Monahan, FOTC 14:187–88.

THE TWO CITIES IN HUMAN HISTORY

In Books 11 and 12, Augustine explores the foreshadowing of the two cities in the fall of the angels. In Book 14 he discusses the creation of the world and of Adam and Eve as well as their Fall and its dire consequences for human history. In Book 15, he turns at last to human history, and here gives his classic exposition of the "two cities" theme. From On the City of God, *Book 15:*

(1) Actually, I think I have said enough on the really great and difficult problems concerning the origin of the world, the soul, and the human race. I divide humanity into two orders. On the one side are those who live according to humankind; on the other, those who live according to God. And I have said that in a deeper sense we may speak of two cities or two human societies, the destiny of the one being an eternal kingdom under God while the doom of the other is eternal punishment along with the devil. Of the final consummation of the two cities, I shall have to speak later. Of the cities' origins in the angels (whose number we do not know) and then in the first two human beings, I have already spoken. For the moment, therefore, I must deal with the course of the history of the two cities from the time when children were born to the first couple until the day when human beings shall beget no more. By the course of their history, as distinguished from their original cause and their final consummation, I mean the whole time of world history in which human beings are born and take the place of those who die and depart.

Now the firstborn of the two parents of the human race was Cain. He belonged to the human city. The next born was Abel, and he was of the City of God. Notice here a parallel between the individual and the larger whole. We all experience as individuals what the Apostle says: "It is not the spiritual that comes first, but the physical, and then the spiritual" (1 Cor 15:46). The fact is that every individual springs from a condemned stock and, because of Adam, must be first evil and carnal, only later to become good and spiritual by the process of rebirth in Christ. So too with the human race as a whole: As soon as human birth and death began the historical course of the two cities, the first to be born was a citizen of this world, and only later came the one who was an alien in the human city but at home in the City of God, one predestined by grace and elected by grace. By grace an alien on earth, by grace he was a citizen of heaven. In and of himself, he sprang from the common clay which was totally under condemnation from the beginning, but which God held in His hands like a potter, to borrow the metaphor which the Apostle so wisely and deliberately uses.[33] For God could make "from the same mass one

---

33. "Like a potter": This imagery from Rom 9 would figure prominently in Augustine's articulation of his views on predestination. See *Simpl.* 1.2.20; *nat. et gr.* 5.5; *ep.* 190.3.12; for the texts, see Chapter 10.

vessel for honorable use, another for ignoble use" (Rom 9:21). The first vessel to be made was for ignoble use. Only later was there made a vessel for honorable use. And as with the whole, so, as I have said, with the individual. First comes the clay that is only fit to be thrown away, with which we must begin but in which we need not remain. This does not mean that everyone who is wicked is to become good, but that no one becomes good who was not once wicked. What is true is that the sooner a person makes a change in himself for the better, the sooner he has a right to be called what he has become. The second name hides the first.

Now it is recorded of Cain that he built a city (Gn 4:17), while Abel, as though he were merely a pilgrim on earth, built none. For the true City of the saints is in heaven, though here on earth it produces citizens in whom it wanders as on a pilgrimage through time, looking for the Kingdom of eternity. When that day comes it will gather together all those who, rising in their bodies, shall have that Kingdom given to them in which, along with their Leader, the King of Eternity, they shall reign for ever and ever.[34]

TWO CITIES AS TWO KINDS OF LOVE

For Augustine, our loves define the city to which we have, as it were, pledged our allegiance. Augustine had no illusions about politics: The earthly city, even at its best, sprang from a libido dominandi, a lust for domination. Mention of this sometimes subtle, sometimes brutal lust for domination appears in the preface (as we saw) and runs as a central thread through the whole work. From On the City of God, Book 14:

(28) What we see, then, is that two societies have issued from two kinds of love. Earthly society has flowered from a selfish love which dared to despise even God, whereas the heavenly is rooted in a love of God that is ready to trample on self. In a word, this latter relies on the Lord, whereas the other boasts that it can get along by itself. The one seeks human glory, whereas the height of glory for the other is to hear God in the witness of conscience. The one lifts up its head in its own boasting; the other says to God: "You are my glory, you lift up my head" (Ps 3:4). In the earthly city both the rulers themselves and the people they dominate are dominated by the lust for domination, whereas in the City of God all citizens serve one another in charity, whether they serve by the responsibilities of office or by the duties of obedience. The one city loves its leaders as symbols of its own strength; the other says to its God: "I love you, O Lord, my strength" (Ps 17:2). Hence, even wise

---

34. *Civ. Dei* 15.1 (CCL 48:453-54); trans. Walsh and Monahan, FOTC 14:413-15.

people in the human city live according to human standards, and their only goals have been the goods of their bodies or of the mind or both. Though some of them have reached a knowledge of God, "they did not glorify Him as God or give thanks, but became vain in their reasonings, and their senseless minds have been darkened. For while professing to be wise" (that is to say, while glorifying in their own wisdom, under the domination of pride), "they have become fools, and they have changed the glory of the incorruptible God for the likeness of an image of a corruptible man and birds and four-footed beasts and creeping things" (meaning that they either led their people, or imitated them, in adoring idols shaped like these things), "and they worshiped and served the creature rather than the Creator who is blessed forever" (Rom 1:21–25). In the City of God, on the contrary, there is no mere human wisdom, but there is a piety which worships the true God as He should be worshiped and has as its goal that reward of all holiness, whether in the society of saints on earth or in that of angels of heaven, which is "that God may be all in all" (1 Cor 15:28).[35]

❧

POLEMIC AGAINST PAGAN CRITICS (BOOKS 1–10)

PROVIDENCE AND THE EXPERIENCE OF DISASTER

On the City of God is, in part, theodicy, an attempt to grapple with God's justice, on the one hand, and, on the other, the mystery of evil, especially the seemingly random anguish and evil that take place amid the chaotic brutality of war. In the following passage, Augustine sets out his views on the hidden providence at work in the brutal experience of those who suffered Rome's sack. From On the City of God, Book 1:

(8) But someone will say: "How, then, is it that this divine mercy was bestowed on the impious and ungrateful?" Surely the answer is that mercy was shown by the One who, day by day, "makes His sun to rise upon the good and bad, and rains upon the just and the unjust" (Mt 5:45). For although some who reflect on these truths repent and are converted from their wickedness, others, according to the words of the Apostle, despise "the riches of His goodness and long-suffering, in the hardness of their heart and impen-

35. Civ. Dei 14.28 (CCL 48:451–52); trans. Walsh and Monahan, FOTC 14:410–11. See en. Ps. 64.2 (CCL 39:823–24). For a discussion, O'Donovan, Problem of Self-Love, 93–111.

itence," and treasure up to themselves "wrath against the day of wrath and revelation of the just judgment of God, who will render to everyone according to his works" (Rom 2:5–6). Nevertheless, God's patience is an invitation to the wicked to do penance, just as God's scourge is a school of patience for the good. In a similar way, God's mercy embraces the good with love, just as His severity corrects the wicked with punishment. It has pleased Divine Providence to prepare, for the just, joys in the world to come in which the unjust will have no part, and for the impious, pains which will not afflict the virtuous. But as for the paltry goods and evils of this transitory world, these He allotted alike to just and unjust in order that one not seek too eagerly after these goods which even the wicked possess, nor shrink too readily from those ills which commonly afflict the just.

There is, however, a vast difference between the manner in which we use what we call prosperity and adversity. A good person is neither puffed up by fleeting success nor broken by adversity, whereas a bad one is chastised by failure of this sort because he is corrupted by success. God often shows His intervention more clearly by the way He apportions the sweet and the bitter. For if He visited every sin here below with manifest penalty, it might be thought that no score remained to be settled at the Last Judgment. On the other hand, if God did not plainly enough punish sin on earth, people might conclude that there is no such thing as Divine Providence. So too in regard to the good things of life. If God did not bestow them with patent liberality on some who ask Him, we could possibly argue that such things did not depend on His power. On the other hand, if He lavished them on all who asked, we might have the impression that God is to be served only for the gifts He bestows. In that case, the service of God would not make us religious, but rather covetous and greedy. In view of all that, when good and bad suffer alike, they are not for that reason indistinguishable because what they suffer is similar. The sufferers are different even though the sufferings are the same trials. Though what they endure is the same, their virtue and vice are different. For in the same fire, gold gleams and straw smokes; under the same flail the stalk is crushed and the grain threshed; the dregs are not mistaken for olive oil because they have issued from the press. So, too, the tide of trouble will test, purify, and improve the good, but will beat, crush, and wash away the wicked. So it is that, under the weight of the same affliction, the wicked deny and blaspheme God while the good pray to Him and praise Him. The difference is not in what people suffer but in the way they suffer. The same shaking that makes fetid water stink makes perfume issue a more pleasant odor.

(9) What then did the Christians suffer in the great devastation of Rome which, if taken in a spirit of faith, would not have served for their great-

er good? For one thing, if they humbly call to mind the sins for which God in His anger filled the world with calamities, they will not judge themselves to be so little responsible for these sins as not to have deserved some measure of temporal affliction—even though they were far from being godless and criminals. The fact is that everyone, however exemplary, yields to some promptings of concupiscence—if not to monstrous crimes, abysmal villainy, and abominable impiety, then at least to some sins, however rarely or (if frequently) however venially. Apart from this fact, I say, is it easy to find anyone who treats as he should those whose horrible pride, lust, avarice, damnable depravity, and scoffing impiety caused God to lay desolate the earth, as was threatened in prophecy? Does anyone live with them in a way that life ought to be lived with such people?

For the most part, we hesitate to instruct, to admonish, and, as occasion demands, to correct, and even to reprehend them. This we do either because the effort wearies us, or we fear offending them, or we avoid antagonizing them lest they thwart or harm us in those temporal matters where our selfishness always seeks to acquire things or our faint hearts fear to lose them. Thus, the good shun the wicked and hence will not share in their damnation beyond the grave. Nevertheless, because they wink at their worse sins and fear to frown even on their minor transgressions, the good must in justice suffer temporal afflictions in common with the rest—even though they will escape eternal ones. Thus, when God's hand falls as heavily on them as on the others, it is just that they should taste the bitter things of this earthly life because they loved the sweet things and refused to feel compunction while others sinned.

At times, one hesitates to reprove or admonish evildoers, either because one seeks a more favorable moment or fears that his rebuke may make them worse, and further, discourage weak brethren from striving to lead a good and holy life, or turn them aside from the faith. In such circumstances, forbearance is not prompted by selfish considerations but by well-advised charity. What is reprehensible, however, is that, while leading good lives themselves and abhorring those of the wicked, some, fearing to offend, shut their eyes to evil deeds instead of condemning them and pointing out their malice. To be sure, the motive behind their tolerance is that they may suffer no hurt in the possession of those temporal goods which the virtuous and blameless may lawfully enjoy. Still, there is more self-seeking here than is becoming for people who are mere sojourners in this world and who profess the hope of a home in heaven.

In truth, it is not only people of less lofty virtue, who live in the married state, having (or seeking to have) children, and possessing a home and household of their own—people such as those whom St. Paul, in the first churches, instructed and admonished how to live: wives with husbands and husbands with wives; children with parents and parents with children; servants with masters and masters with servants—it is not only such people who acquire transitory and earthly goods with zest and lose them with chagrin and, because of that, dare not offend those whose immoral and vicious life revolts them. Even those who profess a more perfect life and are free from conjugal bonds and content with poorer food and dress are also over-solicitous for their good name and security and frequently forbear to reprehend the wicked because they fear their snares and violence. Though the good do not fear the wicked to the point of stooping under intimidation to their villainies and knavery, they often are unwilling to denounce such things, even when they might convert some souls as a result. Here again they fear that a possible failure to effect reform might jeopardize their security and reputation. It is not that they are convinced that these latter are an indispensable means for people's instruction. They are merely victims of that human infirmity which loves the flattering tongue and earthly life and which dreads the censure of the crowd and the anguish and death of the body. In other words, they shirk this duty of fraternal correction because of a certain slavishness to avarice, not because of the obligations of charity.

Hence, this seems to me sufficient reason why the good are scourged with the wicked as often as it pleases God to punish degenerate morals with temporal sufferings. Both are scourged not because both lead a bad life, but because both love an earthly life; not, indeed, to the same extent, but yet both together—a life which the good should think little of in order that the bad, by being admonished and reformed, may attain to eternal life. If the wicked refuse to be joined in the blessed endeavor, they should be brought along and loved as enemies are loved in Christian charity, since as long as they live there is always the possibility that they may come to a better mind. In this respect, the good to whom the Prophet addresses these words, "He is indeed taken away in his iniquity, but I will require his blood at the hand of the watchman" (Ezek 33:6), have not merely an equal but a far graver reason for concern or reflection. For this reason, overseers or rulers are set over the churches, to reprimand sin, not to spare it.[36] Nor is one fully free from blame who is not in authority, but who notices in those persons he meets in social life many faults he should censure and admonish. He is blameworthy if he fails to do this out of fear of hurting feelings or losing such things as he may legitimately enjoy

---

36. "Overseers . . . reprimand sin": The image of the watchman from Ezekiel 33 and the task of reprimanding sin figure prominently in Augustine's self-conception as a bishop. See s. 339.

in this life but to which he is unduly attached. Finally, there is another reason, well known to Job, why even the good must drink the bitter cup of temporal adversity: in order that the human spirit may test its mettle and come to know whether it loves God with the virtue of religion and for His own sake.[37]

ROME NEVER A COMMONWEALTH

In Book 2, Augustine sets forth his core polemic against those who blamed Christianity for Rome's downfall. He argues that the Republic had already lost its legitimacy well before Christ's coming since it lacked social justice. This argument highlights Augustine's strategy as an apologist: drawing on classical authors widely esteemed by his pagan audience and using them against his opponents. From On the City of God, Book 2:

(19) Take a look at your Roman republic. I am not the first to paint this picture. The writers whose works we studied in school for a fee told the tale before Christ's coming. Remember? [As Cicero notes,] "from a state of virtuous splendor [Rome] sank by gradual change to one of shameful corruption."[38] It was before Christ's coming and after the destruction of Carthage that [according to Sallust] "the morals of our forefathers declined, not little by little as before, but rushing headlong like a torrent. So deep into immorality and avarice did the younger generation sink."[39] Let our critics read to us any commandments which the gods ever gave to their Roman people, setting bounds to debauchery and greed. It is not merely that [the gods] had abstained from any mention of chastity and modesty to the people. They went so far as actually to demand lewdness and indecency. They gave those things the sanction of divine approval. As against all this, let [our opponents] turn to our moral teachings. The Prophets, the Gospels, the Acts of the Apostles, and the Epistles have thundered their condemnation of greed and lust into the ears of the throngs assembled in every part of the empire for the very purpose of hearing them. Sublime and divinely inspired utterances, they are not like the cackle of contentious philosophers, but like oracles from God's heaven. But strangely enough, while our pagan foes are slow to impute to their gods the fact that immodesty, avarice, brutal and shameful living turned the Roman commonwealth into [what Sallust called] a "sink of corruption" before the advent of Christ, they loudly reproach the Christian religion for whatever bitter pill their arrogance and their love of pleasure have to swallow at the present time. . . .

37. *Civ. Dei* 1.8–9 (CCL 47:7–10); trans. Zema and Walsh, FOTC 8:28–33.
38. Cicero, *In Catilinam* 5.9.
39. Sallust, *Historiae* 1.16.

(21) If my opponents, content if [Rome] can but endure, are not moved by the shame and ignominy of utter degeneration that flood it, let them note that it had not merely become the "sink of iniquity" described by Sallust, but that, as Cicero maintains, it had long since perished and no longer endured as a state. Cicero lets that same Scipio who had destroyed Carthage voice his opinion of the state at a time when there were warning signs that it would soon be brought low by the rottenness which Sallust describes . . . :

In playing the lute, or the flute, or even in vocal music, the different notes should be kept in harmony. If they are changed into discord, the trained ear cannot endure it. That agreeable harmony, however, is produced by the modulation of tones that are very dissimilar. In like manner, as in music, out of the highest and the lowest classes, and out of those that lie between, by a reasonable control, the State is fashioned into a concordant whole by the consent of very diverse elements. What musicians call harmony in music, in the State is known as concord, the closest and strongest bond of security in any commonwealth, and which can in no way exist without justice.[40]

. . . After the pros and cons of this question had been examined, Scipio again took up the broken threads of the discussion, and, going back to his definition of the republic, he endorsed in a few words the stand that "the commonwealth is the wealth and welfare of the people." He defines the people as "not any mass gathering, but a multitude bound together by a mutual recognition of rights and a mutual cooperation for the common good."[41] . . . But if the king is unjust, or a tyrant (to use the Greek word), or if the aristocrats are unjust (in which case their group is merely a faction), or if the people themselves are unjust (and must be called, for lack of a better word, a tyrant also), then the commonwealth is not merely bad . . . but is no commonwealth at all. The reason for that is that there is no longer the welfare of the people, once a tyrant or a faction seizes it; nor would the people, if unjust, be any longer a people, because they would not then be regarded as a multitude bound together by a common recognition of rights, and a mutual cooperation for the common good, as the standard definition of a people demands.

When, therefore, the Roman republic was such as Sallust describes it, it was not only "very wicked and corrupt"—"a sink of iniquity," as he puts it— it was no republic at all, if measured by the criterion established by its ablest representatives when they met to debate the nature of a republic. . . . Tullius

40. Cicero, *De re publica* 2.42. On Augustine's use of Cicero's treatise, see Hagendahl, *Augustine and the Latin Classics*, 540–43.

41. Cicero, *De re publica* 1.25. It is difficult to capture the rich spectrum of connotations that *res publica* has for Cicero and for Augustine. It literally means "public thing." It could refer more narrowly to "the state," the apparatus of government. But Cicero (as well as Augustine) often uses it in a broader sense of "what belongs to the people," what is best translated into English as "commonwealth." See Paul Weithman, "Augustine's Political Philosophy," in Stump and Kretzmann, *Cambridge Companion to Augustine*, 240–45.

[Cicero] himself, at the beginning of his fifth book [of the *Republic*], quotes the verse of the poet Ennius declaring: "The Roman state rests on men and on the ancient way of life," and in his own words, not those of Scipio or any other, remarks:

That line for its conciseness and truth sounds to me like the utterance of an oracle. For, had not the state been blessed with a wholesome body of citizens, and had not those men stood at the head, neither men nor morals could have availed to found or so long maintain a republic of such might to rule so far and wide and so justly. Indeed, long before our time, it was the custom of the land to appoint distinguished men who held fast to the ancient traditions and the institutions of our forefathers. Our own generation inherited the republic, an exquisite masterpiece, indeed, though faded with age; but it failed to restore its original colors. Worse, alas; it did not even move a finger to preserve as much as its form, or its barest outlines. What is there left of the ancient virtue which the illustrious poet Ennius declared was the mainstay of the Roman state? We are aware only that it has been so utterly cast to the winds that morals are not merely unobserved, but are positively ignored. What can we say of the men? Precisely for want of men the good old customs have been lost, and for so great an evil not only are we responsible but we should face judgment like culprits fearing the penalty of death. By our own vices, not by chance, we have lost the republic, though we retain the name.[42]

All this, Cicero avowed many years ... before the coming of Christ. If such reproaches were expressed or entertained after the triumphant advance of the Christian religion, there is not a pagan who would not think of charging them to the Christians. Why, then, did their gods not save from disaster that republic which, long before Christ appeared in the flesh, Cicero mournfully deplores as lost? Let its panegyrists really take a look at the republic in the day of those ancient men and customs. Let them ask whether true justice flourished and inspired morality or was merely a colored painting of justice, as Cicero himself unwittingly suggests, while meaning to praise it. . . .

I shall endeavor to show later that that ancient creation was never a true republic, because in it true justice was never practiced. I shall base my position on Cicero's own definitions, in the light of which he briefly determined, through the mouth of Scipio, what was a republic and what was a people. There are many confirmatory opinions expressed in that discussion both by himself and by the interlocutors he introduced. According to some definitions, however, that are nearer the truth, it was a commonwealth of a sort, and it was better governed by the earlier Romans than by those who came later. But true justice is to be found only in that commonwealth—if we may so

---

42. Cicero, *De re publica* 5.1.

call it that—whose Founder and Ruler is Christ, for no one can deny that this is people's real wealth. This name [of Christ], with its varied meanings, is perhaps not quite in tune with our language, but this at least is certain: True justice reigns in that City of which Holy Scripture says: "Glorious things are said of you, O City of God" (Ps 86:3).

(22) But concerning the subject under discussion, however deserving of praise they say the republic once was or still is, the fact remains that by the testimony of their most well-informed writers it had, long before Christ's coming, become a "sink of iniquity." Never a true republic, it had fallen through the foulness of its morals.[43]

KINGDOMS AS BANDS OF ROBBERS

Augustine debunks the myth of empire at numerous junctures. He notes that one would think that the Empire would instill in its inhabitants a sense of peace and security, but, in fact, its happiness is as fragile as glass. He goes on to mock Roman claims of justice, noting that the Empire is little more than organized crime draped in the artifice of legitimacy. From On the City of God, *Book 4:*

(3) I would first like to find an answer to this question: Is it reasonable and wise to glory in the extent and greatness of the Empire when you can in no way prove that there is any real happiness in people perpetually living amid the horrors of war, perpetually wading in blood? Does it matter whether it is the blood of their fellow citizens or the blood of their enemies? It is still human blood, in those perpetually haunted by the gloomy specter of fear and driven by murderous passions. The happiness arising from such conditions is a thing of glass, of mere glittering brittleness. One can never shake off the horrible dread that it may suddenly shatter into shards. In order to be perfectly clear on this point, we must not be carried away by hollow verbal blasts and allow our judgment to be confused by the high-sounding words of prattlers about nations, kingdoms, and provinces. . . .

(4) In the absence of justice, what is sovereignty but organized brigandage? For what are bands of brigands but petty kingdoms? They also are groups of people, under the rule of a leader, bound together by a common agreement, dividing their booty according to a settled principle. If this band of criminals, by recruiting more criminals, acquires enough power to occupy

---

43. *Civ. Dei* 2.19–22 (CCL 47:50–55); trans. Zema and Walsh, FOTC 8:102–13. On the centrality of this passage, see Robert Dodaro, *Christ and the Just Society in the Thought of Augustine* (Cambridge: Cambridge University Press, 2004), esp. 10–26, 72–114.

regions, to capture cities, and to subdue whole populations, then it can with fuller right assume the title of kingdom, which in the public estimation is conferred upon it, not by the renunciation of greed, but by the increase of impunity. The answer which a captured pirate gave to the celebrated Alexander the Great was perfectly accurate and correct. When that king asked the man what he meant by infesting the sea, he boldly replied: "What you do by warring on the whole world, I do by fighting on a tiny ship, and they call me a pirate; you do yours with a large fleet, and they call you Commander."[44]

A Philosophy of Religion

Pagans argued that Rome's destruction came because traditional sacrifices to the gods had been outlawed. This charge brought to the fore a debate on the nature of religious sacrifice, ritual, and worship. Augustine was attuned to concerns of educated pagans (such as those in Volusianus's circle) and confronted arguments by Platonists such as Porphyry who had extolled theurgy, that is, sacrificial rites addressed to lesser spirits, or daemons, who, it was believed, acted as mediators in bridging the cosmic gap between the divine realm and humanity.[45] In Book 9, Augustine meditates at length on mediation and mediators. He agreed with Platonists that there exists a vast ontological gap between the divine and the human and that we require a mediator to bridge it, but denounced pagan sacrifices to daemons as useless and as demonic. He also denied Platonist claims that humanity and divinity could have "no immediate communication" since in Christ humankind had a mediator at once fully divine and fully human. In Book 10, Augustine sketches a philosophy of religion, spelling out the deeper purpose of rites and sacrifices, arguing that religion is not for God's sake, but for ours, and that while sacrifice may use visible signs, its real intent is to shape the individual's and the broader community's character. Volusianus's circle had complained of the inconsistency of Old Testament commandments requiring animal sacrifice and the New Testament rejection of such sacrifice. To address all this, Augustine appeals to his theory of sign and sacrament. Medieval and Reformation theologians routinely appealed to this text in their debates and formulations on sacraments and eucharistic sacrifice. From On the City of God, *Book 10:*

(3) If the Platonists and others who, like them, have a knowledge of God would only glorify Him as such and render Him thanks and not become vain

44. Civ. Dei 4.3–4 (CCL 47:100–102); trans. Zema and Walsh, FOTC 8:193–95.

45. We saw mention of Porphyry in Chapters 1 and 2, with regard to those "books of the Platonists" that had played a role in Augustine's conversion. Porphyry was a leading neo-Platonist philosopher who served as Plotinus's biographer and the editor of Plotinus's Enneads. Much of civ. Dei 10 addresses Porphyry's views on theurgy that appear in a lost treatise, On the Return of the Soul (De regressu animae), which may have been part of a larger work, Philosophy from Oracles. See Frederick Van Fleteren, "Porphyry," in AugEncy, 661–63; John J. O'Meara, 'Philosophy from Oracles' in Augustine, CEASA 9 (Paris: Institut d'Études Augustiniennes, 1959).

in their thoughts, whether by starting errors among the people or by failing to correct them, surely they would acknowledge that, in order to be immortal and blessed, both immortal blessed spirits and we miserable mortals must worship the one God of gods who is our God as well as theirs. Both in outward signs and inner devotion, we owe to God that service which the Greeks call latreía. Indeed, all of us together, and each one in particular, constitute His temple because He deigns to take as a dwelling both the whole community and the person of each individual. Nor is He greater in the whole than in each, since He cannot be extended by numbers nor diminished by being shared. When raised to Him, our heart becomes His altar; His only-begotten Son is the priest who wins for us His favor. It is only by the shedding of our blood in fighting for His truth that we offer Him bloody victims. We burn the sweetest incense in His sight when we are aflame with holy piety and love. As for the best gifts, we consecrate and surrender to Him our very selves which He has given us. We dedicate and consecrate to Him the memory of His bounties by establishing appointed days as solemn feasts lest the lapse of time, ingratitude, and forgetfulness should steal upon us. On the altar of our heart, we offer to Him a sacrifice of humility and praise, aglow with the fire of charity. In order to see Him as, one day, it will be possible to see and to cling to Him, we cleanse ourselves from every stain of sin and evil desire, sanctifying ourselves by His name. For He is the source of our happiness and the very end of all our aspirations. We choose Him (or rather, re-choose Him whom, by neglect, we had lost). We offer Him our re-chosen allegiance, for "re-choosing" (religentes) and "religion" (religio) are, at root, the same term. We pursue Him with our love so that when we reach Him we may rest in perfect happiness in the One who is our goal. For our goal . . . is nothing else than union with the One whose spiritual embrace alone can impregnate—so to speak—the intellectual soul and fill it with true virtue.

It is this Good which we are commanded to love with our whole heart, with our whole mind, and with all our strength. It is toward this Good that we should be led by those who love us, and toward this Good we should lead those whom we love. In this way, we fulfill the commandments on which depend the whole Law and the Prophets: "You shall love the Lord your God with your whole heart, and your whole soul, and with your whole mind"; and "You shall love your neighbor as yourself" (Mt 22:37, 39). For in order that a person might learn how to love himself, a standard was set to regulate all actions on which happiness depends.[46] For to love one's own self is nothing but to wish to be happy, and the goal is to cling to God. When, therefore, a person

---

46. "How to love himself": On this theme, see O'Donovan, Problem of Self-Love, 112–36.

who knows how to love himself is commanded to love his neighbor as himself, is he not, as a result, commanded to persuade others, as far as he can, to love God? This, then, is the worship of God. This is true religion and the right kind of piety. This is the service that is due only to God. It follows, therefore, that if any immortal power, however highly endowed with virtue, loves us as itself, it must wish us to be subject, for our own happiness, to the One in submission to whom it finds its happiness. If, then, this spirit does not worship God, it is unhappy because deprived of God, and if it worships God, it itself cannot wish to be worshiped instead of God.[47] . . .

(5) Of course, no one is foolish enough to think that God has any need of the things that are offered in sacrifice. . . . It is true that, in former times, our fathers offered up animals as victims. Today, however, we Christians read about such sacrifices but do not imitate them, and we understand them simply as symbols of the efforts we make to cling to God and to assist our neighbor to the same end. A sacrifice, therefore, is a visible sacrament (that is, sacred sign) of an invisible sacrifice. That is why the penitent in the Psalms—perhaps David means himself—who asks God to have mercy on his sins exclaims: "For if you had desired sacrifice, I would certainly have given it: with burnt offerings you find no delight. A sacrifice to God is a contrite spirit; a contrite and humbled heart, O God, you will not despise" (Ps 50:18–19).

Notice how the Prophet, in saying that God does not want sacrifice, shows that God does want it. What he means is that God does not desire the sacrifice of a slaughtered animal but rather the sacrifice of a contrite heart. Thus the Prophet says that what God does not want is a symbol of what He does want. What the Prophet means is that such things do not please God in the way that foolish people imagine, namely, to satisfy His pleasure. Of course, unless God had wanted sacrifices which seemed to minister to His pleasure, but which really symbolized the sacrifices that are truly pleasing to Him, such as a contrite heart humbled by the sorrow of repentance, then, indeed, in the Old Law, He would not have commanded such things to be offered to Him. . . . We read in the Epistle to the Hebrews: "And do not forget kindness and charity, for by such sacrifices is God pleased" (Heb 13:16). That is why the words, "For I desired mercy and not sacrifice" (Hos 6:6), must be understood to mean that one sacrifice is to be preferred to another, since what is commonly called a sacrifice is merely a symbol of the true sacrifice. For mercy is the true sacrifice. Hence the words just quoted: "By such sacrifices is God pleased" (Heb 13:16). All the divine precepts, therefore, which re-

---

47. Augustine here contrasts the angels, who, while "immortal powers," wish humans to worship God alone, and the demons, who, while also "immortal powers," wish humans to worship them rather than God.

fer, under different forms, to sacrifices in the service either of the tabernacle or of the temple, are to be understood, in the light of symbolism, to refer to the love of God and neighbor. For "on these two commandments depend the whole Law and the Prophets" (Mt 22:40).

(6) There is, then, a true sacrifice in every work which unites us in a sacred communion with God, that is, in every work that is aimed at that final Good in which alone we can be truly blessed. That is why even mercy shown to others is not a sacrifice unless it is done for God. A sacrifice, even though *we* offer it, is something divine—which is what the ancient Latins meant by the word *sacrificium*, "a making holy." For this reason, a person consecrated to God and vowed to God is himself a sacrifice, inasmuch as he dies to the world that he may live for God. For this is a part of that mercy which each one has on himself, according to the text: "Have pity on your own soul, pleasing God" (Eccli 30:24).

Our body, too, is a sacrifice when, for God's sake, we chastise it by temperance as we should, that is, when we do not yield our members as "weapons of wickedness for sin" (Rom 6:13) but as instruments of righteousness for God. The Apostle exhorts us to this when he says: "I exhort you, therefore, brethren, by the mercy of God to present your bodies as a sacrifice, living, holy, pleasing to God—your spiritual service" (Rom 12:1). If, then, the body, which is less than the soul and which the soul uses as a servant or a tool, is a sacrifice when it is used well and rightly for the service of God, how much more so is the soul when it offers itself to God so that, aflame in the fire of divine Love, and with the dross of worldly desire melted away, it is remolded into the unchangeable form of God and becomes beautiful in His sight by reason of the bounty of beauty which He has bestowed upon it. This is what the Apostle implies in the next verse: "And be not conformed to this world, but be transformed in the newness of your mind that you may discern what is the good and acceptable and perfect will of God" (Rom 12:2).

Since, therefore, true sacrifices are works of mercy done to ourselves or our neighbor and directed to God, and since works of mercy are performed that we may be freed from misery and, thereby, be happy, and since happiness is only to be found in that Good of which it is said: "But it is good for me to adhere to my God" (Ps 72:28), it follows that the whole of that redeemed city, that is, the gathering or society of saints, is offered as a universal sacrifice to God through the High Priest who, taking the "form of a servant" (Phil 2:7), offered Himself in His Passion for us that we might be the body of so glorious a Head. For it was this form of a servant He offered; it was in this form that He was the victim since it is in the form of a servant that He is the Mediator; in it He is the Priest, in it He is the Sacrifice.

When, therefore, the Apostle had exhorted us to present our bodies as a sacrifice, living, holy, pleasing to God—our spiritual service—and not to be conformed to this world but be transformed in the "newness of our minds, that we might discern what is the good and acceptable and perfect will of God," he went on to remind us that it is we ourselves who constitute the whole sacrifice: "For I say, by the grace of God given to me, to everyone among you: not to think of oneself more highly than one ought to think, but to deal soberly, each according to the measure of faith that God has apportioned. For as in one body we have many parts, and all the parts do not have the same office, so we, though many, are one body in Christ, and all are members of one another, having gifts that differ according to the grace given to us" (Rom 12:3–6). Such is the sacrifice of Christians: "We, the many, are one body in Christ." This is the sacrifice, as the faithful know well, which the Church continues to celebrate in the sacrament of the altar, in which it is clear to the Church that she herself is offered in the very offering she makes to God.[48]

THE INCARNATION IN GOLD LETTERS

Through the course of his debate with the Platonists in Book 10, Augustine marks out where Christians and Platonists converge and diverge. At one point, he tells a famous anecdote about what separates the two, namely, the Incarnation. From On the City of God, Book 10:

(29) It is, I suppose, humiliating for learned people to leave the school of Plato to enter that of Christ, who inspired a fisherman with wisdom enough to say: "In the beginning was the Word, and the Word was with God; and the Word was God. He was in the beginning with God. All things were made through Him, and without Him was made nothing that has been made. In Him was life, and the life was the light of humanity. And the light shines in the darkness; and the darkness grasped it not" (Jn 1:1–5). This is that beginning of the holy Gospel according to John which, according to a Platonist philosopher, as I often heard from that holy old man Simplicianus,[49] afterwards bishop of the Church at Milan, ought to be written in letters of gold and posted high in a prominent place in all the churches. But the reason why

48. *Civ. Dei* 10.3–6 (CCL 47:274–79); trans. Walsh and Monahan, FOTC 14:120–27. On Augustine's defining of religion, see Madec, "Le *De civitate Dei* comme *De vera religione*," in *Petites Études Augustiniennes*, 189–213. On the issue of sacramentality, see especially Cutrone, "Sacraments," AugEncy, 741–47; Basil Studer, "*Sacramentum et Exemplum chez saint Augustin*," *Recherches Augustiniennes* 10 (1975): 87–141.
49. "Holy old man Simplicianus": Simplicianus was bishop of Milan from 397–400. On his role in Augustine's conversion, see Chapter 1; on his inquiries to Augustine about Paul, see Chapter 10.

the proud despise this divine Teacher is because "the Word was made flesh, and dwelt among us" (Jn 1:14). For such unfortunates it is not enough to be sick; they must take pride in their sickness and think it below their dignity to take the medicine which could cure them. The result is that, instead of being cured, they suffer a serious relapse.[50]

✥

ORIGINAL SIN AND ITS CONSEQUENCES (BOOK 14)

Human Nature: Flesh ≠ Body

Book 14 opens with a meditation on human nature. It is hard to underestimate the significance of what, at first sight, seems an abstract discussion. Augustine here overturns 800 years of thinking about the human person, thinking as old as Plato, namely, that the body is the ultimate source of human downfall. He also rejects reading Scripture from that vantage point, noting that when the Bible speaks of "flesh" it is not referring simply to "body." As Paula Fredriksen notes, "Augustine held not only that the soul, not the flesh, was the seat of sin but also that, after the Fall, the soul was divided against itself. The fault line caused by Adam's sin not only violated man's nature, sundering the fundamental unity of body and soul; it also ran right through the soul, separating intention and affect, dividing man's will from man's loves, the loves that escape his conscious control. Accordingly, the nature of both body and soul, of flesh and spirit, was vitiated by the Fall, Augustine held, because it is one nature, human nature. . . . After the Fall, both the body and soul are 'carnal' because human loves are oriented away from God and toward the self."[51] From On the City of God, Book 14:

(1) I have already said, in previous Books, that God had two purposes in deriving the whole human race from one human being. His first purpose was to give unity to the human race by the likeness of nature. His second purpose was to bind humankind by the bond of peace, through blood relationship, into one harmonious whole. I have said further that no member of this race would ever have died had not the first two—one created from nothing and the second from the first—merited this death by disobedience. The sin which these two committed was so great that it impaired all human nature—in this sense: that the nature has been transmitted to posterity with a propensity to

---

50. *Civ. Dei* 10.29 (CCL 47:306–7); trans. Walsh and Monahan, FOTC 14:173–74 (modified).

51. Paula Fredriksen, "A Response to 'Vitiated Seeds and Holy Vessels' by Elizabeth A. Clark," in *Images of the Feminine in Gnosticism*, Studies in Antiquity and Christianity, ed. Karen L. King (Philadelphia: Fortress Press, 1988), 402–3. See also Brown, *Body and Society*, 418.

sin and a necessity to die. Moreover, the kingdom of death so dominated humankind that all would have been hurled, by a just punishment, into a second and endless death had not some been saved from this by the gratuitous grace of God. This is the reason why, for all the differences of the many and very great nations throughout the world in religion and morals, language, weapons, and dress, there exist no more than the two kinds of society, which, according to our Scriptures, we have rightly called the two cities. One city is that of human beings who live according to the flesh. The other is that of those who live according to the spirit. Each of them chooses its own kind of peace, and, when they attain what they desire, each lives in the peace of its own choosing.

(2) Our immediate task, then, must be to see what it means to live, first, according to the flesh and, second, according to the spirit. It would be a mistake for anyone to take what I have said at face value and without recalling or sufficiently considering the manner of speech used in Holy Scripture. . . . Scripture uses the word "flesh" not only in reference to the body of an earthly and mortal animal, but also to a person, that is, to human nature. . . .

(3) Should anyone say that the cause of vices and evil habits lies in the flesh because it is only when the soul is influenced by the flesh that it lives in such a manner, he cannot have sufficiently considered the entire scope of human nature. It is true that "the corruptible body is a load upon the soul" (Wis 9:15). . . . On the one hand, our corruptible body may be a burden on our soul; on the other hand, the cause of this encumbrance is not in the nature and substance of the body, and, therefore, aware as we are of its corruption, we do not desire to be divested of the body but rather to be clothed with its immortality. In immortal life we shall have a body, but it will no longer be a burden since it will no longer be corruptible. Now, however, "the corruptible body is a load upon the soul, and the earthly habitation presses down the mind that muses upon many things" (Wis 9:15). Yet it is an error to suppose that all the evils of the soul proceed from the body. . . . Our faith teaches something very different [from the Platonists]. For the corruption of the body, which is a burden on the soul, is not the cause, but the punishment of Adam's first sin. Moreover, it was not corruptible flesh that made the soul sinful; on the contrary, it was the sinful soul that made flesh corruptible. . . .

(5) We ought not, therefore, to blame our sins and defects on the nature of the flesh, for this is to disparage the Creator. The flesh, in its own kind and order, is good. But what is not good is to abandon the Goodness of the Creator in pursuit of some created good, whether by living deliberately according to the flesh, or according to the soul, or according to the entire person. . . . Anyone, then, who extols the nature of the soul as the highest good and con-

demns the nature of the flesh as evil is as carnal in this love for the soul as in this hatred for the flesh, for these thoughts flow from human vanity, not from divine truth. . . .

(6) The human will, then, is all-important. If it is badly directed, the emotions will be perverse; if it is rightly directed, the emotions will be not merely blameless but even praiseworthy. The will is in all of these affections; indeed, they are nothing else but the inclinations of the will. For what are desire and joy but the will in harmony with things we desire? And what are fear and sadness but the will in disagreement with things we abhor? The consent of the will in the search for what we want is called desire; joy is the name of the will's consent to the enjoyment of what we desire. So, too, fear is aversion from what we do not wish to happen, as sadness is a disagreement of the will with something that happened against our will. . . .

(7) Anyone who resolves to love God and to love his neighbor as himself, not in a purely human way but according to the will of God, may certainly, because of this love, be called a person of good will.[52]

UNFALLEN HUMANITY

Augustine was convinced that if one reflects only on human beings as we now experience them, one completely misunderstands human nature in its original God-given character, so dire have been the consequences of the Fall. If we want to reflect on what it really is to be human, we must therefore think about either our primeval beginnings or our ultimate end, that is, either about Adam and Eve before the Fall or about redeemed humanity on the far side of the Last Judgment. Only then can human nature, as God made it and intended it, be glimpsed. Thus in Book 14, Augustine reflects at length on Adam and Eve and speculates on what the world would have looked like if the Fall had not occurred. From On the City of God, *Book 14:*

(10) It is quite a different question, and one that deserves attention, whether, even before there was any sin, the first human being, or rather our first parents—since there was a marriage of two—experienced any of those passions in their animal body, from which we shall be free in our spiritual bodies, once all sin has been purged and brought to an end. If they did, how could they have been perfectly happy in that marvelous place called Paradise? . . . The love of our first parents for God was perfectly serene, and their mutual affection was that of a true and faithful married couple. And their love

---

52. *Civ. Dei* 14.1–7 (CCL 48:414–21); trans. Walsh and Monahan, FOTC 14:347–59.

brought them immense joy since the object of their love was always theirs to enjoy. There was a calm turning away from sin, which, so long as it lasted, kept evil of every other kind from saddening their lives. . . . Now, this happiness of our first parents, undisturbed by any passion and undiminished by any pain, is the measure of the happiness which the entire human race would have enjoyed if Adam and Eve had not been guilty of the evil which they have transmitted to posterity or if no one of their descendants had committed any wickedness worthy of damnation. And this happiness would have continued until, in virtue of God's blessing, "Be fruitful and multiply" (Gn 1:28), the number of elect had been completed; after which, another, even more perfect, happiness was to be given, like that which the blessed angels enjoy, a happiness which would have excluded even the possibility of sin or of death, so that the saints would have lived on earth exempt from all labor, pain, and death, just as will now be their lot to live only after all such things have been suffered and they shall be clothed with incorruptible bodies in the final resurrection. . . .

(26) Now the point about Eden was that a person lived there so long as he or she desired what God commanded. In Eden one lived enjoying God, drawing one's own goodness from God's goodness. One's life was free from want, having within one's powers life eternal. There were food and drink to keep away hunger and thirst, and the tree of life to stave off old age. There was not a sign or a seed of decay in the body that could be a source of any physical pain. No sickness assailed from within, and one feared no harm from the outside. One's body was perfectly healthy, and one's soul completely at peace. And as in Eden itself there was never a day too hot or too cold, so in Adam, who lived there, no fear or desire was ever so passionate as to worry his will. Of sorrows there was none at all, and of joys none that was vain, for a perpetual joy that was genuine flowed from the presence of God, because God was loved with a "charity from a pure heart and a good conscience and faith unfeigned" (1 Tm 1:5). Family affection was ensured by purity of love; body and mind worked in perfect accord; and there was an effortless observance of the law of God. Finally, neither leisure nor labor had ever to suffer from boredom or sloth.[53]

HONORABLE MARRIAGE IN PARADISE

Augustine has often been blamed for Western attitudes on sexuality. That blame is largely wrong-headed and misplaced. Moreover, as Robert Markus has insisted, "To understand

---

53. Civ. Dei 14.10–26 (CCL 48:430–49); trans. Walsh and Monahan, FOTC 14:373–406.

Augustine we need to disentangle what he was telling his contemporaries from that which he shared with them and questioned no more than did most of them. What we must listen to is the quiet debate between him and them, indeed a debate within his own mind, concerning the right attitude to take on questions on which his predecessors had already reflected deeply."[54] One of those shifts concerned sexuality. The early Augustine, like his Christian contemporaries, held that Adam and Eve had been created sexless, that, had they not sinned, sexual intercourse would have been unnecessary. But between 400 and 410, Augustine quietly revised these views, recording his new perspectives in his Literal Interpretation of Genesis. There he announced one sharp reversal: "I see no reason why there should not have been honorable marriage in paradise."[55] In Book 14 of On the City of God, Augustine speculates at length on unfallen sexuality and this "honorable marriage in paradise." As Markus notes, *"we need hardly underline the gulf that divides Augustine from, for instance, Jerome, or even Ambrose or the Cappadocian Fathers on the subject. . . . His change of view is remarkable, an impressive result of the independence of mind which enabled him to break from some of the deep-seated ideas current in his circle. . . . [H]e had come to assert that human sexuality was a part of man's created nature, not a result of its corruption through sin. Henceforth sexual existence was no longer a problem for Augustine. What had to be accounted for was no longer the existence of sex, but rather, now, its mode of functioning; and the effect of Adam's sin on the sexuality of his heirs."*[56] From On the City of God, Book 14:

(21) Unfortunately, there are some people today who know so little of the graces that were given in the Garden that they can imagine no other way of begetting children except by arousing that lust which they themselves have experienced, but which involves, as everyone knows, an element of shame even in the most high-minded marriages. There are other people who have no faith in the Scriptures and who simply laugh at the story that it was only after the fall into sin that Adam and Eve were ashamed of their nakedness and covered their shamed parts. A third class accepts and reveres the Scriptures but insists on giving an allegorical interpretation to the text: "Increase and multiply" (Gn 1:28). They say there is no more reference here to increase in population than there is in the words: "You increased strength in my soul" (Ps 137:3). So, too, with the rest of the text in Genesis: "and fill the earth and subdue it" (Gn 1:28). On the theory of spiritual interpretation, they take "earth" to mean the body which is "filled" by the presence of the soul and which is most perfectly "subdued" when the soul is increased in virtue. They also hold that birth could no more take place then than now without that pas-

54. Robert A. Markus, *The End of Ancient Christianity* (Cambridge: Cambridge University Press, 1990), 59.
55. Gn. litt. 9.3.6 (BA 49:96).
56. Markus, *The End of Ancient Christianity*, 59–60.

sion which, as soon as it began with the Fall, made Adam and Eve so self-conscious, so confused, and so eager for concealment. In any case, they say, there would never have been any intercourse in the Garden but only outside, as, in fact, turned out to be the case, since it was only after the expulsion that children were conceived and born.

(22) For ourselves, we do not have the slightest doubt that to "increase and multiply and fill the earth" in obedience to the blessing and command of God is the very mission which God gave to marriage as He instituted it from the beginning and, so, before the Fall. That is why He made the bodies of the two sexes, male and female, so clearly different. And it was precisely on the conjugal duty itself that God's blessing was handed down, for as soon as Scripture notes, "Male and female He created them," the text continues: "And God blessed them, saying: Increase and multiply and fill the earth and subdue it" (Gn 1:27–28), and so on. True—much of what is here said is susceptible of a spiritual interpretation, but it makes no sense to say that "male" and "female" are allegories of two qualities in a single person: that, for example, "male" stands for the part that rules and "female" for the part that is ruled. The simple truth is—as is luminously clear from the bodies of the different sexes—that males and females were made as they were for the purposes of increasing and multiplying and filling the earth by becoming fathers and mothers. To deny this would be utterly absurd. . . . It is, therefore, certain that male and female were created in the beginning exactly as we see and know them now, as human beings of different sexes. If the two are spoken of as "one," that is explained either by their unity in marriage or by the fact that the first woman was made from the side of the man. To confirm this we have the Apostle appealing to this first marriage as a model, as the marriage instituted by God from the beginning, when he calls upon the husbands in every family to love their wives.

(23) The view that there could have been no procreation in Paradise if there had been no sin amounts to this: that humankind had to sin to fill up the number of the saints [in the City of God]. The argument runs: If no sin, then no procreation; but if no procreation, only two saints; but more than two saints were necessary; therefore, sin was necessary. Now this conclusion is an absurdity. Hence, we must believe that the number of saints required to populate the city of the blessed would have been brought into existence even if no one had sinned, and this number equals the number of those who, as things are now, continue to be gathered by God's grace from the multitude of sinners and will continue to be gathered so long as there are parents and babies among the children of this world. We conclude, therefore, that even if there had been no sin in the Garden, there would still have been marriag-

es worthy of that blessed place, and that lovely babies would have flowered from a love untainted by lust. Unfortunately, to show just how that could be we have no present experience to help us.[57]

ORIGINAL SIN

For Augustine, the problem was the will, not the body. He came to define original sin as narcissism, the turning-in of the will "to live according to oneself" (secundum se vivere). Here is his classic account from On the City of God, *Book 14:*

(13) Moreover, our first parents fell openly into the sin of disobedience only because, secretly, they had begun to be guilty. Actually, their bad deed could not have been done had not bad will preceded it. What is more, the root of their bad will was nothing else than pride. For "pride is the beginning of all sin" (Sir 10:13). And what is pride but an appetite for inordinate exaltation? Now exaltation is inordinate when the soul cuts itself off from the very Source to which it should keep close and somehow makes itself—and thus becomes—an end in itself. This takes place when the soul becomes inordinately pleased with itself, and such self-pleasing occurs when the soul falls away from the unchangeable Good which ought to please the soul far more than the soul can please itself. Now this falling away is the soul's own doing, for if the will had merely remained firm in the love of that higher immutable Good which lighted its mind into knowledge and warmed its will into love, it would not have turned away in search of satisfaction in itself and, by so doing, have lost that light and warmth. And thus Eve would not have believed that the serpent's lie was true, nor would Adam have preferred the will of his wife to the will of God nor have supposed that his transgression of God's command was venial when he refused to abandon the partner of his life even if it meant a partnership of sin.

Our first parents, then, must already have fallen before they could do the evil deed, before they could commit the sin of eating the forbidden fruit. For such bad fruit could come only from a bad tree. That the tree became bad was contrary to its nature, because such a condition could come about only by a defect of the will—and a defect is whatever goes against nature. Notice, however, that such worsening by reason of a defect is possible only in a nature that had been created out of nothing. In a word, a nature is a nature because

57. *Civ. Dei* 14.21–23 (CCL 48:443–45); trans. Walsh and Monahan, FOTC 14:396–99. On the broader context of Augustine's meditation here, see David G. Hunter, *Marriage, Celibacy, and Heresy in Ancient Christianity: The Jovinianist Controversy*, OECS (New York: Oxford University Press, 2007).

it is something made by God, but a nature falls away from That Which Is because the nature was made out of nothing.

Yet the human person did not fall away from Being so that he completely disintegrated into non-being. But insofar as he turned himself toward himself, he became less than he was when he used to cling to the One who is supreme Being. Thus, no longer to exist in God but to exist in oneself is to approach nothingness. For this reason, Holy Scripture gives another name to the proud. They are called "rash" and "self-willed" (2 Pt 2:10). Certainly, it is good for the heart to be lifted up, not to oneself (for this is the mark of pride), but to God (for this is a sign of obedience which is precisely the virtue of the humble).

There is, then, a kind of lowliness which in some wonderful ways causes the heart to be lifted up, and there is a kind of loftiness which makes the heart sink lower. This seems to be a sort of paradox, that loftiness should make something lower and lowliness lift something up. The reason for this is that holy lowliness makes us bow to what is above us, and, since there is nothing above God, the kind of lowliness that makes us close to God exalts us. On the other hand, the kind of loftiness that is both defective and a defection refuses this subjection to God and so falls down from the One who is supreme, as Scripture says, that "when they were lifting themselves up you cast them down" (Ps 72:18). Here the Psalmist does not say: "When they had been lifted up," as though they first lifted themselves up and afterwards were cast down, but: "when they are lifting themselves up, at that moment they were cast down," which means that their very lifting themselves up was itself a fall.

Hence, humility is the virtue especially esteemed in the City of God and thus recommended to its citizens in their present pilgrimage on earth, precisely because it is particularly outstanding in Christ its King; just so, pride, the vice contrary to this virtue, is, as Holy Scripture tells us, especially dominant in Christ's adversary, the devil. In fact, this is the main difference which distinguishes the two cities we are speaking of. The humble City is the society of holy human beings and good angels; the proud city is the society of wicked human beings and evil angels. The one City began with the love of God; the other had its beginning in the love of self.

The conclusion, then, is that the devil would not have begun by an open and obvious sin to tempt humanity into doing something which God had forbidden, had not humanity already begun to seek satisfaction in itself and, consequently, to take pleasure in the words: "You shall be as gods" (Gn 3:5). The promise of these words, however, would much more truly have come to pass if, by obedience, Adam and Eve had kept close to the ultimate and true Source of their being and had not, by pride, imagined that they were themselves the source of their being. For created gods are gods not in virtue of their own being but by a participation in the being of the true God.[58]

Thus, there is a wickedness by which a human being, who is self-satisfied as if he were the light, turns himself away from that true Light which, had humanity loved it, would have made us a sharer in the Light; it was this wickedness which secretly preceded and was the cause of the bad act which was committed openly.[59]

THE DIVIDED SELF: HOW THE PUNISHMENT FITS THE CRIME

Augustine argues that the sin of disobedience shaped God's punishment: As we had once disobeyed God, so our wills and our bodies now disobey us. We desire eternal life, but our bodies disobey us by corrupting and dying, while our wills disobey us by our out-of-control desires (evident in sexuality as well as our routine anxieties). From On the City of God, Book 14:

(15) For many reasons, then, the punishment meted out for disobeying God's order was just. It was God who had created humanity. He had made human beings to His own image, set them above all other animals, placed them in Paradise, and gave them an abundance of goods and well-being. God had not burdened them with many precepts that were heavy and hard, but had propped them up with a single precept that was momentary and utterly easy and that was meant merely as a medicine to make human obedience strong, and as a reminder that it was good for one who is a creature to give service freely to God who is our Master.

This just punishment involved many consequences. Humanity, which would have become spiritual even in its flesh—if only it had kept the commandment—became, instead, fleshly even in its soul. [Adam] who, by human pride, had had his own way was, by divine justice, abandoned to his own resources—not, that is, to power but to weakness. The very self that had once been obeyed now became, once he had sinned, a tyrant to torment and, in place of the liberty he longed for, he had to live in the misery of servitude. He had chosen freely the death of his soul; he was now condemned, unwillingly, to the death of this body. He had been a deserter from eternal life; he

---

58. "Participation in the being of the true God": Here is one side of Augustine's doctrine of deification. He plays here off the serpent's temptation ("You shall be as gods," Gn 3:5) to distinguish between a false deifying of self (i.e., pride) and true deification ("participation" in the "being of God" as a fruit of obedience). For more on this issue, see the sources cited above in n. 31.

59. *Civ. Dei* 14.13 (CCL 48:434–35); trans. Walsh and Monahan, FOTC 14:380–83.

was now doomed to eternal death, from which nothing could save him but grace. . . .

Actually, in the punishment for that sin the only penalty for disobedience was, to put it in a single word, more disobedience. There is nothing else that now makes a person more miserable than his own disobedience to himself. Because he would not do what he could have, he can no longer do what he should. It is true that even in the Garden, before sinning, he could not do everything; but he could still do all he desired to do, since he had no desire to do what he could not do. It is different now. As Scripture says, "Human beings are like a breath of air" (Ps 143:4). That is what we see in Adam's progeny. In too many ways to mention, we cannot do what we desire to do, for the simple reason that our very self refuses to obey us; that is to say, neither the self nor even the body obeys the will. For in spite of the will, the self is frequently troubled and the body feels pain, grows old, and dies. Now if only our nature, wholly and in all its parts, would obey our will, we would not have to suffer these and all our other ills so unwillingly.[60]

POLITICS AND THE EARTHLY CITY (BOOK 19)

TORTURE AND TRUTH

Book 19 is perhaps the most studied book of On the City of God. In it, Augustine meditates on political realities within human cities, on the anguishing and often dangerous compromises that their politics require, their often subtle power plays and brutal mechanisms of repression. How, given the social nature of human beings, can one really find happiness and truth and justice? Augustine catalogs the anxious instabilities and everyday betrayals within even the best of human relationships, that is, within families and among friends. He goes on to think about the run-of-the-mill violence that plagues even the best cities, and so examines the Roman judicial system that claimed to punish criminals and dispense justice. He notes how ancient judges routinely had both the accused and the witnesses tortured to extract the truth. For Augustine, this serves as a sort of brutal parable of life in the earthly city. From On the City of God, Book 19:

---

60. Civ. Dei 14.15 (CCL 48:436–37); trans. Walsh and Monahan, FOTC 14:385–86. See also Gn. litt. 9.11.19; pecc. mer. 1.16.21.

(6) Even when a city is enjoying the profoundest peace, some people must sit in judgment on fellow citizens. Even at their best, what misery and grief they cause! No human judge can read the consciences of those before him. That is why so many innocent witnesses are tortured, to find what truth there is in the alleged guilt of others. It is even worse when the accused himself is tortured to find out if he be guilty. Here someone still unconvicted must undergo certain suffering for an uncertain crime—not because his guilt is known, but because his innocence is unproven. Thus it often happens that the ignorance of the judge turns into tragedy for the innocent party. There is something still more insufferable, deplorable beyond all cleansing with our tears. Often enough, when a judge tries to avoid putting someone to death whose innocence is not manifest, he has him put to torture, and so it happens, because of woeful lack of evidence, that he both tortures and kills someone blameless whom he tortured lest he kill him without just cause. And if, on Stoic principles, the innocent man chooses to escape from life rather than endure such torture any longer, he will confess to a crime he never committed. And when it is all over, the judge will still be in the dark whether the man he put to death was guilty or not guilty, even though he tortured him to save his innocent life, and then condemned him to death. Thus, to gather evidence, he tortures an innocent man, and, lacking evidence, kills him.

Such being the effect of human ignorance even in judicial procedure, will any philosopher-judge dare to take his place on the bench? You may be sure, he will. He would think it very wrong indeed to withdraw from his bounden duty to society. But that the innocent should be tortured as witnesses in trials not their own; that the accused should be so overcome by pain as falsely to plead guilty and then die, as they were tortured, in innocence; that many should die as a result of or during their torturings, prior to any verdict at all—in all this our philosopher-judge will condemn to death, as sometimes happens, ones who had nothing but the good of society at heart. To prevent crimes from going unpunished, people go to court; but the witnesses lie and the guilty party holds out inhumanly under the torture and makes no confession; the accusation, in spite of the facts, is not sustained, and it is the accuser who is condemned. No, our philosopher-judge does not reckon such abuses as burdens on his conscience because he has no intention of doing harm. Often, he would say, he cannot get at the truth, yet the good of society demands he hand down decisions. My only point is that, as a man, surely his cannot be the "happy life" even though his philosophy may save him from a sense of wrongdoing. Granted his ignorance and his office are to blame for the torture and death of the innocent, is it any consolation to feel free of the responsibility? Is he really happy? Surely it would be more compassionate and more worthy of human dignity, if he acknowledged this necessity is wretch-ed, if he hated his role in it, and, if he is godly, in crying out to God: "Deliver me from my necessities" (Ps 24:17).[61]

WAR AND PEACE

Augustine has been called the architect of "just war" theory. This is not really accurate. His reflections were but one touchstone for the medieval theorists who actually formulated the theory.[62] Herbert Deane once summarized Augustine's views this way: "In none of Augustine's writings on the subject of war can we find a trace of militarism or of glorification of the struggles that states and groups wage against each other with so much ferocity. Almost every one of his references to civil or international war is bitterly sorrowful; he always remembers the suffering and misery that war brings in its wake, especially for its innocent victims. . . . His own experiences and the age of plundering and slaughter in which he lived left him with a deep hatred of war and a great scorn for those who thought that conquest and military victories were glorious and noble accomplishments."[63] The following passage comes after Augustine's reflections on the diversity of language and the divisions that this causes; he reflects here on the violence that underlay the now peaceful channels of communication that the peace of the Roman Empire made possible. From On the City of God, Book 19:

(7) It will be answered that the Roman Empire, in the interests of peace-ful collaboration, imposes on nations it has conquered the yoke of both law and language, and thus has an adequate, or even an overflowing, abundance of interpreters. True enough. But at what cost! There is one war after another, havoc everywhere, tremendous slaughterings of human beings. All this for peace. Yet when the wars are waged, there are new calamities brewing. To be-gin with, there never has been, nor is there today, any absence of hostile for-eign powers to provoke war. What is worse, the very development of the Em-pire accruing from their incorporation has begotten still worse wars within. I refer to the civil wars and social uprisings that involve even more wretched anxieties for human beings, either shaken by their actual impact or living in fear of their renewal. Massacres, frequent and sweeping, hardships too dire

61. *Civ. Dei* 19.6 (CCL 48:670–71); trans. Walsh and Honan, FOTC 24:204–5.

62. On Augustine's influence on medieval theorists, see Jonathan Barnes, "The Just War," in Norman Kretzmann, Anthony Kenny, and Jan Pinborg, eds., *The Cambridge History of Late Medieval Philosophy* (Cambridge: Cambridge University Press, 1982), 771–84. For an overview of Augustine's own views, see Robert A. Markus, "Saint Augustine's Views on the 'Just War,'" *Studies in Church History* 20 (1983): 1–13; reprinted in *Sacred and Secular: Studies on Augustine and Latin Christianity* (London: Variorum, 1994).

63. Herbert Deane, *The Political and Social Ideas of St. Augustine* (New York: Columbia University Press, 1963), 154.

to endure, are but a part of the ravages of war. I am utterly unable to describe; and even if I should try to begin, where could I end? I know the objection that a good ruler will wage wars only if they are just. But surely if he will only remember that he is a human being, he will begin by bewailing the necessity he is under of waging even just wars. A good person would be under compulsion to wage no wars at all, if there were not such things as just wars. A just war, moreover, is justified only by the injustice of an aggressor; and that injustice ought to be a source of grief to anyone good, because it is human injustice. It would be deplorable in itself, apart from being a source of conflict. Anyone who considers sorrowfully evils so great, such horrors and such savagery, will admit a deep sense of misery. And if there is anyone who can endure such calamities, or even contemplate them without feeling grief, that person's condition is all the more wretched for that. For it is only the loss of all humane feeling that could make anyone call such a life "the happy life."[64]

REDEFINING CIVIL SOCIETY

While City of God is not, technically speaking, a work of political theory, it does take up those issues at key points. In the following passage, Augustine famously returns to his discussion in Book 2 (cited above) about whether or not Rome was truly a republic. He returns to Cicero's definition (placed in the mouth of Scipio) and argues that, if one takes it seriously, Rome was never really a "commonwealth" and never really a "republic" because it lacked justice. Augustine goes on to redefine civil society as an association of people bound by common values ("loves" is Augustine's word). From On the City of God, *Book 19:*

(21) I have arrived at the point where, as I promised in the second book of this work, I will prove, as briefly and clearly as I can, that if we accept the definitions of Scipio (as cited by Cicero in his book *On the Republic*), there never existed any such thing as a Roman Republic.[65] Scipio gives a short definition of a commonwealth as "the wealth and welfare of the people." Now, if this is a true definition, there never was any republic because there never was in Rome any true "wealth and welfare of the people."[66] Scipio defines the "people" as a "multitude bound together by a mutual recognition of rights and a mutual co-operation for the common good." As the discussion progresses, he explains what he means by "mutual recognition of rights," going on to show that a republic cannot be managed without justice, for where there is no

64. *Civ. Dei* 19.7 (CCL 48:671–72); trans. Walsh and Honan, FOTC 24:206–7.
65. "As I promised in the second book": Here Augustine returns to *civ. Dei.* 2.19–22, cited earlier.
66. Cicero, *De re publica* 1.25.

true justice, there is no recognition of rights. For what is rightly done is justly done; what is done unjustly cannot be done by right. We are not to reckon as right such human laws as are iniquitous, since even unjust lawgivers themselves call "a right" (jus) only what derives from the fountainhead of justice, and [we must] brand as false the wrong-headed opinion of those who keep saying that "a right" is "whatever is advantageous to the one in power."

It follows that wherever true justice is lacking, there cannot be a multitude of human beings bound together by a mutual recognition of rights; consequently, neither can there be a "people" in the sense of Scipio's or Cicero's definition. Further, if there is no "people," there is no "wealth and welfare of the people," or commonwealth, but only the wealth and welfare of a nondescript mob undeserving of the designation "the people." To resume the argument: If a commonwealth is "the wealth and welfare of the people," and if there is no people where there is no union "bound together by a mutual recognition of rights," and if there are no rights where there is no justice, it follows beyond question that where there is no justice, there is no commonwealth. Now justice is the virtue which accords to each and every one his due.[67] What, then, shall we say of a person's "justice" when that person takes himself away from the true God and hands himself over to dirty demons? Is this a giving to each his due? Now we would consider it unjust if someone takes away a farm from its purchaser and hands it over to someone who has no claim upon it. How then can someone who removes himself from the overlordship of the God who created him and goes into the service of wicked spirits be counted just?

To be sure, in [Cicero's] *Republic*, there is a hard-fought and powerful debate in favor of justice over against injustice. First, the side of injustice was taken. At that point it was claimed that only by injustice could the republic stand firm and be efficiently managed. And this was put forward as the most telling proof: that it is unjust that some human beings should have to serve others as masters; that, nevertheless, the capital of the Empire to which the commonwealth belongs must practice such injustice or surrender her provinces. Then the side of justice made the following rebuttal: that such procedure is, in fact, just because such submission is advantageous to the men in question, that it is for their own good when such sovereignty is properly managed, that is, when the lawless marauding of criminals is repressed and order is established. Conquered peoples thereafter are better off than they were in liberty. Next, to bolster this reasoning, a new argument was brought forward in the form of an admirable example taken, so they said, from nature itself:

---

67. Aristotle, *Nicomachean Ethics* 5.5. Cf. *De libero arbitrio* 1.13.27 (CCL 29:228).

"Why, otherwise, does God have mastery over humankind, the mind over the body, reason over lust and the other wrongful movements of the soul?" Surely, now, this example teaches plainly enough for anyone that it is for the good of some to be in an inferior position, and that it is good for all without exception to be subject to God. The soul that is submissive to God justly lords it over the body; in the soul itself, reason, bowing down before its Lord and God, justly lords it over lust and every other evil tendency. Because this is so, what fragment of justice can there be in a human being who is not subject to God, if, indeed, it is a fact that such a one cannot rightfully exercise dominion—soul over body, human reason over sinful propensities? And if there is no justice, either, in an assembly made up of such people? As a result, there is lacking that mutual recognition of rights which makes a mere mob into a "people," a people whose common welfare is a commonwealth. What shall I say of the common good whose common pursuit knits human beings together into a "people," as our definition teaches? Careful scrutiny will show that there is no such good for those who live irreligiously, as all do who serve not God but demons and, particularly, those filthy spirits that are so defiant of God that they look to receive sacrifices as if they were gods. Anyway, what I have said with regard to mutual recognition of rights I consider sufficient to show that, on the basis of the definition itself, a people devoid of justice is not such a people as can constitute a commonwealth. . . .

(23) To sum up: Where the civil community does not take its orders from the one supreme God and carry them out with the help of His grace; where sacrifice is offered to something other than God alone; where, as a result, the civil community is such that not everyone obeys God in this respect; where the soul does not control the body; where reason does not control our evil urges as proper order and faith require; where neither individuals nor the whole community, "the people," live by that faith of the just who do good works through love (Gal 5:6), loving God as He should be loved and one's neighbor as oneself—in other words, wherever justice is lacking, I maintain—there does not exist "a multitude bound together by a mutual recognition of rights and a mutual co-operation for the common good." This being so, there is no proper "people"—if Scipio's definition is correct—nor a commonwealth. For where there is no "people," there is no "people's" wealth or welfare.

(24) It is possible to define a "people" not as Cicero does, but as "a multitude of reasonable beings voluntarily associated in the pursuit of common interests which they love." In that case, one need only consider what these interests are in order to determine of what kind any particular people may be. Still, whatever these interests are, so long as we have a multitude of rational

beings—and not irresponsible cattle—who are voluntarily associated in the pursuit of common interests, we can reasonably call them a "people," and they will be a people, for better or worse, according to the interests, whether better or worse, which have brought them together.

This definition certainly makes the Roman people a "people" and their wealth and welfare a "commonwealth" or "republic." We know, however, from history what kind of interest this people had, both in primitive times and more recently, and also what kind of morals brought on the rupture and corruption of their voluntary association (which is the health, so to speak, of any community), first, by bloody seditions, and later, by social and civil war. On this subject, I had a good deal to say earlier in this work. I would, however, still call the Romans a "people" and their affairs a "commonwealth," so long as they remain a multitude of reasonable beings voluntarily associated in the pursuit of common interests. Of course, what I have said of the Romans and their Republic applies not less to the Athenians and other Greek communities, to the Egyptians, to the early Assyrians of Babylonia, and, in general, to any other pagan people whose government exercised real political control, however much or little. The fact is that any civil community made up of pagans who are disobedient to God's command that He alone receive sacrifices, and who, therefore, are devoid of the rational and religious control of soul over body and of reason over sinful appetites, must be lacking in true justice.[68]

THE PEACE OF BABYLON

In Book 19, Augustine meditates on peace and sketches what peace looks like here in the earthly city to those whose citizenship belongs to the City of God. Augustine neither sacralized nor demonized the Roman Empire. He saw it—and all earthly kingdoms—as venues where, at best, the citizens of the two cities worked toward their distinct ends and yet shared a common concern for peace. This passage is one of the climaxes of the entire work, setting out how Christians fit into the saeculum, the world. From On the City of God, *Book 19:*

(17) While the households of people who live without faith are intent upon acquiring temporal peace for the possessions and comforts of this temporal life, the families who live according to faith look ahead to the good things of heaven promised as imperishable and use material and temporal goods in the

68. *Civ. Dei* 19.21–24 (CCL 48:687–96); trans. Walsh and Honan, FOTC 24:232–44 (modified). On this passage, see Oliver O'Donovan, "Augustine's *City of God* XIX and Western Political Thought," *Dionysius* 11 (1987): 89–110; also Mikka Ruokanen, *Theology of Social Life in Augustine's De Civitate Dei*, Forschungen zur Kirchen- und Dogmengeschichte 53 (Göttingen: Vandenhoeck & Ruprecht, 1993), 96–131.

spirit of pilgrims, not as snares or obstructions to block their way to God, but simply as helps to ease and never to increase the burdens of this corruptible body which weighs down the soul. Both types of homes and their homeowners have this in common: that they must use things essential to this mortal life. But the respective purposes to which they put them are very different and unique to their character. So, too, the earthly city which does not live by faith seeks only an earthly peace, of its harmony of authority and obedience among its citizens, for the sake of the voluntary and collective attainment of objectives necessary to mortal existence. The heavenly City, meanwhile—or, rather, that part that is on pilgrimage in mortal life and lives by faith—must use this earthly peace until such time as our mortality, which needs such peace, has passed away. As a consequence, so long as her life in the earthly city is that of a captive and an alien (although she has the promise of ultimate delivery and the gift of the Spirit as a pledge), she has no hesitation about keeping in step with the civil law, which governs matters pertaining to our existence here below. For as mortal life is the same for all, there ought to be common cause between the two cities in what concerns our purely human living. . . .

So long, then, as the heavenly City is wayfaring on earth, she invites citizens from all nations and all tongues, and unites them into a single pilgrim band. She takes no issue with that diversity of customs, laws, and traditions whereby human peace is sought and maintained. Instead of nullifying or tearing down, she preserves and appropriates whatever in the diversities of diverse races is aimed at one and the same objective of human peace, provided only that it does not stand in the way of the faith and worship of the one supreme and true God. Thus, the heavenly City, so long as it is wayfaring on earth, not only makes use of earthly peace but fosters and actively pursues, along with other human beings, a common platform in regard to all that concerns our purely human life and does not interfere with faith and worship. Of course, though, the City of God subordinates this earthly peace to that of heaven. For this is not merely true peace, but, strictly speaking, for any rational creature, the only real peace, since it is, as I said, the perfectly ordered and harmonious communion of those who find their joy in God and in one another in God. When this peace is reached, we will be no longer haunted by death, but plainly and perpetually endowed with life; nor will the body, which now wastes away and weighs down the soul, be any longer animal, but spiritual, in need of nothing, and completely under the control of our will. This peace the pilgrim City already possesses by faith, and it lives justly and according to this faith so long as, to attain its heavenly completion, it refers every good act done for God or—since community life must emphasize social relationships—for one's neighbor. . . .

(26) Meanwhile, it is to our advantage that there be such peace in this life. For as long as the two cities are mingled together, we can make use of the peace of Babylon, but our pilgrim status, for the time being, makes us neighbors. All of this was in St. Paul's mind when he advised the Church to pray for this world's kings and high authorities in order that "we may lead a quiet and peaceful life in all piety and worthy behavior" (1 Tm 2:2). Jeremiah, too, predicting the Babylonian captivity to the ancient People of God, gave them orders from God to go submissively and serve their God by such sufferings and meanwhile to pray for Babylon. "For in its peace," he said, "shall be your peace" (Jer 29:7)—referring, of course, to the peace of this world which the good and bad share in common.

(27) The City of God, however, has a peace of its own, namely, peace with God in this world by faith, and in the world to come, by sight (2 Cor 5:7). Still, any peace we have on earth, whether the peace we share with Babylon or our own peace through faith, is more like a solace for unhappiness than the joy of beatitude.[69]

※

THE HEAVENLY CITY (BOOK 22)

Our Faith Praises the Body

The final book of On the City of God focuses on heaven and especially on the resurrection of the body. In his ordinary sermons, Augustine offered simplified versions of ideas that appear at length in erudite works such as On the City of God. One year, during Easter Week, Augustine gave a lecture series on the resurrection of the body (Sermons 240–242), covering topics that parallel those in Book 22. His concern, as he notes, was not only to bolster his congregation's faith but to equip them to get out into city squares and evangelize educated pagans. In this passage, he spells out the centrality of the doctrine of the resurrection. From Sermon 241:

(1) The belief in the resurrection is the distinctive belief of Christians. Christ our Head in his own person revealed this to us, that is, the resurrection of the dead, and He furnished us an example of this belief, so that His members might hope for themselves in regard to that which had already happened to their Head. Yesterday I informed you that wise men of the pagans whom they call "philosophers," and who were outstanding among their own people, had made a thorough investigation of nature and had come to know the Creator from His works. . . .

---

69. *Civ. Dei* 19.17–27 (CCL 48:683–97); trans. Walsh and Honan, FOTC 24:226–29 (modified).

(6) You who are a philosopher here, that is, on this earth (for the sake of a name, I mention Pythagoras, Plato, Porphyry, or some other of the philosophers), why do you philosophize? He answers: "Because of the happy life." And when will you possess that happy life? He replies: "When I shall have abandoned this body on earth.". . .

(7) Porphyry, a later but important member of that group of philosophers, one who lived in the Christian era, was a bitter enemy of the Christian faith.[70] Although through shame he abjured his mad ravings to a certain extent, yet, when censured by the Christians, he said and wrote: "Every kind of body must be avoided." He said "every kind of body" as if every body were a wretched prison of the soul. And certainly, if we must escape from every kind of body, there is no opportunity for one to praise that body to him and to say that, according to the teaching of God, our faith praises the body, because, although we draw punishment from sin from the body which we now possess, and although "the corruptible body is a load upon the soul" (Wis 9:15), nevertheless, the body has its own beauty, its own arrangement of members, its differentiation of senses, its erect posture, and other qualities which evoke admiration from those considering it. Furthermore, it is destined to be completely incorruptible, completely immortal, completely agile and quick in movement. Porphyry, however, says: "You praise the body to me without good reason. No matter what kind of body it is, you must escape from it if you wish to be happy." Philosophers say this, but they are wrong; they are raving.[71]

PAGAN OBJECTIONS TO THE RESURRECTION OF THE BODY

Augustine, both in this sermon series and again in On the City of God, lists pagan arguments against the core Christian doctrine of the resurrection. Many were stock objections cited and replied to by the earlier apologists Athenagoras and Origen.[72] Like them, Augustine cites objections (the issues raised by miscarriages, deformities, and cannibalism) posed by Platonists who held that eternal life meant only a disembodied soul. From On the City of God, Book 22:

70. On Porphyry, see note 45 above. Here Augustine quotes Porphyry's lost *On the Return of the Soul*, a work he also discusses in *civ. Dei* 10.29 and 22.26.

71. S. 241.1–7 (PL 38:1136–37); trans. Muldowney, FOTC 38:255–62 (modified). See Pierre Courcelle, "Propos antichrétiens rapportés par S. Augustin," *Recherches augustiniennes* 1 (1958): 149–86.

72. See, for example, Athenagoras, *De resurrectione* 8.4, and Origen, *De principiis* 1.6.4 and *Contra Celsum* 5.18. For a selection of texts, see Joanne E. McWilliam Dewart, *Death and Resurrection*, Message of the Fathers of the Church 22 (Wilmington: Michael Glazier, 1986). For an analysis, see Brian Daley, *Hope of the Early Church: A Handbook of Patristic Eschatology* (Cambridge: Cambridge University Press, 1991); on Augustine, pp. 131–50.

(12) Under the pretense of scrupulous inquiry, the pagans have a trick of ridiculing the belief in the resurrection of the body. Thus they will ask with mock seriousness: Do miscarried fetuses share in this resurrection? And taking a cue from our Lord's words, "Not a hair of your head shall perish" (Lk 21:18), they ask whether strength and stature of body are to be the same for all or different. For if all bodies are to be the same, and if miscarriages are to be resurrected, where will they get the stature they lacked on earth? And even if miscarriages are not to rise inasmuch as they were not really born, the same difficulty arises in regard to small children. How are they to make up the full measure of stature which they lack by reason of dying in childhood? (And, of course, Christians will not deny the resurrection of children who were not merely born but reborn in baptism.) How, then, can equality of stature be achieved? If all are to have the stature of the tallest and broadest specimens of humanity, then not merely children but many besides will have to make up for what they lacked on earth; and, it will be asked, how can this be possible if each of us is to have the stature he had on earth? . . .

And the matter of hair may be urged: Will all the hair cut off by the barbers be restored? And if it is, is there anyone who will not dread such a deformity? And then there are the fingernails that have been clipped. Must not everything be restored that was sacrificed to personal appearance? And, then, where will be the physical beauty which, in immortal life, should be greater than in this corruptible life? And if the fingernails are not to be restored, they will have perished. How, then, can it be true that not a hair of the head is to perish? And as with stature, so with skinniness and plumpness. If we are all to be the same, then there can be no one who is thinner or fatter than others. Some then must be reduced and some must put on flesh. Hence, not all can be as they were on earth. Some must gain and some must lose.

Then there is the serious and perplexing problem of physical disintegration after death. Some parts of the body turn to dust and other parts are exhaled off into the air. Some bodies are devoured by wild beasts and others are consumed by fire. Some perish by shipwreck and others are drowned, and such bodies rot and dissolve into liquid. Many who reflect on such facts refuse to believe that all these elements will be reintegrated into the original bodies. The pagans like to recall the blotches and blemishes that occur at birth or later, all the human monstrosities that are born, and then mockingly ask: "What kind of resurrection will there be in cases like these?" If we say that no such blotches are to reappear, they will confound us by boldly asking: "What did we hear you say of the place of the wounds with which the Lord Christ rose from the dead?"

In the whole matter, there is one very difficult problem that can be proposed. Supposing a starving man eats the body of a fellow man, whose body will belong to whom in the resurrection?[73] It became the flesh of the starving man who fed upon it, as was clear when his emaciated frame became filled out. This case is often used not only to make fun of our faith in the resurrection, but also to bolster either the Platonic theory of human souls alternately living in real miseries and imaginary blessedness, or the Porphyrian idea that the soul transmigrates from body to body, but finally, after many vicissitudes, ends all miseries, never to return to them. Of course, in Porphyry's view there was no question of an immortal body, but only of a disembodied spirit.

(13) Such, then, in summary, are the objections to our faith in the resurrection. With God's grace aiding my efforts, I shall reply to them.[74]

GOD THE ARTIST

The heart of Augustine's reply is that God's approach will be like that of a master artist. In Augustine's view, a God who could create the world from nothing could remake the world he had made—and remake it more gloriously than it was originally. From On the City of God, *Book 22:*

(19) I still think that nothing that is a natural part of the human body will be lost. As for deformities—which have the purpose of reminding us of the penal conditions of mortal life—they will be so integrated into the substance of the whole that no deformity will appear in any part. After all, if a human artist happens to make a flawed statue, he can always recast it and restore its beauty without losing any material. If there happens to be something out of proportion in that original figure, or something that does not fit in with the rest, he does not have to chisel it off or separate it off from the matter. Instead, he simply melts the whole thing down and remolds the same mass of material so as to remove the ugly defect and not lose any of the substance. So what are we to think about an omnipotent Artist? Can He not eliminate any deformity in the human body, not only normal ones, but especially those that are rare and monstrous, which may be congruent with the miseries of this life but not with that future happiness enjoyed by the saints? . . . Therefore, let those who, on earth, are too thin or too fat take comfort. They would not choose to be that way now if they could avoid it. They will certainly not be that way in eternity. For what makes a human body beautiful is its harmoni-

---

73. The issue of cannibalism, while meant as a mocking objection by pagans, may well have been a real issue. Jerome reports in *ep.* 127.12 that during Alaric's siege, incidents of cannibalism took place.

74. *Civ. Dei* 22.12-13 (CCL 48:832–33); trans. Walsh and Honan, FOTC 24:457–60 (modified).

ous contours combined with a pleasing color. Now this harmony is lacking whenever some part or other of the body is ugly in itself or is disproportionate with the rest. All ugliness arising from any lack of harmony, however, will disappear in that age. There every deformity will be corrected, and every less-than-fitting element will be readjusted as God-knows-how from what is supplied, and every larger-than-fitting element will be removed without altering the integrity of the body as a whole.[75]

WOMEN AND THE RESURRECTION OF THE BODY

A widespread view in antiquity was that only men were fully human, that women were "misbegotten men," as Aristotle would put it. Thus certain Christians had speculated that the saved would all be raised as men. Augustine strongly disagreed. His principle was based, in part, on his reading of Genesis: as in the beginning, so in the end. From On the City of God, Book 22:

(17) There are some who think that in the resurrection all will be men, and that women will lose their sex. This view springs from an interpretation of the texts: "Until we all attain . . . to perfect manhood, to the mature measure of the fullness of Christ" (Eph 4:13) and "conformed to the image of the Son of God" (Rom 8:29). The interpretation is based on the fact that the man alone was made by God out of the "slime of the earth," whereas the woman was made from the man. For myself, I think that those others are more sensible who have no doubt that both sexes will remain in the resurrection. After all, there will then be none of that lust which is the cause of shame in connection with sex, and so all will be as before the first sin, when the man and the woman were naked and felt no shame (Gn 2:25). In the resurrection, the blemishes of the body will be gone, but the nature of the body will remain. And certainly a woman's sex is her nature and no blemish; only in the resurrection, there will be no conception or childbearing associated with her nature. Her members will remain as before, with the former purpose sublimated to a newer beauty. There will be no concupiscence to arouse, and none will be aroused, but her womanhood will be a hymn to the wisdom of God, who first made her a woman, and to the clemency of God, who freed her from the corruption into which she fell. . . .

God, then, who made us man and woman, will raise us up as man and

---

75. *Civ. Dei* 22.19 (CCL 48:838–39); my trans. Cf. *Enchiridion* 88–91 (CCL 46:97–98). On this issue, see Brian Schmisek, "Augustine's Use of 'Spiritual Body,'" *Augustinian Studies* 35 (2004): 237–52.

woman. This is proved by Christ's own words. He was asked by the Sadducees, who denied the resurrection: "At the resurrection, of which of the seven will she be the wife?" . . . Jesus answered: "You err because you know neither the Scriptures nor the power of God. For at the resurrection they will neither marry nor be given in marriage, but are as the angels of God in heaven" (Mt 22:23–30). Notice that He did not say: The wife you ask about will no longer be a woman but a man. . . . What our Lord said was that in the resurrection there would be no marriage. He did not say that there would be no women.[76]

THE SPIRITUAL BODY AND REPAIRING THE DIVIDED SELF

Augustine often took his cues from St. Paul's letters, and in meditating on the resurrection, he routinely turned to 1 Cor 15. There Paul speaks of a "spiritual body." Augustine came to believe that this phrase did not mean that the resurrection was simply a matter of eternal souls. He came to use the phrase as a code word to describe God's repairing the divided self. We saw earlier how Augustine interpreted the punishment of original sin, that the punishment for disobedience of God was that our bodies and wills disobey us. At the final resurrection that split is repaired. From Sermon 242:

(8) Not without reason have those [risen] bodies been termed "spiritual." They have not been called "spiritual" because they will be spirits and not bodies. As a matter of fact, those bodies which we now possess are called "soul-infused" bodies, yet they are not souls, but bodies. Just as our bodies are now called "soul-infused," yet are not souls, so those [resurrected] bodies are called "spiritual" without being spirits, because they will be bodies. Why, then, is it called a "spiritual body," my dearly beloved, except because it will obey the direction of the spirit? Nothing in yourself will be at variance with yourself; nothing in yourself will rebel against yourself. No longer will there be that which the Apostle laments in the passage: "The flesh lusts against the spirit, and the spirit against the flesh" (Gal 5:17). No longer will the words of the same Apostle be true: "I see another law in my members, warring against the law of my mind" (Rom 7:23). Those conflicts will not exist there; but peace, perfect peace, will be there. Wherever you wish to be, there you will be; but wherever you go, you will possess your God. You will always be with Him in whom your happiness consists.[77]

76. *Civ. Dei* 22.17 (CCL 48:835–36); trans. Walsh and Honan, FOTC 24:463–65.
77. S. 242.8 (PL 38:1142–43); trans. Muldowney, FOTC 38:270–71. On this, see Henri I. Marrou, *The Resurrection and Saint Augustine's Theology of Human Values,* Saint Augustine Lecture 1965 (Villanova: Villanova University Press, 1966).

Imagining Heaven

To help people imagine the grandeur of the new creation, Augustine traced out the magnificence of earthly creation. He begins by recounting the beauties and gifts of the human person, both physical and psychological, then the beauties and gifts of human civilization, and finally the beauties and gifts of the natural world. He mentions especially the beauty of the ocean, something he could easily and routinely enjoy in Hippo. At the end, he notes how these great beauties are savored by a humanity that lives here and now under a death sentence. These are, in a sense, the joys of death row. His argument here relies on a how-much-more logic: that is, if all this is beautiful, how much more beautiful is life with God. All these beauties are at best the faintest glimmerings of the beauties of heaven. From On the City of God, *Book 22:*

(24) We have looked at the human race's misery, a punishment whose justice deserves praise, but we must now consider how God has filled the creation that He administers with so many and such great goods. First, think of the blessing He spoke before the Fall into sin: "Be fruitful and multiply and fill the earth" (Gn 1:28). That blessing did not cease because we sinned, for God wished that the fruitfulness remain even after humanity's gifted rootstalk was condemned. . . . My purpose now is to speak of the gifts of human nature which, by God's generosity, have been lavished on us and continue to be lavished on us, even though we have been wounded by sin and condemned to pay its penalties. . . . God infused into human life a capacity for reasoning and understanding. In infancy, this mental capacity seems, as it were, asleep and practically non-existent, but over the course of years it awakens into a life that involves learning and education, the perception of the true and the pursuit of the good. This capacity flowers into that wisdom and virtue that enable the soul to battle with the arms of prudence, fortitude, temperance, and justice against error, waywardness, and other inborn weaknesses, and to conquer them with a purpose that is none other than that of reaching the supreme and immutable Good. Even when this Good is not attained, there still remains, rooted in all rational nature, a God-given capacity for goods so high that the wonders of God's omnipotence are beyond any tongue to express or any mind to comprehend.

And quite apart from the artistry of living in virtue and of reaching immortal beatitude, which nothing but the grace of God which is in Christ can communicate to the children of promise and heirs of the kingdom, there have been discovered and perfected by natural human genius innumerable arts and skills which serve not only the necessities of life but also human enjoyment (*voluptariae*). And even in those arts where the purposes may seem superfluous, perilous, even pernicious, people exercise an acuteness of intelligence of so high an order that it reveals how richly endowed our human nature is. For our intelligence has the power of inventing, learning, and applying all such arts. Just think of the progress and perfection which human skill has reached in the astonishing achievements of cloth-making, architecture, agriculture, and navigation. Or think of the originality and range of what has been done by experts in ceramics, by sculptors, and by painters. Think of dramas and theatrical spectacles so stupendous that those who have not seen them simply refuse to believe the accounts of those who have. Think of the tricks and traps devised for capturing, killing, or training wild animals. Or think of numerous drugs and devices that medical science has discovered in its zeal for preserving and restoring health. Or, again, of the poisons, weapons, and equipment used in wars devised by military science for defense against enemy attack. Or even of the endless variety of seasonings and sauces which culinary artistry has discovered to be of service to the pleasures of the palate.

It was human ingenuity, too, that devised the multitude of signs we use to express and communicate our thoughts, especially in speech and in writing. The arts of rhetoric and poetry bring delight to hearts by their ornaments of style and the richness of their musicality. Instrumentalists soothe our ears by inventing new variations on old songs. Both theoretical and applied mathematics have made great progress. Astronomy has been most ingenious in tracing the movements of the stars and in distinguishing their magnitudes. In general, the richness of scientific knowledge is beyond all words and becomes all the more astonishing when one pursues any single aspect of this immense corpus of information. . . .

Let us turn now to the body itself. It is true that it is no better than the body of a beast as far as dying is concerned, and, in life, it is even weaker than that of many animals. Nevertheless, the human body is a revelation of the goodness of God and of the providence of the body's Creator. It is a body obviously meant to serve a rational soul, as you can see from the arrangement of the senses and limbs and other parts. This is obvious, too, in our whole appearance, form, and stature. The bodies of irrational animals are bent toward the ground, whereas the human person was made to walk upright with eyes on heaven, as though to remind us to keep our thoughts on things above. And if we need further evidence to show what kind of mind the body was meant to serve, we have only to think of the marvelous dexterity of tongue and hands, so perfectly suited for speaking and writing, for the arts, and for countless other tasks.

What is more, quite apart from these practical purposes, there is in the body such a rhythm, poise, symmetry, and beauty that it is hard to decide whether it was the body's uses or its beauty that the Creator had more in mind.

It is clear that every organ whose function we know adds to the body's beauty, and this beauty would be still more obvious if only we knew the precise proportions by which parts were fashioned and interrelated. I do not mean merely the parts on the outside, which, no doubt, can be accurately measured by anyone with proper skill. I mean the parts hidden below our skin, the intricate complex of veins and nerves, the inmost elements of the human viscera and vital parts, whose rhythmic relationships have not yet been revealed. Surgeons, of course, have done something in their relatively crude anatomical study of corpses (and in the course of their almost inhuman operations on living bodies) to explore the last recesses of the organs they have had to handle in order to learn the best technique in dealing with this or that disorder. But what I have in mind is the rhythm of relationships, the *harmonia*, as the Greeks would say, whereby the whole body, inside and out, can be looked upon as a kind of musical instrument with a melody all its own. The beauty of this music no one has yet discovered, because no one has dared to look for it. Nevertheless, if this total organic design could only be discerned, even in the seemingly ugly elements of the human viscera, there would be revealed to the soul so ravishing a beauty that no visible shapeliness of form that delights the eye—the mere minister of our mind—could be compared with it.

Of course, some parts of the human body appear to have no other purpose than to add to beauty, such as the mammillae on a man's chest or the beard on his face. Certainly, if the beard were meant for protection rather than for beauty, it would have served a better purpose for the weaker sex, whose face remains uncovered. If, then, we argue from the facts, first, that, as everyone admits, not a single visible organ of the body serving a definite function is lacking in beauty, and, second, that there are some parts which have beauty and no apparent function, it follows, I think, that in the creation of the human body God put form before function. After all, function will pass, and the time will come when we shall delight solely in the contemplation of one another's beauty without any lust, knowing that our joy will be giving glory to the Creator, of whom the Psalmist says: "You have put on praise and beauty" (Ps 103:1).

Turn now to the beauties and great usefulness of the rest of creation—what words can describe the riches God has scattered for us to behold and consume, a divine largesse amid the weariness and miseries of our fallen and punished lot in life? What words can describe the myriad beauties of land and sea and sky? Just think of the boundless abundance and the marvelous loveliness of light, or of the beauty of the sun and moon and stars, of shadowy glades in the woods and of the colors and perfume of flowers, of the songs and plumage of so many varieties of birds, of the innumerable animals of every species that amaze us most when they are smallest in size. The activity of ants and bees, for example, seems more stupendous than the sheer immensity of whales. Or take a look at the grandiose spectacle of the open sea, clothing and reclothing itself in changing shades of green and purple and blue. And what a delight when the ocean breaks into a storm and can be enjoyed—at least from the shore where there is no fear of the fury of the waves! Or think of God's overflowing outpourings. There are the never-ending stores of foods that banish hunger; the variety of flavors which nature generously provides without calling on the skill of cooks to stimulate our sluggish appetite; the medicinal value of so many foods, whether we are sick or healthy. We have to thank God too for the alternations of day and night, for the solace of soothing breezes, and for the plants and animals that provide the linen and wool for making our clothing.

No one could catalogue all of God's bounties. Each of the blessings which I have, as it were, piled up in a heap, contains a multitude of lesser blessings wrapped up within it; and if I were to unfold each of these packages and deal with the blessing in detail, I should never end. And, remember, all these favors taken together are but the fragmentary solace allowed us in a life condemned to misery. What, then, must be the consolations of the blessed, seeing that those on earth enjoy so much of so many and of such marvelous blessings? What good will God not give to those predestined to eternal life if He gives so much to those who are doomed to death? What joys in the life of beatitude will God not shower on those for whom, in that life of misery, He allowed His only-begotten Son to suffer so many sorrows, even unto death? It was this that St. Paul had in mind when he wrote: "He who has not spared even His own Son but delivered him for us all, how can He fail to grant us also all things with Him?" (Rom 8:32) When this promise is fulfilled, what will *we* be? What will *we* be like? What good things will we receive in that kingdom since we have already received Christ's death here as a downpayment? Just imagine how perfectly at peace and how strong will be the human spirit when there will be no passion to play the tyrant or the conqueror, no temptation even to test the spirit's strength. And think of the mind's universal knowledge in that condition where we shall drink, in all happiness and ease, of God's own wisdom at the very source. Think how great, how beautiful, how certain, how unerring, how easily acquired this knowledge then will be. And what a body, too, we shall have, a body utterly subject to our spirit and one kept so alive by spirit that there will be no need of any other food. For it will be a spiritual body, no longer merely animal, one composed, indeed, of flesh but free from every corruption of the flesh.[78]

78. *Civ. Dei* 22.24 (CCL 48:846–52); my trans., based on Walsh and Honan, FOTC 24:481–89.

SEEING GOD IN ALL THINGS

Augustine had long wrestled with what the Scriptures meant by "seeing God face-to-face" and what Jesus had, in the Sermon on the Mount, promised: that the pure in heart will "see God." How, Augustine asked, could we see God if God is bodiless, utterly immaterial? He had once considered that that seeing was "intellectual," but as he got older, he came to assert that we might come to see God with transfigured eyes in our transfigured resurrected bodies. In the work's closing pages, Augustine boldly asserts this daring view, that we will indeed come to see God in and through all creation. From On the City of God, Book 22:

(29) What is possible—even highly probable—is that we shall be able to see the material bodies of the new heaven and the new earth in such a way that, by means of our own bodies and of all the others which we shall see wherever we turn our eyes, we shall see God, and we shall see Him with the utmost clarity as being everywhere present and as regulating the whole universe, including material things. We shall see Him in a way different from the way in which His "invisible attributes" are now seen, "being understood by the things that are made" (Rom 1:20), for "we see now through a mirror in an obscure manner" and only "in part" (1 Cor 13:12), and we must rely more on the eyes of faith, whereby we believe, than on the eyes of the body, whereby we see the beauty of the material universe. Think about human beings with whom we now live, how their very movements pulse with life, so that, as soon as we turn our eyes to them, we do not merely *believe* that they are alive; we *see* it. Even though we now have no power to see "living-ness" apart from the "living bodies," nevertheless, we shall then see with the eyes of our spiritual bodies. We shall see the immaterial God, ruling all things, and we shall see Him by means of our bodies. . . . He will be seen in the spirit, and each of us will see Him within our own selves and in one another. He will also be seen in Himself, be seen in the new heaven and the new earth and in every creature then existing. And by means of our [resurrected] bodies, He will be seen in every material object towards which the eyes of our spiritual bodies happen to direct their gaze.[79]

79. *Civ. Dei* 22.29 (CCL 48:861–62); trans. Walsh and Honan, FOTC 24:503–5.

CHAPTER 10

CONTROVERSIES (IV)

Against the Pelagians

Augustine's final controversy centered on the issue of grace. This debate, more than any other, would come to define his legacy to later ages, earning him the title *doctor gratiae* ("teacher of grace"). For Augustine, grace was no wispy abstraction. It lay at the very heart of his life story. In *Confessions*, he set out the high drama of his conversion, how, after hearing stories of converts, this one-time-Manichee-turned-indecisive-Catholic-catechumen wandered into a garden in turmoil and tears, heard a child's voice, a call to "pick up, read," prompting him to seize a book of letters from another convert, St. Paul, and experienced, after reading just a few words from the Letter to the Romans, a profound conversion. In its wake, despite his successful secular career and a promising future, he chose to walk away, to abandon "the world," renouncing fame and power, wealth and marriage. Augustine the bishop, writing *Confessions* more than a decade later, looked back on that scene as an act of God, a moment of unmerited grace.

In the long interval between his experience in the garden in 386 and his writing of it in the late 390s, Augustine meditated deeply on Paul's letters and their intricate assertions on grace. Thinking through the implications came slowly.[1] A grand commentary on Paul's letters never got beyond the opening verses of Romans. Around 394, he published a miscellany of reflections on Paul, drawn from a question-and-answer session held in Carthage.[2] But in

---

1. For an analysis of the sometimes subtle, but significant shifts and stages in Augustine's thinking on grace, see the seminal work of J. Patout Burns, *The Development of Augustine's Doctrine of Operative Grace*, CEASA 82 (Paris: Institut d'Études Augustiniennes, 1980).

2. Augustine published this as *Commentary on Statements in the Letter of Paul to the Romans (Expositio quarundam propositionum ex epistula apostoli ad Romanos*, CSEL 84: 3–52). For the text and an analysis, see Paula Fredriksen Landes, *Augustine on Romans*, 2–49.

396, soon after his installation as bishop of Hippo, he got a letter from an old friend, Simplicianus, the elderly presbyter who had played a passing role in his conversion and who soon succeeded Ambrose as bishop of Milan. Simplicianus wanted help on interpreting certain thorny biblical texts, particularly from Paul's Letter to the Romans. Augustine's reply, *To Simplicianus, on Various Questions*, marked a quiet but decisive revolution in his thought, a landslide of new perspectives on grace and free will, on the history of salvation and the mystery of God's foreknowledge.[3] When, soon after, he set about writing *Confessions*, those new perspectives wove their way into the very fabric of his autobiography.[4] He came to see Paul's message of grace encapsulated in a single verse: "What do you have that you have not received? And if you have received it, why do you glory as if you did not receive it?" (1 Cor 4:7)[5] Augustine thus looked back on his life not as a story of a man coming to truth after a hard-fought intellectual quest nor coming to a more just way of life by willing his way to hard-earned virtues. He saw it, instead, as a story of grace, a mysterious, miraculous series of unearned gifts, graced insights allowing him to grasp some measure of truth and a graced fire of love fueling his heart to live out, however haltingly, some measure of virtue. In the 410s, this reading of the Bible and of his life—and of Christian life—would come under severe fire during the Pelagian controversy.

Pelagius (c. 350–c. 425) was of British origin, a lay ascetic who spent much of his career, from the 380s to around 410, in the city of Rome. The recovery of his writings in the early twentieth century, as well as the discovery in the late nineteenth century of a large dossier authored by allies and sympathizers, known as the Caspari corpus, has enabled historians to strip away centuries of polemic and sketch out a better grounded view of the man and the movement associated with his name.[6] Pelagius moved among Rome's aristocratic families, serving as a tough-minded, no-nonsense, but deeply in-

3. Peter Brown's classic chapter, "The Lost Future," in *Augustine of Hippo*, 139–50, has been widely influential as an interpretation of this phase of Augustine's career. Goulven Madec, *Saint Augustin et la philosophie*, 69–75, and Carol Harrison, *Rethinking Augustine's Early Theology*, 14–19, have challenged this interpretation, stressing greater continuity before and after Ad Simplicianum. Despite their helpful caveats, most scholars remain in agreement with Brown's reading, not to mention Augustine's own self-assessment (*retr.* 2.1.3 [27]; *praed. sanct.* 4.8) that Ad Simplicianum was just such a decisive moment.

4. On this, see Paula Fredriksen, "Paul and Augustine: Conversion Narratives, Orthodox Traditions, and the Retrospective Self," *Journal of Theological Studies* 37 (1986): 3–34.

5. *Simpl.* 1.2.9 (CCL 44:34). On Augustine's appeal to this verse and its place within his broader theology, see Pierre-Marie Hombert, *Gloria Gratiae: Se glorifier en Dieu, principe et fin de la théologie augustinienne de la grâce*, CEASA 148 (Paris: Institut d'Études Augustiniennes, 1996).

6. On these discoveries and their implications, see Gerald Bonner, *Augustine and Modern Research on Pelagianism* (Villanova, PA: Villanova University Press, 1972); see also his further reflections: "Pelagianism and Augustine," *Augustinian Studies* 23 (1992): 33–51, and "Augustine and Pelagianism," *Augustinian Studies* 24 (1993): 27–47. Other recent perspectives are in Mathijs Lamberigts, "Pelagius and Pelagians," in *Oxford Handbook of Early Christian Studies*, 258–79.

spiring spiritual guide.[7] Rome's elite had been among the last in the Empire to come over to the Christian faith. Pelagius and his circle had little patience with their often lukewarm, politically correct conversions: "If it pleases you to be a Christian, then perform the works of Christ and adopt the name of Christian deservedly. Or perhaps you do not wish to be a Christian, but just to be called one!"[8] He railed against a growing gap in moral expectations, a two-tier morality with one standard for monks and another for the average Christian: "I have said and I will repeat: In the matter of righteousness we all have the same obligations: virgins, widows, or married women, men of high, middle, or low class, are equally bidden to obey the commandments."[9] Pelagius's high standards and moral egalitarianism had momentous implications. As Peter Brown has noted, "the stream of perfectionism which," in the ascetic movement, "had flowed in a concentrated jet, will be widened by Pelagius and his followers into a flood into whose icy puritanism they would immerse the whole Christian community."[10] Gerald Bonner has added: "The Pelagians did not build monasteries. Rather, they sought to make the Christian Church one great monastery."[11]

Like Augustine, Pelagius had meditated at length on Paul's letters. His longest surviving work is a verse-by-verse commentary.[12] Like Augustine of the 390s, Pelagius positioned himself as an opponent of the Manichees and worried greatly about Manichean denial of moral freedom. Pelagius laid great stress on free will, on our power of choice, whether for good or for ill. He knew of Augustine's early anti-Manichean treatise, On Free Will, and quoted it to buttress his own views.[13] But what he knew of Augustine's later writings left him uneasy. He nearly came to blows with a bishop who quoted Confessions to him (see below). Pelagius's controversial treatise, On Nature,

7. On this aristocratic social context, see the classic studies of Peter Brown, "Pelagius and His Supporters: Aims and Environment," and "The Patrons of Pelagius: The Roman Aristocracy between East and West," in Religion and Society in the Age of Saint Augustine, 183–226.

8. Pelagius, De vita christiana 1.1–1.2 (PL 40:1033); trans. B. R. Rees, Pelagius: Life and Letters (Rochester, NY: Boydell Press, 1991), 2:108. Some have disputed the attribution of this work to Pelagius; for a discussion, see Robert F. Evans, Four Letters of Pelagius (New York: Seabury Press, 1968), 18–20; Rees, Pelagius, 105–6. If not by Pelagius himself, the work is certainly from his circle and articulates core Pelagian concerns and spirituality.

9. Pelagius, Ad Demetriadem 10 (PL 30:25); trans. Markus, End of Ancient Christianity, 42.

10. Brown, "Pelagius and His Supporters," 194.

11. Bonner, Augustine and Modern Research, 14.

12. Pelagius, Expositiones XIII epistularum Pauli. For the text, see A. Souter, Pelagius's Expositions of Thirteen Epistles of St. Paul, Texts and Studies 9.2 (Cambridge, 1926), reprinted in PLS 1:1110–374; for a partial translation, see Theodore DeBruyn, ed., Pelagius's Commentary on St. Paul's Epistle to the Romans, OECS (New York: Oxford University Press, 1993).

13. Pelagius in De natura quoted Augustine's De libero arbitrio 3.18.50 (CCL 29:304). Augustine strongly defended himself in nat. et gr. 67.80–81 (BA 21:400–406) against what he saw as Pelagius's biased editing. Bonner, Modern Research, 41–42, has argued that this quotation proved a turning point in Augustine's view of Pelagius.

written sometime between 406 and 410, marked his measured response to high-pitched theological debates that had raged in the city of Rome for two decades, debates on marriage and virginity and our capacity for moral excellence.[14] In Pelagius's mind, human nature and moral exhortation were intimately linked. As he stressed in a letter to one of his aristocratic advisees:

Whenever I have to discuss principles of morality and the conduct of the life of holiness, it is my approach to begin first by demonstrating the power and quality of human nature, to show what it is capable of. And from this I then encourage the soul of my hearer to various kinds of virtues. It would do no good to call a person to something when one strongly presumes it to be impossible, for we would never set out on the road to virtue unless hope were our guide and companion. Despairing of reaching it otherwise undermines every effort in pursuing it.[15]

Like a coach of elite athletes, Pelagius called those he directed to re-imagine and exploit to the full their untapped God-given potential. Yet the choices were stark, and the stakes were high:

The Lord of justice wanted human beings to act freely and not under compulsion. It was for this reason He left each person in the hands of his or her own counsel. He placed before them life and death, good and evil. Whatever pleased one, one was given (Sir 15:14–17). Thus we read in Deuteronomy: "I have set before your face blessing and curse. Choose life that you may live" (Dt 30:19).[16]

The consequences for failure were also clear: "On the day of judgment no mercy will be shown to the wicked and the sinners, but they will be consumed in the eternal fires."[17]

Pelagius held a definite, if circumscribed, theology of grace.[18] First, he stressed that creation itself is graced. In particular, God had gifted the human person with great powers, inscribing them into the marrow of our God-imaged nature. Adam's sin, Pelagius argued, hurt only Adam, not human nature. We do not inherit original sin; we imitate the original sinner. Second, Pelagius emphasized the Law as a gift of God's beneficence. The history of human sin had drawn "a dark veil, as it were, over human reason." The Law "filed off" a corrosive "rust of ignorance," restoring our nature's "primordial

14. This has been traditionally dated later, around 413 or 414. Yves-Marie Duval, "La date du *De Natura de Pélage*," *Revue des Études Augustiniennes* 36 (1990): 257–83, has argued in an influential study for the earlier date, placing this work in the aftermath of the Jovinian controversy. On this, see below.

15. Pelagius, *ep. ad Demetriadem* 2 (PL 30:17); my trans.

16. Pelagius, *ep. ad Demetriadem* 2 (PL 30:17); my trans.

17. Pelagius, quoted in Augustine, *De gestis Pelagii* 3.9 (BA 21:450). At his trial at Diospolis in 415, Pelagius acknowledged that the sentence was drawn from one of his writings.

18. For a fair-minded overview of Pelagius's theology, see Robert Evans, *Pelagius: Inquiries and Reappraisals* (New York: Seabury, 1968), esp. 90–121.

brilliance."[19] Third, there is the grace of Christ, who redeemed humankind from sin and who both taught and embodied a just way of life, serving as an exemplar of righteousness and a model for our imitation. Finally, there is the grace of baptism, which cleanses us of sin. But, on the far side of baptism, we have no excuses. We have the power; we need to just do it, do good and spurn evil. He suggested an analogy: We have eyes, the power (*posse*) of sight. That sight is God's gift, God's grace. But what we do with our eyes is our business. We do the willing (*velle*), whether for good or for evil.[20] Given this view of human psychology, it is hard to imagine Pelagius lamenting, as Paul did, "I do not do the good I will, but I do the evil that I do not will" (Rom 7:19); nor could he have written anything like *Confessions*, portraying the will, as Augustine did, as a labyrinth of contrary forces and unfathomable depths.

The Pelagian controversy, as it unfolded from 411 to 431, was more than a duel between two theologians. It was a drama played out on the world stage. It enlisted a large and international cast of characters. There were rapid changes of scene and of fortune, chance events, unexpected collisions, complex personalities facing off over tenacious ideas. To appreciate the texts that follow, I need to sketch out the complicated course of the controversy. Its prelude begins in 410, with the sack of Rome. Pelagius joined the flood of refugees fleeing Italy and the Goths. His ship docked for a time at Hippo, but Augustine happened to be out of town. The two caught brief glimpses of one another in Carthage, but Augustine was busy dealing with the Donatists and the momentous Conference of 411. Pelagius did not linger and soon sailed off to Palestine.

The controversy erupted a year later, in 411, sparked not by Pelagius, but by his sharp-witted disciple and fellow refugee, Caelestius. When Caelestius applied for ordination in Carthage, he was accused of heterodoxy by Paulinus of Milan, Ambrose's former secretary and later his biographer. At an ecclesiastical tribunal presided over by Aurelius of Carthage, Caelestius was convicted and excommunicated (see excerpts below). He too sailed off and got himself ordained in Ephesus, much to the chagrin of the North Africans. Augustine had not been in town for the trial, but Flavius Marcellinus, the imperial commissioner who had overseen the forced reunion of the Donatists and who had prompted Augustine to begin composing *City of God*, pressed him to answer Caelestius. One hot-button issue had been Caelestius's denial that infants inherit Adam's sin. Augustine answered with a two-volume treatise, *On the Merits and Forgiveness of Sins and On Infant Baptism* (*De peccatorum meritis et*

---

19. Pelagius, *ep. ad Demetriadem* 8 (PL 30:23).
20. Pelagius, *Pro libero arbitrio*, Book 3, quoted in Augustine, *gr. et pecc. or.* 1.4.5 (CSEL 42:127–28).

remissione et de baptismo parvulorum). Here he introduced into the conversation a term ever after linked with his name: "original sin."[21] He went on to give voice to tenacious North African convictions about infant baptism, echoing those articulated 150 years earlier by Cyprian.[22]

The controversy in those first years was anti-Caelestian, not anti-Pelagian. Augustine remained cautious in confronting Pelagius. The two men shared a wide network of aristocratic friends, and while Augustine may have heard worrisome rumors, he mostly heard high praise. Soon after publishing *On the Merits,* he came across Pelagius's commentary on Paul's letters. Certain passages troubled him, but Pelagius had subtly worded things and appeared to report rather than assert or defend controversial exegeses. But certain exegeses troubled Augustine enough to append a third volume to *On the Merits,* an extended postscript in the form of a letter to Marcellinus. Properly speaking, the controversy's second phase began in 414 when two ex-disciples of Pelagius sent Augustine a copy of *On Nature.* Its ideas confirmed Augustine's earlier suspicions and led to his carefully crafted rebuttal, *On Nature and Grace* (*De natura et gratia*). While he quoted Pelagius's treatise repeatedly, he never named its author, hoping, he said, to win him over.

At almost the same moment, at the other end of the Mediterranean, these North African concerns erupted into an international *cause célèbre.* Augustine would see his ideas thrust onto the world stage, in debates waged in courtrooms and councils and the corridors of imperial power, in venues across North Africa, Palestine, Italy, and Gaul. The controversy took its international turn in Palestine, thanks to the zealous tactlessness of Paul Orosius, a bright, young Spanish presbyter whom Augustine had encouraged to go to the Holy Land to study with Jerome.[23] In the summer of 415, at a synod held in Jerusalem, presided over by Bishop John of Jerusalem (d. 417), Orosius informed the gathered bishops of Caelestius's condemnation and read out a letter Augustine had written against Pelagian sympathizers in Sicily. Pelagius was summoned, and when asked if he taught what Augustine denounced, he answered: "Who is Augustine to me?" John stepped in: "It is I who am Augustine here." Orosius undiplomatically shot back at John: "If you represent Augustine, follow his faith."[24] John invited Orosius to take up the official role of prosecu-

21. *Pecc. mer.* 1.9.9 (CSEL 60:10–11). Augustine first uses the term "original sin" in 396, in *Simpl.* 1.1.10 and 11 (CCL 44:15–16). See below.

22. Bonner, "Pelagianism and Augustine," 198 ff., stresses the tenacity of these North African theological commitments, for example, Aurelius's remarks at Caelestius's trial (*grat. et pecc. or.* 2.3.3). Aurelius also pressed Augustine on June 27, 413, to preach in Carthage on the issue. In the sermon (*s.* 294), Augustine reads at length from Cyprian's *ep.* 59.5 to Fidus (PL 3:1054).

23. For a helpful reconstruction and analysis of events in Palestine, see Roland Teske, *Answer to the Pelagians* [I], WSA I/23:319–35 and 385–402; also Bonner, *St. Augustine,* 332–39.

24. Orosius, *Liber apologeticus* 3 (CSEL 5:607–8).

tor, but he refused, insisting that the African condemnation and the views of a leading Latin theologian sufficed, and Greek bishops needed to yield to their authority. A verdict exonerating Pelagius was avoided when Orosius appealed to the bishop of Rome, arguing this was a case for the Latin church.

Six months later, formal charges were again brought against Pelagius, this time by two Gallic bishops, Heros and Lazarus. When a synod of bishops met in Diospolis in December 415, the accusers failed to show up (one claimed ill health), and Pelagius was able to defend himself without serious cross-examination. He addressed the long list of written accusations, mostly quotations from his writings that minimized the need for grace. He answered skillfully, and perhaps disingenuously.[25] He felt no qualms anathematizing his one-time disciple, Caelestius. The bishops accepted the explanations, denials, and anathemas and declared themselves satisfied. Pelagius acted quickly, advertising the verdict, sending a digest of the proceedings far and wide, quietly editing out embarrassing moments and boasting: "The statement in which I maintained that 'a person can be without sin and *easily* keep the commandments of God if he wishes,' has been approved by the verdict of fourteen bishops. This verdict has spread confusion over the faces of my opponents."[26] The moment of triumph turned violent. Pelagius's supporters, it was said, torched Jerome's monastery in Bethlehem. A deacon was killed, and Jerome and the nuns under his direction, many from Rome's leading families, barely escaped with their lives.

Pelagius's acquittal was a serious blow to Augustine and the wider North African episcopate. It seemed an affront to their claim against their Donatist rivals that they were in union with the *catholica*, the worldwide consensus of churches. In a newly discovered sermon published by François Dolbeau, we hear Augustine speaking anxiously, right after getting news of Pelagius's vindication. He denounces Pelagius publicly for the first time and warns his congregation of "this new heresy . . . spreading its tentacles far and wide."[27] He tells them that he has just received Pelagius's own digest, that he is suspicious of its accuracy, and that he has written for a full transcript. In a second recent discovery, we now know where he finally got his copy: from Cyril, the formidable patriarch of Alexandria (d. 444).[28] With the full text in hand, Au-

---

25. See Robert F. Evans, "Pelagius's Veracity at the Synod of Diospolis," in *Studies in Medieval Culture*, ed. John R. Sommerfeldt (Kalamazoo: Western Michigan University, 1964), 21–30.

26. Pelagius, quoted in *De gestis Pelagii* 30.54 (CSEL 42:107); trans. Mourant and Collinge, FOTC 86:163. Augustine attacked Pelagius's hyperbole, noting that the word "easily" never appeared in the transcript of the tribunal.

27. S. 348A.5 (= Dolbeau 30). For the text, see François Dolbeau, "Le sermon 348A de saint Augustin contre Pélage: Édition du texte intégral," *Recherches Augustiniennes* 28 (1995): 37–63; reprinted in *Augustin et la prédication en Afrique*, 241–67; trans. Hill, WSA III/11:312.

28. Ep. 4* (BA 46B:108–12). Before its discovery, we had known that Augustine had sent John of Jeru-

gustine wrote a detailed commentary, *On the Deeds of Pelagius* (*De gestis Pelagii*), trying to excuse his Palestinian colleagues and to analyze what he perceived as Pelagius's evasiveness and deceptions.

In 416, the North African bishops, gathering in two province-wide councils, one in Carthage and another in Milevis, formally condemned both Pelagius and Caelestius, then forwarded their judgments to Pope Innocent I, asking him to lend his authority to their decisions. The pope was sent a hefty dossier. It included the statements of both councils and a long private letter, cosigned by Aurelius, Augustine, Alypius, Possidius, and Evodius. It also included copies of Pelagius's *On Nature* and Augustine's *On Nature and Grace*, with key passages marked for quick perusal. Innocent answered decisively on January 27, 417, officially excommunicating Pelagius and Caelestius. Two months later, Innocent was dead, and his successor, Zosimus (d. 418), reopened the case. Caelestius came to Rome, while Pelagius sent in a formal profession of faith, professing loyalty. Zosimus vindicated both men and sent a curt letter to the North Africans, scolding them for their rash judgments. Again, there was violence, this time in Rome, some riots as well as an attack on a local dignitary. Because of this and because of lobbying from the North Africans, the imperial court at Ravenna stepped in, and on April 29, 418, issued a rescript. The Emperor sentenced Pelagius and Caelestius to exile and attributed their attitudes to the movement's aristocratic origins: "This subtle heresy considers it a particular mark of low breeding to agree with other people, and the palm of outstanding good sense to destroy what is generally approved."[29] One day later, on May 1, 418, hundreds of North African bishops met in council in Carthage and passed nine anathemas pertaining to issues of grace, free will, and infant baptism. This legislation would come to define for later ages the official theology on the matter. Pope Zosimus abruptly reversed himself, issuing in the summer of 418 his own condemnation, the *Tractoria*. Pelagius was forced to leave Palestine. He disappears from history, likely spending his final years in Egypt. Caelestius fled Rome, and was taken in by the Antiochene theologian, Theodore of Mopsuestia (d. 428).

The condemnations of 418 were decisive, but hardly the last word. The controversy entered a third phase. Zosimus had required the bishops of Italy to sign his *Tractoria*. A handful of bishops, led by the recently ordained Bishop Julian of Eclanum (c. 380–c. 445), opposed him. For his opposition, Julian was exiled to the Greek East, where he joined Caelestius under Theodore's protec-

---

salem at least one letter (*ep.* 179), requesting a copy of the transcript. This new letter proves that Cyril (at least) sent him an official copy. For more on what this letter reveals about the sequence of events, the ecclesiastical diplomacy, and the theological exchanges, see Geoffrey D. Dunn, "Augustine, Cyril of Alexandria, and the Pelagian Controversy," *Augustinian Studies* 37 (2006): 63–88.

29. Honorius, *Ad Palladium* (PL 48:379–81); trans. Bonner, *Modern Research*, 50–51.

tion. Over the next decade, he became Augustine's most relentless and eloquent critic. He was a masterful writer and a skilled polemicist, tarring Augustine with religious slurs (such as "the new Manichee") and an array of ethnic epithets (such as "Punic debater").[30] Julian waged what Peter Brown has called a "Punic war of the mind,"[31] lambasting Augustine's views on free will, grace, marriage, sexuality, and much else, in a four-volume work, *To Turbantius* (*Ad Turbantium*). Augustine felt compelled to answer, initially in book 2 of *On Marriage and Concupiscence* (*De nuptiis et concupiscentia*), then in a point-by-point rebuttal in *Against Julian* (*Contra Julianum*). Julian answered back with the eight-volume *To Florus* (*Ad Florum*). Augustine again responded, this time with a work that occupied his energies virtually to the day he died, the massive six-volume *Against Julian, an Incomplete Work* (*Contra Julianum opus imperfectum*), which, as its posthumous title indicates, was left unfinished. The final condemnation of Pelagianism came only after Augustine's death. In 431, Cyril of Alexandria presided over the ecumenical Council of Ephesus, best known for its condemnation of Nestorius and its affirmation of the Virgin Mary as *Theotokos* ("Mother of God"). The Council also condemned Caelestius's teaching, and in a letter to the West confirmed its condemnations of Pelagius, Caelestius, and Julian. Julian reportedly lived his last years in Sicily, working as a schoolteacher.

A fourth phase occurred in Augustine's final years. Two groups of monks, one in Hadrumetum in North Africa, another in southern Gaul, had followed the course of controversy. While they had little sympathy with Pelagius, they became alarmed at Augustine's increasingly pungent views on grace and predestination, which seemed to render monks' ascetical efforts useless and to make moral exhortations, whether of the Bible or their abbot, irrelevant. Since the seventeenth century, this final phase has been called "the semi-Pelagian controversy." The term is a misnomer.[32] There is nothing either Pelagian or semi-Pelagian about these monks. The most prominent was John Cassian (c. 360–c. 435), a monk who had settled in Marseilles after spending long years in the Greek East, especially in Egypt, and who, more than anyone else, would translate the spirituality of the Desert Fathers for the Latin West.[33] Widely admired, his works would be commended in Benedict's *Rule*

30. Julian, *Ad Florum*, quoted in Augustine, *c.* Jul. imp. 1.7, 1.32, 1.48, 5.11; cf. 4.56 ("patron of asses," *patronus asinorum*). On this, see Dorothea Weber, "'For What Is So Monstrous as What the Punic Fellow Says?': Reflections on the Literary Background of Julian's Polemical Attacks on Augustine's Homeland," in *Augustinus Afer*, 75–82; also Mathijs J. G. P. Lamberigts, "The Italian Julian of Aeclanum about the African Augustine of Hippo," 83–94.

31. Brown, *Augustine of Hippo*, 385.

32. On this, see Rebecca Harden Weaver, *Divine Grace and Human Agency: A Study of the Semi-Pelagian Controversy*, Patristic Monograph Series 15 (Macon, GA: Mercer University Press, 1996); and Conrad Leyser, "Semi-Pelagianism," *AugEncy*, 761–66.

33. See Columba Stewart, *Cassian the Monk*, Oxford Studies in Historical Theology (New York: Oxford University Press, 1998); Harmless, *Desert Christians*, 373–409.

and powerfully shape medieval monasticism. Cassian insisted on the constant necessity of grace. In his *Conferences* (*Collationes*), he alluded to Augustinian views, and if at times he disagreed, he did so politely and without polemic. One of Cassian's contemporaries in Marseilles, Prosper of Aquitaine, wrote Augustine a letter, complaining that local holy men were questioning his views. Augustine responded with two treatises, *On the Predestination of the Saints* (*De praedestinatione sanctorum*) and *On the Gift of Perseverance* (*De dono perseverantiae*). He stated his own views sharply, but stressed seeing these monastic critics as "brothers," not heretics. Over the next century, Gallic monks and bishops, for all their genuine respect for Augustine, stood closer to Cassian and would struggle to reconcile this dual theological inheritance.

Almost everything about the Pelagian controversy is complicated. First, the volume of surviving documents is enormous. Augustine's anti-Pelagian writings alone are several times the length of *City of God*. Second, the unfolding of events is both crucial and intricate. That should be evident from my cursory summary, which glosses over the often intense dramas that both preceded and played themselves out when those tribunals and councils and popes set out their momentous, but nuanced decisions. As in modern court cases, it is one thing to recognize the big issues being fought over, and quite another to follow the back-and-forth of the courtroom battles. For that, one has to plunge into technical arguments on disputed evidence, to be sensitive to precedents and procedures, and to be attuned to what final verdicts say and do not say. Third, there is the large cast of characters who, at one point or another, take center stage in the drama. One has to be alert to their often hard-to-decipher personal motives and their often limited knowledge of one another and of what was happening elsewhere. Fourth, there is the wide array of theological issues. While grace remained the point of contention, around it and flowing from it other theological issues came to the fore: human nature and free will; virtue and holiness; infant baptism and original sin; the origin of the soul; marriage, sexuality, and carnal desire; salvation history and God's predestining will; and, at the very outset and beneath it all, the fundamental Christian claim that Jesus is the one and only Savior of the world. Finally, because this controversy set off reverberations that have rumbled down through the centuries, notably during the Protestant Reformation, when similar debates on grace, free will, and predestination, repeated themselves with new variations and in new contexts, it is difficult to step back and see the original dispute with fresh eyes and savor its unique contours. Scholars have sifted through the huge mass of evidence, and on this controversy, perhaps more than on any other of Augustine's career and thought, interpretations vary widely, as scholars work to reconstruct lost theologies, chart events, diagnose personalities, and speculate discerningly on behind-the-scenes happenings and beneath-the-surface motives. Therefore, this chapter, despite its length, has quite modest aims: providing the basics of and a framework for following this many-sided debate. To capture the back-and-forth of the debate and Augustine's unfolding response to events and ideas, I have organized the texts under its four phases: (1) the debate against Caelestius, (2) the debate against Pelagius, (3) the debate against Julian, and (4) the discussion with the monks. These are not evenly distributed. The second phase gets the bulk of attention not because it has the bulkiest texts (the third has that claim to fame), but because it proved the most consequential.

❧

BACKGROUND TEXTS
PELAGIUS ANTICIPATED

Augustine's old mentor, Simplicianus, had read some of his early exegetical works and asked his perspectives on two perplexing texts from Paul's Letter to the Romans. In 396, Augustine answered with his first work after becoming bishop of Hippo, To Simplicianus on Various Questions. Thirty years later, on the far side of the Pelagian controversy, Augustine looked back on these essays as a watershed moment, as a collection of breakthrough insights into Paul's teaching on grace, free will, and divine election. The work seemed, in retrospect, a God-inspired rebuttal to Pelagius years before he had ever heard of Pelagius. Thus, its place in this chapter. However much it anticipates the later debate, we need to bear in mind that it comes from Augustine of 396, that is, Augustine the new bishop struggling to pastor an all-too-human congregation; Augustine the exegete returning to Pauline texts he had wrestled with earlier; Augustine the polemicist worried about defending free will against the Manichees; and Augustine the convert deeply aware of his own graced conversion experience and his ongoing struggles. To Simplicianus, while a watershed, is not an easy one to savor. It is, first and foremost, a work of exegesis. To appreciate it, one first needs to ruminate on the same biblical texts that so puzzled Simplicianus and Augustine. It is also not an easy work to excerpt, given its tightly threaded arguments. Its insights appear within a dense exegetical shorthand, and their scope would require the later Pelagian controversy to let them unfold into a fuller symphonic exposition.

(i) Grace and the Will

Simplicianus's first question concerned Rom 7:7–25. In answer, Augustine summarizes insights he had honed in prior works and, momentously, coins a term that would loom large in the later debate: original sin. From To Simplicianus, Book 1, Question 1:

(1.11) "To will," Paul says, "is close to me, but to do the good is not" (Rom 7:18). For those who do not correctly understand these words, Paul seems to be eliminating free choice. But how does he eliminate it since he says, "To will is close to me"? For certainly willing itself is in our power, but what is not in our power is doing what is good. This [inability] is among the results of original sin. This comes not from our original human nature, but rather is the penalty for our guilt through which mortality itself has become a sort of second nature. It is from this that the grace of our Creator liberates those of us who submit ourselves to Him by faith. But these words [of Paul] are the voice of a person who is under the law and not yet under grace. He who is not yet under grace does not do the good he wills but does the evil he does not will, being overwhelmed by a concupiscence whose oak-hard strength not only binds us in a chain of mortality, but also weighs us down with a mill-stone of habit. But if he does what he does not will, it is no longer he who does it, but the sin that dwells in him. . . .

(1.14) Humankind—conquered, condemned, held captive—must, there-fore, speak humbly, and, after having received the Law, not as a victor but rather a law-breaker, must humbly cry out: "O, what a wretched man I am! Who will liberate me from the body of this death? The grace of God through Jesus Christ our Lord" (Rom 7:24–25). What is left in this mortal life to our free choice is this: Not that a person can fulfill righteousness when he wants to, but that with a humble piety he may turn to the One by whose gift he can have the power to fulfill it.[34]

(ii) Grace Precedes, Good Works Follow

Simplicianus's second question, on Rom 9:10-29, pressed Augustine to new and dramatic assertions about grace which laid the groundwork for his later positions during the Pelagian controversy. Early in the essay, he insists that we need to read Romans 9 in terms of Paul's broader theology of grace. From On Simplicianus, Book 1, Question 2:

34. Simpl. 1.q.1.11–14 (CCL 44:15–18); my trans. Burns, *Development*, 30–51, traces how Simpl. overturns certain earlier reflections; Burns also highlights how it differs in subtle, yet vital ways from Augustine's later views, especially those after 418 (see pp. 7–8, 121–24). See also James Wetzel, "Pelagius Anticipated: Grace and Election in Augustine's Ad Simplicianum," in *Augustine: From Rhetor to Theologian*, ed. Joanne Mc-William (Waterloo, Ontario: Wilfrid Laurier University, 1992), 121–32.

(2.2) First I will try and grasp the Apostle's main idea, which runs through the entire letter that I will be considering here. It is this: that no one should glory in the merits of his good deeds. The Israelites dared to glory in theirs on the grounds that they had served the Law given to them, and for that reason received the grace of the Gospel as though it were due them, as something they merited because they had observed the Law. . . . They did not understand that the grace of the Gospel, of its very nature, is not given because of good works. Otherwise, grace is no longer grace (Rom 11:6).

(2.3) . . . Grace, therefore, is from the One who calls; the good works that result are from the one who receives that grace. These good works do not produce grace; they are produced by grace. Fire, after all, does not heat in order to burn, but because it burns; a wheel does not roll well in order to be round, but because it is round. So no one does good works in order that one may receive grace, but only because one has received grace. How, after all, can one who had not been justified live justly? Or can one who has not been sanctified live in a saintly way? Or, for that matter, how can one live at all if one has not been given life? Grace justifies so that the one justified can live justly. Grace, therefore, comes first; good works, second.[35]

(iii) Jacob vs. Esau

In Rom 9:6–14, Paul alludes to the Old Testament story of God's election of Jacob over Esau (Gn 25:19–34). For Augustine and his contemporaries, this story became a sort of test case, challenging any commonsense understanding of divine justice—as though God took no initiative, but stood back as a dispassionate judge, either rewarding the good or punishing the bad. In the following passage, Augustine states the acute nature of the problem. Meditating on these unborn twins provides the dynamic of the rest of Augustine's essay. Jacob's case becomes a way to think through whether we contribute anything to our salvation; Esau's case becomes a way to think about why some are damned. From To Simplicianus, *Book 1, Question 2:*

(2.4) If Jacob, not yet born and having done nothing, was chosen without any merit, then there could be no difference at all in existence between the two by which Jacob might be chosen. Likewise, if Esau was rejected without any cause—after all, he himself was not yet born and had done nothing—how, when it says: "The elder shall serve the younger" (Rom 9:12), can Esau's rejection be called "just"? How are we to understand what follows: "Jacob I have loved, but Esau I have hated" (Mal 1:3; Rom 9:13)? . . . On what basis,

35. Simpl. 1.q.2.2-3 (CCL 44:24–27); my trans.

therefore, is this choice or any choice made if the not-yet-born and not-yet-active have no opportunity for merits?[36]

(iv) Grace of the Call

In thinking about Jacob, Augustine raises the question: While the good works we do are permeated by grace, what about faith itself? Can we even, at a minimum, lay claim to willing the initial decision for faith? Here he quotes 1 Cor 4:7, the text that he later saw as encapsulating the whole issue. From To Simplicianus, Book 1, Question 2:

(2.7) The question now is: Whether faith merits a person's justification, or whether or not the merits of faith precede God's mercy, or whether, in fact, faith itself is to be numbered among the gifts of grace? . . . No one believes who is not called. But the merciful God does call, giving lavishly and not as a merit for faith, because the merit of faith follows rather than precedes the calling. After all, "how will they believe him whom they have not heard of? And how will they hear without a preacher?" (Rom 10:14) Unless, therefore, God's mercy in calling us precedes, no one can believe so that one can begin to be justified and begin to receive the capacity for doing good works. Thus, before any merit, there is grace; the fact is, "Christ died for the ungodly" (Rom 5:6). . . .

(2.9) If someone boasts that he merits [God's compassion] by believing, let him understand that God inspired his faith, having mercy on whom He is merciful by giving him, while still an unbeliever, a share in this calling. This, then, distinguishes the believer from the ungodly. "For what do you have," Paul says, "that you did not receive? And if you have received it, why do you glory as if you had not received it?" (1 Cor 4:7)[37]

(v) "Lump of Sin"

Thinking about Esau leads Augustine to the issue of the judgment of sinners. In Rom 9:21–23, Paul compares God to a potter who makes pottery from a single lump of earth, using some of it to make fine china ("vessels of honor") and some of it to make discardable everyday dishware ("vessels of wrath"). Augustine would seize upon this as a master-metaphor. Here he accents the fallenness of humanity as a "lump of sin" (massa peccati). From To Simplicianus, Book 1, Question 2:

(2.16) Since, as the Apostle says, "in Adam all die" (1 Cor 15:22), and from Adam that offense's origin spread to the entire human race, all human be-

36. Simpl. 1.q.2.4 (CCL 44:28–29); my trans.
37. Simpl. 1.q.2.7–9 (CCL 44:31–34); my trans.

ings are, as it were, one mass of sin owing a debt of punishment to that divine and highest justice. No matter whether the debt is exacted or waived, there is no injustice. . . . God Himself forces no one to sin, but simply does not lavish the mercy of justification on certain sinners, and for this reason is said "to harden" certain sinners, not because He compels them to sin, but because He does not have mercy on them. For those He is not merciful to, He judges that mercy should not be shown according to a deeply hidden standard of justice far removed from human sensibilities. For "inscrutable are His judgments, and unsearchable His ways" (Rom 11:33). . . .

(2.20) There is a certain passage from Scripture that I take as absolutely necessary to what is being interpreted here, which marvelously confirms what has been explained. It comes from the book that some call "Jesus Sirach" and others call "Ecclesiasticus." In it is written: "All human beings are from the ground, and from earth was Adam created. In an abundance of discipline, the Lord separated them and altered their pathways. Some He blessed and exalted, and these He sanctified and brought to Himself. Some He cursed and humbled, and turned them to dissension among themselves. As clay in a potter's hand, to be molded and arranged in every way according to his good pleasure, so is the human being in the hand of the One who made him according to His judgment. Opposed to evil, there is good; set against death, there is life; so too is the sinner opposed to the just. And so look upon the work of the Most High, two by two, one against the other" (Sir 33:10–15). First, God's discipline is commended here. "In the abundance of discipline," he says, "the Lord separated them"—from what if not from the blessings of paradise? "And he altered their ways"—so that they would now live as mortal beings. Then one mass was made of all of them, coming from inherited sin and its penalty of mortality, though in terms of God's forming them and creating them, they are good. . . . Human nature as a whole is fine-tuned in a marvelous way, the spirit of life vivifying earthly limbs, the soul as ruler, the body as subject. But the concupiscence of the flesh, now reigning as a result of the penalty for sin, has thrown everything into confusion, with the whole human race, because of original guilt, made as though one permanent lump. And yet [Sirach] goes on: "Some He blessed and exalted, and these He sanctified and brought to Himself. Some He cursed and humbled, and turned them to dissension among themselves" (Sir 33:12)—as though saying as the Apostle does: "Or does not the potter have power over the clay, to make out of the same lump one vessel for honor and another for ignominy?" (Rom 9:21)[38]

---

38. Simpl. 1.q.2.16–20 (CCL 44:41–52); my trans.

(vi) The Mystery of Election

Augustine, at the midpoint of the essay, wrestles with Jesus' statement, "Many are called but few are chosen" (Mt 20:16), and argues that the elect receive a "suitable calling" (vocans congruens) in which each of the saved is drawn to God in some unique, decisive way. At the end of the essay, Augustine acknowledges the limits of the free choice of the will and the radical mystery of God's election, noting that such a "suitable calling" comes by providential arrangement, a mysterious intertwining of inner delight and an exterior environment of choice. In closing, he turns from Paul's words to Paul's life story and sees it as a paradigm of the mystery of election that defies all human standards of fair play. From To Simplicianus, Book 1, Question 2:

(2.21) The Apostle's main idea . . . is nothing other than this: that the one who glories should glory in the Lord. Who, after all, will question the work of the Lord, who from the same lump damns one and justifies another? Free choice of the will has great value. It certainly exists, but what value is it for those who have been put up for sale due to [the debt of] sin? "The flesh," Paul says, "lusts against the spirit and the spirit against the flesh so that you do not do what you will" (Gal 5:17). It is commanded that we live uprightly, and this reward has been set out: that in eternity we shall merit to live in happiness. But who can live uprightly and do good works unless he has been justified by faith (Rom 5:1)? It is commanded that we believe that, in receiving the gift of the Holy Spirit, we can, through love, do good works. But who is able to believe unless touched by some calling, that is, by a certain testimonial to things? Who has it in his power that some vision touch his mind in a way that his will may be moved to faith? Who embraces, in his core self, something that does not first stir him to delight? But then who has it in his power such that either something happens that is able to delight him or something that delights him happens? Thus when these things by which we make progress delight us, that is because it is inspired and set up by God's grace. It is not acquired by our nodding and our hard labor or the merits of our works because, whether it be the nodding assent of our will, or it be the diligence of hard labor, or it be the works of fervent charity, He bestows it, He lavishes it on us. . . .

(2.22) That if some choice is to be made here, as we understand by what Paul says, that "a remnant was formed through the choice of grace" (Rom 11:5), it is not that the justified are choosing life eternal, but that those who will be justified are chosen. Clearly that choice is so hidden that it does not appear obvious to those of us in that same lump. Or if it appears obvious to others, I for my part confess my own weakness in this matter. . . . Do we not see certain people of both sexes living in marital chastity without complaint, whether heretics or pagans or even the lukewarm, even if they hold the true faith and are in the true Church, that we are amazed at how they are surpassed not only in patience and sobriety but also in faith, hope, and love by prostitutes and actors who undergo sudden conversions? What's left, therefore? That wills are chosen. But the will itself cannot be moved in any way unless something happens that delights and invites our core self. That that occur is not in any person's power. What did Saul want to do except attack, arrest, tie up, kill Christians? How rabid a will, how enraged, how blind! Yet it took one voice from on high, and he was laid prostrate and met such a vision that his mind and will, shattered by savagery, were twisted round the right way and set straight towards the faith—he it was who went from being the Gospel's extraordinary persecutor to being its even more extraordinary preacher. And yet, "what shall we say? Is there injustice with God" (Rom 9:14), who exacts payment from whom He pleases and gives to whom He pleases, who never exacts anything un-owed and never gives anything foreign? "Is there injustice with God? Of course not!" (Rom 9:14) Why, then, this one this way and that one that way? "O man, who are you?" (Rom 9:20) If you do not have to repay the debt, you have something to be grateful for. If you have to, you have nothing to complain about. Let us believe this much, even if we cannot grasp it: that the One who founded and made the created universe, both spiritual and physical, arranges everything in its number and weight and measure (Wis 11:20). But "inscrutable are His judgments, and unsearchable His ways" (Rom 11:33). Let us say, "Alleluia," and let us together give praise in song, and let us not say: "Why's this?" or "Why's that?" For everything has been created, each in its own time.[39]

❧

PHASE ONE: THE DEBATE WITH CAELESTIUS (411–413)

CAELESTIUS ON TRIAL (411)

The controversy erupted dramatically in Carthage in 411.[40] Augustine was not present; nor was Pelagius. At the center of the storm was Pelagius's disciple, Caelestius, who applied to become a presbyter in the Carthaginian church. Paulinus of Milan, Ambrose's one-time deacon, knew of Caelestius and charged him with heterodox views. A formal

---

39. Simpl. 1.q.2.21–22 (CCL 44:53–56); my trans.

40. On this, see F. Refoulé, "Datation du premier concile de Carthage contre les Pélagiens et du Libellus fidei de Rufin," *Revue des études augustiniennes* 9 (1963): 41–49.

tribunal was held in Carthage, with Paulinus acting as prosecutor and Aurelius, bishop of Carthage, serving as judge. In the following passage, Augustine writes to Aurelius and recalls six heterodox positions that Caelestius was accused of holding. From On the Deeds of Pelagius:

(11.23) For there follow certain objections made against Pelagius, which are said to have been found in the doctrine of his disciple Caelestius:

"That Adam was created mortal, and, whether he had sinned or not, he would have been going to die."

"That the sin of Adam injured only himself and not the human race."

"That the Law leads to the Kingdom just as does the Gospel."

"That before the coming of Christ there were men without sin."

"That newborn infants are in the same condition in which Adam was before his transgression."

"That the human race as a whole does not die through the death or transgression of Adam, nor does the human race as a whole rise again through the resurrection of Christ."

These statements were raised in objection, just as also they are said to have been heard and condemned at Carthage by your Holiness and other bishops with you. As you will recall, I was not present there myself, but later, on my arrival in Carthage, I examined the acts of the synod, some of which I remember.[41]

Augustine has preserved one segment of the tribunal's record. This verbatim transcript allows us to hear the sometimes tense exchanges between Paulinus, Caelestius, and Aurelius. Quoted by Augustine in On the Grace of Christ and Original Sin, *Book 2:*

(3.3) *Bishop Aurelius:* "Let what follows be read out." And it was read out: "That the sin of Adam injured himself alone and not the human race."

Caelestius: "I said I was in doubt about the transmission of that sin, but that I would agree to it should someone bestowed with the grace of knowledge explain it, since I've heard various views from those who hold positions as presbyters in the Catholic Church."

Deacon Paulinus: "Tell us their names."

Caelestius: "The holy presbyter Rufinus, who stayed in Rome along with the holy Pammachius. I heard him say that there was no transmission of sin."

Deacon Paulinus: "Is there anyone else?"

---

41. *De gestis Pelagii* 11.23 (CSEL 42:76–77); trans. Mourant and Collinge, FOTC 86:134–35. See also Augustine's discussion in *ep.* 157.3.22 (BA 21:78–80). The same six charges appear in a slightly different order in Marius Mercator, *Commonitorium super nomine Coelestii* (PL 48:69–70).

Caelestius: "I heard various others say it as well."

Deacon Paulinus: "State their names!"

Caelestius: "Isn't one priest enough for you?"

Bishop Aurelius: (a little later): "Let the rest of the charges be read." And it was read out: "That infants who are newborns are in the same state that Adam was in before the transgression." And so on to the end of the list of charges.

(3.4) *Bishop Aurelius:* "Caelestius, did you ever teach, as Deacon Paulinus claims, that newborn infants are in the same state that Adam was in before the transgression?"

Caelestius: "Let him explain what he means by 'before the transgression.'"

Deacon Paulinus: "You deny you taught this? [Turning to the court:] One of two options: Either let him deny that he used to teach this or let him condemn it here and now."

Caelestius: "I just said: Let Paulinus explain what he meant by 'before the transgression.'"

Deacon Paulinus: "Deny you taught this!"

Bishop Aurelius: "I ask you what I am to gather from this objection of yours. Here's what I say: Adam, as constituted in paradise, was made imperishable. Afterwards, through the transgression of [God's] command, he was made corruptible. Do you say this, brother Paulinus?"

Deacon Paulinus: "Yes, my lord."

Bishop Aurelius: "What is the state of unbaptized infants today? Is it the same as Adam's was before the transgression? Or does it bring along the guilt of the transgression from the same sinful origin from which it is born? That is what Deacon Paulinus wants to hear."

Deacon Paulinus: "Did he teach this? Or does he deny it now?"

Caelestius: "I have said that concerning the transmission of sin, I have heard different people within the Catholic Church argue against it, and some others defend it. It is an open question, not a matter of heresy. I have always said that infants need baptism and ought to be baptized. What more does he want?"[42]

RUFINUS THE SYRIAN

In his testimony, Caelestius appealed to a certain "holy presbyter Rufinus" to justify his stance on the sin of Adam. Scholars presume that Caelestius was referring to Rufinus the Syrian, who, it seems, had once been a monk in Jerome's monastery in Bethlehem and who later settled in Rome. Some scholars have suggested that Rufinus, not Pelagius, was the real founder of what became the Pelagian movement.[43] During his stay in Rome in the

42. *Gr. et. pecc. or.* 2.3.3–3.4 (CSEL 42:168–69); my trans.
43. This claim dates back to the 5th-century historian Marius Mercator. On Rufinus's role in the contro-

390s, Rufinus authored a work entitled The Book of Faith (Liber de fide), *in which he explicitly denies original sin along the lines that Caelestius spoke of. From Rufinus the Syrian,* Book of Faith:

(39) They are insane, those who, on account of one human being, Adam, condemn the entire world of injustices and of crimes. People who say this proclaim an unjust God or at least estimate that the devil is stronger than God, implying that the nature which God created good the devil could make evil through the transgression of Adam and Eve. Were it the case that the transgression of the first human being, Adam, and his wife, Eve, made all human beings accountable for the sin, then they certainly ought to acknowledge their [own] lusts for criminal offenses. But inasmuch as they themselves are lovers of pleasure and of the flesh, they should not latch onto others as the cause for things they themselves are seen to be the authors of. Or, should we let those who think themselves prudent and who can neither understand things they are saying nor comprehend things they argue about tell us why Adam and Eve, once they fell the first time, never fell a second time, if their nature, made inwardly sinful by their transgression, had become unable to keep itself away from evils? For nowhere does sacred Scripture remember them as having sinned a second time, while concerning Cain, it did not hesitate to narrate that he sinned a second time, and yet concerning Abel, it also taught that he was a stranger to sins. . . .

(40) But if, as they themselves assert, infants die on account of Adam's sin, let them tell us why those infants who have just been baptized are allowed to taste death, since all who have been baptized and, because of this, have become sons and daughters of God, cannot have any sin. If it were really the case that infants are baptized on account of Adam's sin, then those born of Christian parents should not be baptized at all and should be regarded just as if they too were holy ones because they have been begotten of faith-filled parents, for the blessed Paul teaches this in this way, saying: "Otherwise, your children would be unclean, whereas in fact they are holy" (1 Cor 7:14). In a similar way, blessed John too teaches concerning newborn children that, as soon as they are born, they take in an enlightening sanctification from the only-begotten Word, as he says: "It was the true light who enlightens every person coming into the world" (Jn 1:9). Therefore, infants take in baptism not on account of sins but in order to be created in Christ through baptism, having a spiritual procreation, and so themselves are made partakers in His heavenly kingdom, for the blessed Paul teaches this in this way: "Whoever is in Christ is a new creation" (2 Cor 5:17), and again: "If children, then heirs as well, indeed heirs of God, co-heirs with Christ" (Rom 8:17).[44]

versy, see Gerald Bonner, "Rufinus the Syrian and African Pelagianism," *Augustinian Studies* 1 (1970): 31–47; Eugene TeSelle, "Rufinus the Syrian, Caelestius, Pelagius: Explorations in the Pre-History of the Pelagian Controversy," *Augustinian Studies* 3 (1972): 61–95.

44. Text in Mary W. Miller, ed., *Rufini Presbyteri: Liber de Fide: A Critical Text and Translation with Introduction and Commentary*, Patristic Studies 96 (Washington, DC: The Catholic University of America Press, 1964), 112–14; my trans.

CHRIST THE PEDIATRICIAN

After the tribunal, Marcellinus wrote Augustine, asking him to respond to Caelestius's assertions. Augustine replied with On the Merits and Forgiveness of Sins and On Infant Baptism. *Note three points: First, Augustine did not initiate the controversy; his close friends and colleagues did. We need to appreciate to what degree Augustine's role was thrust upon him. Second, the controversy at this juncture was anti-Caelestian. The condemnation of Caelestius said nothing about Pelagius. Only in retrospect would Augustine see this as his first anti-Pelagian treatise. Third, while Caelestius took a stand on infants, Pelagius (at least in his surviving writings) shows no interest in them. This highlights what scholars now emphasize: Pelagianism is not a single, coherent body of ideas, even if Augustine treated it as such, but rather "a loose confederation of theologies taking their name, but not necessarily their inspiration, from the British moralist."[45] In this initial work, Augustine focuses on two issues that came up during Caelestius's trial. The first is original sin and its implications for infant baptism. As Augustine sees it, the underlying yet central theological issue is Christology.[46] To declare infants innocent implicitly denies that Christ is the one and only Savior of the world. Note how Augustine gives his stock image of Christ the Doctor a new twist: that Jesus is also a baby doctor, a pediatrician. From* On the Merits and Forgiveness of Sins and On Infant Baptism, *Book 1:*

(18.23) Those people raise a question and seem to offer something worth considering and discussing: They say that little ones, newly born from their mothers' wombs, receive baptism not for the remission of sin, but in order that, through "spiritual procreation," they may be created in Christ and become partakers of the kingdom of heaven and, by this, children and "heirs of God, co-heirs with Christ" (Rom 8:17).[47] Yet when one asks them whether those who are not baptized and not made co-heirs with Christ and partakers of the kingdom of heaven have the benefit of eternal salvation at the resurrection of the dead, they labor furiously but find no way out. After all, would any Christian allow it to be said that one can attain eternal salvation without being reborn in Christ? Christ willed that rebirth to take place through baptism when he established just such a sacrament for regenerating us for the hope of eternal salvation. For this reason, the Apostle said: "Not because of any righteous deeds we have done but according to His mercy, He saved us through the bath of rebirth" (Ti 3:5). . . . Who would dare claim that without

45. James Wetzel, "Snares of Truth: Augustine on Free Will and Predestination," in Dodaro and Lawless, *Augustine and His Critics,* 126.

46. Burns, *Development,* 96.

47. "Not for the remission of sin, but . . . partakers of the kingdom": Augustine is here quoting nearly word-for-word Rufinus's text. It is possible either that Augustine had the text or that Caelestius had quoted it in the documents that he formally submitted on the occasion of the ecclesiastical tribunal.

this rebirth infants are able to be saved, as if Christ had not died for them? For "Christ died for the ungodly" (Rom 5:6). But as for these infants, who, as is clear, have done nothing ungodly in their lives, if they are not held prisoner by any chain of ungodliness from the outset, originally, then how did He who died for the ungodly die for them? If they are not wounded by that disease of original sin, then why are they carried to Christ the Doctor, that is, carried by those running[48] in pious fear so that these infants might receive the sacrament of eternal health and well-being? Otherwise, why would [those who bring them] not be told when they come to church: "Get these innocents out of here! It's not the healthy who need a doctor, but the sick; Christ came to call not the righteous, but sinners"? Never was such nonsense said, never is it said, never will it be said, not ever in the Church of Christ.

(19.24) . . . The Doctor does indeed call infants—the Doctor who is not needed by the healthy but by the sick, the One who came to call to repentance not the just, but sinners (Lk 5:31-32). And since infants are as yet held debt-bound by no sin from their own lives, then it must be the disease of original sin that is cured in them, cured by that grace of His which makes them healthy through the bath of rebirth. . . .

(22.33) Let us consent to and yield to the authority of Holy Scripture, which knows not how to deceive nor be deceived. And just as we believe that those not yet born have done nothing good or bad to make any discernible difference in what they merit, so let us not have the slightest doubt that all are under the sin which, through one man, entered into the world and has been passed on to all humanity (Rom 5:12), something from which only "the grace of God through our Lord Jesus Christ" (Rom 7:25) can liberate us.

(23.33) This medicinal coming [of Christ] is a deed done "not for the healthy but for the sick," because He "came to call not the righteous, but sinners" (Lk 5:31–32). Into His Kingdom, one will not enter unless one has been born again of water and of the Spirit (Jn 3:5), nor will one possess eternal life and well-being other than in His kingdom since those who have not eaten His flesh (Jn 6:54) and who have not believed in the Son will not have life (Jn 3:36), but the anger of God remains upon them. From this sin, from this sickness, from this anger of God, only the "Lamb of God who takes away the sins of the world" (Jn 1:29) can deliver them; only the Doctor who came "not for the healthy but for the sick" (Lk 5:31); only the Savior of whom it was said to the

48. "Carried by those running": The Maurist edition has "those running" (*currentium*, PL 44:122), whereas Zycha, the editor of the critical edition, suggests "those caring" (*curantium*, CSEL 60:23). The Maurist version is correct: Augustine routinely speaks of mothers (and others) "running" with their infants to church to get them baptized. Given the high incidence of infant mortality in the ancient world, coupled with the North African conviction that there is no salvation outside of baptism, it is little wonder parents ran to church with dying babies in their arms.

human race, "Today a savior has been born to you" (Lk 2:11); *only a Redeemer whose blood has paid off our debts.* These children, even if they have no sin of their own because of age, have original sin and are, "by nature, children of wrath" (Eph 2:3). Now who would dare to say that Christ is not the Savior of infants nor their Redeemer? From what does He rescue them if they do not have within them the disease of original sin? From what does He redeem them if they have not been put up for sale through their sin-subjected origin from the first human being? In our judgment, therefore, one should not go promising infants eternal salvation outside the bounds of Christ's baptism— nothing beyond what Holy Scripture promises, preferring it over all human ingenuity.[49]

SIN AND THE WILL

The second issue from Caelestius's trial was the place of the will in the Christian pursuit of holiness. The circle around Pelagius was fond of citing Old Testament notables as possible candidates for sinlessness. Augustine granted sinlessness as a theoretical possibility, but insisted that such an unlikely possibility would only be possible with the infused grace of God. Both Augustine and his opponents located the problem of sin in the will. But for Augustine, moral decision-making always seemed more subtle than it was for others. Knowing moral rules was not enough. We need God to enlighten our minds and to ignite our hearts. From On the Merits and Forgiveness of Sins and On Infant Baptism, *Book 2:*

   (17.26) Since human beings are able to live in this life without sin so long as divine grace helps the human will, then why don't we? This I can easily and truthfully answer: Because people are unwilling to. But if I am asked why they are unwilling, . . . I would briefly say this: People do not will to do what is right either because they do not know what is right or because they find no delight in it. For we will something more passionately depending on how much certainty we have in knowing that it is good and how burning our delight in it is. Therefore, ignorance and weakness are faults that hinder the will either from being moved to do a good work or to refrain from an evil one. But that what was hidden may come to light and what did not delight us may become sweet, this belongs to the grace of God, which helps people's wills. The reason why they are not helped by grace lies in them, not in God, whether they be predestined to be condemned on account of the sin of pride or wheth-

49. *Pecc. mer.* 1.18.23–23.33 (CSEL 60:23–33); my trans. On this, see William Harmless, "Christ the Pediatrician: Augustine on the Diagnosis and Treatment of the Injured Vocation of the Child," in *The Vocation of the Child*, ed. Patrick McKinley Brennan (Grand Rapids: Eerdmans, 2008), 127–53.

er they are to be judged and corrected over their pride if they are children of mercy. . . .

(18.28) We human beings struggle to find in our will some good that is ours, some good in us not from God, but I do not know how one can possibly find it. For the Apostle says this, when speaking of human goods: "For what do you have that you have not received? And if you have received it, why do you glory as if you did not receive it?" (1 Cor 4:7)[50]

⊰⊱

PHASE TWO: THE DEBATE WITH PELAGIUS (414–418)

EARLY IMPRESSIONS OF PELAGIUS

Augustine had close friends in Italy who knew Pelagius well and who had spoken highly of him. Even after the affair of Caelestius, Augustine was wary of attributing the disciple's failings to his spiritual mentor. In this passage, Augustine speaks of his brief glimpses of Pelagius and his own early hesitations. From On the Deeds of Pelagius:

(22.46) To refer especially to my own case, I first became acquainted with Pelagius's name and the great reputation he had, when he was away and established at Rome. Later, reports began to reach us that he was arguing against the grace of God. Although I deplored this and believed those who told it to me, I still desired to observe something of this sort from him directly, or in one of his books, so that if I began to refute it, he could not disavow it. But afterwards, when he arrived in Africa during my absence, he was received on our coast, that is, that of Hippo, where, as I learned from our friends, nothing of this nature was heard from him, for he left from there more quickly than was expected. Later, as I remember, I saw his face once or twice at Carthage, when I was preoccupied with preparations for the conference which we were about to have with the heretical Donatists,[51] but he had hastened away from there across the sea. Meanwhile, these doctrines were seething, spread by the mouths of those who were regarded as his disciples, to the point where Caelestius appeared before an ecclesiastical tribunal and incurred a verdict worthy of his perverse opinions. At any rate, we thought it a more helpful way of proceeding against them if, without mentioning the names of any individuals, we were to challenge and refute the errors them-

---

50. *Pecc. mer.* 2.17.26–18.28 (CSEL 60:98–100); my trans.
51. "Preparations for the conference . . .": Augustine is referring to the Conference of Carthage in 411, which ended the Donatist schism. On this, see chapter 7.

selves. Thus the individuals might be brought to their senses by a fear of ecclesiastical judgment rather than punished by a judgment itself. Hence, we did not cease to argue against these evil doctrines either through books or by instructions to the people.[52]

PELAGIUS DENOUNCES CONFESSIONS

In Rome, probably around 405, a bishop who was a friend of Augustine happened to be speaking with Pelagius and quoted from Augustine's Confessions, *Book 10. Pelagius was, to put it mildly, irritated. Here is Augustine's account. From* On the Gift of Perseverance:

(20.53) And which of my works has been able to be more widely known and more popular than the books of my *Confessions*? Although I published this work before the Pelagian heresy arose, certainly I said in it to God, and said it often: "Give what you command, and command what you will."[53] When these words of mine were quoted one day at Rome in Pelagius's presence by a fellow bishop and brother of mine,[54] Pelagius was not able to bear them and, attacking them with considerable emotion, came close to fighting with the one who had quoted them. Yet what does God command first and foremost but that we believe in him? And this, therefore, he gives, if it is well said to him, "Give what you command." And also in this same work, when I recounted my conversion, how God converted me to this faith that I was laying waste to with a most miserable and raging loquacity, do you not remember how I told the story in such a way as to show that it was granted to the faithful and daily tears of my mother that I should not perish? Certainly I was taught there that God, by his grace, converts people's wills, not only those turned away from right faith but also those turned against right faith. And I begged God for growth in perseverance, you know, and you can review [my words] when you wish. But as for all the gifts of God which in that work I either requested or praised, who would dare to deny or even to doubt that God foreknew that He would give them and could never have failed to know to whom He would give them? This is the evident and certain predestination of the saints, which necessity

52. *De gestis Pelagii* 22.46 (BA 21:532–34); trans. Mourant and Collinge, FOTC 86:157–58.

53. "Give what you command, and command what you will" (*da quod iubes et iube quod uis*): This phrase appears at key junctures as a sort of refrain: *conf.* 10.29.40 (twice), 10.31.45 and 10.37.60 (CCL 27:176, 179, 188). On this, see Cornelius Mayer, "Da quod iubes et iube quod uis," *Aug-Lex* 2: 211–13; for a complete listing of the phrase in Augustine's works, see Hombert, "Appendice," *Gloria Gratiae*, 593–94.

54. "Fellow bishop and brother of mine": Augustine does not identify him. O'Donnell, 3:201, suggests two possibilities: Evodius of Uzalis, who was in Italy in 404–5; and Possidius of Calama, who was in Italy in 408. Brown, *Augustine of Hippo*, 343, suggests Paulinus of Nola.

later compelled me to defend more carefully and laboriously when I began arguing against the Pelagians.[55]

PELAGIUS THE SPIRITUAL DIRECTOR

In the 390s and 400s, Pelagius moved among aristocratic circles of the city of Rome and was a respected spiritual guide. One of the wealthiest and most powerful families in the Empire was the Anicii. When one of the Anicii, Demetrias, decided at age 14 to take the veil as a consecrated virgin, the family invited famous theologians from around the Latin-speaking world to compose exhortations. Jerome was invited; so was Augustine. So too was Pelagius. Pelagius's exhortation—really a sort of manifesto—was written around 413, when he was settled in Palestine. We get a glimpse here of Pelagius the tough-minded spiritual director. From Pelagius, Letter to Demetrias:

(16.1) We need to pause here for a little while, virgin, and think about the precious pearls within each word of the Apostle [Paul], pearls with which the bride of Christ is to be adorned. He says, "Do everything" (Phil 2:14). So we ought not to pick and choose from God's commandments, but fulfill every one of them without exception. Nor should we scorn certain precepts as mere tokens or trivial matters. We should regard all of them in terms of the imperial majesty of the Ruler. No command of God can seem to us disdain-able if we bear in mind its author, and we should do it without grumbling and stammering. We see worthless, ignoble masters publicly scoffed at by their slaves who are used to resisting even minimal orders right to their face. But this is not permitted to happen with noble personages. The more powerful the lord, the quicker the slaves are to obey; the harder the orders, the more cheerfully they are heard. Certainly, at the king's command, all stand alert, geared and battle-ready to obey, such that they even desire to receive their orders, and they believe themselves fortunate not only when they do what is commanded but even that they are considered worthy of being commanded. Just serving a high dignitary is esteemed as a position of privilege.

(16.2) God Himself, the God of eternal, ineffable majesty and of incalculable power, has sent us sacred writings, the summit of his precepts, truly worthy of our worship, and yet we do not immediately receive them with joy and reverence, nor do we esteem it a great privilege to be ruled by such a great and such an illustrious power, especially when what is being sought for is advantageous not to the One giving the orders but to the ones carrying them out. On the contrary, we, in fact, behave like arrogant, worthless slaves. With a disdainful and lazy mindset, we cry in protest before the Lord's face and say: "That's too hard! That's too tough! We can't do it; we're only human. We're wrapped up in this fragile flesh." What insane blindness! What reckless profanity! We

---

55. *De dono perseverantiae* 20.53 (BA 24:730–32); trans. Mourant and Collinge, FOTC 86:323–24.

accuse the God of knowledge of a twofold ignorance: that He appears not to know what He has made and not to know what He has commanded—as if He has forgotten human frailty (something He Himself is the author of) and imposed commands on humanity that we cannot bear. At the same time (and this is really horrible!) we ascribe iniquity to the Just One and cruelty to the Holy One when we complain that, first, He commands something impossible and that, then, He damns human beings for something they cannot avoid such that God seems to be seeking not so much our salvation as our damnation—something that is even a sacrilege to suspect.

(16.3) The Apostle, therefore, knowing that the Lord of justice and majesty commands nothing impossible, snatches away from us this vice of grumbling—something that tends to come up when what is ordered is either unfair or when the one giving orders is a less respected person. Why do we uselessly turn our back on this challenge? And why do we complain to the Lawgiver about the frailty of our nature? No one knows better the scope of our strength than the One who gave us our strength. Nor does anyone understand what we are capable of better than the One who gave us the capacity for virtue. The Just One would neither command the impossible nor would the Holy One intend to damn a person for something that he could not avoid.[56]

A Man Inflamed

In 414, Augustine was given a copy of Pelagius's treatise On Nature *by two of Pelagius's disciples—or rather, ex-disciples. It proved eye-opening. In the preface of his rebuttal, Augustine speaks of how the treatise revealed Pelagius's fiery temperament as a reformer. From* On Nature and Grace:

(1.1) The book which you have sent to me, dearly beloved sons Timasius and James, I have read through somewhat rapidly . . . but with considerable attention. I saw [in it] a man inflamed with a very ardent zeal against those who, although they ought, when they sin, to censure the human will, try instead to accuse the nature of human beings and thus to excuse themselves. He has flared up excessively against this plague, which even writers of secular literature have strongly censured, exclaiming: "The human race wrongly brings a complaint against its own nature."[57] With all his strong intellectual talents, your author also has piled up support for precisely this judgment. I fear, nevertheless, that he will instead give support to those "who have a zeal for God, but not according to knowledge; for they, not knowing the justice of God and seeking to establish their own, have not submitted themselves to the

56. Pelagius, Ad Demetriadem 16 (PL 30:31–32); my trans. Augustine eventually obtained a copy and commented on it notably in *gr. et pecc. or.* 1.37.41–40.44; also *ep.* 188.

57. Sallust, Bellum Iugurthinum 1.1.

justice of God" (Rom 10:2–3). The Apostle makes clear the meaning of "justice of God" in this passage by adding immediately: "For the end of the law is Christ, to justice for everyone who believes" (Rom 10:4). . . .

(7.7) Therefore, however great the zeal with which the author of this book you sent is inflamed against those who base a defense plea for their sins on the infirmity of human nature, with an equal and more burning zeal must we be inflamed so that the cross of Christ not be made void.[58]

PELAGIUS'S ON NATURE

Augustine's tactic of quoting opponents has, as we have seen, made it possible for scholars to reconstruct lost works by Manichees and Donatists. In the same way, we can assemble fragments of Pelagius's lost treatise On Nature.[59] The work dates, it seems, from his time in Rome, likely between 405 and 410. Augustine quotes this work in a scattered fashion so that it is not possible to reconstruct the entire text. Still, certain key themes emerge:

(i) The Possibility of Sinlessness

Pelagius was, at heart, a moral theologian. He insisted that we can only be held morally responsible for our misdeeds if we are really and truly free. Without such freedom, we cannot fairly be judged culpable. So he argued at length that sinlessness must exist, at least as a theoretical possibility. From Pelagius, On Nature, as quoted in Augustine, On Nature and Grace:

(7.8) It is one thing to ask whether something *can be* (what has to do only with its possibility), and it is another thing to ask whether it *is*. . . . Here we are treating only possibility . . . I say that it is possible for a person to be without sin. And what do you say? "That it is impossible for a human being to be without sin." I am not saying that there is a human being without sin, nor do you say that there is not a human being without sin. We are disputing about what is possible and impossible, not about what is and is not. . . . [Scripture says:] "There is no just person on earth" (Eccl 7:21), and, "There is no one who does good" (Ps 13:3). By [such] passages, it can be shown how some human beings were at a given time, not whether they could not have been something else. For this reason, they were justly found to be guilty. But if they were as they were because they could not have been otherwise, then they would be free from any blame. . . .

(42.49) All right, suppose I grant that the Apostle [Paul] teaches us that all have

---

58. *Nat. et gr.* 1.1–7.7 (BA 21:244–54); trans. Mourant and Collinge, FOTC 86:22–26.
59. For a gathering of the fragments of Pelagius's *De natura*, see PL 48:598–606.

been sinners. He declares what they have been, not that they could not have been otherwise. Therefore, even if all human beings could be proved to be sinners, that would not in any way prejudice our position, since we insist not so much on what human beings *are* as on what they *are able to be*. (43.50) God, being as good as He is just, created human beings with sufficient ability to be without the evil of sin—if only they had been willing. . . . Natural ability does not come from will. . . .

(44.52) But what disturbs many people, you will say, is that I do not maintain that it is by the grace of God that a person can be without sin. . . . O blindness of ignorance, O listlessness of an inexperienced mind, to suppose that I defend without the grace of God what one hears should be attributed only to God. (45.53) But when it is said that this very ability does not come from human choice but from nature, from the author of nature, namely, God, is there any way that what is considered to belong to God particularly can be regarded as without God's grace? . . . We affirm then that the possibility of anything lies not so much in the power of the human choice as in the necessity of nature . . . For instance, I can speak. That I can speak is not up to me, but that I do speak is up to me, that is, it is due to my own will. And because choosing to speak is up to me, I can do either, that is, either speak or not speak. But because the fact that I *am able* to speak is not up to me, that is, does not belong to my choice and will, it is necessary that I always be able to speak. And even if I wished that I could not speak, still, I cannot become unable to speak unless I were to remove the organ by which I carry out the task of speaking. . . . (49.57) Because not sinning is up to us, we can either sin or not sin.[60]

(ii) Imitating the Original Sinner

Pelagius, given his moral rigorism, was outraged by those who blamed the sin of Adam for human sinfulness. He insisted that we do not inherit original sin; we imitate the original sinner. From Pelagius, On Nature, *as quoted in Augustine,* On Nature and Grace:

(9.10) [A human being] is not damned just because it is said, "All have sinned in Adam." One is damned not because of sin contracted in the origin of one's birth, but rather because of an imitation of Adam.[61] If one was as one was because one could not have been otherwise, then one would have to be free of blame. . . . (19.21) First,

60. Quoted in Nat. et gr. 7.8–49.57 (BA 21:254–350); trans. Mourant and Collinge, FOTC 86:27–64 (modified). Here Pelagius uses the example of speaking to distinguish between the ability (*posse*), which comes from God, and the willing (*velle*), which comes from us. In Book 3 of On Free Choice (Pro libero arbitrio), as preserved in Augustine's gr. et pecc. or. 1.3.3–5.6, Pelagius uses a similar example of seeing.

61. "Imitation of Adam": Pelagius, In Romanos, commenting on Romans 5:12 ("Through one man, sin came into the world, and through sin death"), tersely notes: "By example or by pattern. . . . As long as they sin the same, they likewise die" (trans. DeBruyn, *Pelagius's Commentary*, 92–93). See Augustine's very different reading of this text below.

we must dispute the view that maintains that our nature has been weakened and changed through sin. I think, therefore, that before all else we must inquire what sin is. Is it some substance? Or is it a name wholly lacking substance, by which is expressed neither a thing nor an existent nor some kind of body, but the action of doing something evil? I believe it is the latter, and, if it is, how could that which lacks substance have weakened or changed human nature? . . .

(21.23) Those for whom you seek a physician are in good health. And not even the first man was condemned to death for such a reason, for he did not sin afterwards. . . . His descendants also are not only not weaker than he, but have actually fulfilled more commandments, since he neglected to obey even the one. . . . (30.34) How can people be answerable to God for the guilt of a sin which they know is not theirs? For if it is necessary, it is not theirs. Or if it is theirs, it is voluntary; and if it is voluntary, it can be avoided.[62]

(iii) Salvation Outside Christianity

Pelagius argued for the possibility of salvation beyond the borders (whether temporal or geographical) of Christianity. From Pelagius, On Nature, *as quoted in Augustine,* On Nature and Grace:

(2.2) Even if, in some nature or in some past time, faith in the blood of Christ was not known to [humanity], God is not unjust and would not deprive the just of their reward for justice if the mystery of Christ's nature as both human and divine, which was manifest in the flesh, had not been proclaimed to them. . . . For there still exist some people in remote places, although it is said that they are few in number, to whom the Gospel has not yet been preached—what should human nature do or what has it done, either before, when it had not yet heard that salvation was to come to pass, or now, if it has not learned that it was accomplished? What should it do except fulfill God's will by believing in the One who made heaven and earth and who created human nature itself (as it is naturally perceived), and by living rightly, even though it has not been tinged with any faith in the Passion and Resurrection of Christ?[63]

---

62. Quoted in *nat. et. gr.* 9.10–30.34 (BA 21:258–306); trans. Mourant and Collinge, FOTC 86:28–47. Note the final syllogism. Caelestius, in a book of syllogisms entitled *Definitiones,* argued in a similar vein: "We must ask whether a person ought to be without sin. Undoubtedly, one ought to be. If one ought to be, one can be. If one cannot be, then one should not have to be. And if a person ought not to be without sin, then the person, therefore, ought to be with sin; and then sin will no longer be sin. . . . Or if it is absurd to say that, then it is necessary to admit that a person ought to be without sin, and it is obvious that one is not obliged to do more than one's ability" (quoted by Augustine, *De perfectione justitiae hominis* 3.5, CSEL 42:6; my trans.).

63. Quoted in *nat. et. gr.* 2.2 (BA 21:246–48); trans. Mourant and Collinge, FOTC 86:23–24.

AUGUSTINE'S VIEW BRIEFLY STATED

The Pelagian controversy drew out Augustine's tenacious long-windedness, but he was also capable of stating his views with cogent brevity. He opens his rebuttal to Pelagius's On Nature *with a survey of his own core positions on creation, sin, and redemption. What undergirds Augustine's logic here are two fundamental convictions: (i) Christ is the one and only savior; and (ii) there is no salvation outside the Church. Note his appeal to Romans 5:12, what would become his favorite text to justify the North African view on the universal scope of original sin. From* On Nature and Grace:

(3.3) In the beginning humanity's nature was created without any fault and without any sin; however, this human nature in which we are all born from Adam now requires a physician because it is not healthy. Indeed, all the good qualities that it has in its organization, life, senses, and understanding, it possesses from the most high God, its Creator and Shaper. On the other hand, the defect—which darkens and weakens all those natural goods so that there is a need for illumination and for healing—is not derived from its blameless Maker, but from that original sin that was committed through free will. Consequently, that criminal nature draws upon itself the most righteous punishment. For if we are now a new creation in Christ, "we were," nevertheless, "children of wrath, even as the rest. But God, who is rich in mercy, because of the great love with which He loved us, even though we were dead through our offenses, has given us life together with Christ, by whose grace you have been saved" (Eph 2:3–5).

(4.4) This grace of Christ, then, without which neither children nor adults can be saved, is given gratuitously and not for our merits, and for this reason is called "grace." "[They are] justified," says the Apostle, "freely by His blood" (Rom 3:14). As a result, those who are not liberated through grace—either because they have not yet been able to hear or because they have not wished to obey or because, when on account of their age they were not capable of hearing, they did not receive the bath of rebirth, which they could have received and by means of which they would have been saved—are justly condemned. For people are not without sin, whether the sin they contracted originally or sins they added through their own misconduct. "For all have sinned," either in Adam or in themselves, "and are deprived of the glory of God" (Rom 3:23).

(5.5) As a result, the whole human mass[64] ought to be punished, and if the punishment of damnation were rendered to all, beyond all doubt it would be justly rendered. This is why those who are liberated from it by grace are

---

64. "The whole human mass": This imagery, drawn from Rom 9:21, first appears in Simpl. 1.q.2.19, cited earlier.

not called vessels of their own merits, but "vessels of mercy" (Rom 9:23). But whose mercy was it but the One who sent Jesus Christ into this world to save sinners, whom He foreknew, predestined, called, justified, and glorified? Who then is so insane, so demented, as not to give ineffable thanks to the mercy of God, who liberates those He wills, considering that one could in no way complain against God's justice had He condemned absolutely everyone?

(6.6) If we understand this according to Scripture, we are obliged not to dispute against the grace of Christ nor to try to show that human nature, in infancy, needs no physician because it is healthy and, in adults, can be sufficient, if it wishes, to obtain justice for itself. . . .

(8.9) Notice what [the author of *On Nature*] said [about salvation outside Christianity]. I, however, for my part, say that an infant born where it was not possible for him to be rescued through the baptism of Christ, having been overtaken by death, was thereby in such a state—that is, of having departed without the "bath of rebirth" (Ti 3:5)—because he could not have been otherwise. Therefore, our author would absolve this infant and, contrary to the statement of the Lord, would open to him the kingdom of heaven. But the Apostle does not absolve him when he says: "Through one man sin entered the world, and through sin death, and thus it was passed on to all human beings, in whom all have sinned" (Rom 5:12).[65] Justly, therefore, because of the condemnation that runs through the whole mass of humanity, one is not admitted into the kingdom of heaven, even though one not only was not a Christian but could not have been one.

(9.10) But they say, "One is damned not because it is said, 'All have sinned in Adam,' not because of sin contracted in the origin of one's birth, but rather because of imitation of him." If, therefore, it may be said that Adam is the author of all sins that followed his own, since he was the first sinner in the human race, how then does it happen that Abel is not placed at the head of the just rather than Christ, because Abel was the first just man? I leave aside the case of infants. Consider instead the case of a young man or an old man who died in a place where he could not have heard the name of Christ. Could he, or could he not, have become just by his own nature and free will? If they say he could have, then see what amounts to rendering the cross of Christ void (1 Cor 1:17): to contend that without the cross anyone can be justified by the law

65. "By one man sin entered into this world, and by sin, death, and so death passed upon all men, in whom all have sinned" (Rom 5:12): This is one of Augustine's key proof texts, but his Old Latin version says "in whom all have sinned" (*in quo omnes peccaverunt*), that is: in Adam, all humanity sinned. But that does not match Paul's original Greek, which says "inasmuch as all have sinned." Pelagius himself has the same inaccurate Latin translation; and Jerome maintained it in his Vulgate. On this issue, see Bonner, *St. Augustine*, 372–74; also J. Patout Burns, "The Interpretation of Romans in the Pelagian Controversy," *Augustinian Studies* 10 (1979): 43–54.

of nature and the choice of his will. And so we would be able to say, "Then Christ died in vain" (Gal 2:21), for this [salvation by one's nature and free will] would be something that everyone could do, even if Christ had not died. And if they were unjust, it would be because they wished to be, and not because they could not be just. If, however, one could not be justified in any way without the grace of Christ, let [the author of *On Nature*] absolve him, if he dares, in accordance with his statement that, "If one was as one was because one could not have been otherwise, then one would have to be free from blame."[66]

WOUNDED HUMAN NATURE

The debate between Augustine and Pelagius was, in part, a debate about the human condition. In On Nature, *Pelagius argued that the healthy do not need a doctor. This turn-of-phrase provided Augustine an opening to draw on his image of Christ the Doctor. Augustine invokes the image repeatedly throughout* On Nature and Grace *(as well in other anti-Pelagian treatises) to articulate his view of our current condition and Christ's saving action. Augustine argues as much by image as by logic, using medical metaphors to draw out his theological stance. In what follows, I have highlighted this essential thread with excerpts that run the length of the treatise. Note how Augustine invokes Jesus' parable of the Good Samaritan to speak of Christian life as a convalescence within the "Inn" of the Church. From* On Nature and Grace:

(30.34) What does [Pelagius] mean in the following passage?[67] "Next, how can people be answerable to God for the guilt of some sin which they know is not theirs? For if it is necessary, it is not theirs. Or if it is theirs, it is voluntary; and if it is voluntary, it can be avoided." We answer: Beyond all doubt [Adam's sin] is theirs, but the fault through which it was committed has not yet been completely healed. And the fact that it increases in us happens because we have abused the good health we were endowed with. Because of this injury, people are now increasingly in bad condition and, through weakness or blindness, commit more sins. They ought to pray that they may be healed and that from here on they may enjoy a life of unending good health, not becoming proud, as if human beings could be healed by the very same power [of will] they became injured by. . . .

(34.39) When [Pelagius] thinks that he is pleading God's case by defend-

---

66. *Nat. et. gr.* 3.3–9.10 (BA 21:248–52); trans. Mourant and Collinge, FOTC 86:24–26 (modified).

67. "[Pelagius]": Augustine consciously chose not to cite Pelagius's name, speaking only of "the author," "he," "him," etc. Translators typically insert Pelagius's name here and elsewhere for clarity's sake. I have added square brackets to try and balance Augustine's concern to protect the anonymity of his opponent with contemporary readers' need for clarity of reference.

ing nature, he forgets that in declaring this nature to be healthy he rejects the mercy of the Doctor. But the God who created [Pelagius] is also his Savior. Therefore, we should not so praise the Creator that we are compelled to say (or rather be convicted of saying) that there is no need for a Savior. Therefore, let us honor human nature with fitting praise and let us attribute these praises to the glory of the Creator, but let us not be grateful to Him for having created us in such a way that we seem ungrateful to Him for having healed us. Let us attribute our defects . . . not to God's actions, but to the human will and God's just punishment. Nevertheless, we must admit that it was once in our power that these defects should not have come about, just as we confess that their cure depends upon His mercy more than upon our own power. [Pelagius], however, reduces this mercy and healing aid of the Savior to the fact "that He forgives the transgressions of the past, not that He will help us to avoid sins in the future." Here he is most dangerously mistaken, for without realizing it, he hinders us from being careful and from praying that we enter "not into temptation," (Mt 6:13) since he maintains that it is entirely within our power that it should not happen to us. . . .

(39.46) Let [Pelagius] faithfully and obediently listen to what [Scripture] says: "Through one man sin entered the world, and through sin death, and thus it was passed on to all human beings, in whom all have sinned" (Rom 5:12), and let him not weaken the grace of so great a Doctor in refusing to admit that human nature has been corrupted. How I wish he would read [Scripture] as a Christian should: that apart from that of Jesus Christ, "there is no other name under heaven in which we can be saved" (Acts 4:12), and not defend the power of human nature to the point of believing that human beings can be saved by free will even without that name [of Christ]. . . .

(43.50) For who does not know that humankind was created healthy and faultless, endowed with a free will and a free ability to live a just life? But now we are concerned with human beings [like the man in Jesus' parable] whom the thieves left half-dead on the road, who, being injured and pierced with serious wounds, cannot ascend to the heights of justice as they were once able to descend from [the City of God], even though they are now undergoing treatment in the inn [of the Church] (Lk 10:33–35). God then does not command the impossible, but by His commandments He counsels you to do what you can do and to pray for His aid for what you cannot do. Now let us see where the ability comes from and where the inability comes from. [Pelagius] declares, "Natural ability does not come from the will." But I say: A human being is not just as a result of the will if he can be so by nature, but one will be able to be just as a result of the medicine [of grace], something one cannot be [on one's own] as a result of one's injury. . . .

(52.60) "How can it be," he asks, "that to any baptized person, the flesh is contrary?" So flesh *can* be contrary to those who have not been baptized. Let him explain this somehow, since that [same] nature he has strongly defended also exists in them. He certainly concedes that at least in the non-baptized it has been injured, even if now that wounded man, now among the baptized, has left the inn healthy, or is healthy while still in the inn where the compassionate Samaritan took him to be healed. Now if [Pelagius] will concede that in the non-baptized the flesh is contrary, let him tell us what happened to cause this, since both the flesh and the spirit alike are the creation of one and the same Creator and, since God is good, both are undoubtedly good. It must be that the injury that has been inflicted came from humanity's own will. That this defect in our nature may be healed, we need that same Savior who, as Creator, brought forth our nature. If we confess that all, both great and small, from crying infants to white-haired elders, require this Savior and that medicine of His, that is, the Word who was made flesh to dwell among us, then all controversy between us on this question will be resolved.[68]

PREVENIENT GRACE

As Augustine thought through the implications of grace, he came to stress how God's grace not only works within us and imbues all our good deeds, but that that grace even anticipates those deeds. Later theologians came to refer to this as "prevenient grace," noting Augustine's appeal to Ps 58:11: "His mercy shall come before (praeveniet) me." From On Nature and Grace:

(31.35) And I would have said these things in such a way as to confess my ignorance of the profound judgment of God, why He does not immediately cure this pride which, even in doing good deeds, lies in ambush for the human spirit. It is for this cure that pious souls beg him with tears and great sighs, imploring Him to extend a hand to them in their efforts in order to conquer this pride and in some way beat it down and crush it. . . . "Reveal your way to the Lord, and hope in Him, and He will do it" (Ps 36:5)—and not as some think: that they themselves do it. For when the Psalmist said, "and He will do it," he evidently had no one else in mind other than those [like the Pelagians] who declare, "We do it," that is, we ourselves justify ourselves. We do, in fact, work, but when we work, we cooperate with God who works, for his mercy comes before us. It comes before us, however, that we may be healed, as it will also follow us so that being healed we may gain strength. It

68. *Nat. et. gr.* 30.34–52.60 (BA 21:306–58); my trans., based on Mourant and Collinge, FOTC 86:47–67.

comes before us so that we may be called, and it will follow us so that we may be glorified. It comes before us so that we may lead pious lives; it will follow us so that we may always live with Him, for without Him we can do nothing (Jn 15:5). For Scripture says both, "He is my God, His mercy shall come before me" (Ps 58:11), and, "Your mercy will follow me all the days of my life" (Ps 22:6). Therefore, let us reveal to Him our way in confession, rather than praise it in self-defense. For if it is not His way, but our way, then it certainly is not the right way. Let us reveal it to Him by our confession, for it is not hidden from Him even if we try to conceal it. For "it is good to confess to the Lord" (Ps 91:2).[69]

FREE WILL VS. FREE CHOICE

Pelagius and his circle defined free will in a conventional way: the ability to choose good or evil.[70] This implies that sinning is a sign of our freedom. Augustine disagreed. If defined that way, then God would not be free since God cannot sin.[71] Augustine distinguished freedom of will (libertas) from free choice (liberum arbitrium). True freedom cannot include the ability to choose evil, for the saved in the City of God after the resurrection will not be able to choose evil. Choosing evil diminishes freedom. A modern analogy: Think of those who dabble with heroin. They may be "free" the first time; but thereafter, as the drug works its chemistry into their system, they become less and less free in their descent into addiction. That is how Augustine thinks about freedom of will vs. free choice: Our wills, on the far side of Adam's Fall, simply do not work right. Left to our own devices, we inevitably (one might even say "addictively") choose the sinful course. Thus our wills need God's grace to repair their marred operation, to restore their primordial freedom, that we might again have the ability to choose wisely among goods. From Letter 157 to Hilary of Syracuse:

(8) This free will will be free to the extent that it is healthy, and healthy to the extent that it is submissive to divine mercy and grace. Therefore, it prays with faith and says, "Direct my journeying according to your word, and let no iniquity have dominion over me" (Ps 118:133). For in what way is free will free if iniquity has dominion? But in order that it may not have dominion over it, see whom it invokes. For it does not say, "Direct my journeying according to free choice because no iniquity has dominion over me," but says rather: "Di-

---

69. Nat. et gr. 31.35 (BA 21:308–10); trans. Mourant and Collinge, FOTC 86:47–48 (modified).

70. Pelagius, *De natura*, quoted in *nat. et gr.* 49.57. Julian of Eclanum, *Ad Florum* (quoted in Augustine, c. Jul. imp. 6.9 [PL 45:1515]) puts it clearly: "Free choice . . . is nothing but the possibility of sinning or not sinning."

71. Augustine makes this point repeatedly to Julian of Eclanum: see c. Jul. imp. 1.81; 3.120; 6.10 (PL 45:1103, 1299, 1518); also *nat. et gr.* 49.57.

rect my journeying according to your word, and let no iniquity have dominion over me" (Ps 118:133). It prays, it does not promise; it confesses, it does not make claims for itself; it begs for fullest freedom, it does not boast of its own power. . . . (10) The freedom of the will is not destroyed by being helped; it is rather helped because it is not destroyed. The one who says to God, "Be my helper" (Ps 26:9), confesses that he wishes to carry out what is commanded but asks help of the One who gave the command so that he may be able to do it.[72]

PELAGIUS VINDICATED IN THE EAST (415)

When Pelagius was acquitted in Palestine, it set off a complex chain of events. Here is a recently discovered letter of Augustine to his powerful colleague in the Greek East, Cyril of Alexandria, who sixteen years later oversaw the formal ecumenical condemnation of Pelagianism at the Council of Ephesus. This letter fills in one factual tidbit: Cyril was the one who sent Augustine the complete transcript of Pelagius's trial. Before its discovery, we did not know that Cyril and Augustine had ever been in direct contact. From Letter 4* *(Divjak):*

(2) Your Sincerity recalls, I think, that you sent us the transcript (*acta*) of the council held in the province of Palestine where the supposedly Catholic Pelagius was acquitted, when he succeeded in concealing himself within the clever hiding places of his words and deceived our brothers who then presided as judges when no one representing the other side came forward to expose him. When I read and studied these proceedings as carefully as I could, I wrote a book about them[73] for our venerable brother and fellow bishop, Aurelius, bishop of the church of Carthage, in which, as much as the Lord permitted, it was demonstrated how it was that Catholic judges understood Pelagius's answers so that they came to the verdict that he was a Catholic. For many who were caught in that error of his were boasting that, since he had been acquitted, his heretical teachings had been confirmed as Catholic by the judgment of Catholic bishops, and with these people spreading this story just about everywhere, very many, not knowing what had really happened, believed what they were saying to the great scandal of the churches.

(3) In order to get rid of this misconception, I wrote the book mentioned above. Here, to the best of my ability, I showed that, even though Pelagius had been acquitted—not by God, whom no one can deceive, but in a human court

---

72. Ep. 157.8–10 (BA 21:44–48); my trans., based on Parsons, FOTC 20:323–25. See also *Contra duas epistulas Pelagianorum* 1.25 (CSEL 60:445). On this issue, see Burns, *Development*, 109–19.

73. "Wrote a book about them": Augustine is referring to *On the Deeds of Pelagius* (*De gestis Pelagii*).

which he was able to deceive—still those pestiferous teachings of his were condemned; even he himself anathematized them.[74]

ATTACK ON JEROME'S MONASTERY

After Pelagius's trial, some of his supporters reportedly attacked monks at Jerome's monastery in Bethlehem. This violence was one factor in a turning of the tide against Pelagius and his allies. We have several reports of the incident. Here is Augustine's, which he added as an appendix to his account of Pelagius's trial in Diospolis (or Lydda; today: Lod, Israel). From The Deeds of Pelagius:

(35.66) After this judgment [in favor of Pelagius], certain crimes are said to have been committed with incredible audacity by some band of rabble, who were held to have strongly supported Pelagius in his perversity. It is said that the servants and handmaidens of God, residing under the direction of the holy priest Jerome, were set upon in a most wicked onslaught, that a deacon was killed, that the buildings of the monastery were burned, and that only a well-fortified tower managed to protect Jerome himself, by the mercy of God, from the attack and assault of these impious people. About these matters, my view is that it is best for us to remain silent, and wait and see what our brother bishops there think should be done about such evils. For who would think they could ignore them? After all, the impious teachings of such persons [as Pelagius] ought to be refuted by all Catholics, even those who live far away from these lands, so that they cannot do damage wherever they have been able to spread. But impious actions, whose suppression belongs to episcopal discipline in the place where they are committed, should ordinarily be punished there, with pastoral diligence and pious severity, by those in authority in that place or nearby. Therefore, we, who live so far away, can only hope that such an end be put to these matters, that there be no necessity for further adjudication about it anywhere else, but rather an end which it is fitting for us to proclaim, so that the souls of all who have been seriously wounded by the report, winging about everywhere, of those crimes, may be healed by the mercy of God, following afterward.[75]

74. Ep. 4*.2–3 (BA 46B:108–10); trans. Eno, FOTC 81:41–42. On this, J.-P. Bouhot, "Une lettre d'Augustin d'Hippone à Cyrille d'Alexandrie (Epist. 4*)," in Lepelley, *Les lettres de saint Augustin découvertes par Johannes Divjak*, 147–54; Bonner, "Some Remarks on Letters 4* and 6*," in Lepelley, 155–64; and especially Dunn, "Augustine, Cyril of Alexandria, and the Pelagian Controversy," 63–88.

75. *De gestis Pelagii* 35.66 (BA 21:576–78); trans. Mourant and Collinge, FOTC 86:176–77.

MAKING THE CASE TO ROME (416)

After Pelagius's vindication, the North African bishops formed a united front. In 416, two regional councils were held, one in Carthage and one in Milevis, and both sent letters to Pope Innocent I, asking him to second their condemnations of Pelagius and Caelestius. To these letters, other documents were added, notably, copies of Pelagius's On Nature *and Augustine's* On Nature and Grace. *These conciliar letters help highlight that the Pelagian controversy was much more than Augustine's personal battle with Pelagius. Augustine saw himself and was seen by his colleagues as the spokesman for North African theology. The following letter offers a compact summary of the theological issues as the North Africans saw them. Among the long list of signatories were Augustine, Alypius, and Possidius. From the Council of Milevis, preserved in Augustine's corpus as* Letter 176:

(2) A new and very dangerous heresy is trying to break out through the efforts of the enemies of the grace of Christ, who seek by their wicked arguments to deprive us even of the Lord's Prayer. For though the Lord taught us to say, "Forgive us our debts as we also forgive our debtors" (Mt 6:12), they say that it is possible for a human being in this life, simply by knowing God's commandments, to attain to such perfection of holiness solely by the force of free will, and without the help of the Savior's grace, that it is not even necessary to say: "Forgive us our debts." In that case, the words that follow, "Lead us not into temptation" (Mt 6:13), are not to be taken in the sense that we ought to ask for divine help lest we be tempted to fall into sin, but that this is in our own power and the human will alone suffices to fulfill it—as if it were in vain that the Apostle said: "It depends not upon the one willing or the one running, but upon God who shows mercy" (Rom 9:16); and, "God is faithful and will not let you be tested beyond what you can do, but will, with the temptation, provide you a way out so that you may be able to endure it" (1 Cor 10:13). If all this lay within human power, in vain would the Lord have said to the Apostle Peter, "I have prayed for you that your faith not fail" (Lk 22:32), and, "Keep vigil and pray that you not enter into temptation" (Mt 26:41). They also claim with wicked presumption that the little ones will possess eternal life even without the sacraments of Christian grace, thus emptying [the meaning out of] what the Apostle says: "By one man sin entered into the world, and by sin death, and so it was passed on to all human beings, in whom all have sinned" (Rom 5:12), and in another passage: "Just as in Adam all die, so also in Christ all shall be made alive" (1 Cor 15:22). . . .

(4) The authors of this destructive error are said to be Pelagius and Caelestius, and we would rather see them cured of it in the Church than cut off from the Church and without hope of salvation (unless necessity requires it). It is reported that one of them, Caelestius, even entered the presbyterate in Asia, but your Holiness has probably been better informed by the church of Carthage on the action taken in his re-

gard a few years ago.[76] Pelagius, however, as we learn from letters sent by some of our brethren, has set up residence at Jerusalem and is said to lead many astray. But many more, who have been able to examine more carefully the meaning of his teaching, are actively opposing him in defense of the grace of Christ and the truth of the Catholic faith; in the vanguard of these is your holy son, our brother and fellow priest, Jerome.[77]

ROME'S REPLY (417)

On January 27, 417, Innocent answered the North African councils with letters confirming their condemnations. From Pope Innocent I, Letter to Silvanus, Primate of Numidia, preserved as Letter 182 in Augustine's corpus:

(3) The authors of the new heresy should be shunned. What more bitter attack could they imagine against the Lord than to take away the reason for daily prayer, after having nullified divine assistance? This is the same as saying: "What need have I of God?" Let the Psalmist say of them with good reason: "Behold human beings who have not made God their helper!" (Ps 51:9) Therefore, by denying the help of God they say that a human being is self-sufficient, that he has no need of divine grace, the deprivation of which necessarily entangles him in the snares of the devil and makes him fall, while at the same time they claim that human liberty alone is enough to enable him to fulfill all the commandments of life. O perverse doctrine of utterly depraved minds! . . .

(4) When we read on every divine page nothing else except that the help of God must be added to our free will, and that, deprived of these heavenly safeguards, it can do nothing, how can Pelagius and Caeléstius so obstinately defend the power of the will alone, persuading themselves of its truth, as you assert? . . .

(5) That other doctrine which your Fraternity claims that they preach, that little children can attain the reward of eternal life without the grace of baptism, is very foolish. . . . Those who claim this [eternal life] for them without rebirth seem to me to want to nullify baptism, since they teach that these children have what faith holds is bestowed on them only by baptism. If, then, they do not wish anything to stand in their way, let them confess that there is no need for rebirth and that the sacred stream of regeneration has no effect. But in order to disarm the vicious doctrine of useless human beings by the swift reasoning of truth, the Lord proclaims this in the Gospel by saying: "Let the little children come to me and do not prohibit them from me" (Mt 19:4).

76. "On the actions taken . . . a few years ago": Caelestius's trial in 411.
77. Ep. 176.2–4 (CSEL 44:664–67); my trans., based on Parsons, FOTC 30:91–93.

(6) Therefore, concerning Pelagius and Caelestius, that is, the inventors of these new ideas, which, as the Apostle says, are of no profit, but tend to generate utterly vain questions, we decree, relying on the strength of apostolic authority, that they are deprived of communion with the Church until "they recover themselves from the snares of the devil, by whom they are held captives at his will" (2 Tm 2:26), that they are not to be received within the Lord's flock, which they have chosen to forsake by following the path of a crooked way.[78]

Causa Finita Est

We have seen certain of Augustine's famous one-liners (e.g., "Love, and do what you will") taken out of context. Here is another. To Augustine has long been attributed the statement: "Rome has spoken; the matter is settled" (Roma locuta est; causa finita est). Defenders of universal papal jurisdiction over the centuries have cited this phrase as though it were really Augustine's and as though Augustine accepted the pope's word as the last word. It turns out that the first phrase is not his; the second is his, but needs to be seen in context. Augustine was an African bishop deeply committed to African traditions of conciliar decision-making. He deeply respected the prestige of the bishop of Rome, but hardly thought papal decisions were the last word. The famous phrase occurs in a sermon, delivered in Carthage on September 23, 417. Augustine alludes to the condemnations of the African councils of Carthage and Milevis. It is in this light that he says, "The case is closed" (causa finita est). The case, it turns out, had not only been reopened but reversed by Pope Zosimus, and the North Africans would have to work around the pope and win over imperial authorities. Augustine's famous text appears in the closing words of a lengthy sermon on John's Gospel. From Sermon 131:

(10) "For being ignorant of the justice of God, and wishing to establish their own, they have not submitted themselves to the justice of God" (Rom 10:3). My brothers and sisters, come and share in my sorrow. Wherever you find such people, do not hide them. Let there be no misplaced mercy in you. Wherever you find such people, you don't want to hide them. Argue against the naysayers. Bring those resistant to us. For two councils on this case have already been sent to the Apostolic See. And rescripts have come back to us. The case is closed! Would that the error come to a close as well! Therefore, we advise that they pay attention; we teach that they be instructed; we pray that they be changed.[79]

---

78. Ep. 182.3–6 (CSEL 44:717–21); trans. Parsons, FOTC 30:129–31.

79. S. 131.10 (PL 38:734); my trans. See Cornelius Mayer, "Causa finita est," Aug-Lex, 1:827. For a new critical edition, see G. Partoens, "Le sermon 131 de saint Augustin: Introduction et édition," Augustiniana 54 (2004): 35–77.

THE COUNCIL OF CARTHAGE (418)

After Innocent's death, his successor, Pope Zosimus, reopened the case, acquitted Pelagius and Caelestius, then sent a brusque letter to the North African bishops. The North Africans were not cowed. They lobbied the imperial government in Ravenna and won harsh sanctions against Pelagius and Caelestius. Zosimus quickly reversed course and published his own condemnation. On May 1, 418, the day after the imperial government issued its condemnation, the North African bishops, meeting in council at Carthage, promulgated a set of influential canons denouncing Pelagian views on original sin, grace, and free will. The hand of Augustine is clearly visible in their wording. From the Council of Carthage (418):

(Canon 1) All gathered in the holy synod of the church of Carthage agreed that anyone who said that Adam was made mortal in such a way that he would have died physically whether he had sinned or not, that is, he would have left the body not as punishment for sin, but from the necessity of nature, let him be anathema.

(Canon 2) They also agreed that if anyone denies that infants newborn from their mothers' wombs should be baptized, or if anyone says that infants are baptized for the forgiveness of sins but contract nothing from Adam, no original sin expiated by the bath of rebirth, such that, as a result, the formula of baptism "for the forgiveness of sins" is understood not as true but as false, let him be anathema. What the Apostle said: "Through one man sin entered the world and through sin death so that it passed on to all human beings, in whom all have sinned" (Rom 5:12) is not to be understood in any way other than as the Catholic Church spread across the world has always understood it. On account of this rule of faith, even little ones who have been able to commit no sins of their own are truly baptized for the remission of sins so that what they contracted by their birth might be cleansed by their rebirth. . . .

(Canon 5) They also agreed that anyone who says the grace of God through Jesus Christ our Lord helps us in being sinless only because it reveals and opens up to us an understanding of the commandments so that we know what to desire and what to avoid, but that it does not give us the gift to love and to be strong enough to do what we know we should do, let him be anathema. Since the Apostle says, "Knowledge puffs up, love builds up" (1 Cor 8:1), it is impious for us to believe that we have the grace of Christ for what puffs up, but do not have it for what builds up, since both of these are a gift of God: to know what we should do and to love doing it so that what loving builds up in us, knowledge is not able to puff up. Just as it is written of God, "He is One who teaches human beings knowledge" (Ps 93:10), so it is also written: "Love is from God" (1 Jn 4:7).

(Canon 6) They also agreed that if anyone says that we are given the grace of justification so that we can more easily fulfill through grace what we are commanded to do through free choice, as though, even if grace were not given, we could still fulfill the divine commandments without it, let him be anathema. For when the Lord spoke about the fruits of the commandments, He did not say "Without me you can do so, but only with more difficulty," but rather said: "Without me you can do nothing" (Jn 15:5).[80]

�֎

PHASE THREE: THE DEBATE WITH JULIAN OF ECLANUM (418–430)

ANGUISHING OVER INFANTS

From an early date, Augustine refused to take a stand on one of the burning philosophical questions of his age: the origin of the soul. Two common views at that time were "traducianism" and "creationism." Traducianists argued that we get our souls passed down to us from our parents just as we get our bodies passed down from them. This view could have supported Augustine's view of original sin, but he rejected it because it implied that the soul, like the body, was material. Creationists argued that God created a new soul for each new person. This view, favored by Jerome, did not square well with the idea of an inherited original sin. Augustine eventually published a book-length treatise, On the Soul and Its Origin (De anima et eius origine), *defending his agnosticism. Before this, in 415, Augustine wrote a long letter to Jerome discussing the question of the soul's origin and, in the process, expressed his personal anguish over his own teaching that God justly condemned unbaptized infants. He also anguished over the sufferings of infants. While convinced that his teaching was, in its fundamentals, correct, he sought some way of articulating how all this squared with God's goodness and justice. He begged Jerome for an answer to these anguishing questions. Jerome never answered. From* Letter 166:

(4.10) Teach me, I beg of you, what I am to teach. Teach me what I am to hold, and tell me, if souls are individually created today for individuals at birth, how these souls commit sin in infants so as to need the remission of sin in the sacrament of Christ since they sin in Adam from whom the flesh of sin is derived; or, if they do not sin, how can it be just of the Creator to bind them by another's sin when they are joined to mortal bodies descended from him so that damnation is their lot unless help is given them by the Church since it is not in their power to be helped by the grace of baptism? What kind of justice is it that so many thousands of souls should be damned because they departed from their bodies by death in infancy, without the grace of the

---

80. Council of Carthage (418), *Canons* 1–5 (CCL 149:69–71); my trans.

Christian sacrament, if new souls, created separately by the will of the Creator, are joined to separate bodies at birth, with no previous sin of their own, souls which He created and gave to animate these bodies, when He certainly knew that each one of them by no fault of its own would leave the body without the baptism of Christ? Since, therefore, we cannot say of God that He either forces souls to become sinful or punishes the innocent, and we must necessarily assert that souls, even those of infants, which leave the body without the sacrament of Christ are subject to damnation, how are we to defend this opinion which holds that other souls do not come into being from that of the first man, but are thus created separately as that first one was? . . .

(6.16) But when I come to the question of the sufferings of infants, believe me, I am greatly upset, and I find no ready answer. I mean not only those suffering what damnation brings after this life and what must necessarily come upon those who leave the body without the grace of the Christian sacrament, but also those who are presented in this life to our grieving eyes, so numerous that the time for narrating it, rather than examples, fails me. They pine away with illness, they are racked with pains, they are tortured with hunger and thirst, they are weak of limb, they are deprived of their faculties, they are tormented by unclean spirits. Certainly, there must be a proof that they suffer all this justly, without any evil cause on their part. It is not permissible to say either that these things happen without God's knowledge, or that He is unable to hinder those who cause them, or that He causes or permits them unjustly. Of irrational animals we say rightly that they are given over to be used by higher beings, even sinful ones, as we see in the Gospel, where the devils were allowed to use the swine for their intended purpose. But how can we rightly say the same of a human being? The human being is an animal, but a rational (though mortal) one. There is a rational soul in his members that pays the penalty by such sufferings. God is good, God is just, God is almighty. Only a madman doubts this. Therefore, a just cause must be assigned to these great sufferings that befall little children. Doubtless, when their elders suffer these afflictions, we are wont to say either that their goodness is being tested, as in the case of Job, or that their sins are being punished, as happened to Herod; and from the examples that God has willed to make clear, it is granted to us to conjecture about other cases that are hard to understand. But these are older people. Tell me what we are to answer about children if there are no sins to be punishcd in them by such sufferings, since there obviously is no virtue to be tested at their age.[81]

81. Ep. 166.4.10–6.16 (CSEL 44:530–70); trans. Parsons, FOTC 30:15–22.

INFANTS LOST BY ORIGINAL SIN

That anguishing is one side of Augustine. There is another, tougher side. Around 418, both before and after Pelagius's final condemnation, Augustine and his North African colleagues conducted a wide-ranging letter-writing campaign, spelling out and defending their views to friends and allies across the Empire. Gerald Bonner has argued that in this period one sees Augustine hardening his position.[82] The following is an example in which he summarizes the logic of predestination in its most unbending terms. From Letter 190 to Optatus of Milevis:

(3.12) But God willed that so many He created be born whom He fore-knew would have no part in His grace so that by their countless multitude they might outnumber those whom He has deigned to predestine to the king-dom of His glory as children of promise. Thus, He even willed to show by this very multitude of rejected [infants] how the mere number, whatever it may be, of the justly damned is of no account with a just God. And those who are re-deemed from that damnation may understand that what they see meted out to so large a part is owed to the whole lump of clay. And in this part are in-cluded not only those who add many sins to the original sin by the free choice of an evil will, but even many infants, bound only by the fetter of original sin, who are carried off from this life without the grace of the Mediator. Indeed, the whole mass would have received for its debt a just damnation, if the pot-ter, who is not only just but merciful, had not made of it vessels for honor, ac-cording to grace (Rom 9:21), not according to their due, when He both comes to the aid of the little ones who have no merits to speak of and predisposes their elders that they may have some merits.[83]

PERSECUTOR OF NEWBORNS?

After 418, the Pelagian controversy entered its third phase. Here Augustine faced off with his most tenacious critic, Julian of Eclanum, who from his exile in the Greek East had the leisure to pen long and venomous treatises against his African adversary. Lancel has referred to the two men's voluminous and no-holds-barred exchanges as "a dialogue of the deaf," while Brown has called these a "slogging-match."[84] We cannot begin to survey here the range of issues they slogged over. Some of the back-and-forth arguments are ones we have already seen. In this section, I want to highlight two issues. The first is this debate about unbaptized infants. In the two previous passages, we saw Augustine's sometimes

---

82. Bonner, "Augustine and Pelagianism," 28–30.
83. Ep. 190.3.12 (CSEL 57:146–47); my trans., based on Parsons, FOTC 30:277–78.
84. Lancel, Saint Augustine, 417; Brown, Augustine of Hippo, 389.

anguished and sometimes hard-hearted articulations. In the following, we hear Julian's outraged response, a sentiment perhaps shared by many modern readers. From Julian of Eclanum, To Florus, quoted in Augustine, Against Julian, An Unfinished Work, Books 1 and 3:

(1.48) "Little babies," you say, "are weighed down not by some sin of their own, but are loaded down by another's."[85] It is not clear what evil you are thinking of. . . . Tell us, then: Who is this punisher of innocents? You answer: God! . . . What God do you call upon for such crimes? You, this very religious priest, this highly learned orator, spew out the gloomiest, most horrid-smelling stuff. . . . God, you say? The very One who commended His love to us, who loves us, and who "did not spare his own Son, but handed Him over for us" (Rom 8:32)? God Himself judges this way? He is a persecutor of newborns? He, out of some evil will, hands over tiny babies to eternal fires, babies He knows could have neither a good nor an evil will? After statements so monstrous, so sacrilegious, so deadly, I should demand, if we had sane judges, nothing less than your public condemnation. With a gravity both just and proper, I should assess you as unworthy of argument, you who have fled so far from religious feeling, from erudition, even from common sense, that you think your God capable of crimes a barbarian would scarcely do. . . .

(3.67) We are asked why we do not agree that there is a sin that is part of nature. Here is our answer: It has no semblance of reality—let alone, of truth; it is unjust; it has no shred of piety. It makes it seem the devil is humanity's founder. (3.68) It affixes to God as judge a charge of criminal unfairness. (3.69) It breaks down and destroys free choice. . . . (3.70) by saying that all human beings are so utterly incapable of virtue that in their mothers' wombs, they are implanted with long-past crimes (3.71) and that the force of that villainy not only expunges nature's innocence, but also compels people ever after, throughout the entirety of their lives, into vices of every sort.[86]

LEX ORANDI, LEX CREDENDI

In defending original sin against Julian, Augustine repeated his standard arguments. He also argued that he was defending the apostolic tradition and quoted long passages from venerable predecessors and contemporaries, such as Cyprian, Ambrose, Gregory of Nazianzus, and John Chrysostom. He also appealed to the rite of baptism itself, arguing that the liturgy embodied the Church's hidden wisdom. He pointed especially to one of baptism's preparatory rites, "exsufflation" (exsufflatio), a breathing upon or hissing at the candidate meant to exorcise demonic influences. For Augustine, this liturgical practice

85. "'Little babies,' you say . . .": Julian is quoting Augustine, De nuptiis et concupiscentia 1.20.22.
86. Quoted in c. Jul. imp. 1.48–3.71 (CSEL 85.1:37–403); my trans.

implied that infants needed such an exorcism, just as adults did, to release them from the devil's power. Augustine thus worked from the principle of lex orandi, lex credendi *("what the Church prays is what the Church believes"). In fact, this famous principle was first articulated by Augustine's disciple, Prosper of Aquitaine, precisely in reference to Augustine's appeal to exsufflation.*[87] From Against Julian, Books 1, 3, and 6:

(1.4.14) The original sin which you deny, to the destruction of other infants, at whatever age you were baptized, was itself remitted for you, or, at any rate, was also remitted. But if it is true, as we have heard, that you were baptized as an infant, then even you, although innocent of personal sins, yet because you were born physically of Adam, contracted the contagion of the ancient death by your first birth, and you were conceived in iniquity and then exorcised and exsufflated so that, rescued from the power of darkness, you might be transferred into the kingdom of Christ. O my son, ill born of Adam but well reborn in Christ, you attempt to take from your Mother the sacraments by which she bore you. . . .

(3.3.9) Without a glance you pass by the evils which befall infants. . . . You pass by, exercising your learned wit and skillful tongue in praise of nature, but that nature, fallen into such great and obvious misery, must necessarily have Christ for its Savior, Liberator, Cleanser, Redeemer—not Julian, not Caelestius, not Pelagius as the singer of its praises. . . .

(6.5.11) [Original sin] has been proclaimed throughout the whole Church and believed from ancient times as the true Catholic faith. The Church would not exorcise nor exsufflate the infants of the faithful if she were not rescuing them from the power of darkness and from the prince of death. I wrote this in my book which you are supposedly refuting,[88] but you were afraid to mention it, as though you yourself would be exsufflated by the whole world if you were to contradict this exsufflation by which, even from infants, the prince of this world is cast out. Your meaningless arguments are not against me, but against our common spiritual Mother. You would not have her bring forth children now in the way she brought you forth. You strike her very womb by what you regard as adequately sharp weapons, summoning arguments from the justice of God against the justice of God, from the grace of God against the grace of God. This, then, is the true justice of God: that the heavy yoke

---

87. Prosper of Aquitaine, *Auctoritates* 8–9 (PL 51:209–10). Prosper plays a key role in the final phase. See below.

88. "I wrote this in my book": Augustine is referring to *De nuptiis et concupiscentia* 1.20.22, which also discusses this same issue. Augustine had first written this work in response to a letter that Julian had sent Count Valerius, a powerful figure at the imperial court at Ravenna. Julian had first composed his *Ad Turbantium* against this work of Augustine's, and Augustine challenges Julian for skipping over that passage. Augustine regularly refers to the *exsufflatio* as evidence of original sin: *pecc. mer.* 1.34.63; *De symbolo ad catechumenos* 1.2; *ep.* 194.46; *c. Jul. imp.* 3.144.

upon the children of Adam from the day of their coming out of their mother's womb is not unjust. How is that heavy yoke not unjust if there is no evil in infants which makes it just that a heavy yoke oppress them? This is the true grace of God: when reality and word are in agreement. How could this be if grace exsufflates one in whom it knows there is nothing to expel, if it washes one in whom it knows there is nothing to wash away?[89]

JULIAN ON MARRIAGE AND CONCUPISCENCE

A second important issue in the clash between Julian and Augustine was their respective evaluations of sexuality and marriage. Julian had gotten married as a young man, and one of Augustine's good friends, Paulinus of Nola, had even composed a poem for the occasion. Julian, at some point, chose a life of continence, likely when he was ordained. We need to bear in mind that both Julian and Augustine spoke from experience; both had lived in long-standing committed sexual relationships, but their respective evaluations were very different. Julian argued for the unequivocal goodness of "concupiscence," of sexual desire, within the confines of marriage. At the same time he ridiculed and caricatured Augustine's views, branding them as a sort of disguised Manicheism in which marriage and sexuality are treated as the devil's making. Here is a sample of Julian's positive (if somewhat clinical) teaching. From Julian, To Turbantius, as quoted by Augustine, Against Julian, Book 3:

(3.13.25) It is correct to state that the origin of concupiscence is in the fire of life. It follows that the concupiscence of the flesh must be attributed to the fire through which the life of the flesh is put together. (3.13.26) Its genus is in the vital fire; its species is in the movement of the genitals; its moderation is in the marital act; its excess is in the intemperance of fornication. . . . (3.13.27) The guilt of such appetite is not in its genus or its species or its moderation, but in its excess, because the genus and species are the work of its Maker, and its moderation pertains to its appropriate use, but its excess comes from the fault of the will. . . . (3.14.28) In the married it is exercised appropriately; in the chaste it is restrained by virtue. . . . The excess of that pleasure is practiced by the lascivious; and because this is done in insolence, not from nature, it is condemned by law. . . . (3.15.29) [Marital chastity] is opposed to the unlawful acts of the one extreme and marvels at the other's rejecting even the lawful. Its own domain lies on the farthest boundary. From there it despises the barbarism of those who go beyond the limit and venerates the striking brilliance of those [celi-

89. Contra Julianum 1.4.14–6.5.11 (PL 44:649–829); trans. Schumacher, FOTC 35:16–321.

bates] above itself. It modestly soothes those burning [in passion] and praises those who do not need this cure.[90]

AUGUSTINE ON MARRIAGE
AND CONCUPISCENCE

Augustine had staked out his basic position on marriage well before the Pelagian controversy. In the 390s, in Rome, there had been a fierce debate over marriage and virginity. A monk named Jovinian had argued that the married life and the celibate life were equally good. His opponent, Jerome, had tenaciously insisted on the radical superiority of celibacy and had asserted—infamously—that the only good of marriage was that it produced virgins.[91] Both were rejected as extremist. Augustine entered the fray with his book On the Good of Marriage. *The title is crucial: marriage is "good." Thus its real, but unstated, title is "Against Jerome."[92] Augustine was one of those authors who plotted out what became the moderate middle ground: that while Christians see the life of continence as superior, marriage must be valued for its undeniable goods: not only children, but also the couple's lifelong union and partnership.*

As the Pelagian controversy unfolded, however, Augustine came to locate the propagation of original sin from generation to generation in the couple's mutual sexual desire. He used the term "concupiscence" not only for sexual desire, but more broadly, for the disordering of the human will on the far side of Adam's fall. Our disordered sexual desires, he argued, are both emblematic and symptomatic of the disobedience of our lower self (not just body but also will), a just punishment meted out as a result of humanity's disobedience to God. (We saw this idea in Book 14 of City of God*). In this passage, Augustine sets out his later understanding of marriage and sexuality. From* Against Julian, *Book 3:*

(13.26) You divide, you define, you give a kind of clinical dissertation on the genus, the species, the moderation, and the excess of concupiscence. . . . Yet after all this supposedly subtle and long-winded disputation of yours, I ask you briefly and openly why this vital fire plants the root of warfare in human beings, so that the flesh lusts against the spirit and the spirit necessarily lusts against the flesh (Gal 5:17), why one who wills to consent to the vital fire receives a mortal wound. I presume the black ink in your book must be turning red with blushing. . . .

90. For the fragments of Julian's Ad Turbantium, see Lucas de Coninck, ed., Iuliani Aeclanensis: Expositio Libri Iob, CCL 88:340–96. The passage here is from Ad Turbantium, frag. 44–45, 47–49 (CCL 88:351–52); trans. Schumacher, FOTC 35:130–33 (modified).

91. On this Roman debate, see Hunter, Marriage, Celibacy, and Heresy in Ancient Christianity: The Jovinianist Controversy; on Augustine's contributions, see pp. 269–84.

92. See Markus, "Augustine: A Defense of Christian Mediocrity," End of Ancient Christianity, 45–62.

(15.29) . . . As you say, very well and truly, the reason why marital modesty praises those living in continence is that they do not need the cure that it sees itself needing, as the Apostle says: "But if they do not have self-control, let them marry" (1 Cor 7:9). Why do you acknowledge need for a cure for concupiscence, yet contradict me when I say concupiscence is a disease? If you acknowledge a cure, acknowledge the disease. If you deny the disease, deny the cure. I ask you at last to yield to the truth that speaks to you even through your own mouth. No one provides a cure to the healthy.

(16.30) You say correctly: "On close examination, we see that marriage cannot be pleasing if it is praised only by comparing it with something evil." This is true. Marriage is by all means good in its own kind, but the reason it is good is because it preserves the fidelity of the marriage bed, because it unites the two sexes for the purpose of raising offspring, and because it is terrified of the impiety of separation. These are the goods of marriage that make marriage itself good.[93] As we have often said, such marriage could have existed even if no one had sinned. After sin, however, and not because of happiness, but of necessity, a struggle came to marriage so that it, by its very goodness, must now battle against the evil of concupiscence, not allowing it to do anything unlawful, though concupiscence itself, acting now gently and relaxed, now with rapid waves of intense passion, never ceases to urge it on, and marriage makes good use of its evil in the propagation of children. Who can deny that this is an evil except one unwilling to hear the Apostle's warning: "But this I say as a concession, not as a command" (1 Cor 7:6)? When married couples have sexual intercourse, overcome by desire not for having offspring, but for the sheer physical pleasure of it, this is not to be praised, but is excused in comparison with what is worse because marriage intercedes and pleads on their behalf.

(22.51) Since this is so, we see that marriage as marriage is good and that a human being as a human being, whether born of marriage or of adultery, is good because as human, one is God's creation. And yet because one is born with and from the evil that marital chastity uses well, it is necessary that one be freed from the bond of this evil by rebirth. Why do you ask, "Where is original evil?" when the sexual desire you fight against in yourself speaks to you more eloquently than you yourself speak when you praise it? Why do you ask, "How does a human being whom God made come under the devil's power?" How, then, is one in [the power of] death, something God did not

---

93. "The goods of marriage . . .": Augustine refers here to his treatise *On the Good of Marriage* (*De bono conjugali*), in which he outlines several goods: (1) friendship and fidelity of the couple; (2) the propagation of children, raised in the social framework of the family; (3) the sacramental indissolubility, symbolic of God's faithfulness. On this, see David G. Hunter, "*Bono conjugali, De*" and "Marriage," *AugEncy*, 110–11; 535–37. For a collection of texts with commentary, see Elizabeth A. Clark, ed., *St. Augustine on Marriage and Sexuality* (Washington, DC: The Catholic University of America Press, 1996).

make? "What," you ask, "does the devil recognize there as his own if he made neither what is made nor what it is made from?" Clearly, what is made is the human being; what one is made from is the human seed. Both are good. The devil made neither, but sowed the seed's defect. The devil does not recognize there some good of his because the good we both praise is not his, but he recognizes his own evil against which we both fight. And it is not right that what we both fight against is praised by just one of us. Look carefully at the very matter you asked me about: "Among so many good things, where does the evil in infants come from?" And you are silent about what I put in that very same book you are answering. And among the words you are now rebutting, there is what the Apostle says: "Through one man sin entered into the world, and through sin death, and thus it was passed to all human beings, in whom all have sinned" (Rom 5:12). You do not want anyone to hear or read this passage—there where it matters most—lest they recognize their own faith and hold your arguments in contempt.

(23.53) If the goodness of marriage were only the good use of a good, we might well wonder how evil can be derived from it. But since the goodness of marriage is the good use of an evil, it does not surprise us that the evil that is original sin is derived from the evil of concupiscence, which the goodness of marriage uses well. . . . Marital union was not instituted, as you think, for the sake of carnal concupiscence, but for the sake of the good which is made from that evil. This good would exist without that evil if no one had sinned, but, as it is, this good cannot exist without that evil; yet the good is not therefore evil. Conversely, there can be no evil without some good; yet evil is not therefore good, for the work of God in nature is a good, without which, however, there cannot be an evil will. Just as adultery cannot exist without the good of nature, yet adultery is not therefore good, so marriage cannot now exist without the evil of concupiscence, yet it does not follow that marriage is evil. Even if we should grant you that "every cause of evil is destitute of good," this does not apply to marriage, which is not a cause of evil. Marriage did not produce the evil of concupiscence, but only found it there to be used well.[94]

A LIFELONG STRUGGLE

From Confessions onward, Augustine wrote against any false optimism of born-again Christianity, as if conversion and baptism marked the cessation of one's inner troubles. In the Pelagian controversy, he came to articulate the often tedious, lifelong struggles that remained in the convert on the far side of baptism. From Against Julian, Book 2:

94. *Contra Julianum* 3.13.26–23.53 (PL 44:715–30); my trans., based on Schumacher, FOTC 35:129–55.

(9.31) Now let us sum up as best we can what we have discussed through-out this whole book. . . . You say:

If God creates human beings, they cannot be born with any evil. If marriage is good, nothing evil arises from it. If all sins are forgiven in baptism, those born of the reborn cannot contract original sin. If God is just, He cannot condemn in the children the sins of the parents, since He forgives the parents their sins as well. If human nature is capable of perfect justice, it cannot have natural faults.

To this we reply: [1] that God is the Creator of human beings, that is, of both soul and body; and [2] that marriage is good; and [3] that through the baptism of Christ all sins are forgiven; and [4] that God is just; and [5] that human nature is capable of perfect justice. Yet although all these are true, human beings are born subject to the vitiated origin which is contracted from the first human being, and therefore go to damnation unless they are reborn in Christ. And this we have proved by the authority of Catholic saints who assert what we say about original sin and also confess that all five of these statements are true.

(9.32) Blessed Ambrose says that only that man, the "mediator between God and human beings" (1 Tm 2:5), because He was born of a virgin and did not experience sin in His birth, was not subject to the chains of the bound generation. But all human beings are born under sin, and their very origin is in evil, because they are formed in the pleasure of concupiscence, as the law of sin, in the body of this death, wars against the law of the mind, so that not only all the good and faithful but also the great strength of the Apostle fought against it, so that the flesh being subjected to the spirit by the grace of Christ may be brought back into harmony, because through the transgression of the first man discord was brought about between these two who were first created without sin. Who is it that says this? Ambrose, a man of God, a Catholic, and a most keen defender of the Catholic truth against heretics, even risking his life, one so highly praised by the testimony of your teacher that he said, "Not even an enemy would dare find fault with his faith and his clear understanding of the Scriptures."[95] . . . Ambrose placed human justice in this life in a kind of warfare and battle not only against the hostile [demonic] powers of the air, but also against our own lusts, through which those external enemies strive to overthrow us or enter into us. In this war, he says, the flesh itself is a dangerous adversary, whose nature as it was first created would have remained in harmony with us if it had not been vitiated by the sin of the first man, but it now strives against us in a kind of sickness. In this

---

95. "Your teacher": Pelagius. Augustine is quoting here from Pelagius's Pro libero arbitrio, Book 3; also cited in gr. et pecc. or. 1.42.46.

war the holy man warns us to flee from the world, and shows the great difficulty—rather, the very impossibility—of this flight, unless we are aided by the grace of God. He says that our faults are dead through the forgiveness of all our sins in baptism, but that we must take care, as it were, of their burial. In this same work he recounts that we have such a conflict with our dead faults that we do not do what we wish, but do what we hate; that sin works many things in us while we struggle with it; that pleasures often revive and rise again; that we must struggle against the flesh, against which Paul was struggling when he said: "I see another law in my members warring against the law of my mind" (Rom 7:23). He teaches us not to trust our flesh, not to rely on it, since the Apostle exclaims: "I know that the good does not dwell in me, that is, in my flesh. To will is close to me, but to do the good is not" (Rom 7:18). See what a fight we have with our dead sins, as that active soldier of Christ and faithful teacher of the Church shows. For how is sin dead when it works many things in us while we struggle against it? What are these many things except foolish and harmful desires which plunge those who consent to them into death and destruction (1 Tm 6:9)? And to bear them patiently and not to consent to them is a struggle, a conflict, a battle. And between what parties in this battle if not between good and evil, not of nature against nature, but of nature against fault, which is already dead but still to be buried, that is, entirely healed? How, then, do we say this sin is dead in baptism, as this man also says, and how do we confess it dwells in our members and causes many desires against which we struggle and which we resist by not consenting to them, as this man also confesses, except that it is dead in that guilt by which it held us, and until it is healed by the perfection of its burial it rebels even though dead? It is, however, called sin, not in such a way that it makes us guilty, but because it is the result of the guilt of the first man and because by rebelling it strives to draw us to guilt, unless we are aided by the grace of God through Jesus Christ our Lord, lest even the dead sin so rebel that, by conquering, it revives and reigns.[96]

᭢

---

96. *Contra Julianum* 2.9.31–9.32 (PL 44:694–96); trans. Schumacher, FOTC 35:92–93 (modified).

PHASE FOUR: DISCUSSION WITH MONKS (427–430)

Concerns of Gallic Monks

The final phase was sparked by Augustine's reading public, notably two groups of monks. One group was based at Hadrumetum in North Africa. These were concerned that Augustine's views seemed to make their personal ascetical practices useless and to render their abbot's admonitions equally useless. To these concerns, Augustine addressed two treatises, On Grace and Free Will (De gratia et libero arbitrio) and On Admonition and Grace (De correptione et gratia). After their publication, further concerns were expressed by influential monks in southern Gaul, especially in the port city of Massilia (modern Marseilles). Around 427, Augustine received letters from two laymen from the area, Hilary and Prosper of Aquitaine. We know almost nothing of Hilary, but Prosper later served as secretary to Pope Leo the Great (d. 461), assisting Leo behind-the-scenes in the great debate on Christology that took place at the Council of Chalcedon in 451. While neither letter names the real dissenters, we know of one very well-respected and influential monastic theologian, John Cassian (d. c. 435), who expressed a quiet cautionary disagreement with certain Augustinian views. From Prosper of Aquitaine, preserved in Augustine's corpus as Letter 225:

(2) Many of the servants of Christ who live in the city of Marseilles, having read the writings that your Holiness published against the Pelagian heretics, think that your argument on the calling of the elect according to the design of God is contrary to the opinions of the Fathers and the view of the Church. . . . We have to fear this sharp dissent of theirs, first for their own sake, lest the spirit of Pelagian impiety trick men who are so clear-minded and so exemplary in their pursuit of all the virtues; and second, for less sophisticated people, who hold these others in high esteem because they see their uprightness, for these ordinary people think that the safest opinion they can hold is the one they hear asserted by others whose authority they follow without reflection.

(3) This is a summary of what [these critics] profess: Every human being has sinned in the sin of Adam and no one can be saved through his or her own efforts, but only by rebirth through the grace of God. Moreover, the propitiation which is present in the sacrament of the blood of Christ was offered for all human beings, without exception, such that all who are willing to come to faith and to baptism can be saved. But God foresaw before the foundation of the world (Eph 1:4; Mt 25:34) those who would believe or who would stand firm in the faith (a faith helped afterwards by grace); and He predestined to His kingdom those freely called, those He foresaw would be worthy of election and would depart this life by a good death. Therefore, every human being is warned by divine instructions to believe and to act accordingly so that no one need despair of laying hold of eternal life, since a reward has been prepared for those

with willing devotion. But [they claim] this design of God's calling, by which, it is said, a distinction is made between the chosen and the rejected (either before the beginning of the world or in the act of creating the human race such that, according to the Creator's pleasure, some are created "vessels of honor," others, "vessels of dishonor" [Rom 9:21]) deprives the fallen of any motive for rising up from their sins and allows the holy an excuse for lukewarmness. In both cases, all effort is useless if the rejected cannot enter [the Kingdom] no matter how they work, nor if the chosen fall away no matter how negligent. For however they act, the outcome for them cannot be other than what God has determined, and in this uncertainty of hope there can be no consistent course of action because the effort of human striving is useless if the choice of God's predestination rules otherwise. This has the effect of undermining effort and doing away with the virtues if God's ordering comes prior to human willing, and thus under the name of "predestination" a certain inevitability of fate is introduced; or else the Lord is said to be the Creator of different natures if no one can become other than what God has made. . . .

(5) When one raises as an objection to these arguments the countless multitude of little ones who have as yet no will, no actions of their own, ones who, in any case, are set aside by God's judgment for no reason except for original sin (under which all human beings are similarly born to share in the condemnation of the first human being), who are carried off before any experience of this life gives them a discernment of good and evil, some of whom are enrolled among the heirs of the heavenly kingdom because of their rebirth, while others, without baptism, pass over as debtors to eternal death. They say that such children are lost or saved according to what the divine knowledge foresees they would have been in their adult years if they had reached such an age and become active. . . .

(6) Our Lord Jesus Christ, they say, died for the whole human race, and that no one is excluded from the redemption wrought by His blood, not even someone who spends his whole life with a mindset utterly alienated from God, because the sacrament of divine mercy belongs to all human beings. The reason why many are not renewed is because God foresees that they do not have the will to receive it. Therefore, as far as God is concerned, eternal life is prepared for all, but as far as the freedom of choice is concerned, eternal life is grasped by those who believe in God by their own free choice and who receive the help of grace as a reward for their belief. The main reason these people, whose counter-arguments upset us (though they earlier had a better sense of it), preach grace in such a way is this: because if they were to admit that grace comes before all those good merits and that grace makes them possible and confers them, these people would necessarily have to concede that, according to His plan and the determination of His will, by a hidden judgment but by clear action, God "makes one vessel for honor, another for dishonor" (Rom 9:21) since no one is justified except by grace and no one is born except in sin. But they shrink from ad-

mitting this, and they have a dread of designating the merits of the saints as the work of God. Nor do they agree that the predestined number of the elect can neither be increased nor decreased because [that would mean that] the incentives in their exhortations would have no place, whether among the nonbelieving or the negligent, or because speaking out about being diligent and working hard would be useless for any whose striving would be frustrated by not being among the elect. For they assert that one can only be called to correction or to progress if one knows that one can be good by one's own effort, and that one's freedom of will will be assisted by the help of God if one chooses to do what God commands. And so [they argue that] for those who have reached the age of free will, there are two elements which bring about human salvation: namely, the grace of God and the obedience of a human being. These people want obedience to come before grace such that we would have to believe that salvation is initiated by the one who is saved, not by the One who saves, and we would have to believe that the will of a human being brings forth the help of divine grace for itself, not that that grace subjects the human will to itself.[97]

FAITH AS GIFT

These monastic critics in Gaul were no Pelagians. They shared Augustine's conviction that God's grace imbues our minds and hearts, giving us the strength to do the right thing. But they argued that we at least deserve credit for freely choosing to believe, that the initial saying "yes" to faith is our own free choice. In other words, they did not accept Augustine's notion of prevenient grace. Augustine here clarifies this: faith itself, even in its very beginnings, is a gift. To justify it, he cites both the example of and key words from St. Paul. Note also in this passage how he expands on his earlier views on the relationship between faith and reason by speaking of belief as "thinking with assent." From On the Predestination of the Saints:

(1.1) Now I confess that it troubles me that people do not yield to so many and such clear words from sacred Scripture in which the grace of God is preached, a grace that would in no way be grace were it given according to our merits. Still, I love the zeal and fraternal affection, my most beloved sons Prosper and Hilary, which makes you wish such persons not be in error, so that after so many books and letters of mine on this subject, you would have me write on it again. . . .

(1.2) After having closely read your letters, it seems to me that these brothers, on whose behalf you show such pious solicitude, should be treated as the Apostle treats those to whom he said, "And if on some matter you see differ-

97. Ep. 225.2–6 (BA 24:392–406); my trans., based on Parsons, FOTC 32:120–26.

ently, this also God will reveal to you" (Phil 3:15). Certainly they still remain in the dark concerning the question of the predestination of the saints, but they have the source from which, if on this matter they see differently, God may reveal this also to them if they keep walking on [the road] to which they have come. . . . These truths, to which they have come and which they hold fast, separate them considerably from the error of the Pelagians. . . .

(2.3) Now I see that I must reply to those who claim that the divine testimonies which we have cited on this issue mean [simply] that we [supposedly] know that faith itself comes from us, but its increase is from God, as if He did not give us faith, but only increased it in us, an increase merited because it started from our initiative. Now this does not differ from that opinion which Pelagius himself, before the tribunal of the bishops of Palestine, as its own Proceedings testify, was required to condemn: "That the grace of God is given according to our merits"[98]—as if our beginning to believe does not belong to God's grace, but rather grace is an additive given to us so that we may believe more fully and perfectly. . . .

(2.4) But against this idea, why do we not instead listen to the words [of Paul]: "Who has first given to Him and may be repaid in turn? For from Him and through Him and in Him are all things" (Rom 11:35–36)? And therefore, that very beginning of our faith: From whom does it come if not from Him? For it is not the case that all *other* things are from Him, and this is the sole exception. But "from Him and through Him and in Him are all things." Who would say that one who has already begun to believe deserves nothing from the One in whom he has believed? From this, it ends up that other divine gifts are said to be added in repayment to one who has some merit, and thus that God's grace is given according to our merits—a statement which Pelagius himself, when it was raised to him as an objection, condemned so that he himself might not be condemned. Therefore, whoever wants to avoid, in every sense, this condemnable view, let him understand that the Apostle spoke truly when he said, "To you it is given for Christ's sake not only to believe in him but also to suffer for him" (Phil 1:29). Both of these he shows to be the gifts of God, because he says both are given. He does not say, "to believe in him *more fully and perfectly*," but "*to believe* in him." Nor does he say that he himself had obtained mercy in order to be *more* faithful, but simply *to be faithful*, because he knew that he had been made faithful by God, the One who also made him an apostle. For the beginning of his faith is recorded in Scripture (Acts 9:1–9), and the account is very well known, for it is read in our churches on a solemn occasion. Once turned away from the faith—one that

98. "Pelagius . . . was required to condemn": See *De gestis Pelagii* 14.30.

he used to devastate and had been angrily turned against—he was suddenly converted to it by a more powerful grace. He was converted by the One to
whom the prophet said, just as it was about to happen: "You will turn us and
bring us to life" (Ps 84:7). So he not only went from being one who refused to
believe to becoming a willing believer, but even from being a persecutor to
becoming one who suffered persecution in defense of that faith he once used
to persecute. It was a gift given him by Christ: not only to believe in Him, but
also to suffer for Him.

(2.5) And therefore commending this grace—which is not given according to merits, but rather causes all good merits—he says: "Not that we are
sufficient to think anything as from ourselves, but our sufficiency is from
God" (2 Cor 3:5). Let them consider this well and weigh these words, those
who believe that the beginning of faith is our doing and that only the supple-
menting of faith is from God. For who would not see that thinking comes before believing? For no one believes anything unless one has first thought that
it is to be believed. However hastily, however speedily, some of our thoughts
fly before the will to believe, and even if this will follows them in such a way
that it appears to accompany them, as though they were inseparable, still it
is necessary that all things that are believed are believed after thought has
preceded. Yet even to believe is, in fact, nothing other than to think with assent. For not everyone who thinks believes, for many think in order that they
may not believe, but everyone who believes thinks, and in believing, thinks,
and in thinking, believes. So in what concerns religion and piety (of which
the Apostle was speaking), if we are not "sufficient to think anything as from
ourselves but our sufficiency is from God" (2 Cor 3:5), it follows that we are
not capable of believing anything, as though from ourselves, for we cannot
believe anything without thought, but "our sufficiency," by which we begin
to believe, "is from God." Therefore, just as no one is sufficient to himself for
the beginning or the completion of any good work (which these brothers, as
your letters indicate, already believe is true), so that in the beginning as well
as in the perfecting of every good work, our sufficiency is from God, so no
one is sufficient to himself either to begin or to perfect faith, but "our sufficiency is from God." For without thinking, there is no faith, and we are not
"sufficient to think anything as from ourselves, but our sufficiency is from
God."[99]

---

99. *De praedestinatione sanctorum* 1.1–2.5 (BA 24:468–74); my trans., based on Mourant and Collinge,
FOTC 86:218–22. Cf. *gr. et pecc. or.* 1.31.34 (CSEL 42:152).

PREDESTINATION

Few elements of Augustine's teaching would be more controversial in his time—and ever since—than his views on predestination. Predestination is hardly Augustine's invention. It is, first and foremost, biblical and appears explicitly in Pauline letters. Both opponents (such as Pelagians) and sympathizers (such as Prosper) had their own speculative theories. Here Augustine gives his classic articulation. As James Wetzel has noted, "predestination, to hear Augustine tell of it, is simply grace from God's point of view."[100] *From* On the Predestination of the Saints:

(10.19) If it is discussed and is asked how anyone can be worthy, there is no lack of those who will say: "by the human will." But we say: it is by grace or by divine predestination. And between grace and predestination the only difference is this: that predestination is the preparation for grace, while grace is the gift itself. Thus, when the Apostle says, "It is not from works so that no one may boast. For we are his workmanship, created in Christ Jesus for good works" (Eph 2:9–10), he speaks of grace, but when he says what follows, "which God has prepared that we should walk in them" (Eph 2:10), he speaks of predestination. Predestination cannot exist without foreknowledge, though there can be foreknowledge without predestination. By predestination God indeed foreknew that which He Himself was going to do; for this reason, it was said, "He has made that which shall be" (Is 45:11, LXX). Furthermore, He can foreknow even those things that He Himself does not do, such as whatever sins there may be. For even though there are certain things that are sins and at the same time punishment for sins, so that it is written, "God delivered them up to a reprobate mind to do those things which are not fitting" (Rom 1:28). This is not the sin of God, but the judgment of God. Therefore, the predestination of God, which has goodness as its goal, is, as I have said, the preparation for grace, and grace in turn is the effect of that predestination. Hence, when God promised Abraham that the faith of the nations was in his seed, saying, "I have established you as a father of many nations" (Gn 17:5)— and this is the basis on which the Apostle says, "For this reason, it depends on faith that according to grace the promise might be firm for every descendant" (Rom 4:16)—such a promise was based not upon the power of our will, but upon [God's] predestination. For He promised what He Himself would do, not what human beings would do. For even though human beings do good works which pertain to honoring God, it is He who brings it about that they do what He has ordered. It is not they who bring it about that He does what He has

---

100. Wetzel, *Augustine and the Limits of Virtue,* 9.

promised. Otherwise, the accomplishment of God's promises would not be in the power of God, but in that of human beings, and what was promised by the Lord would be rendered to Abraham by human beings themselves. This was not what Abraham believed, but rather "he believed, giving glory to God, that whatsoever He has promised, He is able also to perform" (Rom 4:20–21). He does not say "to foretell," he does not say "to foreknow"—because God can foretell and foreknow also what others do. But he says: "He is able also to perform." And thus the deeds are not those of another, but His own.[101]

Jesus as Predestination Incarnate

In his later years, Augustine began quietly wrestling with the same issue that was beginning to boil over in the Greek East and would come to a crisis in the clash between Nestorius and Cyril of Alexandria in 431, namely, what it means to speak of Christ as truly human. Augustine never devoted an entire treatise to Christology, but the ever-so-gradual evolution of his thinking through the questions appears both in sermons and in passing remarks in various treatises. In the following passage, Augustine boldly speaks of Christ as the exemplar of predestined humanity. From On the Predestination of the Saints:

(15.30) There is another most illuminating example of predestination and grace, and that is the Savior Himself, "the mediator between God and human beings, the man Christ Jesus" (1 Tm 2:5). By what prior merits of His, whether of works or of faith, did the human nature which is in Him come to attain this status? Let there be an answer to my question: How did this human being merit that He be assumed by the Father's co-eternal Word, the only-begotten Son of God, into the unity of the one person? What good of His, of whatever kind, preceded this? What did He do beforehand, what did He believe, what did He ask for in order to arrive at this ineffable excellence? Did He not begin to be the only Son of God from the moment He himself began to be a human being by the Word creating and assuming Him? Did not that woman, full of grace, conceive the only Son of God? Was not the only Son of God born of the Holy Spirit and the Virgin Mary, not by a desire of the flesh but by a unique gift of God? Was it to be feared that this human being as He grew older might sin through free will? Or for that reason was His will not free—or rather,

---

101. *De praedestinatione sanctorum* 10.19 (BA 24:522–24); trans. Mourant and Collinge, FOTC 86:241–42. On the reception of such views in North Africa, see J. Patout Burns, "The Atmosphere of Election: Augustinianism as Common Sense," *Journal of Early Christian Studies* 2 (1994): 325–39.

was it not so much freer because He was that much more unable to be a slave to sin? Certainly, human nature—that is, our nature—received uniquely in Him, without any prior merits of its own, all these uniquely admirable gifts and whatever other gifts may most truly be said to be proper to Him. . . .

(15.31) Therefore, in Him who is our Head, let there appear for us the very fountain of grace, from which He pours Himself out through all His members according to the measure of each one. For the grace that makes any human being a Christian from the time one begins to believe is the same grace by which that man from his beginning became the Christ. The Spirit by whom a Christian is reborn is the same Spirit who brings about in us the remission of sins and is also the Spirit who brought it about in Christ that He had no sin. These things God, beyond all doubt, foreknew that He would accomplish. This then is that predestination of the saints, which appeared most clearly in the Saint of saints. Who can deny this predestination, who rightly understands the words of the truth? For we learn that the very Lord of glory was predestined inasmuch as He who was Son of God became human. This is what the teacher of the Gentiles proclaims in the beginning of his Epistles: "Paul, a servant of Jesus Christ, called to be an apostle, set apart for the Gospel of God, which He had promised before, by His prophets, in the holy Scriptures, concerning his Son, who was born of Him, according to the flesh from the seed of David, who was predestined to be the Son of God in power, according to the Spirit of holiness, by the resurrection from the dead" (Rom 1:1–4).

Therefore, Jesus was predestined so that He who was to be the Son of David according to the flesh should nonetheless be the Son of God in power according to the Spirit of holiness, because He was born of the Holy Spirit and the Virgin Mary. This is the assumption by God the Word of a human being that ineffably occurred so that He might truly and properly be called at the same time the Son of God and the Son of Man, Son of Man because of the man who was assumed, the Son of God because of the only-begotten God who assumed him. Otherwise, a quaternity, not a Trinity, would be believed in. Such an uplifting of human nature was predestined, an elevation so great, so lofty, and so sublime that our nature could not be raised higher, just as for us the divinity could not humble itself more profoundly than by taking on human nature with the infirmity of the flesh, even to death on a cross. Therefore, just as that One was predestined to be our Head, so we, being many, are predestined to be His members. Here let human merits, which perished through Adam, be silent, and let that grace of God reign which reigns through Jesus Christ our Lord, the only Son of God, and the one Lord. Anyone who can discover in our Head the merits that preceded his unique birth, let

that person seek in us, His members, those merits which preceded our multiple rebirth. For that birth was not given to Christ as recompense, but rather
was given so that He should be born of the Spirit and the Virgin, apart from
all the bonds of sin. And likewise our being born again by water and the Spirit is not a recompense for any merit but is freely given to us. And if faith has
led us to the bath of rebirth, we ought not for that reason to think that we
have first given something to God so that our saving rebirth might be given
to us in return. For the One who has made us believe in Christ is the One who
made for us the Christ in whom we believe. He who made in human beings
the beginning (principium) and the perfection of their faith in Jesus, made the
man Jesus "the author (principem) and perfecter of faith" (Heb 12:2), for this is
what He is called, as you know, in the Epistle to the Hebrews.[102]

MAKING PROGRESS

Augustine recognized that his thinking on grace and on many other issues, both large and
small, had shifted over time. At the very moment when he was responding to Prosper's
and Hilary's concerns, he was also in the process of reviewing his vast output and his
long career as an author and recording his reflections in his Reconsiderations. Here he
reflects on his search. From The Gift of Perseverance:

(21.55) For at this moment I am writing a treatise in which I have begun
to reconsider my works[103] in order to show that I have not followed myself in
all matters, but rather I think that, through the mercy of God, I have made
progress in writing and did not begin at the point of perfection. For that matter, I would be speaking with more arrogance than truth if I were to say that
even now, at my present age, I have arrived at perfection, in writing without
any errors. But it makes a difference to what extent and in what matters one
has erred, and how easily one corrects one's error, or with what obstinacy one
attempts to defend it. Certainly there is high hope for a man, if the last day
of this life finds him making such progress that whatever was lacking in his
progress is supplied to him, and that he is judged as worthy to be perfected
rather than punished.[104]

102. De praedestinatione sanctorum 15.30–31 (BA 24:252–56); my trans., based on Mourant and Collinge,
FOTC 86:253–56. On this theme, see Réné Bernard, "La prédestination au Christ total selon saint Augustin," Recherches augustiniennes 3 (1965): 1–58; on its place within Augustine's broader Christology and theology of grace, see Hombert, Gloria Gratiae, 439–508.
103. "Reconsider my works": Augustine is referring to retr.
104. De dono perseverantiae 21.55 (BA 24:736); trans. Mourant and Collinge, FOTC 86:326.

CONQUERED BY THE GRACE OF GOD

Augustine tells his correspondents that the turning point in his career had been his first work he wrote as a bishop, To Simplicianus, On Various Questions, *in which his old mentor from Milan had asked him to wrestle with certain texts from Paul's Letters. From* On the Predestination of the Saints:

(3.7) I did not think that faith was preceded by the grace of God, so that through it, it might be given to us that we might ask usefully. Except for the fact that we could not believe unless the proclamation of the truth had preceded, I thought that, once the Gospel was preached to us, our assent was our own doing and came to us from ourselves. This error of mine is sufficiently evident in some small works of mine written before my episcopate. Among these is that which you mentioned in your letters, that is, my *Commentary on Statements in the Letter of Paul to the Romans*. . . .

(4.8) I see those brothers of ours [in Marseilles] are now of that opinion, because they did not take the same care with which they read my books also to join me in my progress in them. For if they had taken such care, they would have discovered that this question is resolved in accordance with the truth of the divine Scriptures in the first of the two books which I addressed at the very beginning of my episcopate to Simplicianus of blessed memory, bishop of the Church of Milan and successor to blessed Ambrose. Unless perhaps they did not know of this work—in this case, see to it that they do know it. . . . In the second book of my *Reconsiderations*, what I have said is as follows:[105]

The first two books which I wrote as a bishop are addressed to Simplicianus, bishop of the Church in Milan, who succeeded the most blessed Ambrose. They deal with various questions. . . . The second question deals with the passage where the Apostle says: "Not only Sarah, but also Rebecca who conceived in one act of intercourse [two sons] of Isaac our father" (Rom 9:10), up to where he says, "Unless the Lord of Hosts had left us a posterity, we should have become as Sodom and should have been like Gomorrah" (Rom 9:29). In the solution of this question, I indeed labored in defense of the free choice of the human will, but the grace of God conquered, and only thus was I able to arrive at the point where I understood that the Apostle spoke with the clearest truth, "For who singles you out? Or what do you have that you have not received? And if you have received it, why do you glory as if you had not received it?" (1 Cor 4:7). . . .

---

105. "Second book of my *Reconsiderations*": He quotes here from *retr.* 2.1.1 (CCL 57:89–90).

It was especially this testimony of the Apostle by which I myself was convinced when I thought otherwise about this matter. God revealed this to me, as I have said, when I was writing to Bishop Simplicianus, trying to resolve this question. Therefore, this testimony of the Apostle, when, in order to suppress human conceit, he said, "What do you have that you have not received?" does not permit any believer to say, "I have faith which I did not receive" [as a gift of God]. These words of the Apostle completely suppress all the pride of such a reply. Nor can even this be said: "Although I have not a perfected faith, yet I have its beginning, by which I first believed in Christ." For here also the reply is "But what do you have that you have not received? And if you have received it, why do you glory as if you had not received it?" (1 Cor 4:7)[106]

106. *De praedestinatione sanctorum* 3.7–4.8 (BA 24:484–88); trans. Mourant and Collinge, FOTC 86:224–28. On this, see Wetzel, *Augustine and the Limits of Virtue*, 161–81.

EPILOGUE

Around 421, a man named Laurentius wrote Augustine and asked him to set out the essentials of Christianity. He wanted something brief, "not a work that would tax a whole bookcase," but rather a work like what Greek writers of his day used to call "an *enchiridion*, a 'handbook,'" quite literally, "a book the hand can hold."[1] By this point in his career, Augustine had authored enough books to tax several bookcases. Yet for all his eloquent long-windedness, he remained capable of brilliant brevity and answered Laurentius with a modest-sized *Enchiridion*, drawing his outline and overview of Christianity from the core virtues of faith, hope, and love.

This book that you have in your hand is, in its own way, an *enchiridion*. I have tried here to gather together the many Augustines—the philosopher and bishop, the preacher and exegete, the theologian and controversialist—within the covers of a single volume, something that might not tax a whole bookcase, but instead be something the hand can hold. We have explored, or at least scanned, the best-known dimensions of his life and work, but there are others, facets we caught brief glimpses of: the monk, the teacher of prayer, the sacramental theologian, the moralist. My hope is that this survey might help readers discern where they desire to turn to next. In the introduction, I spoke of mosaics, of the way that mosaic was one of the great art forms of Augustine's world, of the way that fourth-century North African mosaic-artists used to create portraits from seemingly haphazard little stones known as *tesserae*, gem-like tidbits that, when properly arranged, once one stood back, came together to create colorful portraits. My hope is that all these many, many fragmentary quotations, these tiny verbal *tesserae*, tidbits at once colorful and sharp and gemlike, have begun to come together, to create a mosaic portrait

---

1. *Enchiridion* 1.6 (BA 9:108–10); trans. Peebles, FOTC 2:372.

of Augustine, something whole from something fragmentary. Other *tesserae* deserving inclusion have had to be excluded, but let these final few suffice.

෫෧

CONFESSIONS OF AUGUSTINE THE THEOLOGIAN

In one of the newly discovered Dolbeau sermons, at its very close, Augustine spells out how he wanted to be read and remembered as an author. From Sermon 162C:

(15) I have said what I thought had to be said with great care. Long have I held on to your love, and long has care for you held on to me. We who debate things and write books, we write in a very, very different way from all that is written in the holy canonical books. We make progress as we write. Every day we learn, we explore as we dictate [our books]. We knock [on God's door] as we speak. Certainly I will not keep silent, but as much as I can, where I can, I try to be useful to the brethren, both by speaking and by writing. To me, as far as it's up to me, I advise your Charity: Do not treat as canonical Scripture some theological debate or a book of some such debate. In the sacred writings of Scripture we learn to judge; in terms of our own writings, we are not above being judged. Certainly, what we'd choose, of the two options, is that we'd much rather speak accurately, whether in writing or in giving talks, and never make a mistake. But since this is hard to do, it is for that reason there is the firm foundation of the canon of the Scriptures, like that other firmament of the sky where luminous bodies are fixed between the waters above and the waters below, between nations of angels and nations of human beings, these above, those below (Gn 1:6). Let us treat the Scriptures as Scriptures, as God speaking. Let us not seek out an error-prone human being. After all, it is to spare us such frustration that the canon has been established in the Church. If someone, therefore, reads a book of mine, he may criticize me. If I speak in a reasonable way, let him follow not me, but reason itself. If I prove something by citing some clear and divine testimony, let him follow not me, but the sacred Scriptures. If, however, someone wants to criticize what I have rightly said, then he is not acting rightly; but I get more irritated with those lavishers of praise who treat my books as though a canonical text than with those who criticize my books for what's not criticize-able. Although I see you so eager, as though newly arrived, I do not wish to say anything more now so that what I've said here at the end you may hold on to more tenaciously. Turning to the Lord. . . .[2]

2. S. 162C = Dolbeau 10 (Dolbeau, VSS, 55–56); my trans. In this sermon, Augustine publicly discusses his dispute with Jerome on Galatians. (We saw this debate in Chapter 5.) François Dolbeau, VSS, 37–45, dated the sermon to 397, that is, soon after Augustine became bishop, but Hombert, *Nouvelles recherches*, 347–54, argues that it dates from 405, that is, contemporary with *ep.* 82 to Jerome. On the broader theme, see

THE DEATH OF AUGUSTINE

Augustine died at the age of 76, just as the Vandal army was laying siege to Hippo. From Possidius of Calama, Life of St. Augustine:

(31) Now, that holy man in the long life God gave him for the Church's welfare and happiness (indeed, he lived seventy-six years, almost forty of them as bishop or presbyter) used to say to us in intimate conversation that, even after receiving baptism, praiseworthy Christians and priests should not depart from the body without worthy and proper repentance. This he himself performed in the last illness that caused his death. He commanded the very brief penitential Psalms of David to be written out, and during the days of his illness, as he lay in bed, he looked at the pages which were opposite him on the wall and read them with overflowing and constant weeping. Moreover, in order that no one might hinder his purpose, about ten days before he departed from the body, he asked those of us who were present not to allow anyone to come to him except at the hours when the physician came to examine him or when nourishment was brought to him. His request was respected and fulfilled, and during all that time he had leisure for prayer. Up to his very last illness he preached the word of God in church incessantly, vigorously, and forcefully, with clear mind and sound judgment. With all the limbs of his body intact, his sight and hearing unimpaired, while we looked on and prayed at his bedside, "he slept with fathers," as we read, "well-nourished in a good old age" (1 Kgs 2:10). After the Holy Sacrifice was offered, he was buried in our presence as we commended the repose of his body.[3]

READING AUGUSTINE VS. HEARING HIM

By no small miracle, Augustine's works were preserved. We do not know the full circumstances, but Possidius certainly played a key role. We have Possidius's Index (Indiculus), an invaluable catalog of Augustine's library. But Possidius was acutely aware of the difference between reading Augustine and hearing him live. From the conclusion of Possidius of Calama, Life of St. Augustine:

(31) It is clear from his writings that this priest, so valued and accepted by God, lived rightly and wisely in the faith, hope, and love of the Catholic Church, as far as he could, seeing things in the light of truth. Those who read what he has written in his

---

Isabelle Bochet, "*Le Firmament de l'Écriture*": *L'herméneutique augustinienne*, CEASA 172 (Paris: Institut d'Études Augustiniennes, 2004). "Turning to the Lord . . .": Augustine ended his sermons with a prayer that began with these words; his stenographers recorded not the full prayer, but only the opening words. On this, see François Dolbeau, "L'oraison 'Conuersi ad dominum. . . .' Un bilan provisoire des recensions existants," *Archiv für Liturgiewissenschaft* 41 (1999): 295–321; reprinted in *Augustin et la prédication en Afrique*, 127–54.

3. Vita 31 (Geerlings, 102); trans. Muller and Deferrari, FOTC 15:122–23 (modified).

works on theological matters profit greatly, but I believe that the ones who really profited were those who actually heard him and saw him speak in church, and especially those who got to know him in conversations when he was among us. Not only was he a scribe well-instructed in the kingdom of heaven, bringing forth from his storehouse treasures new and old (Mt 13:52), and one of those merchants who, once he had found the precious pearl, sold what he had and bought it (Mt 13:45–46); he was also one of those about whom we read: "So you speak, and so you do" (Jas 2:12).'[4]

OF USEFUL LENGTH

Augustine concluded his "handbook" to Laurentius with the following remarks. It seems a fitting end to this volume. From Enchiridion:

(33) But there must be an end somewhere to this volume. It is for you to see whether you ought to call it a handbook or use it as such. As for myself, since I thought that your zeal in Christ was not to be despised, believing and hoping good things for you with the help of our Redeemer, and loving you greatly among the members of His body, I have written for you, as well as I could, this book on faith, hope, and love. May it be as useful as it is lengthy.[5]

4. Vita 31 (Geerlings, 104); my trans., based on Muller and Deferrari, FOTC 15:124.
5. Enchiridion 33 (BA 9:326); trans. Peebles, FOTC 2:471–72.

CHRONOLOGY
The Life and Major Works of Augustine

Scholars have been able to plot out the chronology of Augustine's life and works with remarkable precision, one virtually impossible with any other figure from antiquity. Three major things make this possible: the volume of his surviving works which contain scattered cross-references and chronological markers; the dates and autobiographical comments in *Confessions*, and his scrupulous listing and ordering of his books in *Reconsiderations*. While one does find, in the scholarly literature, occasional variations on the dating of this or that work (generally with a year or two's difference), there is, on the whole, surprisingly broad consensus on most matters. (I should add that it remains difficult to date the majority of his sermons, though certain ones can be pinpointed with some precision.) On the chronology of Augustine's life and works, see Goulven Madec, *Introduction aux 'Revisions' et à la Lecture des Œuvres de saint Augustin* (1996), esp. 159–65; Serge Lancel, *Saint Augustine* (1999; English: 2002), esp. 531–36; and Allan Fitzgerald, *Augustine through the Ages* (1999), xliii–il.

EARLY CAREER: THAGASTE, CARTHAGE, MILAN (354–387)

354 (Nov. 13)	Born in Thagaste
366–369	Studies in grammar at Madaura
369–370	Studies interrupted; idle year in Thagaste
370	Begins studies in rhetoric at Carthage; begins living with mistress
c. 371	Death of Augustine's father Patricius; birth of Adeodatus
c. 373	Reads Cicero's *Hortensius*; joins Manichees
373–374	Teaches in Thagaste
374–383	Teaches in Carthage
383	Meets Faustus of Milevis
383–384	Teaches in Rome
384	Appointed orator for Milan; meets Ambrose of Milan

386 | Reads Platonist books

386 (August) | Conversion in garden in Milan

386 (Sept.) | Withdraws to Cassiciacum; writes:
Against the Skeptics (*Contra Academicos*, 386)
On the Happy Life (*De beata vita*, Nov. 386)
On Order (*De ordine*, 386)
Soliloquies (*Soliloquia*, 386–387)

387 (Mar.) | Returns to Milan for Lenten training for baptism; writes:
On the Immortality of the Soul (*De immortalitate animae*, 387)

387 (April) | Baptized in Milan by Ambrose

ROME AND THAGASTE (387–391)

c. 387 | Vision at Ostia; death of Augustine's mother Monnica

387–388 | Spends year in Rome; writes:
On the Catholic and Manichean Ways of Life (*De moribus ecclesiae Catholicae et de moribus Manichaeorum*, 388–389)
On the Greatness of the Soul (*De animae quantitate*, 388)
On Free Will, Bk. 1 (*De libero arbitrio*, begun: 388)

388 | Leaves Italy; sails with family and friends to North Africa

388–391 | Establishes and leads monastic community in Thagaste; writes:
On Genesis against the Manichees (*De Genesi adversus Manichaeos*, 388)
On Music (*De musica*, c. 388 or 389)
On the Teacher (*De magistro*, 389)
On True Religion (*De vera religione*, c. 390)

390 | Death of Adeodatus; death of Nebridius

391 | Aurelius becomes Catholic bishop of Carthage

PRESBYTER: HIPPO REGIUS (391–395)

391 | Ordained presbyter for Hippo Regius; soon after writes:
On the Advantage of Believing (*De utilitate credendi*, 391)
On the Two Souls (*De duabus animabus*, 391–392)

392 (August) | Debates Fortunatus the Manichee (*Acta contra Fortunatum Manichaeum*)

393 (October) | Council of Hippo; Augustine addresses bishops on creed, published as:
On Faith and the Creed (*De fide et symbolo*, 393)

393–395   Other major works written (or completed or begun) in this
        period:
           Expositions on the Psalms, 1–32 (Enarrationes in Psalmos,
              begun: c. 393)
           Psalm against the Donatists (Psalmus contra partem Donati, c. 393)
           On the Lord's Sermon on the Mount (De sermone Domini in monte,
              394)
           Commentary on Statements in the Letter of Paul to the Romans
              (Expositio quarundam propositionum ex epistula apostoli ad
              Romanos, 394)
           Against Adimantus (Contra Adimantum Manichei discipulum, 394)
           On Free Will, Bks. 2–3 (De libero arbitrio, completed c. 395)
           Commentary on the Letter to the Galatians (Expositio epistulae ad
              Galatas, c. 395)

c. 395   Initiates correspondence with Jerome (*Letter 28*)

c. 395   Initial exchange of letters with Paulinus of Nola, beginning a
        25-year correspondence

BISHOP: HIPPO REGIUS (396–430)

c. 395   Ordained coadjutor bishop for Hippo Regius

c. 396   Succeeds Valerius as bishop of Hippo Regius; writes soon after:
        To Simplicianus, on Various Questions (Ad Simplicianum, 396)

397   Death of Ambrose of Milan

397 (June, Aug.)   Attends Councils of Carthage; preaches there during summer

397–400   Major works composed (or begun) during this period:
           Against the "Foundation Letter" of Mani (Contra epistulam
              Manichaei quam vocant fundamenti, 396–397)
           Rule (Regula: Praeceptum, c. 397)
           On Christian Teaching, Bks. 1–3 (De doctrina christiana, begun
              397)
           Confessions (Confessiones, 397–401)
           Against Faustus, a Manichee (Contra Faustum Manichaeum,
              397–398)
           On the Trinity (De Trinitate, begun 399 or 400)
           On the Nature of the Good (De natura boni, 399)
           On Catechizing Beginners (De catechizandis rudibus, c. 399)

400   Death of Simplicianus

400–403   Major works composed during this period:
           On the Agreement among the Evangelists (De consensu evangelista-
              rum, 400)
           Against the Letter of Parmenian (Contra epistulam Parmeniani, 400)
           On Baptism (De baptismo, 400–401)

400–403 (cont.)	Responses to Januarius (Ad inquisitiones Januarii, 400) (= Letters 54–55)
	On the Good of Marriage (De bono conjugali, 401) On the Literal Interpretation of Genesis (De Genesi ad litteram, begun 401) Against the Letters of Petilian (Contra litteras Petiliani, 400–403)
403	Attends Council of Carthage. Escapes assassination.
405	Government issues Edict of Unity (against Donatists)
405–410	Major works composed (or begun) during this period: Against Cresconius (Contra Cresconium, 405) Tractates on the Gospel of John 1–16 (In Johannis evangelium tractatus, begun late 406) Expositions of the Psalms 119–133 (Enarrationes in psalmos, late 406–407) Tractates on the First Letter of John (In epistulam Johannis ad Parthos tractatus, begun Easter Week, 407) On One Baptism in Answer to Petilian (De unico baptismo contra Petilianum, 410)
410	Alaric and the Goths sack Rome; Pelagius and Caelestius flee to North Africa
411 (June 1–8)	Participates in Conference of Carthage (with Donatists); publishes précis: Summary of the Meeting with the Donatists (Breviliculus conlationis cum Donatistis)
411 (fall)	Tribunal in Carthage convicts Caelestius of heresy
412–413	Major works composed (or begun) during this period: On the Merits and Forgiveness of Sins and On Infant Baptism (De peccatorum meritis et remissione et de baptismo parvulorum, 412 On the Spirit and the Letter (De spiritu et littera, 412) On the City of God, Bks. 1–3 (De civitate Dei, begun 413)
413 (Sept.)	Flavius Marcellinus executed
414	Receives a copy of Pelagius's On Nature from former disciples of Pelagius
415 (July)	Paul Orosius accuses Pelagius of heresy at synod in Jerusalem
415 (Dec.)	Pelagius vindicated at Synod of Diospolis in Palestine
415–416	Major works composed (or completed) during this period: On the Literal Interpretation of Genesis (De Genesi ad litteram, completed 415) On Nature and Grace (De natura et gratia, 415) On the Perfection of Human Righteousness (De perfectione justitiae hominis, 416) On the Deeds of Pelagius (De gestis Pelagii, late 416–early 417)

416	Councils of Carthage and Milevis (Augustine attends latter); dossier of documents sent to Pope Innocent I
417 (Jan. 27)	Innocent I condemns Pelagius and Caelestius
417 (March)	Death of Innocent I; Zosimus becomes pope
417	Initial contacts with Count Boniface; Augustine responds to his inquiries with: On the Correction of the Donatists (De correctione Donatistarum = Letter 185)
417 (Sept.)	Zosimus clears Pelagius and Caelestius of charges of heterodoxy
418 (Apr. 29)	Imperial rescript issued against Pelagius and Caelestius
418 (May 1)	Council of Carthage issues canons on original sin, grace, and infant baptism
418 (summer)	Zosimus issues Tractoria against Pelagians
419	Julian of Eclanum writes initial works against Augustine
c. 420	Death of Jerome
418–422	Major works composed (or completed) during this period: On the Grace of Christ and Original Sin (De gratia Christi et de peccato originali, 418) On Marriage and Concupiscence (De nuptiis et concupiscentia, 419–421) On the Trinity (De Trinitate, completed: 419 or 420) On the Soul and Its Origin (De anima et eius origine, 419–420) Against Gaudentius (Contra Gaudentium Donatistarum episcopum, 419) Against Two Letters of the Pelagians (Contra duas epistulas Pelagianorum, 421) Against Julian (Contra Julianum, 421) Enchiridion (Enchiridion, c. 421–422)
423	Affair of Antoninus of Fussala
426	Travels to Milevis to settle succession of Severus
426	Announces retirement; Eraclius nominated as Augustine's successor
426–428	Major works composed (or completed) during this period: On Grace and Free Will (De gratia et libero arbitrio, 426–427) On Admonition and Grace (De correptione et gratia, 426–427) On the City of God (De civitate Dei, completed c. 426) Reconsiderations (Retractationes, 426–427) On Christian Teaching, Bk. 4 (De doctrina christiana, completed 427) On Heresies (De haeresibus, 428)
427	Revolt of Count Boniface

427 Public disputation against the Arian Maximinus; published as:
Debate with Maximinus (Conlatio cum Maximino Arianorum
episcopo, 427–428)

428 Receives letter from Prosper of Aquitaine about complaints in
Gaul

428–430 Final writings:
On the Predestination of the Saints (De praedestinatione sanctorum,
428–429)
On the Gift of Perseverance (De dono perseverantiae, 428–429)
Against Julian, an Unfinished Work (Contra Julianum opus
imperfectum, 429–430)

430 Vandals lay siege to Hippo

430 (Aug. 28) Death of Augustine

431 Council of Ephesus condemns Pelagianism

Note: Pierre-Marie Hombert, in his Nouvelles recherches de chronologie augustinienne
(2000), has argued that in light of the recent discoveries of the Divjak letters and
the Dolbeau sermons, there needs to be a thorough revision of the dating of Augustine's works, especially from his mid-career. Of the works listed above, Hombert
has proposed the following modifications:

Confessions   397–400 (for Bks. 1–9), 403 (for Bks. 10–13)

Against Faustus, a Manichee   400–402

On Catechizing Beginners   403

On the Trinity   400–403 (Bk. 1), 411–422 (Bks. 2–15)

Against the Letter of Parmenian   403–404

Letters 54–55   403

On the Good of Marriage   403–404

Literal Interpretation of Genesis   404–405 (Bks. 1–3a), 412–414 (Bks. 3b–12)

Against the Letters of Petilian   400–401 (Bks. 1–2), 403–405 (Bk. 3)

SUGGESTIONS FOR
FURTHER READING

LIFE OF AUGUSTINE

The starting point for any study of Augustine is Peter Brown's landmark biography, *Augustine of Hippo: A Biography*, rev. ed. (Berkeley: University of California Press, 2000). Originally published in 1968, this brilliant work, written in masterful prose and with masterful insights, brings alive all the richly human tensions and depths of Augustine's personality and the intricacies of his world. The 2000 revised edition has added chapters that discuss the newly discovered Dolbeau sermons and Divjak letters. Also excellent is Serge Lancel, *Saint Augustine*, trans. Antonia Nevill (London: SCM Press, 2002). Lancel's work has its distinctive strengths: an extraordinary command of the archeological data from Roman North Africa; cogent analyses of the course of the Donatist controversy, especially the Conference in Carthage in 411; overviews of each of Augustine's major works. See also:

Bonner, Gerald. "Augustinus (uita)." In *Augustinus-Lexikon*, 1:519–50. Ed. Cornelius Mayer. Basel: Schwabe, 1986.
Chadwick, Henry. *Augustine of Hippo: A Life*. New York: Oxford University Press, 2009.
Harrison, Carol. "Augustine." In *The Early Christian World*, 2:1205–27. Ed. Philip Esler. New York: Routledge, 2001.
Marrou, Henri. *Saint Augustine and His Influence Through the Ages*. Trans. Patrick Hepburn-Scott. 1957; reprint in *Personalities of the Early Church*, ed. Everett Ferguson, 271–352. New York: Garland Publishing, 1993.

THEOLOGY OF AUGUSTINE

Augustine's theology is so rich and so many-sided that it is difficult to survey well within a single volume. It is easier, in some ways, to absorb Augustine's thought topic by topic, controversy by controversy. Therefore, the more focused studies listed under Chapters 6–10 may provide easier starting points. Nonetheless, there are several one-volume surveys of Augustine's theology that may prove helpful for first-time readers of Augustine. One up-to-date survey is Carol Harrison's *Augustine: Christian Truth and Fractured Humanity*, Christian Theology in Context (New York: Oxford University Press, 2000). A helpful, though somewhat dated, overview is Gerald Bonner's

St Augustine of Hippo: Life and Controversies (1963; reprint with new preface: Norwich: Canterbury Press, 1986, 2002). See also:

Burnaby, John. Amor Dei: A Study of the Religion of St. Augustine. 1938; reprint: Eugene, OR: Wipf & Stock, 2007. A classic.

Chadwick, Henry. Augustine: A Very Short Introduction. New York: Oxford University Press, 2001.

Hombert, Pierre-Marie. Nouvelles recherches de chronologie augustinienne. Collections des Études Augustiniennes, Série Antiquité 163. Paris: Institut d'Études Augustiniennes, 2000.

Madec, Goulven. Introduction aux 'Revisions' et à la lecture des oeuvres de saint Augustin. Collection des Études Augustiniennes, Série Antiquité 150. Paris: Institut d'Études Augustiniennes, 1996.

Mandouze, André. Saint Augustin: L'aventure de la raison et de la grâce. Collection des Études Augustiniennes 31. Paris: Institut d'Études Augustiniennes, 1968.

TeSelle, Eugene. Augustine the Theologian. 1970; reprint: Eugene, OR: Wipf & Stock, 2004. Dated in certain respects.

REFERENCE WORKS

For an excellent up-to-date reference work, see Allan Fitzgerald, ed., Augustine Through the Ages: An Encyclopedia (Grand Rapids, MI: Eerdmans, 1999). Over 900 pages, this surveys every aspect of Augustine's life, writings, theology, and influence; articles are written by the leading English-speaking Augustinian scholars. Also excellent, but incomplete, is the Augustinus-Lexikon, ed. Cornelius Mayer (Basel: Schwabe, 1986–), 3 vols. to date; this massive encyclopedia, with individual articles written in either German or English or French, is admirably ambitious but seems likely to take decades to complete.

JOURNALS AND COLLECTIONS OF ESSAYS

There are major journals that specialize in the study of Augustine, notably, Augustinian Studies, Revue des Études Augustiniennes, Recherches Augustiniennes, and Augustiniana. Other major journals regularly include essays on Augustine, notably, Journal of Early Christian Studies, Journal of Theological Studies, Revue Bénédictine, and Vigiliae Christianae. Valuable essays appear also in various festschrifts, compilations, and conference proceedings. Those focused on individual topics or individual texts are listed later under the appropriate chapter. Listed below are those that cover a wide miscellany of topics:

Bonner, Gerald. Church and Faith in the Patristic Tradition: Augustine, Pelagianism and Early Christian Northumbria. Collected Studies. London: Variorum Reprints, 1996.

Brown, Peter. Religion and Society in the Age of St. Augustine. 1972; reprint: Eugene, OR: Wipf & Stock, 2007.

Bruning, Bernard, ed. Collectanea Augustiniana: Mélanges T. J. van Bavel. 2 vols. Louvain: Leuven University Press, 1990.

Dodaro, Robert, and George Lawless, eds. *Augustine and His Critics: Essays in Honour of Gerald Bonner*. New York: Routledge, 2000.

Fux, P.-Y., J.-M. Roessli, and Otto Wermelinger, eds., *Augustinus Afer: Saint Augustin, africanité et universalité*. Actes du colloque international, Alger-Annaba, 1–7 avril 2001. Fribourg: Éditions universitaires, 2003.

Klingshirn, William E, and Mark Vessey, eds. *The Limits of Ancient Christianity: Essays on Late Antique Thought and Culture in Honor of R. A. Markus*. Ann Arbor: University of Michigan Press, 1999.

Madec, Goulven. *Lectures Augustiniennes*. Collections des Études Augustiniennes, Série Antiquité 168. Paris: Institut d'Études Augustiniennes, 2001.

———. *Petites Études Augustiniennes*. Collections des Études Augustiniennes, Série Antiquité 142. Paris: Institut d'Études Augustiniennes, 1994.

Markus, Robert A. *From Augustine to Gregory the Great: History and Christianity in Late Antiquity*. Collected Studies 169. London: Variorum Reprints, 1983.

———. *Sacred and Secular: Studies on Augustine and Latin Christianity*. Collected Studies 465. Brookfield, VT: Variorum Reprints, 1994.

Markus, Robert A., ed. *Augustine: A Collection of Critical Essays*. Garden City, NJ: Anchor Books, 1972.

Mayer, Cornelius, ed. *Homo Spiritualis: Festgabe für Luc Verheijen OSA*. Würzburg: Augustinus-Verlag, 1987.

Schnaubelt, Joseph C., and Frederick Van Fleteren, eds. *Augustine: Second Founder of the Faith*. Collectanea Augustiniana. New York: Peter Lang, 1990.

———. *Augustine in Iconography: History and Legend*. Augustinian Historical Institute Series, vol. 4. New York: Peter Lang Publishing, 1999.

Van Fleteren, Frederick, Joseph C. Schnaubelt, and Joseph Reino, eds. *Augustine: Mystic and Mystagogue*. Collectanea Augustiniana. New York: Peter Lang, 1994.

Zumkeller, Adolar, ed. *Signum Pietatis: Festgabe für Cornelius Petrus Mayer OSA*. Würzburg: Augustinus Verlag, 1989.

Augustinus Magister. Congrès internationale augustinien, 1954. 3 vol. Collection des Études Augustiniennes, Série Antiquité 1–3. Paris: Institut d'Études Augustiniennes, 1954.

EARLY CHRISTIANITY: HISTORY AND THEOLOGY

It is vital to see Augustine's life and thought within the broader history and theology of early Christianity. The scholarly literature is obviously vast, but what follows are some essentials. There are several excellent (and massive) overviews of the history: Henry Chadwick, *The Church in Ancient Society: From Galilee to Gregory the Great*, Oxford History of the Christian Church (New York: Oxford University Press, 2001); Frances Young and Margaret Mitchell, eds. *Origins to Constantine*, Cambridge History of Christianity, vol. 1 (Cambridge: Cambridge University Press, 2005); and Augustine Casiday and Frederick W. Norris, eds., *Constantine to c. 600*, Cambridge History of Christianity, vol. 2 (Cambridge: Cambridge University Press, 2007). For a survey of the literature and theology of early Christianity, see Frances Young, Lewis Ayres, and Andrew Louth, eds., *The Cambridge History of Early Christian Literature* (Cambridge: Cambridge University Press, 2004). Also excellent is Philip F. Esler, ed., *The Early Christian World*, 2 vols. (New York: Routledge, 2000). See also:

Brown, Peter. *The Rise of Western Christendom: Triumph and Diversity, AD 200–1000*. 2nd ed. Oxford: Blackwell Publishers, 2003.

DiBerardino, Angelo, ed. *Encyclopedia of the Early Church*. 2 vol. Trans. Adrian Walford. New York: Oxford University Press, 1991.

Drobner, Hubertus. *The Fathers of the Church: A Comprehensive Introduction*. Trans. Siegfried Schatzmann; bibliographies for the English edition, William Harmless, SJ, and Hubertus Drobner. Peabody, MA: Hendrickson, 2007.

Ferguson, Everett, Michael P. McHugh, and Frederick W. Norris, eds. *Encyclopedia of Early Christianity*. 2nd ed. New York: Garland Publishing, 1998.

Harvey, Susan Ashbrook, and David G. Hunter, eds. *The Oxford Handbook of Early Christian Studies*. New York: Oxford University Press, 2008.

Kelly, J. N. D. *Early Christian Doctrines*. 5th ed. New York: Continuum, 2000.

Roldanus, Johannes. *The Church in the Age of Constantine: The Theological Challenges*. New York: Routledge, 2006.

Wilken, Robert L. *The Spirit of Early Christian Thought: Seeking the Face of God*. New Haven: Yale University Press, 2003.

LATE ANTIQUITY: HISTORY AND SOCIAL WORLD

Just as it is important to situate Augustine's life and thought within the history and theology of early Christianity, so it is important to situate him within the history and social world of Late Antiquity. Brown's and Lancel's biographies do this in very helpful ways. Still, readers may find it helpful to see things in a broader context. Listed below are a mix of surveys and specialized studies:

Beard, Mary, John North, and Simon Price. *Religions of Rome*. 2 vols. Cambridge: Cambridge University Press, 1998.

Bowersock, G. W., Peter Brown, and Oleg Grabar, eds. *Late Antiquity: A Guide to the Postclassical World*. Cambridge, MA: Belknap Press/Harvard University Press, 1999.

Cameron, Averil, and Peter Garnsey, eds. *The Late Empire, A.D. 337–425*. Cambridge Ancient History, vol. 13. Cambridge: Cambridge University Press, 1998.

Clark, Gillian. *Women in Late Antiquity: Pagan and Christian Lifestyles*. New York: Oxford University Press, 1994.

Dominik, William, and John Hall, eds. *A Companion to Roman Rhetoric*. Blackwell Companions to the Ancient World. Oxford: Blackwell, 2007.

Elsner, J. R. *Imperial Rome and Christian Triumph: The Art of the Roman Empire AD 100–450*. New York: Oxford University Press, 1998.

Finn, Richard, ed. *Almsgiving in the Later Roman Empire: Christian Promotion and Practice (313–450)*. Oxford Classical Monographs. New York: Oxford University Press, 2006.

Glancy, Jennifer A. *Slavery in Early Christianity*. New York: Oxford University Press, 2002.

Hadot, Pierre. *What Is Ancient Philosophy?* Trans. Michael Chase. Cambridge, MA: Harvard University Press, 2002.

Haines-Eitzen, Kim. *Guardians of Letters: Literacy, Power, and the Transmitters of Early Christian Literature*. New York: Oxford University Press, 2000.

Harrison, Stephen, ed. *A Companion to Latin Literature*. Blackwell Companions to the Ancient World. Oxford: Blackwell, 2006.

Hunt, E. D. *Holy Land Pilgrimage in the Later Roman Empire, AD 312–460*. Oxford: Clarendon Press/New York: Oxford University Press, 1984.

Jones, A. H. M. *The Later Roman Empire, 284–602: A Social, Economic, and Administrative Survey*. 2 vols. 1964; reprint: Baltimore: Johns Hopkins, 1978.

Kaster, R. A. *Guardians of Language: The Grammarian and Society in Late Antiquity*. Berkeley: University of California Press, 1988.

Kelly, Christopher. *Ruling the Later Roman Empire*. Cambridge, MA: Harvard University Press, 2004.

Lenski, Noel, ed. *The Cambridge Companion to the Age of Constantine*. New York: Cambridge University Press, 2006.

Lepelley, Claude. *Les cités de l'Afrique romaine au Bas-Empire*. 2 vols. Collection des Études Augustiniennes, Série Antiquité 80–81. Paris: Institut d'Études Augustiniennes, 1979–1981.

Long, A. A. *Hellenistic Philosophy: Stoics, Epicureans, Skeptics*. 2nd ed. Berkeley: University of California Press, 1986.

Marrou, Henri I. *A History of Education in Antiquity*. Trans. George Lamb. 1956; reprint: Madison: University of Wisconsin Press, 1982.

Monceaux, Pierre. *Histoire littéraire de l'Afrique chrétienne*. 7 vols. Paris: Leroux, 1901–1923.

Rüpke, Jörg, ed. *A Companion to Roman Religion*. Blackwell Companions to the Ancient World. Oxford: Blackwell, 2006.

Salzman, Michele Renee. *The Making of a Christian Aristocracy: Social and Religious Change in the Western Roman Empire*. Cambridge, MA: Harvard University Press, 2004.

Swain, Simon, and Mark Edwards, eds. *Approaching Late Antiquity: The Transformation from Early to Late Empire*. New York: Oxford University Press, 2004.

Veyne, Paul, ed. *The History of Private Life*, Vol. 1: *From Pagan Rome to Byzantium*. Cambridge, MA: Harvard University Press, 1987.

CHAPTER 1

Confessions: Studies

The major biographies of Augustine do a fine job of guiding readers through the story recorded in *Confessions*, both setting episodes within the context of late antiquity and of North African Christianity and adding critical perspectives to Augustine's self-presentation: see Brown, *Augustine of Hippo* (pp. 7–124 and 151–75); Lancel, *Saint Augustine* (pp. 3–120); and Bonner, *St. Augustine* (pp. 36–103). For an introduction to the literary character of the text, see Gillian Clark, *Saint Augustine: The Confessions*, Landmarks of World Literature (Cambridge: Cambridge University Press, 1993). For a detailed paragraph-by-paragraph commentary, see J. J. O'Donnell, *Augustine: Confessions*, 3 volumes (New York: Oxford University Press, 1991); O'Donnell presumes readers have command of Latin. Also valuable is the introduction and commentary by Aimé Solignac in the French edition of *Confessions*, BA 13–14, rev. ed. (Paris: Desclée de Bouwer, 1992). *Confessions* is certainly Augustine's most studied book. Here is a very small selection of both classic and recent studies:

Burns, J. Patout, "Ambrose Preaching to Augustine: The Shaping of Faith." In *Augustine: Second Founder of the Faith*, 373–86. Ed. Joseph C. Schnaubelt and Frederick van Fleteren. New York: Peter Lang, 1990.

Burton, Philip. *Language in the Confessions of Augustine*. New York: Oxford University Press, 2007.

Cavadini, John C. "Time and Ascent in *Confessions* XI." In *Augustine: Presbyter Factus Sum*, 171–85. Ed. Joseph T. Lienhard et al. Collectanea Augustiniana. New York: Peter Lang, 1993.

Chadwick, Henry. "History and Symbolism in the Garden at Milan." In *From Augustine to Eriugena: Essays on Neoplatonism and Christianity in Honor of John O'Meara*, 42–55. Ed. F. X. Martin and J. A. Richmond. Washington, DC: The Catholic University of America Press, 1991.

Courcelle, Pierre. *Recherches sur les Confessions de saint Augustin*. 2nd ed. Paris: E. de Boccard, 1968.

———. *Les Confessions de saint Augustin dans la tradition littéraire: Antécédents et postérité*. Collection des Études Augustiniennes, Série Antiquité 15. Paris: Études Augustiniennes, 1963.

Feldman, E. "Confessiones." *Augustinus-Lexikon*, 1:1134–94. Ed. Cornelius Mayer. Basel: Schwabe, 1986.

Fredriksen, Paula. "Paul and Augustine: Conversion Narratives, Orthodox Traditions, and the Retrospective Self." *Journal of Theological Studies* n.s. 37 (1986): 3–34.

Kenney, John Peter. *The Mysticism of Saint Augustine: Re-Reading the Confessions*. London and New York: Routledge, 2005.

Kotzé, Annemaré. *Augustine's Confessions: Communicative Purpose and Audience*. Supplements to Vigiliae Christianae 71. Leiden and Boston: Brill, 2004.

Madec, Goulven. "Le néoplatonisme dans la conversion d'Augustin: État d'une question centenaire (depuis Harnack et Boissier, 1888)." In *Petites Études Augustiniennes*, 51–69. Collection des Études Augustiniennes, Série Antiquité 142. Paris: Institut d'Études Augustiniennes, 1994.

O'Connell, Robert J. *St. Augustine's Confessions: The Odyssey of Soul*. Cambridge, MA: Harvard University Press, 1969. Controversial, but full of insights.

———. *Images of Conversion in Saint Augustine's Confessions*. New York: Fordham University Press, 1995.

O'Meara, John J. *The Young Augustine: An Introduction to the Confessions of St. Augustine*. 2nd ed. 1956; reprint: New York: Alba House, 2001. A classic.

———. "Augustine's *Confessions*: Elements of Fiction." In *Augustine: From Rhetor to Theologian*, 77–96. Ed. Joanne McWilliam. Waterloo: Wilfrid Laurier University Press, 1992.

Paffenroth, Kim, and Robert Peter Kennedy, eds. *A Reader's Companion to Augustine's Confessions*. Louisville: Westminster John Knox, 2003.

Ramsey, Boniface. *Ambrose*. The Early Church Fathers. New York: Routledge, 1997.

Young, Frances. "The *Confessions* of St. Augustine: What Is the Genre of this Work?" 1998 St. Augustine Lecture. *Augustinian Studies* 30 (1999): 1–16.

Le Confessioni di Agostino (402–2002): Bilancio e prospettive: XXXI Incontro di studiosi dell'antichità cristiana, Roma, 2–4 maggio 2002. Rome: Institutum Patristicum Augustinianum, 2003.

CHAPTER 2

Augustine the Philosopher: Studies

Augustine's lifestyle and mood in this transitional period from Cassiciacum to Thagaste (387 to 391) are well evoked in Brown, *Augustine of Hippo*, pp. 115–37. A good introduction to the philosophical dimensions of Augustine's thought is the collection of essays edited by Eleonore Stump and Norman Kretzmann, eds., *The Cambridge Companion to Augustine* (Cambridge: Cambridge University Press, 2001). For brief, cogent perspectives, see Goulven Madec, *Saint Augustin et la philosophie: Notes critiques*, Collections des Études Augustiniennes, Série Antiquité 149 (Paris: Institut d'Études Augustiniennes, 1996). Also excellent is John M. Rist, *Augustine: Ancient Thought Baptized* (Cambridge: Cambridge University Press, 1994). Below I have listed two types of works: (i) ones that focus on Augustine's more philosophically oriented early treatises; (ii) ones that more broadly examine underlying philosophical concerns spanning the course of his career:

Bouton-Touboulic, Anne Isabelle. *L'ordre caché: La notion d'ordre chez saint Augustin*. Collection des Études Augustiniennes, Série Antiquité 174. Paris: Institut d'Études Augustiniennes, 2004.

Conybeare, Catherine. *The Irrational Augustine*. Oxford Early Christian Studies. New York: Oxford University Press, 2006.

Hadot, Pierre. *Plotinus or the Simplicity of Vision*. Trans. Michael Chase. Chicago: University of Chicago Press, 1993.

Hagendahl, Harald. *Augustine and the Latin Classics*. Studia Graeca et Latina XX. Guteborg: Acta Universitatis Cothoburgensis, 1967.

Harrison, Carol. *Rethinking Augustine's Early Theology: An Argument for Continuity*. New York: Oxford University Press, 2006.

Holte, Ragnar. *Béatitude et sagesse: Saint Augustin et le problème de la fin de l'homme dans la philosophie ancienne*. Collection des Études Augustiniennes, Série Antiquité 14. Paris: Études Augustiniennes, 1962.

Madec, Goulven. "Augustine et son fils: Le Christ Maître intérieur." In *Lectures Augustiniennes*, 43–58. Collection des Études Augustiniennes, Série Antiquité 168. Paris: Institut d'Études Augustiniennes, 2001.

Matthews, Gareth B. *Augustine*. Blackwell Great Minds. Oxford: Blackwell Publishing, 2005.

———. *Thought's Ego in Augustine and Descartes*. Ithaca: Cornell University Press, 1992.

Marrou, Henri-Iréné. *Saint Augustin et la fin de la culture antique*. 4th ed. Paris: de Boccard, 1958. A classic.

McWilliam, Joanne. "The Cassiciacum Autobiography." *Studia Patristica* 18/4 (1990): 14–43.

O'Connell, Robert J. *St. Augustine's Early Theory of Man, A.D. 386–391*. Cambridge,

MA: Belknap Press, 1968. Controversial, but threaded with valuable insights.

———. *Art and the Christian Intelligence in St. Augustine.* Cambridge, MA: Harvard University Press, 1978.

O'Daly, Gerard J. P. *Augustine's Philosophy of Mind.* Berkeley: University of California Press, 1987.

O'Meara, Dominic J. *Plotinus: An Introduction to the Enneads.* New York: Oxford University Press, 1995.

O'Meara, John J. *Studies in Augustine and Eriugena.* Ed. Thomas Halton. Washington, DC: The Catholic University of America Press, 1992. Valuable essays on Augustine's Neoplatonism.

Pollman, Karla, and Mark Vessey, eds. *Augustine and the Disciplines: From Cassiciacum to Confessions.* New York: Oxford University Press, 2005.

Rombs, Ronnie J. *Augustine and the Fall of the Soul: Beyond O'Connell and His Critics.* Washington DC: The Catholic University of America Press, 2006.

Teske, Roland J. *To Know God and the Soul: Essays on the Thought of St. Augustine.* Washington, DC: The Catholic University of America Press, 2008.

Testard, Maurice. *Saint Augustin et Cicéron.* 2 vols. Collection des Études Augustiniennes, Série Antiquité 5–6. Paris: Institut d'Études Augustiniennes, 1958.

Wetzel, James. *Augustine and the Limits of Virtue.* New York: Cambridge University Press, 1992.

CHAPTER 3

Augustine the Bishop: Studies

Peter Brown's and Serge Lancel's biographies offer helpful portraits of Augustine the bishop. Brown captures the mood and atmosphere of Augustine's congregation and North African Christianity (pp. 183–206); Lancel does an excellent job on matters of archeology and incorporates perspectives from the recent Divjak letters (pp. 235–70). The classic study is by Frederic van der Meer, *Augustine the Bishop: The Life and Work of a Father of the Church,* trans. B. Battershaw and G. R. Lamb (London: Sheed and Ward, 1961); while badly dated in certain ways, it still has much to offer. The publication of 31 letters discovered by Johannes Divjak has opened new perspectives, especially on Augustine's later years; see the studies in Claude Lepelley, ed., *Les Lettres de saint Augustin découvertes par Johannes Divjak,* Collection des Études Augustiniennes, Série Antiquité 98 (Paris: Études Augustiniennes, 1983). See also:

Chadwick, Henry. "The New Letters of St. Augustine." *Journal of Theological Studies,* n.s. 34 (1983): 425–52. Reprinted in *Heresy and Orthodoxy in the Early Church.* London: Variorum Reprints, 1991.

Doyle, Daniel E. *The Bishop as Disciplinarian in the Letters of St. Augustine.* Patristic Studies 4. New York: Peter Lang, 2002.

Hermanowicz, Erika. *Possidius of Calama: A Study of the North African Episcopate in the Age of Augustine.* Oxford Early Christian Studies. New York: Oxford University Press, 2008.

Lawless, George. *Augustine of Hippo and His Monastic Rule.* Oxford: Clarendon Press, 1990.

LeMoine, Fannie, and Christopher Kleinhenz, eds. *Saint Augustine the Bishop: A Book of Essays.* New York: Garland Publishing, 1994.

Lienhard, Joseph T., Earl C. Muller, Roland J. Teske, eds. *Augustine: Presbyter Factus Sum.* Collectanea Augustiniana. New York: Peter Lang, 1993.

Merdinger, Jane E. *Rome and the African Church in the Time of Augustine.* New Haven: Yale University Press, 1997.

Perler, Othmar. *Les voyages de saint Augustin.* Collection des Études Augustiniennes, Série Antiquité 36. Paris: Études Augustiniennes, 1969.

Verheijen, Luc. *Saint Augustine's Monasticism in the Light of Acts 4:32–35.* Villanova: Villanova University Press, 1979.

CHAPTER 4

Augustine the Preacher: Texts and Studies

For a one-volume selection drawn from Augustine's massive *Sermones ad populum*, see Daniel H. Doyle, ed., *Saint Augustine: Essential Sermons*, trans. Edmund Hill (Hyde Park, NY: New City Press, 2007). For a study of Augustine the preacher, see William Harmless, *Augustine and the Catechumenate* (Collegeville, MN: The Liturgical Press [A Pueblo Book], 1995). This focuses on the way Augustine preached to both catechumens preparing for baptism and to neophytes who had just been baptized. On the recently discovered Dolbeau sermons, see especially Goulven Madec, ed., *Augustin Prédicateur (395–411): Actes du Colloque International de Chantilly (5–7 Sept, 1996)*, Collection des Études Augustiniennes, Série Antiquité 159 (Paris: Études Augustiniennes, 1998). See also:

Chadwick, Henry. "The New Sermons of St. Augustine." *Journal of Theological Studies*, n.s. 47 (1996): 69–91.

Deferrari, Roy. "St. Augustine's Method of Composing and Delivering Sermons." *American Journal of Philology* 43 (1922): 97–123, 193–219.

———. "Verbatim Reports of Augustine's Unwritten Sermons." *Transactions and Proceedings of the American Philological Association* 46 (1915): 35–45.

Dolbeau, François. *Augustin et la prédication en Afrique: Recherches sur divers sermon authentiques, apocryphes ou anonymes.* Collection des Études Augustiniennes, Série Antiquité 179. Paris: Institut d'Études Augustiniennes, 2005.

Drobner, Hubertus R. *Augustinus von Hippo: Sermones ad Populum; Überlieferung und Bestand, Bibliographie-Indices.* Supplements to Vigiliae Christianae 49. Leiden: Brill, 2000.

Harmless, William. "The Voice and the Word: Augustine's Catechumenate in Light of the Dolbeau Sermons." *Augustinian Studies* 35 (2004): 17–42.

LaBonnardière, Anne-Marie. "Augustine, Minister of the Word of God." In *Augustine and the Bible*, ed. Pamela Bright, 245–51. Notre Dame: Notre Dame University Press, 1999.

Marec, Erwan. *Monuments chrétiens d'Hippone: Ville épiscopale de saint Augustin.* Paris: Arts et Métiers Graphiques, 1958.

Mohrmann, Christine. "Saint Augustin prédicateur," *La Maison Dieu* 39 (1954): 83–96. Reprinted in *Études sur le latin des Chrétiens*, 2nd ed., 1:391–402. Rome: Edizioni di Storia e Letteratura, 1961.

————. "*Praedicare-tractare-sermo*." *La Maison Dieu* 39 (1954): 96–107. Reprinted in *Études sur le latin des Chrétiens*, 2nd ed., 2:63–72. Rome: Edizioni di Storia e Letteratura, 1961.

O'Connell, Robert J. *Soundings in Augustine's Imagination*. New York: Fordham University Press, 1994. A study of image patterns in Augustine's sermons.

Poque, Suzanne. *Le langage symbolique dans la prédication d'Augustin d'Hippone: Images héroïques*, 2 vols. Collection des Études Augustiniennes, Série Antiquité 105. Paris: Institut d'Études Augustiniennes, 1984.

Rebillard, Eric. "Sermones." In *Augustine Through the Ages: An Encyclopedia*, 773–92. Ed. Allan Fitzgerald. Grand Rapids: Eerdmans, 1999.

Verbraken, Pierre-Patrick. *Études critiques sur les sermons authentiques de saint Augustin*. Instrumenta Patristica XII. Steenbrugis: In abbatia S. Petri, 1976.

CHAPTER 5

Augustine the Exegete: Studies

For a lively and sympathetic introduction to early Christian exegesis, see John O'Keefe and Russell R. Reno, *Sanctified Vision: An Introduction to Early Christian Interpretation of the Bible* (Baltimore: Johns Hopkins University Press, 2005). For an overview of Augustine's biblical concerns and interpretative practices, see Michael Cameron, "Augustine and the Bible," *A Companion to Augustine*, Blackwell Companions to the Ancient World, ed. Mark Vessey (Oxford: Blackwell, forthcoming). See also Frederick Van Fleteren and Joseph C. Schnaubelt, eds., *Augustine: Biblical Exegete*, Collectanea Augustiniana (New York: Peter Lang, 2001); and Pamela Bright, ed., *Augustine and the Bible* (Notre Dame: University of Notre Dame Press, 1999), which partially translates and partially expands upon an earlier French collection by Anne-Marie LaBonnardière, ed., *Saint Augustin et le Bible*, Bible de tous les temps (Paris: Beauchesne, 1986). For essays on Augustine's *On Christian Teaching*, see Duane W. H. Arnold and Pamela Bright, eds., *De Doctrina Christiana: A Classic of Western Culture* (Notre Dame: University of Notre Dame Press, 1995). See also:

Berrouard, Marie-François. *Introduction aux Homélies de saint Augustin sur l'Évangile de saint Jean*. Collection des Études Augustiniennes: Série Antiquité 170. Paris: Institut d'Études Augustiniennes, 2004.

Bochet, Isabelle. *"Le Firmament de l'Écriture": L'herméneutique augustinienne*. Collection des Études Augustiniennes: Série Antiquité 172. Paris: Institut d'Études Augustiniennes, 2004.

Burton, Philip. *The Old Latin Gospels: A Study of Their Texts and Language*. Oxford Early Christian Studies. New York: Oxford University Press, 2001.

Cain, Andrew. *The Letters of Jerome: Asceticism, Biblical Exegesis, and the Construction of Christian Authority*. Oxford Early Christian Studies. New York: Oxford University Press, 2009.

Cameron, Michael. "*Totus Christus* and the Psychagogy of Augustine's Sermons." *Augustinian Studies* 36 (2005): 59–70.

Fiedrowicz, Michael. *Psalmus vox totius Christi: Studien zu Augustins Enarrationes in Psalmos*. Freiburg: Herder, 1997.

————. "General Introduction." In *Augustine: Exposition of the Psalms, 1–32*, trans. Maria Boulding, WSA III/15: 13–66. Hyde Park, NY: New City Press, 2000.

Gamble, Harry Y. *Books and Readers in the Early Church: A History of Early Christian Texts.* New Haven: Yale University Press, 1995.

Jackson, B. Darrell. "The Theory of Signs in St. Augustine's *De doctrina christiana*." *Revue des Études Augustiniennes* 15 (1969): 9–49. Reprint: *Augustine: A Collection of Critical Essays*, 92–147. Ed. R. A. Markus. Garden City, NJ: Anchor Books, 1972.

Kelly, J. N. D., *Jerome: His Life, Writings, and Controversies.* New York: Harper & Row, 1975.

LeLandais, M. "Deux années de prédication de saint Augustin. Introduction a la lecture de l'In Joannem." In *Études Augustiniennes*, 1–95. Théologie 28. Ed. H. Rondet. Paris: Aubier, 1953.

Lienhard, Joseph T. *The Bible, the Church, and Authority: The Canon of the Christian Bible in History and Theology.* Collegeville, MN: Liturgical Press, 1995.

Markus, Robert A. "St. Augustine on Signs." In *Augustine: A Collection of Critical Essays*, 61–91. Ed. R. A. Markus. Garden City, NJ: Anchor Books, 1972.

Martin, Thomas. "*Vox Pauli*: Augustine and the Claims to Speak for Paul: An Exploration of Rhetoric at the Service of Exegesis." *Journal of Early Christian Studies* 8 (2000): 237–72.

McCarthy, Michael C. "An Ecclesiology of Groaning: Augustine, the Psalms, and the Making of the Church." *Theological Studies* 66 (2005): 23–48.

Plumer, Eric, ed. and trans. *Augustine's Commentary on Galatians.* Oxford Early Christian Studies. New York: Oxford University Press, 2003.

Pollmann, Karla. *Doctrina Christiana: Untersuchungen zu den Anfängen der christlichen Hermeneutik unter besonderer Berücksichtigung von Augustinus, De doctrina christiana.* Freiburg: Universitätverlag, 1996.

Pontet, Maurice. *L'exégèse de s. Augustin prédicateur.* Paris: Aubier, 1946.

Simonetti, Manlio. *Biblical Interpretation in the Early Church: An Historical Introduction to Patristic Exegesis.* Edinburgh: T&T Clark, 1994.

Williams, Megan Hale. *The Monk and the Book: Jerome and the Making of Christian Scholarship.* Chicago: University of Chicago Press, 2006.

CHAPTER 6

Mani and Manicheism: Texts and Studies

In the last 100 years, there has been a series of key archeological discoveries that have provided wide-ranging new insights into Mani and the religion he founded. For a remarkable collection of Manichean texts, together with a valuable introduction, see Iain Gardner and Samuel N. C. Lieu, eds., *Manichaean Texts from the Roman Empire* (Cambridge: Cambridge University Press, 2004). Much of this material had been available previously only to specialists. For an overview and a history of Manichaeism, see Samuel N. C. Lieu, *Manichaeism in the Later Roman Empire and Mediaeval China* (Manchester: University of Manchester Press, 1985; 2nd ed. Tübingen: Mohr, 1992). See also:

BeDuhn, Jason D. *The Manichaean Body in Discipline and Ritual.* Baltimore: Johns Hopkins University Press, 2000.

Coyle, J. Kevin. *Manichaeism and Its Legacy.* Nag Hammadi and Manichaean Studies 69. Leiden and Boston: Brill, 2009.

Decret, F. *L'Afrique manichéenne (IVᵉ–Vᵉ siècles): Étude historique et doctrinale,* 2 vols. Collection des Études Augustiniennes, Série Antiquité 74–75. Paris: Études Augustiniennes, 1978.

Franzmann, Majella. *Jesus in the Manichaean Writings.* London: T&T Clark, 2003.

Lieu, Samuel N. C. *Manichaeism in Mesopotamia and the Roman East.* Religions in the Graeco-Roman World 118. Leiden: Brill, 1997.

———. "Manichaeism." In *The Oxford Handbook of Early Christian Studies,* ed. Susan Ashbrook Harvey and David G. Hunter, 221–36. New York: Oxford University Press, 2008.

Augustine against the Manichees: Studies

These new perspectives on Manicheism have, in turn, altered earlier estimates of Augustine's anti-Manichean works. See Johannes Van Oort, Otto Wermelinger, and Gregor Wurst, eds., *Augustine and Manichaeism in the Latin West: Proceedings of the Fribourg-Utrecht International Symposium of the IAMS,* Nag Hammadi and Manichaean Studies, vol. 49 (Leiden: Brill, 2001). See also:

BeDuhn, Jason D. *Augustine's Manichaean Dilemma.* Vol. 1: *Conversion and Apostasy: 373–383 C.E.* Divinations: Rereading Late Ancient Religion. Philadelphia: University of Pennsylvania Press, 2009.

Clark, Elizabeth A. "Vitiated Seeds and Holy Vessels: Augustine's Manichean Past." *Ascetic Piety and Women's Faith: Essays on Late Ancient Christianity,* 291–349. Studies in Women and Religion, vol. 20. Lewiston: Edwin Mellen Press, 1986.

Coyle, J. Kevin. *Augustine's "De Moribus Ecclesiae Catholicae": A Study of the Work, Its Composition and Its Sources.* Paradosis 25. Fribourg: Fribourg University Press, 1978.

———. "Saint Augustine's Manichean Legacy." *Augustinian Studies* 34 (2003): 1–22.

Evans, G. R. *Augustine on Evil.* Cambridge: Cambridge University Press, 1982.

Fredriksen, Paula. *Augustine and the Jews: A Christian Defense of Jews and Judaism.* New York: Doubleday, 2008.

Harrison, Simon. *Augustine's Way into the Will: The Theological and Philosophical Significance of De libero arbitrio.* Oxford Early Christian Studies. New York: Oxford University Press, 2006.

Madec, Goulven. "Vnde malum? Le livre I du *De libero arbitrio.*" In *Petites Études Augustiniennes,* 121–35. Collection des Études Augustiniennes, Série Antiquité 142. Paris: Institut d'Études Augustiniennes, 1994.

Teske, Roland J. "Augustine, the Manichees and the Bible." In *Augustine and the Bible,* ed. Pamela Bright, 208–21. Notre Dame: Notre Dame University Press, 1999.

Torchia, N. Joseph. *"Creatio Ex Nihilo" and the Theology of St. Augustine.* Collectanea Augustiniana. New York: Peter Lang, 1999.

CHAPTER 7
Donatism: Texts and Studies

For a brief overview of the history of Donatism, see James Alexander, "Donatism," in Philip F. Esler, *The Early Christian World* (New York: Routledge, 2000), 2:952–74. For a sympathetic reading of the Donatist concerns and perspectives, especially as they evolve over time, see Maureen A. Tilley, *The Bible in Christian North Africa: The Donatist World* (Minneapolis: Fortress Press, 1997). See also:

Brown, Peter. "Religious Dissent in the Later Roman Empire: The Case of North Africa." In *Religion and Society in the Age of Saint Augustine*, 237–59. 1972; reprint: Eugene, OR: Wipf & Stock, 2007.

Burns, J. Patout. *Cyprian the Bishop.* Routledge Early Church Monographs. New York and London: Routledge, 2002.

Edwards, Mark, trans. and ed. *Optatus: Against the Donatists.* Translated Texts for Historians, vol. 27. Liverpool: Liverpool University Press, 1997.

Frend, W. H. C. *The Donatist Church: A Movement of Protest in Roman North Africa.* Oxford: Clarendon Press, 1952; reprint: 1972. A classic, superbly detailed, but dated in some broader claims.

Lancel, Serge, and James S. Alexander. "Donatistae." In *Augustinus-Lexikon*, 2:606–38.

Monceaux, Paul. *Histoire littéraire de l'Afrique chrétienne: Depuis les origines jusqu'à l'invasion arabe.* 7 vols. 1912–1923: reprint: Bruxelles: Culture et Civilisation, 1966. Vols. 4–6 survey the major writers and the history of the controversy up to Augustine. Dated, but a classic study. In Vol. 5, Monceaux appends a reconstruction of some key Donatist documents.

Tilley, Maureen A., trans. and ed. *Donatist Martyr Stories: The Church in Conflict in Roman North Africa.* Translated Texts for Historians, vol. 24. Liverpool: Liverpool University Press, 1997.

Augustine against the Donatists: Studies

Fine overviews of Augustine's clash with the Donatists are found in both Brown (pp. 212–43) and Lancel (pp. 169–73, 270–305). Brown does especially well evoking the contrasting moods and deeper outlooks; Lancel ably summarizes Augustine's treatises and the Conference of 411. See also:

Berrouard, Marie-François. "Un combat pour l'honneur du Christ: La controverse antidonatiste des Tractatus." In *Introduction aux Homélies de saint Augustin sur l'Évangile de saint Jean*, 55–78. Collection des Études Augustiniennes: Série Antiquité 170. Paris: Institut d'Études Augustiniennes, 2004.

Brown, Peter. "St. Augustine's Attitude to Religious Coercion." In *Religion and Society in the Age of Saint Augustine*, 237–59. 1972; reprint: Eugene, OR: Wipf & Stock, 2007.

Congar, Yves. "Introduction générale." *Traité anti-Donatistes, Volume 1. Oeuvres de saint Augustin.* BA 28: 9–133. Paris: Desclée de Brouwer, 1963.

Cranz, F. E. "The Development of Augustine's Ideas on Society before the Donatist Controversy." In *Augustine: A Collection of Critical Essays*, 366–403. Ed. R. A. Markus. Garden City, NJ: Anchor Books, 1972.

Markus, Robert A. "*Afer scribens Afris*: The Church in Augustine and the African Tradition," and "*Coge Intrare*: The Church and Political Power." In *Saeculum: History and Society in the Theology of St. Augustine*, 105–53. Cambridge: Cambridge University Press, 1970.

Monceaux, Paul. *Saint Augustin et le Donatisme*. Vol. 7 of *Histoire littéraire de l'Afrique chrétienne: Depuis les origines jusqu'à l'invasion arabe*. 1923: reprint: Bruxelles: Culture et Civilisation, 1966. Dated, but an unusually thorough overview.

Willis. G. G. *St. Augustine and the Donatist Controversy*. London: SPCK, 1952; reprint: Eugene, OR: Wipf & Stock, 2005. A classic, now dated.

CHAPTER 8

Trinitarian Theology before Augustine: Studies

Orthodox positions on the divinity of Christ and the doctrine of the Trinity were forged during the fourth-century "Arian Controversy" (as it is inaccurately but still widely called). Recent studies have thoroughly revised older perspectives. The most comprehensive study is R. P. C. Hanson, *The Search for the Christian Doctrine of God: The Arian Controversy, 318–381 AD* (Edinburgh: T & T Clark, 1988). For a major rethinking of the categories and course of the controversy, see Lewis Ayres, *Nicaea and Its Legacy: An Approach to Fourth-Century Trinitarian Theology* (New York: Oxford University Press, 2004). The classic orthodox position was forged by Athanasius and the Cappadocians. On Athanasius, see Thomas G. Weinandy, *Athanasius: A Theological Introduction*, Great Theologians (Burlington, VT: Ashgate, 2007), and Khaled Anatolios, *Athanasius*, Early Church Fathers (New York and London: Routledge, 2005). On the Cappadocians, see Stephen M. Hildebrand, *The Trinitarian Theology of Basil of Caesarea: A Synthesis of Greek Thought and Biblical Truth* (Washington, DC: The Catholic University of America Press, 2007); and Christopher A. Beeley, *Gregory of Nazianzus on the Trinity and the Knowledge of God: In Your Light We Shall See Light*, Oxford Studies in Historical Theology (New York: Oxford University Press, 2008). See also:

Anatolios, Khaled. *Athanasius: The Coherence of His Thought*. Routledge Early Church Monographs. New York: Routledge, 1998.

Barnes, Michel R., and Daniel H. Williams, eds. *Arianism after Arius: Essays on the Development of the Fourth-Century Trinitarian Conflicts*. Edinburgh: T & T Clark, 1993.

Daley, Brian E. *Gregory of Nazianzus*. Early Church Fathers. New York: Routledge, 2006.

Gavrilyuk, Paul L. *The Suffering of the Impassible God: The Dialectics of Patristic Thought*. Oxford Early Christian Studies. New York: Oxford University Press, 2004.

Kelly, J. N. D. *Early Christian Creeds*, 3rd edition. London: Longman, 1972.

Lyman, J. Rebecca. "Arius and Arians." In *The Oxford Handbook of Early Christian Studies*, 237–57. Ed. Susan Ashbrook Harvey and David G. Hunter. New York: Oxford University Press, 2008.

McGuckin, John. *Saint Gregory of Nazianzus: An Intellectual Biography*. Crestwood, NY: St. Vladimir's Seminary Press, 2001.

Robinson, Jon M. *Christ as Mediator: A Study of the Theologies of Eusebius of Caesarea, Marcellus of Ancyra, and Athanasius of Alexandria.* Oxford Theological Monographs. New York: Oxford University Press, 2007.

Roldanus, Hans. *The Church in the Age of Constantine: The Theological Challenges.* New York: Routledge, 2006.

Studer, Basil. *Trinity and Incarnation: The Faith of the Early Church.* Ed. Andrew Louth. Collegeville, MN: Liturgical Press, 1993.

Turcescu, Lucian. *Gregory of Nyssa and the Concept of Divine Persons.* AAR Academy Series. New York: Oxford University Press, 2005.

Vaggione, Richard Paul. *Eunomius of Cyzicus and the Nicene Revolution.* Oxford Early Christian Studies. New York: Oxford University Press, 2001.

Weedman, Mark. *The Trinitarian Theology of Hilary of Poitiers.* Supplements to Vigiliae Christianae 89. Leiden: Brill, 2007.

Williams, Daniel H. *Ambrose of Milan and the End of the Nicene-Arian Conflicts.* Oxford Early Christian Studies. New York: Oxford University Press, 1995.

Williams, Rowan. *Arius: Heresy and Tradition.* Rev. ed. Grand Rapids, MI: Wm. B. Eerdmans, 2002.

Augustine's Theology of Trinity: Studies

The starting point for any serious study of Augustine's *On the Trinity* is Lewis Ayres's *Augustine and the Trinity* (Cambridge: Cambridge University Press, 2010). This represents a significant advance on many fronts, illustrating, for example, how deeply exegetical concerns (rather than simply philosophical ones) shaped the contours of Augustine's Trinitarian thought and how deeply Christology remained Augustine's abiding focus. Michel Barnes has also been at the forefront of this area of Augustinian studies. For a good sample of Barnes' approach, see "Re-reading Augustine's Theology of the Trinity," in S. T. Davis, D. Kendall, and G. O'Collins, eds., *The Trinity: An Interdisciplinary Symposium on the Doctrine of the Trinity* (New York: Oxford University Press, 1999), 145–76. I have listed other important studies by Ayres and Barnes below. One other recent comprehensive interpretation of Augustine's *On the Trinity* is Luigi Gioia's study, *The Theological Epistemology of Augustine's De Trinitate*, Oxford Theological Monographs (New York: Oxford University Press, 2008). See also:

Ayres, Lewis. "'Giving Wings to Nicaea': Reconceiving Augustine's Earliest Trinitarian Theology." *Augustinian Studies* 38 (2007): 19–40.

———. "'Remember That You Are Catholic' (*serm.* 52.2): Augustine on the Unity of the Triune God." *Journal of Early Christian Studies* 8 (2000): 39–82.

———. "The Christological Context of Augustine's *De trinitate* XIII: Toward Relocating Books VIII–XV." *Augustinian Studies* 29 (1998): 111–39.

Barnes, Michel René. "*De Trinitate* VI and VII: Augustine and the Limits of Nicene Orthodoxy." *Augustinian Studies* 38 (2007): 189–202.

———. "Exegesis and Polemic in Augustine's *De Trinitate* I," *Augustinian Studies* 30 (1999): 43–60.

———. "The Arians of Book V, and the Genre of *De Trinitate*." *Journal of Theological Studies*, n.s. 44 (1993): 185–95.

———. "Augustine in Contemporary Trinitarian Theology." *Theological Studies* 56 (1995): 237–50.

Cavadini, John. "The Structure and Intention of Augustine's *De trinitate*." *Augustinian Studies* 23 (1992): 103–23.

Louth, Andrew. "Love and the Trinity: Saint Augustine and the Greek Fathers." *Augustinian Studies* 33 (2002): 1–16.

Madec, Goulven. *Le Christ de saint Augustin: La patrie et la voie*. Paris: Desclée, 2001.

———. "*Christus, scientia et sapientia nostra*: Le principe de cohérence de la doctrine augustinienne." *Recherches augustiniennes* 10 (1975): 77–85.

Roy, Olivier du. *Intelligence de la foi en la Trinité selon saint Augustin*. Paris: Etudes Augustiniennes, 1966. A classic; some of its perspectives have been strongly criticized.

Studer, Basil. *Augustinus: De Trinitate: Eine Einführung*. Paderborn: Ferdinand Schöningh, 2005.

———. "History and Faith in Augustine's *De Trinitate*." The 1996 Saint Augustine Lecture. *Augustinian Studies* 28 (1997): 7–50.

———. "La foie de Nicée selon saint Augustin." *Revue des Etudes Augustiniennes* 19 (1984): 133–54. Reprint in *Dominus Salvator: Studien zur Christologie und Exegese der Kirchenvater*, 369–400. Studia Anselmiana 107. Rome: 1992.

Wilken, Robert Louis. "*Spiritus sanctus secundum scripturas sanctas*: Exegetical Considerations of Augustine on the Holy Spirit." 1999 St. Augustine Lecture. *Augustinian Studies* 31 (2000): 1–18.

Williams, Rowan. "*Sapientia* and Trinity: Reflections on the *De Trinitate*." In Bernard Bruning et al., *Collectanea Augustiniana: Mélanges T. J. Van Bavel* (Leuven, 1990) vol. 1:317–32.

CHAPTER 9

On the City of God: Studies

For an introduction, see Gerard G. P. O'Daly, *Augustine's City of God: A Reader's Guide* (New York: Oxford University Press, 1999). Also valuable is the chapter "The Two Cities," in Carol Harrison, *Augustine: Christian Truth and Fractured Humanity*, 194–220. A classic is that of Robert A. Markus, *Saeculum: History and Society in the Theology of Saint Augustine*, 2nd ed. (Cambridge: Cambridge University Press, 1988). Theological perspectives are highlighted in Robert Dodaro, *Christ and the Just Society in the Thought of Augustine* (Cambridge: Cambridge University Press, 2004). See also:

Brown, Peter. "Saint Augustine." *Religion and Society in the Age of St. Augustine*, 25–45. 1972; reprint: Eugene, OR: Wipf & Stock, 2007.

Cranz, F. E. "*De Civitate Dei* XV, 2, and Augustine's Idea of the Christian Society," *Speculum* 25 (1950): 215–25. Reprinted in *Augustine: A Collection of Critical Essays*, 404–21. Ed. R. A. Markus. New York: Doubleday, 1972.

Curbelié, Philippe. *La justice dans la cité de Dieu*. Collection des Études Augustiniennes, Série Antiquité 171. Paris: Institut d'Études Augustiniennes, 2004.

Deane, Herbert A. *The Political and Social Ideas of St. Augustine*. New York: Columbia University Press: 1963. Dated, but still of value.

Donnelly, Dorothy F., ed. *The City of God: A Collection of Critical Essays.* New York: Peter Lang, 1995.

Gorman, M. M. "A Survey of the Oldest Manuscripts of St. Augustine's *De Civitate Dei.*" *Journal of Theological Studies* n.s. 33 (1982): 398–410.

Guy, J.-C. *Unité et structure logique de la 'Cité de Dieu' de saint Augustin.* Collection des Études Augustiniennes, Série Antiquité 12. Paris: Institut d'Études Augustiniennes, 1961.

Lauras, A., and H. Rondet. "Le thème des deux cités dans l'oeuvre de saint Augustin." In *Études Augustiniennes,* 97–160. Théologie 28. Ed. H. Rondet. Paris: Aubier, 1953.

Madec, Goulven. "Le *De ciuitate Dei* comme *De uera religione.*" In *Petites Études Augustiniennes,* 189–213. Collection des Études Augustiniennes, Série Antiquité 142. Paris: Institut d'Études Augustiniennes, 1994.

Markus, Robert A. "'*Tempora christiana*' Revisited." In *Augustine and His Critics,* ed. Robert Dodaro and George Lawless, 201–13. New York: Routledge, 2000.

O'Donovan, Oliver. "Augustine's *City of God* XIX and Western Political Thought." *Dionysius* 11 (1987): 89–110.

O'Meara, John. *Charter of Christendom: The Significance of the City of God.* Saint Augustine Lecture 1961. New York: Macmillan, 1961.

Ruokanen, Mikka. *Theology of Social Life in Augustine's De civitate Dei.* Forschungen zur Kirchen- und Dogmengeschichte, Band 53. Göttingen: Vandenbork & Ruprecht, 1993.

Van Oort, Johannes. *Jerusalem and Babylon: A Study into Augustine's City of God and the Sources of His doctrine of the Two Cities.* Supplements to Vigiliae Christianae 14. Leiden: Brill, 1991.

Vessey, Mark, Karla Pollmann, and Allan Fitzgerald, eds. *History, Apocalypse, and the Secular Imagination: New Essays on Augustine's City of God. Augustinian Studies* 30.2 (1999). Bowling Green: Philosophy Documentation Center, 1999.

Weithman, Paul. "Augustine's Political Philosophy." In *The Cambridge Companion to Augustine,* ed. Eleonore Stump and Norman Kretzmann, 234–52. New York: Cambridge University Press, 2001.

CHAPTER 10

Pelagius and the Pelagians: Texts and Studies

Historical scholarship over the last 80 years has done much to strip away centuries of misunderstanding fostered by medieval and Reformation anti-Pelagian polemic. Drawing on Pelagius's genuine works, a more balanced (and more sympathetic) view of Pelagius and of those he inspired has emerged. For an overview of recent research and perspectives, see Mathijs Lamberigts, "Pelagius and Pelagians," in *The Oxford Handbook of Early Christian Studies,* ed. Susan Ashbrook Harvey and David Hunter (New York: Oxford University Press, 2008), 258–79. For a translation of key writings of Pelagius and his allies, see B. R. Rees, *Pelagius: Life and Letters* (Rochester, NY: Boydell Press, 1991). For a balanced presentation and assessment of Pelagius's theology, see Robert F. Evans, *Pelagius: Inquiries and Reappraisals* (New York: Seabury Press, 1968).

On his aristocratic social milieu, see Peter Brown, "Pelagius and His Supporters: Aims and Environment," in *Religion and Society in the Age of Saint Augustine* (reprint: Eugene, OR: Wipf & Stock, 2007), 183–207. See also:

Bonner, Gerald. *Augustine and Modern Research on Pelagianism*. Saint Augustine Lecture 1970. Villanova: Villanova University Press, 1972.
———. "Pelagianism and Augustine," *Augustinian Studies* 23 (1992): 33–51; and "Augustine and Pelagianism," *Augustinian Studies* 24 (1993): 27–47. Reprint in *Church and Faith in the Patristic Tradition: Augustine, Pelagianism and Early Christian Northumbria*. London: Variorum Reprints, 1996.
Brown, Peter. "The Patrons of Pelagius: The Roman Aristocracy between East and West." In *Religion and Society in the Age of Saint Augustine*, 208–26. 1972; reprint: Eugene, OR: Wipf & Stock, 2007.
DeBruyn, Theodore, trans. *Pelagius' Commentary on St. Paul's Epistle to the Romans*. Oxford Early Christian Studies. New York: Oxford University Press, 1993.
Duval, Yves-Marie. "La date du De Natura de Pélage." *Revue des Études Augustiniennes* 36 (1990): 257–83.
Hunter, David G. *Marriage, Celibacy, and Heresy in Ancient Christianity: The Jovinianist Controversy*. Oxford Early Christian Studies. New York: Oxford University Press, 2007.
Lamberigts, Mathijs. "The Italian Julian of Aeclanum about the African Augustine of Hippo." In *Augustinus Afer: Saint Augustin: africanité et universalité, Actes du colloque international Alge—Annaba, 1–7 avril 2001*, 83–93. Edited by P.-Y. Fux, J.-M. Roessli and O. Wermelinger. Fribourg: Éditions Universitaires Fribourg Suisse, 2003.
———. "Recent Research into Pelagianism with Particular Emphasis on the Role of Julian Aeclanum." *Augustiniana* 52 (2002): 175–98.
———. "Competing Christologies: Julian and Augustine on Jesus Christ." *Augustinian Studies* 36 (2005): 159–94.
Lössl, Josef. *Julian von Aeclanum: Studien zu seinem Leben, seinem Werk, seiner Lehre und ihrer Überlieferung*. Supplements to Vigiliae Christianae 60. Leiden: Brill, 2001.
Nuvolone, F. G, and A. Solignac. "Pélage et pélagianisme." *Dictionnaire de spiritualité* 12B (1986): 2889–942.
Refoulé, F. "Datation du premier concile du Carthage contre les Pélagiens et du Libellus fidei de Rufin." *Revue des études augustiniennes* 9 (1963): 41–49.
TeSelle, Eugene. "Rufinus the Syrian, Caelestius, Pelagius: Explorations in the Pre-History of the Pelagian Controversy." *Augustinian Studies* 3 (1972): 61–95.
Wermelinger, Otto. *Rom und Pelagius*. Päpste und Papsttum 7. Stuttgart: Hiersemann, 1975.

Augustine against the Pelagians: Studies

On Augustine's role in the anti-Pelagian controversy, see Lancel, *Saint Augustine*, pp. 325–65 (on Pelagius) and 413–38 (on Julian of Eclanum and the monastic reaction); and Brown, *Augustine of Hippo*, pp. 340–77 (on Pelagius) and 383–410 (on Julian and the monastic reaction), as well as 465–68 and 491–93 (Brown's "reconsiderations" of his 1968 portrait of the late Augustine). On Augustine's theology of grace and predestination, see J. Patout Burns, *The Development of Augustine's Doctrine of Operative Grace*, Collection des Études Augustiniennes, Série Antiquité 82 (Paris: Études Augustiniennes, 1980), which skillfully traces the often subtle evolution of Augustine's theology of grace prior to, during, and through the Pelagian Controversy. See also:

Bonner, Gerald. *Freedom and Necessity: St. Augustine's Teaching on Divine Power and Human Freedom*. Washington, DC: The Catholic University of America Press, 2007.

Burns, J. Patout. "The Interpretation of Romans in the Pelagian Controversy." *Augustinian Studies* 10 (1979): 43–54.

———. "Augustine's Role in the Imperial Action against Pelagius." *Journal of Theological Studies* n.s. 30 (1979): 67–83.

———. "The Atmosphere of Election: Augustinianism as Common Sense," *Journal of Early Christian Studies* 2 (1994): 325–39.

Dodaro, Robert. "*Sacramentum Christi*: Augustine on the Christology of Pelagius." *Studia Patristica* 27 (1993): 274–80.

Dunn, Geoffrey D. "Augustine, Cyril of Alexandria, and the Pelagian Controversy." *Augustinian Studies* 37 (2006): 63–88.

Harmless, William. "Christ the Pediatrician: Augustine on the Diagnosis and Treatment of the Injured Vocation of the Child." In *The Vocation of the Child*, ed. Patrick McKinley Brennan, 127–53. Grand Rapids: Eerdmans, 2008.

Hombert, Pierre-Marie. *Gloria Gratiae: Se glorifier en Dieu, principe et fin de la théologie augustinienne de la grâce*. Collection des Études Augustiniennes, Série Antiquité 148. Paris: Institut d'Études Augustiniennes, 1996.

O'Connell, Robert J. *The Origin of the Soul in St. Augustine's Later Works*. New York: Fordham University Press, 1987.

Wetzel, James. "Snares of Truth: Augustine on Free Will and Predestination." In *Augustine and His Critics*, 124–41. Ed. Robert Dodaro and George Lawless. New York: Routledge, 2000.

———. "Pelagius Anticipated: Grace and Election in Augustine's *Ad Simplicianum*." In *Augustine: From Rhetor to Theologian*, 121–32. Ed. Joanne McWilliam. Waterloo: Wilfrid Laurier University, 1992.

The Monastic Reaction: Studies

Recent studies have rendered the terminology of the "semi-Pelagianism" out of date and have stressed seeing the reaction of the Gallic monks in terms both of local concerns and of emerging Christian monasticism. On developments in Gaul, see Conrad Leyser, *Authority and Asceticism from Augustine to Gregory the Great*, Oxford Historical Monographs (New York: Oxford University Press, 2001). One major monastic leader based in Marseilles who disagreed with Augustine was John Cassian. On his life and spiritual theology, see Columba Stewart, *Cassian the Monk*, Oxford Studies in Historical Theology (New York: Oxford University Press, 1998). See also:

Casiday, A. M. C. *Tradition and Theology in St. John Cassian*. Oxford Early Christian Studies. New York: Oxford University Press, 2007.

Harmless, William. *Desert Christians: An Introduction to the Literature of Early Monasticism*. New York: Oxford University Press, 2004.

Weaver, Rebecca H. *Divine Grace and Human Agency: A Study of the Semi-Pelagian Controversy*. Macon, GA: Mercer University Press, 1996.

INDICES

INDEX OF SCRIPTURE

Citations in Augustine's Writings

Old Testament

Genesis
1:1: 4, 38
1:3: 77
1:6: 438
1:26: 16
1:27: 303
1:27–28: 224, 350
1:28: 348, 349, 368
1:31: 224
2:2: 38
2:19–20: 129
2:24: 195
2:25: 366
3:5: 129, 352,
    353n58
4:17: 331
6:14: 261
11:1–9: 172
12:1–3: 227
17:5: 431
22:6: 227
22:13: 227
22:18: 270
25:19–34: 385
28:11: 227
28:11–18: 228
32:24–31: 227

Exodus
3:14: 19, 30n52,
    76
11:2–3: 183

12:35–36: 183
34:28: 178

Deuteronomy
6:4: 283
25:4: 173

1 Kings
2:10: 439
19:8: 178

2 Kings
1:9: 14

Job
12:13, 16: 9
28:28: 307

Psalms[1]
2:8: 259
3:4: 331
4:5–6: 68
4:8: 13
6:3: 35
6:4: 26
17:2 (LXX) = 18:1:
    331
18:6 (LXX) = 19:6:
    129
18:7 (LXX) = 19:7: 36
18:15 (LXX) = 19:15: 26
21:27 (LXX) = 22:27: 3

22:6 (LXX) = 23:6:
    408
24:7 (LXX) = 25:6: 9
24:17 (LXX) = 25:17: 356
25:7 (LXX) = 26:7: 38
26:9 (LXX) = 27:9: 409
28:9 (LXX) = 29:9: 37
29:11 (LXX) = 30:11: 19
32:3 (LXX) = 33:3: 199,
    200
32:11 (LXX) = 33:11: 31
33:2 (LXX) = 34:2: 324
34:10 (LXX) = 35:10: 26,
    35
35:7 (LXX) = 36:7: 12
35:10 (LXX) = 36:10: 30
36:5 (LXX) = 37:5: 407
38:12 (LXX) = 39:12: 19
39:5 (LXX) = 40:5: 21
41:4 (LXX) = 42:4: 19
41:6 (LXX) = 42:6: 12
44:2 (LXX) = 45:2: 37
45:5–6 (LXX) = 46:5–6
    329
47:2 (LXX) = 48:2: 3, 37,
    329
47:3 (LXX) = 48:3: 329
47:9 (LXX) = 48:9: 329
49:1 (LXX) = 50:1: 270
50:8 (LXX) = 51:8: 36
50:15 (LXX) = 51:15: 12,
    27

1. As noted in the Introduction, the numbering of the Psalms throughout this volume has followed the numbering Augustine knew, namely, that of the Septuagint (LXX). Septuagint numbering of Psalms 9 through 147 is one behind the modern numbering. Therefore, in this listing I have given Augustine's (Septuagint) numbering first, then the modern equivalent.

50:18–19 (LXX) = 51:18–19 342
50:19 (LXX) = 51:19: 26
58:11 (LXX) = 59:11: 94n23, 407–8
58:18 (LXX) = 59:18: 8

60:2 (LXX) = 61:2: 37
60:9 (LXX) = 61:9 : 13
68:3 (LXX) = 69:3: 10
71:8 (LXX) = 72:8 : 270
71:18 (LXX) = 72:18: 36
72:18 (LXX) = 73:18: 352
72:23 (LXX) = 73:23: 308
72:28 (LXX) = 73:28: 343
73:16 (LXX) = 74:16: 37
78:5 (LXX) = 79:5: 26
78:8 (LXX) = 79:8: 26
79:2 (LXX) = 80:2: 30
80:17 (LXX) = 81:17: 13
81:6 (LXX) = 82:6: 329n31
83:11 (LXX) = 84:11: 82
84:7 (LXX) = 85:7: 430
85:1 (LXX) = 86:1: 37
86:3 (LXX) = 87:3: 316, 329, 339
87:3 (LXX) = 88:3: 10
89:1 (LXX) = 90:1: 290
91:2 (LXX) = 92:2: 408
93:1 (LXX) = 94:1: 12
93:15 (LXX) = 94:15: 328
95:4 (LXX) = 96:4: 3, 37
95:9–10 (LXX) = 96:9–10: 254
99:3 (LXX) = 100:3: 31
102:2–3 (LXX) = 103:2–3: 147
102:3 (LXX) = 103:3: 141, 308
103:1 (LXX) = 104:1: 370
104:3–4 (LXX) = 105:3–4: 313

104:4 (LXX) = 105:4: xii, 287, 288, 313, 314
105:2 (LXX) = 106:2: 12
111:10 (LXX) = 112:10: 21
113:5 (LXX) = 115:5: 323
116:2 (LXX) = 117:2: 31
117:1 (LXX) = 118:1: 37
118:18 (LXX) = 119:18: 38
118:34 (LXX) = 119:34: 3
118:85 (LXX) = 119:85: 229
118:133 (LXX) = 119: 133: 408, 409
118:155 (LXX) = 119:155: 14
121:2 (LXX) = 122:2: 198
123:1 (LXX) = 124:1: 198
126:1 (LXX) = 127:1: 322
137:3 (LXX) = 138:3: 349
138:8 (LXX) = 139:8: 4
143:4 (LXX) = 144:4: 354
144:3 (LXX) = 145:3: 3
146:2 (LXX) = 147:2: 322
146:5 (LXX) = 147:5: 3
147:14: 13

Proverbs
9:9: 269
18:21: 35
24:35 (LXX): 264
26:27: 270
29:19: 269

Song of Songs
4:2: 173

Wisdom
7:16: 127
7:27: 31, 282
9:15: 346, 363
11:20 : 54n37, 389
14:11: 8

Sirach (Ecclesiasticus)
2:10: 7
5:8: 25, 94
5:8–9: 94
10:13: 351
18:6: 163
23:3: 18
29:12: 153
30:24: 343
33:10–15: 387
33:12: 387
39:36: 7

Isaiah
7:9 (LXX): 216
40:4: 28
45:11 (LXX): 431
52:7: 147
53:8: 129
55:6–7: 313
58:7: 153, 181
58:8: 181
61:10: 192

Jeremiah
21:1–10: 320
23:24: 5
25:12: 321
29:5–7: 320–21
29:7: 362
29:10: 321

Lamentations
5:17: 12

Ezekiel
33:6: 335

Hosea
6:6: 342

Malachi
1:3: 385

New Testament

Matthew
3:12: 253
4:2: 178
5:3: 23
5:3–9: 37
5:8: 128, 197, 294
5:9: 247

5:17: 179
5:34–35: 223
5:39: 72
5:44: 73
5:45: 151, 332
6:8: 37, 151
6:9: 151

6:11: 151
6:12: 152
6:19–21: 72
7:7: 37
7:12: 296
9:12: 140, 141
9:21: 172

10:19–20: 127
11:12: 25
11:25 : 20, 134
12:42–44: 180
13:4: 179
13:8: 322
13:24–30: 253
13:47–48 : 244, 253
15:16: 152
17:1–3: 178
19:21: 27
20:2: 178
20:9–10: 178
20:12–15: 92
20:16: 388
22:23–30: 367
22:37–39: 181, 341
22:37–40: 169, 180
22:40: 296, 343
23:10: 162
25:21: 31
27:60: 295
28:19: 259
28:20: 194

Mark
8:1–9: 127
12:42–44: 180
13:8: 322
14:30: 142

Luke
1:33: 322
2:11: 395
5:31: 394
5:31–32: 394
8:5: 253
10:30–35: 145, 180
10:33–35: 406
11:12–13: 321
11:20: 223
12:35–36: 322
13:34: 323
14:10: 83
14:11: 72
14:16–23: 273
14:25: 161n18
14:25–35: 161–62
14:28: 24
16:10: 137
17:21: 73
21:18: 364
21:33: 322

24:37: 144
24:37–40: 144
24:38–39: 144

John
1:1: 128–29, 160, 197
1:1, 3: 285
1:1–3: 72, 128, 176, 285
1:1–5: 344
1:14: 19, 128, 129, 143, 148,
    160, 197, 306, 345
1:18: 181
1:29: 394
1:32–33: 257
1:33: 258, 258n40
1:51: 228
3:5: 93, 394
3:21: 36
3:36: 394
4:2: 254
4:40: 180
5:1–18: 176
5:5: 177
5:6: 180
5:8: 180
6:54: 394
7:16: 312
7:18: 319
8:31–32: 197
10:16: 270
10:30: 195, 285
10:34: 329n31
11:1–44: 295
12:3–7: 172
14:6: 54, 133, 197, 228
14:9: 285
14:28: 285
15:2: 264
15:5: 308–9, 408
15:13: 251
15:26: 312
16:8: 60
20:17: 285
20:22: 312

Acts of the Apostles
1:9–12: 295
1:14: 126
2:1–4: 178
4:12: 406
4:32: 82, 108
4:35: 108
9:1–9: 329

9:4: 195, 196
15:9: 197
17:27–28: 307

Romans
1:1–4: 433
1:3: 320
1:20: 20, 168, 372
1:21–25: 332
1:28: 431
2:4: 319–20
2:5–6: 333
3:14: 403
3:23: 403
4:16: 431
4:20–21: 432
5:1: 388
5:5: 11, 179, 296
5:6: 386, 394
5:12: 394, 404, 406, 423
6:6: 74
6:13: 343
6:21: 7
7:7–25: 384
7:18: 384, 425
7:19: 377
7:23: 367, 425
7:24–25: 384
7:25: 394
8:17: 393
8:23: 31
8:26: 258
8:28: 296
8:29: 366
8:32: 371
9:5: 320
9:6–14: 385
9:10: 435
9:10–29: 384–85
9:12: 385
9:13: 385
9:14: 389
9:20: 389
9:21: 331, 387, 417
9:21–23: 386
9:23: 404
9:28: 180
9:29: 435
10:2–3: 399–400
10:3: 413
10:4: 400
10:8: 197
10:12: 37

Romans (cont.)
10:13: 146
10:14: 3, 386
10:14–15: 147
11:5: 388
11:6: 385
11:33: 387, 389
11:35–36: 429
11:36: 4, 283, 308
12:1ff.: 136
12:1: 343
12:2: 343
12:3–6: 344
12:21: 100
13:1: 101
13:4: 98
13:9–10: 169
13:10: 179
13:13–14: 27
14:1: 91

1 Corinthians
1:22: 273
1:23–24: 70
1:24: 290
1:25: 168
2:8: 148
2:9: 30
3:1–3: 228
3:6–7: 255
3:16: 68
4:5: 91
4:7: 374, 386, 396, 435
7:6: 422
7:9: 422
8:3: 296
9:9: 173
10:4: 181, 262n41
10:17: 153–54
10:33: 84
11:3: 284, 285
11:7: 302, 303, 304
11:27: 155
12:7–8: 305–6
12:12: 195
13:3: 264
13:2: 309
13:3: 264
13:12: 36, 294, 311, 372
15:1–57: 367
15:5: 141
15:22: 141, 386
15:28: 285, 332

15:46: 330
15:47: 74
15:48–49: 74
15:51: 31, 75
15:55: 198

2 Corinthians
3:5: 430
3:6: 14, 17, 157, 226
3:14: 17, 226
3:16: 226
3:18: 309
4:10: 3
4:16: 308
4:18: 73
5:6: 168, 197
5:7: 197, 294, 362
5:13: 228
5:14–15: 228
5:20: 145
6:2–11: 136
6:16: 109
10:6: 273
11:2: 130
11:10: 210

Galatians
1:20: 189, 190
2:14: 189, 263
2:20: 194
2:21: 405
3:16: 195
3:24: 226
3:26–28: 304
3:29: 192
4:4–5: 228
4:9: 60
4:21–26: 136
5:4: 226
5:6: 359
5:14: 296
5:17: 367, 388, 421
6:2: 182, 296
6:8: 72

Ephesians
2:3: 395
2:3–5: 403
2:9–10: 431
2:10: 431
2:19–22: 181
3:14–17: 70
3:17: 68

4:2–3: 182
4:3: 273
4:11–16: 154n63
4:13: 366
4:23–24: 304
4:24: 74
5:19: 29
5:27: 36, 232
5:32: 195
6:16, 17: 223

Philippians
1:29: 429
2:6: 285
2:6–7: 149
2:7: 246, 285, 343
2:21: 114
3:13: 30
3:15: 428–29

Colossians
1:5: 284
1:18: 154n63
1:24: 194
2:1–3: 305
2:3: 306
2:8: 20
3:9–10: 304
3:10: 292, 304

1 Timothy
1:5: 311, 348
1:13: 91
2:1–2: 321
2:2: 362
2:5: 180, 424, 432
6:9: 425

2 Timothy
2:15: 16
2:19: 259
4:3–4: 228

Titus
2:12: 178
2:13: 178
3:5: 150, 393, 404

Hebrews
12:2: 434
12:22: 320
13:16: 342

James
  1:17: 210
  4:6: 328

1 Peter
  2:5: 261
  4:8: 264
  5:5: 3, 19

2 Peter
  2:10: 352

1 John
  1:8: 152
  1:8–9: 149
  2:1–2: 149
  2:15–16: 73
  4:6: 270, 271

4:7: 271, 296
4:8: 271
4:16: 181, 296, 297
4:18: 272
4:20: 181

Citations in Other Ancient Authors and Texts

Old Testament

Leviticus
  19:2: 239 (Cyprian)

Numbers
  19:22: 239 (Cyprian)

Deuteronomy
  30:19: 376 (Pelagius)

Psalms
  13:3: 400 (Pelagius)
  41:4: 120 (Possidius)
  51:9: 412 (Innocent I)

93:10: 414 (Council of
    Carthage)
118:137: 121 (Possidius)

Proverbs
  14:30: 120 (Possidius)

Song of Songs
  6:8: 238 (Cyprian)

Ecclesiastes
  1:18: 120 (Possidius)
  7:21: 400 (Pelagius)

Sirach (Ecclesiasticus)
  15:14–17: 376 (Pelagius)
  34:40: 195 (Petilian)

Isaiah
  66:24: 242 (Petilian)

Jeremiah
  2:13: 239 (Cyprian)

Ezekiel
  36:25–26: 239 (Cyprian)

New Testament

Matthew
  5:39, 40, 41: 325 (Flavius
    Marcellinus)
  6:12, 13: 411 (Council of
    Milevis)
  7:16, 17: 241 (Petilian)
  8:21–22: 241 (Petilian)
  12:30: 239 (Cyprian)
  12:35: 241 (Petilian)
  12:45: 241 (Petilian)
  13:45–46: 440 (Possidius)
  13:52: 440 (Possidius)
  19:4: 412 (Innocent I)
  25:34: 426 (Prosper of
    Aquitaine)
  26:41: 411 (Council of
    Milevis)
  27:4–5: 241 (Petilian)

Mark
  1:1: 206–7 (Faustus of
    Milevis)

Luke
  22:32: 411 (Council of
    Milevis)

John
  1:1: 206 (Faustus of
    Milevis)
  15:5: 415 (Council of
    Carthage)
  17:12: 241 (Petilian of
    Constantine)

Romans
  5:12: 401n61 (Pelagius),
    411 (Council of
    Milevis), 414 (Council
    of Carthage)
  8:17: 392 (Rufinus the
    Syrian)
  8:32: 418 (Julian of
    Eclanum)
  9:16: 411 (Council of
    Milevis)

9:21: 427 (Prosper of
    Aquitaine)

1 Corinthians
  6:1–5: 96 (Possidius)
  7:14: 392 (Rufinus the
    Syrian)
  8:1: 414 (Council of
    Carthage)
  10:13: 411 (Council of
    Milevis)
  15:22: 411 (Council of
    Milevis)

2 Corinthians
  5:17: 392 (Rufinus the
    Syrian)

Ephesians
  1:4: 426 (Prosper of
    Aquitaine)
  4:4–6: 238 (Cyprian)
  4:5: 242 (Petilian)

Philippians
  2:14: 398 (Pelagius)
  2:21: 104 (Possidius)

1 Timothy
  4:4–5: 104 (Possidius)
  6:16: 207 (Faustus)

2 Timothy
  2:26: 413 (Innocent I)

James
  2:12: 440 (Possidius)

1 John
  4:7: 414 (Council of
      Carthage)

INDEX OF AUGUSTINIAN TEXTS

Ad Catholicos fratres (To the
Catholic Members of the Church)
  5.9: 243

Ad inquisitiones Januarii
(Responses to Januarius)
  1.1.1–2.3: 88–89

Ad Simplicianum de diversis
quaestionibus (To Simplicianus,
on Various Questions)
  1.q.1.10, 11: 378n21
  1.q.1.11–14: 384
  1.q.2.2–3: 385
  1.q.2.4: 385–86
  1.q.2.7–9: 386
  1.q.2.20: 330n33
  1.q.2.16–20: 386–87
  1.q.2.19: 403n64
  1.q.2.21–22: 388–89

Confessiones (Confessions)
  1.1.1–2.2: 3–5
  1.6.7–7.11: 5
  1.8.13: 6
  1.11.17: 15n22
  2.1.1: 35, 37n63
  2.4.9–9.17: 7–8
  3.1.1: 8
  3.2.2–2.4: 172n37
  3.4.7: 39n1, 43n16
  3.4.7–5.9: 9–10
  3.6.10–6.11: 209–10
  3.11.20: 204n8
  3.11.20–12.21 10–11
  4.4.7–8.13: 11–13
  5.1.1: 35–36
  5.6.10: 14n20
  5.6.10–7.13: 212n20
  5.10.19–10.20: 211
  5.13.23–6.5.7: 13–17

6.3.4: 223n31
6.4.6: 226n35
6.13.23–15.25: 17–18
7.2.3: 216–17
7.9.13–17.23: 19–20
8.2.3–2.5: 20–22, 146n49
8.6.14–6.15: 22–24
8.7.17–12.29: 25–27
9.2.4: 44n21
9.4.7–4.8: 27–28
9.5.13–6.14: 28–29
9.10.23–10.25: 30–31
9.12.32: 54n39
10.1.1–2.2: 36
10.8.12–8.15: 32–33
10.27.38: 33–34
10.29.40: 397n53
10.31.45: 397n53
10.37.60: 397n53
11.1.2–2.3: 36–38
12.15.20: 9n12
13.11.12: 286
13.28.43–32.47: 224–25

Contra Academicos (Against the
Skeptics)
  1.1.4: 43n16
  2.2.4–2.6: 45–46
  2.3.7: 39
  2.5.11–5.12: 47–48
  3.7.15: 44n21
  3.9.21–11.25: 48
  3.14.30–14.31: 49–50
  3.15.34: 50–51
  3.18.41–20.43: 52–53

Contra adversarium legis
et prophetarum (Against
Adversaries of the Law and the
Prophets)
  1.18: 316n3

Contra Cresconium (Against
Cresconius)
  3.49.54: 262n41

Contra duas epistulas
Pelagianorum (Against Two
Letters of the Pelagians)
  1.25: 409n72

Contra epistulam Parmeniani
(Against the Letter of Parmenian)
  1.1.1: 191n67
  2.13.29: 256n37
  3.6.29: 262n41

Contra Faustum Manichaeum
(Against Faustus, a Manichee)
  2.1–3.1: 206–7
  4.1: 207
  5.1: 205–6
  12.7: 227
  12.25–27: 227–29
  20.2: 207
  20.11: 207n14, 229–30
  26.7: 230

Contra Julianum (Against
Julian)
  1.4.14: 419
  2.9.31–9.32: 424–25
  3.3.9: 419
  3.13.26: 421
  3.13.27–15.29: 420–21
  3.15.29–23.53: 422–23
  6.5.11: 419–20

Contra Julianum opus
imperfectum (Against Julian, an
Unfinished Work)
  1.7: 381
  1.32: 381n30

Contra Julianum opus
imperfectum (Against Julian, an
Unfinished Work) (cont.)
   1.48: 381n30, 418
   1.81: 408n71
   3.67–71: 418
   3.120: 408n71
   3.144: 419n88
   4.56: 381n30
   5.11: 381n30
   6.10: 408n71

Contra litteras Petiliani (Against
the Letters of Petilian)
   1.24.26: 262n41
   2.1.2–108.246: 240–43
   3.23.27: 240n18

De baptismo (On Baptism)
   1.3.4–4.5: 256
   1.12.28: 256–57
   3.10.15: 255n34

De beata vita (On the Happy
Life)
   1.1–1.5: 43–45
   4.33–35: 45n23, 53–54

De catechizandis rudibus (On
Catechizing Beginners)
   3.6: 170n36
   11.48: 172n37
   12.17: xix, 145–46
   19.31–21.37: 319–21

De civitate Dei (The City of God)
   praef.: 328
   1.8–9: 332–36
   1.35–36: 326n27
   2.19–22: 336–39, 357n65
   2.21: 316n5
   4.3–4: 339–40
   8.14–22: 325n23
   9.8–16: 325n23
   10.3–6: 340–44
   10.7: 316n5
   10.29: 344–45, 363n70
   10.32: 326n27
   11.1: 156, 316n5, 329
   11.18: 318–19
   11.26: 300n40
   14.1–7: 345–47

14.10: 347–48
14.13: 351–53
14.15: 353–54
14.21–23: 349–51
14.26: 348
14.28: 331–32
15.1: 330–31
18.1: 326n27
18.18: 325n23
18.43: 187n59
19.6: 100n33, 355–56
19.7: 356–57
19.17: 360–61
19.21–24: 357–60
19.26–27: 362
22.12–13: 364–65
22.17 : 366–67
22.19: 365–66
22.24: 368–71
22.26: 363n70
22.29 : 372
22.30: 315

De correctione Donatistarum (On
the Correction of the Donatists)
   22–24: 272–73
   23: 255n35, 256n37

De diversis quaestionibus
octoginta tribus (Eighty-Three
Different Questions)
   31: 301n42

De doctrina christiana (On
Christian Teaching)
   praef. 1–9: 163–64
   1.1.1: 127n15, 164
   1.3.3–11.11: 167–68
   1.26.27–36.40: 169–70
   2.1.1–5.6: 171–72
   2.6.7–6.8: 173–74
   2.8.12–9.14: 165–67
   2.10.15: 172–73
   2.15.22: 184–85
   2.16.25: 174–75
   2.18.28: 182–83
   2.40.60: 183
   3.10.14–15.23: 170
   3.27.38: 190–91
   3.30.42: 158
   3.30.42–31.44: 191–93
   4.2.3: 130–31

4.10.25: 134
4.11.26: 131
4.12.27–13.29: 135–36
4.15.32: 126–27
4.17.34–26.56: 137–40

De dono perseverantiae (On the
Gift of Perseverance)
   20.53: 397–98
   21.55: 434

De excidio urbis Romae (On
the Sack of the City of Rome =
Sermon 397)
   1.1–8.9: 321n18

De fide et symbolo (On Faith and
the Creed)
   3.3–3.4: 282
   9.16–9.17: 283–84
   9.18: 284–85

De Genesi ad litteram (On the
Literal Interpretation of Genesis)
   4.3.7–6.12: 54n37
   9.3.6: 349
   9.11.19: 354n60
   11.15.20: 317

De Genesi adversus Manichaeos
(On Genesis, Against the
Manichees)
   1.17.28–17.29: 223–24
   2.29.43: 231

De gestis Pelagii (On the Deeds of
Pelagius)
   3.9: 376n17
   11.23: 390
   14.30: 429n98
   22.46: 396–97
   35.66: 410

De gratia Christi et de peccato
originali (On the Grace of Christ
and Original Sin)
   1.4.5: 377n20
   1.31.34: 430n99
   1.37.41–40.44: 399n56
   1.42.46: 424n95
   2.3.3: 390–91

De haeresibus (On Heresies)
  praef.: 46n24
  46: 209n16

De immortalitate animae (On the
Immortality of the Soul)
  16.25: 66

De libero arbitrio (On Free Will)
  1.1.1: 221
  1.2.4: 215–16
  1.13.27: 358n67
  2.19.53–20.54: 222–23
  3.18.50: 375n13

De magistro (On the Teacher)
  1.1–3.5: 67–69
  11.36–12.40: 69–70

De moribus ecclesiae Catholicae et
de moribus Manichaeorum (On
the Catholic and the Manichean
Ways of Life)
  1.2: 205n12
  2.2.2–7.9: 217–20

De natura et gratia (On Nature
and Grace)
  1.1: 399–400
  3.3–5.5: 403–4
  5.5: 330n33
  7.7.: 400
  8.9–9.10: 404–5
  30.34: 405
  31.35: 407–8
  34.39–52.60: 406–7
  43.50: 145n45
  49.57: 408n70, 408n71
  52.60: 145n45
  67.80–81: 375n13

De nuptiis et concupiscentia (On
Marriage and Concupiscence)
  1.20.22: 418n85, 419n88

De ordine (On Order)
  1.1.1: 55
  1.1.2: xvii, 56
  1.2.5: 44n21
  1.11.31: 45n15
  1.11.32: 39n1
  2.10.29: 40–41

2.12.35–18.47: 65n52
2.17.45: xi n4
2.18.47: 58n45

De origine animae et de sententia
Jacobi (On the Origin of the Soul
and On a Verse in James = Letters
166–167)
  4.10–6.16: 415–16

De peccatorum meritis et
remissione et de baptismo
parvulorum (On the Merits and
Forgiveness of Sins and on Infant
Baptism)
  1.9.9: 378
  1.16.21: 354n60
  1.18.23–23.33: 393–95
  1.19.24: 5n6
  1.34.63: 419n88
  2.17.26–18.28: 395–96
  3.4.7: 5n6

De perfectione justitiae hominis
(On the Perfection
of Human Righteousness)
  3.5: 402n62

De praedestinatione sanctorum
(On the Predestination of the
Saints)
  1.1–2.5: 428–30
  3.7–4.8: 435–36
  4.8: 374n3
  10.19: 431–32
  15.30–31: 432–34

De symbolo ad catechumenos
(On the Creed to Catechumens =
Sermon 398)
  1.2: 419n88
  8.16: 256n37

De Trinitate (On the Trinity)
  1.2.4–3.5: 287–88
  1.3.5: xii
  1.4.7: 274
  8.3.4–3.5: 293
  8.4.6: 294
  8.4.7–5.7: 295
  8.5.8: 274n1, 294
  8.7.10–10.14: 296–97

9.2.2: 298
9.4.7: 40
9.5.8: 299
10.10.14: 300
10.11.17–11.18: 301–2
12.7.9–8.13: 303–5
13.4.7: 43n16
13.9.12: 316n
13.19.24: 305–6
14.8.11–17.23: 307–9
14.9.12: 43n16
14.19.26: 43n16
15.2.2: 313–14
15.3.4–4.6: 289–92
15.6.10: xv, 274n1
15.7.11: 309
15.11.20: 282n23
15.12.21: 300n40
15.14.24–15.25: 282n23
15.17.28: xv, 274n1
15.22.42–24.44: 310–11
15.27.48: 312–13

De unitate ecclesiae (On the Unity
of the Church)
  5.9: 243

De utilitate credendi (On the
Advantage of Believing)
  1.2: 204n8, 212
  3.9: 225–27
  8.20: 212–13
  9.21–12.26: 214–15

De vera religione (On True
Religion)
  3.3–4.7: 71–74
  5.8: 39
  26.48–27.50: 74–75
  27.50: 317
  49.97: 76
  55.112–13: 76–77

Enarrationes in Psalmos
(Expositions of the Psalms)
  3.1–10: 190n70
  10.8: 174n40
  29.2.22: 35n57
  32.2.8: 199–200
  39.10: 122–23
  41.9: 159
  42.1: 159

Enarrationes in Psalmos
(Expositions of the Psalms)
(cont.)
   56.1: 193–94
   61.23: 92n21
   64.2: 317n9, 332n35
   78.17: 135n26
   84.10: 317n9
   94.4: 135n26
   95.11: 254
   96.2: 159n13
   99.4: 200n76
   99.12: 90
   102.5: 141
   123.1–4: 196–98
   123.2: 168n33
   126.3: 87–88
   141.19: 35n57, 135n26
   142.3: 194–95
   149.7: 318

Enchiridion / De fide, spe, et
caritate (Enchiridion / On Faith,
Hope, and Love)
   1.6: 437
   5.17: 267
   13.42–43: 5n6
   33: 440
   88–91: 366n75

Epistulae (1–270) (Letters
1–270)
   3.1–4: 62–64
   10.2: 41
   11.2–4: 279–81
   18.2: 65
   21.1–6: 83–85
   28.3.3: 187
   33.5: 246
   36.14.32: 89n18
   40: 187n60
   43.1.2–9.27: 247–50
   43.4: 234n4
   43.8.24: 262n41
   50: 97
   52: 232n1
   54.1.1–2.3: 88–89
   59.1–2: 107–8
   71: 188n60
   71.2.3–4.6: 185–87
   73.2.5: 157
   82: 438n2
   82.1.2–2.8: 188–90

82.5.34–5.35; 187n59
85.2: 79n3
87.1–5: 249n28, 251–52
93.5.16–5.19; 268–70
93.10.36–10.40; 263–64
102.32: 325n23
105.1.1: 256n37
105.2.3–2.5: 263–65
105.5.16: 253
134.1–4: 97–100
135: 326n24
136.1–3: 325–26
137: 326n24
137.1.3–5.18; 162–63
137.13: 325n23
138: 326n24
138.18–19: 325n23
139.3: 115
149.7: 318
154.2: 315, 318n15
157.3.22: 390n41
157.8–10: 408–9
166.4.10–6.16; 415–16
169: 116n59, 274, 318n15
169.1: 316n3
173.3: 256n37
174: 274, 286–87
176.2–4: 411–12
182.3–6: 412–13
184A.3.5: 316n3, 318n15,
   326n27
185.22–24: 272–73
185.23: 255n35, 256n37
190: 116n55
190.3.12: 330n33, 417
192: 116n57
194.96: 419n88
209: 110n48
211: 109n45
213.1–7: 117–19
220: 121n63
224: 116n59
225.2–6: 426–28
236.1–3: 208–9

Epistulae 1*–29* (Letters
1*–29* [Divjak])
   1*.1–2: 316n3
   1*.1–3: 326–27
   2*.1: 316n3
   2*.3: 326n25
   2*.3–7: 92–94
   2*.7: 70n58

   4*.2–3: 409–10
   10*.2–8: 102–3
   20*.2–32: 111–14
   23*A.3–4: 116
   28*.2–3: 236n8
   28*.7: 267n49

In epistulam Johannis ad Parthos
tractatus (Tractates on the First
Letter of John)
   6.10–13: 250–51
   7.4–8: 270–71
   9.4: 142–43

In Johannis evangelium tractatus
(Tractates on the Gospel of John)
   1.7: 175n43
   1.8–12: 282n23
   2.16: 143
   3.15: 70n58
   5.1: 132–33
   5.6–15: 254–55
   6.1–24: 257–63
   9.7: 181n48
   11: 178n46
   12: 178n46
   13: 178n46
   15.1: 159, 175n43
   15.26: 181n48
   15.33: 180n47
   16.3: 180n47
   17.1–9: 176–82
   25.16: 142
   36.1: 175–76
   41.13: 144–45
   99.7–9: 312–13

Psalmus contra partem Donati
(Psalm Against the Donatists)
   7–33: 244–45
   23, 30, 293: 234n4
   270–97: 245

Quaestiones expositae contra
paganos numero sex (Six
Questions Against Pagans =
Letter 102)
   32: 325n23

Regula: Praeceptum (The Rule)
   1.1–8: 108–9

Retractationes (Reconsiderations)
  prol. 3: 41–42
  1.4.2: 60n47
  1.4.3: 62n49
  1.4.4: 69n57
  1.5.1: 41
  1.6: 64–65
  1.9: 221n28
  1.20: 244
  2.1.1: 435
  2.1.3: 374n3
  2.4.1: 158
  2.6.1: 38
  2.20: 88n17
  2.37: 115n53
  2.42.2: 166n29
  2.48: 273n58
  2.69: 316n3, 326n27

Sermones ad populum (1–396)
(Sermons to the People)
  46.2: 79n4
  52.19–23: 302n43
  56.4–11: 151–53
  57: 153n58
  58: 153n58
  58.10: 153n57
  59: 153n58
  67.1: 35n57, 134–35
  81: 321n18
  88.1–7: 141
  95.1–2: 88n16, 127
  96.4: 133
  101.4: 156n1
  105.9–13: 321–24
  123.3: 168n33
  131.10: 413
  134.1.1: 70n58
  155.15: 25n44
  188.1–4: 128–30
  210.10–11: 95
  211.1–7: 95
  212: 150n56
  213.1–9: 146–50

  214: 150n56
  215: 150n56
  220: 132, 323n20
  227: 73n60, 153–55
  237.1–3: 143–44
  241.1–7: 362–63
  242.8: 367
  272: 153n59
  275.1: 124n6
  276.1: 124n6
  278.4–5: 143n41
  280.1: 124n6
  288.3–4: 282n23
  296: 321n18
  302.1: 124n6
  302.10–21: 100–102
  339: 335n36
  339.1: 79
  339.3: 156
  339.4: 127n15
  355.2: 82–83
  355.5: 100n33, 106
  356.13: 104–5
  359.5: 256n37
  397.1.1–8.9: 321n18
  398.1.2: 419n88
  398.8.16: 256n37

Sermones (Caillau, Denis,
Guelferbytanus, Morin, etc.)
(Miscellaneous Sermons)
  179A.8 (= s. Wilmart 2):
    156n1
  213 (= s. Guelf. 1): 146–47
  260D.2 (= s. Guelf. 18):
    156n1
  279.10–12 (= s. Morin 1):
    91–92
  229O.1 (= s. Guelf. 17):
    141–42
  301A.1–2 (= s. Denis 17):
    161–62
  313D.1–2 (= s. Guelf. 27):
    124n6

Sermones (Dolbeau) (Dolbeau
Sermons)
  29B.1–6 (= s. Dolbeau 8):
    35n57, 135n26
  162C.3–4 (= s. Dolbeau
    10): 190n64
  162C.15 (= s. Dolbeau
    10): 438
  198 (= s. Dolbeau 26):
    321n17
  198.45 (= s. Dolbeau 26):
    267–268n51
  293A.5–13 (= s. Dolbeau
    3): 282n23
  293A.6 (= s. Dolbeau 3):
    70n58
  299A (= s. Dolbeau 4):
    321n17
  299A.2 (= s. Dolbeau 4):
    256n37
  299A.5 (= s. Dolbeau 4):
    142n39
  299A.8 (= s. Dolbeau 4):
    317
  348A.5 (= s. Dolbeau 30):
    379
  359B (= s. Dolbeau 2):
    133n22
  374.23 (= s. Dolbeau 23):
    144n44

Soliloquia (Soliloquies)
  1.1.1: 57–58
  1.1.2–1.3: 59–60
  1.2.7: 58
  1.6.12–7.14: 61–62
  1.12.21: 46n24
  2.7.14: 57
  2.20.35: 69n57

INDEX OF OTHER ANCIENT AUTHORS
AND TEXTS

Ambrose, *Hymns*
Deus Creator omnium: 54n39
Splendor paternae gloriae: 13

Caelestius, *Definitiones* (in
Augustine, *De perfectione
justitiae hominis*)
3.5: 402n62

Cicero, *De re publica*
1.25: 337, 357
2.42: 337
5.1: 338

Cicero, *Hortensius*
frag. 101: 25

Cicero, *Orator*
69: 135
101: 137

Coptic Manichean Psalm Book
223.2–3: 202
223.26–27: 203
248.26–27: 203

Council of Milevis, *ep.* (=
Augustine, *ep.* 176)
176.2.3: 411–12

Council of Carthage (418),
Canons
1–6: 414–15

Cyprian, *De unitate ecclesiae*
(*On the Unity of the Church*)
4–6: 238–39

Cyprian, *Epistulae* (*Letters*)
70.1–3: 239–40
73.21.2: 237

Faustus of Milevis, *Capitula*
(*Chapters*) (in Augustine,
Contra Faustum)
2.1–3.1: 206–7
4.1: 207
5.1: 205–6
20.2: 207

Flavius Marcellinus, *ep.* (=
Augustine, *ep.* 136)
136.1–3: 325–26

Innocent I, *ep. ad Silvano* (=
Augustine, *ep.* 182)
182.3–6: 412–13

Julian of Eclanum, *Ad Florum*
(*To Florus*) (in Augustine,
*Contra Julianum opus
imperfectum*)
1.7: 381
1.48: 418
3.67–71: 418
6.9: 408n70

Julian of Eclanum, *Ad
Turbantium* (*To Turbantius*) (in
Augustine, *Contra Julianum*)
frag. 44–49: 420–21

Macedonius, *ep.*
(= Augustine, *ep.* 154)
154.2: 315

Optatus of Milevis, *De
schismate Donatistarum* (*On the
Schism of the Donatists*)
1.15: 234
3.12: 269n53

Petilian of Constantine, *ep.
ad Presbyteros et Diaconos* (*Letter
to the Presbyters and Deacons*)
(in Augustine, *Contra litteras
Petiliani*)
2.1.2–108.246: 240–42

Pelagius, *ep. ad Demetriadem*
(*Letter to Demetrias*)
2: 376
8: 376–77
10: 375
16: 398–99

Pelagius, *De natura* (*On
Nature*) (in Augustine,
De natura et gratia)
2.2: 402
7.8: 400
9.10: 401
19.21: 401–2
21.23: 402
30.34: 402
42.49–49.57: 400–401

Pelagius, *De vita Christiana*
(*On Christian Life*)
1.1–1.2: 375

Pelagius, *In Romanos*
5:12: 401n61

Pelagius, *Pro libero arbitrio*
(*In Favor of Free Choice*) (in
Augustine, *De gratia Christi et
de peccato originali*)
   1.4.5: 377
   1.42.46: 424n95

Possidius of Calama, *Vita s.
Augustini* (*Life of St. Augustine*)
   4: 81–82
   5–7: 85–86
   8: 86–87
   10: 265
   11: 109–10
   12: 267

18: xiii
19: 96
22: 104
24: 105–6
31: 122, 439–40

Prosper of Aquitaine, *ep. ad
Aug.* (=Augustine, *ep.* 225)
   225.2–6: 426–28

Prudentius, *Contra
Symmachum* (*Against
Symmachus*)
   I.506–II.641: 318

Rufinus the Syrian, *Liber de
fide* (*Book of Faith*)
   39–40: 392
Sermo Arrianorum (*Arian
Sermon*)
   17–27: 277

Tyconius, *Liber regularum*
(*Book of Rules*)
   praef.: 158, 192

Vergil, *Aeneid*
   1.278–79: 322
   6.853: 328

INDEX OF PERSONS AND SUBJECTS

Academics, 15, 40, 44, 46–51, 53, 212

Ad inquisitiones Januarii (Responses to Januarius), 88–89

Ad Simplicianum (To Simplicianus), 20n32, 160, 374, 383–89, 435–36, 443

Adam, 75, 140, 141, 151, 174, 330, 354, 387, 390, 403, 408, 411, 419–20, 421, 433; Pelagius on, 376, 401–2; sin of, 7, 345–46, 349, 353, 376, 377, 386, 390–92, 403–4, 405, 414, 415, 426

Adeodatus, 2, 17–18, 29, 41, 67–69, 442; in De magistro, 29, 67–69

Africa Proconsularis, 79, 80, 106

Against Faustus, a Manichee. See Contra Faustum Manichaeum

Against Julian. See Contra Julianum

Against Julian, an Unfinished Work. See Contra Julianum opus imperfectum

Against the Letters of Petilian. See Contra litteras Petiliani

Against the Skeptics. See Contra Academicos

agentes in rebus (special agents), 79, 80

Alaric, 316, 317, 321, 365n73, 444

Alexander of Alexandria, 274–75, 276

Alexandria, 13, 22, 165n26, 183, 274, 276, 323, 379, 381, 409, 432

Alfaric, Prosper, 42

allegory, 13–14, 17, 38n64, 157–58, 182, 349–50

almsgiving, 106, 152–53

Alypius of Thagaste, 22–23, 25–27, 28, 29, 46–47, 49–50, 80, 102–3, 109n45, 110, 121n63, 380, 411

Ambrose of Milan, 4n4, 13–17, 20, 23, 28–29, 44n19, 88–89, 136, 213, 235, 276, 305n45, 317, 349, 374, 377, 389, 418, 435, 441–43; De fide (On the Faith), 278; De spiritu sancto (On the Holy Spirit), 278; as exegete, 13–17, 157, 226n35; hymns, 53, 54; as preacher, 13–17, 40, 153, 157, 204

angel(s), 21, 31, 175, 293, 297, 309, 367, 438; Christ as, 227; and the City of God, 75, 317, 320, 329, 330, 332, 343n47, 348, 352; evangelists as, 228

Annaba. See Hippo Regius

anti-Nicenes, 275–78, 290n31

Antoninus of Fussala, 110–14, 445

Antony (of Egypt), 22–24, 27

Apollonius of Tyana, 325

Apringius, 97–100

Apuleius of Madauros, 325

Arian Sermon, 276–77

Arians, 80, 116, 275–77. See also anti-Nicenes

Arius, 274–75

asceticism, 108, 374, 375, 381, 426; and baptism, 21n34, 146; Manichean, 204, 205–6; and the philosophical life, 39, 41

Athanasius, 22, 275–76; Vita Antonii (Life of Antony), 22

Augustine of Hippo (life), ix–xi, 1–2, 5–20, 24–31, 39–41, 43–46, 64–65, 67, 78–87, 115–21, 373–74, 437–38; baptism, xiv, 1, 17, 27n46, 28–30, 40, 41, 64, 159, 204, 217, 221, 442; as biblical interpreter, xiv, xxi, 125–26, 156–61, 257–63, 373–74, 383–89, 438; as bishop, ix–xi, xiv, 1–2, 11, 78–81, 86–88, 106–8, 111–14, 122, 125, 160, 172n37, 204, 267, 373, 374, 383, 437, 439, 443–45; as catechumen, xiv, 15, 28–29, 42, 59, 213, 373; clothing, ix–xi, 104–5; confrontation with Donatism, 235–36, 243–44, 246, 267–68; confrontation with paganism, 316–18, 321–24, 326–28; confrontation with Pelagianism, 377–82, 393, 396–97, 399–400, 409–13, 414, 426, 434–36; conversion, xiv, 1, 13, 22, 24–27, 40, 44n21, 45–46, 69n57, 157, 160, 211–13, 340n45, 344n49, 373–74, 383, 397, 442; dealings with imperial officials, 80, 97–103; dealings with military, 100–102, 121n63; death, 381, 439; as doctor *gratiae*, 373; iconography of, ix–xi, 104–5; as judge, xi, 96; as a Manichee, xv, 10–11, 14–15, 40, 159, 204, 209–10, 212, 373, 381, 420, 441; as monastic legislator, 108–9; as monk, xi, 104, 108; as North African, ix–xi, 8, 78–80, 106, 109–14, 122–25, 157, 199, 232, 235, 378, 380, 403, 411, 413, 414, 417; as orator, xi, xiv, xix–xx, 6, 13, 27, 31–32, 44n21, 78, 80, 85, 122, 125, 130, 204, 281, 418, 441; ordination of, 78, 81–84, 118; as preacher, xi, xiv, 81, 85–86, 87–88, 90–92, 95, 122–26, 128–35, 140–55, 161–62, 175–82, 193–200, 257–63, 321–24, 437, 438, 439–40, 443; as presbyter, 78, 81–86, 150n56, 204, 211, 222, 235, 243, 281, 439, 442; retirement, 117–19; as *servus Dei*, 78; as teacher of rhetoric, xix–xx, 22, 27, 39, 65, 130, 135; as writer, ix–xi. *See also Vita s. Augustini*

Aurelius of Carthage, 80, 90–91, 106, 116n58, 235, 274, 286–87, 288, 377, 378n22, 380, 390–91, 409, 442

Auxentius of Milan, 276

baptism, 15n22, 21, 27n46, 88, 146, 150, 153, 242, 249, 254–57, 260, 304, 426; of Augustine, xiv, 1, 17, 28–30, 40, 41, 64, 159, 204, 217, 221, 442; Augustine's preparing candidates for, 79, 85, 145–53; character of, 255–56; Christ's power in, 254–55, 257, 258–59; Cyprian's view of, 238–40, 242, 250–51, 263–64, 378; Donatist view of, 232, 239–43, 254–56; delay of, 92–94; Easter, 146, 153; emergency, 12, 15n22; and the Eucharist, 153–54; for the forgiveness of sins, 147, 149–50, 152, 239–40, 242, 256–57, 308, 377, 393, 424–25; formula of, 414; fruitfulness of, 256–57, 260–62; and the Holy Spirit, 232, 239–40, 250–51, 258, 260–61; infant, 15n22, 115, 378, 380, 382, 391–95, 404, 412, 414–16; Lord's Prayer as daily, 150, 152–53; and love, 250–51, 261; military tattoo as analogy for, 255–56; minister of, 254–55, 258n40, 259–60; necessity of, 394–95, 404, 412, 415–16, 427; one, 150, 239–40, 242, 255; outside of the Church, 243, 255–57, 260; as rebirth, 151, 364, 393; as Red Sea, 149–50; rite of, 21n35, 28, 93n22, 153, 250, 414, 418–19; secrecy of, 28, 146, 150; signed with the cross of Christ, 150; turn in one's name for, 21, 28–29, 92, 93n22,

146; unrepeatability, 255–56; validity of, 255, 256–57, 259; as washing, 150, 173, 174, 239, 240; white robes, 27n46, 250. *See also* catechumen; *disciplina arcani*; *exsufflatio*; rebaptism

Basil of Caesarea, 108, 277

Basilica Major, xvii, 87, 122–23, 162, 250

Basilica Pacis, 117, 122–23

beauty, 18, 40, 65, 145; of the body, 63, 224, 363, 364, 365–66, 369–70; of creation, 56, 59, 133, 167, 210, 225, 368, 370–72; God as, 33, 59, 61, 66, 133, 210; as harmony, 63, 224, 365–66, 369–70; mosaic analogy, xvii, 56; of music, 199–200; in rhetoric, 137–38, 139, 140, 319; of the soul, 162, 343

Bible, xi, xii, 9, 345, 374, 381; Ambrose's interpretation of, 13–14, 16–17, 157, 226n35; and the ascent of the mind, 157, 158, 167; Augustine's commentaries on, 158–61, 373–74, 383; Augustine as interpreter of, xiv, 125–26, 156–61, 257–63, 383–89; canon of, 88, 158, 164–67, 184, 188, 190, 263, 438; Christological interpretation of, 194–98, 227–29; figurative interpretation of, 157–58; as food, 152, 156; Greek translation of, xxi, 157, 183–87; hidden meanings of, 190–93, 226; Latin translation of, xxi, 9, 157, 195; love command as hermeneutical key, 169–70, 176, 180–82, 296, 343; Manichean attacks on, 10, 207–8, 223–24, 227; memorizing, xi, 31, 164; as mirror, 161–62, 196–98; obscurity of, 14, 16, 162–63, 164, 166, 173–74, 176, 190–92, 226; pagan disrespect of, 162–63; and the persecution of Diocletian, 233; polysemy of, 190–91; and preaching, 133–34, 140, 156; prosopological interpretation, 193–94; and sign theory, 167–73; "speaking," xx–xxi, 2, 156; truth of, 16, 163, 188–90, 192, 226–27, 230, 435, 438; Tyconius's view of, 158, 191–92; unity of the Testaments, 225–27. *See also* allegory; *De doctrina christiana*; Septuagint; *Vetus Latina*

bishop(s), 10–11, 50, 82, 107, 120–21, 186, 375, 380, 382, 397, 410; Augustine's view of, 79, 83–85, 87–88, 104–6, 335n36; canons of Nicaea on, 87, 110, 113, 118; coadjutor, 78, 86–87, 117–18; Cyprian's view of, 238–39, 263–64; dealings with the imperial government, 80, 97–103, 236–37, 266, 268–70, 271–73; Donatist view of, 232–34, 236, 240–43, 253; election of, 117–19;

bishop(s) (cont.)
  ecumenical councils, 87, 275, 278, 381; as
    episkopos (overseer), 81, 161–62; financial
    duties, 79–80, 105–6; as judge, 80, 96,
    113–14, 246, 247–49, 382–83, 390–91, 409;
    liturgical duties, 28, 79, 123–24, 127, 146,
    153, 155, 233, 239, 242; Manichean, 14n20,
    205, 208; misbehavior, 110–14; as monk,
    78, 82–83, 108–10, 114; North African, xi,
    80, 106–8, 186, 411, 413–14; ordination of,
    106, 111, 233; as preacher, 13–14, 85–86,
    124; as priest, 81n7; regional councils of,
    xi, 80, 106–7, 118, 150n26, 165, 233, 234,
    236, 238, 247–49, 275, 281, 378–81, 382,
    411, 429; as sinner, 152; training catechu-
    mens, 28, 79, 92–94, 146–53; training
    neophytes, 153–55; as watchman, 335
body, 6, 12, 15, 37, 71, 86, 99, 141, 196, 241,
    264, 295, 308; beauty of, 63, 224, 363,
    365–66, 369–70; before the Fall, 347–51;
    Christ's human, 52 130, 140, 144, 229–30;
    Church as Christ's, 16, 90, 153–55,
    158–59, 174, 191–98, 228–29, 238, 251,
    373, 323–24, 343–44, 440; death of, 74,
    335, 353, 364–65, 384, 414, 416, 424, 439;
    Eucharist as Christ's, 88, 89, 153–55, 172,
    273; not same as "flesh," 345–46; God
    beyond corporeality, 16, 44, 223, 294, 304,
    307; harmony of, 63, 224, 363, 365–66,
    369–70; Manichean view of, 203–4, 206,
    208, 222, 230; and mind, 40, 71, 282, 304,
    348–49, 359–60, 354, 359, 369; Platonic
    view of, 42, 52, 346, 362–63; resurrected /
    spiritual, 309, 346, 346, 361, 362–67, 371;
    senses, 32, 61, 291–92, 300, 310; and soul,
    61, 62–66, 120, 210, 343, 345–46, 359–61,
    369, 387, 424; of women, 22, 366–67
Boniface (Roman general), 121, 271–72, 445
Boniface I (Pope), 110, 113
Bonner, Gerald, 205n9, 329n31, 375, 378n22,
    392n43 404n65, 410n74, 417
Brown, Peter, ix n2, 1n1, 25n43, 78n1, 236n9,
    237n13, 243, 374n3, 375, 381, 397n54,
    417

Caecilian of Carthage, 233–34, 247–49, 268,
    270
Caelestius, xvi, 377–78, 379, 380–81, 383,
    389–96, 402n62, 411–14, 419, 444–45
Caesarius of Arles, 88n16
canon law, 86, 87, 110, 113, 118n60, 165n25,
    414–15, 445

canon of scriptures, xiii, 88, 158, 164–67,
    184–86, 187n59, 188, 190, 263, 438. See
    also Bible
Cappadocians, 252, 277–78, 349. See also
    Basil of Caesarea; Gregory of Nazianzus;
    Gregory of Nyssa
Carneades, 15n21, 46–47
Carpaccio, Vittore, ix–xi
Carthage, xvi, xviii, 80, 116, 120, 145, 233,
    319, 324, 326, 327, 336, 337, 377, 389–90,
    411; Augustine in, xi, 8–9, 41, 80, 90, 116,
    160, 172n37, 204, 205, 216, 247, 373, 377,
    378n22, 396, 413, 441; Conference of (year
    411), xv, 236, 272, 396n51, 444; Council of
    (year 397), 165n25, 443; Council of (year
    407), 112n49; Council of (year 416), 118,
    380, 411, 413, 416; Council of (year 418),
    380, 418, 445
Caspari corpus, 374
Cassian. See John Cassian
Cassiciacum, 27–28, 40, 41, 43, 55, 62
catechumen(s), 28, 92, 146, 153, 240, 326;
    Augustine as, xiv, 15, 28–29, 42, 59, 213,
    373; Augustine's training of, 79, 85,
    92–93, 146–53
cathedra, 113, 123, 137n32, 161–62
Catholic, 98n32, 114, 235, 240, 266, 312, 373,
    409; Augustine as, 15, 17, 42, 80, 82, 373,
    439; clergy, 80, 97, 99, 209, 234, 265, 390,
    409, 424; church in North Africa, 80, 81–
    82, 86, 107, 232–36, 264, 267, 268; con-
    version to, 14–17, 42, 116, 234, 266, 268;
    clash with Donatists, xv, 56n56, 97–99,
    116, 191n67, 232, 234–38, 244–45, 250–52,
    254–56, 260–61, 265–66, 268–69, 270–72;
    faith, 14, 16, 116, 195, 269, 279, 280, 391,
    412, 419, 424; clash with Manichees, xvii,
    14, 214, 218, 230–31; teaching, 17, 109,
    209, 213, 218–20, 223, 410, 439; as world-
    wide communion, 15, 23, 42, 90, 165, 239,
    250, 251–53, 379, 409, 414
Celestine I (pope), 110
celibacy, 25n43, 73, 204, 421
Chalcedon, Council of (year 451), 426
Christ, 9, 15, 16, 27, 65, 86, 88, 91–92, 100,
    117–18, 127, 139, 245, 257–58, 304, 318,
    323–24, 336, 338, 404, 419; authority of,
    68, 69–70; as banker, 92; blood of, 88,
    89, 150, 153, 155, 172, 241, 259, 341, 395,
    402–3, 426–27; Church as body of, 16, 90,
    153–55, 158–59, 174, 191–98, 228–29, 238,
    251, 373, 323–24, 343–44, 440; as confes-

sor, 134–35; death of, 132, 143–44, 148–49, 150, 230, 371, 386, 394, 402, 404–5; as doctor (*medicus*), 132, 140–45, 176–77, 393–95, 405–6; Donatist view, 240–42; as enfleshed, 144, 148, 229, 251; as founder of the City of God, 338–39, 352; as God, xv, 128, 180, 195, 197, 274–76, 278, 282, 285, 305–6; as Good Samaritan, 144–45, 405; grace of, 222, 226, 368, 377, 384, 403–5, 411–12, 414, 424–25; as Head, 154–55, 192–96, 227, 228, 238, 246, 343, 362, 433; as human, 4, 19, 128–30, 132, 148–49, 168, 175, 176–77, 180, 194–95, 197, 230, 275, 279–81, 285, 295, 305–6, 432; as judge, 21, 79, 146, 149, 245; as lawyer, 146, 149; Manichean view of, 201, 205–7, 208, 211, 227, 229–30; as mediator, 18, 180, 309, 340, 343, 417, 424, 432; as pediatrician, 393–95; as predestined, 432–34; presence in Old Testament, 159, 226, 227–29, 320; as Redeemer, 132, 148, 272, 395, 419, 440; resurrection of, 89, 143–44, 149, 176, 178, 208, 312, 362, 390, 402; as rock, 181–82, 262n41; as Savior, 148, 176–78, 181, 382, 393, 395, 403, 419; as *scientia* (knowledge), 305–6; as Teacher, 42, 68, 69–70, 88, 129, 161–62, 180, 345; *totus Christus*, 158–59, 193–96; as Truth, 37, 54, 69–70, 71, 76, 132–33, 168, 196–97, 306; as Wisdom (*sapientia*), 9, 53, 70, 72, 76, 168, 207, 230, 282, 285, 290, 305–6, 323; the Word (Jn 1:1), 72, 128–30, 153, 160, 161, 175–76, 195, 197, 206, 229, 281–82, 285, 306, 320, 344; the Word-made-flesh (Jn 1:14), 19, 128–30, 143, 148, 160, 197, 206, 306, 344, 345. *See also* Christology

Christmas, 128–30

Christology, 128n16, 168n33, 194, 393, 426, 432. *See also* Christ

Church, 15, 21–22, 29, 130, 195–96, 237; as Body of Christ, 16, 90, 153–55, 158–59, 174, 191–98, 228–29, 238, 251, 373, 323–24, 343–44, 440; and the care of the poor, 79, 83, 105–6, 111, 114, 153; catholicity, 23, 73, 81, 86, 89, 90, 109, 165, 193, 214, 218, 232, 235–36, 245, 249–54, 260, 263–64, 379, 391, 414, 439; of Christ, 21, 85, 106, 155, 173, 321, 394; as *corpus permixtum*, 90, 158, 237, 253, 259, 260; finances of, 79, 105–6; holiness of, 253; as hospital, 144–45, 405–6; Mother, 16, 53, 93, 99, 150, 151, 244–45; no salvation outside, 249, 256,

403; as Noah's ark, 238, 257–62; oneness of, 238–40, 250–51, 257, 264, 265; purity of, 243, 253

Cicero, Marcus Tullius, 9–10, 25, 39–40, 43, 52, 156, 157, 213, 214, 301n42, 336, 338, 441; political philosophy, 315, 337, 338, 357–59; rhetorical theory, 51n32, 135–37. *See also* Hortensius

Circumcellions, 98, 116n57, 234, 264–67

city of God, xvi, 38n64, 74–75, 93, 195–96, 316, 318, 320, 328–32, 338–39, 350, 352, 360–62, 406. *See also* De civitate Dei; earthly city

coercion, 235–37, 268–70, 271–73

Cologne Mani Codex, 204

competentes, 21nn34–35, 146, 150, 153

concubine, 17–18, 121n63

concupiscence, 334, 366, 384, 387, 420–23, 424

Conference of Carthage (year 411). *See* Carthage

confession, 211, 256, 328, 408, 438; of faith, 2, 35, 36–37, 224, 228; of praise, 2–5, 35–36, 38, 134–35; of sin, 2, 7–8, 35, 134–35

Confessiones (*Confessions*), xii, xiv, xv, xvii, xxi, 1–38, 42, 43, 57, 64, 67, 71, 75, 157, 159, 205, 211, 274, 294, 328, 373, 423, 441; as anti-Manichean, 10–11, 204–5, 209–12, 216–17; ascents of mind in, 18–20, 30–31, 60–61, 289; as autobiography, 1–2, 160; date of composition, 2, 443, 446; as exegesis of Genesis, 224; outline of, 31, 34–35; Pauline perspectives, 373–74; and the Pelagian controversy, 160, 375–76, 377, 397–98; Trinitarian theology, 285–86; as prayer, 2–5, 33–34, 37, 58–59; unity of, 34–35; use of Psalms, 2, 24, 159

Constantine, 96, 233–34, 236, 237, 247–49, 268, 275, 317

Constantinople, 312, 323; Council of (year 381), 275, 278

continence, 109, 111, 259, 265, 420, 421, 422

Contra Academicos (*Against the Skeptics*), xiv, 15n21, 40, 45–63

Contra Faustum Manichaeum (*Against Faustus, a Manichee*), 205–7, 227–30, 443

Contra Julianum (*Against Julian*), 381, 410–25, 445

Contra Julianum opus imperfectum (*Against Julian, an Unfinished Work*), xiii, 381, 417–18, 446

Contra litteras Petiliani (*Against the Letters of Petilian*), 235, 240–42, 262n41 444, 446

conversion, 160, 211–13, 340n45, 344n49, 373–74, 383, 397, 442; of Augustine, xiv, 1, 13, 22, 24–27, 40, 44n21, 45–46, 69n57, 157, 160, 211–13, 340n45, 344n49, 373–74, 383, 397, 442; suspicious, 90–92, 268, 375; of Victorinus, 20–22

council, xi, 80, 87, 88–89, 106, 107, 165, 233, 238, 239, 263, 275, 276, 281, 378, 380, 382, 409, 411, 413, 414. See also Carthage; Constantinople; Ephesus; Milevis; Nicaea

Courcelle, Pierre, 19n29, 24n41, 42, 46n24, 363n71

creation, xvii, 3, 36, 56, 159, 210, 282, 330, 363, 376, 403; God as author of, 320, 370, 407, 422; goodness of, 205, 224–25, 368; Manichean view of, 202–3

creationism, 415–16

creed, xv, 21n35, 146–50, 154, 234, 275–76, 278, 281, 312

Crispinus of Calama, 266

Cyprian of Carthage, 80, 136, 153n58, 237–38, 243, 250, 256, 378, 418; Augustine's view of, 124n6, 237, 250, 256, 263–64, 378; De unitate ecclesiae (On the Unity of the Church), 238–39

Cyril of Alexandria: Augustine's correspondence with, 379–80, 409; condemns Pelagianism, 381, 409; and Council of Ephesus (year 431), 381, 409, 432

Cyril of Jerusalem, 153

De baptismo (On Baptism), 235, 255n34, 255–57, 263, 443

De beata vita (On the Happy Life), 40, 43–45, 53–54, 442

De catechizandis rudibus (On Catechizing Beginners), xviii–xix, 145–46, 170n36, 172n37, 225, 319–21, 443, 446

De civitate Dei (On the City of God), xiii, xiv, xv–xvi, 71, 74, 92, 98n32, 116, 156, 159, 315–19, 326–72, 377, 382, 421; occasion, xvi, 316–17; outline, 326; polemic against paganism, 316, 340–45, 363–66; as political philosophy, 315–16, 318, 336–40, 354–62; title, 316, 328–29; two cities theme, xvi, 74, 316–17, 327–32, 352, 362. See also city of God; earthly city

De doctrina christiana (On Christian Teaching), xiv, 161, 443, 445; on the canon of Scripture, 164–67; date of composition, 125–26, 158; theory of exegesis, xv, 126, 157–58, 161, 169–75, 176, 182–85, 190–93; theory of

preaching, 125–27, 130–31, 134, 135–40; three aims of eloquence, 135–36; three styles, 136–40; Tyconius's influence, 158, 191–93; use / enjoy distinction, 167–68

De dono perseverantiae (On the Gift of Perseverance), 382, 397–98, 434, 446

De Genesi ad litteram (On the Literal Interpretation of Genesis), 158, 317, 349, 444

De Genesi adversus Manichaeos (On Genesis, Against the Manichees), 158, 223–24, 230–31, 442

De gestis Pelagii (On the Deeds of Pelagius), 376, 379–80, 390, 396–97, 409n73, 410, 444

De gratia Christi et de peccato originali (On the Grace of Christ and Original Sin), 377, 390–91, 399n56, 401n60, 424n95, 430n99, 445

De libero arbitrio (On Free Will), 43n14, 215–16, 221–23, 375, 442, 443

De magistro (On the Teacher), 29, 40, 67–70, 442

De moribus ecclesiae Catholicae et de moribus Manichaeorum (On the Catholic and the Manichean Ways of Life), 42, 205n12, 217–20, 442

De musica (On Music), 40, 64–65, 442

De natura et gratia (On Nature and Grace), 145n45, 330n33, 375n13, 378, 380, 399–408, 411, 444

De ordine (On Order), xi n4, xviii, 39n1, 40–41, 43n14, 44n21, 55–56, 58n45, 59n46, 65n52

De peccatorum meritis et remissione et de baptismo parvulorum (On the Merits and Forgiveness of Sins and On Infant Baptism), 5n6, 115n53, 354n60, 377–78, 393–96, 419n88, 444

De praedestinatione sanctorum (On the Predestination of the Saints), 382, 428–34, 435–36, 446

De Trinitate (On the Trinity), xii, xv, 274, 277, 278, 285, 286–314, 318, 443, 445

De utilitate credendi (On the Advantage of Believing), 204n8, 211–15, 227

De vera religione (On True Religion), xiv, 39, 40, 71–77

deacon, 81n9, 83, 105, 112, 124, 145, 233, 240, 287, 319, 379, 389–91, 410; Manichean, 208

defender of the Church (defensor ecclesiae), 112

Deogratias of Carthage, xviii, 81n8, 145–46, 319–21

Descartes, René, 76, 299

Diocletian, 232, 233

disciplina arcani (discipline of secrecy), 28, 93n22, 146, 153

Divjak, Johannes, 81, 92, 102, 110, 115, 236n8, 267n49, 326, 409, 446

Dolbeau, François, xii n7, 35n57, 124n8, 125, 133n22, 135n26, 142n39, 144n44, 190n64, 256n37, 267n51, 282n23, 316, 317n7, 321n17, 379, 438, 439n2, 446

Donatus, 233–34, 245, 248, 252, 254, 264, 269

Donatist(s), xiv, xvi, 107, 114, 158, 191, 192, 232–73, 316, 379, 400; Augustine's polemic against, xv, 80, 199n75, 235, 243–64, 268–73, 396, 443–45; as "church of the martyrs," 232–33, 234, 241–42, 262n41; conversion to the Catholics, 111, 236, 268; end of schism, 98n32, 236, 324, 377, 396n51, 444; history, 232–34, 247–49; imperial government action against, xv, 234, 235–36, 268–73; leadership, 116, 234–36, 240; as majority church of North Africa, xv, 232; scholarly interpretations of, 234n5, 237; view of baptism, 232, 239–43, 254–56; view of Catholics, 232, 240, 243; view of the Church, 233–35, 237, 238, 240–43, 253; violence, xv, 97, 98n31, 234, 264–67. See also Circumcellions

earthly city, xvi, 74–75, 316, 318–19, 328–31, 354–61; of God, xvi, 38n64, 74–75, 93, 195–96, 316, 318, 320, 328–32, 338–39, 350, 352, 360–62, 406. See also city of God; De civitate Dei

Easter, 85, 132, 143, 146, 153, 178, 250, 270, 362, 444; baptism at Vigil, xiv, 28–29, 79, 146, 153, 250

Edict of Unity, 235, 265n46, 268, 444

eloquence, 13–14, 129, 130–31, 192, 212, 264; Augustine's reputation for, xi, 122n2, 325, 437; Cicero as model, 9, 135n27, 137; three aims, 135–36; three styles, 136–40. See also rhetoric

Emeritus of Caesarea, 251–52

Enarrationes in Psalmos (Expositions of the Psalms), xiii, 87–88, 90, 124n8, 125, 141, 159, 161, 254, 443, 444; Head / Body theme, 154n63, 193–98

Enchiridion, 5n6, 267, 366n75, 437, 440, 445

Ephesus, 165, 249n28, 377; Council of (year 431), 381, 409

Epicurus of Samos, 63

Epistulae (Letters), 62–64, 65, 83–85, 88–89, 92–94, 97–100, 102–3, 107–8, 110–14, 115–19, 162, 185–90, 208–9, 247–53,

263–70, 272–73, 279–81, 286–87, 324–27, 408–13, 415–17, 426–28; newly discovered, 81; numbering, 81n8

Eraclius (successor of Augustine), 117–19, 445

eternal life, 30, 71, 72, 74, 75, 76, 96, 98, 152, 177, 207, 256, 292, 353, 363, 368, 371–72, 394, 411–12, 426–27

Eucharist, 79, 123n15, 269n53, 340; frequency of, 89, 150, 151–52; and lifting up the heart, 73, 154, 308; North Africa liturgy, 73n60, 122–24, 150–53, 308; secrecy of, 15n22, 93n22, 150, 153

Eunomius of Cyzicus, 278

evil, 18, 40, 43, 57, 60, 95, 99, 109, 112, 114, 115, 138–39, 151, 152, 159, 205, 241, 245, 265, 267, 269, 273, 324, 326, 332, 352, 357, 359, 384, 387, 395, 410, 427; Church as mix of good and, 158, 245, 252, 259, 260, 261; concupiscence as, 422–23; confession of, 7–8, 11, 26, 38, 64; as corruption, 219–20; and embodiment, 345–47, 402; as free will misused, 56, 70, 220–22, 231, 341, 377, 402, 408; God not author of, 59, 218, 221, 418; God's permitting of, 59, 151–52, 231; as insubstantial, 217–20, 402; Manichean view of, 202, 209, 216–19, 231; mosaic analogy, 56; as nothing, 56, 59, 217, 222; and original sin, 330, 348, 351–53, 416, 417, 418, 419–20, 422–23, 424; Pelagian view of, 375–77, 392, 400–402, 408, 418, 424; as privation of being, 210n18, 217–19; problem of, 55–56, 215–16, 220–21; return of evil for, 100–101, 325; as turning from God, 222, 231, 351–53

Evodius of Uzalis, 116n59, 215–16, 221, 274, 318n15, 380, 397n54

exegesis, 187; Ambrose's principles of, 157; Augustine's practice of, xv, 126, 153n58, 156–61, 175, 176–82, 193–200, 256–63; Augustine's theory of, xv, 126, 156–61, 163–64, 167–75, 182–83; and the canon, 164–65; figurative, 157–58, 170–75; of Genesis, 158–59; of John's Gospel, 128, 132–33, 159–60, 175–82, 257–63, 312; and the love command, 164–70; of Paul's letters, 74–75, 160, 187–90, 302, 373–74, 375, 383–89, 404n65; Pelagius's, 375, 401n61, 404n65; of the Psalms, 2, 28, 159, 193–200; and sign theory, 167–68, 170–75; and the totus Christus, 158–59, 193–96. See also allegory, Bible

exercitatio mentis, 18–20, 30–31, 60–62, 289
exorcism, 154, 418–19
Expositions of the Psalms. See also Enarrationes in Psalmos
exsufflatio, 418–20

faith, xiv, 17, 23, 28, 54, 72, 89, 93, 98, 114,
    126, 132, 150, 159, 162, 163, 183, 188, 191,
    230, 238–39, 240–41, 261–62, 270, 273,
    279, 273, 287, 294, 295, 304, 309, 311,
    325, 333, 334, 348, 360, 361, 362, 372,
    375, 384, 389, 402, 423, 426, 430, 431,
    434; and authority, 49–50, 52–53, 77, 212–
    15; Catholic, 14, 16, 116, 195, 266, 269, 412,
    419; and children, 392, 412, 419; cleansed
    by, 197, 306; confession of, 2, 35, 36–37,
    224, 228; converted to, 74, 91–92, 397,
    426; creed as rule of, 147, 275–75, 414; en-
    emies of, 91–92, 363; as gift, 4, 386, 428–
    30; and hope and love, 54, 60, 61–62, 110,
    130, 294, 389, 437, 439, 440; journeying
    by, 197, 328, 408; and justification, 386,
    388; and morals, 89, 166, 170; Platonism
    and, 183; in praise of the body, 362–63;
    preceded by grace, 386, 388–89, 426–27,
    428–30, 435–36; predestined to, 431–32;
    profession of, 21–22, 380; and reason, 45,
    205, 212, 213–15; in the resurrection, 346,
    362–63, 365; seeking understanding, 287;
    versus sight, 197, 212, 294; that works
    through love, 359; turning away from, 11,
    120, 397, 429–30; and works, 96, 432
fasting, 94–95, 154, 177–79
Faustinus (Carthaginian banker), 90–92
Faustus of Milevis, 14, 205–7, 212, 227, 441;
    Capitula (Chapters), 205–7. *See also Contra Faustum Manichaeum*
Felix of Abthungi, 233, 247–48
filioque, 312–13
Fortunatus (Manichean priest), 205, 442
freedom, 56, 89, 253, 272; Manichean denial
    of, 43, 56, 200–223, 375–76; Pelagius's
    views on, 376–77, 400–402, 408; of the
    will, 40, 42, 43, 205, 220–23, 408–9,
    427–28
frui (enjoyment), 167–68

Gaudentius of Thamugadi (Timgad), 116, 236
Genesis, xvii, 34, 42, 56, 165, 303;
    Augustine's commentaries on, 42, 158–59,
    223–24, 230–31, 317, 349; in *Confessiones*,
    34, 159, 224–25, 285; in *De civitate Dei*,

159, 230–31, 345–54, 366; on goodness of
    creation, 159, 224–25; vehicle to counter
    Manichees, 158–59, 223–25
gnosticism, xv, 10, 165, 201–2
God, xii, xiv, 18, 40, 83, 94, 114, 117, 168,
    176–77, 251, 270, 286, 316, 325, 329, 332,
    340–44, 351–53, 361, 426–28, 431–32; as
    all-powerful, 54, 55, 76, 147–48, 216–17,
    365, 416; as Beauty, 33, 59, 61, 66, 133, 210;
    Christ as, xv, 128, 180, 195, 197, 228, 274–
    76, 278, 281–86, 305–6, 312–13, 320, 432–
    34; *Confessiones* addressed to, 2–3, 33–37;
    as creator, xvii, 4, 30–31, 38, 56, 59, 72, 77,
    141, 146, 320, 322, 347–51, 353, 365–66,
    368–71, 376–77, 407, 422, 424; as Father,
    45n23, 59, 76–77, 99, 128, 147–48, 150–52,
    176, 195, 238, 264, 275–92; as food, 8,
    19–20, 30–31, 127, 152; foreknowledge of,
    374, 431, 433; as the Good, 55, 59, 76, 210,
    218–20, 222, 231, 288, 292–93, 341–43,
    351, 368, 401, 407; as Happiness, 53, 54,
    59; Holy Spirit as, xv, 168, 277–78, 283–84,
    288, 290, 291, 310, 312–13; Homoian view
    of, 276–77; as incorporeal, 44, 66, 223–4l;
    as incorruptible, 217, 218–20, 332; as inef-
    fable, 94, 199–200; journey to, 57, 167–68,
    195–200, 293–94; judgment of, 12, 91, 99,
    101, 102, 121, 146, 318, 332–36, 353–54,
    367, 406, 407–8, 415–17, 421; as Love, 19,
    181, 270–71, 296–98; love of, 57, 144, 169–
    70, 176, 179, 181, 296–98, 331, 343, 352;
    Manichean view of, 159, 216–17, 201–2,
    207, 208–9, 211, 217–20, 231; Neoplatonic
    view of, 18, 20, 30n52, 340–45; not au-
    thor of evil, 55, 59, 151–52, 218, 221, 231,
    392, 418; as omnipresent, 3–5; one, 54,
    72, 73, 75, 76, 77, 80, 195, 238, 242, 275,
    283–84, 309–11, 320, 329, 341; problem of
    knowing, 3–5, 57–58, 61–62, 65, 293–94,
    309–11, 313–14, 332; providence of, 1–2,
    43, 55, 56, 75, 83, 267, 332–36; as thing
    to be enjoyed, 167–68, 169, 170, 348, 361;
    as rest, 2–3, 38; seeing, 60–62, 128, 143,
    181, 196–97, 293, 294, 372; as Supreme
    Measure, 45, 54; as Trinity, xv, 168, 274,
    279–81, 286, 287–88, 289, 307–11; as
    Truth, 19, 30, 59, 76, 168, 209–10, 212, 291,
    306; as unchangeable, 65, 77, 132, 168,
    197, 275, 285, 289, 291, 293, 311, 343, 351;
    as Wisdom, 30, 31, 39, 53–54, 59, 72, 290,
    311; within, 34, 54, 68, 69–70, 73, 92, 173,
    181, 286, 289, 297, 306–7, 372

gospel(s), 27, 29, 85, 124, 130–31, 134, 147, 160, 175–76, 178, 183, 193, 223, 229–31, 240, 241, 244, 262, 272–73, 295, 317, 336, 385, 389, 390, 402, 435; apocryphal, 165; four, 166, 179; Manichean view of, 205–7; as mirror, 161–62; the Psalms as, 159, 193–95; truth of, 189–90, 230

Gospel of John, 116, 124–25, 128, 132–33, 142–43, 144, 159–61, 175–82, 235, 254–55, 257–63, 312, 444. See also In evangelium Johannis tractatus

Goths, xvi, 120–21, 316, 321, 377, 444

grace, xvi, 20, 72, 195, 199, 226, 304, 311, 359, 412, 414; in Ad Simplicianum, 20n32, 160, 383–89; Augustine's theology of, xvi, 20n32, 92, 160, 373–74, 378–82, 403–9, 423–25, 428–36; of baptism, 16, 20, 21, 28, 29, 92, 94, 394, 403, 412, 415–16, 420; as calling, 92, 386; Christ as, 77, 306; of Christ, 222, 226, 394, 403, 406, 411–12, 414, 417, 424–25; of election, 388–89; of God, 82, 86, 250, 295, 327, 328, 334, 346, 350, 368, 396, 401, 419–20, 425, 426; and good works, 427–28, 429–30; of the Holy Spirit, 11, 179, 296; of justification, 414; Pauline basis for theology of, 373–74, 383–89, 403–5, 411, 414, 425, 428–30, 431–32, 433, 435–36; Pelagius's view of, 376–77, 379; predestination and, 330, 407–8, 417, 428, 431–34; prevenient, 94n23; and the will, 374, 375–77, 383–84, 395–96, 397, 408–9, 427

Gregory of Nazianzus, 277–78, 284n25, 418

Gregory of Nyssa, 277–78

Hadrumetum, 381, 426

Hanson, R. P. C., 275

happy life, 37, 43–45, 53–54, 59, 61, 62–64, 65, 168, 308, 343, 355–56, 357, 363

heart, 6, 7, 9, 12, 17, 18, 22, 24–27, 29, 30, 31, 32, 35, 36, 37, 39, 68, 87, 88, 109, 114, 120, 127, 130, 136, 139, 143, 144, 153, 154, 155, 158, 161, 175, 179, 181, 183, 191, 206, 229, 239, 250, 251, 272, 305, 313–14, 323, 332, 334, 342, 369, 374; Christ diagnoses and heals, 141–42, 144; cleansed to see God, 128, 177,197, 294, 311, 372; as cubiculum, 25, 68; enlightened by God, 7, 27; God sees into, 37, 126; love of God poured into by Spirit, 179, 296; hiddenness of, 91, 113, 282; Holy Spirit delights, 395–96, 428; lifting up in Eucharist, 73, 154–55, 323,

352; love God with whole mind and, 169, 179, 181, 182, 341; jubilation as song of, 199–200; preacher links to hearers', 145–46; Psalms touch, 159, 194–200; restless, 2–3; stairway in, 195–96; and the tongue, 15, 27, 126, 128, 209, 217, 254, 260, 310; as treasury, 72, 241

Hilary (Gallic correspondent), 426, 428, 434

Hilary of Poitiers, 278, 290, 312

Hilary of Syracuse, 408

Hippo Regius, ix, xi, 2, 78–80, 81, 87, 90, 100, 109, 110, 111, 112, 113, 122–23, 232, 267, 326, 368, 374; Augustine as bishop, ix–xi, 86, 87, 111–14, 122, 125, 160; Augustine ordained in, 40, 78, 81–83, 204; Christian majority in 100, 101–2; Council of (year 393), 150n56, 165, 281, 283, 284, 442; Donatist majority in, 232, 243, 246–47; as port, ix, 78–80, 102, 103, 377, 396; sack by Vandals, 119–21, 439

Holy Spirit, 89, 127, 129, 178, 232, 251, 259, 279, 289, 298, 313; in baptism, 173, 257–58; chrismation as sacrament of, 154; Christ born of, 148, 432, 433; Cyprian's view of, 238–40; distinct Person, 283, 291, 310; Donatist view of, 242, 247n27; equal to the Father and the Son, 283, 291; as fire, 154, 258, 263; in the form of a dove, 257–60, 263; gifts of, 127, 250–51, 388; as God, xv, 168, 277–78, 283–84, 288, 290, 291, 310, 312–13; inspired the Scriptures, 174, 184, 188, 191; Manichean view of, 201–2, 207, 209, 229; one power with the Father and the Son, 279–81, 290; of one substance with the Father and the Son, 279, 288; at Pentecost, 89, 154, 250; poured into the heart, 11, 179, 296; proceeds from the Father and the Son, 312–13; teaches prayer, 258

Homoians, 276–77, 284

Honoratus, 211, 213

Honorius (emperor), 96n28, 235, 380

Hortensius, 9–10, 25, 39–40, 43. See also Cicero

human being(s), 14, 72, 74, 91, 92, 95, 97, 141, 189, 215, 271, 293, 309, 345–47, 354, 364, 369–70, 372, 382, 384, 387, 411, 412, 416, 422–23, 424, 426–28, 438; bound together by mutual rights, 357–60; Christ as, 4, 19, 128–29, 132, 148–49, 168, 175, 176–77, 180, 194–95, 197, 230, 275, 279–81, 285, 295, 305–6, 432–33; before the Fall, 347–51, 353, 403;

human being(s) (cont.)
  in the image and likeness of God, 16,
    223–24, 225, 285, 291–92, 298, 302–5,
    306–9, 310–11, 353, 366, 376; image of
    the Trinity within, 31–32, 285, 289, 291,
    310; Manichean view of, 202–3, 208, 222,
    231; Pelagius's view of, 376–77, 396–97,
    400–402; as sign makers, 171–72, 281; as
    sinner, 152–53; as subject to God, 359;
    violence of, 356–57; women as, 302–5,
    366–67. See also body; freedom; heart;
    mind; soul; sexuality; will
humanity, 52, 72, 74, 75, 104, 215, 231, 315,
    353, 354, 368–69; desire for God, 2–3,
    308; divided between two cities, 316–17,
    319–21, 330–32, 352, 361; divided into two
    sexes, 302–5, 349–51; in exile, 167–68;
    as fallen, 129, 140–41, 142, 143, 172, 229,
    308, 319–20, 352, 368, 384, 386–87, 392,
    395–96, 403–7, 414, 421–22, 424–25; need
    for grace, 18, 222–23, 311, 328, 426–28,
    431–32; need for healing, 141–45, 180, 196,
    394–95, 404–7, 433; need for a mediator,
    340, 432–33; as proud, 129, 142, 215, 328;
    as unfallen, 347–51, 353, 403
hymns, 13n19, 29, 53, 54n39, 90, 120,
    283n24, 366

image(s), xvii, xx, 12, 63, 90, 156, 197, 292;
    Christ as Father's, 284, 290; human be-
    ings as, 16, 223–24, 225, 285, 291–92, 298,
    302–5, 306–9, 310–11, 353, 366, 376; in
    the mind, 32–33, 71, 210, 295
In epistulam Johannis ad Parthos tractatus
    (Tractates on the First Letter of John), 125,
    142–43, 250–51, 444
In Johannis evangelium tractatus (Tractates on the
    Gospel of John), 70n58, 116n57, 124, 132–33,
    142, 143, 144–45, 159, 161, 175–82, 199n75,
    254–55, 257–63, 282n23, 312–13, 444
Incarnation, 176, 205, 229, 279–81, 344;
    Manichean denial of, 144, 204, 206, 211,
    229; pagan denial of, 324–25, 326n24
Indiculum (Index), xiii. See also Possidius of
    Calama
infant(s), 5, 6, 16, 377, 393, 407; baptism,
    15n22, 115, 378, 380, 382, 391–95, 404,
    412, 414–16, 419, 445; and original sin,
    5, 378, 393–95, 404–7, 414–17, 418–20,
    423
infantes (newly baptized), 153
Innocent I (pope), 380, 411–12, 414, 445

interiority, 10, 30, 42, 54, 69–70, 76, 195–96,
    223, 281, 289, 292, 296–97, 298
Isidore of Seville, xiii

Jerome, 157, 185–90, 316, 349, 365n73, 378,
    398, 421; Augustine's correspondence
    with, 157, 185–90, 415, 438n2; in Pelagian
    controversy, 378–79, 391–92, 410, 412. See
    also Vulgate
Jerusalem, 87, 108 165n26, 174, 259, 322–23,
    378, 412, 444; as the city of God, 195, 198,
    316–17, 319, 320–21, 323
Jesus, 128, 132, 140, 160, 161, 175, 180, 201,
    254, 382, 393; miracles of, 127, 324,
    325n23; parables of, 144–45, 209–10, 244,
    253, 272, 405–6; picturing the face of, 295;
    words of, 140, 160, 205, 321, 329n31, 367,
    372, 388. See Christ; Christology
Jews, 114, 164, 184, 186, 187n59, 189–90, 195,
    227, 242, 320; Manichean view of, 201,
    207, 208n15, 229
John Cassian, 381–82, 426
John Chrysostom, 51n32, 108, 135n25, 153,
    418
John of Jerusalem, 378–79
Jovinian, 351n57, 376n14, 421
Judas, 241–42, 258; Catholics as church of,
    232, 233, 242, 254
Julian of Eclanum, xvi, 380–81, 383, 408n70,
    415, 417–25, 445, 446; Ad Florum (To
    Florus), 381, 408n70, 418; Ad Turbantium (To
    Turbantius), 381, 419n88, 420–21

language, 6, 40, 67–69, 130–31, 158, 163, 166,
    172, 310, 346, 356
Latin (language), ix–xi, xx , 3, 9, 19, 20,
    31–32, 33, 85, 87, 131, 132, 146, 157, 173,
    184, 185, 186, 237, 243, 244, 257, 276, 339,
    343, 356, 398
Lent, 21n34, 21n35, 28, 85, 94–95, 143, 146,
    178, 236n8, 442
Leo I (pope), 426
Letters (of Augustine). See Epistulae
lex orandi, 418–20
liberal arts, 40, 64–65, 182–83
liturgy, 81, 88–89, 123, 134, 278, 418–19; of
    baptism, 150, 173, 250, 414, 418–19; of the
    Eucharist, 15n22, 153–55; of the Word,
    15n22, 79, 123–24, 153
Lord's Prayer, 150–53, 155, 411
love, 22, 23, 28, 36, 65, 72, 84, 91–92, 90,
    115, 169–70, 179–82, 199, 215, 241, 244,

253, 261, 262, 293, 318, 333, 341, 347, 389, 414, 418, 428; of Christ the Head, 193–95, 228; definition of, 170; ". . . and do what you will," 270–71; earthly city bound by, 357–60; of enemy, 73, 100, 335; of evil, 7–8; faith and hope and, 54, 60, 61–62, 110, 130, 166, 222–23, 294, 389, 437, 439, 440; as gift of the Holy Spirit, 11, 179, 251, 258, 261, 388; God as, 19, 181, 270–71, 296–98; of God, 19–20, 28, 31, 33–34, 35, 36, 37–38, 57–58, 59–60, 133, 144, 169–70, 173–74, 176, 179, 181, 210, 288, 294, 295, 296–98, 331, 336, 341–43, 347, 352; as hermeneutic for interpreting the Bible, 169–70; in love with, 8; of neighbor, 144, 169–70, 173–74, 176, 180–82, 296, 308, 341–43, 347, 359, 361; original sin as self-ish, 351–53; of peace, 250, 251; of preacher and audience, 145–56, 257–58, 438; triad of mind, knowledge and, 299, 301, 307–8; the Trinity and, 291, 294, 296–98, 307–8, 310–11; two cities defined by, 317, 321–22, 329, 331–32, 352; of unity of the Church, 154, 251, 266, 268; of wisdom, 9, 25, 39, 43–45; of the world, 133, 334–35

Mani, xv, 201–4; biography of, xv, 201; Concerning the Origin of His Body, 204; as Paraclete, 201, 202; religious teaching, 201–3; writings, 203–4

Manichean Psalm Book, 202, 203, 204

Manichee(s), xiv, xv, xvii, 12, 316, 400; asceticism of, 204, 205–6; Augustine as, xv, 10–11, 14–15, 40, 159, 204, 209–10, 212, 373, 381, 420, 441; Augustine's debates with, 80, 122n2, 204, 205, 246, 442; in China, 203, 204; as Christians, 203, 205–7, 208–9; clergy, 14n20, 205, 208; the Elect, 10, 203, 208; Hearers, 203, 208–9; as missionaries, 203, 205, 208–9, 215, 220–21; secrecy of, 208–9

Manicheism, xv, 10, 13, 86, 201–31, 279; appeal to reason, 17, 212–15; Augustine's polemic against, xvii, 14, 42–43, 44n17, 65, 86, 158, 159, 204, 209–31, 279, 383; Augustine's summaries of, xvii, 208–9, 230–31; on the body, 203–4, 206, 208, 222, 230; cosmogony, 201–2, 216–17, 231; dualism, 55, 201–2; on evil, 202, 209, 216–19, 231; God of, 159, 216–17, 201–2, 207, 208–9, 211, 217–20, 231; Pelagius as opponent of, 375–76; rejection of the Old Testament,

10, 203, 207–8, 223–24, 227; veneration of the sun and moon, 44n18, 203, 208–9; view of Christ, 201, 205–7, 208, 211, 227, 229–30; view of the human person, 202–3, 208, 222, 231; view of salvation, 202, 204, 207, 211

Marcellinus, Flavius, 81n8, 98, 115, 162, 324–26; and Conference of Carthage (year 411), 98n32, 236, 272, 377; as dedicatee of City of God, 98n32, 327–28; execution of, 98n32, 327–28, 444; and the Pelagian controversy, 98n32, 115n53, 377, 378, 393

Marcellus of Ancyra, 276

marriage, 17–18, 73, 121n63, 129–30, 347–51, 367, 373, 376, 381, 382, 420; Augustine's view of, 129–30, 347–51, 421–24; Julian of Eclanum's view of, 420–21, 424

martyr(s), 73, 99, 124n6, 232, 237; Cyprian as, 263–64; Donatists and, 232, 233, 234, 262, 267; as forerunners, 196–98; suicidal, 262n41

Mauretania Caesarensis, 208, 251

Mauretania Tingitania, 116

Mauretanias (Roman provinces), 107, 120, 232, 234

Maurists, 65n52, 81n8, 92n21, 125n9–10, 147n54, 221n27, 394n48

Maximinus (Donatist bishop), 234

Maximinus (Homoian bishop), 277, 446

memory, xi, 1, 6, 20, 21, 27, 29, 31–33, 54, 57, 67–68, 133–34, 139, 146–47, 167, 179, 186, 190, 195, 244, 289, 292, 341; triad of understanding, will, and, 291, 300–302, 306, 310–11

Mensurius of Carthage, 233

Milan, xiv, 13, 17, 18, 20, 22, 23, 28, 29, 40, 41, 42, 43, 44n21, 64, 65, 78, 80, 89, 160, 204, 213, 217, 235, 249, 251, 276, 344, 374, 377, 389, 435, 441, 442

Milevis, Council of (year 416), 380, 411–12, 413, 445

Miltiades (pope), 233, 248

monastery, 375, 381; in Hippo Regius, xi, 78, 82–83, 104, 108–12, 114; Jerome's in Bethlehem, 157, 379, 391, 410; Manichean, 204; in Milan, 23; in Thagaste, 78, 81, 279, 442

monasticism, xi, 23–24, 108–9, 120, 375, 382, 426, 428

Monnica, 1–2, 5, 9, 10–11, 12, 17–18, 28, 30–31, 53–54, 89, 397, 442

mosaic, xvii–xviii, 56, 122, 150n55, 437–38

music, 34n56, 65n52, 67, 159, 182, 199–200, 337, 370
mystagogy, 153–55

Nebridius, 2, 22, 27, 40, 41, 62–64, 216, 279–80, 442
Neoplatonism, 18–20, 30–31, 40, 42, 56, 66. See also Platonism
New Testament, 75, 96, 164–65, 166, 176, 203, 205, 207, 223, 255, 295, 340
Nicaea, Council of (year 325), xv, 87n14, 110, 113n50, 118, 275–76, 278; creed of, 278. See also anti-Nicene; pro-Nicene
North Africa, ix–xi, xvii, 8, 78, 119, 122, 199, 378, 437, 444
North African Christianity, xi, xv, 80, 90, 106, 109, 122–23, 134, 157, 165, 232–37, 238–39, 377–81, 394n48, 403, 411–14, 426
notarius. See stenographer
Novatianists, 238, 239
Numidia, 87, 103, 106–7, 118, 232, 233, 234, 247, 412

Old Testament, 75, 124, 160, 223–24, 243, 285, 340; Ambrose as interpreter of, 13–14, 157–58, 213; canon of, 164–66; Christ's presence in, 159, 227–29; Greek version of, xxi, 184–87; Manichean rejection of, 10, 203, 207, 211n18, 223; pagan objections to, 325; Pelagius's appeal to, 395; Vetus Latina translations of, xxi, 84–87
On Baptism. See De baptismo
On Catechizing Beginners. See De catechizandis rudibus
On Christian Teaching. See De doctrina christiana
On Free Will. See De libero arbitrio
On Genesis, Against the Manichees. See De Genesi adversus Manichaeos
On Nature and Grace. See De natura et gratia
On Order. See On Order
On the Advantage of Believing. See De utilitate credendi
On the City of God. See De civitate Dei
On the Deeds of Pelagius. See De gestis Pelagii
On the Gift of Perseverance. See De dono perseverantiae
On the Happy Life. See De beata vita
On the Literal Interpretation of Genesis. See De Genesi ad litteram
On the Merits and Forgiveness of Sins and On Infant Baptism. See De peccatorum meritis et remissione et de baptismo parvulorum

On the Predestination of the Saints. See De praedestinatione sanctorum
On the Teacher. See De magistro
On the Trinity. See De Trinitate
On True Religion. See De vera religione
Optatus of Mauretania Tingitana, 116
Optatus of Milevis, 234, 262n41, 269n53, 417
Optatus of Thamugadi, 234
oratory, xix–xx, 9, 31–32, 39, 51n32, 80, 125–26, 130–31, 135–40. See also rhetoric
Origen, 13, 182, 185n57, 187, 275n6, 316, 363
original sin, 5, 56, 159, 318, 345, 351–54, 367, 378, 382, 384, 393–95, 403–7, 414, 427, 445; definition of, 351–53; and exsufflatio, 418–20; and infants, 5, 378, 393–95, 404–7, 414–17; and the origin of the soul, 415; Pelagian opposition to, 376, 392, 401–2, 417–18, 424
Ostia, 31, 41, 442
Our Father. See Lord's Prayer

pagan(s), 42, 86, 114, 153, 172n37, 182–83, 241, 326, 360, 389; Augustine's reply to objections from, 90–92, 156 316, 318, 319–21, 332–45; conversion of, 90–92, 317, 319–21, 362; monotheism, 42, 344–45; in North Africa, 80, 96–97, 101–2; objections to Christianity, 162, 275, 316, 324–26, 332, 363–66; suppression of, 97n28, 236, 317; views on the sack of Rome, xvi, 316, 321–24, 340; violence of, 96–97; worship, 21n33, 122, 269n53, 316, 340–44
paradox of inquiry, 293–94
Parmenian of Carthage, 191n67, 234, 235, 237
Paul (apostle), 9n12, 20n32, 91, 96, 124, 166, 144–45, 147n51, 148, 203, 207, 226, 238, 242, 255, 258, 262n41, 295, 309, 321; Augustine's clash with Jerome over, 187–90; Augustine's commentaries on, 160, 344n49, 373–74, 383, 435–36; as convert, 91, 272–73, 388–89; influence of Augustine's conversion, 23, 27, 46, 160, 373; influence on Augustine's view of grace, 374, 386, 435–36; influence on Augustine's view of original sin, 394, 404, 406, 411, 414, 423; influence on Augustine's view of predestination, 431–32; Pelagius's commentaries on, 375, 378, 398, 400
Paul Orosius, 378–79, 444
Paulinus of Milan, 377, 389–91
Paulinus of Nola, 79n3, 397n54, 420, 443

Pelagius, xvi, 92, 160, 374–81, 383, 389–90, 391, 393, 396–415, 419, 424n95, 444; commentaries on Paul's letters, 375, 378, 398, 400, 401n61; condemnations of, xvi, 380, 411–14, 417, 445; *De natura* (*On Nature*), 375–76, 378, 380, 400–408, 444; *De vita Christiana* (*On Christian Life*), 375; denounces *Confessiones*, 92, 375, 397–98; *ep. ad Demetriadem* (*Letter to Demetrias*), 375, 376–77, 375, 398–99; as moralist, 375–76, 400, 401; as opponent of Manicheism, 375–76; quoting Augustine, 221n28, 375; *Pro libero arbitrio* (*In Favor of Free Choice*), 377, 424n95; in Rome, xvi, 374–76, 377, 396, 397–98, 400; as spiritual director, xvi, 374–75, 376, 378, 398–99; on trial in the Holy Land, 376n17, 378–80, 409–11, 429, 444; view of Adam, 376, 401–2; view of evil, 375–77, 392, 400–402, 408, 418, 424; view of free will, 375–77, 400–402, 408, 411–12; view of grace, 376–77, 379; view of the human person, 376–77, 396–97, 400–402

Pelagian controversy, 98n32, 145n45, 160, 221n28, 373–436; complexity of, 382; four phases of, 377, 378, 380, 381, 383, 417; international character, 378–81, 409–13; issues in, 382

Pelagian movement, xiv, xvi, xvii, 56, 195, 277n16, 375, 377–78, 381, 389–91; as confederation of theologies, 393. *See also* Caelestius; Julian of Eclanum; Rufinus the Syrian

Petilian of Constantine, 236, 240–42, 243, 254, 444

Petrarch, 32

philosophic dialogue, xiv, 27, 29, 40–42, 43, 45, 46, 50, 53, 55, 57–58, 61, 62, 67–69, 193, 215–16, 221

philosophy, xiv, 2, 6, 9–10, 15, 21, 27, 39–77, 158, 167, 170, 183, 205, 209, 216, 236, 279, 289, 299, 315–16, 336, 344, 355, 362–63, 415, 437; Christianity as, 39, 71–74; conversion to, 39, 42, 43–46; of language, 6–7, 67–69; as love of wisdom, 9, 39, 43–45; Platonism as truest, 20, 52–53, 71–74, 183; of religion, 340–44; *See also* Academics; Neoplatonism; Platonism; skepticism; Stoicism

Plato, 15n21, 40, 44n20, 50, 52, 62

Platonism, 18–20, 52, 53, 60, 74, 183, 204, 217, 340, 344, 346, 363. *See also* Neoplatonism

Plotinus, 18–19, 40, 42, 44, 52, 57, 158, 168n32, 340n45

Ponticianus, 22–25

Porphyry of Tyre, 18, 40, 42, 158, 340, 363, 365

Possidius of Calama, xiii, xiv, 81–82, 85–87, 96, 104, 105–6, 109–10, 115, 119–21, 122, 265–66, 267, 380, 397n54, 411, 439–40

prayer, 2, 10, 23, 68, 85, 97, 104, 151, 229, 412; Augustine's appeal to congregation for, 85, 91–92, 117, 119, 177; Augustine's practices of, 2, 437, 439; Eucharistic, 73n60, 154–55, 323; examples of Augustine's, 33–34, 58–60, 438n2; of the Faithful, 154; teaching of the Lord's, 147, 150–53, 411; preaching and, 124, 126–27, 438n2

preaching, 3–4, 72, 99, 175–76, 179, 183; of Ambrose, 13–17, 40, 153, 157, 204; audience for, 91n20, 122–23, 126–27, 130–31, 132, 133–35, 136, 139, 150, 159, 173, 257; Augustine's practice of, xi, xiv, 81, 85–86, 87–88, 90–92, 95, 122–25, 128–35, 140–55, 161–62, 175–82, 193–200, 257–63, 321–24, 437, 438, 443; Augustine's theory of, xiv, 125–27, 130–31, 135–40, 145–46, 158; biblical focus of, xiv–xv, 126, 127–28, 156, 159–60, 161–62, 164, 428; to catechumens, 85, 146–53; Christological themes in, 69, 128–30, 140–45, 193–200; against Donatists, xv, 235, 254, 265–66; episcopal duty of, 79, 85–86, 88n16; liturgical setting, 122–24; preparation for, 126–27; rhetorical techniques in, 130–33, 135–40; on the sack of Rome, 321–24; two cities theme, 316–17, 319–21. *See also De doctrina christiana*; sermons

predestination, 92, 330, 371, 381–82, 395, 397, 404, 417, 426–28, 429–34

presbyter, 20, 22, 81n9, 83, 98, 105, 111, 112, 114, 117–19, 123, 155, 208, 240, 266, 274, 374, 378, 389, 390, 391, 411; Augustine as, 78, 81–86, 150n56, 204, 211, 222, 235, 243, 281, 439, 442

prevenient grace, 94n23, 407–8, 428

pride, 10, 11, 19, 27, 28, 53, 109, 129, 139, 142, 168, 172, 173, 209, 245, 262, 270, 297, 319, 320, 328, 332, 334, 395–96, 407, 436; as beginning of sin, 351–53; cured by Christ's humility, 129, 142, 345, 352

primate, provincial, 80, 86–87, 106–7, 111, 113, 233, 412

Primian of Carthage, 234
pro-Nicenes, 276–77, 279, 284, 290n31
Prosper of Aquitaine, 382, 419, 426–28, 431, 434, 446
Psalms, 147, 159, 166, 342; of Ascent, 195; Augustine's preaching on, xiii, 125, 159, 254; City of God theme from, 328–29; in *Confessiones*, 2, 24, 28, 159; in North African liturgy, 124; prosopological exegesis of, 158, 193, 194, 195; Septuagint numbering of, xxi; singing as therapeutic, 159, 196–98, 229; as voice of Christ, 158, 159, 193, 195, 196. See also *Enarrationes in Psalmos*
Psalmus contra partem Donati (Psalm Against the Donatists), 243–45, 443

Ravenna, 80, 380, 414, 419n88
rebaptism, 239–40, 249, 255–56, 263–64, 272
Reconsiderations. See Retractationes
redditio symboli (handing back of the creed), 21, 22n35, 146
Regula (Rule), 83n11, 108–9, 443
resurrection, 177, 208, 306, 348, 362–63, 365, 393, 408, 433; of the body, 144n43, 309, 346, 361, 362–67, 371; of Christ, 89, 143–44, 149, 176, 178, 208, 312, 362, 390, 402; of women, 366–67
Retractationes (Reconsiderations), xiii, 38, 43, 64–65, 243–44, 326, 434, 435, 441, 445
rhetoric, 65, 318–19, 369; Augustine's practice of, xx, 42, 71, 128, 131–33; Augustine as teacher of, 22, 27, 39, 65, 130, 135; Ciceronian, 9–10, 43, 135; and figures of speech, 131–33, 138–39, 318–19; as tool for Christian preaching, 130–31. See also *De doctrina christiana*; eloquence
Romanianus, 45–46
Rome, 20–21, 40–41, 88–89, 124, 185, 187n60, 204, 217, 221, 276, 312, 390, 391, 421; bishop of, 233, 248–49, 379, 380, 411–14; Christian views on, 317–18; as commonwealth, 336–39, 357–60; Pelagius in, 374–76, 396, 397–98, 400; sack of, xvi, 316–17, 321–24, 332–34, 340, 377
Rufinus the Syrian, 390, 391–92, 393n47

sacrament, 29, 88, 120, 153, 154n60, 155, 253, 255, 261, 264, 340, 411, 419, 426–27; Augustine as minister of, 37, 79, 84; baptism as, 92, 93, 256–57, 393, 394, 415; chrismation as, 154; Eucharist as, 153–54, 172, 273, 344, 426; of exorcism, 154; few,

88; necessary for salvation, 415–16; as sacred sign, 154n60, 342
Sallust, 336, 337, 339
salvation, 14, 22, 29, 39, 73, 83, 84, 94, 146, 163, 177, 249, 253, 279, 295, 385, 393, 399, 402, 428; history of, 72, 169, 172, 285, 317–18, 374, 382; Manichean view of, 202, 204, 207, 211; not outside the Church, 237, 239, 256, 261, 394n48, 395, 403, 404, 411
schism, xv, 80, 98n32, 232–34, 246, 247–49, 250, 251, 252, 253, 256–57, 272–73, 312; Cyprian on, 238–39
Scriptures. See Bible.
Secundus of Tigisis, 233, 247–48
semiotics, 170–73. See also sign(s)
Septuagint, xxi, 164, 183–87, 195, 213
sermon(s), xiv, xv, 81, 82–83, 90, 100, 116, 123, 136, 160, 161, 174, 281n22, 282n23, 318, 362–63, 432; Ambrose's, 13, 17, 44; Augustine's surviving corpus, xiii, 124–25; biblical focus of, xiv–xv, 126, 127–28, 156, 159–60, 161–62, 164, 428; catechetical, 146–53; Christmas, 128–30; *Christus medicus* theme, 140–45; *conversi ad Dominum* prayer at close, 438n2; on the First Epistle of John, 235, 250–51, 270–71; on the Gospel of John, 159–60, 161, 175–82, 198n75, 257–63, 413; hour-long, 124; mystagogical, 153–55; newly discovered, 80n5, 125, 190n64, 316, 321n17, 379, 438; as oral performances, 2n3, 80, 86, 124, 131–33, 159; polemical, 86, 235, 257, 276; on the Psalms, 87–88, 159, 161, 193–200; on the sack of Rome, 321–24; recorded by stenographers, 85–86, 116, 124, 147, 159. See also *Enarrationes in Psalmos*; *In Johannis evangelium tractatus*; mystagogy; preaching; *Sermones ad populum*
Sermones (Dolbeau), xxvii, 35n57, 70n58, 124n8, 125, 133n22, 142n39, 144n44, 190n64, 256n37, 267–268n51, 282n23, 316–17, 321n17, 379, 438, 446
Sermones (Denis, Guelf., Morin, Wilmart) (Miscellaneous Sermons), 91–92, 124n6, 141–42, 146–47, 156n1, 161–62
Sermones ad populum (Sermons to the People), xiii, xix, 82–83, 90–92, 94–95, 100–102, 104–5, 106, 125, 127, 128–30, 132–35, 140–41, 143–44, 146–55, 321–24, 362–63, 367, 413; chronology, 124n8; numbers, 124n8, 125
sexuality, 25n43, 39, 113, 225, 230, 303–5, 348–51, 353, 366–67, 381, 382, 420–21

sign(s), 42, 47, 48, 67, 170–75, 176, 177, 179, 182, 250–51, 320, 341, 369; ambiguous, 172–73; baptism as, 150; the Bible as, 167, 170, 179; conventional, 171–72; in the Eucharist, 155, 340; gestures as, 171–72; natural, 171; obscure, 173–75; spoken words as, 6, 31, 68–69, 70, 172, 282; writing as, 172; sacrament as sacred, 154n60, 342

Simplicianus, 20–22, 160, 344, 374, 383–89, 435–36, 443

sin, 3, 7, 60, 73, 75, 82, 84, 111, 142, 149, 152, 172, 226, 231, 244, 249, 253, 264, 341, 347, 359, 403, 431, 432; of Adam, 7, 345–47, 349, 353, 376, 377, 386, 390–92, 401–5, 414, 415, 426; after baptism, 150, 152–53, 377; baptism for the forgiveness of, 149–50, 153, 232, 239–40, 256–57, 308, 377, 393–94, 414, 415, 424–25; confession of, 2, 7–8, 14, 18, 29, 35, 134–35, 149; Cyprian's view of, 239, 263; body's disobedience as punishment for, 343, 353–54, 367, 424–25; of disobedience, 351–54, 367; Donatist view of, 232, 233, 240–42, 264; free will and, 216, 222–23, 231, 345–47, 384, 395–96, 399, 408–9, 417; God's blessings despite, 368–71; God's forgiveness of, 147–50, 177, 231, 377, 433; humanity before, 347–51, 363; infants and, 5, 390–95, 414, 415–17, 418; Manichean view of, 231; massa peccati, 386–88, 417; mortality result of, 394, 404, 406, 411, 414, 423; Pelagius's view of, 376–77, 400–402, 405–6; and Romans 5:12, 394, 404, 406, 411, 414, 423; sexuality and, 18, 29, 348–51, 420–23; soul, not body, as source of, 345–47; of traditio, 233, 250. See also original sin; sinlessness

sinlessness, 135, 348–51, 390, 395–96, 400–401, 403, 414, 424, 434

skepticism, 15n21, 40, 46–51, 299

slavery, 102–3, 215, 246, 271, 272, 398

Soliloquia (Soliloquies), 27n47, 40, 46n24, 57–62, 63, 64, 65, 69n57, 71, 442

Souk Ahras. See Thagaste.

soul, 7, 12, 18, 25, 36, 40, 43, 44, 45, 53, 54, 57–58, 70, 71, 72, 109, 120, 126, 161, 177, 181, 208, 213, 214, 217, 220, 225, 267, 282, 291, 293, 341, 353, 359, 368, 369, 370, 387, 410; Augustine's agnosticism about the origin of, 116, 415–16; and the body, 61, 62–66, 120, 210, 343, 345–46, 349,

359–61, 363, 367, 369, 387, 424; eye of, 19, 61–62, 70; healed by faith, hope, and love, 61–62, 294; in the hierarchy of being, 65; immortality of, 64; made by God, 141, 216; Manichean view of, 203, 208, 217; movement to God as love, 170; original sin and, 351, 353; Platonist view, 69n57, 363, 365; pre-existence of, 69n57; unhealthy, 8, 15, 18, 35, 52, 141, 240

stenographer(s), xi, 85–86, 117–18, 124, 147, 159, 439n2

Stephen I (pope), 239

Stoicism, 47, 355

symbolum, 22n35, 146–47, 150n56, 281. See also creed

tattoo (stigma, puncta), 255–56, 272

Teske, Roland, 33n54, 66, 75, 174n40, 230–31, 387n23

Thagaste, ix, xiv, 11n15, 40, 41, 42, 67, 78, 80, 81, 268n52, 279, 441–42

Theodore of Mopsuestia, 153, 380

Theodorus, Manlius, 19n29, 43

time, 13, 30n52, 40, 65, 75–76, 129, 225, 290, 310–11, 321, 330–31, 341, 370

To Simplicianus, on Various Questions. See Ad Simplicianum

torture, 8n10, 97–98, 100n33, 106, 120, 245, 265, 354–55

Tractates on the First Letter of John. See In epistulam Johannis ad Parthos tractatus

Tractates on the Gospel of John. See In Johannis evangelium tractatus

Tractoria, 380, 445. See also Zosimus

traditio, 233, 247n27, 250

traditio orationis (handing over the Prayer), 147n53, 150–53

traditio symboli (handing on of the Creed), 146–50

traditor (betrayer), 233, 241–43, 247, 252, 253

traducianism, 415

Trinity, xv, 53–54, 76, 88, 168, 274–78; analogies for, 281–84, 291–92, 296–99, 300–302, 306–11; Cappadocian view of, 277–78, 290; distinction of persons, 276, 278, 283–84, 286, 298, 309–10; equality of Father and Son, 128, 149, 176, 195, 277, 284–85, 289–90, 298; God who is, xv, 274, 289, 309–11; Homoian view of, 276–77; human being as an image of, 285–86, 291, 292, 302–5, 306–9, 310; inseparability, 279–81, 286, 299, 310–11; and love, 296–97;

Trinity (cont.)
as single operation, 279–81, 289; un-
changeability, 77, 275, 285, 289, 291–92,
310–11; unity of substance, 76–77, 283–84,
298–311. See also filioque
truth, 2, 14, 16, 21, 29, 40, 45, 47, 48–53, 57,
64, 69–70, 71, 109, 131, 209, 211, 212, 213,
224, 347, 424; Christ as, 37, 54, 69–70,
71, 76, 132–33, 168, 196–97, 306; God as,
19, 30, 59, 76, 168, 209–10, 212, 291, 306;
hiddenness of, 47, 163, 213, 226–27; in the
liberal arts, 182–83; rhetoric and, 130–31;
in Scripture, 163, 188–90, 191, 226–27, 435
Tyconius, 158, 191–93, 194, 237

uti (use), 167–68

Valerius (bishop of Hippo), 78, 81, 83–87,
117–18, 443
Vandals, 119–21, 439, 446
Verbraken, Pierre-Patrick, 124n9, 125n9–10
Vergil, 69, 156, 322, 328
Vetus Latina, xxi, 9–10, 75n62, 157–58,
174n40, 178n45, 195, 198n74, 404n65
Victorinus (Manichee), 208–9
Victorinus (Numidian bishop), 106–8
Victorinus, Marius, 20–22, 278, 283n24, 312
Vincent of Cartenna, 263–64, 268–70
virgin(s), 73, 120, 130, 375, 398
Virgin Mary, 129–30, 148, 206, 208, 211, 230,
381, 424, 432–34
virginity, 24, 130, 376, 421
vision of God, 19, 30–31, 60–62, 286, 309,
311, 388–89, 442
Vita s. Augustini (Life of St. Augustine), xiii n8,
xiv, 80–82, 85–87, 96, 104, 106, 109–10,
122, 265, 267, 439–40. See also Possidius
of Calama
Vulgate, 75n62, 157, 185, 187n59, 198n74,
404n65. See also Jerome

war, xvi, 80, 120–21, 138, 315, 325, 332, 339,
356–57, 360, 369, 424
will (voluntas), 6, 20, 43, 70, 94, 112, 171, 172,
270–71, 286, 397, 399; as cause of original
sin, 351–53, 417, 421; and the City of God,
319; evil, 5n6, 220–21, 231, 423; freedom
of, 40, 42, 43, 205, 220–23, 374, 380, 381,
382, 383–84, 388–89, 403, 404–6, 408–9,
414, 428, 432, 435; of God, 55, 94, 120,
166, 172, 231, 344, 347, 382, 402, 404,
431; healed by grace, 412, 428, 430, 435; of
infants, 5n6, 427; as locus of divided self,
345–47, 353–54, 367; Pelagius on, 375–76,
377, 400–401, 411–12; and predestination,
417, 426–27, 431; triad of memory, understanding, and, 300–302, 306–9; unfallen,
348
wisdom, 3, 30, 53, 116, 307, 322, 344, 366,
368, 418; Christ as, 9, 53, 70, 72, 76, 168,
207, 230, 282, 285, 290, 305–6, 323; as
contemplation of eternal, 292, 305; distinguished from knowledge, 292, 305–6;
God as, 30, 31, 39, 53–54, 59, 290, 311;
knowledge of, 49–50; life of, 9, 39–40, 62;
Manichean view of, 207; philosophy as
love of, 9, 25, 39; quest for, 25, 39, 53; and
skepticism, 49; as supreme good, 46n24;
wise man's dialogue with, 49–50
Wittgenstein, Ludwig, 6
women, 18, 28, 93, 112, 375; Augustine's view
of, 93, 129–30, 225, 302–5, 348–51, 366–
67; before the Fall, 348–51; as images of
God, 225, 302–5; in late antiquity, 18n25;
and the resurrection, 366–67

Xanthippius of Tago, 107

Zeno of Citium, 47, 48
Zenobius, 55
Zosimus (pope), 380, 413, 414, 445

Augustine in His Own Words was designed in Quadraat and MetaPro and
typeset by Kachergis Book Design of Pittsboro, North Carolina.
It was printed on 50-pound Natures Book Natural and bound
by Thomson-Shore of Dexter, Michigan.